Brief Review

PRENTICE HALL
GLOBAL HISTORY AND GEOGRAPHY

Steven Goldberg
Judith Clark DuPré

PEARSON

Prentice
Hall

Boston, Massachusetts
Upper Saddle River, New Jersey

13-digit ISBN 9780-13-365317-5

ISBN 0-13-365317-X

2 3 4 5 6 7 8 9 10   11 10 09 08

Contents

ABOUT THIS BOOK

This book has been written to help you, the student, review your two-year global history and geography course. Its purposes are to:

- Help you focus on the key facts, themes, and concepts that you need to know to succeed on the Regents Examination in global history and geography.
- Allow you to become familiar with the format of the Regents Examination.
- Provide you with the test-taking skills you will need to apply your social studies knowledge to the Regents Examination.

In this book, the ninth- and tenth-grade global history and geography curriculum is presented chronologically. In other words, it is presented in time order, from earliest times to the present. Within this organization, there has been a careful attempt to group the material in meaningful eras, or periods of time in which certain types of activity were going on all over the world. For example, Unit 5 covers the period from 1750 through 1914. During this period of more than 160 years, revolutions were occurring all over the world, and nations formed and grew strong.

The book highlights the key themes and concepts that are woven throughout the global history and geography curriculum. Concentrating on themes and concepts will help you organize the global history and geography that you have studied. It will also start you thinking about history in ways that will help you excel on the Regents Examination.

Four overall themes—history; geography; economics; and civics, citizenship, and government—draw these units together. As you review and study, these themes will help you make connections between different times and places. In the side column, several types of help are available.

- **The Big Idea** notes at the beginning of each section organize the section content at a glance. This feature highlights key content in list form.
- **Preparing for the Regents** notes provide questions, explanations, and activities that will give you practice in applying your knowledge to Regents-type questions.
- **Key Themes and Concepts** notes summarize important content and link it to key themes and concepts.

Other sections of this book are also important.

- **Preparing for the Regents** provides instructions and hints for Regents success, using questions like those you will see on the test.
- **Questions for Regents Practice,** found at the end of each unit, will help you figure out your strengths and weaknesses as you practice taking the test.
- **Four sample Regents Examinations** also appear at the back of the book.

- **Thematic Review** reviews key content within those themes that the Regents Examination may focus on.

The goal of this book is to help you attain success on the Regents Examination. It will focus your efforts in areas that will pay off on exam day. With this book, you will have the tools to master the material and present it effectively. Best of luck on exam day!

ABOUT THE CONSULTING AUTHORS

Steven Goldberg is the District Chairperson of Social Studies for the City School District of New Rochelle. He received his bachelor's degree in history from the University of Rochester, a master's degree in East Asian Studies from Yale University, and an administrative certificate from Teachers' College, Columbia University. He was a Fulbright Fellow to the Netherlands and studied at Sophia University in Tokyo. He is past president of both the New York State Council for the Social Studies and the New York State Social Studies Supervisory Association and has served on the executive board of the Westchester Council of the Social Studies. A consultant to the State Education Department, he has been on numerous Regents Examination committees, as well as the design team for Global History and Geography. In addition, he is a charter member of the Westchester Holocaust Education Center planning commitee. He has traveled through Eastern and Western Europe, Japan, Mexico, and Israel.

Judith Clark DuPré is a social studies teacher in the Fairport School District. She received her bachelor's and master's degrees from the State University of New York, Brockport. She is president of the Rochester Area Council for the Social Studies, a member of the New York State Council for the Social Studies Board of Directors, and serves on the Advisory Council of the International Studies Program at St. John Fisher College. She had been named to Who's Who Among America's Teachers and has received the Rochester area Outstanding High School Social Studies Classroom Teacher Award. She was a Fulbright fellow in Japan. She has contributed to several curriculum development projects in Global Studies and Global History and Geography. She has traveled throughout Western and Eastern Europe, Africa, and Australia.

The Social Studies Standards

STANDARD 1: HISTORY OF THE UNITED STATES AND NEW YORK

Students will use a variety of intellectual skills to demonstrate their understanding of major ideas, eras, themes, developments, and turning points in the history of the United States and New York.

STANDARD 2: WORLD HISTORY

Students will use a variety of intellectual skills to demonstrate their understanding of major ideas, eras, themes, developments, and turning points in world history from a variety of perspectives.

STANDARD 3: GEOGRAPHY

Students will use a variety of intellectual skills to demonstrate their understanding of the geography of the interdependent world in which we live—local, national, and global—including the distribution of people, places, and environments over Earth's surface.

STANDARD 4: ECONOMICS

Students will use a variety of intellectual skills to demonstrate their understanding of how the United States and other societies develop economic systems and associated institutions to allocate scarce resources, how major decision-making units function in the United States and other national economies, and how an economy solves the scarcity problem through market and nonmarket economies.

STANDARD 5: CIVICS, CITIZENSHIP, AND GOVERNMENT

Students will use a variety of intellectual skills to demonstrate their understanding of the necessity for establishing governments; the governmental system of the United States and other nations; the U.S. Constitution; the basic civic values of American constitutional democracy; and the roles, rights, and responsibilities of citizenship, including avenues of participation.

Key Themes and Concepts

Global history and geography can be best understood if it is organized by studying key themes and key concepts that recur in many times and places. Themes and concepts are mental images and classifications that help you to:
- understand important ideas.
- recognize global connections and linkages.
- see similarities and differences among events.
- determine the causes that lead up to events and the effects that result from events.

The Regents Examination uses a number of themes and concepts in constructing questions for the test. They are listed and explained below in four categories: history; geography; economics; and civics, citizenship, and government.

HISTORY: SOME KEY THEMES AND CONCEPTS

- **Belief Systems** means the established, orderly ways in which groups or individuals look at religious faith or philosophical tenets.
- **Change** is the basic alterations in things, events, and ideas.
- **Choice** means the right or power to select from a range of alternatives.
- **Conflict** is disagreement or opposition between ideas or groups, which may lead to an armed struggle.
- **Culture and Intellectual Life** means the patterns of human behavior that include ideas, beliefs, values, artifacts, and ways of making a living that any society transmits to succeeding generations to meet its fundamental needs. It also includes ways of thinking, studying, and reflecting on ideas and life.
- **Diversity** means understanding and respecting others and oneself, including any similarities or differences in language, gender, socioeconomic class, religion, and other human characteristics and traits.
- **Empathy** means the ability to understand others through identifying in oneself responses similar to the experiences, behaviors, and responses of others.
- **Identity** means awareness of one's own values, attitudes, and capabilities as an individual and as a member of various groups.
- **Imperialism** means the domination by one country of the political and/or economic life of another country or region.
- **Interdependence** means reliance upon others in mutually beneficial interactions and exchanges.

- **Movement of People and Goods** is the exchange of people, ideas, products, technologies, and institutions from one region or civilization to another, a process that has existed throughout history.
- **Nationalism** means a feeling of pride in and devotion to one's country or the desire of a people to control their own government, free from foreign interference or rule.
- **Urbanization** means movement of people from rural to urban (city) areas.

GEOGRAPHY: SOME KEY THEMES AND CONCEPTS

The six essential elements of geography follow.
- **The World in Spatial Terms**—Geography studies the relationships among people, places, and environments by mapping information about them in a spatial context.
- **Places and Regions**—The identities and lives of individuals and peoples are rooted in particular places and in those human constructs called regions.
- **Physical Systems**—Physical processes, such as erosion and flooding, shape Earth's surface and interact with plant and animal life to create, sustain, and modify ecosystems.
- **Human Systems**—People are central to geography in that human activities help shape Earth's surface, human settlements and structures are part of Earth's surface, and humans compete for control of the Earth's surface.
- **Environment and Society**—Environment means the surroundings, including natural elements and elements created by humans. The physical environment is modified by human activities, largely as a consequence of the ways in which human societies value and use Earth's natural resources, and human activities are also influenced by Earth's physical features and processes.
- **The Uses of Geography**—Knowledge of geography enables people to develop an understanding of the relationships between people, places, and environments over time—that is, of Earth as it was, is, and might be.

ECONOMICS: SOME KEY THEMES AND CONCEPTS

- **Economic Systems** include traditional, command, market, and mixed systems. Each must answer the three basic economic questions: What goods and services are to be produced and in what quantities? How shall these goods and services be produced? For whom shall goods and services be produced?

- **Factors of Production** are human, natural, and capital resources that, when combined, can be converted to various goods and services (for example, land, labor, and capital are used to produce food).
- **Needs and Wants** means those goods and services that are essential, such as food, clothing, and shelter (needs), and those goods and services that people would like to have to improve the quality of their lives, such as education, security, health care, and entertainment (wants).
- **Scarcity** means the conflict between unlimited needs and wants and limited natural and human resources.
- **Science and Technology** means the tools and methods used by people to get what they need and want.

CIVICS, CITIZENSHIP, AND GOVERNMENT: SOME KEY THEMES AND CONCEPTS

- **Citizenship** means membership in a community (neighborhood, school, region, state, nation, world) with its accompanying rights, responsibilities, and dispositions.
- **Civic Values** are those important principles that serve as the foundation for our democratic form of government. These values include justice; honesty; self-discipline; due process of law; equality; majority rule with respect for minority rights; and respect of self, others, and property.
- **Decision Making** means the process through which people monitor and influence public and civil life by working with others, clearly articulating ideals and interests, building coalition, seeking consensus, negotiating compromise, and managing conflict.
- **Government** means the formal institutions and processes of a politically organized society with authority to make, enforce, and interpret laws and other binding rules about matters of common interest and concern. Government also refers to the group of people—acting in formal political institutions at national, state, and local levels—who exercise decision-making power or enforce laws and regulations.
- **Human Rights** are those basic political, economic, and social rights to which all human beings are entitled, such as the right to life, liberty, security of person, and a standard of living adequate for the health and well-being of oneself and one's family. Human rights are inalienable and are expressed in various United Nations documents, including the United Nations Charter and the *Universal Declaration of Human Rights.*
- **Justice** means fair, equal, proportional, or appropriate treatment rendered to individuals in interpersonal, societal, or government interactions.

- **Nation-State** means a geographic/political organization that unites people through a common government.
- **Political Systems** include monarchies, dictatorships, and democracies and address certain basic questions of government, such as: What should a government have the power to do? What should a government not have the power to do? A political system also provides for ways in which parts of that system interrelate and combine to perform specific functions of government.
- **Power** is the ability of people to compel or influence the actions of others. Legitimate, or rightful, power is called authority.

Preparing for the Regents

This section of the book provides you with strategies for success on the Regents Examination in Global History and Geography. Because you will need to pass the examination in order to graduate from high school, these strategies are important for you to learn and master. They will also help you to succeed in other types of academic work.

UNDERSTANDING SOCIAL STUDIES

To do well in your study of global history and geography and to pass the Regents Examination, you need to understand three related elements of social studies. On the Regents Examination, you will be asked to demonstrate your mastery of the *factual content* of the global history and geography course, the *concepts* that recur over time, and the *skills* you have mastered.

Specific Factual Content

In a social studies course, you learn about specific historical events and figures. For example, you learn that the French Revolution occurred in 1789 and that Napoleon carried its ideals throughout much of Europe. This is part of the specific content of the global history and geography course you are taking.

Concepts

In social studies courses, you also learn about themes and concepts such as *change* and *nationalism.* (See "Key Themes and Concepts," which begins on page 2 of this book.) You learn how the French Revolution brought change to France and other lands. You also examine the role that this revolution played in developing and spreading nationalism. In addition, you link developments in France to developments in other places and at different times. You may discuss the similarities and differences in other revolutions, or the types of factors that lead to revolutionary movements. Understanding these connections across place and time is as important as knowing facts about the events themselves.

Skills

In a social studies course, you acquire skills. These skills help you to gather, organize, use, and present information. For example, you learn to interpret various types of documents. Historical documents include maps, graphs, and political cartoons. When you read a circle graph that illustrates class structure and land ownership in France, or when you interpret a political cartoon about Napoleon, you are using social studies skills.

A GLOSSARY OF SKILL WORDS

Following is a glossary of skill words that you will see often on the Regents Examination and in other social studies materials. Comprehending these words will help you do well on the Regents Examination.

Analyze to break an idea or concept into parts in order to determine their nature and relationships

Assess to determine the importance, significance, size, or value of

Categorize to place in a class or group; to classify

Classify to arrange in classes or to place in a group according to a system

Compare to state the similarities between two or more examples

Contrast to differentiate; to state the differences between two or more examples

Define to explain what something is or means

Describe to illustrate in words; to tell about

Develop to explain more clearly; to reveal bit by bit

Differentiate to state the difference or differences among two or more examples

Discuss to make observations using facts, reasoning, and argument; to present in some detail

Evaluate to examine and judge the significance, worth, or condition of; to determine the value of

Explain to make plain or understandable; to give reasons for

Generalize to reach a broad conclusion, avoiding specifics, or to base an overall law on particular examples

Hypothesize to present an explanation or an assumption that remains to be proved

Identify to establish the essential character of

Illustrate to make clear or obvious by using examples or comparisons

Incorporate to introduce into or include as a part of something

Infer to conclude or judge from evidence; to draw a conclusion through reasoning

Investigate to research; to inquire into and examine with care

Organize to arrange in a systematic way

Recognize to identify by appearance or characteristics

Restate to say again in a slightly different way

Scrutinize to investigate closely; to examine or inquire into critically

Show to point out; to set forth clearly a position or idea by stating it and giving data that support it

STRUCTURE OF THE REGENTS EXAMINATION

You will have three hours to complete the Regents Examination. The test will include three types of questions.

Multiple-Choice Questions

Together, the multiple-choice questions will account for 55 percent of the points to be earned. There are usually about 50 multiple-choice questions on the Regents Examination. Four possible choices will be provided for each question, only one of which is correct.

Thematic Essay Question

There will be one question of this type on the test, and it will account for 15 percent of the points to be earned. You will be asked to write a thematic essay on a particular topic. Clear and definite directions will be provided to guide you in writing your essay.

Document-Based Question

There will be one multisection document-based question, and it will account for 30 percent of the points to be earned. This question has two major parts. Part A requires that you look at several historical documents and answer one or more questions about each one. Part B requires that you write a clear essay, using evidence from these documents and your knowledge of global history and geography.

You will find examples of all of these types of questions at the end of every unit, in the sample tests, and in the part of the book you are now reading. By working with these examples, you will become familiar with the Regents Examination and build skills for approaching these types of questions. This work will help you get the highest score possible.

STRATEGIES FOR THE REGENTS EXAMINATION

The Regents Examination will cover material that you studied in your Global History and Geography course. Some subjects are more likely to appear on the test than others, however. This book will help you review these topics thoroughly.

This book will also teach you how to approach the topics in ways that will help you succeed on all parts of the Regents Examination. Several concepts are especially important.

Understanding the Themes

The test will be built around major themes that recur throughout history. Many themes are listed and defined for you in the Key Themes and Concepts portion of this book. The most common

Regents themes are reviewed with examples in the Thematic Review section of this book. As you prepare for the Regents Examination, keep in mind the themes that are most likely to appear on the test. Make sure that you understand these themes and can provide examples of each. Some of the most important themes are listed below.

Belief Systems

Change

Conflict

Culture and Intellectual Life

Diversity

Economic Systems

Geography and the Environment

Imperialism

Interdependence

Justice and Human Rights

Movement of People and Goods (Cultural Diffusion)

Nationalism

Political Systems

Science and Technology

Urbanization

Making Connections Across Place and Time

You will do well on the test if you can make connections among events and developments in different parts of the world and in different time periods. As you study various regions and eras, try to see similarities and differences in events that took place. For example, revolutions occurred in many parts of the world in the 1700s and 1800s. How were these revolutions similar? How were they different? How did earlier revolutions have an impact on later ones? As you review global history and geography, look for patterns and generalizations that hold true across place and time.

Understanding Causes and Impacts

The Regents Examination will also require that you understand the cause-and-effect links between events. As you review major events and turning points, make sure that you understand the factors and conditions that caused them. Then

make sure that you can explain the impacts that these events had on later developments.

Practice in Analyzing Documents

This review book provides you with many historical documents, including written documents, maps, tables, charts, graphs, and political cartoons. The multiple-choice and document-based parts of the test will require you to analyze many types of documents. You will be expected to take into account both the source of each document and the author's point of view.

Developing Your Writing Skills

You will earn a higher score on the test if you practice and improve your ability to communicate through writing. Essay-writing skills are required for both the thematic essay and the document-based question. It is most important to write essays that demonstrate a logical plan of organization and include a strong introduction and conclusion.

MULTIPLE-CHOICE QUESTIONS

More than half of the points to be earned on the Regents Examination (55 percent) are earned by answering multiple-choice questions. You will therefore want to get the highest possible score in this section.

Strategies for Multiple-Choice Questions

Keep several points in mind when you are answering the multiple-choice questions on the Regents Examination.

1. Read the entire question carefully. Read all the choices before you make a decision.

2. Eliminate any choices that you are sure are not true, crossing them out in the test booklet.

3. Remember that in the Regents Examination, there is no penalty for guessing. (This is *not* true of all multiple-choice tests.) Therefore, you should make your best guess at an answer to *every* question.

4. See if there is a key phrase that signals what you should be looking for in the question. Not

all questions have such phrases. However, you should be aware of certain signal words and phrases.

Signals for Questions About Cause and Effect: *one effect, one result, is most directly influenced by, have led directly to, have resulted in, a major cause of, are a direct result of*

Signals for Questions That Require an Example: *best illustrates, best reflects, are all examples of, best explains, is an example of*

Signals for Questions That Ask for a Main Idea: *main idea, primarily characterized by, formed the basis for*

Signals for Questions That Ask About Similarities or Differences: *are similar, one similarity, one difference between*

Types of Multiple-Choice Questions

Although you will see many types of multiple-choice questions on the Regents Examination, all fall into one or more of the following general categories.

UNIT CONTENT QUESTIONS The test will include multiple-choice questions that cover material from each of the eight units in this book.

CROSS-UNIT QUESTIONS Questions that ask you to respond to historical situations or people discussed in several different units will also appear on the test. These questions often ask you to make a deduction that is *valid* (true) about the situations or people, find a *similarity* between them, or identify a *characteristic* that is common to all.

THEMATIC QUESTIONS Some questions will address general social studies themes such as nationalism, imperialism, political systems, or economic systems. These questions often ask you to provide *the best example of* something, explain *how it developed,* or describe *characteristics of* a particular concept or system. The themes that these questions may deal with are listed in the Key Themes and Concepts section of this book and highlighted in the Thematic Review.

QUESTIONS BASED ON DOCUMENTS Some multiple-choice questions are based on documents. Types of documents that may appear include:

- A short passage
- A map
- A graph
- A table or chart
- A political cartoon

Such document-based questions often ask for the *main idea* of a passage or cartoon. Sometimes they ask you to identify an *accurate statement* or the statement *best supported by the data.* They may also ask you to choose the *valid conclusion* drawn from the document. These types of questions often require both skills in interpreting documents and factual knowledge of global history and geography.

Sample Unit Content Questions

Each of the next two questions tests your knowledge of content from a specific unit of the Global History and Geography course.

1 A negative effect of the partitioning of India in 1947 was that
   1 foreign rule was reestablished in India
   2 Hinduism became the only religion practiced in India
   3 the government policy of nonalignment further divided Indian society
   4 civil unrest, territorial disputes, and religious conflict continued throughout the region

You know from the question that the answer must be an *effect* and that it must be *negative.* Choice 1 cannot be the answer, since British rule ended in 1947. Choice 2 is incorrect because Islam, Sikhism, and other religions besides Hinduism are practiced in India. Choice 3 cannot be correct, since nonalignment was a reaction to the Cold War, not to partition. Choice 4 is the correct answer because the creation of Pakistan and India increased tensions and conflicts between Hindus and Muslims in the region.

2 Which group had the greatest influence on early Russian culture?
1 Franks
2 Ottoman Turks
3 Byzantine empire
4 Roman Catholic Church

The important words in this question are *the greatest influence.* The Franks (Choice 1) were a Germanic tribe of the early Middle Ages. They had a strong effect on Western Europe but not on Russia. The Ottoman Turks (Choice 2) had an influence on Russia, but their influence occurred later. The Roman Catholic Church (Choice 4) had little influence because the Orthodox Christian Church was adopted by Russia. The Byzantine empire (Choice 3), however, is the correct answer because it had an enormous impact on early Russia.

Sample Thematic Questions

Each of the next two multiple-choice questions deals with a specific theme or concept.

3 Which aspect of a nation's culture is most directly influenced by the physical geography of that nation?
1 form of government
2 population distribution
3 religious beliefs
4 social class system

The question involves physical geography and its influence on a nation. The key phrase in the question is: *is most directly influenced.* If you understand physical geography, you know that it has a great influence on where people live. For example, people tend to live near sources of water. Large populations live where the geography easily allows settlement. The answer to this question would therefore be Choice 2. Geography sometimes influences forms of government (Choice 1), as in the Greek city-states, but it has a more direct influence on population distribution. It has even less influence on religious beliefs (Choice 3) and the social class system (Choice 4).

4 Which quotation best reflects a feeling of nationalism?
1 "An eye for an eye and a tooth for a tooth."
2 "A person's greatest social obligation is loyalty to the family."
3 "For God, King, and Country."
4 "Opposition to evil is as much a duty as is cooperation with good."

This question is about nationalism, a theme you need to understand to prepare for the Regents Examination. First, you must know what nationalism is: a feeling of pride in and devotion to one's country. Then you must decide which of the possible answers best expresses that idea. Choice 1 has to do with justice, not nationalism. Choice 2 has to do with social behavior and Choice 4 with moral behavior. Only Choice 3 expresses the idea of devotion to one's nation, so Choice 3 is the correct answer.

Sample Cross-Unit Questions

Each of the next two questions deals with content from two or more units of the Global History and Geography course.

5 One similarity found in the leadership of Peter the Great of Russia, Kemal Atatürk of Turkey, and Jawaharlal Nehru of India is that each leader
1 expanded his territory by invading Greece
2 borrowed ideas and technology from Western Europe
3 supported equal rights for women
4 increased the power of religious groups in his nation

Each of these leaders appears in a different unit of this book. Note that this question asks for *one similarity.* This means that the answer must be true for all three leaders. Therefore, if you know that a choice is not true of even one leader, it cannot be the right answer. Choice 1 is not correct because none of the three leaders invaded Greece. Although each of these leaders supported some reforms or societal changes that involved women, none called for equal rights for women, so Choice 3 is incorrect. Peter the Great and Kemal Atatürk actually decreased the power of religious groups in their nations, so Choice 4 cannot be correct. All of these leaders did, however, borrow ideas and technology from the West, making Choice 2 the correct answer.

6   The societies of traditional China, feudal Japan, and czarist Russia were all characterized by
   1   a rigid class structure
   2   much interaction with other cultures
   3   great economic change
   4   rapidly changing social values

This question also asks you about content from several units of your Global History and Geography course. Familiarity with all three cultures would help you select Choice 1. None of the other choices is characteristic of *any* of the civilizations, so even if you were familiar only with czarist Russia, you would still be able to choose the correct answer (1).

Sample Document-Based Questions

The remaining sample questions are based on historical documents.

Base your answer to question 7 on the poem below and on your knowledge of social studies.

> May our country
> Taking what is good
> And rejecting what is bad
> Be not inferior
> to any other
> —Mutsuhito

7   According to this Japanese poem, Mutsuhito believed that Japan should modernize by
   1   completely changing Japanese society
   2   borrowing selectively from other societies
   3   controlling other cultures that were superior
   4   rejecting foreign influence

Here, you are asked to demonstrate understanding of Mutsuhito's poem. Choice 1 is not appropriate because the poem does not indicate whether Mutsuhito favored just a little change or massive change. Choice 3 is incorrect because the poem talks about borrowing from other cultures, not controlling them. Choice 4 is wrong because the poem advises rejection only of "what is bad." Choice 2 correctly summarizes the meaning of the poem.

Base your answer to question 8 on the map below and on your knowledge of social studies.

African Kingdoms, 1000 B.C.–A.D. 1600

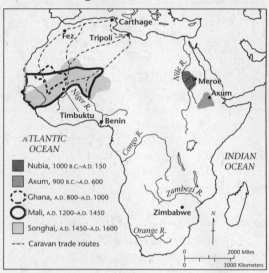

8   Which conclusion regarding early African trade is supported by the information provided by this map?
   1   The kingdom of Zimbabwe grew rich from trade with Egypt.
   2   The kingdoms of West Africa traded with the city-states of East Africa.
   3   The Congo and Zambezi Rivers played an important role in Africa's early trade.
   4   The West African kingdoms had trading contacts with the cities of the Mediterranean.

The question asks which conclusion can be supported by information provided in the map. Only Choice 4 can be supported by information from the map. Trade routes are shown linking the West African kingdoms with the Mediterranean cities of Carthage and Tripoli. Even if any of the other selections are true, they *are not supported* by evidence in this map. The map provides no information about how rich Zimbabwe was, about trade with East African cities, or about the role of the Congo and Zambezi Rivers.

Base your answer to questions 9 and 10 on the table below and on your knowledge of social studies.

Statistics for Selected Nations of South Asia

Nations	Population Density (per sq mi)	Per Capita Income (dollars)	Percentage of Labor Force in Agriculture	Literacy Rate (percentage)
Bangladesh	2,294	1,260	65	38
Malaysia	164	10,750	21	83
Myanmar	181	1,120	67	83
Pakistan	440	2,300	47	38
Thailand	303	7,700	43	94

Source: *The World Almanac, 1999.*

9   Which nations have more than half of the labor force engaged in agriculture?
1   Bangladesh and Myanmar
2   Pakistan and Bangladesh
3   Thailand and Malaysia
4   Myanmar and Thailand

Question 9 asks you to examine one column of the table. Choices 2 and 3 are incorrect because none of the nations mentioned has more than 50 percent of the labor force engaged in agriculture. Choice 4 is incorrect because only Myanmar has the appropriate percentage. Choice 1 is correct, listing the two nations with more than half of the labor force in agriculture.

10   Which is a valid conclusion, based on the information in the table?
1   Bangladesh has the highest per capita income.
2   Myanmar has the smallest percentage of workers involved in farming.
3   Malaysia has the highest population density.
4   Thailand has the highest percentage of children enrolled in school.

For question 10, the correct answer is Choice 4. A high literacy rate (94 percent) indicates that a high percentage of children are learning to read in school. Choice 1 is not true: Bangladesh has nearly the lowest per capita income of the nations shown. Choice 2 is incorrect, since Myanmar has the highest percentage of workers involved in farming. Choice 3 is incorrect because Malaysia actually has the lowest population density, not the highest.

Base your answer to question 11 on the graph below and on your knowledge of social studies.

Population Projections for Selected East and Southern African Nations

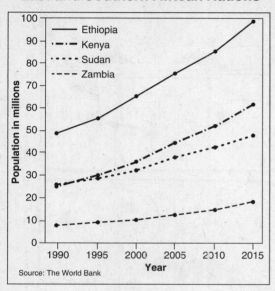

Source: The World Bank

11   Based on the information in the graph, which is a valid conclusion about the populations of East and Southern African nations?
   1 The nation with the largest population in 1990 will have the lowest population in 2015.
   2 Population will rise in all countries, but it will rise fastest in Ethiopia.
   3 Populations will level off in all of these nations after the year 2005.
   4 In 1995, the population of Zambia was approximately 28 million people.

You can rule out Choice 1 because the ranks of the nations changed very little if at all. You can eliminate Choice 3 because one glance at the lines shows all four populations continuing to rise more steeply after 1995. You can rule out Choice 4 by reading the graph and seeing that Zambia's population in 1995 was about 10 million. Choice 2, however, is a valid conclusion to draw from this graph.

Base your answer to question 12 on the cartoon below and on your knowledge of social studies.

THE OLD MAN AND THE SEA

By permission of Rex Babin, *Times Union*, Albany, NY.

12   What is the main idea of the cartoon?
   1 Cuba's fishing industry is suffering a decline.
   2 Castro rode the wave of world communism to a successful conclusion.
   3 Cuba is isolated without Soviet economic support.
   4 Castro bears responsibility for the failure of communism in Eastern Europe.

Questions on political cartoons require skill in interpreting such cartoons as well as knowledge of global history. When you look at a political cartoon, make sure that you can identify its elements. Many are symbolic. For example, the small boat marked *Cuba* represents the country of Cuba. The figure in it is a caricature of Fidel Castro, the president of Cuba. The carcass of the fish has a hammer and sickle, the national symbol of the former Soviet Union. The image communicates the idea that the Soviet Union is dead.

Choice 1 is incorrect because the cartoon is clearly about political issues, not about the Cuban fishing industry. You can rule out Choice 2 because the figure in the boat does not look happy. Also, you have read that Cuba has experienced difficulty since the fall of communism. Choice 4 is not correct because Castro is feeling the *effects* of change; he was not the *cause*. That leaves only Choice 2, which you know to be true: Cuba has had difficulties without Soviet support.

Base your answer to question 13 on the cartoon below and on your knowledge of social studies.

13 Which conclusion is best supported by the cartoon?

1 Imprisonment of political dissidents rarely ends opposition to the government.
2 The United Nations supports punishment of acts of civil disobedience.
3 Better media coverage would prevent the imprisonment of protesters.
4 Mistreatment of political prisoners often results in their acceptance of government policies.

Again, you must first examine the cartoon and analyze its elements. The name *Mandela* and your knowledge of global history tell you that this cartoon shows the time when Nelson Mandela was in prison in South Africa. You notice that Mandela is of normal size when he enters prison in 1962 but has grown greatly by the time he emerges in 1990. His increased size represents his increased world stature during the time of his imprisonment. You can eliminate Choice 2 because it is untrue and because the United Nations is not featured in this cartoon. Choice 3 can be ruled out because media coverage is not shown by the cartoon. Choice 4 is also not supported by the cartoon, since there is no indication that Mandela accepted government policies. Instead, Mandela's changed size indicates that Choice 1 is the answer. Instead of stopping opposition by imprisoning Mandela, the South African government only succeeded in furthering his cause of opposition to apartheid.

THEMATIC ESSAY QUESTION

There will be one thematic essay question on the Regents Examination. It will count for 15 percent of the total points you may receive. This section of the exam requires you to understand, interpret, and explain a key social studies theme or concept. In your essay, you should be able to:

- State a main idea in a thesis statement.
- Develop it and add supporting details.
- Summarize it with an effective conclusion.

Basic Characteristics

The directions for thematic essay questions always consist of three parts: a theme, a task, and suggestions.

THE THEME This part of the question identifies a broad social studies theme that will be the general topic of your essay. The theme is given more focus by a brief explanatory statement that follows the statement of the theme. (To review the most common themes tested in Regents Examinations, see the Thematic Review section at the end of this book.)

THE TASK The second part of a thematic essay question is the task. The task section usually has three parts and presents the instructions you will need to write your essay. Generally, you will be asked to define or describe a theme or concept, to give a specific number of examples or results, and then to evaluate the theme or concept in some way. Typical forms of evaluation include describing causes or effects and evaluating positive or negative aspects.

SUGGESTIONS The final part of a thematic essay question is the suggestions section. This part lists specific areas that you might choose to discuss in your essay. The suggestions might name people, nations, or civilizations, depending on the topic of the question. These are, of course, only suggestions, and you may choose to write about other examples that are relevant to the essay topic. Often, the suggestions will caution you not to choose the United States as your topic. If this warning is present, pay attention to it. You will not receive full credit for an answer that does not follow the directions.

Strategy for the Thematic Essay Question

Keep the following strategies in mind as you approach a thematic essay question.

1. Read the entire question through first.

2. After you have read the question, begin jotting down any ideas you have.

3. After you have jotted down your initial ideas, begin to make a brief outline. Organization is important in writing a good essay. The outline does not need to be very detailed, but it should include enough information to help you remember all the points that you want to use in the essay. It should also help you to see whether your essay has a logical organization.

4. Use the suggestions to help you recall the importance of the theme in different places and times.

5. Develop your essay logically.

6. Do not merely list facts. Analyze and evaluate the information, and compare or contrast various aspects.

7. Make sure that you provide examples to support your ideas.

8. Make sure that you have completed each of the items listed in the task section.

9. Make sure that your essay has both a strong introduction and a strong conclusion. You cannot get full credit for your essay if either of these elements is missing or weak.

SAMPLE THEMATIC ESSAY QUESTIONS

The thematic essay questions included throughout this book will provide you with insight into the types of questions you will see on the actual Regents Examination. Below are two sample thematic essay questions. They follow the same format as those that will appear on the actual Regents Examination.

Directions

Read the following instructions that include a theme, a task, and suggestions. Follow the instructions to create a well-organized essay that has an introduction with a thesis statement, several paragraphs explaining the thesis, and a conclusion.

Theme: Change

The Industrial Revolution in Europe made great changes in the lives of individuals and nations.

Task

- Define the term *Industrial Revolution.*
- Select a nation you have studied, and describe three changes brought about by the Industrial Revolution in that country.
- Describe a situation in which the Industrial Revolution had a positive effect and one in which it had a negative effect.

Suggestions

You may discuss any nation or empire that you have studied, except the United States. Some suggestions you may wish to consider are Britain, France, Germany, and Japan. You are not limited to these suggestions.

Directions

Read the following instructions that include a theme, a task, and suggestions. Follow the instructions to create a well-organized essay that has an introduction with a thesis statement, several paragraphs explaining the thesis, and a conclusion.

Theme: Civilization

Throughout history, great civilizations have existed in various parts of the world. The cultural and intellectual achievements of these civilizations contributed to the advancement of humankind.

Task

- Define the term *civilization.*
- Describe some examples of cultural or intellectual achievements made by past civilizations. Identify each example with the particular civilization that made the contribution.
- Explain the lasting importance of each of these achievements or contributions to global history.

Suggestions

You may discuss any civilization from your study of global history, except the United States. Some civilizations you might wish to consider include ancient Egypt, classical Rome, the Gupta empire, classical China, or the Muslim golden age. You are not limited to these suggestions.

THEMATIC ESSAY SCORING

Knowing how your essay will be scored will help you write it effectively. Essays are scored with point values from 0 to 5. An essay receiving a score of 5 answers the question in a complete, comprehensive manner. You would receive a score of 0 only if you failed to address the theme at all, wrote an essay that was completely illegible, or turned in a blank paper.

The scoring rubric that follows represents the generic criteria on which your essay will be scored.

GENERIC SCORING RUBRIC

THEMATIC ESSAY

SCORE OF 5:
- Thoroughly develops all aspects of the task evenly and in depth
- Is more analytical than descriptive (analyzes, evaluates, and/or creates information)
- Richly supports the theme with many relevant facts, examples, and details
- Demonstrates a logical and clear plan of organization; includes an introduction and a conclusion that are beyond a restatement of the theme

SCORE OF 4:
- Develops all aspects of the task but may do so somewhat unevenly
- Is both descriptive and analytical (applies, analyzes, evaluates, and/or creates information)
- Supports the theme with relevant facts, examples, and details
- Demonstrates a logical and clear plan of organization; includes an introduction and a conclusion that are beyond a restatement of the theme

SCORE OF 3:
- Develops all aspects of the task with little depth or develops most aspects of the task in some depth
- Is more descriptive than analytical (applies, may analyze, and/or evaluate information)
- Includes some relevant facts, examples, and details; may include some minor inaccuracies
- Demonstrates a satisfactory plan of organization; includes an introduction and a conclusion that may be a restatement of the theme

SCORE OF 2:
- Minimally develops all aspects of the task or develops some aspects of the task in some depth
- Is primarily descriptive; may include faulty, weak, or isolated application or analysis
- Includes few relevant facts, examples, and details; may include some inaccuracies
- Demonstrates a general plan of organization; may lack focus; may contain digressions; may not clearly identify which aspect of the task is being addressed; may lack an introduction and/or a conclusion

SCORE OF 1:
- Minimally develops some aspects of the task
- Is descriptive; may lack understanding, application, or analysis
- Includes few relevant facts, examples, or details; may include inaccuracies
- May demonstrate a weakness in organization; may lack focus; may contain digressions; may not clearly identify which aspect of the task is being addressed; may lack an introduction and/or a conclusion

SCORE OF 0:
- Fails to develop the task or may only refer to the theme in a general way; *OR* includes no relevant facts, examples, or details; *OR* includes only the theme, task, or suggestions as copied from the test booklet; *OR* is illegible; *OR* is a blank paper

DOCUMENT-BASED QUESTION

This type of question presents you with up to eight historical documents on a single subject. The documents may be letters, speeches, or other written records; maps; charts; political cartoons; graphs; or tables.

Basic Characteristics

Questions based on historical documents have several characteristics. The documents provided give information or express viewpoints about a common theme. For space reasons, the samples you will see here and at the end of each unit will include only a few documents. Those on the test, however, may include up to eight documents.

A document-based question always has two parts. Part A requires short answers to specific questions about the documents. Part B requires you to write an essay. The themes for these essays are based on the same social studies themes and concepts as are used for thematic essays. Refer to the sample shown on the following pages as you read this information about document-based questions.

GENERAL DIRECTIONS The question will begin with a set of directions. These directions will tell you what to do for each part of the question.

HISTORICAL CONTEXT Each question will contain a short statement that defines the historical context for the question. Read this statement carefully. It will help you understand the main topic to be discussed.

TASK This statement defines the overall task that you will perform as you examine the documents provided.

PART A: SHORT ANSWER In this part of the question, you will be presented with the documents themselves. Documents that are quotations will be enclosed within boxes. The author of the quotation will be clearly identified. Documents may also be maps, charts, or political cartoons. Each document will be followed by one or possibly more questions. The questions will ask you to consider the viewpoint and source of the document. This is important because the author of a document may have a bias or a special motive that makes it difficult to accept his or her words as the whole truth. For example, a person who is trying to persuade soldiers to go into battle will not present the point of view of the opposing side very completely. Skills in interpreting the information in documents are very important.

PART B: ESSAY The essay portion of the question includes a set of general instructions and repeats the historical context. Pay very close attention to the instructions. Note that they call for a well-organized essay with both an introduction and a conclusion. They require you to use evidence from the documents to support your response. You should not, however, merely repeat the contents of the documents. Be sure also to include specific, related information from your knowledge of global history and geography. You must use information beyond that included in the particular documents. Otherwise you will not receive full credit for your essay. For the highest possible score, refer to all of the documents provided in the question, and include additional information from your knowledge of global history.

Strategy for the Document-Based Question

ANSWERING PART A Your first task is to answer each of the questions about the documents. Examine each passage carefully, and look closely at each image. Read the question or questions and then reexamine the documents. Keep in mind the historical context. Recognize the various viewpoints that are being expressed. Finally, write a clear answer to each question.

ANSWERING PART B You can approach this part much as you would a thematic essay, except that you need to consider how to incorporate evidence from the documents provided as well as knowledge from your Global History and Geography course.

You will find it useful to make a brief outline as you did for the thematic essay, showing what you plan to use as a thesis statement, what your supporting facts will be, where you will use various documents for support, and what your conclusion will be.

Take a look at the scoring rubric that follows the sample document-based question. A rubric like this one will be used to score Part B of the document-based question.

To get a high score on the essay portion of the test, do the following:

- Complete all parts of the task thoroughly.
- Provide analysis and interpretation of all or most of the documents supplied in the question.

Information from the documents must be included within the body of your essay.

- Include as much related outside information as you can. Relevant outside information is crucial to a high score. Support your essay with related facts, examples, and details.
- Write an essay that is organized clearly and logically. Outlining your essay will help you maintain a clear organization.
- After you have finished writing, check to be sure that you have included a strong introduction and a strong conclusion.

SAMPLE DOCUMENT-BASED QUESTION

The following sample of a document-based question includes three documents. As already noted, a document-based question on the Regents Examination could show up to eight documents. Otherwise, the short-answer questions and essay question in this sample are similar to what you will see on the Regents Examination. For additional practice with questions based on documents, see the Questions for Regents Practice at the end of each unit as well as the sample tests.

Directions
Read the documents in Part A and answer the question or questions after each document. Then read the directions for Part B and write your essay.

Historical Context
Throughout history, leaders have had vastly differing viewpoints on whether violence or war is ever justified. Some leaders, for example, have felt that violence is justified for certain purposes. Others have believed that violence against others is never the right choice. These viewpoints have had powerful effects on historical events.

Task
Evaluate several viewpoints on whether violence or war is ever justified in order to achieve a desired goal.

Part A: Short Answer
Directions: Analyze the documents and answer the question or questions that follow each document, using the space provided.

DOCUMENT 1

What difference does it make to the dead, the orphans and the homeless, whether the mad destruction is wrought under the name of totalitarianism or the holy name of democracy and liberty?

—Mohandas Gandhi, 1948

1 Does Gandhi think that violence may be justified if the cause is a good one? Explain your answer, referring to the quotation.

_____

_____

_____

_____

_____

DOCUMENT 2
The Atomic Bomb

PROBLEM
Should U.S. President Truman use the atomic bomb against Japan?

Reasons FOR	Reasons AGAINST
• It would save American lives. • It would bring a quick end to the war. • It would show the power of the United States to any future enemies.	• It would cause massive destruction. • Once used, it would more likely be used again. • It would release deadly radioactivity.

Decision
Truman orders atomic bomb dropped on Hiroshima and Nagasaki.

RESULTS
• More than 110,000 die. • Japan surrenders.

2 List two reasons why President Truman decided to use atomic bombs against Japan.

_____

_____

_____

_____

_____

3 Describe two reasons why some Americans disagreed with President Truman's decision.

_____

_____

_____

_____

_____

DOCUMENT 3

Brutality is respected. Brutality and physical strength. The plain man in the street respects nothing but brutal strength and ruthlessness—women, too, for that matter, women and children. The people need wholesome fear.

—Adolf Hitler, 1936

4   How did Adolf Hitler justify his inhumanity? Explain your answer, referring to the quotation.

_____

_____

_____

_____

_____

_____

DOCUMENT 4

A government should not mobilize an army out of anger, military leaders should not provoke a war out of wrath. Act when it is beneficial, desist when it is not. Anger can revert to joy, wrath can revert to delight, but a nation destroyed cannot be restored to existence, and the dead cannot be restored to life.

—Sun Tzu, *The Art of War*, c. 300 B.C.

5   Why should Sun Tzu say it is bad to start a war out of anger? Explain your answer, referring to the quotation.

_____

_____

_____

_____

_____

_____

DOCUMENT 5

> *A revolution is not a dinner party, or writing an essay, or painting a picture or doing embroidery;*
> *it cannot be so refined, so leisurely and gentle, so kind, courteous, restrained, and generous. A*
> *revolution is an insurrection, an act of violence by which one class overthrows another.*
>
> **—Mao Zedong, leader of the Communist Revolution in China**

6 According to Mao, what means are necessary in order for a revolution to succeed? Explain your
   answer, referring to the quotation.

   _____

   _____

   _____

   _____

   _____

   _____

Part B: Essay

Directions:
- Write a well-organized essay that includes an introduction, several paragraphs, and a conclusion.
- Use evidence from the documents to support your response.
- Do not simply repeat the contents of the documents.
- Include specific, related outside information.

Historical Context

Throughout history, leaders have had vastly differing viewpoints on whether violence or war is ever justified. Some leaders, for example, have felt that violence is justified for certain purposes. Others have believed that violence against others is never the right choice. These viewpoints have had powerful effects
on historical events.

Task

Using information from the documents and your knowledge of global history and geography, write an essay that evaluates the differing views people have regarding whether violence or war can be justified. Take
a position, stating whether you think violence or war is ever justified. Support your position effectively.

   **Be sure to include specific historical details. You must also include additional information from
your knowledge of global history.**

DOCUMENT-BASED QUESTION SCORING

Knowing how your document-based essay will be scored will help you write it effectively. Like thematic essays, document-based essays are scored with point values from 0 to 5. An essay receiving a score of 5 answers the question in a complete, comprehensive manner. You would receive a score of 0 only if you failed to address the theme at all, wrote an essay that was completely illegible, or turned in a blank paper.

The scoring rubric that follows represents the generic criteria on which your document-based essay will be scored.

GENERIC SCORING RUBRIC

DOCUMENT-BASED QUESTION

SCORE OF 5:
- Thoroughly develops all aspects of the task evenly and in depth
- Is more analytical than descriptive (analyzes, evaluates, and/or creates information)
- Incorporates relevant information from at *least* **xxx** documents
- Incorporates substantial relevant outside information
- Richly supports the theme with many relevant facts, examples, and details
- Demonstrates a logical and clear plan of organization; includes an introduction and a conclusion that are beyond a restatement of the theme

SCORE OF 4:
- Develops all aspects of the task but may do so somewhat unevenly
- Is both descriptive and analytical (applies, analyzes, evaluates, and/or creates information)
- Incorporates relevant information from *at least* **xxx** documents
- Incorporates relevant outside information
- Supports the theme with relevant facts, examples, and details
- Demonstrates a logical and clear plan of organization; includes an introduction and a conclusion that are beyond a restatement of the theme

SCORE OF 3:
- Develops all aspects of the task with little depth *or* develops most aspects of the task in some depth
- Is more descriptive than analytical (applies, may analyze, and/or evaluate information)
- Incorporates some relevant information from some of the documents
- Incorporates limited relevant outside information
- Includes some relevant facts, examples, and details; may include some minor inaccuracies
- Demonstrates a satisfactory plan of organization; includes an introduction and a conclusion that may be a restatement of the theme

SCORE OF 2:
- Minimally develops all aspects of the task *or* develops some aspects of the task in some depth
- Is primarily descriptive; may include faulty, weak, or isolated application or analysis
- Incorporates limited relevant information from the documents *or* consists primarily of relevant information copied from the documents
- Presents little or no relevant outside information
- Includes few relevant facts, examples, and details; may include some inaccuracies
- Demonstrates a general plan of organization; may lack focus; may contain digressions; may not clearly identify which aspect of the task is being addressed; may lack an introduction and/or a conclusion

SCORE OF 1:
- Minimally develops some aspects of the task
- Is descriptive; may lack understanding, application, or analysis
- Makes vague, unclear references to the documents or consists primarily of relevant and irrelevant information copied from the documents
- Presents no relevant outside information
- Includes few relevant facts, examples, or details; may include inaccuracies
- May demonstrate a weakness in organization; may lack focus; may contain digressions; may not clearly identify which aspect of the task is being addressed; may lack an introduction and/or a conclusion

SCORE OF 0:
- Fails to develop the task or may only refer to the theme in a general way; *OR* includes no relevant facts, examples, or details; *OR* includes only the historical context and/or task as copied from the test booklet; *OR* includes only entire documents copied from the test booklet; *OR* is illegible; *OR* is a blank paper

A FEW FINAL WORDS

You have learned a number of strategies to help you prepare for the multiple-choice, thematic essay, and document-based questions on the Regents Examination in Global History and Geography. Try out these strategies on the practice tests included in the book and on the questions at the end of each unit. This practice will help you find out what works best for you and will allow you to become comfortable with the various types of questions found in the Regents Examination. As you practice more, you will also become confident of your ability to do well on the test.

Make sure you are well rested on the day of the examination. If you have devoted serious effort to your study of global history and geography, reviewed the material in this book, and used the many test items provided here for practice, you will be thoroughly prepared for the exam.

UNIT OVERVIEW

Over the first thousands of years of human existence, people advanced in many different areas. A new era of human development began when humans discovered how to plant crops and domesticate animals. A more settled life and more dependable food sources allowed people to build civilizations with complex political, social, and religious structures. Civilizations began to interact with each other. They shared ideas and technology through such means as trade and conquest. Classical civilizations arose in Africa, Asia, and Europe. These civilizations made contributions in art, architecture, law, government, and other fields. Their achievements continue to affect society today. Ancient civilizations also made an impact on each other and on today's world through the development of powerful belief systems. These belief systems have spread throughout the world and affected cultural development and the course of history.

THEMATIC TIME LINE ACTIVITY

Some of the many themes developed in Unit 1 are:

change	movement of people and goods
geography	culture and intellectual life
urbanization	economic systems
political systems	belief systems

Choose one of the themes listed above. As you review Unit 1, create a thematic time line based on the theme you have chosen. Your time line should stretch from 4000 B.C. to A.D. 500 and include major developments and key turning points having to do with your theme.

1 Early Peoples and River Civilizations

SECTION OVERVIEW

Scientists believe that humans first appeared over two million years ago. The first humans were wandering hunters and gatherers. They made simple tools and weapons from stone, bone, and wood.

With the development of farming, ancient peoples gave up their no-madic lifestyles and established permanent settlements, which grew over time into civilizations. Early civilizations developed in river val-leys. As populations grew, these peoples developed systems of govern-ment, social structures, and belief systems. Migration, trade, and warfare helped ideas move from one culture to another.

KEY THEMES AND CONCEPTS

As you review this section, take special note of the following key themes and concepts:

Environment How did the earliest people adapt to their environment?

Urbanization How did the development of agriculture change the way early people lived?

Political Systems What types of government and social structure were created by early civilizations?

Culture and Intellectual Life What contributions did early people make to later civilizations?

Movement of People and Goods How did trade, warfare, and migration spread ideas among early civilizations?

KEY PEOPLE AND TERMS

As you review this section, be sure you understand the significance of these key people and terms:

nomad	technology	pharaoh	empire
cultural diffusion	civilization	Fertile Crescent	Middle Kingdom
Neolithic	polytheistic	cuneiform	dynasty

★ **THE BIG IDEA**
The Agricultural Revolution led to the first civilizations. These early civilizations:

- relied on a traditional economy based on farming.

- were often located in river valleys.

- developed cities, systems of government, social structures, and belief systems.

- made contributions to later civilizations in tech-nology, the arts, law, and other areas.

- exchanged ideas and de-velopments with other cultures.

EARLY PEOPLES

The first people lived more than two million years ago, in prehistoric times. Prehistory is the time before people invented writing.

Hunters and Gatherers

The earliest people lived during the Old Stone Age, also called the Paleolithic age, which began more than two million years ago. Paleolithic people were **nomads,** or people who moved from place to place, hunting and gathering their food. Their simple social structure consisted of small groups of people who traveled together.

Adapting to Their Environment

Stone Age people adapted to their environment. They made simple tools and weapons, such as digging sticks and spears, from stone, bone, or wood. During Paleolithic times, people developed language, which allowed them to communicate and cooperate during a hunt. Paleolithic people invented clothing made of animal skins. They used fire for warmth as well as for cooking food.

Spiritual Beliefs

Paleolithic people developed some spiritual beliefs. Toward the end of the Old Stone Age, people began burying their dead with care, a practice suggesting that they believed in an afterlife. They buried tools and weapons with their dead.

Migration

Evidence supports the theory that the earliest people lived in East Africa. Their descendants spread to every part of the world. During the Old Stone Age, people migrated north and east into Europe and Asia. After many years, some migrated over a land bridge into North America. Others migrated by boat to islands in the Pacific. Migration led to **cultural diffusion,** or the exchange of ideas, customs, and goods among cultures. Cultural diffusion also occurred through trade and warfare.

THE NEOLITHIC REVOLUTION

Environmental changes brought new climate patterns that contributed to the end of the Old Stone Age. Warmer weather allowed plants to grow where, previously, sheets of ice had dominated the landscape.

Around 10,000 B.C., people made two important discoveries. They learned to plant seeds to grow food, and they learned to domesticate animals. These discoveries meant that people no longer had to wander in search of food. They could live in permanent settlements. This change marked the beginning of the New Stone Age, or **Neolithic** period. Historians call these discoveries the Neolithic Revolution, or the Agricultural Revolution, because farming and domestic animals changed the way people lived.

PREPARING FOR THE REGENTS

How did Paleolithic people acquire food from their natural environment?

KEY THEMES AND CONCEPTS

Movement of People and Goods Three important ways in which cultural diffusion occurs are through migration, trade, and warfare.

The Impact of Agriculture

After the Neolithic Revolution, more abundant food helped the population to increase. Humans' lives changed in many ways:

- **Permanent Settlements** People settled together in villages.
- **New Social Classes** When resources were scarce, groups went to war. Chiefs or headmen emerged. Some men gained prestige as warriors and had great power.
- **New Technology** People began to develop **technology,** or tools and skills they could use to meet their basic needs, such as calendars and plows. Other new technology included the wheel, metal weapons, and metal tools.

These changes paved the way for civilization to emerge.

THE RISE OF CIVILIZATION

About 5,000 years ago, the first civilizations began to develop along river valleys. The rich, fertile farmlands of river valleys helped these civilizations to thrive. Most early **civilizations** were characterized by several basic features:

- Cities
- Central governments
- Traditional economy
- Organized religion
- Social classes
- Art and architecture
- Roads, bridges, and other public works
- System of writing
- Specialized jobs

Cities and Central Government

Cities emerged as farmers cultivated land along river valleys and produced surplus food. Surplus food led to increased population. More systematic leadership than just a headman or council of elders was needed. Governments developed to make sure that enough food was produced and that the city was protected. Rulers also ordered that public works such as roads, bridges, and defensive walls be built.

Traditional Economy

Traditional economies, based primarily on farming, grew up in early civilizations. Skilled craftsworkers made pottery, cloth, and other goods.

Organized Religion

Ancient peoples were **polytheistic,** believing in many gods. Priests and worshipers tried to gain the favor of these gods through complex rituals. They hoped that the gods would ensure plentiful crops and protect their cities.

Job Specialization and Social Classes

People began to specialize in certain jobs because no one person could master all the necessary skills to provide for himself or herself. People became ranked in classes according to their jobs. Priests and nobles

PREPARING FOR THE REGENTS

List and explain five characteristics of early civilizations.

1.

2.

3.

4.

5.

were usually at the top of these societies, followed by warriors and merchants, with peasant farmers and slaves at the bottom.

Art and Architecture

Much early art and architecture consisted of temples and palaces, symbols of the power of rulers.

System of Writing

Writing may have first developed in temples, where many types of records were kept. Early writing was picture writing, consisting of simple drawings. Over time the writing became more symbolic.

EGYPT

One of the earliest civilizations arose in Egypt about 5,000 years ago.

Geographic Setting

Since most of Egypt is a desert, people settled along the Nile River. The Nile provided water for drinking and for irrigation of crops. Yearly floods soaked the land and left rich deposits of silt that kept the agricultural areas fertile. The river also served as a highway for travel.

Religion

Egyptians were polytheistic. The sun god Amon-Re was the chief god. Osiris was the god of the Nile. Osiris controlled the annual flood that made the land fertile. The Egyptians also believed in a host of other gods who served specific functions.

The cornerstone of the religious faith of the Egyptians was a belief in life after death. Egyptians prepared their dead for the afterlife through a preservation process called mummification.

PREPARING FOR THE REGENTS

The Egyptians formed a centralized government with the pharaoh as its focus. As in many ancient civilizations, the pharaohs claimed divine support for their rule and eventually claimed that they themselves were gods. This claim was an effective way to maintain power.

Government

The Egyptian ruler was called a **pharaoh.** Egyptians believed that the pharaoh was both a god and a king. In fact, when a pharaoh died, he was buried in a majestic pyramid. The pyramids took years to build and required enormous planning and organization. When the mummies of pharaohs were buried in pyramids, they were surrounded by possessions for use in the afterlife. After the death of a pharaoh, power usually passed to another member of the family. These ruling families were called dynasties.

Social Structure

Egyptian society was divided into classes. The pharaoh held the highest position in society. Next were the priests, who served the gods and goddesses. Third were the nobles, who fought the pharaoh's wars, followed by the craftspeople and merchants. Near the bottom was the biggest group, the peasant farmers. Beneath the peasants were the slaves.

Women had a higher status in Egyptian society than in any other ancient civilization. A woman could own property, enter business deals, and obtain a divorce.

The Ancient Middle East

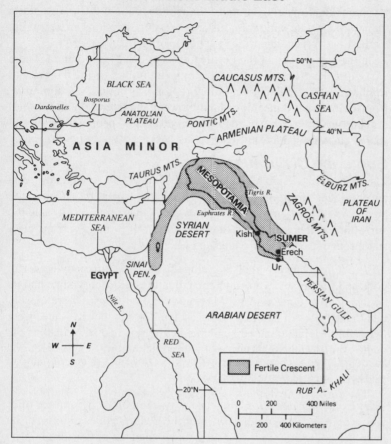

 PREPARING FOR THE REGENTS

Practice your map skills by answering the following questions about the map.

1. Which two rivers ran through the Fertile Crescent?

2. Which two river valley civilizations are shown on this map?

Contributions

The Egyptians made many advances in science and art. The process of mummification helped them learn much about the human body, allowing them to diagnose many illnesses and perform surgery. Egyptians developed a calendar very similar to the one we use today. They also created a system of picture writing called hieroglyphics. Egyptian temples and monuments, as well as the pyramids, have survived thousands of years. Egyptian statues and paintings show daily life, ceremonies, and military victories.

MESOPOTAMIA

Geographic Setting

To the north and east of Egypt, the **Fertile Crescent,** a crescent-shaped region of good farmland created by the Tigris and Euphrates Rivers, stretches from the Persian Gulf to the Mediterranean. The lack of

 PREPARING FOR THE REGENTS

The tools and other technology that a civilization develops tells much about what is important to that culture. Early river valley civilizations developed methods of flood control and irrigation.

 PREPARING FOR THE REGENTS

What geographical features of the Fertile Crescent helped civilization to grow and ideas to spread between cultures?

natural barriers in the Fertile Crescent allowed frequent migrations and invasions, while the diversity of the people made it difficult to unite them into a single nation. In this area great civilizations arose, giving the Fertile Crescent the name "the cradle of civilization."

In the eastern end of the Fertile Crescent lies Mesopotamia. There early civilizations developed, along the banks of the Tigris and Euphrates Rivers. This river valley region was called Mesopotamia, from a Greek word meaning "land between the rivers." With few natural barriers, this area became a crossroads where people mingled and shared customs and ideas.

Sumerian Civilization

The first civilization in Mesopotamia was Sumer. By about 5,000 years ago, villages along the Tigris and Euphrates Rivers had grown into busy cities. These city-states, political units made up of a city and the surrounding land, made up the civilization of Sumer. Various city-states fought each other for land and water.

RELIGION   The polytheistic Sumerians believed in many powerful gods and goddesses, who had human qualities. Each city-state had its own special god or goddess. Most gods and goddesses were closely tied to the forces of nature. The largest buildings in the city-states were pyramidlike temples called ziggurats. A ziggurat had steps that people could climb to reach the shrine of that particular city-state's chief god or goddess. Keeping these divine beings happy was considered important to the well-being of the city-state.

GOVERNMENT   Each Sumerian city-state had a hereditary ruler who was seen as the chief servant of the gods. Besides enforcing the laws and collecting taxes, the ruler maintained the city walls and irrigation systems.

SOCIAL STRUCTURE   Every city-state had distinct social classes. The ruling family, officials, and high priests of a city-state formed the highest social class. There was a small middle class that included merchants and artisans and a large lower class of peasant farmers.

ECONOMY   Sumer grew rich from trade. Traders traveled along rivers and over the desert. Historians know that Sumerian trade was extensive because evidence of goods from as far away as Egypt and India has been found there.

CONTRIBUTIONS   The Sumerians made important contributions to the world. They built the first wheeled vehicles. They also had irrigation systems, dikes, and canals to provide protection from floods as well as water for crops. By 3200 B.C., the Sumerians had invented an early form of writing. **Cuneiform** was wedge-shaped writing formed by pressing a penlike instrument into clay. The Sumerians also developed algebra and geometry. Invaders conquered the Sumerians, but

KEY THEMES AND CONCEPTS

Belief Systems Many early peoples had polytheistic belief systems. The gods were seen as closely tied to the forces of nature, and keeping them happy was essential to agriculture. Therefore, religious leaders became very important in early societies.

PREPARING FOR THE REGENTS

Compare Sumerian society to Egyptian society. How were they alike? How were they different?

they often adopted many Sumerian ideas and passed them down to later civilizations.

Other Civilizations of the Fertile Crescent

Many outside groups invaded the Fertile Crescent. Some invaders destroyed city-states. Others stayed to rule. Some of these rulers created large, well-organized **empires,** or groups of states or territories governed by one ruler.

STRONG RULERS AND EMPIRES   The Assyrians lived in the upper Tigris region. By the 600s B.C., they had conquered the entire Fertile Crescent. However, after Assyria's enemies united and destroyed the Assyrian capital in 612 B.C., the empire collapsed. Then, around 500 B.C., the peoples of the Middle East were united in a single empire by the Persians under Darius. Darius divided his empire into provinces, and he built roads to aid travel and communication.

HAMMURABI: GREAT LAWGIVER   Another early empire was Babylon. Babylon's powerful ruler, Hammurabi, conquered much of Mesopotamia. Hammurabi is best known for his set of laws, called the Code of Hammurabi. This was the first major collection of laws in history. Although these laws favored higher classes over lower ones, they established standards of justice for all classes. Punishment was harsh, however.

ADVANCES IN LEARNING AND TECHNOLOGY   The many peoples of the Fertile Crescent made advances in learning. In what is now Turkey, the Hittites mined iron ore to produce iron. This allowed the Hittites to make stronger plows and weapons. Over time this knowledge passed throughout the region, bringing the world into the Iron Age. In addition, the Babylonians' observations of the heavens added new knowledge to the science of astronomy. The Lydians developed a system of coined money.

 PREPARING FOR THE REGENTS

Hammurabi used law to unite his empire. Later empires, including the Byzantine and Muslim empires, also used systems of law as unifying forces. To learn more about the Byzantine empire, see Unit 2, Section 3. To learn more about Muslim empires, see Unit 2, Section 4.

INDUS RIVER VALLEY

Like the civilizations that developed in Mesopotamia and the Nile Valley, Indian civilization evolved in a fertile river valley.

Geographic Setting

The Indian subcontinent is a large, wedge-shaped peninsula that extends southward into the Indian Ocean. This peninsula is surrounded on the north and northwest by huge mountains, which often limited India's contacts with other cultures.

Winds called monsoons bring rain every summer. India depended on monsoons to grow their crops. When there was not enough rain, people could not grow crops. When there was too much, rivers rose to cause deadly floods.

⚷ KEY THEMES AND CONCEPTS

Political Systems The well-planned cities of Harappa and Mohenjo-Daro suggest that these people must have had well-organized governments. Government officials probably planned these cities and made sure that there was a steady food supply.

Indus Valley Cities

About 2500 B.C., at about the time when the pyramids were rising in Egypt, the first Indian civilization arose in the Indus River valley. Archaeologists have found remains of impressive cities, but little is known about the civilization that produced them. However, it is clear that the Indus Valley civilization covered a large area and that its cities were well planned.

The two main cities of this civilization were Harappa and Mohenjo-Daro. Roads were laid out in a grid pattern, and each city was dominated by a structure built on a hill, probably a fortress or temple. Enormous granaries stored crops that were grown in outlying villages. Houses, which were made of bricks, had plumbing with baths and chutes that led to sewers.

Most Indus Valley people were farmers. They were the first to grow cotton and weave it into cloth. Merchants traveled far, trading even with the cities of Sumer.

Aryan Invaders

Around 1750 B.C., for unknown reasons, Indus Valley civilization began to decline. Then, in about 1500 B.C., nomadic warriors called Aryans conquered the Indus Valley.

CHINA

⚷ KEY THEMES AND CONCEPTS

Environment and Political Systems The Huang He flooded when heavy rains swelled the river. The need to control the river through public works may have contributed to the rise of a strong central government in China.

Geographic Setting

Chinese civilization grew up in the river valleys of the Huang He, or Yellow River, and the Yangzi. Geography—mountains, deserts, jungles, and an ocean—isolated Chinese culture more than it did many other early civilizations. Having little contact with other cultures, the early Chinese believed that their culture was the center of the Earth, so they called it the **Middle Kingdom.** Although China covers a huge area, until recent times most people lived only along the east coast or in the river valleys. Despite its isolation, China traded with other cultures. Chinese goods reached the Middle East and even beyond.

Government

About 1650 B.C., a Chinese people called the Shang gained control of part of northern China. Although there was a king in Shang China, clans—groups of families—controlled most of the land. In this way Shang China was more similar to the small kingdoms of Aryan India or Sumer's city-states than to the centralized government of Egypt. The Shang set up the first **dynasty,** or ruling family, in China.

Social Structure

Shang society resembled that of other ancient cultures. A class of noble warriors owned the land. Merchants and craftspeople earned a living in cities. Most people, however, were peasants and lived in farming villages.

Religion

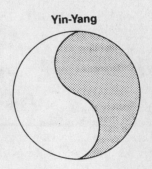

Yin-Yang

The Shang Chinese prayed to many gods and nature spirits. The Chinese looked to their dead ancestors to intercede with the gods to help the living, offering them sacrifices of food and other objects. The ancient Chinese also believed that the universe was held in a delicate balance between two forces, the yin and the yang. When these forces were in balance, peace and prosperity would result.

Contributions

One of the most important achievements of China was written Chinese, which developed about 4,000 years ago. The ancient Chinese used a system of writing that included both pictographs (drawings of objects) and ideographs (drawings of thoughts and ideas). Because the Chinese writing system consisted of tens of thousands of characters, only the upper classes had the time to learn to read and write.

DEMOGRAPHIC PATTERNS & MIGRATION

Demography is the study of human populations. Demographic patterns, or changes in populations over time, are often influenced by geographic features such as rivers. For example, ancient civilizations in Egypt, Mesopotamia, and India all developed in fertile river valleys. Rivers provided water for drinking and irrigation. Rivers also served as highways for the transport of people and goods.

Bantu Migrations

As populations grew, some groups began to migrate in search of new lands to settle. The Bantu migrations are an example of this movement. The Bantu peoples originally lived in West Africa. Then, as the Sahara region began to dry out, these skilled farmers and herders migrated south and east in search of fertile land. Between 500 B.C. and A.D. 1500, Bantu settlers spread their knowledge of farming and ironworking, as well as their language, across the continent. Today, about a third of all Africans speak a language in the Bantu family.

SUMMARY

The earliest people were nomadic hunters and gatherers. When they learned how to grow food, they settled in villages. These changes led to the growth of civilization. Early civilizations grew up in river valleys. Civilizations developed governments, economic systems, and social structures. Early civilizations also had complex systems of belief and made advances in technology, architecture, and legal systems. These advances were spread among early civilizations by migration, trade, and warfare.

 PREPARING FOR THE REGENTS

What were some important contributions of early river civilizations? How are these advances important today?

⭐ **THE BIG IDEA**

The classical civilizations of India, China, Greece, and Rome:

- had strong governments.

- developed ideas and technology that were important contributions to later civilizations.

- developed trade networks that enriched their economies and allowed them to exchange goods and technology.

SECTION OVERVIEW

The classical civilizations of China, India, Greece, and Rome have had a strong impact on the world. Each of these civilizations was influenced by its particular geographic setting. Each had a strong, well-organized government and a prosperous economy that allowed it to thrive. Each civilization made important contributions in such areas as art, science, architecture, and law. The growth of global trade routes during this period allowed classical civilizations to share ideas and technology.

KEY THEMES AND CONCEPTS

As you review this section, take special note of the following key themes and concepts:

Geography How did geographic conditions influence the development of classical civilizations?

Government What features of government allowed the classical civilizations of India, China, Greece, and Rome to remain strong?

Culture and Intellectual Life What contributions have the classical civilizations of India, China, Greece, and Rome made to later civilization?

Movement of People and Goods How did trade routes link civilizations and lead to cultural diffusion?

KEY PEOPLE AND TERMS

As you review this section, be sure you understand the significance of these key people and terms:

Mandate of Heaven	bureaucracy	Hellenistic	Pax Romana
feudalism	Asoka	republic	Laws of the
Qin	polis	Senate	Twelve Tables
Han dynasty	aristocracy	patrician	aqueduct
Maurya dynasty	direct democracy	plebeian	Silk Road

38

CHINA (c. 1027 B.C.–A.D. 220)

Geographic Setting

China was the most isolated of all ancient civilizations. China's culture developed separately from the civilizations of Egypt, the Middle East, and India. China was separated from these civilizations not only by long distances but by physical barriers. For example, high mountains existed to the west and southwest of China. Also, the Gobi Desert lay to the north and the Pacific Ocean to the east. After the Shang united the area around the Huang He and Yangzi, civilization prospered there.

Zhou Dynasty (1027 B.C.–221 B.C.)

Between 1100 and 1000 B.C., the Zhou people overthrew the Shang and set up their own dynasty, which lasted nearly 800 years. The Zhou told the people that the gods had become angry at Shang cruelty and now had chosen the Zhou to rule. This right to rule was called the **Mandate of Heaven,** a divine right to rule. From that time on, each new dynasty would claim the Mandate of Heaven. The Chinese later expanded this idea to explain the dynastic cycle, the rise and fall of dynasties.

 PREPARING FOR THE REGENTS

Practice your chart reading skills by describing how a dynasty might lose the Mandate of Heaven.

The Mandate of Heaven

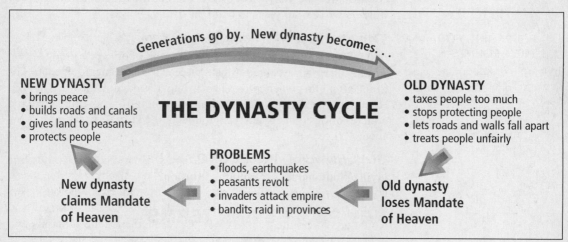

Generations go by. New dynasty becomes. . .

THE DYNASTY CYCLE

NEW DYNASTY
• brings peace
• builds roads and canals
• gives land to peasants
• protects people

OLD DYNASTY
• taxes people too much
• stops protecting people
• lets roads and walls fall apart
• treats people unfairly

PROBLEMS
• floods, earthquakes
• peasants revolt
• invaders attack empire
• bandits raid in provinces

New dynasty claims Mandate of Heaven

Old dynasty loses Mandate of Heaven

A FEUDAL GOVERNMENT The Zhou kings granted control of large areas of land to their supporters. In a system called **feudalism,** local lords controlled their own regions but owed military service to the ruler. Over time, feudal lords came to hold the real power in China.

ECONOMY The economy grew under the Zhou. After the Chinese began using iron to make tools, they could produce more food. Irrigation projects also increased crop yields. Trade expanded along new roads and canals built by feudal lords. The Chinese began for the first time to use money, which spurred the development of trade.

ZHOU CONTRIBUTIONS   Under the Zhou, the Chinese made the first books. They also made progress in other areas. Astronomers studied planet movements and eclipses, developing an accurate calendar. The Chinese discovered how to make silk from the cocoons of the silkworm. Silk became a valuable Chinese export.

○
╟ **KEY THEMES AND**
╟ **CONCEPTS**

Government Shi Huangdi was able to attain power because of divisions in the feudal Zhou government. He moved quickly to centralize his own government through political, economic, and cultural means.

Shi Huangdi and the Qin Dynasty *(221 B.C.–206 B.C.)*

By 221 B.C., a leader of the **Qin** people proclaimed himself Shi Huangdi, meaning "First Emperor."

CENTRALIZED GOVERNMENT   After conquering the Zhou empire, Shi Huangdi centralized his power.

- He abolished the old feudal states and divided the country into military districts, each ruled by an appointed official.
- He standardized measurements.
- He created national coins.
- He promoted uniformity in Chinese writing.
- He repaired canals and roads.

THE GREAT WALL   Shi Huangdi's greatest achievement was the Great Wall. The wall was built to keep out invaders. Thousands of workers worked for years to build the wall.

The Han Dynasty *(206 B.C.–A.D. 220)*

After Shi Huangdi's death in 210 B.C., the people revolted. A new dynasty, the Han, emerged. A peasant leader, Liu Bang, took control of China after Qin power collapsed. As emperor, he took the title Gao Zu. He reduced taxes and eased the harsh policies of the Qin. Gao Zu's policies allowed the dynasty he founded, the **Han dynasty,** to last for about 400 years.

▨ **PREPARING FOR**
  THE REGENTS

To learn more about the rise and fall of the Han dynasty, see Section 3 of this unit.

GOVERNMENT AND ECONOMY   The most famous Han emperor, Wudi, began his reign in 141 B.C. Wudi strengthened Chinese government by establishing a civil service system. Examinations based on the teachings of Confucius, not family influence, determined who would get government jobs. Wudi also strengthened the economy and improved canals and roads.

▨ **PREPARING FOR**
  THE REGENTS

To learn more about Confucianism, see Section 4 of this unit.

HAN SOCIETY   The civil service system had an impact on Han society and China for years to come. It established Confucian values in government and in daily life. Confucianism spelled out proper behavior for all parts of society. Men were thought to be superior to women. Because men were considered superior, women were excluded from taking civil service examinations and, thus, from holding positions in government. A few women, including religious recluses and noblewomen, did receive an education, however.

HAN CONTRIBUTIONS   The Han period was a golden age in China.

- **Technology** The Chinese made technological advances such as learning how to make paper out of wood pulp. They also invented the wheelbarrow; the fishing reel; and the rudder, a device used to steer ships.
- **Science** In medicine the Han developed acupuncture, a technique in which needles are inserted under the skin to relieve pain or treat illness. The Chinese also experimented with herbal remedies and anesthesia. Furthermore, Han scholars wrote texts on chemistry, zoology, and botany.
- **Arts** Some craftsworkers created jade and ivory carvings. Other artisans worked in bronze, ceramics, and silk.

INDIA (c. 1500 B.C.–185 B.C.)

Geographic Setting

The subcontinent of India juts out from the Asian continent. The Indian subcontinent includes three major geographic regions:

- The northern plain, fertile and well watered by the Indus and the Ganges
- The Deccan Plateau, dry and sparsely populated

Ancient India

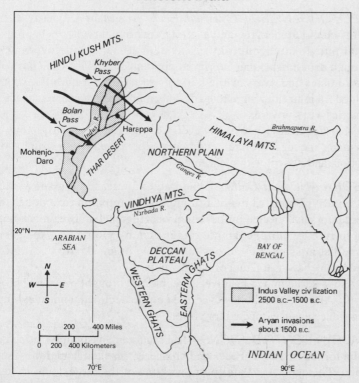

PREPARING FOR THE REGENTS

Practice your map skills by locating the Indus and Ganges Rivers and describing the invasion route used by the Aryans.

- The coastal plains, flat land along the east and west coasts where farming, fishing, and trading can occur

This varied geography has made the subcontinent difficult to unite.

Aryans and the Vedic Age (c. 1500 B.C.–500 B.C.)

The Aryans were Indo-European warriors who moved into India from Europe and Asia. Early Aryans built no cities and left few artifacts. Most of what is known of them comes from the Vedas, a collection of sacred writings. The Vedas portray the Aryans as fierce warriors who loved food, music, and chariot racing. Aryan priests recited the Vedas from memory before they were written down. The period from 1500 B.C. to 500 B.C., the Vedic age, is named for those writings.

Over the years, the Aryans mingled with the people they conquered. The Aryans also began to build cities. By 500 B.C., a new Indian civilization had come into being.

Mauryan Empire (321 B.C.–185 B.C.)

Many competing kingdoms were spread across the northern plains. Into this battleground of rival kingdoms came Chandragupta Maurya. Chandragupta first gained power in the Ganges Valley, but with his army he soon conquered much of northern India. His descendants moved southward, dominating the Deccan Plateau. From about 321 B.C. to 185 B.C., the **Maurya dynasty** ruled over the first united Indian empire.

WELL-ORGANIZED GOVERNMENT   The Maurya dynasty set up an efficient bureaucracy and a strong government with its capital at Pataliputra. A **bureaucracy** is a system of managing government through departments that are run by appointed officials. Officials collected taxes and oversaw the building of roads and harbors, which helped trade to flourish. Other officials managed government-owned factories and shipyards.

Maurya rule was harsh, however. Chandragupta was suspicious of his many enemies. A brutal secret police force reported on crime, corruption, and dissent within his empire.

ASOKA AND REFORM   Chandragupta's grandson **Asoka** ruled differently. Horrified by the brutality of a campaign to conquer the Deccan, Asoka rejected further conquest. He turned to Buddhism, hoping to rule by moral example rather than by violence. Asoka sent Buddhist missionaries across India. Despite his desire to promote Buddhism, he was tolerant of other beliefs.

Asoka's rule united his diverse people and brought peace and prosperity. After his death, however, the empire declined, and rival kingdoms once again competed for power.

MAURYA CONTRIBUTIONS   The Maurya dynasty united much of India for the first time. Peace and prosperity resulted, and trade flourished. The capital at Pataliputra was one of the largest and richest

PREPARING FOR THE REGENTS

To learn more about the extent of the Mauryan empire, see the map in Unit 2, Section 1.

PREPARING FOR THE REGENTS

To learn more about Buddhism, see Section 4 of this unit.

cities of its time. The capital had schools and a library; learning was highly advanced. One of the most lasting contributions of the Maurya dynasty was the spreading of the Buddhist religion by means of missionary activity.

GREECE (c. 1750 B.C.–133 B.C.)

The ancient Greeks adapted ideas from many earlier cultures, such as those of Mesopotamia and Egypt. However, they also developed their own ideas about the role of the individual and how society is best governed.

Geographic Setting

Greece, located in southeastern Europe, is made up of many mountains, isolated valleys, and small islands. This geography prevented the Greeks from building a large empire like that of Egypt or Mesopotamia. Instead the Greeks created many small city-states.

The Aegean and Mediterranean Seas were an important link to the rest of the world. The Greeks became skilled sea traders. They exchanged not only goods but ideas and technology as well. For example, the Greeks adapted the Phoenician alphabet for their own use.

Early Civilizations

Around 1750 B.C., the Minoans built the first Greek civilization on the island of Crete. The Minoans traded with Egypt and Mesopotamia. Through these exchanges they gained new ideas and technology. The Mycenaeans, also sea traders, conquered Crete around 1400 B.C. From the Minoans they learned writing and other skills.

The Rise of City-States

As you know, Greece is divided by mountains into isolated valleys. In addition, hundreds of scattered islands exist off its coast. As a result, Greece did not form a large, unified empire, but existed as a collection of small city-states. A city-state was also known as a **polis.**

A polis typically was made up of two parts. There was a hilltop acropolis, which included marble temples. On the flatter ground below was the main city, within a wall. This area included the marketplace, theater, other public areas, and homes.

Between 750 B.C. and 500 B.C., the Greek city-states had several different types of government. At first, kings ruled the city-states. Over time, landowning nobles gained power, creating an **aristocracy,** a government ruled by the landholding elite.

The two most powerful city-states were Sparta and Athens. Though they shared Greek culture, they developed different ways of life.

Militarism in Sparta

Sparta was a warrior society, and from an early age, boys trained for a lifetime in the military. At the age of seven, boys were moved into

PREPARING FOR THE REGENTS

How were the roles of women in the Athenian and Han societies similar?

PREPARING FOR THE REGENTS

In what ways were the city-states of Sparta and Athens similar? In what ways were they different?

PREPARING FOR THE REGENTS

What impact did classical Greece have on the development of modern political systems?

barracks, where they were toughened by a coarse diet, hard exercise, and rigid discipline. Girls were also trained to exercise rigorously and strengthen their bodies in order to give birth to healthy boys for the army. Although Sparta was an excellent military state, its power declined as a result of its rigid ways and its inability to change.

Limited Democracy in Athens

A wise leader named Pericles ruled Athens from 460 B.C. to 429 B.C. Under Pericles, Athens had a **direct democracy,** in which a large number of the male citizens actually took part in the day-to-day running of the government. Women, however, did not participate, since Athenians believed that women were inferior to men and needed male guidance. Another group that did not participate in the Athenian democracy was made up of slaves. Slaves had neither political rights nor any personal freedom. Even so, Athens gave a greater number of people a voice in government than did any other culture of its time.

Athens prospered during this time and became the cultural center of Greece. Great buildings were built; many thinkers, writers, and artists came to Athens.

Alexander the Great and the Hellenistic Age

Macedonia was a mountain kingdom north of Greece. In the 300s B.C., Philip of Macedonia conquered Greece, which had been weakened by years of civil war. His son, Alexander the Great, went on to build an empire that included the Nile Valley, Persia, and parts of India. Through his conquests Alexander spread Greek culture. A new **Hellenistic** culture arose that blended aspects of Greek, Persian, Egyptian, and Indian life. This culture gave more rights and opportunities to women, who even gained some political power.

Athens and Sparta

ATHENS

- Limited democracy
- Laws made by assembly
- Only male citizens in assembly
- Trade with other city-states
- Education for boys
- Women inferior

- Common language
- Shared heroes
- Olympic Games
- Same gods and religious beliefs

SPARTA

- Monarchy with two kings
- Military society
- Trade and travel not allowed
- Military training for all boys
- Girls trained to be mothers of soldiers
- Women obey men
- Women own property

The Greek Philosophers

SOCRATES	PLATO	ARISTOTLE
Developed Socratic method: learning about beliefs and ideas by asking questions	Believed government should control lives of people	Believed one strong and good leader should rule
Government put him to death	Divided society into three classes: workers, philosophers, and soldiers	Believed people learned through reason

Although Alexander's empire fell apart soon after his death. Hellenistic culture had a lasting impact on the regions he had ruled.

Greek and Hellenistic Contributions

Ancient Greek and Hellenistic culture left an enduring legacy. In addition to their ideas about government, Greeks made contributions in philosophy, literature, science, and the arts.

PHILOSOPHY   Greek thinkers tried to use observation and reason to understand why things happened. The Greeks called these thinkers philosophers, a word that means "lovers of wisdom." Three of the most famous Greek philosophers were Socrates, Plato, and Aristotle.

LITERATURE   The first Greek plays developed from religious festivals. Stories of the gods usually served as the basis for plays. Aeschylus, Sophocles, and Euripides wrote tragedies, plays that told stories of human conflict. Other Greek playwrights wrote comedies. In addition, the Greek poet Homer wrote epic poems that inspired many later writers. Greeks applied observation and logic to their writing of history. The Greek historian Herodotus is often called the Father of History because of his careful historical writing.

ART AND ARCHITECTURE   The Greeks believed in beauty, balance, and order in the universe. Greek art and architecture reflected those ideas. Greek paintings and statues were lifelike, but they also showed the human body in its most perfect form. The most famous Greek building was the Parthenon. Architects today still use ancient Greek ideas, such as Greek column styles, in their buildings.

SCIENCE   The astronomer Aristarchus discovered that the earth rotates on its axis and moves around the sun. Archimedes explored the principles of the lever and pulley. Hippocrates, a Greek physician, studied the causes of illness and looked for cures.

MATHEMATICS   Greek and Hellenistic thinkers made great strides in mathematics. Pythagoras developed a formula to measure the sides of a right triangle; Euclid wrote a book that became the basis for modern geometry.

⚷ KEY THEMES AND CONCEPTS

Culture and Intellectual Life Greek art portrayed individuals in perfect form, a reflection of the Greek belief in beauty, balance, and order in the universe.

ROME (c. 509 B.C.–A.D. 476)

KEY THEMES AND CONCEPTS

Geography The location of Rome helped the Romans to carry on trade and build an empire around the Mediterranean Sea.

PREPARING FOR THE REGENTS

What impact did Rome have on the development of later political systems?

PREPARING FOR THE REGENTS

To learn more about the rise and fall of the Roman empire, see Section 3 of this unit.

Geographic Setting

Rome is located near the center of Italy, a peninsula located in the Mediterranean. Unlike the geography of Greece, Italy's geography helped its people to unite. Low mountains presented fewer natural barriers. Fertile plains supported a growing population. In addition, the location of the Italian peninsula helped Romans to move easily through the lands of the Mediterranean.

The Roman Republic

The traditional date given for the founding of Rome is 509 B.C., when the Romans drove out the Etruscans who had ruled them. The Romans established a new form of government called a republic. In a **republic,** officials were chosen by the people. The most powerful governing body was the **Senate.** Senators were members of the landholding upper class, called **patricians.** These officials elected two consuls, who supervised the business of government and commanded the armies. The **plebeians**—farmers, merchants, artisans, and traders, who made up most of the population—had little power.

Under Roman law, the male head of the household had authority over his wife and family. During the late years of the republic and early years of the empire, however, women gained greater freedom. Roman women held prominent public roles and owned successful businesses.

The Roman Empire

By 270 B.C., Rome had conquered all of Italy. The Romans went on to conquer Carthage, Macedonia, Greece, and parts of Asia Minor. This expansion, however, led to a widening gap between rich and poor and also to increased corruption. Attempts at reform led to a series of civil wars. Out of this period of chaos, Julius Caesar came to power in 48 B.C. Caesar made new conquests as well as important reforms.

After Caesar was murdered, his grandnephew Octavian—later called Augustus—became ruler. Augustus ruled with absolute power, thus bringing the republic to an end. The age of the Roman empire had begun. The 200-year peace that began with Augustus is called the **Pax Romana,** or Roman peace. During this time, the Roman empire spread stability over a large area of the world, including parts of Europe, North Africa, and Southwest Asia.

Roman Contributions

Roman civilization spread to other lands. The Romans also absorbed the ideas of other cultures.

LAW A system of laws was Rome's greatest achievement. It applied to all people and created a stable Roman empire. Many of its basic principles—including equality under the law, the right of the accused to face one's accusers and mount a defense, and the idea of being considered innocent until proven guilty—are the basis for systems of justice to this day.

In 450 B.C., the plebeians demanded written laws, saying that they could not know what the laws were if they were not written down. These **Laws of the Twelve Tables,** inscribed on twelve tablets, were displayed in the marketplace. Later, plebeians won the right to elect their own officials and serve in all kinds of government jobs.

ART AND ARCHITECTURE   The Romans borrowed many Greek concepts in the arts and architecture. They used Greek-style statues in their homes and public buildings. Roman buildings were mighty and grand, however, instead of simple and elegant. Roman writers used the Latin language, which united the empire, to write great poetic, historical, and philosophical works.

ENGINEERING   The Romans were very practical. They built excellent roads, bridges, harbors, and **aqueducts**—bridgelike stone structures that carried water from the hills to the cities. The Romans also improved the arch and the dome.

THE GROWTH OF GLOBAL TRADE ROUTES

The classical civilizations engaged in trade with one another. These exchanges of goods, technology, and culture expanded from the time of the first Indian empire to the time of the Romans.

Phoenician Trade

The Phoenicians were one of the earliest trading empires of the ancient Middle East. Phoenicia was made up of small city-states in the lands known today as Lebanon and Syria. Phoenicians made glass from sand, manufactured a purple dye from the sea snail, and created scrolls from Egyptian papyrus. Their ships carried valuable goods across the Mediterranean. As trade expanded, Phoenicia founded colonies throughout the region. The most important Phoenician contribution to history was the alphabet, developed to record business transactions. It is the basis of the alphabet we use today.

India's Role in Trade

Even during early Indus Valley civilization, trade had gone on between the peoples of the Indian coast and Mesopotamian civilizations such as Sumer. During the 300s B.C., when Alexander expanded his territory into India, he opened a trade corridor between India and the Mediterranean. By 100 B.C., Indian goods such as textiles, gems, and spices were in great demand. Some goods were sent overland into central Asia and China. Others went by ship to the Middle East, Egypt, East Africa, and Southeast Asia. Rome later became an eager market for Indian goods.

PREPARING FOR THE REGENTS

The blending of Greek, Hellenistic, and Roman traditions is often referred to as Greco-Roman civilization. It has had a great impact on the western world.

PREPARING FOR THE REGENTS

List three contributions of each of the classical civilizations listed below.

India:

China:

Greece:

Rome:

Mediterranean Trade Routes

Map labels:
10° W
ATLANTIC OCEAN
EUROPE
ITALIAN PENINSULA
Adriatic Sea
CRIMEAN PENINSULA
Sea of Azov
Byzantium
Black Sea
40° N
CORSICA
Rome
Aegean Sea
ASIA MINOR
IBERIAN PENINSULA
SARDINIA
Athens
GREECE
Strait of Gibraltar
CYPRUS
Carthage
SICILY
Syracuse
CRETE
Alexandria
Tyre
Mediterranean Sea
Cyrene
NORTH AFRICA
EGYPT

Legend:
Roman trade routes
Greek trade routes
Grain-producing regions

PREPARING FOR THE REGENTS

Practice your map skills by locating three grain-producing regions that were part of Mediterranean trade routes.

KEY THEMES AND CONCEPTS

Movement of People and Goods In the ancient world, goods moved both overland and over the seas. Rulers saw the value of improving transportation. Governments built roads, bridges, ships, and canals to benefit trade.

China and the Silk Road

The Han dynasty opened a trade route called the **Silk Road** that eventually linked China with lands as far west as Mesopotamia. Silk and other Chinese goods moved west, while products such as muslin, glass, and new foods flowed into China.

The Silk Road eventually stretched for 4,000 miles. Few merchants traveled the entire distance. Most goods were traded at various markets along the way. In the west, groups such as the Persians controlled the Silk Road.

Roman Trade

During the Pax Romana, trade flowed freely among the peoples of the Roman empire and other parts of the world. Egyptian farmers supplied grain; other Africans supplied ivory, gold, and even lions. Indians exported cotton and many spices to the Roman empire, and the Chinese supplied silk and other exotic goods.

SUMMARY

Great civilizations arose in India, China, Greece, and Rome from the 300s B.C. through about A.D. 500. Strong, centralized governments allowed these civilizations to rise and remain strong. Their cultural contributions in the arts and architecture, science and engineering, and law have lasted to the present day. As global trade began to develop, these civilizations shared ideas and technology.

3 Rise and Fall of Great Empires

SECTION OVERVIEW

The rise and fall of the Han dynasty and the Roman empire followed remarkably similar courses. Both empires gained power through conquest, strong central government, and profitable trade. Both eventually fell because of weak leadership, internal dissent, and aggressive invaders.

KEY THEMES AND CONCEPTS

As you review this section, take special note of the following key themes and concepts:

Political Systems What factors contributed to the rise of both the Han dynasty and the Roman empire?

Economic Systems What was the importance of trade to the Han and Roman empires?

Change What factors contributed to the decline of both the Han and Roman empires?

KEY PEOPLE AND TERMS

As you review this section, be sure you understand the significance of these key people and terms:

Wudi	Silk Road	Pax Romana
monopoly	Augustus	

FACTORS LEADING TO GROWTH

Both the Han and the Roman empires reached their height between 200 B.C. and A.D. 200. Both empires began by throwing off oppressive rulers: the Qin in China and the Etruscans in Rome. Although many elements contributed to the growth of these two empires, the most important factors that sustained them were strong government and profitable trade.

★ **THE BIG IDEA**
The Han and Roman empires:

- grew through military expansion.
- were supported by strong government and thriving trade.
- fell as a result of internal weakness and invading forces.

The Han Empire

MILITARY POWER   The most famous of the Han emperors, **Wudi,** conducted many military campaigns to secure and expand China's borders. Many of the battles he fought were attempts to drive nomadic peoples beyond the Great Wall.

GOVERNMENT   Wudi worked to strengthen the Chinese government. He removed many harsh laws. Also, the civil service system helped him to choose wise officials. He set up an imperial university to train scholars in Confucian teachings.

ECONOMY AND TRADE   Initially, Wudi improved the economy internally by adding canals and roads to ease the movement of goods. He also had storage areas for grain set up throughout his empire. When grain was plentiful, the government would buy and store it. Then, when it became scarce, the government could sell it.

Another source of government revenue was income from the sale of iron and salt. Wudi created a government monopoly on these items. A **monopoly** is the complete control of a product or business by one person or group—in this case, the Han government. Sales of iron and salt allowed the government to have a source of income besides taxes. Wudi and other, later emperors also developed the **Silk Road,** a caravan route stretching from the Chinese capital to the Mediterranean Sea.

The Roman Empire

MILITARY POWER   The Romans were able to conquer partly because they had a strong, well-disciplined army. However, they also treated conquered peoples well, allowing them to keep their own governments and customs. In return, conquered lands were required to supply soldiers for the Roman army and pay taxes to Rome.

GOVERNMENT   Emperor **Augustus,** who ruled the Roman empire from 31 B.C. to A.D. 14, stabilized the government. He, like the Han emperors, created a civil service system that ensured a supply of well-trained and well-educated government officials.

Both good and bad emperors followed Augustus. However, the 200-year period called the **Pax Romana,** or Roman Peace, began with his reign. During this time Roman rule brought order and prosperity to the empire. Roman legions maintained the road system and guarded the borders.

ECONOMY AND TRADE   Roman expansion allowed the empire to take over prosperous trade routes throughout the Mediterranean. The Mediterranean served as a natural highway for trade. In addition, the Romans built miles of fine roads that promoted trade and brought wealth into the empire. Grain from the Nile Valley, ivory and gold from Africa, spices and gems from India, and silk that came from China via the Silk Road flowed into the empire. Under Augustus the tax system was reformed, and new coins were issued to make trade easier.

♀ KEY THEMES AND
⚲ CONCEPTS

Political Systems Both the Han empire and the Roman empire instituted civil service systems. Working properly, such systems assured that officials were not just the most privileged or powerful people in the empire but instead were also skilled in government.

♀ KEY THEMES AND
⚲ CONCEPTS

Economic Systems Trade was encouraged in both the Han and Roman empires by extensive road systems.

The Roman Empire, 44 B.C.

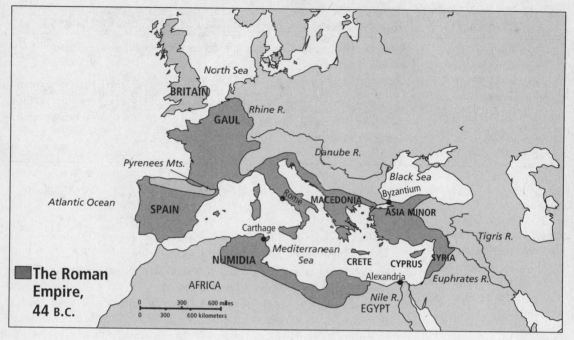

GEOGRAPHIC SETTING

The Han and Roman empires arose on opposite sides of the Eurasian landmass. Both, however, expanded their borders over time.

Extent of the Han Empire

The Han empire was first located where the Qin had ruled: in eastern China. However, the empire expanded during Han times as Wudi secured and expanded China's borders. To the north, the Han moved into Manchuria and Korea. To the south, the empire moved into northern Vietnam. To the west, the Han gained territory in Tibet and central Asia.

Extent of the Roman Empire

Rome also expanded from its initial location in central Italy. The powerful Roman military first took over the Italian peninsula. By about 44 B.C., Roman power extended throughout the Mediterranean, from Spain to parts of Asia Minor. To the north, the Roman empire spread to what is now France as well as into parts of Britain.

CAUSES OF DECLINE

Both the Han and Roman empires grew weak as a result of internal problems and external pressures.

PREPARING FOR THE REGENTS

Name three lands that were part of the Roman empire in 44 B.C.

1.

2.

3.

The Fall of Rome

Military causes	Economic causes	Political causes	Social causes
• Visigoths and other Germanic peoples invade the empire. • Roman army lacks training and discipline. • Romans forced to hire foreign soldiers to defend borders.	• Heavy taxes necessary to support the government. • Farmers leave land. • Middle class disappears. • Romans use too much slave labor.	• Government becomes too strict. • People stop supporting government. • Many corrupt officials. • Divided empire becomes weak.	• Population declines because of disease and war. • People become selfish and lazy.

KEY THEMES AND CONCEPTS

Change Expansion often helps an empire to grow, but it can also lead to decline. The more an empire expands, the more difficult it can be to keep together. Wealth from trade can make an economy grow, but it can also lead to great class differences, greed, and corruption.

PREPARING FOR THE REGENTS

To learn more about the Byzantine empire, see Unit 2, Section 3.

PREPARING FOR THE REGENTS

Write an essay that compares and contrasts the rise and fall of the Han and Roman empires.

The Han Empire

Expansion helped to strengthen the Han empire but also led to its decline.

- **Political Causes** Rulers that followed Wudi were unable to control powerful warlords in outlying areas.
- **Economic Causes** Some rulers did not maintain the systems of canals and roads, which were vital routes of commerce. As a result, the economy suffered. High taxes oppressed the peasants and thus led to a revolt.
- **Military Causes** In A.D. 220, warlords overthrew the last Han emperor, and the empire was split into several kingdoms. Invaders overran the Great Wall and set up their own kingdoms.

The Roman Empire

Some of the same factors that led to the Han decline also led to the Roman decline. Overexpansion of the empire, high taxes, and foreign invasions all weakened the empire.

Roman emperor Diocletian divided the empire into two parts in a failed attempt to restore order. Although the decline of the Roman empire was a long, slow process, the year A.D. 476, when Germanic leader Odoacer ousted the emperor in Rome, is the date generally considered to mark its fall. The Eastern Roman empire survived, however, and became known as the Byzantine empire.

SUMMARY

At opposite ends of the Eurasian landmass, two great empires thrived between 200 B.C. and A.D. 200. The Han empire in China and the Roman empire in the lands around the Mediterranean Sea shared many characteristics. Both grew through conquest and were supported for centuries by strong central governments. Far-flung trade thrived in both empires and led to prosperity. Eventually, however, internal weakness and external invasions brought about the decline of these two great empires.

SECTION 4
Emergence and Spread of Belief Systems

SECTION OVERVIEW

Belief systems developed with the earliest humans, who saw the world as being full of spirits. With the rise of civilization, more complex belief systems developed. Hinduism and Buddhism emerged in India. In China, Confucianism and Taoism developed. In the Middle East, three great world religions—Judaism, Christianity, and Islam—grew. Each of these religions had its own beliefs and sacred texts, though all shared some concepts. Several of these religions spread and had an impact far beyond their places of origin.

KEY THEMES AND CONCEPTS

As you review this section, take special note of the following key themes and concepts:

Belief Systems What are the characteristics of the major religions? How are they similar and different?

Culture How did major religions affect cultures?

Movement of People and Goods How did belief systems spread over large areas?

KEY PEOPLE AND TERMS

As you review this section, be sure you understand the significance of these key people and terms:

animism	Buddha	hijra
brahman	nirvana	Quran
reincarnation	monotheistic	Sharia
karma	Torah	missionary
dharma	Messiah	diaspora
Upanishads	Bible	

★ **THE BIG IDEA**
As civilizations developed and spread, so did belief systems and religions. These belief systems include:

- animism
- Hinduism
- Buddhism
- Confucianism
- Taoism
- Judaism
- Christianity
- Islam

MAJOR BELIEF SYSTEMS

Religious beliefs developed even in very early cultures. As civilizations arose in Africa, Europe, and Asia, more complex systems of belief developed.

Animism

The belief that every living and nonliving thing in nature has a spirit is called **animism.** Animism was a feature of the belief systems of many early people. Stone Age paintings on the walls of caves probably express these early beliefs.

Religions of some early civilizations combined animism with reverence for ancestors. People in Shang China and in some traditional African societies, for example, believed that the spirits of deceased ancestors could affect life in a positive or negative way. The prayers of ancestors were thought to be an important way to influence the gods. Therefore, people would offer food and other necessities to their ancestors' spirits.

Hinduism

KEY THEMES AND CONCEPTS

Belief Systems Define each of the following terms:

1. brahman

2. reincarnation

3. karma

4. dharma

Hinduism is one of the oldest and most complex religions in the world. Unlike most major religions, Hinduism has no single founder. Hinduism developed and changed over 3,500 years, growing out of the diverse peoples who settled India. These groups include the original inhabitants of the Indus Valley as well as the nomadic Aryans who entered India in about 1500 B.C.

UNIVERSAL SPIRIT   Hindus believe in one unifying spirit, **brahman.** Because brahman is too complex for humans to understand, Hindus worship gods that give a more concrete form to brahman. The three most important Hindu gods are Brahma the Creator, Vishnu the Preserver, and Shiva the Destroyer. The goal of life is to achieve union with brahman.

REINCARNATION   Achieving union with brahman is said to occur as people free themselves from the selfish desires that separate them from the universal spirit. Most people cannot achieve this union in one lifetime. The concept of **reincarnation,** the rebirth of the soul in a new body, allows people to continue their journey toward union with brahman. People get closer to this union by being born into higher and higher levels of existence.

KARMA AND DHARMA   In each lifetime, a person can come closer to union with brahman by obeying the law of karma. **Karma** consists of all the deeds of a person's life that affect his or her existence in the next life. By living in a right way, a person will be reborn at a higher level. Evil deeds cause people to be reborn into a lower level. Good deeds involve following **dharma,** the moral and religious duties that are expected of an individual. A person's gender, class, age, and occupation all affect his or her dharma.

The Caste System

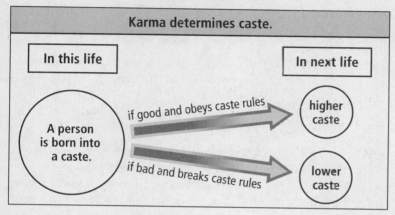

Karma determines caste.

| In this life | | In next life |

A person is born into a caste.

if good and obeys caste rules → higher caste

if bad and breaks caste rules → lower caste

CASTES The caste system is an important part of Hinduism. Castes are social groups into which people are born and out of which they cannot move during a lifetime. A person may, however, by acquiring good karma, be born into a higher caste in the next life. The three basic caste groups during Aryan times were priests (Brahmins), warriors (Kshatriyas), and a group that included herders, farmers, artisans, and merchants (Vaisyas). Later, a separate group was created for non-Aryans. This group (Sudras) included farm workers and servants. The lowest-ranked people, called Untouchables, were at the bottom of the social system.

SACRED TEXTS Over several thousand years, Hindu teachings were developed and recorded in a number of sacred texts. These include the Vedas, collections of prayers and sacred verses, and the **Upanishads,** philosophical dialogues about Hindu beliefs.

Buddhism

Buddhism also developed in India but later spread into other areas, such as China. Its founder, a prince named Siddhartha Gautama, was born a Hindu in the 500s B.C.

THE ENLIGHTENED ONE Siddhartha Gautama left his wealthy home to search for the meaning of human suffering. While meditating under a sacred tree, he found the answer to his question, and he was thereafter referred to as the **Buddha,** or the Enlightened One.

THE FOUR NOBLE TRUTHS The central philosophy of Buddhism revolves around the Four Noble Truths. Briefly, these are:

1. All life is suffering.
2. Suffering is caused by desire for things that are illusions.
3. The way to eliminate suffering is to eliminate desire.
4. Following the Eightfold Path will help people overcome desire.

 PREPARING FOR THE REGENTS

Millions of Hindus and Muslims live on the Indian subcontinent today. Over the years, there have been conflicts between these groups. To learn more about conflicts today on the Indian subcontinent, see Unit 7, Section 4.

PREPARING FOR THE REGENTS

List two similarities and two differences between the Hindu and Buddhist religions.

Similarities:

1.

2.

Differences:

1.

2.

Proper Relationships

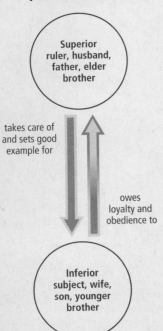

THE EIGHTFOLD PATH The Eightfold Path involves right views, right intentions, right speech, right conduct, right livelihood, right effort, right mindfulness, and right meditation. The ultimate goal is **nirvana,** union with the universe and release from the cycle of death and rebirth.

COMPARISON WITH HINDUISM Buddhism accepts the Hindu concepts of karma, dharma, and reincarnation. However, Buddhism rejects the many Hindu gods as well as the rituals and priesthood of Hinduism. Buddhists do, however, accept the idea of religious communities that include monks and nuns. Buddhism also rejected the caste system.

SACRED TEXTS After the Buddha died, his teachings were collected into the *Tripitaka*, or "Three Baskets of Wisdom." This collection is made up of rules for Buddhist monks; sermons; and discussions of Buddhist beliefs. Later, other Buddhists added many more scriptures.

Two Philosophies of China

The late Zhou dynasty was a troubled time in China. There were many wars, and economic and social changes disrupted everyday life. Beginning in the 500s B.C., several major Chinese philosophies developed. Two of the most important were Confucianism and Taoism. These philosophies shared the common purpose of restoring harmony.

CONFUCIANISM Confucius, born in 551 B.C., was China's most influential thinker. Confucius's teachings, collected in *The Analects*, taught people to accept their given places in society. These individual places were expressed through five key relationships.

Confucius believed that, except for friendships, none of these relationships was equal. Older people were superior to younger, for example, and men were superior to women. Every person had duties and responsibilities that depended on his or her position.

Other ideas of Confucius include the following:

- People are naturally good.
- Education should be the road to advancement in society.
- To ensure social order, the individual must find and accept his or her proper place in society.

TAOISM Another influential Chinese philosophy was Taoism (often spelled *Daoism*). Taoism sought to help people to live in harmony with nature. Laozi, who founded Taoism, taught people to contemplate the Tao, or the "way" of the universe. Important virtues in Taoism are yielding and acceptance. Followers of Laozi rejected the world and human government and often withdrew to become hermits, mystics, or poets.

Taoists also believe in a balance between yin and yang. The yin stands for Earth, darkness, and female forces. The yang stands for Heaven, light, and male forces. The peace and well-being of the universe depend on harmony between yin and yang.

The beliefs of Taoism are collected in two works. Laozi is traditionally thought to be the author of the first, *The Way of Virtue*. A second text is the *Zhuang-zi,* written several centuries later. It contains fables, sayings, and dialogues.

Judaism

The Hebrews were one of the nomadic groups who lived in the Fertile Crescent. According to Hebrew tradition, the Hebrews became enslaved in Egypt, and God helped them escape this slavery. By about 1000 B.C., the Hebrews had set up the kingdom of Israel with Jerusalem as its capital. They believed that God had promised them this land. Over time, Hebrew beliefs evolved into the religion we today call Judaism. Several beliefs are very important to Judaism.

BELIEF IN ONE GOD   Judaism is **monotheistic,** teaching a belief in one God. Most other religions of the time worshiped many gods and goddesses. The Hebrews believed that God was their special protector and was all-knowing, all-powerful, and present everywhere.

SACRED TEXTS AND MORAL TEACHINGS   According to the sacred scriptures of the Hebrews, the **Torah,** God made a covenant, or a binding agreement, to be the God of the Hebrews. Jews also believe that God gave them the Ten Commandments through Moses. These are laws that describe how people should behave toward God and each other. The Old Testament of the Bible includes the Torah, which is made up of five books. The Torah also sets out many other laws that establish the moral basis for Judaism.

 PREPARING FOR THE REGENTS

Make a chart comparing the basic ideas of Confucianism and Taoism.

KEY THEMES AND CONCEPTS

Belief Systems Judaism influenced the development of two later monotheistic world religions: Islam and Christianity.

Judaism

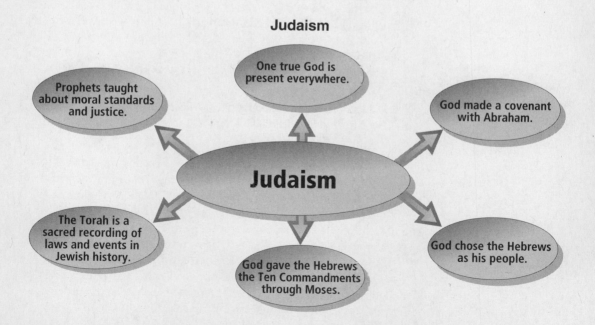

Prophets taught about moral standards and justice.

One true God is present everywhere.

God made a covenant with Abraham.

Judaism

The Torah is a sacred recording of laws and events in Jewish history.

God gave the Hebrews the Ten Commandments through Moses.

God chose the Hebrews as his people.

Hebrew sacred scriptures also include the writings of spiritual leaders called prophets, who urged Hebrews to act according to God's teachings. The prophets preached a strong code of ethics, or moral standards of behavior. Judaic thought had a strong influence on two other world religions: Christianity and Islam.

📝 **PREPARING FOR THE REGENTS**

Prepare a time line that shows events in the growth of Christianity as well as several other global events of the same period.

Christianity

Christianity began in Palestine with the teachings of a Jew named Jesus in about A.D. 30. Beginning with a small group of followers, Christianity grew and spread to become the official religion of the Roman empire by A.D. 392.

LIFE AND DEATH OF JESUS According to Christian tradition, Jesus' mother, Mary, had been told before his birth that he would be the Messiah. **Messiah** is the Jewish word, derived from Hebrew, for a savior sent by God. Jesus grew up worshiping God and following Jewish law. At about age 30, he began to travel through the countryside preaching and teaching new beliefs.

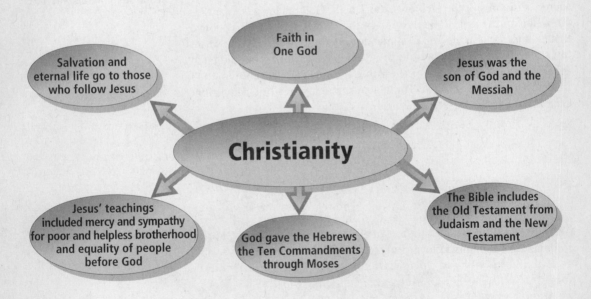

Many Jews and Romans worried that Jesus was dangerous. Around A.D. 29, the Romans arrested Jesus, tried him, and executed him by crucifixion. By this method a person was tied or nailed to a cross and left to die. After Jesus' death, many of his followers said that he had risen from the grave. His followers worked to spread his teachings. The Romans persecuted Christians, who set up an organized church. In A.D. 313, Roman Emperor Constantine ended the persecution of Christians. In A.D. 392, Christianity became the official religion of the Roman Empire.

TEACHINGS OF JESUS   The teachings of Jesus were rooted in Jewish tradition. For example, Jesus accepted the Ten Commandments that God had given to the Jews through Moses. At the same time, he preached new ideas. According to his followers, he was the son of God and the savior that the Jews had been expecting. His mission was to bring salvation and eternal life to anyone who would follow his teachings. Jesus taught mercy and sympathy for the poor and helpless. Jesus also preached brotherhood and the equality of people before God.

SACRED TEXT   The sacred text of Christianity is the Christian **Bible.** It has two parts. The Old Testament includes the Hebrew scriptures, books of law, history, prophetic writing, and poetry. The New Testament includes the Gospels (describing Jesus and his teachings) and other writings, mostly letters written by Christians that explain Christian doctrine.

Islam

In A.D. 622, a new religion called Islam arose in Arabia. Like Christians and Jews, people who follow Islam believe in one God.

LIFE OF MUHAMMAD   In about 570, an Arab named Muhammad was born in Mecca. Muhammad became a caravan merchant, married, and had children. He was troubled, however, by the idol worship of the Arabs of the time. According to Muslim tradition, the angel Gabriel commanded Muhammad to spread the message of Islam.

Muhammad obeyed this command. Soon Meccan merchants sought to kill him. In 622, Muhammad and his followers left Mecca for Yathrib (later named Medina) on a journey known as the **hijra** (often spelled hegira). The hijra was a turning point for Islam. Muslim converts in Medina welcomed Muhammad, and the religion grew.

MUSLIM BELIEFS   The followers of Islam are called Muslims. All Muslims accept five basic duties, known as the Five Pillars. First, Muslims believe in one God, Allah, who is compassionate and all-powerful. Muhammad is God's greatest prophet. Second, Muslims are expected to pray five times daily. Third, Muslims are expected to give

⚲ KEY THEMES AND CONCEPTS

Belief Systems Jews, Christians, and Muslims all believe in one God, and their holy writings share many themes and ethics. Despite these similarities, the three groups have often come into conflict, as they did during the Crusades in the 1000s. Even today, especially in the Middle East, these groups do not always coexist peacefully. To learn more about the Crusades, see Unit 2, Section 6. To learn more about conflicts in the Middle East today, see Unit 7, Section 5.

The Five Duties of Islam

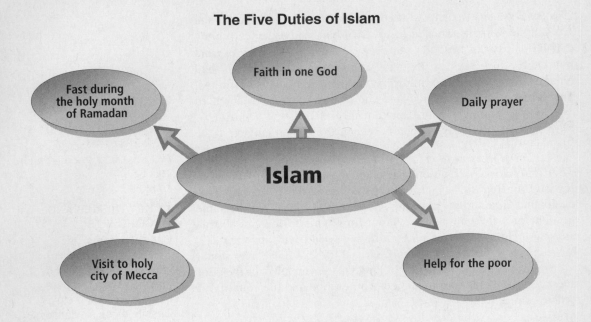

PREPARING FOR THE REGENTS

Describe a major belief of each of the belief systems that follows.

Hinduism:

Buddhism:

Confucianism:

Taoism:

Judaism:

Christianity:

Islam:

PREPARING FOR THE REGENTS

The Muslim code of law is called the Sharia. To learn more about the Sharia and its effect on the Muslim empire, see Unit 2, Section 4.

money to the poor. Fourth, Muslims are expected to fast from sunrise to sunset during the holy month of Ramadan. Fifth, Muslims are supposed to visit Mecca at least once in their lives.

SACRED TEXT   The sacred scriptures of Islam are contained in the **Quran.** The Quran is the final authority on all matters and provides a guide to life for Muslims. Muslim scholars have also developed an immense body of laws, called the **Sharia,** that covers all aspects of life. Over time, this system of law acted as a means to unite Muslims of differing backgrounds.

EXPANSION OF WORLD RELIGIONS

Some of the religions discussed here, such as Confucianism and Taoism, remained within a fairly limited geographical area. Hinduism spread throughout India and into Southeast Asia. Other religions spread more widely.

Spread of Buddhism

Over the centuries, the Buddha's teachings won wide acceptance. The Mauryan ruler Asoka converted to Buddhism and sent messengers to spread Buddhist beliefs. Over time, traders and **missionaries,** or people dedicated to spreading a religion, spread Buddhism far beyond India to many parts of Asia, including China, Japan, Korea, and Southeast Asia. In India, where Buddhism started, it eventually declined.

Spread of Judaism

Judaism spread in a unique way. The Romans expelled the Jews from Palestine in A.D. 135. This event became known as the **diaspora,** or scattering of people. Wherever Jews settled, they lived in close-knit communities and maintained their identity through the careful preservation of tradition.

Spread of Christianity

Christianity first spread through the work of Christian missionaries such as Paul. Even though Roman rulers persecuted Christians, the religion continued to spread throughout the Roman empire. This occurred for many reasons. The poor and oppressed found comfort in Jesus' message of love and a better life after death. Also, Christian missionaries often added Greek concepts to their teaching of the religion, appealing to educated Romans as well as others. In 313, Emperor Constantine allowed freedom of worship throughout the Roman empire. Later, Emperor Theodosius made Christianity the official religion of the empire.

After the fall of the Western Roman empire, missionaries continued to spread Christianity through Europe. Trading networks also spread Christianity, especially as Europe began voyages of exploration and expansion in the 1400s. Europeans took Christianity with them when they established settlements in the Americas, Africa, and Asia.

 KEY THEMES AND CONCEPTS

Movement of People and Goods Although Christians were initially persecuted, Christianity spread throughout the Roman empire. Eventually, Christianity became the official religion of the empire.

Spread of Islam

In the 150 years after the death of Muhammad, Islam spread over three continents. Skillful Arab fighters spread Islam through military conquest. Because the Arabs treated conquered peoples in a fair way, many people converted to Islam willingly. The teaching of Islam appealed to many because it emphasized honesty, generosity, and social justice.

Trade had always been considered an honorable occupation for Muslims. Muslims built vast trading empires. Merchants established trading networks with Africa, China, and India. In India, Muslim traders were an important means of spreading Islam. At the other end of the Eurasian landmass, Islam spread from North Africa into Spain.

KEY THEMES AND CONCEPTS

Movement of People and Goods Three ways in which religions spread were through missionary activity, military conquest, and trade.

PREPARING FOR THE REGENTS

To learn more about the spread of Islam, see Unit 2, Section 4.

SUMMARY

Many belief systems emerged over time in various parts of the world. In India, Hinduism and Buddhism developed. In China, Confucianism and Taoism were significant philosophies. In the Middle East, Judaism, Christianity, and Islam developed. All of these belief systems had important effects on the civilizations of their time as well as later on. Several belief systems spread widely through missionary effort, conquest, and trade.

Questions for Regents Practice

Review the Preparing for the Regents section of this book. Then answer the following questions, which include multiple-choice questions, a thematic essay, and a series of document-based questions.

MULTIPLE CHOICE

Directions

Circle the *number* of the word or expression that best completes the statement or answers the question.

1 One result of the Neolithic Revolution was
   1 an increase in the number of nomadic tribes
   2 a reliance on hunting and gathering for food
   3 the establishment of villages and the rise of governments
   4 a decrease in trade between cultural groups

2 The ancient civilizations of Mesopotamia and Egypt were similar in that both cultures
   1 established trade routes to China
   2 used the ziggurat form for their temples
   3 developed along rivers
   4 used a hieroglyphic writing system

3 "If a seignior [noble] has knocked out the tooth of a seignior of his own rank, they shall knock out his tooth. But if he has knocked out a commoner's tooth, he shall pay one-third mina of silver."

   —Code of Hammurabi

   Which idea of Babylonian society does this portion of the Hammurabi code of law reflect?
   1 All men were equal under the law.
   2 Fines were preferable to corporal punishment.
   3 Divisions existed between social classes.
   4 Violence was always punished with violence.

4 The early civilizations of the Nile River valley, Mesopotamia, and the Huang He were similar because they were
   1 dependent on fertile land
   2 monotheistic
   3 industrialized societies
   4 dependent on each other for trade

5 All citizens in ancient Athens had the right to attend the assembly, where they could meet in the open to discuss and cast votes. This situation is an example of
   1 direct democracy
   2 totalitarianism
   3 parliamentary democracy
   4 absolutism

6 A major contribution of the Roman empire to western society was the development of
   1 gunpowder
   2 the principles of feudalism
   3 monotheism
   4 an effective legal system

7 A major impact of ancient Greece and Rome on western civilization was that
   1 the Greeks and Romans achieved a classless society, which was later copied in Western Europe
   2 Greek sculpture and Roman architecture were much admired and copied in Western Europe in later centuries
   3 Greece and Rome transmitted Islamic philosophy to the areas they conquered
   4 Greek and Latin are still widely spoken in universities throughout the West

8 In traditional India, the caste system and the Hindu beliefs in karma and dharma most directly resulted in
1 the establishment of a set of rules for each individual in society
2 the rapid industrialization of the economy
3 a strong emphasis on the acquisition of wealth
4 a strong belief in the importance of education

9 According to the teachings of Confucius, the key to the successful organization of society is that
1 the ruler should be chosen democratically
2 the evil in humans must be eliminated
3 ancestor worship should be discontinued
4 individuals should know and do what is expected of them

10 The Quran, Mecca, and the hijra (hegira) are most closely associated with the practice of
1 Islam
2 Judaism
3 Christianity
4 Buddhism

11 One similarity between the Five Pillars of Islam and the Ten Commandments is that both
1 support a belief in reincarnation
2 promote learning as a means to salvation
3 encourage the use of statues to symbolize God
4 provide a guide to proper ethical and moral behavior

THEMATIC ESSAY

Directions

Read the following instructions that include a theme, a task, and suggestions. Follow the instructions to create a well-organized essay that has an introduction with a thesis statement, several paragraphs explaining the thesis, and a conclusion.

Theme: Civilization

Throughout history, great civilizations have existed in various parts of the world. The cultural and intellectual achievements of these civilizations contributed to the advancement of humankind.

Task

• Define the term *civilization.*
• Describe some examples of cultural or intellectual achievements made by past civilizations. Identify each example with the particular civilization that made the contribution.
• Explain the lasting importance of each of these achievements or contributions to global history.

Suggestions

You may discuss any civilization from your study of global history, except the United States. Some civilizations you might wish to consider include ancient Egypt, classical Rome, the Gupta empire, classical China, or the Muslim golden age. You are not limited to these suggestions.

QUESTIONS BASED ON DOCUMENTS

The following exercise asks you to analyze three historical documents and then write an essay using evidence from those documents. This exercise is similar to the document-based question that you will see on the Regents Examination, which may include six or more documents. For additional practice with historical documents, see the Preparing for the Regents section and the sample examinations in this book.

This task is based on the accompanying documents. Some of these documents have been edited for the purposes of this task. This task is designed to test your ability to work with historical documents. As you analyze the documents, take into account both the source of each document and the author's point of view.

Directions
Read the documents in Part A and answer the question or questions after each document. Then read the directions for Part B and write your essay.

Historical Context
Throughout global history, people have established different systems of government. They have been based on different views of how people should be ruled.

Task
Understand and evaluate various viewpoints on how government should work. Evaluate the effects that these viewpoints have had on the people of a society.

Part A: Short Answer
Directions: Analyze the documents and answer the question or questions that follow each document, using the space provided.

DOCUMENT 1
The Mandate of Heaven

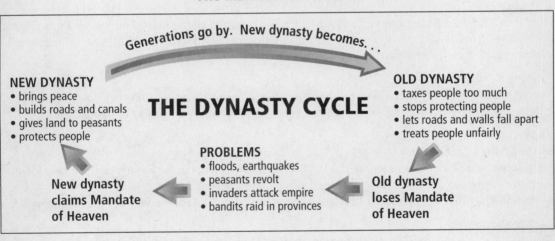

1 According to this chart, how did Chinese rulers lose power?

_____

_____

2 How did Chinese rulers show that they had the Mandate of Heaven?

_____

_____

DOCUMENT 2

People become naturally spoiled by love, but are submissive to authority. . . . That being so, re-wards should be rich and certain so that the people will be attracted to them; punishments should be severe and definite so that the people will fear them; and laws should be uniform and steadfast so that the people will be familiar with them.

—Hanfeizi, 200s B.C.

3 According to this philosophy, what is the best way to make sure that people will respect and obey government?

_____

_____

DOCUMENT 3

We differ from other states in regarding the man who holds aloof from public life not as "quiet" but as useless; we decide or debate, carefully and in person, all matters of policy, holding, not that words and deeds go ill together, but that acts are foredoomed to failure when undertaken undiscussed.

—Speech of Pericles (431 B.C.) in Thucydides, *History of the Peloponnesian War*

4 According to Pericles of Athens, what was the best way for a government to make decisions?

_____

_____

Part B: Essay
Directions:
- Write a well-organized essay that includes an introduction, several paragraphs, and a conclusion.
- Use evidence from the documents to support your response.
- Do not simply repeat the contents of the documents.
- Include specific, related outside information.

Historical Context
Throughout global history, people have established different systems of government. They have been based on different views of how people should be ruled.

Task
Using information from the documents and your knowledge of global history and geography, write an essay that evaluates different perspectives on government. Develop a position on what is the best kind of government.

  Be sure to include specific historical details. You must also include additional information from your knowledge of global history.

  Note: The rubric for this essay appears in the Preparing for the Regents section of this book.

2 Expanding Zones of Exchange
(500–1200)

UNIT OVERVIEW

During the period from about 500 to 1200, civilizations matured in various regions of the world. The Gupta dynasty united northern India. The Tang and Song dynasties each ruled a unified China. In southeastern Europe and the Middle East, the Byzantine empire carried on the traditions of Greece and Rome. The first Russian state was founded in Kiev. Islamic civilization flourished across several continents. In Europe, Christianity, feudalism, and the manor system dominated life.

As civilizations expanded, they often encountered one another. Sometimes the encounters were peaceful; at other times, violent. Always, however, encounters led to exchanges of people, goods, and ideas.

THEMATIC TIME LINE ACTIVITY

Some of the many themes developed in Unit 2 are:

economic systems	diversity	interdependence
culture and intellectual life	power	political systems
movement of people and goods	belief systems	

Choose one of the themes listed above. As you review Unit 2, create a thematic time line based on the theme you have chosen. Your time line should stretch from 500 to 1200 and include major developments and key turning points having to do with your theme.

SECTION 1   The Gupta Empire in India

SECTION OVERVIEW

The Gupta dynasty came to power in India in A.D. 320 and ruled until 550. The strong Gupta government, which gave power to local leaders, united much of the Indian subcontinent and ensured peace and prosperity. Hinduism had a very strong impact on Gupta society and cultural life. Gupta scientists and mathematicians made important discoveries and advances.

KEY THEMES AND CONCEPTS

As you review this section, take special note of the following key themes and concepts:

Political Systems What were some key characteristics of Gupta rule?

Belief Systems How did Hinduism influence Gupta society and culture?

Culture and Intellectual Life What advances did people of the Gupta empire make in the arts and sciences?

KEY PEOPLE AND TERMS

As you review this section, be sure you understand the significance of these key people and terms:

Gupta dynasty	Untouchables	patriarchal	Arabic numerals
Pataliputra	joint family	decimal system	stupa

GEOGRAPHIC SETTING

About 500 years after the rule of the Maurya dynasty in India, the **Gupta dynasty** came to power. The Mauryas and the Guptas were the only early Indian civilizations to be able to unite the subcontinent under their rule. Both arose in the north and spread southward. Geography benefited the northern empires in various ways. Mountains helped protect these civilizations from foreign invaders. In addition, the Indus and Ganges

<aside>
⭐ **THE BIG IDEA**
During Gupta rule, the people of India:

- experienced peace and prosperity under a strong government.

- were influenced greatly by Hindu ideas.

- produced many achievements in the arts and sciences.
</aside>

PREPARING FOR THE REGENTS

What geographic features of India were beneficial to both the Maurya and Gupta empires? Explain.

The Maurya and Gupta Empires

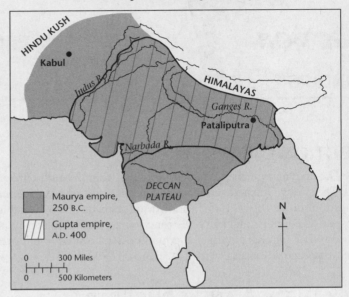

Maurya empire, 250 B.C.

Gupta empire, A.D. 400

0   300 Miles
0   500 Kilometers

Rivers flowed through the northern region, providing water and fertile soil. The Gupta period was one of peace and prosperity for India.

THE INFLUENCE OF HINDUISM

Hinduism had a strong impact on all areas of Gupta life. The Gupta dynasty adopted and actively promoted Hinduism. This set of beliefs affected the social life of Gupta villages through the caste system. Hinduism also had a strong effect on the flowering of cultural and intellectual achievements during the Gupta era.

GUPTA GOVERNMENT

KEY THEMES AND CONCEPTS

Political Systems Gupta emperors established a stable central government but also shared power with local leaders. The resulting peace and prosperity contributed to a golden age in India.

Central Government

Gupta emperors ruled over a spectacular court at **Pataliputra,** the former Mauryan capital on the Ganges River. An efficient central government allowed farming and trade to prosper and provided a stable background for advances in learning and the arts.

Local Government

Although the Gupta rulers maintained a strong central government, they also gave great power to local leaders. These leaders were elected by merchants and artisans. In each village, a headman and council made decisions for the village. The most respected people of the village served on the council.

Role of Women

In earlier times, women were allowed to serve on the councils. Over time, however, Hindu law placed greater restrictions on women, excluding them from participation.

HINDUISM AND GUPTA SOCIETY

Society came to be ordered by Hindu concepts during the Gupta period. Most Indian people lived in small villages, where Hindu ideas about caste and family regulated society.

The Caste System

Caste had originated in early Aryan times, and by the time of Gupta rule, the system had expanded from four basic castes to include many more groupings. People believed that their karma, all the good and bad things they had done in life, determined their caste. People could not change their caste in one lifetime, but they could be born into a higher caste in the next life by fulfilling moral duties, or dharma.

Organization of Village Life

The village was the center of Indian life during Gupta times. A cluster of homes built of earth and stone was surrounded by fields, where farmers grew their crops. Villages ran their own affairs and faced little interference from the central government as long as they paid their taxes.

Village life was governed by caste rules and traditions. These strong traditions created a stable society. People in the higher castes had the strictest rules, which were designed to keep them from being contaminated by people from lower castes. The **Untouchables** were outcasts who lived harsh lives. They were given the jobs that were considered "impure," such as cleaning the streets or digging graves. Untouchables had to live apart from the other members of Gupta society.

Organization of Family Life

In villages, wealthier persons often lived in **joint families,** where parents, children, grandparents, uncles, and their children shared a common home.

PATRIARCHAL STRUCTURE   Indian families were **patriarchal,** with the father or oldest male heading the household. Heads of families had great authority.

CHILDREN AND MARRIAGE   Indian children learned the family trade or worked in the fields and were taught what would be expected of them as adults. An important duty for parents was to arrange the marriage of their children. Hindu law required that people marry only within their own caste.

ROLE OF WOMEN   Although the status of women varied throughout India, the role of women generally became more restricted over time

PREPARING FOR THE REGENTS

To learn more about Hinduism and the caste system, see Unit 1, Section 4.

KEY THEMES AND CONCEPTS

Belief Systems Hindu beliefs governed village life, creating a stable society.

PREPARING FOR THE REGENTS

How did the Hindu caste system affect village and family life in Gupta India?

PREPARING FOR THE REGENTS

Examine the role of women in Gupta life. How does it compare to the role of women in other civilizations and societies you have studied?

because of the development of Hindu law. By the end of Gupta rule, upper-class women were largely restricted to their homes and had to cover themselves from head to foot when they went out. Lower-class women worked in the fields or did spinning and weaving.

SCIENTIFIC AND ARTISTIC CONTRIBUTIONS

An environment of peace and prosperity allowed scientific and artistic achievements to flourish during the Gupta dynasty. Education took place at religious institutions. At Hindu and Buddhist centers, students learned subjects such as mathematics, medicine, physics, and languages.

Mathematics

KEY THEMES AND CONCEPTS

Culture and Intellectual Life Religion was a strong influence in Indian art and architecture. Gupta architects built beautiful temples for both the Buddhist and Hindu religions.

ZERO AND THE DECIMAL SYSTEM   Indian mathematicians developed the concept of zero as well as the decimal system. The **decimal system** is the system we use, based on the number 10.

ARABIC NUMERALS   Gupta mathematicians developed the system of writing numerals that we use today. They are known as **Arabic numerals** because Arabs brought them from India to the Middle East and Europe.

Medicine

Gupta physicians began to use herbs and other remedies to treat illnesses. Surgeons were able to set bones and repair facial injuries with plastic surgery. Furthermore, Gupta physicians vaccinated people against smallpox approximately 1,000 years before this practice began in Europe.

Architecture

Architects built beautiful stone temples for Hindu worship. A typical shape was a square (symbolizing the Earth) within a circle (which stood for eternity). Hindu temples were filled with carvings of gods and goddesses, animals such as elephants and monkeys, and ordinary people.

Buddhist architects constructed **stupas,** large dome-shaped shrines that contained the remains of holy people. These Buddhist shrines were plain but included gateways with elaborate carvings that depicted the life of Buddha.

PREPARING FOR THE REGENTS

Describe the achievements of the Gupta dynasty in each of the categories listed.

Mathematics:

Medicine:

Architecture:

Literature:

Literature

Extraordinary works of literature were created during the Gupta dynasty. Fables and folk tales in the Sanskrit language were collected and recorded. These stories were carried west to Persia, Egypt, and Greece.

The most famous of Gupta writers was the poet and playwright Kalidasa. His best-known play is *Shakuntala.* In this play a king marries a beautiful orphan, Shakuntala. Later, an evil spell causes him to forget his bride. By the end of the story, however, he recovers his memory, and the two are happily reunited.

END OF GUPTA RULE

After about 200 years, the Gupta empire declined because of weak rulers and foreign invasions. The invaders were the White Huns from central Asia, nomads who destroyed villages and disrupted trade in the Gupta empire.

SUMMARY

The Gupta dynasty reigned successfully through a strong central government that also gave great power to local leaders. Gupta rule helped India to enjoy peace and prosperity for 200 years. The rules and rituals of Hinduism governed daily life. The Gupta era became known for its significant contributions to science, medicine, mathematics, architecture, art, and literature.

2 Tang and Song Dynasties in China

★ **THE BIG IDEA**
During Tang and Song rule:

- China had a strong government and a strictly ordered social structure.

- the economy was strong.

- there were great achievements in the arts and architecture.

- China influenced other cultures, including that of Japan.

SECTION OVERVIEW

The Tang dynasty came to power in China in 618 and ruled until 907. This dynasty unified China and expanded the empire. The Song dynasty ruled China from 960 to 1279. Under the Tang and Song dynasties, government was efficient and society was well structured and stable. Farming and trade flourished. China produced great advances in literature, art, and architecture. During this period, Chinese culture spread to Japan.

KEY THEMES AND CONCEPTS

As you review this section, take special note of the following key themes and concepts:

Political Systems How did the Tang dynasty unite China and keep it strong?

Economic Systems How did Tang and Song rulers help the economy to flourish?

Culture and Intellectual Life What were the Tang and Song dynasties' contributions to the arts and architecture?

Movement of People and Goods How did Tang and Song China influence Japanese culture?

KEY PEOPLE AND TERMS

As you review this section, be sure you understand the significance of these key people and terms:

Tang dynasty	gentry	pagoda
tributary state	calligraphy	porcelain
Song dynasty		

THE RISE AND FALL OF DYNASTIES

After the Han dynasty declined in the A.D. 200s, China was divided for nearly 400 years. Then, in the 600s, a young general came to power. He took the name Tang Taizong and established the **Tang dynasty,** a powerful dynasty that ruled China from 618 to 907.

The Tang dynasty built a vast empire with its capital at Xian (Changan). Tang rulers forced Vietnam, Korea, and Tibet to become **tributary states.** These states remained independent, but their rulers had to acknowledge China's greater power and send tribute, or regular payment. Japan sent missions to China to conduct trade and study Chinese culture.

Government corruption, drought, and rebellions all contributed to the collapse of the Tang dynasty in 907. Then, in 960, a scholarly general named Zhao Kuangyin reunited China under the **Song dynasty.** China prospered under Song rule, but the dynasty was weakened by invaders. The Song dynasty was finally conquered by the Mongols in 1279.

GOVERNMENT AND SOCIETY

Confucianist beliefs guided both the nature of the government and the structure of the society. Confucian thought stressed social order based on duty, rank, and proper behavior.

Skillful Government

Tang rulers revived the civil service system that had first been developed during the Han dynasty. People who wanted to hold office had to pass difficult examinations that emphasized Confucian philosophy. Rulers set up schools that prepared male students to take these exams. This system gave Tang and Song China a highly educated ruling class.

Strict Social Order

China had a strict social structure under the Tang and Song dynasties. Chinese social structure consisted of three main classes: the gentry, the peasantry, and the merchants.

The Tang and Song Dynasties, 618–1215

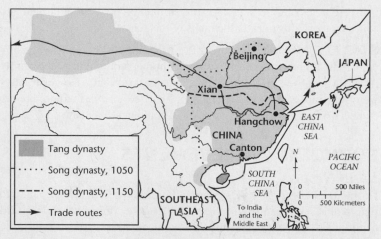

 PREPARING FOR THE REGENTS

To learn more about Confucianism, see Unit 1, Section 4.

 KEY THEMES AND CONCEPTS

Government The Tang dynasty revived and improved the civil service system. As a result, both Tang and Song China had a highly educated ruling class.

PREPARING FOR THE REGENTS

Use the map to explain how the extent of Song rule changed between 1050 and 1150.

PREPARING FOR THE REGENTS

Describe the role and status of each of the following groups in Tang and Song China.

Gentry:

Peasants:

Merchants:

Women:

Chinese Society

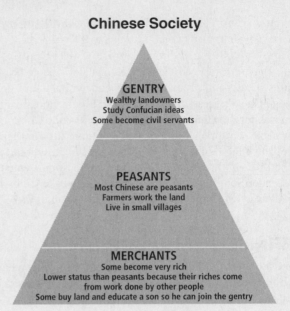

GENTRY
Wealthy landowners
Study Confucian ideas
Some become civil servants

PEASANTS
Most Chinese are peasants
Farmers work the land
Live in small villages

MERCHANTS
Some become very rich
Lower status than peasants because their riches come
from work done by other people
Some buy land and educate a son so he can join the gentry

GENTRY   The **gentry** were wealthy landowners who preferred scholarship over physical labor. Confucian thought was valued, and members of the gentry sometimes spent years studying it. The gentry had to pass a civil service examination to obtain honored positions in government.

PEASANTS   Most Chinese were peasants. They worked the land and lived on what they produced. To supplement their income, they sometimes sold or traded handicrafts. Peasants lived in small villages that managed their own affairs.

MERCHANTS   Although some merchants acquired vast wealth, they held a lower social status than the peasants because their wealth came from the labor of others. As a result, some merchants bought land and educated their sons to enter the ranks of the gentry.

STATUS OF WOMEN   Under the Tang and Song dynasties, many women held great authority. Within the home, women managed family finances, imposed discipline, and supervised servants. However, boys were still valued over girls. When a girl married, she was required to become a part of her husband's family and could never remarry.

ECONOMIC ACHIEVEMENTS
Land Reform
During the Tang dynasty, a system of land reform redistributed land to peasants. Large landowners had less power, and peasants could contribute to government revenue by paying taxes.

Japan Adapts Chinese Ideas

600s–700s	800s	900s–1200s
• Japanese study Chinese civilization. • Emperor builds capital city modeled on Chinese capital. • Japanese nobles adopt Chinese language, food, and style of dress. • Japanese nobles adopt Chinese tea ceremony, music, dance, and gardens.	• Japanese stop traveling to China.	• Japanese keep some Chinese ways but build their own civilization. • Japanese artists develop their own styles. • Japanese change the Chinese system of writing.

Expanded Trade

Foreign trade expanded under both the Tang and Song dynasties. Chinese merchants traded with India, Persia, and the Middle East. The Chinese became expert shipbuilders and emerged as a naval power. To improve trade, the government issued paper money—the world's first.

Canals

Canals were built to encourage trade and improve transportation. The Grand Canal was the largest, linking the Huang He and the Yangzi. This canal allowed food from farms in southern China to be sent north.

LITERATURE AND ARTS

The arts were important during the Tang and Song dynasties. Chinese writers wrote short stories and poetry. Chinese landscape painting became popular during the Song period, and **calligraphy**—fine handwriting—flourished. Chinese architects created the **pagoda,** a temple with a roof that curved up at the corners. The Chinese became experts at making **porcelain,** a hard, shiny pottery.

CHINESE INFLUENCE ON JAPAN

The Japanese first learned about Chinese culture through Korea. During the Tang dynasty, a Japanese prince sent nobles to China to study. Japanese nobles continued to bring Chinese ideas and technology back to Japan. By the 800s, as the Tang dynasty began to decline, the Japanese had begun to blend Chinese ideas with their own to create a unique culture.

SUMMARY

Chinese civilization flourished under the Tang and Song. Efficient government was fueled by an educated ruling class, thanks to the revival of the civil service system. A fixed social structure added stability. Land reform, advances in farming, canals, and increased trade helped the empire economically. China made contributions in art, literature, and architecture. Chinese culture influenced other lands, including Japan.

⚷ KEY THEMES AND CONCEPTS

Economic Systems Many aspects of Tang and Song rule benefited the economy. Land reform created more tax revenue. Improvements in farming increased productivity. The expansion of trade brought money into the empire from outside China. Better transportation improved economic efficiency.

 PREPARING FOR THE REGENTS

List one achievement of the Tang or Song dynasty in each of the following categories.

Government:

Economy:

Art:

SECTION 3

The Byzantine Empire and Russia

⭐ THE BIG IDEA
The Byzantine empire:

- had a strong government and a uniform code of laws under Justinian.

- was closely tied to the Orthodox Christian Church.

- made contributions in architecture, engineering, and art.

- affected the later development of Russia and other nations of Eastern Europe.

SECTION OVERVIEW

The Roman empire had been divided since the 200s. As the western half declined, the eastern half rose in importance. The emperor Constantine founded a capital on the site of Byzantium. Justinian, the greatest of the Byzantine emperors, ruled a vast empire with a centralized government and a codified set of laws. The Orthodox Christian Church became powerful as the official church of the Byzantine empire. The Byzantine empire blended Greek, Roman, and Christian influences and produced art and architecture that have lived on through the centuries. The empire also left a legacy in Russia. The Byzantines gave Russia a written language, and influenced Russian religion, government, art, and architecture.

KEY THEMES AND CONCEPTS

As you review this section, take special note of the following key themes and concepts:

Government How did Justinian organize his government and code of law?

Belief Systems What was the significance of the Orthodox Christian Church in the Byzantine empire and Russia?

Culture and Intellectual Life How was the Byzantine empire able to preserve and spread Greek and Roman knowledge and culture?

Movement of People and Goods What influence did the Byzantine empire have on Russia and other areas of Eastern Europe?

KEY PEOPLE AND TERMS

As you review this section, be sure you understand the significance of these key people and terms:

Justinian	icon	schism
autocrat	mosaic	Kiev
Justinian's Code	patriarch	czar

GEOGRAPHIC SETTING

The Roman empire had been divided since the reign of Diocletian in the late A.D. 200s. As Germanic invaders weakened the western half, power shifted to the east. By 330, the emperor Constantine had built a splendid new capital in Constantinople, on the site of the Greek city of Byzantium. The Byzantine empire, as it came to be called, drew its name from this ancient city.

Greatest Extent

At its height, the Byzantine empire covered an area from Rome through southeastern Europe and Asia Minor, down to Egypt and across North Africa. Even a portion of southern Spain was once part of the empire.

Preserving and Spreading Culture

The city of Constantinople was on a peninsula overlooking the Bosporus, a strait connecting the Black Sea to the Mediterranean. The city possessed an outstanding harbor and was protected on three sides by water. From its central location Constantinople controlled key trade routes that linked Europe and Asia. Heir to Rome, the Byzantine empire blended Greek, Roman, and Christian influences and helped spread them to other regions of the world. In Russia, thriving trade with Constantinople helped Kiev become the center of the first Russian state.

KEY THEMES AND CONCEPTS

Culture Constantinople was also known as New Rome. This name emphasized the role of the Byzantine empire as the bearer of the Roman heritage. The Byzantine empire blended ancient Greek, Roman, and Christian influences and spread them to the regions they conquered.

PREPARING FOR THE REGENTS

Practice your map skills by using the map to describe the extent of the Byzantine empire in 1000.

The Byzantine Empire

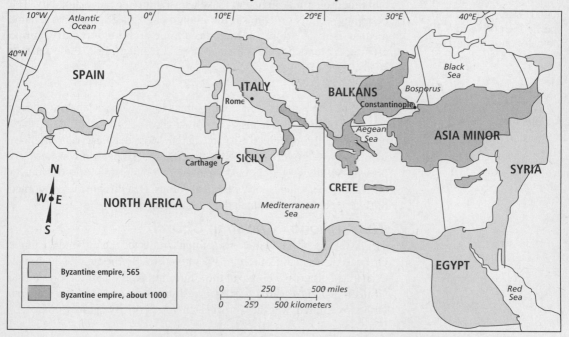

ACHIEVEMENTS OF THE BYZANTINE EMPIRE

The Byzantine empire reached its peak under the emperor **Justinian,** who reigned from 527 to 565. Like other Byzantine rulers, Justinian was an **autocrat,** a single ruler with complete authority. Justinian hoped to recover the western Roman provinces that invading tribes had seized. During his reign, Byzantine armies did reconquer parts of North Africa, Italy, and southern Spain. These conquests were expensive, however, and they were temporary. The achievements of the Byzantine empire were in other areas.

Justinian's Code of Law

Emperor Justinian is probably best known for his code of law. Soon after he became emperor, he set up a team of scholars to gather and organize the ancient laws of Rome. His collection became the "body of civil law," known today as **Justinian's Code.** His code included Roman laws, legal writings, and even a student handbook. Later emperors continued to update the code. By the 1100s, it had reached Western Europe, where it became the basis of law for both the Roman Catholic Church and medieval rulers. Even today, international law is influenced by Justinian's Code.

Engineering and Architecture

The Byzantine empire extended Roman knowledge of engineering, especially in the area of architecture. Justinian launched an impressive building program designed to make Constantinople a dazzling city. The best known of his structures is the Church of Hagia Sophia, whose name means "Holy Wisdom." It includes a huge arching dome. Byzantine architects blended Greek, Roman, Persian, and other Middle Eastern styles.

Art

Byzantine artists made great contributions to religious art that influenced styles for many years. **Icons** were holy images of Jesus, the Virgin Mary, or saints of the Orthodox Christian Church. More than just paintings, they were supposed to create a sense that the sacred person was actually present. **Mosaics,** pictures or designs formed by inlaid pieces of stone or other materials, often showed biblical scenes. Beautiful mosaics adorned the interiors of churches, including the Hagia Sophia.

The Orthodox Christian Church

The art and architecture of Constantinople reflected the importance of the Orthodox Christian Church in Byzantine life. By the time of Justinian, divisions had grown between the Church in Rome and the Byzantine Church. The Orthodox Christian Church, also called the Eastern Orthodox Church, was the Christian Church of the Byzantine empire.

PREPARING FOR THE REGENTS

How did Justinian go about reforming the law of the empire? What impact did Justinian's Code have on later legal systems?

PREPARING FOR THE REGENTS

Describe how the Byzantine empire preserved and transmitted Greek and Roman knowledge and culture in the categories named.

Law:

Architecture:

IMPERIAL AUTHORITY OVER THE CHURCH   The Byzantine emperor controlled the business of the Church and appointed the **patriarch,** the highest church official, in Constantinople. The emperor was considered Jesus' co-ruler on earth. Byzantine Christians did not believe that the pope in Rome had supreme authority over them.

DIFFERENCES WITH THE WEST   Other divisions widened over time between the Church in the East and the Roman Church. Byzantine priests could marry, while Roman Catholic priests could not. Also, Greek (instead of Latin) was the language of the Byzantine Church. A major disagreement arose over the use of icons. Some people believed that the importance placed on them by the Orthodox Christian Church bordered on idolatry.

CHRISTIAN SCHISM   In 1054, there was finally a permanent split, or **schism,** between the Orthodox Christian Church in the East and the Roman Catholic Church in the West.

Preservation of Greco-Roman Culture

The Byzantine empire remained a political and cultural force nearly 1,000 years after the fall of Rome. To Europe it was a symbol of the power and glory of Rome long after the Roman empire had faded. Justinian's Code preserved Roman law, and the accomplishments of Roman engineers were preserved and extended in Byzantine architecture.

Furthermore, Byzantine culture was strongly rooted in Greece. The Byzantine empire preserved Hellenistic (Greek) science, philosophy, arts, and literature. The empire even served to preserve some of the ancient texts of Greece, which were carried to the West as the Byzantine empire declined in the 1400s.

DECLINE AND FALL OF THE EMPIRE

The Byzantine empire had reached its height under Justinian. In the centuries after his reign, the empire lost much land to invading armies. It was also weakened by internal court struggles and constant warfare. During the Fourth Crusade in the early 1200s, western Christians took Constantinople and ruled it for 50 years. The final blow to the empire was the taking of Constantinople by the Ottoman empire in 1453.

RUSSIA AND EASTERN EUROPE

The first Russian state was established in the 800s. This early Russian state was centered in the city of **Kiev,** in present-day Ukraine. Kiev's location on the Dneiper River made the city easily accessible to Byzantine traders.

♀ KEY THEMES AND CONCEPTS

Political Systems In the Byzantine empire, the power of both state and Church was centered in the emperor.

♀ KEY THEMES AND CONCEPTS

Belief Systems The Roman and Byzantine Churches shared many common beliefs, yet their differences became too difficult to overcome. Many world religions have experienced schisms over time.

▨ PREPARING FOR THE REGENTS

The fall of Constantinople was a turning point in global history. It marked a change in power in the region from the Christian Byzantine empire to the great Muslim trading empire of the Ottomans. To learn more about the effects of the Ottomans on global history, see Unit 4, Section 3.

Around this time, states such as Poland, Hungary, and Serbia were established in Eastern Europe. Settlers arrived from Western Europe, Russia, and Asia, giving the region a wide variety of languages and cultural traditions. As in Russia, trade with the Byzantine empire helped bring Eastern Europe into the Byzantine sphere of influence. The Byzantines influenced both Russia and Eastern Europe in a variety of ways.

Written Language

The Byzantines gave Russia a written language. Two Byzantine missionaries adapted the Greek alphabet in order to translate the Bible into Slavic languages as early as the 800s. This alphabet, called the Cyrillic alphabet after Cyril, one of the monks, is still used in Russia and other countries of Eastern Europe today.

Orthodox Christianity

Byzantine missionaries carried Orthodox Christianity to Russia and other countries of Eastern Europe. The Orthodox Christian faith remains a powerful force through much of the region today. The close church-state relationship in the Byzantine empire also became a model for Russian government and religion. The Russian Orthodox Church became an important arm of state power.

Autocratic Government

One Byzantine tradition that continued was that of autocratic rule, which became the norm in Russian government. Autocratic rulers in Russia were known as **czars.** *Czar* is the Russian word for "Caesar."

Art and Architecture

Russians adopted the religious art, music, and architecture of the Byzantine empire. Byzantine domes were transformed into the onion domes of Russian architecture.

 PREPARING FOR THE REGENTS

Describe how the Byzantine empire affected Russia in the areas listed.

Language:

Religion:

Government:

Art and architecture:

SUMMARY

As the Roman empire in the West declined, the Byzantine empire grew in power. The lasting heritage of the Byzantine empire lay in its preservation of classical culture, its traditions of law and government, and its spreading of Christian beliefs. The Orthodox Christian Church, a powerful force in the empire, developed its own practices and traditions and split from the Roman Catholic Church. The Byzantine empire provided Russia and other Eastern European lands with a written language, art and architecture, and an autocratic style of government.

SECTION 4 Islamic Civilization

SECTION OVERVIEW

In the years after the death of Muhammad, Islam spread across parts of three continents. Muslim empires ruled over vast areas of land that included parts of Europe, Africa, and Asia. The Muslim world was influenced by many cultures, including those of ancient Greece, Rome, and India. During the 700s and 800s, Islam experienced a golden age. A diverse society, an economy based on flourishing trade, and achievements in the arts and sciences characterized this era. The achievements of Islam's golden age reached Europe through Muslim Spain and Italy as well as through the Crusades.

KEY THEMES AND CONCEPTS

As you review this section, take special note of the following key themes and concepts:

Diversity What lands and peoples came under Muslim rule?

Economic Systems What was the importance of trade in the Muslim empires?

Culture and Intellectual Life What achievements did Muslim society produce in the arts and sciences?

Interdependence How did Islamic civilization interact with Christian Europe?

KEY PEOPLE AND TERMS

As you review this section, be sure you understand the significance of these key people and terms:

caliph	Shiite	Abbassid dynasty
Sharia	Umayyad dynasty	Averröes
Sunni		

★ **THE BIG IDEA**
The Muslim world:

- included lands and peoples from parts of three continents.

- preserved, blended, and spread the cultures of classical Greece, Rome, India, and other civilizations.

- enjoyed a prosperous golden age with advances in art, literature, mathematics, and science.

- spread new learning to Christian Europe.

PREPARING FOR THE REGENTS

To learn more about the beliefs of Islam, see Unit 1, Section 4.

PREPARING FOR THE REGENTS

To learn more about the extent of the Muslim world, see the map "The Spread of Islam" in the Questions for Regents Practice at the end of this unit.

THE SPREAD OF ISLAM

Islam arose in the Arabian peninsula in the early 600s. In 632, the founder of Islam, Muhammad, died. Abu Bakr was elected the first **caliph,** or successor to Muhammad. The period when Muslims were ruled by caliphs, from Muhammad's death until the 900s, was called the caliphate. The Muslim world expanded during the caliphate.

Diverse Lands and Peoples

In the years after Muhammad's death, Islam spread rapidly. Abu Bakr was successful in uniting Arabs in the Islam faith. His forces began an extraordinary military campaign that conquered parts of the Byzantine empire, the Persian empire, Egypt, and Spain. Their push into Europe was stopped only at Tours in 732. Over the following centuries, more and more people embraced Islam.

MIDDLE EAST   Arab armies took control of the Middle East in the early 600s. Syria and Palestine were quickly defeated by Arab forces. Persia and Egypt were conquered soon after.

NORTH AFRICA   Muslim armies carried Islam into North Africa in the mid- to late 600s. Muslim invaders initially fought African forces. Eventually, however, Muslims and North Africans joined forces to conquer Spain. Islam continued to spread to other parts of North and West Africa.

SPAIN AND SICILY   Muslim conquests included parts of southern and western Europe, especially Spain and the island of Sicily. Muslim Arabs and their North African allies attacked Spain in the early 700s. When Europe was weak, during the Middle Ages, the Muslims seized control of Sicily.

INDIA   In the early 700s, Muslim armies conquered the Indus Valley. For several hundred years, Islam did not spread beyond western India. In the 1000s and 1100s, however, Turkish converts to Islam conquered most of northern India. By the 1200s, the Turks had created a great Muslim empire on the subcontinent, with its capital at Delhi.

SOUTHEAST ASIA   After Muslims took control of northern India in the 1200s, Islam was carried into Southeast Asia. Islamic beliefs and civilization were spread mainly through trade. As Islam gradually spread to lands surrounding the Indian Ocean, thriving trade networks were established.

Reasons for Muslim Success

One reason for the spread of Islam was that the Arabs were strong fighters. Their cavalry, mounted on camels and horses, overwhelmed their opponents. The Muslims were also successful partly because the Byzantine and Persian empires were weak from fighting wars against each other. Another important factor was that the Muslims were united by their belief in Islam. In addition, Muslim rulers often treated conquered peoples fairly. People in defeated empires welcomed Muslim rule after years of living under harsh rulers. Many converted to Islam.

ISLAMIC LAW AND ITS IMPACT

As Islam spread, Islamic scholars developed a system of laws to help people interpret the Quran and apply it to everyday life. The **Sharia**—the Islamic system of law—regulated moral behavior, family life, business, government, and other areas of community life. The Sharia acted as a uniting force for Muslims. Unlike laws in the western world, the Sharia did not separate religious and worldly matters. It applied the Quran to all situations and aspects of life.

DIVISIONS WITHIN ISLAM

Several decades after the death of Muhammad, divisions grew among Muslims about who should be Muhammad's successor. Followers split into two groups: Sunni and Shiite. **Sunnis** believed that the caliph should be chosen by Muslim leaders. Sunni Muslims did not view the caliph as a religious authority. **Shiites** believed that only the descendants of the prophet Muhammad should be his successors. They believed that the descendants of the prophet were divinely inspired.

The split between Sunni and Shiite Muslims continues to this day. Like the differing branches of Christianity, these branches of Islam share many basic beliefs, such as devotion to the same God and reverence for the same scriptures.

SOCIAL PATTERNS

Social Mobility

In some ways, Muslim society allowed more social mobility than did medieval European society. Under earlier dynasties, Arabs had considered themselves superior to non-Arabs, but this belief declined with later dynasties. It became possible to move up in the social order, especially through religious, scholarly, or military achievements.

Treatment of Conquered Peoples

Islamic leaders imposed a special tax on non-Muslims, but they allowed people to practice their own faiths. Christians and Jews often served as doctors, officials, and translators in Muslim communities.

Slavery

As in Greece and Rome, slavery was common in the Muslim world. Slaves from Spain, Greece, Africa, India, and central Asia were brought to Muslim cities. Most slaves worked as house servants, and some were

KEY THEMES AND CONCEPTS

Justice Islamic law was an important unifying element in the Muslim empires. Justinian had also unified his empire through a uniform code of law.

PREPARING FOR THE REGENTS

Write a paragraph that describes several similarities and differences between the splits in the Christian Church and the division in Islam.

skilled craftspeople. It was possible for slaves to buy their freedom. Also, if a slave converted to Islam, his or her children would be free.

Status of Women

Islam teaches the spiritual equality of men and women. The Quran protected women of the time in ways that some societies did not. For example, it prohibited the killing of daughters and protected the rights of widows. Women had inheritance rights, could be educated, and had to consent to marriage freely. Nevertheless, in Muslim society, the roles and rights of women differed from those of men. For example, a daughter's inheritance was less than a son's.

As Islam spread, Muslims adopted some beliefs of non-Arab people. In Byzantium and Persia, for example, Arabs veiled women and secluded them in a separate part of their homes. Restrictions on women varied by region and class in Muslim civilization. Upper-class women were more likely to be restricted. In rural areas, women continued to participate in the economy.

MUSLIM EMPIRES

After the death of the fourth caliph in 661, the Umayyad family established a dynasty that ruled the Muslim world until 750. After that, the Abbassid dynasty took over control of the Muslim world.

The Umayyad Dynasty

The Muslim world grew under the **Umayyad dynasty,** spreading Islam to the Atlantic in the west and to the Indus Valley in the east. It was based in Damascus rather than in Mecca. While conquests brought wealth, the Umayyad dynasty also faced the challenge of ruling large cities and territories. They often relied on local officials to help govern their empire. This reliance allowed Byzantine and Persian traditions of government to influence Islamic leaders.

As conquests slowed in the 700s, tensions developed between rich and poor. There was criticism that the Umayyad family had left the simple ways of Islam. Non-Arab Muslims complained that they had fewer rights than Arab Muslims. In addition, the Shiites opposed the Umayyads because the Umayyads had killed a descendant of Muhammad. Over time, anger over these inequities developed into a rebellion.

The Abbassid Dynasty

Unhappy Muslims found a leader in Abu al-Abbas, who in 750 captured the Umayyad capital of Damascus. Abu al-Abbas then founded the **Abbassid dynasty,** which ruled until the mid-1200s.

One consequence of Abbassid rule was that it ended Arab domination of Islam. The Abbassid court ruled from Baghdad. Early Abbassid rulers enjoyed great wealth and power, and the Muslim world experienced a

PREPARING FOR THE REGENTS

What was the status of women under ancient Islamic law?

KEY THEMES AND CONCEPTS

Diversity The diversity of the Umayyad empire was one cause of its decline. Rich and poor, Sunni and Shiite, and Arab and non-Arab disagreed about important issues.

PREPARING FOR THE REGENTS

How was life under Abbassid rule different from life under Umayyad rule?

golden age. Baghdad exceeded the size and wealth of Constantinople under Abbassid rule. It was a beautiful city with gardens and magnificent buildings.

Political Divisions

Around 850, Abbassid rule of Islamic civilization began to decline. Independent dynasties began to rule separate Muslim states. In the 900s, the Seljuk Turks adopted Islam and built their own empire. They took control of the Arab capital, Baghdad. Then, in the 1200s, the Mongols destroyed Baghdad. Even so, the Muslim religion continued to link people over three continents.

ISLAM'S GOLDEN AGE

At its height under the Abbassids, the Muslim world was composed of people from many cultures, including Arabs, Persians, Egyptians, and Europeans. Muslims absorbed and blended customs and traditions from many of the peoples they ruled. The glory of the empires was reflected in their emphasis on learning, achievements in the arts and sciences, and flourishing economies based on trade.

Preservation of Greco-Roman Culture

Muslim scholars translated the works of many of the Greek scholars. Muslim advances in mathematics, astronomy, and medicine were also based partly on their study of Greek and Indian knowledge.

Education

The prophet Muhammad taught a respect for learning that continued to characterize Muslim culture throughout the ages. The Muslim empires

⚷ KEY THEMES AND CONCEPTS

Culture and Intellectual Life Education was an important part of Muslim culture. Cities such as Baghdad, Cairo, and Cordoba were powerful centers of learning.

The Golden Age of Muslim Civilization

Art	Literature
• Use beautiful writing and patterns to decorate buildings and art • Adapt Byzantine domes and arches • Paint people and animals in nonreligious art	• Consider Quran most important piece of Arabic literature • Chant oral poetry • Collect stories from other people

Muslim Civilization

Learning	Medicine
• Translate writings of Greek philosophers • Develop algebra • Observe Earth turning and measure its circumference	• Require doctors to pass difficult tests • Set up hospitals with emergency rooms • Study diseases and write medical books

included dazzling centers of learning such as Baghdad, Cairo, and Cordoba. The vast libraries and universities of these cities attracted a large and diverse number of well-paid and highly respected scholars.

Art and Architecture

MOSQUES AND PALACES   Muslim architects were influenced by Byzantine domes and arches. The walls and ceilings of mosques and palaces were decorated with elaborate abstract and geometric patterns. Muslim religious leaders forbade artists to portray God or human figures in religious art.

CALLIGRAPHY   Muslim artists were highly skilled in calligraphy, or artistic writing. Calligraphy decorated buildings and pieces of art. Often, Muslim calligraphers used verses from the Quran.

DRAWINGS AND PAINTINGS   In nonreligious art, some Muslim artists portrayed animal or human figures, although this was usually discouraged. Persian and Turkish artists adorned books with beautiful miniature paintings.

Literature and Philosophy

POETRY   A wide variety of themes dominated written Muslim poetry, from praise of important leaders to contemplation of the joys and sorrows of love. In addition, because the Quran was the most important piece of Muslim literature, many writers wrote poems based on this holy book.

TALES   Muslim storytellers adapted stories from Greek, Indian, Jewish, and Egyptian culture, as well as others. The most famous collection of Muslim stories is *The Thousand and One Nights,* which includes fables, romances, and humorous anecdotes.

PHILOSOPHY   Muslim scholars translated the philosophical works of Greek, Indian, and Chinese writers. In fact, the scholar Ibn Rushd, who was known in Europe as **Averröes,** strongly influenced medieval Christian scholars with his writings on Aristotle. The Jewish rabbi Maimonides influenced Christian scholars of the Middle Ages in much the same way.

Mathematics and Science

ALGEBRA   Muslims studied Indian and Greek mathematics before making their own contributions. Muslims pioneered the study of algebra. Eventually, the works of some Muslim mathematicians were translated into Latin and studied in Europe.

ASTRONOMY   Greek and Indian astronomical discoveries resulted in Muslim development of astronomical tables. Muslim astronomers also observed the Earth's rotation and calculated the circumference of the Earth within a few thousand feet.

KEY THEMES AND CONCEPTS

Belief Systems Muslim religious art rarely depicted God or human figures because the Quran prohibited the worship of idols.

KEY THEMES AND CONCEPTS

Culture and Intellectual Life Modern mathematics and science can trace many of their roots to the achievements of Islamic civilization.

MEDICINE Muslim medicine was remarkably advanced. Doctors were required to pass difficult tests before they could practice. Hospitals were set up. Physicians studied various diseases and wrote books that became standard texts in Europe.

Economic Achievements

The Muslim world developed a prosperous economy. Muslims had an extensive trade network and encouraged manufacturing. Agriculture also flourished.

TRADE Merchants were honored in Muslim society. From 750 to 1350, Muslims established a large trade network across their empire. Traders not only exchanged goods but spread religious belief, culture, and technology as well.

Trading and a money economy allowed Muslims to take the lead in new business practices. They established partnerships, sold goods on credit, and formed banks to exchange different kinds of currency.

MANUFACTURING Guilds organized manufacturing in the Muslim world. Heads of guilds regulated prices, weights, and measurements, and they monitored product quality. Muslim craftworkers produced steel swords in Damascus, leather goods in Cordoba, and carpets in Persia.

AGRICULTURE Muslim farmers grew crops such as sugarcane, cotton, medicinal herbs, fruits, and vegetables. These products were purchased and sold in many world markets.

CHRISTIAN EUROPE ENRICHED BY ISLAMIC CIVILIZATION

The advances of the Muslim world gradually reached Christian Europe through Spain and Sicily. The Crusades also encouraged cultural diffusion.

Muslim Spain

Spain became a magnificent Muslim cultural center. Muslim princes encouraged poetry, the arts, and learning. In Spain, the Muslims continued their policy of toleration, hiring Jewish officials and encouraging Christian students to study Greek thought.

Muslim Sicily

During the early Middle Ages, Arabs gained control of Sicily and other Mediterranean islands. The island was soon regained by Europeans, but a Muslim presence remained. Muslim officials provided effective government, and Arab merchants and farmers helped the economy to grow. Muslim culture graced the courts of the Christian kings.

PREPARING FOR THE REGENTS

List two Islamic achievements in each of the following areas.

Mathematics:

Art:

Literature:

Medicine:

Economics:

KEY THEMES AND CONCEPTS

Interdependence It was through Muslim Spain and Sicily, as well as through the Crusades and the Muslim trading network, that the achievements of Islam's golden age reached European society.

The Crusades

Crusaders came into contact with various Muslim peoples and cultures. Europeans were impressed with Muslim advancements in the arts and sciences as well as with their preservation of Greco-Roman culture. As a result, the advances of the Muslim world gradually influenced Christian Europe.

SUMMARY

The Muslim world was richly diverse. It spread across an extensive area in Europe, Africa, and Asia. Muslim empires had flourishing economies supported by a vast trade network. At its height, the Muslim world made great advances in fields such as literature, mathematics, astronomy, and medicine. In these areas, Muslims were greatly influenced by other cultures, including those of classical Greece and India. In time, Islamic civilization had a great impact on Christian Europe.

SECTION OVERVIEW

The Middle Ages, or **medieval** period, lasted from about 500 to the middle of the 1400s. The collapse of the Roman empire had left Western Europe with no unifying government. In response, political and social systems emerged, such as feudalism and manorialism, that were based on powerful local lords and their landholdings. A strict social hierarchy existed during the Middle Ages. The Christian Church emerged as a unifying force in Western Europe and had great influence over economic and social as well as religious life. Conditions gradually improved, allowing Europeans to build a new civilization based on Greco-Roman and Christian traditions.

KEY THEMES AND CONCEPTS

As you review this section, take special note of the following key themes and concepts:

Interdependence What duties and responsibilities guided people's lives in medieval Europe?

Political Systems What roles did individual citizens play in the medieval feudal systems?

Economic Systems How did manorialism provide for people's basic economic needs?

Belief Systems What roles did the Church play in medieval society?

KEY PEOPLE AND TERMS

As you review this section, be sure you understand the significance of these key people and terms:

medieval	serf	monastery
Charlemagne	secular	anti-Semitism
chivalry	excommunicate	Gothic
manorialism	Pope Innocent III	

★ **THE BIG IDEA**
During the Middle Ages in Europe:

- there was disorder for a time after the collapse of the Roman empire.

- wealthy landowners dominated society and provided people with protection.

- people relied on the Christian Church for spiritual and political guidance.

- achievements in art and architecture centered around Christianity.

GEOGRAPHIC SETTING

The geography of Europe had a powerful effect on the development of the area. Europe's location and resources helped determine the groups of people who settled there and the people who would try to control it.

Location

Europe lay at the western end of the Eurasian landmass, which extends from present-day Portugal to China. Parts of Great Britain, Spain, France, Italy, Greece, and other areas of Eastern Europe had been within the Roman empire. Roman roads had allowed Roman and Christian customs to spread. As you have learned, Germanic tribes overran Europe from about 400 to 700, ending Roman rule.

Resources

FORESTS AND FERTILE SOIL   Europe had many natural resources. Dense forests, with valuable timber, covered much of northern Europe, and the area's fertile soil was well suited for raising crops. In addition, minerals such as iron and coal lay untapped beneath the Earth's surface.

SEAS AND RIVERS   The oceans and seas that surrounded much of Europe were also important resources. People on the coasts fished the waters and used them as a means of trade and transportation. Large rivers in Europe also provided food and a means of travel.

PREPARING FOR THE REGENTS

How did Europeans use natural resources to provide for basic economic needs?

THE FRANKISH EMPIRE

The Germanic people who overran the Roman empire were warriors, farmers, and herders. Their culture differed greatly from that of the Romans they had conquered. Germanic tribes were governed by unwritten laws and customs and ruled by elected kings.

KEY THEMES AND CONCEPTS

Change Clovis, king of the Franks, converted to Christianity. By doing this, he gained the support of the leaders of the Christian Church.

The Rise of the Franks

From about 400 to 700, warrior tribes divided Europe and fought for control of various territories. During this time, the Franks emerged as the most powerful and successful of the tribes in Gaul, or present-day France. In the late 400s, Clovis, a brilliant and ruthless leader, became king of the Franks. Clovis is probably best known for his conversion to Christianity, which gained him a powerful ally in the Christian Church.

Battle of Tours

As you have learned, Muslims had moved into Spain. They tried to advance into France. At the Battle of Tours in 732, the Franks defeated a Muslim army. Although Muslims continued to rule most of Spain, they advanced no farther in Western Europe.

Charlemagne

During the 800s, **Charlemagne,** a Frankish king, built an empire that stretched across modern-day France, Germany, and part of Italy.

Charlemagne's Empire

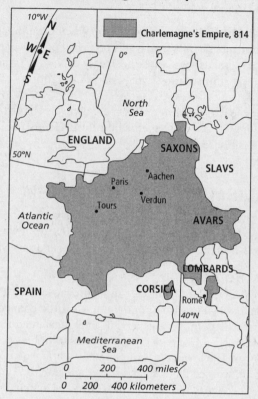

PREPARING FOR THE REGENTS

Practice your map skills by answering the following questions.

1. Name two groups that were part of Charlemagne's empire.

2. Name two modern-day countries that include areas once ruled by Charlemagne.

COOPERATION WITH THE CHURCH In 800, Pope Leo III, the head of the Christian Church of the time, called for help against rebellious nobles in Rome. Charlemagne answered the pope's call and defeated the Roman nobles in battle. To show his gratitude, Pope Leo III, on Christmas Day 800, crowned Charlemagne "Emperor of the Romans." The crowning of Charlemagne helped revive the ideal of a united Christian church and empire.

After being named emperor, Charlemagne strengthened his rule and attempted to create a united Christian Europe. Working closely with the Roman Catholic Church, he helped spread Christianity to the far reaches of his empire.

GOVERNMENT Charlemagne appointed nobles to rule local areas. He gave them land, expecting them in return to help with the defense of the empire. As a way to control these rulers, Charlemagne regularly sent out officials called *missi dominici* to check on conditions throughout the empire.

LEARNING Charlemagne also encouraged learning. He set up a school to ensure the education of government officials. He also established

PREPARING FOR THE REGENTS

Describe several ways in which Charlemagne sought to restore order to medieval Europe.

libraries where scholars copied ancient texts, including the Bible and texts of science and history written in Latin.

END OF CHARLEMAGNE'S REIGN   When Charlemagne died in 814, his empire quickly fell apart as his heirs battled for control. In 843, Charlemagne's grandsons signed the Treaty of Verdun, which divided Charlemagne's empire into three separate kingdoms, one for each grandson.

Charlemagne had a lasting influence, however. His strong government was a model for future medieval rulers. He also helped spread Christianity to northern Europe.

FEUDALISM AND MANORIALISM

During the early part of the Middle Ages, kings were too weak to keep invaders out of their kingdoms. People began to leave towns and cities, banding together in the countryside for protection and survival.

Medieval Society

Everyone had a well-defined place in medieval society. People were born into their social positions, and there was little chance of moving beyond them. The nobility consisted of the kings and queens, greater lords, lesser lords, and knights. The elite class of nobles controlled the land and power. The lower class of peasants, who made up the bulk of the population, worked the land and served the nobles. The clergy was highly respected, due to the fact that the Christian Church dominated life during the Middle Ages.

Feudalism

FEUDAL RESPONSIBILITIES   Feudalism was a loosely structured political system in which powerful lords (nobles) owned large sections of land. They divided their land into estates called fiefs, which were given to lesser lords called vassals. Vassals pledged their loyalty and military support to their lords in return for this land.

KNIGHTHOOD   Because people in medieval Europe were often at war, many nobles trained to become knights, or mounted warriors. They practiced strict discipline and learned how to ride well and handle weapons skillfully. In addition, knights were bound by a code of conduct known as **chivalry.** This code charged them to be brave, loyal, and true to their word. The code also required knights to protect women.

ROLE OF NOBLEWOMEN   Women played an active role in feudal society. A "lady" was in charge of her husband's estate while he was away serving his lord in battle. She was responsible for all household affairs including the raising of children. In preparation for their adult role, girls received training in household arts such as spinning, weaving, and

The Structure of Feudal Society

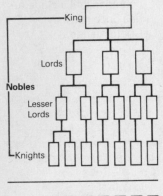

 PREPARING FOR THE REGENTS

Feudalism was based on personal agreements among individuals. This loose system of government differed greatly from the strong centralized government of Rome that existed before the Middle Ages.

PREPARING FOR THE REGENTS

What roles did individual citizens play in feudal society?

the management of servants. Women had limited inheritance rights, however, since most possessions went to the eldest son.

Manorialism

The basis for the medieval economy was **manorialism,** an economic system structured around a lord's manor, or estate. Manors often included one or more villages and the land surrounding them. Under the manorial system, each group in society had a place; each also had certain rights and responsibilities.

PEASANTS AND LORDS   Most of the peasants who lived on the estate were **serfs.** Serfs were not slaves, but they were bound to the land. They could not leave the estate without the lord's permission.

MUTUAL RESPONSIBILITIES   Serfs farmed the lord's land and did other work such as repairing roads and fences. In return for the service provided by peasants, the lord provided them with the use of several acres of land to farm. The lord was also supposed to protect them during times of war.

HARSH LIFE FOR PEASANTS   For peasants, life on the manor was difficult and often harsh. Peasant men, women, and children worked long hours, and few peasants lived past the age of 35. In spite of such hardship, the lives of peasants were held together by the common thread of Christianity. Their celebrations—marriages, births, and holidays such as Christmas and Easter—were centered in the Christian Church.

THE CHURCH IN MEDIEVAL LIFE

During the Middle Ages, two distinct Christian churches emerged: the Orthodox Christian Church in the east and the Roman Catholic Church in the west. (The two branches split permanently in 1054.) The Roman Catholic Church became the main stabilizing force in Western Europe. The Church provided religious leadership as well as **secular,** or worldly, leadership. It also played a key role in reviving and preserving learning.

Church Hierarchy

At the head of the Roman Catholic Church was the pope, whom followers believed to be the spiritual representative of Jesus on earth. Below the pope came archbishops, bishops, and local priests. For peasants and town dwellers, everyday life was closely tied to local priests and the village church.

Spiritual Role of the Church

The main responsibility of the Church was to serve the spiritual needs of medieval society. Local priests instructed peasants and townspeople in the faith and provided comfort to them in troubled times. The Church taught that all men and women were sinners but that Christians could achieve salvation, or eternal life in heaven, through faith in Jesus, good works, and

 **PREPARING FOR THE REGENTS**

What was the most important economic resource in medieval Europe? Who controlled this resource? How did control of economic resources affect the power structure in medieval society?

♀ KEY THEMES AND CONCEPTS

Interdependence
Feudalism and the manor system were both based on mutual responsibility. In feudalism, nobles owed duties to each other. In the manor system, nobles and peasants provided benefits to each other.

♀ KEY THEMES AND CONCEPTS

Belief Systems Religion was an essential part of life for medieval people. The Roman Catholic Church spread the teachings of Jesus and administered the sacraments, including marriage and baptism.

participation in sacraments, or sacred spiritual rituals. To escape the punishment of hell, they needed to take part in the sacraments of the Church.

Secular Role of the Church

ECONOMIC POWER   The Church filled many secular, or worldly, roles during the Middle Ages. As the largest landholder in Europe, the Church had significant economic power. The Church also gained wealth through the tithe, a tax Christians were required to pay that equaled 10 percent of their income.

POLITICAL POWER   The Church had its own set of laws, called canon law, and its own courts of justice. The Church claimed authority over secular rulers, but monarchs did not always recognize this authority. As a result, there were frequent power struggles between the pope in Rome and various kings and emperors.

Popes believed that they had authority over kings. Popes sometimes **excommunicated,** or excluded from the Catholic Church, secular rulers who challenged or threatened papal power. For example, **Pope Innocent III** excommunicated King John of England in the 1200s during a dispute about appointing an archbishop.

Monastic Orders

Some men and women became monks or nuns, leaving worldly society and devoting their lives to God. They entered **monasteries,** communities where Christian men or women focused on spiritual goals. Monks and nuns took vows of chastity, or purity, and of obedience to the abbot, or head of the religious order. They also took an oath of poverty. Monks

PREPARING FOR THE REGENTS

Identify four ways in which the Roman Catholic Church affected economic or political affairs during the Middle Ages.

1.

2.

3.

4.

The Medieval Church

Everyday Life
- Christians attend village churches.
- Some priests run schools in village churches.
- All Christians pay taxes to Church.

Power of Church
- Pope leads Roman Catholic Church.
- Church has its own laws and courts.
- Church excommunicates those who do not obey rules.

Nuns and Monks
- Some set up housing, hospitals, and schools for sick and poor.
- Some become missionaries.
- Some preserve learning.

Reform
- Church becomes rich and powerful.
- Some clergy become corrupt.
- Reformers try to make changes.

and nuns fulfilled many social needs, such as tending to the sick, helping the poor, and educating children.

CENTERS OF LEARNING   In monasteries and convents (religious communities of women), monks and nuns also preserved ancient writings by copying ancient texts. Some monks and nuns taught Latin and Greek classics; others produced their own literary works.

MISSIONARY WORK   Not all monks and nuns remained in monasteries. Some became missionaries, risking their lives to spread the message of Christianity. The Church sometimes honored its missionaries by declaring them saints. St. Patrick was a missionary who set up the Church in Ireland. St. Augustine was sent as a missionary to the Angles and Saxons in England.

Women and the Church

The Church taught that women and men were equal in the sight of God. However, on earth, women were supposed to be subservient to men. There was some effort to protect women in medieval society. For example, the Church set a minimum age for women to marry. However, women were viewed in two opposing ways. On one hand, the Church considered women weak, easily tempted into sin, and dependent on the guidance of men. On the other hand, women were seen as modest and pure in spirit, similar to Mary, the mother of Jesus.

JEWS IN MEDIEVAL EUROPE

Numerous Jewish communities existed throughout Europe during the Middle Ages. While Jews in Muslim Spain and northern areas of Europe were generally tolerated, most Christians persecuted Jews. Not only did the Church bar Jews from owning land or practicing many occupations; many Christians blamed Jews for the death of Jesus. As a result, the foundations for **anti-Semitism,** or prejudice against Jews, were laid. Gradually, Christians began blaming Jews for all kinds of misfortunes, from famines to disease. In time, Jews migrated to Eastern Europe, where they set up communities that survived until modern times.

MEDIEVAL CULTURAL ACHIEVEMENTS

In early medieval times, life was very chaotic. People concentrated on protecting themselves from invasions and taking care of their own physical needs. Toward the end of the Middle Ages, however, European society became more stable and made cultural gains in the fields of literature, art, and architecture.

Literature

Although the language of scholars was Latin, new stories and writings began to appear in the everyday languages of the people. Medieval

 PREPARING FOR THE REGENTS

What role did monks and nuns play in preserving Greco-Roman culture?

 PREPARING FOR THE REGENTS

Compare and contrast the roles of men and women in feudal society.

literature included stories of knights and feudal lords as well as tales about the common people. Authors such as Dante and Chaucer wrote stories about warrior heroes and ordinary people who showed courage, humor, and morality.

Architecture and Art

The architecture and art of the Middle Ages focused on glorifying God. Almost all of the artistic achievements of the time were a reflection of the power of the Church. With money from increased trade in the late Middle Ages, nobles and townspeople alike began contributing to great works of architecture and art.

ROMAN INFLUENCES   Around the year 1000, towns began to build stone churches that reflected the influence of Rome. With thick supporting walls and towers and only small slits in the stone for windows, these structures were fortresslike and dimly lighted.

THE GOTHIC TRADITION   The Gothic style of architecture first appeared in Europe in the early 1100s. These new buildings, unlike those in the Roman style, seemed to soar upward. The **Gothic** style was characterized by pointed arches and by flying buttresses, stone supports that stood outside the building. With this outside support, walls could be built higher, leaving space for huge stained-glass windows. These windows, along with sculptures and carvings inside the churches, often told biblical stories, serving to educate the illiterate people of medieval Europe.

 PREPARING FOR THE REGENTS

Describe the relationship between religion and art in both medieval Europe and Islamic civilization.

PREPARING FOR THE REGENTS

What cultural contributions did medieval Europe make in literature? In architecture?

SUMMARY

The Middle Ages was a troubled period in European history. After the Germanic invasions, society began to come together under the strict political organization supplied by feudalism and the economic system of manorialism. The Christian Church helped to unify Western Europe and touched every aspect of medieval life. Monasteries and convents became centers of learning; monks and nuns preserved ancient writings by copying ancient texts. As conditions improved and life became more stable, medieval Europe began to develop its own unique culture.

SECTION 6 The Crusades

SECTION OVERVIEW

In the 1050s, Seljuk Turks, who were Muslims, invaded the Byzantine empire and conquered Palestine. The Christian Church called for a movement to drive the Muslims out of Palestine. For nearly 200 years, Christians fought a series of religious wars known as the **Crusades.** The wars failed to regain Palestine, and they left a legacy of ill will and distrust between Christians and Muslims. However, the Crusades had other effects as well. Trade increased, and the European economy expanded. Feudal monarchs gained more power, and Europeans learned of the existence of lands beyond their borders. Europeans also benefited from the learning and cultural achievements of Islam.

KEY THEMES AND CONCEPTS

As you review this section, take special note of the following key themes and concepts:

Imperialism Why did Christians and Muslims engage in the Crusades?

Change What effect did the Crusades have on the economy of Europe?

Power How did the Crusades affect the power of the Church and feudal lords?

Culture How did the Crusades expand Europeans' view of the world?

KEY PEOPLE AND TERMS

As you review this section, be sure you understand the significance of these key people and terms:

Crusades	Holy Land
Urban II	Saladin
Council of Clermont	Richard the Lion-Hearted

★ THE BIG IDEA
The Crusades:

- were driven by Christians' desire to force the Muslims from Palestine as well as to gain wealth and power.

- resulted in increased European trade with the Muslim world.

- temporarily increased the power of the Church and greatly strengthened feudal monarchs.

- introduced Europeans to the advances of Byzantine and Muslim civilizations.

BEGINNING OF THE CRUSADES

In the 1050s, the Seljuk Turks invaded the Byzantine empire. Over the next four decades, they overran most Byzantine lands in Asia Minor as well as Palestine. In 1095, the Byzantine emperor asked the pope, **Urban II,** for help. Pope Urban agreed. At the **Council of Clermont,** Urban encouraged French and German bishops to recover Palestine, or the **Holy Land,** as it was called by Christians. Christians referred to this area as the Holy Land because it was where Jesus had lived and taught. Muslims and Jews also considered the land holy. Christians who answered the pope's call were known as crusaders. Men and women from all over Western Europe left their homes to reclaim the Holy Land. Many never returned.

PREPARING FOR THE REGENTS

The Crusades were caused by a variety of factors. Describe several causes of the Crusades.

REASONS FOR THE CRUSADES

There were several other motives for the Crusades, some religious and some secular. These reasons included the following.

- The pope believed that the Crusades would increase his power in Europe.
- Christians believed that their sins would be forgiven if they participated in the Crusades.
- Nobles hoped to gain wealth and land by participating in the Crusades.
- Adventurers saw the Crusades as a chance for travel and excitement.
- Serfs hoped to escape feudal oppression by fighting in the Crusades.

PREPARING FOR THE REGENTS

During the Crusades, how do you think Muslims viewed Christians? How do you think Christians viewed Muslims?

AN INITIAL CHRISTIAN VICTORY

For 200 years, the fighting went on. Only the first of four Crusades, however, came close to achieving its goals. In 1099, Christians captured the city of Jerusalem. They followed the victory with a massacre of Muslim and Jewish inhabitants.

Crusaders divided their conquered lands into four small states called the crusader states. They divided these lands into feudal domains. Muslim leaders tried to regain these kingdoms, and this effort resulted in additional Crusades.

SALADIN AND MUSLIM VICTORY

A Respected Muslim Leader

During the late 1100s, **Saladin** united the Muslim world. Both Muslims and Christians admired and respected Saladin. However, when Saladin marched toward Jerusalem, the Christians were determined to stop him.

The Taking of Jerusalem

A Christian victory did not occur, however. The crusaders in Jerusalem surrendered. Saladin forbade his soldiers to kill, harm, or steal from the defeated crusaders.

Richard the Lion-Hearted became king of England in 1189. He was determined to retake Jerusalem from Saladin. During the Third Crusade, Richard won several victories. Richard's forces advanced to within a few miles of Jerusalem, but were unable to capture the city.

THE END OF THE CRUSADES

Later Crusades also resulted in failure for the Christians. The Fourth Crusade was supposed to regain Jerusalem, but the knights were diverted. After helping Venetian merchants defeat their Byzantine trade rivals, the knights looted Constantinople itself. What had started as a war of Christians against Muslims ended in a battle between rival Christian factions.

In Palestine, Muslims overran the crusader states. They captured Acre, the last city to fall, in 1291. This time the Muslims massacred Christian inhabitants after their victory.

IMPACT OF THE CRUSADES

The crusaders failed to attain their main goal of retaking the Holy Land. Unfortunately, the Crusades left behind a legacy of religious hatred between Christians and Muslims, since each group had committed terrible acts of violence against the other. Crusaders sometimes turned their hatred on Jews in Europe as they traveled to or from Palestine. At times crusaders destroyed entire Jewish communities.

The Crusades did, however, have some positive effects. The European economy began to grow, and Europeans gained an expanded view of the world.

Increased Trade

Trade with the Byzantine empire before the time of the Crusades had sparked the interest of Europeans in goods from the east. The amount of trade increased during the time of the Crusades. Crusaders returning to Europe brought with them interesting new fabrics, spices, and perfumes.

Merchants from the Italian city of Venice had built ships to transport crusaders. After the conflicts, these ships were available to carry products to and from Palestine. After the fall of the Christian states, Italian traders helped keep the trade routes to Palestine open. Sugar, cotton, and rice were just a few of the goods traded. The economies of both East and West benefited from this commerce.

Encouragement of Learning

European interest in learning was stimulated as Europeans were introduced to Byzantine and Muslim culture. Europeans saw how the Byzantines and Muslims had preserved Greco-Roman learning and maintained great universities. Europeans were also exposed to advances these cultures had made in mathematics, science, literature, art, and

📝 **PREPARING FOR THE REGENTS**

To learn more about Constantinople and the Byzantine empire, see Section 3 of this unit.

KEY THEMES AND CONCEPTS

Economic Systems The increase in trade that resulted from the Crusades had a significant impact on Europe. Desire for direct access to the riches of the East was one motive for the overseas explorations that began in the 1400s.

Causes

- People want to free the Holy Land from Seljuk control.
- Many people want to get rich and gain new land.
- Some people want to see new places.

The Crusades

Effects

- Trade increases.
- People of different religions grow to hate each other.
- Popes become more powerful.
- Feudal kings become more powerful.
- Renting land helps to free serfs.
- Europeans become interested in traveling.
- People learn about other cultures.

geographical knowledge. Europeans gained a broader outlook and were introduced to many new ideas.

Changes in the Church

The Crusades temporarily increased the power of the pope. Papal conflicts with feudal monarchs in Europe eventually lessened this power, however. In addition, the rift between the eastern and western churches was not healed. In fact, it was widened after the crusaders' attack on Constantinople.

Changes in the Feudal System

The Crusades increased the power of monarchs, who had gained the right to increase taxes in order to support the fighting. Some feudal monarchs led crusaders into battle and thereby heightened their prestige.

At the same time, the institution of feudalism was weakening. Traditionally, lords had required grain or labor from their serfs. Now, needing money to finance the Crusades, they began to ask for payment of rent in money. Feudalism was weakened, and an economy based on money, not land, took hold.

SUMMARY

The Crusades began in the 1000s for a variety of reasons. For 200 years, Christians and Muslims fought one another and committed terrible massacres. However, both sides also had admirable leaders. The Crusades had several effects on Europe. Trade began to increase, and a money economy emerged. The Church temporarily gained power. Although feudal monarchs were strengthened, feudalism itself was weakened. Christian Europe was influenced by various aspects of Byzantine and Muslim civilization as a result of the Crusades.

PREPARING FOR THE REGENTS

List two ways in which the Crusades had an impact on each of the aspects of medieval life.

Global economy:

1.

2.

European interest in learning:

1.

2.

Christian Church:

1.

2.

Questions for Regents Practice

Review the Preparing for the Regents section of this book. Then answer the following questions, which include multiple-choice questions, a thematic essay, and a series of document-based questions.

MULTIPLE CHOICE

Directions

Circle the *number* of the word or expression that best completes the statement or answers the question.

1 In traditional India, the caste system and the Hindu beliefs in karma and dharma most directly resulted in
   1 the establishment of a set of rules for each individual in the society
   2 the rapid industrialization of the economy
   3 a strong emphasis on the acquisition of wealth
   4 a strong belief in the importance of education

2 In traditional Chinese culture, which philosophy had the greatest influence on the development of social order and political organization?
   1 Taoism
   2 Shintoism
   3 Confucianism
   4 Marxism

3 After the fall of Rome, the eastern portion of the Roman empire became known as the
   1 Persian empire
   2 Byzantine empire
   3 Mongol empire
   4 Gupta empire

4 Which group had the greatest influence on early Russian culture?
   1 Franks
   2 Ottoman Turks
   3 Byzantine empire
   4 Roman Catholic Church

5 An important achievement of the Golden Age of Muslim culture was the
   1 preservation of ancient Greek and Roman ideas
   2 development of gunpowder
   3 establishment of trade with South America
   4 emergence of feudalism as a unifying force

6 Which factor helps explain the scientific and literary achievements of the Muslims during their golden age?
   1 expansion of transatlantic trade
   2 innovations introduced by the Europeans during the Renaissance
   3 cultural diversity accepted by many Islamic governments
   4 legal equality of all people in the Islamic empire

7 Which economic system existed in Europe during the early Middle Ages?
   1 free market
   2 socialism
   3 manorialism
   4 command

8 The growth of feudalism in Europe during the Middle Ages was primarily caused by the
   1 rivalry between the colonial empires
   2 suppression of internationalism
   3 decline of the Roman Catholic Church
   4 collapse of a strong central government

9 Which was a characteristic of feudalism?
   1 Land was exchanged for military service and obligations.
   2 Government was provided by a bureaucracy of civil servants.
   3 Power rested in the hands of a strong central government.
   4 Unified national court systems were developed.

10 "All things were under its domain. . . . Its power was such that no one could hope to escape its scrutiny."

Which European institution during the Middle Ages is best described by this statement?
1 the guild
2 the knighthood
3 the Church
4 the nation-state

11 The art, music, and philosophy of the medieval period in Europe generally dealt with
1 human scientific achievements
2 religious themes
3 materialism
4 classical Greek and Roman subjects

12 Buildings such as the Gothic cathedrals in Western Europe and the Parthenon in ancient Greece reflect each society's
1 imperialist attitudes
2 cultural values
3 belief in democracy
4 rigid social structure

13 As the Middle Ages ended, the rise of a middle class in Western Europe can be attributed partly to the
1 economic policies of the Roman empire
2 increase in trade that resulted from the Crusades
3 strength of Christianity in medieval Europe
4 self-sufficiency of the manor system

14 One major result of the Crusades was
1 permanent occupation of the Holy Land by the Europeans
2 long-term decrease in European trade
3 conversion of most Muslims to Christianity
4 spread of Middle Eastern culture and technology to Europe

15 In Europe, the Crusades resulted in
1 a greater isolation of the region from the world
2 an increased demand for goods from the Middle East and Asia
3 the adoption of Islam as the official religion of many European nations
4 the strengthening of the feudal system

THEMATIC ESSAY

Directions
Read the following instructions that include a theme, a task, and suggestions. Follow the instructions to create a well-organized essay that has an introduction with a thesis statement, several paragraphs explaining the thesis, and a conclusion.

Theme: Culture and Intellectual Life
Throughout global history, political conditions in some civilizations have produced "golden ages."

Task
- Define the term *golden age.*
- Describe a golden age in a specific civilization you have studied. Give specific examples that show why the time is considered such a memorable one in that civilization's history.
- Describe the political, economic, and other conditions that help a golden age to occur.

Suggestions
You may discuss any golden age you have studied. Some golden ages you may wish to consider include classical China, the Hellenistic Age, the Pax Romana, or the Muslim golden age. You are not limited to these suggestions.

QUESTIONS BASED ON DOCUMENTS

The following exercise asks you to analyze three historical documents and then write an essay using evidence from those documents. This exercise is similar to the document-based question that you will see on the Regents Examination, which may include six or more documents. For additional practice with historical documents, see the Preparing for the Regents section and the sample examinations in this book.

This task is based on the accompanying documents. Some of these documents have been edited for the purposes of this task. This task is designed to test your ability to work with historical documents. As you analyze the documents, take into account both the source of each document and the author's point of view.

Directions

Read the documents in Part A and answer the question or questions after each document. Then read the directions for Part B and write your essay.

Historical Context

Throughout global history, interactions between people of different belief systems have had a variety of results. Sometimes the interactions have been peaceful. At other times conflict has occurred.

Task

Examine several examples of interactions between belief systems. Evaluate the effects that these exchanges have had on the cultures involved.

Part A: Short Answer

Directions: Analyze the documents and answer the question or questions that follow each document, using the space provided.

DOCUMENT 1

> *Whoever honors his own [religion] and disparages another man's, whether from blind loyalty or with the intention of showing his own [religion] in a favorable light, does his own [religion] the greatest possible harm. Concord [peaceful harmony] is best, with each hearing and respecting the other's teachings. It is the wish of the [king] that members of all [religions] should be learned and should teach virtue.*
>
> —**Asoka,** *Edicts,* **about 270 B.C.**

1 Explain in your own words how Asoka felt people of one belief system should interact with followers of another belief system.

_____

_____

_____

2 Over what areas did Muslim leaders exert control by A.D. 750?

DOCUMENT 2

The Spread of Islam

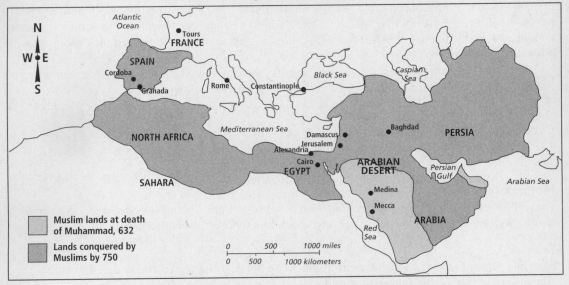

_____

_____

_____

DOCUMENT 3

> For your brethren who live in the east are in urgent need of your help, and you must hasten to give them the aid which has often been promised them. For . . . the Turks and Arabs have attacked them. . . . They have occupied more and more of the lands of those Christians, ... If you permit them to continue . . . the faithful of God will be much more widely attacked by them. On this account I, or rather the Lord, beseech you as Christ's heralds to publish this everywhere and to persuade all people of whatever rank, foot-soldiers and knights, poor and rich, to carry aid promptly to those Christians and to destroy that vile race from the lands of our friends. . . . Christ commands it.
>
> **—Fulcher of Chartres, *Gesta Francorum Jerusalem Expugnantium*, 1095**
> **[A contemporary account of Urban II's speech at the Council of Clermont]**

3   What does the speaker want Christians to do in response to his words?

_____

_____

_____

Part B: Essay

Directions:
- Write a well-organized essay that includes an introduction, several paragraphs, and a conclusion.
- Use evidence from the documents to support your response.
- Do not simply repeat the contents of the documents.
- Include specific, related outside information.

Historical Context

Throughout global history, interactions between people of different belief systems have had a variety of results. Sometimes the interactions have been peaceful. At other times conflict has occurred.

Task

Using information from the documents and your knowledge of global history and geography, evaluate the effects of interaction between people of different belief systems. Discuss both positive and negative effects.

Be sure to include specific historical details. You must also include additional information from your knowledge of global history.

Note: **The rubric for this essay appears in the Preparing for the Regents section of this book.**

3 Global Interactions (1200–1650)

UNIT OVERVIEW

In the years from 1200 through 1650, groups from various parts of the world came into contact with one another. In East Asia, cultural exchange occurred among China, Korea, and Japan. The Mongols established a vast empire that stretched from China westward into Europe. Over time, overland and sea trade routes linked more and more of the world and encouraged diffusion between East and West. In Europe, global interactions led to a new type of economy, based on money, and a new middle class. New ways of thinking emerged, in which old authority was questioned. Nations began to take shape as individual rulers gained power. In Africa, commerce contributed to the rise of powerful trading empires and the spread of Islam.

THEMATIC TIME LINE ACTIVITY

Some of the many themes developed in Unit 3 are:

interdependence   culture

movement of people and goods   change

nationalism   urbanization

economic systems   conflict

Choose one of the themes listed above. As you review Unit 3, create a thematic time line based on the theme you have chosen. Your time line should stretch from 1200 to 1650 and include major developments and key turning points having to do with your theme.

SECTION 1 — Early Japan and Feudalism

SECTION OVERVIEW

Even though Japan was always an island nation, it was not completely isolated. It was influenced by Korea and China. Japan was ruled by an emperor since about A.D. 500, but fights between rival warlords led to the development of feudalism in the 1100s. For several hundred years, military rulers controlled Japan. The dynasty that took power in 1603 brought stability and prosperity to Japan but imposed a rigid political and social order.

KEY THEMES AND CONCEPTS

As you review this section, take special note of the following key themes and concepts:

Geography How did Japan's geographic setting contribute to its development?

Movement of People and Goods What influence did China and Korea have on Japan?

Political Systems How did the system of feudalism work in Japan?

Economic Systems and Culture In what ways did the economy and culture of Japan flourish during its later feudal age?

KEY PEOPLE AND TERMS

As you review this section, be sure you understand the significance of these key people and terms:

Shinto
kami
Zen Buddhism
shogun
daimyo

samurai
bushido
kabuki
haiku

★ **THE BIG IDEA**
Early Japan:

- was strongly influenced by geography.
- borrowed selectively from Chinese culture.
- developed a feudal system.
- experienced stability and strong government during later feudal times.

GEOGRAPHIC SETTING

Major Physical Features

Japan is made up of a chain of mountainous islands in the Pacific Ocean off the coast of mainland Asia. There are four main islands and more than 3,000 smaller islands. The Japanese islands are part of the Ring of Fire, a group of lands around the Pacific Ocean that are vulnerable to earthquakes and volcanoes. Underground earthquakes can cause deadly tidal waves to sweep over the islands, destroying everything in their path.

Impact on Japanese Life

Because the islands of Japan are mountainous, the land was difficult to farm. Most of the population has always lived in narrow river valleys or along the coast. The rugged terrain has sometimes acted as a barrier to political unity.

The Japanese learned to use the sea both as a source of food and as a means of transportation from one island to another. The sea sometimes isolated Japan from other cultures, but it also acted as protection from invasion.

In addition, the experience of living in an unsettled natural environment that could bring volcanoes, earthquakes, and tidal waves taught the Japanese a deep respect for the forces of nature.

SHINTOISM

The traditional Japanese religion is called **Shinto,** meaning "the way of the gods." Shinto was characterized by the worship of the **kami,** or spirits found in all living and nonliving things. Kami were thought to control the powerful forces of nature. Believers respected the kami and tried to win their favor through prayer and offerings. The shared beliefs of the followers of Shinto eventually helped unite all of Japan. Shinto shrines still appear throughout Japan in places of unusual natural beauty or interest.

DIFFUSION FROM KOREA AND CHINA

Japanese culture features a unique blend of its own original traditions and ideas borrowed from the nearby civilizations of Korea and China. Korea often acted as a bridge between China and Japan.

Contact between Korea and Japan occurred as a result of both warfare and trade. Koreans introduced the Japanese to various aspects of Chinese culture.

Great interest in Chinese civilization was sparked among the Japanese. Around 600, a Japanese ruler had sent nobles to study in China. For over a century, during the Tang dynasty, the Japanese upper classes imported cultural traditions and ideas directly from China.

PREPARING FOR THE REGENTS

Describe two effects of geography on the development of Japanese culture.

1.

2.

KEY THEMES AND CONCEPTS

Belief Systems The Shinto belief system reflected the Japanese reverence for nature. Followers of Shintoism believed that all living and nonliving things possessed divine spirits. This belief caused a strong respect for the natural world.

KEY THEMES AND CONCEPTS

Movement of People and Goods The Japanese people borrowed ideas selectively from their mainland neighbors, Korea and China. Korea acted as a bridge between China and Japan.

Between the 700s and the 1100s, the Japanese blended the best of China with their own traditions to produce a distinctly Japanese civilization.

Chinese Influence on Writing

Around 500, the Koreans brought the Chinese system of writing to the Japanese. By the 800s, however, when Tang China began to decline, the Japanese adapted the Chinese system of writing to suit their own language and ideas.

Buddhism

Koreans also brought Buddhism from China. The religion spread quickly, and it flourished alongside traditional Japanese religions. During feudal times, a Chinese sect called **Zen Buddhism** spread throughout Japan. Zen Buddhists value peace, simple living, nature, and beauty.

Confucianism

The Japanese also were influenced by the Chinese philosophy of Confucianism, especially its ideas about proper behavior and social order. Although Buddhism took hold strongly in Japan, many Confucian ideas took root as well. These included ideas about family loyalty, honoring parents, and a respect for learning and the educated class.

Customs and Arts

Japanese courts adopted such Chinese customs as tea drinking and the tea ceremony. Chinese music and dancing, as well as Chinese garden design, became popular. In addition, the Japanese built their Buddhist monasteries to resemble Chinese monasteries.

THE IMPERIAL TRADITION

Early Japanese society was organized into clans with separate rulers and religious customs. One clan, the Yamato, gained control over the largest island of Japan around A.D. 500. Slowly the Yamato extended their rule and established themselves as the royal family of Japan. They claimed to be direct descendants of the sun goddess.

During the Heian period, which occurred between the 700s and the 1100s, the Japanese court was elegant and sophisticated. Nobles draped themselves in layers of fine silk. Elaborate rules of etiquette governed court ceremony. The emperor, who was revered as a god, presided over the Heian court. Although the Japanese emperor today no longer claims divinity, he still traces his roots to the Yamato clan.

FEUDAL JAPAN

In the 1100s, the central authority of the Japanese emperor declined. Local warlords fought one another. While armies battled for power, a feudal system developed. Feudal society had distinct levels. All members of society had a defined place.

PREPARING FOR THE REGENTS

List three ways in which China influenced Japan.

1.

2.

3.

PREPARING FOR THE REGENTS

To learn more about China's effects on Japan during the Tang dynasty see Unit 2, Section 2. To learn more about borrowing during the Ming dynasty, see Unit 4, Section 2.

PREPARING FOR THE REGENTS

For a definition of feudalism, see Unit 1, Section 2.

Landowners and Warriors

Under the Japanese feudal system, the emperor still ruled in name, but powerful warrior nobles actually controlled the country. The Japanese warrior aristocracy consisted of the following groups.

SHOGUNS Under the feudal system, the real power lay in the hands of the **shoguns,** or top military commanders. Shoguns set up dynasties called shogunates.

DAIMYO As in European feudalism, the shogun distributed land to vassal lords, called **daimyo** in Japan. The daimyo received land in exchange for a promise to support the shogun with their armies when needed.

SAMURAI The daimyo, in turn, granted land to lesser warriors called **samurai,** whose name means "those who serve." The samurai promised loyalty to the daimyo and lived by a strict code of conduct known as **bushido,** or "the way of the warrior." The samurai promised to be loyal, brave, and honorable. Honor was supremely important. A samurai who betrayed the code of bushido was expected to commit ritual suicide, an act called seppuku.

Other Classes and Groups

PEASANTS AND ARTISANS Peasants farmed the land, and artisans made weapons for the samurai. For their services, peasants and artisans were granted the protection of the samurai.

MERCHANTS Despite the fact that they might possess more wealth than members of the upper classes, merchants were the lowest social class in medieval Japan. Over time, however, merchants gained more influence.

WOMEN Early in the feudal period, women sometimes became warriors or ran estates. The status of women declined, however. Japanese feudal codes did not place women in high esteem. As time passed, inheritance was passed on to sons only.

THE TOKUGAWA SHOGUNATE

In 1603, the Tokugawa shogunate came to power, bringing peace and stability to Japan for nearly 300 years.

Centralized Feudal Government

The Tokugawa shoguns created a centralized feudal government. They halted the fighting among the powerful daimyo by at times forcing them to live at the capital of Edo (now Tokyo) instead of at their country estates. When the daimyo did leave the capital, their families were forced to stay under the shogun's careful watch.

PREPARING FOR THE REGENTS

How was the structure of Japanese feudalism similar to or different from European feudalism? Were the reasons for the development of feudalism in the two regions the same? Explain your answer.

PREPARING FOR THE REGENTS

How was the position of women different in feudal Japan and medieval Europe?

KEY THEMES AND CONCEPTS

Political Systems The Tokugawa shogunate brought stability to Japan by bringing the warring daimyo under central control.

Economic Prosperity

The stability of the Tokugawa shogunate resulted in economic gains. New seeds, tools, and techniques allowed farmers to grow more food. The population grew, and towns were linked by roads. Trade increased. In the cities, a wealthy class of merchants emerged.

In addition, Tokugawa shoguns became extremely hostile toward foreigners. By 1638, they had barred all western merchants and prohibited Japanese from traveling abroad. During Japan's period of strict isolation, internal trade boomed. The economy prospered.

Cultural Advances

During the Tokugawa shogunate, many Japanese learned Zen Buddhist practices, such as the tea ceremony and landscape gardening. At the same time, the Japanese made advances in the arts and theater. In **kabuki** theater, actors wore colorful costumes and acted out stories about families or events in history. In literature, Japanese poets created a Chinese-influenced form of poetry called **haiku.**

Comparison with Europe

Japanese feudalism was similar to European feudalism. Both systems evolved in response to the basic desire for stability. In both Japan and Europe, emperors and kings were too weak to prevent invasions or halt internal wars. Feudalism provided a way for ruling classes to preserve law and order.

In the feudal systems of both Japan and Europe, everyone had a well-defined place in society. In both societies, power and wealth were concentrated in the hands of an elite land-owning class. As the class of respected warriors, Japanese samurai played a role similar to that of European knights. Peasants in both feudal systems worked the land and served the landowners in exchange for protection.

The position of women was different in Japan and Europe. In Japan, the status of women declined during feudal times. In Europe, the code of chivalry helped raise the status of women. Another difference was the role of religion. Leaders of the Catholic Church in Europe had more political power than Zen Buddhist monks in Japan.

SUMMARY

Japan was strongly influenced by geographic conditions. It borrowed cultural elements from China but adapted them to develop its own unique culture. A decline in the power of the emperor led to the development of feudalism in the 1100s. In the early 1600s, the Tokugawa shogunate emerged, bringing stability and a flowering of culture but also strict government and a social structure consisting of unequal classes. Landowners and warriors dominated Japanese society.

Feudal Society in Japan

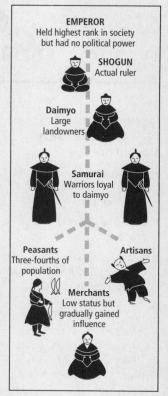

EMPEROR
Held highest rank in society but had no political power

SHOGUN
Actual ruler

Daimyo
Large landowners

Samurai
Warriors loyal to daimyo

Peasants
Three-fourths of population

Artisans

Merchants
Low status but gradually gained influence

SECTION 2

The Mongols and Their Impact

⭐ **THE BIG IDEA**
Mongol rule:

- covered a large area that included diverse lands and peoples.
- provided stability and prosperity.
- encouraged an exchange of goods and ideas between East and West.

SECTION OVERVIEW

Around 1200, the Mongols swept out of the grasslands of central Asia to build the largest empire in the world. Under leaders such as Genghis Khan and Kublai Khan, fierce Mongol fighters conquered an area from China to Persia, entering even Europe. Often, Mongol rulers provided stability, peace, and prosperity. This stability encouraged cultural exchange between East and West. Mongol power declined gradually because of the size and diversity of the area they ruled, poor administration, and internal revolt.

KEY THEMES AND CONCEPTS

As you review this section, take special note of the following key themes and concepts:

Diversity How did diversity both provide benefits and create problems for Mongol rulers?

Culture How did Mongol rule affect cultural development in the lands under their control?

Interdependence How did the exchange of goods and ideas throughout Eurasia increase with Mongol rule?

KEY PEOPLE AND TERMS

As you review this section, be sure you understand the significance of these key people and terms:

Genghis Khan	Yuan dynasty	Pax Mongolia
Golden Horde	Mughal dynasty	Marco Polo
Kublai Khan	Akbar the Great	Ibn Battuta

RISE OF THE MONGOLS

The Mongols of central Asia were nomadic herders who roamed the grasslands with their horses and sheep. The Mongols were skillful riders and fierce fighters and raiders. Under their leader Genghis Khan, the Mongols built the largest empire in the world.

Genghis Khan

Genghis Khan was born Temujin in central Asia in the 1100s. After experiencing a difficult boyhood, Temujin became a courageous warrior and a skilled leader. As supreme ruler of the Mongol clans, he earned the title Genghis Khan, which meant "World Emperor."

With his organized and disciplined armies, Genghis Khan took most of Asia from Korea in the east to the Caspian Sea in the west. His armies advanced into Persia, India, and even northern China.

There were several reasons for these Mongol victories. The Mongols were skilled horsemen and bowmen. They also borrowed new military technology, such as cannons, from the Chinese and the Turks.

Expansion to the West

EASTERN EUROPE   During the time of Genghis Khan, the Mongols invaded Eastern Europe. They even came within reach of the Byzantine city of Constantinople. After the time of Genghis Khan, the Mongols attacked Russia, Hungary, and Poland.

One grandson of Genghis Khan, called Batu, led Mongol armies into Russia and other lands of Eastern Europe between 1236 and 1241. Known as the **Golden Horde** because of the color of their tents, this group conquered many Russian cities. They ruled from a capital on the Volga River for 240 years. Like other Mongols, the Golden Horde were fierce warriors but relatively tolerant rulers.

THE MIDDLE EAST   In the late 1300s, Timur, also called Tamerlane, gathered Mongol groups together and conquered areas of Persia, Mesopotamia, Russia, and India. Eventually a descendent of Tamerlane established the Mughal dynasty in India.

A Mongol Dynasty in China

In 1279, **Kublai Khan,** another grandson of Genghis Khan, completed the job of conquering China by dominating the south. He ruled not only China but also Korea, Tibet, and parts of Vietnam.

Kublai Khan adopted a Chinese name for his dynasty, the **Yuan dynasty.** He did not want the Mongols to become absorbed into Chinese civilization, however. He gave the best government jobs to Mongol workers and allowed only Mongols to serve in the army, although Chinese officials still governed the provinces.

Mughal India

Babur, a descendent of Tamerlane, established India's **Mughal dynasty,** which ruled from 1526 to 1857. Babur's grandson **Akbar the Great** was the greatest Mughal ruler. Although he was a Muslim, Akbar won the support of Hindus because of his tolerant policies.

KEY THEMES AND CONCEPTS

Culture Mongol armies were made up of highly skilled horsemen. Armies were able to travel for days on horseback. The Mongols' expertise in horsemanship contributed greatly to their victories.

PREPARING FOR THE REGENTS

Support this statement in a short paragraph: The Mongol empire in 1279 brought together many different groups and cultures.

PREPARING FOR THE REGENTS

To learn more about Akbar the Great, see Unit 4, Section 5.

THE MONGOL IMPACT

Mongol power reached its greatest extent by about 1300. Mongol rule stretched throughout central Asia and China, into Russia and Europe, and into Southwest Asia and India.

Destruction and Conquest

Fierce Mongol warriors spread terror and destruction throughout the regions they conquered. For example, Mongols devastated the thriving province of Sichuan in China. In Russia, the Golden Horde looted and burned Kiev and other Russian cities, killing countless inhabitants.

Despite brutality in war, most Mongol leaders ruled with tolerance. Genghis Khan respected academics, artists, and artisans. He listened to the ideas of scholars of many religions. His heirs continued both his conquests and his tolerant policies. Conquered peoples were often allowed to live as before, as long as they paid tribute to the Mongols.

Lasting Effects on Russia

The Mongols ruled Russia for about 250 years. Mongol rule had a great long-term impact on Russia.

ABSOLUTIST GOVERNMENT The absolute power of the Mongol rulers served as a model for later Russian rulers who also expected to rule without interference from groups such as nobles or the Church.

ISOLATION Mongol rule also cut Russia off from Western Europe. This isolation deprived Russia of many advances in the arts and sciences of the later Middle Ages and the Renaissance.

Prosperity and Discontent in China

The Yuan dynasty ruled China for 150 years. They established peace and order in their kingdom. Great cities flourished in China under Kublai

The Mongol Empire

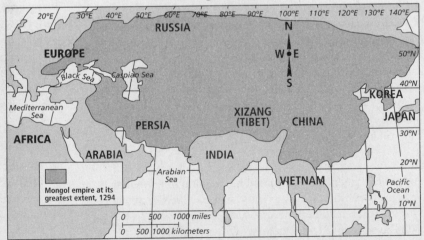

Mongol empire at its greatest extent, 1294

Khan. His capital of Khanbalik (now Beijing) was a large, well-planned city into which riches flowed. The city of Hangzhou was described as 10 or 12 times the size of Venice, one of Italy's richest city-states.

However, only Mongols could serve in the military and hold the best government jobs. Chinese resentment resulted, and uprisings occurred.

Pax Mongolia and Global Trade

Political stability throughout much of Asia resulted from Mongol rule. This period of stability, known as the **Pax Mongolia,** allowed for an exchange of goods and ideas between East and West.

THE SILK ROAD AND TRADE   In the centuries before the rise of the Mongols, the Silk Road, the trade route that linked China to the Middle East, had become dangerous. Traders used it less. The Mongols, however, provided safe passage along the Silk Road; as a result, trade flourished. Products such as gunpowder and porcelain, as well as technology such as papermaking and the use of windmills, flowed west.

MARCO POLO AND IBN BATTUTA   Safer travel meant that people could explore other lands. **Marco Polo,** an Italian merchant, traveled to the court of Kublai Khan in the late 1200s and remained for many years. His writings introduced Europeans to the beauty and riches of China.

Ibn Battuta, a scholar from Morocco, traveled at about the same time. He traveled first to Mecca and then through Asia Minor, Persia, India, Indonesia, and China. Later, he traveled to Spain. The record of his travels is of great interest to historians.

DECLINE OF MONGOL POWER

Mongol power declined for several reasons. Mongol lands were too large and diverse for one power to govern effectively. Although the Mongols were excellent fighters, they had little experience in government. They often depended on other people to do this job. Sometimes the people they chose were incompetent or corrupt.

The death of strong leaders also hurt Mongol power. After the death of Kublai Khan, for example, the Yuan dynasty broke apart. In both China and Russia, there had long been resentment of Mongol rule. In both countries a desire for independence from foreign rule provoked leaders to overthrow the Mongols and establish new dynasties

SUMMARY

The Mongols conquered lands in Asia and Europe. Areas of Mongol rule included people of varied religions and nationalities, most of whom were allowed to continue their own ways of life. Mongol rule provided a period of stability and economic growth. Increased trade encouraged the movement of goods, ideas, and technology between East and West. As the pressures of such a diverse power grew, the Mongols declined.

KEY THEMES AND CONCEPTS

Urbanization As China grew in importance as a center of trade and culture, European travelers such as Marco Polo wrote with awe of the cities of Kublai Khan.

KEY THEMES AND CONCEPTS

Interdependence Marco Polo traveled from West to East and introduced Europeans to advanced Chinese culture. Ibn Battuta traveled from Africa throughout Southwest Asia and even to Spain. Both kept records of their travels. Their writings have been important to scholars all over the world.

 PREPARING FOR THE REGENTS

List two causes of the decline of the Mongol empire.

1.

2.

3 Global Trade and Interactions

⭐ **THE BIG IDEA**
Beginning around 1200, global trade and interactions increased as:

- the Ming dynasty prospered and China traded by both land and sea.
- goods from the East moved to Africa and Asia Minor and then to Europe.
- cities in Asia, Africa, and Europe grew.
- European coastal towns transported goods to the European interior.
- Portugal began to search for new routes to Asia.

SECTION OVERVIEW

In the 1200s, global interactions increased. During the early Ming dynasty in China, trade thrived and cities grew. Goods continued to travel with Muslim traders by sea from China to Africa, where Venetian ships transported goods across the Mediterranean Sea to Europe. The population of Europe began to grow, leading to a revival of European trade and town life. Italian cities became flourishing centers of industry and trade. Also, the Hanseatic League gained control of trade in the Baltic and North Seas. In time, Portugal found a sea route to Asia, providing Europeans with easier access to the riches of the East. Trade and urbanization were slowed, however, by the coming of the bubonic plague in the 1300s. As a result, social, economic, and political upheaval occurred in Asia, Africa, and Europe.

KEY THEMES AND CONCEPTS

As you review this section, take special note of the following key themes and concepts:

Interdependence What factors led to increased global trade from the 1200s to the 1500s?

Movement of People and Goods What were some of the major trade centers and trade routes from the 1200s to the 1500s?

Urbanization Why did cities grow in importance?

Change How did the plague affect the world socially, economically, and politically?

KEY PEOPLE AND TERMS

As you review this section, be sure you understand the significance of these key people and terms:

Zheng He	Cairo	Hanseatic League
Canton	Venice	bubonic plague
Mogadishu	trade fair	epidemic

EXPANSION OF CHINESE TRADE

As you know, trade thrived in China under the Yuan dynasty in the 1200s. Goods traveled west along the Silk Road to Russia, Asia Minor, and lands beyond. Other goods and such travelers as Marco Polo traveled east.

The Ming dynasty took control of China in 1368, overthrowing the Mongols and driving them back behind the Great Wall. A time of economic prosperity and industrial growth followed. Population growth and expanded trade led to the growth of cities.

Ming rulers began a period of overseas expansion. In 1405, **Zheng He,** a Chinese admiral, set out with a fleet of ships. His goals were to promote Chinese trade and to collect tribute from less powerful lands.

The 1405 voyage was one of seven Zheng He would take between 1405 and 1433. During this time, he traveled through Southeast Asia, along the coast of India, around the Arabian Peninsula, and to the port cities of East Africa. He exchanged Chinese silks and porcelain for luxury items, including exotic animals for the imperial zoo. Along the way he convinced many people of the supremacy of Chinese culture.

The Chinese city of **Canton** became an important center for global trade. Canton, known today as Guangzhou, is located more than 90 miles inland from the South China Sea. In the 1500s, the Portuguese sent traders to Canton. In the 1600s, the Dutch and British followed. Europeans were allowed to trade with the Chinese in Canton, but only under strict limits.

MAJOR TRADE ROUTES

Important trade routes enabled people and goods to move across Asia, Africa, and Europe.

Across the Indian Ocean

Sea routes crossing the Indian Ocean and the Arabian Sea allowed easy trade between Asia and East Africa. Trading centers developed in eastern Africa. For example, **Mogadishu** and Great Zimbabwe thrived on trade across the Indian Ocean. European ships on their way to Asia often stopped at East African coastal cities.

Overland Between East and West

A variety of overland trade routes linked Asia with the Middle East, North Africa, and Europe. Trade from China followed the Silk Road and entered Europe through Russia or Constantinople. Goods also traveled between Constantinople and India.

Across the Mediterranean Sea

In the Middle East, Muslim traders brought goods to ports in Egypt, Syria, and Turkey. Major Egyptian ports included **Cairo** and Alexandria. In Egypt, goods could be transferred to Italian ships. Italian merchants carried the goods across the Mediterranean Sea to Europe.

KEY THEMES AND CONCEPTS

Urbanization The prosperity of the Ming dynasty led to population growth and an increase in trade. In China, cities expanded.

PREPARING FOR THE REGENTS

To learn more about the Ming dynasty, see Unit 4, Section 2.

KEY THEMES AND CONCEPTS

Interdependence The trade routes of this era linked Asia, Africa, and Europe. A growing economic interdependence characterized this period of history.

PREPARING FOR THE REGENTS

To learn more about the trade routes of this era, see the map of trade routes that is included in the Questions for Regents Practice at the end of this unit.

RESURGENCE OF EUROPEAN TRADE

Europeans were more and more interested in trade with the East. Improved methods of agriculture during the later Middle Ages allowed the European population to grow, leading to an increase in trade. The Crusades had also had an impact.

Impact of the Crusades

As you have learned, one of the effects of the Crusades was increased European interest in the East. Returning crusaders brought back goods. Ships that had been used to carry crusaders back and forth to the Holy Land could now be used for trade. Even though the Muslims had captured the crusader states, trade continued between the Middle East and Europe through Italy.

Italian City-States

By the late 1300s, northern Italian cities had become flourishing centers of industry and trade. Venice, Genoa, and Florence had grown rich and powerful. Venice in particular took advantage of its location to control the valuable spice trade with Asia. Eventually **Venice,** in partnership with Egypt, came to dominate trade with the East. The Venetians and their Muslim counterparts prospered.

After goods arrived in Venice, traders took them over the Alps and up the Rhine River to Flanders. From there, other traders took the goods throughout Europe, as far as England and to areas along the Baltic Sea.

Trade Fairs and the Growth of Cities

Much trade within Europe went on at **trade fairs.** Trade fairs took place in towns where trade routes met, often on navigable rivers. These fairs contributed to the growth of European cities. Many traders came to settle in these areas, as did craftworkers and merchants. The population of towns increased. In time, some towns developed into large cities populated by thousands of people. The wealthiest cities were at either end of the trade routes: in Flanders in the north and in Italy in the south.

The Hanseatic League

In northern Germany, groups of traders and merchants began to join together in the 1100s. Because central governments were still weak in Europe at this time, merchants sometimes banded together to protect their interests. By the mid-1300s, Lübeck, Hamburg, and many other northern German towns were members of the **Hanseatic League.** Eventually the league monopolized trade in the Baltic and North Seas. The league worked to make navigation safer by controlling piracy, building lighthouses, and training sailors.

Portugal and the Spice Trade

Spices, such as pepper and cinnamon, were extremely valuable during the Middle Ages. Spices served many purposes. Not only were they used to preserve and flavor meats, but they were used in perfumes and

 PREPARING FOR THE REGENTS

To learn more about the Crusades and their impact, see Unit 2, Section 6.

 PREPARING FOR THE REGENTS

Discuss one reason for the growth of cities in each of the following areas.

China:

Italy:

Northern and Western Europe:

KEY THEMES AND CONCEPTS

Economic Systems Weak central governments during the earlier Middle Ages led merchants to band together for protection. The Hanseatic League, an organization made up of German towns and commercial groups, developed for this reason.

Asia and the European Powers

1400s	1500s	1600s
China Ming dynasty ends overseas exploration by the Chinese	**China** Ming allow Europeans to trade only at Canton and force them to leave after each trading season	**China** British pressure Qing dynasty to open up more cities but Qing continue policy of limiting European trade
Korea Korean traders travel all over East Asia	**Korea** Japan conquers Korea	**Korea** Koreans decide to isolate themselves and forbid foreigners from coming to Korea
Japan No contact with Europeans	**Japan** Japanese welcome European traders	**Japan** Shoguns end European trade and foreign travel and Japan remains isolated for next 200 years

medicines as well. The riches that spices could bring prompted many to risk their lives traveling to Asia to acquire them.

As the Ottoman empire expanded into Eastern Europe and the eastern Mediterranean, European trade routes were disrupted. As a result, Portugal, at the southwestern end of Europe, began to look for new routes. In the early 1400s, Portugal began to explore the coast of Africa. The goal was to find a direct sea route to the riches of the East. Before the end of the century, the Portugese found a route around the tip of Africa to the Indian Ocean. In the 1500s, the Portugese established posts in Africa, India, Japan, and China. Trade brought great wealth to Portugal.

THE PLAGUE AND ITS IMPACT

The **bubonic plague,** also called the Black Death, was a highly contagious disease spread by the fleas that lived on rats. Shortly after being bitten by a flea, people developed swellings and black bruises on their skin. Within a few days, victims often died in agony. At the time, there was no cure for the plague, so many of those who became infected died.

Outbreak in China

Although the bubonic plague had previously broken out in parts of Europe, Asia, and North Africa, it had died out on its own without affecting a large area. However, in the early 1300s, the plague appeared in Chinese cities. Rats, common in the cities of the time, carried the disease through the crowded urban centers.

A Global Epidemic

The bubonic plague was a devastating **epidemic,** an outbreak that spreads quickly and affects a large number of people. The resurgence of

♀ KEY THEMES AND CONCEPTS

Movement of People and Goods In the 1400s, Western Europeans were looking for ways to avoid the Muslim and Italian middlemen and obtain direct access to Asia's riches. This is why Portugal was looking for a new route to the East.

 PREPARING FOR THE REGENTS

Increases in trade transmitted not only goods and ideas but diseases as well. The Black Death spread across Eurasia and Africa along the trade routes.

trade that had been occurring since the 1100s had helped the plague to spread. Fleas from rats infested traders in the East, who then carried the plague to the Middle East. North Africa and Italy were hit next. By the mid-1300s, the plague had reached Spain and France. From there it swept across the rest of Europe.

Effects of the Plague

The plague brought terror and devastation to all the regions it struck.

POPULATION LOSSES   In the early 1300s, when the plague first began to spread in China, about 35 million Chinese died. At its peak, the plague killed about 7,000 people a day in Cairo. Other regions of Africa and the Middle East suffered similar fates. By the time the worst of the plague was over, about one-third of the European population had died.

ECONOMIC DECLINE   In killing so many people, the plague devastated economies around the world. In Europe, farm and industrial production declined. The people who were left were in a position to demand higher wages, and prices rose. When landowners and merchants took action to stop this wage increase, peasant revolts occurred.

Because it devastated the economies of Eurasia and North Africa, the plague also disrupted trade. Some cities and provinces that had grown rich through trade struggled to survive.

SOCIAL AND POLITICAL CHANGE   Economic changes had social results, as the strictly defined levels of society that had been in place before began to break down. Feudalism declined as peasant revolts weakened the power of landowners over peasants. The decline of feudalism led to the growth of new political systems. In England and France especially, monarchs gained power and began to build more powerful nations.

CONFUSION AND DISORDER   The plague threw society into disorder. Some people questioned their faith and the Church, turning to magic and witchcraft to try to save themselves. Others blamed local Jews, whom they said had poisoned the wells. As a result, thousands of Jews were murdered.

SUMMARY

Beginning in the 1200s, global trade and other interactions increased. China underwent a period of expanding overseas and overland trade. Trade between Asia, Africa, and Europe increased. The Crusades and a growing population helped European trade. Italian city-states transported goods across the Mediterranean Sea, becoming rich and powerful. Portugal found a direct sea route to the East. In the 1300s, however, the bubonic plague disrupted trade as well as social and political life in Europe, Asia, and parts of Africa.

PREPARING FOR THE REGENTS

Describe three ways in which the plague affected Europe, Asia, and North Africa during the 1300s.

1.

2.

3.

KEY THEMES AND CONCEPTS

Change and Political Systems Many factors led to the decline of feudalism. One was that the social upheaval resulting from the plague led to the breakdown of Europe's strict social hierarchy.

SECTION OVERVIEW

From the 1300s through the 1700s, Europe underwent many changes. An increase in the importance of trade brought Europe not only an economy based on money but also a new middle class. The Renaissance brought new philosophies that emphasized the world and the individual. In art and literature, new styles and ideas emerged. Reformers challenged the power and authority of the Roman Catholic Church in a movement that divided the Church. Throughout this period, feudalism weakened. In England and France, nation-states were forming. In France, the monarchy gained power; in England, the monarch shared power with a representative body.

KEY THEMES AND CONCEPTS

As you review this section, take special note of the following key themes and concepts:

Economics What factors led to the commercial revolution?

Change What were the causes and impacts of the Reformation and Counter-Reformation?

Nationalism How did the governments of France and England differ as they moved toward a stronger sense of nationhood?

KEY PEOPLE AND TERMS

As you review this section, be sure you understand the significance of these key people and terms:

guild	humanism	Ignatius Loyola
apprentice	Michelangelo	common law
capitalism	Leonardo da Vinci	Magna Carta
commercial revolution	95 Theses	Parliament
Renaissance	Protestant Reformation	

THE COMMERCIAL REVOLUTION

⭐ **THE BIG IDEA**
In Europe at the end of the Middle Ages:

- the commercial revolution brought new ways of doing business.

- the Renaissance introduced new ways of thinking and a flowering of culture.

- religious reformers challenged the authority of the Roman Catholic Church.

- monarchs increased their power and formed nation-states.

- limits were placed on the power of monarchs in England.

With the expansion of trade and the growth of cities between about 1000 and 1300, new ways of doing business arose in Europe. Money grew in importance, and a new social class emerged.

Towns and the Middle Class

A growing population and an increase in trade led to the growth of towns and cities. Urban centers based on trade gave new power to a rising new class—a middle class of merchants, traders, and artisans. They were called the "middle" class because they ranked between the older feudal classes of nobles and peasants.

Importance of Guilds

Merchants and craftspeople formed guilds. A **guild** was a type of trade association. All of the people who worked in one craft, such as baking or weaving, would join together. Merchant guilds had great power. Typically, guilds did the following to protect the interests of their members:

- Made sure the quality of goods stayed high
- Provided social services for members, such as hospitals and aid to widows and children of members
- Regulated hours of work and prices of goods
- Ensured a supply of new artisans by training young people, called **apprentices,** in their crafts

Rise of Capitalism

As feudalism was declining all over Europe, a new system called capitalism was emerging. **Capitalism** is based on trade and capital, the name for money used for investment. When the demand for a product is great, prices rise, and traders therefore profit. However, traders can lose everything when the demand falls. Early capitalists devised new business methods to create wealth. This and other changes are known as the **commercial revolution,** or business revolution.

New Business Practices

The new middle class gathered together in various types of organizations. Business people were aided by banking and insurance services.

PARTNERSHIPS AND JOINT STOCK COMPANIES   Merchants sometimes joined together in partnerships. By pooling their capital, they could finance ventures that no single merchant could have afforded. In a partnership, a small group of merchants pooled their funds to finance a large-scale trading venture. A joint stock company allowed many merchants to pool their funds for business ventures. Joint stock companies invested in trading ventures around the world.

BANKING   Banking grew during this period. Individual merchants often did not have the capital they needed for an overseas trading venture. They borrowed from moneylenders, who developed systems of banking.

KEY THEMES AND CONCEPTS

Change Feudalism and the manor economy were based on land. Those who had land held wealth and power. A money economy gave a larger number of people the ability to gain wealth and to rise in society.

PREPARING FOR THE REGENTS

How does capitalism determine what goods and services are to be produced and in what quantities?

PREPARING FOR THE REGENTS

Why were bankers important to the commercial revolution and the development of capitalism?

Bankers also provided bills of exchange. These were needed because it was dangerous to travel over long distances with gold coins. Instead, a merchant deposited money with a banker in his hometown. The banker gave him a bill of exchange. The merchant could exchange this bill for cash in the city where he would be engaging in trade.

INSURANCE   Insurance helped reduce business risks. For a small fee, a merchant's shipment was insured. If the merchant's goods were damaged or lost, the insurer paid the merchant most of the value of the shipment.

Social Changes

The commercial revolution reshaped medieval society. For example, the use of money undermined serfdom and led to the decline of feudalism. Because feudal lords needed money to buy goods, peasants sold their farm products and began paying their lords with money rather than labor.

 PREPARING FOR THE REGENTS

What new business practices developed during the commercial revolution?

THE RENAISSANCE AND HUMANISM

The period from the 1300s to the 1500s was a time of great creativity and change in Europe. This period is called the **Renaissance,** which means "rebirth." It was a golden age in the arts, literature, and sciences.

The Renaissance began in Italy in the mid-1300s and then spread northward. The cities of Italy were thriving centers of trade and manufacturing. Merchants in these cities had great wealth and were willing to use it to promote art and education.

New Ways of Thinking

During the Renaissance, Europeans developed a new way of thinking called **humanism.** During the Middle Ages, philosophers and writers had wondered about life after death. Renaissance humanists, on the other hand, were more curious about life in the present. Another feature of this new way of thinking was an emphasis on the achievements of the individual. Instead of religious issues, humanists examined worldly subjects that the ancient Greeks and Romans had studied. They hoped to use ancient learning to increase knowledge about their own times.

Artistic Achievements

The Renaissance produced some of the greatest paintings, sculptures, and architecture in the history of the world. Renaissance architects rejected medieval forms of architecture. They returned to Greek and Roman styles for columns, arches, and domes. Artists were supported by merchants, popes, and princes.

The art of the time reflected humanist concerns. Many paintings still had religious subjects, but others portrayed important contemporary figures. Renaissance art was very realistic. Renaissance artists learned

KEY THEMES AND CONCEPTS

Change The Renaissance represented a widespread change in worldview. Instead of concentrating on spiritual things, people began to focus more on the world they lived in.

 PREPARING FOR THE REGENTS

Humanist thinkers used the Greeks and Romans as models. They also focused on individual achievement.

the rules of perspective—the technique used to give art a three-dimensional effect. These artists also studied human anatomy and often worked from live models, so they could portray the body in amazingly accurate detail. Two of the most famous artists of the Renaissance were Michelangelo and Leonardo da Vinci.

MICHELANGELO　**Michelangelo** was a sculptor, engineer, poet, painter, and architect. He is probably best known for his enormous mural on the ceiling of the Sistine Chapel in the Vatican. Michelangelo is also well known for his statue of the biblical character David.

LEONARDO DA VINCI　The *Mona Lisa* is **Leonardo da Vinci's** most famous painting. Leonardo da Vinci was very much interested in human anatomy, and he dissected human corpses to see how muscles and bones worked. His sketches for flying machines and underwater boats were made centuries before the first airplane or submarine was actually built.

NORTHERN ARTISTS　In the late 1400s, German artist Albrecht Dürer studied the techniques of Italian masters in Italy. When he returned to his homeland, he helped to spread Italian Renaissance ideas. Dürer's paintings, engravings, and prints portray the religious upheaval

PREPARING FOR THE REGENTS

Name three Renaissance artists, and describe an achievement of each.

1.

2.

3.

Artists of the Italian Renaissance

Leonardo da Vinci
- Painter, sculptor, inventor, architect, musician, engineer
- Painting of *Mona Lisa*
- Sketches and plans for flying machines and submarines

Michelangelo
- Sculptor, engineer, poet, painter, architect
- Statue of *David*
- Dome of St. Peter's Church in Rome

Raphael
- Painter
- Student of Michelangelo and Leonardo da Vinci
- Paintings of the madonna, mother of Jesus

Sofonisba Anguissola
- Woman artist
- Painting of *The Artist's Sisters Playing Cards*
- Painter for King Philip II of Spain

of his age. Flemish painters Jan and Hubert van Eyck developed oil paint in the 1400s. In the 1500s, Pieter Bruegel painted lively, vibrant scenes of daily life. Peter Paul Rubens, another Flemish painter, blended the realism of Bruegel with the classical themes and artistic freedom of the Italian Renaissance in the 1600s.

Literary Achievements

The humanist interest in this world was also expressed in the literature of the day. In the late Middle Ages, people had begun to write in the everyday language of ordinary people. Instead of scholarly Greek and Latin, they used Italian, French, English, and other languages.

DANTE Dante Alighieri was an Italian writer who wrote in the years before the Renaissance took hold. Dante wrote about a journey through hell and heaven in his masterpiece, *The Divine Comedy*. Because he wrote in the language of the Italian people, not in Latin, he is seen as a forerunner of the Renaissance.

CERVANTES Spanish writer Miguel de Cervantes shows the effects of the Renaissance as it moved northward. In the early 1600s, he wrote *Don Quixote*. Cervantes expressed Renaissance ideas by poking fun at the traditions of knighthood and chivalry. For example, Don Quixote, an old man who thinks he is a brave knight in battle with a giant, attacks a windmill.

SHAKESPEARE William Shakespeare, writing in England around 1600, is another figure of the northern Renaissance. Shakespeare wrote extensively about human beings and the joys and sorrows of human life.

MACHIAVELLI Niccolò Machiavelli wrote *The Prince* in the early 1500s. In this book he advises rulers on how to gain and maintain power. He tells rulers that they should use whatever methods are necessary to ensure their success. His work is seen today as a realistic picture of the politics of his time.

Impact of the Printing Press

By 1300, papermaking and printing technology had reached Europe from China. The invention of movable type in the 1400s led to Johann Gutenberg's printing of the Bible on his press in Germany in 1456.

The printing press was important for the Renaissance and later intellectual development.

- **Books became more available.** Books became cheaper and easier to make.
- **Literacy increased.** Because books were more readily available, more people learned to read and write.
- **Ideas spread rapidly.** People also had access to new knowledge about such subjects as medicine and geography. Printed Bibles increased the spread of religious ideas.

 PREPARING FOR THE REGENTS

How did writing in the languages of ordinary people rather than Latin help Renaissance ideas to spread?

KEY THEMES AND CONCEPTS

Culture and Intellectual Life Machiavelli, in writing about court and politics, expressed the Renaissance interest in worldly rather than only spiritual things.

 PREPARING FOR THE REGENTS

List three ways in which the printing press had an impact on European culture.

1.

2.

3.

REFORMATION AND COUNTER-REFORMATION

In the 1500s, great changes occurred in European religious life: the Protestant Reformation and the Counter-Reformation.

Causes of the Reformation

The movement that resulted in the Reformation did not have a simple cause. A number of factors led to its emergence.

- **The Renaissance** Humanism led people to question Church authority. They placed increasing faith in human reason.
- **Strong Monarchs** Strong national monarchs were emerging. Sometimes they increased their own power by supporting reformers against the Church.
- **Problems in the Church** As ordinary people examined the Church, some felt that its leaders were acting more like kings, fighting for power and wealth, than like representatives of God. Others objected to the Church charging increased fees for marriages and baptisms and selling indulgences, or pardons for sins.

Protestant Reformers

MARTIN LUTHER By the 1500s, many Christians wanted to reform the Church. One such person was the German monk Martin Luther. Disgusted over the sale of indulgences, Martin Luther took action in 1517. He posted his famous **95 Theses,** which were 95 arguments against indulgences, on the door of a church in Wittenberg. This event sparked the **Protestant Reformation,** the period when Europeans broke away from the Catholic Church and formed new Christian churches.

Luther believed that people could reach heaven only through faith in God and that the pope could not grant a pardon for sins. He thought that the Bible was the only source of religious truth. Luther was excommunicated, or excluded from the Roman Catholic Church, for his radical views. The ideas of Luther, however, spread throughout northern Europe and Scandinavia, thanks in part to the printing press. Followers of Luther's beliefs were called Lutherans and—eventually—Protestants because they protested papal authority.

JOHN CALVIN John Calvin was another influential reformer. Born in France, Calvin was trained as a priest. Like Luther, Calvin believed that Christians could reach heaven only through faith in God. Calvin, however, had his own views on the power of God and the nature of human beings. He promoted the idea of predestination, the belief that God had determined before the beginning of time who would gain salvation. Calvin's followers lived strict, disciplined, and frugal lives. Calvinism spread to Germany, France, Scotland, England.

Many other reformers also emerged. They included John Knox in Scotland and Huldrych Zwingli in Switzerland.

 **PREPARING FOR THE REGENTS**

How were Lutheranism and Calvinism different from Roman Catholicism?

Leaders of the Protestant Reformation

Martin Luther	John Calvin
• Did not believe in sale of indulgences. • Believed Christians reached heaven only through faith in God. • Did not believe that priests had special powers. • Ideas spread to northern Germany and Scandinavia. • Followers later called themselves Protestants.	• Believed Christians reached heaven only through faith in God. • Believed people are born sinners. • Preached predestination. • Ideas spread to Germany, France, Holland, England, and Scotland. • Led a community in Switzerland.

The Counter-Reformation

As the Protestant Reformation continued to spread, a reform movement was also taking place within the Roman Catholic Church. That movement is called the Counter-Reformation, or the Catholic Reformation. The purpose of the Counter-Reformation was to strengthen the Catholic Church as well as to keep Catholics from converting to Protestantism.

THE COUNCIL OF TRENT   Pope Paul III called the Council of Trent in 1545 to guide the reform movement. The council, which met on and off for 20 years, reaffirmed traditional Catholic beliefs and worked to end abuses in the Church. It also set up schools to assure that the clergy would be well educated.

IGNATIUS LOYOLA AND THE JESUITS   Another strong force in the Counter-Reformation was **Ignatius Loyola.** Loyola founded the Society of Jesus, also called the Jesuits. The Jesuits are a religious order that emphasizes spiritual and moral discipline as well as strict obedience to Catholic authority. Early Jesuits saw themselves as the defenders of the Catholic faith throughout the world. Many Jesuits became advisors to Catholic rulers. Jesuit missionaries spread Catholicism to Asia, Africa, and the Americas.

TERESA OF AVILA   Teresa of Avila, a Spanish noblewoman, became a member of the religious order of nuns called the Carmelites. Disturbed by a lack of severity within the order, she withdrew with a few followers for prayer and meditation. Eventually she set up a new convent. The Catholic Church asked Teresa to reorganize and reform Carmelite monasteries and convents throughout Spain. After her death, the Church made her a saint.

Effects of the Reformation

The Reformation had complex effects. Most obviously, it led to the formation of the Protestant churches. Other effects also occurred over time.

• **Religious and Political Divisions** The Reformation created a loss of religious unity in Western Europe. Political divisions resulted as

KEY THEMES AND CONCEPTS

Belief Systems The Counter-Reformation was both an attempt to keep Catholics from leaving the Church and an effort to reform some aspects of the Church.

The Protestant Reformation

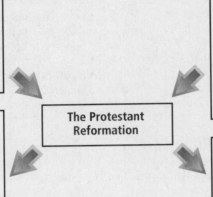

Long-Term Causes
- Roman Catholic Church becomes more worldly
- Humanists urge return to simple religion
- Strong kings emerge and resent power of Church

Short-Term Causes
- Indulgences are sold in Germany
- Martin Luther writes 95 Theses
- Luther translates Bible into German
- Printing press helps spread ideas
- Reformers call for change

The Protestant Reformation

Long-Term Effects
- Religious wars break out in Europe for more than 100 years
- Catholic Reformation takes place
- Inquisition becomes stronger
- Many Jews forced into Eastern Europe

Short-Term Effects
- Peasants revolt
- Lutheran, Calvinist, Anglican, and other Protestant churches founded
- Holy Roman emperor weakened

PREPARING FOR THE REGENTS

List and explain two causes and two impacts of the Reformation.

Causes

1.

2.

Impacts

1.

2.

well. Rulers often chose a religion for their nations. While some states remained Catholic, others became Protestant.

- **Religious Conflicts** For more than 100 years after the Reformation, wars sparked in part by religion raged in Europe. In the 1500s, religious civil wars occurred in Germany and France, and Spanish Catholics battled English Protestants. The Thirty Years' War, involving many European states, occurred in the 1600s.
- **Anti-Semitism** The Reformation brought persecution to several groups, especially the Jews. Over time, restrictions placed on Jews by both Protestants and Catholics increased. For example, in some cities, Jews were forced to live in a separate neighborhood. Some Jews were expelled from their homes; others were murdered.
- **Witch Hunts** Religious fervor sometimes led people to accuse others of being witches, agents of the devil. Thousands of people, especially women, were put to death for this reason.

RISE OF NATION-STATES

During the late Middle Ages, kings, nobles, and the Church struggled for power. Feudalism was on the decline. Kings slowly began to increase their power. This shift occurred first in England and France, taking a somewhat different path in each country. These changes marked the beginning of feelings of nationalism—pride and devotion to one's country.

Kings Increase Their Power

Kings in England

- Decide who can build castles and where
- Force vassals to obey them
- Establish common law so that all people are treated the same
- Collect records of who owns land

(shared)

- Add to their lands
- Set up organized government
- Collect taxes
- Create a royal treasury
- Set up royal courts and royal law

Kings in France

- Make throne hereditary
- Become allies with the Church
- Organize army
- Take French lands from English king

Growth of Royal Power in France

When Hugh Capet became monarch in 987, feudal nobles did not perceive him as a threat to their power. However, Hugh and his heirs, known as the Capetians, slowly increased royal power. The Capetians made the throne hereditary. They also gained vast amounts of land by playing rival nobles against one another. They developed a system of tax collection as well.

The growth of royal power led in part to the Hundred Years' War, a conflict that occurred between England and France from the middle of the 1300s to the mid-1400s. When it looked as if the French would lose the war, a peasant woman named Joan of Arc managed to rally the French to victory. Killed by the English, she became an important focus of French national feeling.

Joan's efforts built up the power of the French monarchs. France's kings developed policies that weakened the power of the nobles and strengthened the power of the crown. The French representative body, the Estates General, did not limit the monarch's power during this period.

Nationhood and Limited Monarchy in England

When the Anglo-Saxon king Edward died in 1066, his brother-in-law was chosen to rule. However, Duke William of Normandy claimed the English throne as well. A battle for the throne began. William invaded England and won the throne. As king, William the Conquerer exerted firm control.

AN ENGLISH LEGAL SYSTEM   William's successors strengthened English finance and law. Under Henry II, **common law**, or law that was the same for all people, was established. Henry broadened the system of royal justice by sending out traveling justices to enforce laws. Henry also developed an early jury system. When justices visited an area, a jury, or group of men sworn to speak the truth, was gathered by local officials. The jury determined which cases should be brought to trial.

♀ KEY THEMES AND ⊦ CONCEPTS

Nationalism During the late Middle Ages, nation-states began to form in France and England. While monarchs gained significant power in France, the English monarchs shared their power with a representative body.

MAGNA CARTA   English rulers clashed with nobles and the Church over efforts to extend royal power. In 1215, the nobility rebelled against King John and forced him to sign the **Magna Carta,** a charter that placed limits on the king's power. The Magna Carta stated, for example, that the monarch must obey the law and that the monarch could not raise taxes without first consulting his Great Council of lords and clergy.

PARLIAMENT   During the 1200s, this council evolved into the representative assembly known as **Parliament.** In order to finance their wars, English monarchs repeatedly had to ask Parliament for funds, thus strengthening the power of Parliament.

AN ENGLISH CHURCH   The final break between the English monarchy and the Catholic Church occurred under Henry VIII in the 1500s. Angered that the pope refused to grant him an annulment of his marriage, Henry consulted Parliament and had a series of laws passed. Under these laws, Henry gained control of the English church. He created the Anglican Church, or Church of England. In 1558, Henry's daughter, Elizabeth I, became queen and firmly established England as a Protestant nation.

SUMMARY

A growing population and an increase in trade led to a commercial revolution in Europe and a rising middle class. At the same time, the Renaissance brought new ideas about the world and the place of people within it. Great works of art and literature emerged from this period. Inventions such as the printing press helped learning and new ideas to spread throughout Europe. There were also religious changes, as Protestant reformers challenged the authority of the Roman Catholic Church and founded new Christian churches. Throughout this period, feudalism weakened, while nations united under strong monarchs. In 1215, England instituted the Magna Carta, which placed limits on royal power. Under the Magna Carta, the English monarch shared power with Parliament, a representative body.

SECTION 5 African Civilizations

SECTION OVERVIEW

Africa's varied climates and terrains contributed to the development of diverse societies on that continent. From about A.D. 800 to 1600, several civilizations rose and fell in Africa. West Africans built the powerful kingdoms of Mali and Songhai as they gained control over internal trade routes. In East Africa, the kingdom of Axum became a center of international trade. Africa played an important role in the global trading network. Trade with the people of Europe, the Middle East, and India encouraged an exchange of ideas between Africa and other lands. During this time, Islam became established in various parts of Africa. Still, traditional patterns of village, family, and religious life remained important through most of Africa.

KEY THEMES AND CONCEPTS

As you review this section, take special note of the following key themes and concepts:

Geography How did the geography of Africa encourage the development of diverse civilizations?

Power What factors contributed to the rise and fall of powerful kingdoms in Africa?

Movement of People and Goods What links did Africa have with global trade routes?

Culture How did traditional art and literary forms reflect the beliefs of African peoples?

KEY PEOPLE AND TERMS

As you review this section, be sure you understand the significance of these key people and terms:

savanna	Ghana	Mansa Musa	Swahili
desert	Mali	Songhai	Axum

★ **THE BIG IDEA**
Prior to 1600, people in Africa:

- formed diverse societies in different geographical areas.

- built trading empires in Ghana, Mali, Songhai, and Axum.

- became part of the global trade network through West African and East African trading states.

- were introduced to the religion of Islam.

- maintained traditions around village, family, and religious belief.

⚷ KEY THEMES AND
CONCEPTS

Geography The geographic diversity and geographic barriers of Africa led to the development of many different cultures on the continent.

⚷ KEY THEMES AND
CONCEPTS

Movement of People and Goods Throughout history, trade had a major impact on the societies of Africa. Trade brought new cultural influences to Africa, adding to its diversity.

AFRICA'S VARIED GEOGRAPHY

The second largest continent in the world, Africa accounts for one-fifth of the land surface on the Earth. Africa includes varied climates and terrains. Much of Africa is made up of **savanna,** or grassy plains. Despite hot weather and occasional droughts, this area generally has good soil and enough rain to support farming. It is therefore the most densely populated climate region. A large part of Africa, however, is made up of **desert,** or dry, barren land. The Sahara in North Africa is the world's largest desert, with extremely hot temperatures during the day and little vegetation. Africa also has a small belt of rain forests along the Equator and small areas of Mediterranean climate along the coast of North Africa and at the southern tip of the continent. In these areas, there is fertile farmland.

Africa has few good natural harbors. Because much of the interior is a high plateau, the rivers that flow down to the coast cascade through a series of rapids. Barriers such as these sometimes made travel difficult for Africans.

Despite geographic barriers, early Africans traveled within and beyond their continent. Much of this movement was linked to trade. Africa's gold, salt, iron, copper, and other minerals were important goods in early trade networks.

TRADITIONAL SOCIETY AND CULTURE

Village Government

In most traditional African communities, power was shared among members of the community rather than exercised by a single leader. Within a village, decisions were often made by a process known as consensus. Village members gathered together for open discussions. Elders and other respected people presented their arguments before a general agreement was reached.

Family Patterns

While the family was the basic unit of society in traditional Africa, patterns of family life varied in several ways. For example, the nuclear family was common in hunting and gathering societies. In a nuclear family, parents and children worked and lived together as a unit. In other communities, and more commonly, several generations lived in one household or near each other as an extended family.

Because traditional African social structures emphasized the group over the individual, extended families who descended from a common ancestor formed clans. Community values were greatly enhanced through identification with a particular clan.

Religious Beliefs

Across Africa, religious beliefs were varied. Like many other ancient peoples, early Africans identified the forces of nature with divine spirits and worshiped many gods and goddesses. Many Africans believed that the spirits of their departed ancestors were present on Earth. They would call on these spirits for help in times of trouble. Some people in these long-ago African societies believed in one supreme being who was the creator and ruler of the universe.

RISE AND FALL OF AFRICAN KINGDOMS

In Africa, towns soon became part of an important trade network. Gold and salt were the most important products that were traded. People needed salt in their diets to prevent dehydration, the dangerous loss of water from the body. There was plenty of salt in the Sahara, but there was little in the savanna. The people of the savanna traded the plentiful gold of their region to obtain salt from the Sahara.

Strong African rulers created powerful kingdoms by gaining control over the most profitable trade routes. Three trading kingdoms of West Africa were Ghana, Mali, and Songhai. The trading kingdom of Axum thrived in East Africa. Over time, Islam became an important social and religious force, particularly in North Africa and West Africa.

Ghana

Around A.D. 800, the rulers of many farming villages united to create the kingdom of **Ghana.** Ghana had a powerful king who ruled over a splendid court in his capital of Kumbi Saleh. Income from the gold trade allowed him to maintain a large army of foot soldiers and cavalry. This army helped the king to control and expand his kingdom.

Muslim merchants brought their religion and ideas when they settled in the kingdom of Ghana. The king had Muslim officials and thus was influenced by Muslim military technology and ideas about government. Ghana also absorbed Muslim cultural influences, such as Arabic writing and Muslim styles of architecture. Most of the people of Ghana, however, kept their traditional religious beliefs. Women in Ghana had a high status and played an active role in the economic life of the empire.

Mali

Mali was also ruled by powerful kings, called mansas. Under **Mansa Musa,** the most powerful ruler, Mali extended its borders and dominated West Africa. Mansa Musa's large army kept order in the empire and protected it from attack. Although warriors were an elite class in Mali, most of its people were farmers and herders.

Mansa Musa ran an efficient government, appointing governors to rule particular areas. Mansa Musa converted to Islam, basing his system of justice on the Quran. He also made the city of Timbuktu a center of Muslim learning. The empire, however, declined in the 1400s, when the people could not agree on who should rule the kingdom.

PREPARING FOR THE REGENTS

As you read, take note of what forces contributed to the rise and fall of the kingdoms of Ghana, Mali, Songhai, and Axum.

KEY THEMES AND CONCEPTS

Belief Systems After Mansa Musa converted to Islam, he traveled to Mecca. In making this trip, he fulfilled one of the Five Pillars of Islam. His pilgrimage had a cultural impact on Mali, since Mansa Musa brought home Muslim scholars and artists and forged new trading ties.

Kingdoms of West Africa

Ghana (800–1000)	Mali (1200–1450)	Songhai (1450–1600)
• Controls trade in gold and salt across West Africa	• Mali conquers kingdom of Ghana	• Songhai grows into largest West African state
• Women work in business and government	• Mansa Musa becomes great emperor	• Controls important trade routes
• King has Muslim advisors	• Mali controls gold trade routes	• Emperor sets up Muslim dynasty
	• Timbuktu becomes a great trading city and center of learning	

KEY THEMES AND CONCEPTS

Government The West African kingdoms were ruled by powerful emperors. They had strong armies to maintain order and protect the kingdoms from attack.

PREPARING FOR THE REGENTS

What influence did Islam have on the kingdoms of West Africa?

Songhai

Like Ghana and Mali, the **Songhai** empire depended on a strong army to control trade routes. The emperor Sonni Ali built Songhai into the largest state that had ever existed in West Africa, bringing the wealthy city of Timbuktu under his control. Songhai established an efficient bureaucracy to govern the kingdom. Its people also expanded trade to Europe and Asia. Songhai prospered until the late 1500s, when civil war broke out. At that time, invaders from the north defeated the disunited forces of Songhai and caused the downfall of the kingdom.

Axum

As in the kingdoms of West Africa, trade helped **Axum** become a powerful kingdom. Axum's location on the Red Sea helped Axumites command a thriving trade network linking Africa, India, and the Mediterranean world. Axum's population was descended from African farmers and from traders who had immigrated from Arabia. This merging of cultures introduced Jewish and Christian religious traditions to Axum. After being weakened by civil war and cut off from its harbors, Axum declined.

AFRICA'S ROLE IN GLOBAL TRADE

African states in both the eastern and western parts of the continent played a significant role in global trade. The Mediterranean and Red Seas linked Africa to the Middle East and Europe. In addition, the Indian Ocean linked East Africa to India and other Asian lands. Products from the African interior were transported overland to the coast and then out of Africa.

Hausa

In the 1300s, the Hausa people built city-states in what became present-day Nigeria. The products of Hausa cotton weavers and leatherworkers

African Kingdoms, 1000 B.C.–A.D. 1600

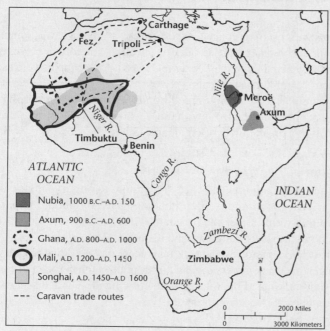

ATLANTIC
OCEAN

- Nubia, 1000 B.C.–A.D. 150
- Axum, 900 B.C.–A.D. 600
- Ghana, A.D. 800–A.D. 1000
- Mali, A.D. 1200–A.D. 1450
- Songhai, A.D. 1450–A.D. 1600
- --- Caravan trade routes

INDIAN
OCEAN

0   2000 Miles
0   3000 Kilometers

KEY THEMES AND CONCEPTS

Geography The bodies of water on Africa's east and west coasts were busy highways for trade with Europe and Asia. These contacts had an effect on Africa's history and culture.

from the city-states traveled on caravans across the Sahara and sometimes were transported as far as Europe. By the 1500s, the Hausa dominated Saharan trade routes.

Benin

In the rain forests on the Guinea coast, the Benin people traded ivory, pepper, and eventually slaves with their northern neighbors in the savanna. Benin traders also dealt with the Portuguese, who began arriving in growing numbers in the 1500s. The people of Benin learned how to cast bronze and brass. Benin bronze sculpture often portrays warriors and Benin rulers.

East African City-States

Around 600, trading cities rose along the coast of East Africa as Arab and Persian merchants established trading communities. By 1000, East African port cities such as Mogadishu, Kilwa, and Sofala conducted a booming trade with India. Part of this commerce system included slaves, who were seized inland and then sold to Persian traders.

Trade led to a mixing of cultures in the city-states of East Africa. Over time, this blending of cultures resulted in the rise of a new language, **Swahili,** in which Arabic words were mixed with Bantu, an African language.

PREPARING FOR THE REGENTS

Describe one positive and one negative effect of global trade on Africa.

Positive:

Negative:

PREPARING FOR THE REGENTS

Traditional arts of Africa have had a lasting impact beyond Africa. Today many African Americans show pride in their heritage by displaying traditional African art in their homes. African music has influenced the development of jazz, rock, blues, and other styles of music.

CONTRIBUTIONS

The Arts

African art, most often created in ivory, wood, and bronze, was sometimes used for decorative purposes, such as jewelry. More often, however, art was closely tied to religion. Statues and masks, for example, were used in religious ceremonies and rituals.

African art also strengthened bonds within the community. Art linked people who created it with those who used it. Moreover, decorative patterns on an object often identified it as the work of a particular clan or as a possession of royalty.

Literary Traditions

Africans used both oral and written literature to preserve their culture. Arabic was a common written language used by people in parts of Africa that were influenced by Islam. Today, Arabic documents offer insight into the laws, religions, and history of African societies.

Most often, histories and folk tales were passed down in oral form from generation to generation. Histories praised the heroism of famous ancestors or kings. Folk tales, on the other hand, blended fantasy and humor to teach important moral lessons.

Education

In most African societies, it was the duty of the elders to teach boys and girls what their special roles would be in the community. The elders also passed down information about their clans' history and religious beliefs.

In the 1400s, Timbuktu in Mali had become a leading center of learning. Manuscripts were brought to Timbuktu to be sold at high prices. The university at Timbuktu, built by Mansa Musa, attracted students from all over the Muslim world.

Commerce

The development of commerce by African kingdoms did much to establish trade routes that would endure for centuries. Commerce also introduced Africa to crops and animals from other lands. In addition, a rich mix of cultures developed. An unfortunate result of commerce, however, was the rise of slave trading.

SUMMARY

Africa's geography encouraged the formation of separate kingdoms. After A.D. 800, powerful trading empires formed in western Africa. Through trade, Africans were introduced to Islam. During the same period, trading kingdoms on Africa's eastern coast were forming ties with India, the Middle East, and the Mediterranean. African societies were exposed to many new influences but retained the traditional importance of village, family, and religion.

PREPARING FOR THE REGENTS

To learn more about global trade routes and the African slave trade, see Unit 4, Section 4 as well as the map of Atlantic Trade Routes in the Questions for Regents Practice at the end of this unit.

Questions for Regents Practice

Review the **Preparing for the Regents** section of this book. Then answer the following questions, which include multiple-choice questions, a thematic essay, and a series of document-based questions.

MULTIPLE CHOICE

Directions

Circle the *number* of the word or expression that best completes the statement or answers the question.

1 One similarity between the cultures of traditional China and traditional Japan was that
 1 the educated class was held in high esteem
 2 religion played a minor role in society
 3 social mobility was encouraged
 4 the people elected the political leaders

2 The code of bushido of the Japanese samurai is most similar to the
 1 belief in reincarnation and karma of Hindus
 2 practice of chivalry by European knights
 3 teachings of Judaism
 4 theory of natural rights of the Enlightenment writers

3 When Russia was under Mongol domination, the effect on Russia was to
 1 end feudalism
 2 convert the Russian people to Hinduism
 3 keep Russia isolated from Western Europe
 4 reunite the Orthodox Christian Church with the Roman Catholic Church

4 Which was a major characteristic of the Renaissance?
 1 conformity
 2 humanism
 3 mysticism
 4 obedience

5 Which long-term effect did the Magna Carta and the establishment of Parliament have on England?
 1 The system of mercantilism was strengthened.
 2 The power of the monarchy was limited.
 3 The new American form of government was adopted.
 4 The influence of the middle class was reduced.

6 Which societal condition was basic to the development of Greek philosophy and Renaissance art?
 1 rigid social classes
 2 emphasis on individualism
 3 religious uniformity
 4 mass education

7 Which factor helped most to bring about the Protestant Reformation?
 1 The Catholic clergy had lost faith in their religion.
 2 Islam had attracted many converts in Western Europe.
 3 Kings and princes in northern Europe resented the power of the Roman Catholic Church.
 4 The exploration of the Americas led to the introduction of new religious ideas.

8 Which was a major result of the Reformation?
 1 New Christian denominations emerged.
 2 Religious teachings were no longer allowed in the universities.
 3 The Crusades were organized.
 4 The power of the pope was strengthened.

Base your answers to questions 9 and 10 on the map below and on your knowledge of social studies.

Trade Routes (13th–15th centuries)

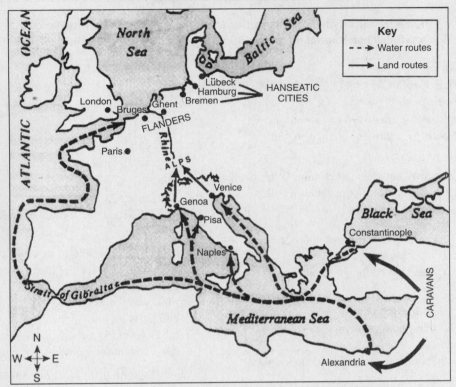

9   One reason Italian city-states were able to dominate the trade pattern shown on the map was that they were
1   centrally located on the Mediterranean Sea
2   situated north of the Alps
3   unified by the Hanseatic League
4   located on the trade routes of the North Sea

10   The development of trade along the routes shown on the map led to the
1   decline of the Greek city-states
2   start of the Renaissance in Italy
3   beginning of the Crusades to the Middle East
4   first religious wars in Europe

11   African kingdoms such as Ghana, Songhai, and Axum flourished mainly because they
1   controlled important trade routes
2   developed self-sufficient economies
3   became religious centers considered sacred by Africans
4   received support from European colonial governments

12   Mansa Musa's journey to Mecca in the 1300s is evidence that
1   the Crusades had a great influence on western Africa
2   most African leaders were educated in the Middle East
3   European culture was superior to the cultures of western Africa
4   Islam had a major influence on the Mali empire

THEMATIC ESSAY

Directions

Read the following instructions that include a theme, a task, and suggestions. Follow the instructions to create a well-organized essay that has an introduction with a thesis statement, several paragraphs explaining the thesis, and a conclusion.

Theme: Change

Throughout global history, events and changes have occurred that historians have considered turning points.

Task

- Describe what would make an event or a change a turning point in global history.
- Identify and describe two specific examples of turning points in global history.
- Explain why each of these events or changes is considered a turning point in global history. Provide specific examples of the impacts each had.

Suggestions

You may discuss any major changes or turning points from any period of global history you have studied. Some periods you might want to consider are prehistoric times or Europe in the 1400s. You are not limited to these suggestions.

QUESTIONS BASED ON DOCUMENTS

The following exercise asks you to analyze four historical documents and then write an essay using evidence from those documents. This exercise is similar to the document-based question that you will see on the Regents Examination, which may include six or more documents. For additional practice with historical documents, see the Preparing for the Regents section and the sample examinations in this book.

This task is based on the accompanying documents. Some of these documents have been edited for the purposes of this task. This task is designed to test your ability to work with historical documents. As you analyze the documents, take into account both the source of each document and the author's point of view.

Directions

Read the documents in Part A and answer the question or questions after each document. Then read the directions for Part B and write your essay.

Historical Context

Throughout global history, cultures and civilizations have held different viewpoints on diversity in society. Diversity has been seen as both positive and negative.

Task

Compare the different viewpoints societies have held about diversity. Evaluate the positive and negative impacts that diversity may have on a society.

Part A: Short Answer

Directions: Analyze the documents and answer the question or questions that follow each document, using the space provided.

DOCUMENT 1

The Mongol Empire

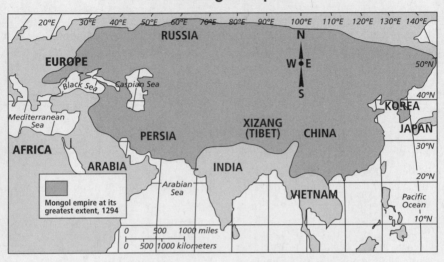

1 Use this map to support the statement that the Mongols ruled a diverse empire.

_____

_____

_____

DOCUMENT 2

> *A nation is an association of those who are brought together by language, by given geographical conditions, or by the role assigned them by history, who acknowledge the same principles and who march together to the conquest of a single definite goal under the rule of a common body of law. . . . It is necessary that [a nation's] ideas be shown to other lands in their beauty and purity, free from any alien mixture.*
>
> **—Giuseppe Mazzini, Italian nationalist leader, 1835**

2 Did Giuseppe Mazzini believe that diversity of ideas within a nation was positive or negative? Explain your answer.

_____

_____

DOCUMENT 3

> *To make our dream of a united, democratic, non-racial, non-sexist South Africa real is an immense challenge. Yet we look forward to the future with confidence and hope because we know that the people of South Africa — every racial group, every faith, every ethnic and language community in our country — are possessed of many talents, skills, and an infinite resourcefulness.*
>
> **— Nelson Mandela, President of South Africa, 1994**

3   Does this document express a positive view of diversity? Explain your answer.

_____

_____

DOCUMENT 4

> *India has not ever been an easy country to understand. Perhaps it is too deep, contradictory, and diverse.*
>
> **—Indira Gandhi, Prime Minister of India, 1970s**

4   What problems caused by diversity does Indira Gandhi refer to in this quotation?

_____

_____

Part B: Essay
Directions:
- Write a well-organized essay that includes an introduction, several paragraphs, and a conclusion.
- Use evidence from the documents to support your response.
- Do not simply repeat the contents of the documents.
- Include specific, related outside information.

Historical Context
Throughout global history, cultures and civilizations have held different viewpoints on diversity in society. Diversity has been seen as both positive and negative.

Task
Using information from the documents and your knowledge of global history and geography, write an essay that evaluates the positive and negative impacts of diversity on a society. Tell whether you think diversity has a positive or negative influence today.

   Be sure to include specific historical details. You must also include additional information from your knowledge of global history.

   Note: **The rubric for this essay appears in the Preparing for the Regents section of this book.**

4 **The First Global Age (1450–1770)**

UNIT OVERVIEW

In the 1400s and 1500s, Europeans began exploring much of the world. These European explorers encountered rich and powerful civilizations in Africa, Asia, and the Americas. Thus began a period of increasing global interaction that continues to the present day. As interaction among civilizations increased, so did conquests and global exchanges. Around the world, these developments had significant impacts on the way people lived. One major result was that, by the 1600s and 1700s, Western European monarchs had increased their power within their own countries and around the world.

THEMATIC TIME LINE ACTIVITY

Some of the many themes developed in Unit 4 are:

economic systems	government
belief systems	change
places and regions	culture
movement of people and goods	political systems

Choose one of the themes listed above. As you review Unit 4, create a thematic time line based on the theme you have chosen. Your time line should stretch from 1450 to 1770 and include major developments and key turning points having to do with your theme.

SECTION 1 Mesoamerican Civilizations

SECTION OVERVIEW

Tens of thousands of years ago, Paleolithic hunters migrated to North America from Asia. People learned to cultivate plants and to domesticate animals. These changes led to an increase in population. In the Americas, complex societies developed. The Olmecs and, later, the Mayas and Aztecs ruled great empires in Mexico. In South America, the Incas conquered a vast area along the western coast. The people in these empires were skilled farmers, were devoted to their religions, and possessed advanced knowledge in many areas.

KEY THEMES AND CONCEPTS

As you review this section, take special note of the following key themes and concepts:

Economic Systems Why was agriculture important to Mesoamerican civilizations?

Belief Systems What significance did religion have in the empires of the Americas?

Government What types of governments allowed Mesoamerican societies to rule large areas?

Culture and Intellectual Life What were the accomplishments and advances of the Mesoamerican empires?

KEY PEOPLE AND TERMS

As you review this section, be sure you understand the significance of these key people and terms:

Olmecs

Mayas

Aztecs

Incas

terraces

quipus

★ **THE BIG IDEA**
The Olmecs, Mayas, Aztecs, and Incas:

- developed agriculture that could support large populations.
- placed great importance on religion.
- formed governments that ruled large empires.
- had advanced knowledge in areas such as agriculture, engineering, and architecture.

PREPARING FOR THE REGENTS

The Agricultural Revolution occurred throughout the world during Neolithic times. To learn more about this turning point in global history, see Unit 1, Section 1.

 PREPARING FOR THE REGENTS

Compare the effects of the Agricultural Revolution that occurred in the Americas with the Agricultural Revolution in Eurasia. What were the similarities and differences?

GEOGRAPHIC SETTING

During the last ice age, large amounts of ocean water froze into thick ice sheets. A land bridge between Siberia and Alaska was created as the ocean levels dropped. Across this bridge, groups of Paleolithic hunters in Asia followed herds of bison and mammoths into North America. Over the following centuries, the nomadic hunter-gatherers in North America migrated eastward and southward. These first Americans settled in many different regions and had to adapt to a variety of climates and landforms, including woodlands, fertile plains, mountain ranges, and thick rain forests.

Slowly, between 8500 B.C. and 2000 B.C., important changes occurred. Groups of Americans learned to cultivate crops. They began to domesticate animals, perhaps in response to the disappearance of large mammals. Neolithic farmers in Mexico raised a variety of crops, including corn, beans, sweet potatoes, peppers, tomatoes, and squash. Farmers in South America domesticated llamas and other animals that were valued for their wool.

In the Americas, as in Africa and Eurasia, this Agricultural Revolution had a major impact on the population. Farmers settled into villages that sometimes developed into large religious centers, which could then grow into major cities. The first great American civilizations developed in Mesoamerica (also called Middle America), the region that includes Mexico and Central America.

Ancient Cultures of Mexico

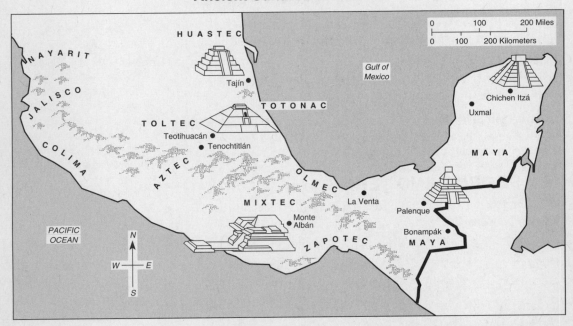

THE OLMECS

The Olmec empire, which lasted from around 1400 B.C. to 500 B.C., was the first major American civilization. It emerged in the tropical forests along the Gulf coast of Mexico. Instead of cities, the **Olmecs** built ceremonial centers comprising pyramid-shaped temples and other buildings. The Olmecs invented a calendar and developed a system of writing made up of carved inscriptions. Through trade links, their influence extended over a large area. Olmec carvings appear in the artwork of later societies. Perhaps the most important legacy of the Olmecs was their devotion to religion and their especially honored class of priests. These characteristics were common in later Mesoamerican civilizations.

THE MAYAS

One major civilization influenced by the Olmecs was that of the **Mayas,** who flourished from about A.D. 300 to 900. During this period, the Mayas developed a complex agricultural society. They established large city-states in southern Mexico and throughout much of Central America.

Farming and Trade

Farmers made up most of the Mayan population. Men usually cultivated the crops, which included maize (corn), beans, and squash. Women were in charge of turning these crops into food. Farmers paid taxes, in the form of food, to support the cities and their temples. The Mayas accumulated much wealth from a profitable trade system. Traders carried valuable honey, cocoa, and feathers across Central America along hard-packed dirt roads.

Religion

Because of the significance of religion to the Mayas, priests occupied an exalted place in the social hierarchy. These religious leaders held such importance because they alone could conduct the elaborate rituals that the Mayas believed would ensure bountiful harvests and victories in battle.

Social Structure

Mayan civilization featured a distinct social hierarchy. Each Mayan city-state had its own ruling chief. Immediately below this chief were the nobles, who served as city officials and military leaders. Although those in the ruling class were usually men, women could occasionally obtain some degree of power. Most Mayas, however, were farmers.

Contributions

ARCHITECTURE   In their cities, the Mayas built giant pyramid temples and large palaces. Elaborate paintings and carvings on the walls depicted events from Mayan history.

KEY THEMES AND CONCEPTS

Belief Systems The importance of religion to the Mayas may be judged from the size of their temples. Priests climbed these tall structures to perform rituals while the common people watched from far below.

KEY THEMES AND CONCEPTS

Economic Systems The Mayas were advanced enough to modify their natural environment to increase their agricultural output. For example, they developed ways to drain excess water from fields.

PREPARING FOR THE REGENTS

Compare the achievements of the Mayas with those of one or more of the classical civilizations of Eurasia and Africa.

AGRICULTURE   Despite the tropical environment, the Mayas grew enough food to support large city populations. Farmers made this possible by clearing out the dense rain forests and then building raised fields that were capable of holding and draining rainwater.

LEARNING AND SCIENCE   Perhaps the most impressive achievement of the Mayas was their advanced learning. Mayas developed a hieroglyphic (picture) system of writing and recorded much of their knowledge in books made of bark. Mayan priests developed a very accurate 365-day calendar. They also used a numbering system and understood the concept of zero before Europeans did.

Decline

Around A.D. 900, the Mayas abandoned their cities. Historians speculate that warfare or overpopulation may have caused agriculture to decline or that there were revolts by the lower classes. Remnants of this great culture remain, however. Today, millions of people in Guatemala and southern Mexico speak Mayan languages.

THE AZTECS

In the late 1200s, a nomadic group migrated from the north into the Valley of Mexico. They settled in the area, establishing their capital at Tenochtitlán. The **Aztecs,** who developed from this group, were fierce warriors. In the 1400s, the Aztecs used conquests and alliances to build a huge empire. Their capital grew to become a magnificent city with temples, palaces, gardens, and zoos.

Aztec Expansion

The Aztecs founded Tenochtitlán in 1315. In the early 1400s, Aztec leaders began forming alliances with neighboring states. The Aztecs soon became the dominant power in what is now central Mexico. Then, though a series of military conquests over hundreds of smaller states, the Aztecs steadily expanded their empire. Each conquered state was given an Aztec governor. The Aztecs became wealthy from tribute, payment they took from conquered peoples. By the early 1500s, the Aztec empire covered most of Mexico and included about 30 million people.

KEY THEMES AND CONCEPTS

Power The Aztecs' ability to collect tribute from so many groups over such a large area illustrates their power in the region.

Social Structure

RULERS, NOBLES, AND PRIESTS   Unlike the Mayas, the Aztecs were ruled by a single emperor, who was chosen by a council of nobles and priests. Below this ruler was the noble class, from which officials, judges, and provincial governors were drawn.

WARRIORS AND TRADERS   The warriors came next in the Aztec class structure. A warrior might rise into the noble class through superior performance on the battlefield. Traders formed another group in Aztec society. They carried goods over long distances to exchange for exotic products from peoples who lived beyond the empire. Traders also scouted distant lands to help plan future conquests.

FARMERS AND SLAVES Most of the people in the empire were farmers. Slaves made up the lowest class in the social structure. Members of this group were mainly criminals or enemy soldiers who had been captured. Despite their lowly status, they still had certain rights guaranteed by Aztec law. Some slaves even owned land and eventually bought their freedom.

Religion

Religion was important to the Aztecs. As in Mayan society, priests gained significance because they led rituals that were believed to appease the gods, who would then prevent disasters. The Aztecs built a huge pyramid in the center of Tenochtitlán to honor their chief deity, the sun god.

To please their gods, Aztec priests offered many thousands of human sacrifices. Both the Olmecs and the Mayas had also practiced human sacrifice, but not on such a large scale. Aztec sacrificial victims were usually captured enemy soldiers.

Contributions

LEARNING AND SCIENCE Aztec priests devised an accurate calendar. They also established schools and recorded historical events. Aztec medical practices were advanced enough that practitioners could set broken bones and treat dental cavities.

ARCHITECTURE AND ENGINEERING The Aztec capital of Tenochtitlán was one of the great achievements of Mesoamerican civilization. Built on the site of present-day Mexico City, Tenochtitlán began as two small islands in Lake Texcoco. Engineers filled in parts of the lake and built wide stone causeways to connect Tenochtitlán to the mainland. Architects designed huge pyramid temples, an elaborate emperor's place, and busy outdoor markets. An estimated 200,000 people lived in Tenochtitlán in 1500, making it the largest and most densely populated settlement in Mesoamerica.

AGRICULTURE As their population grew, the Aztecs found ingenious ways to create more farmland. They used a variety of fertilizers and converted swampy areas into productive farmland. They also built *chinampas,* artificial islands made of earth piled on reed mats that were anchored to the shallow bed of Lake Texcoco. On these "floating gardens" Aztec farmers raised corn, squash and beans. The Aztecs' ability to produce an abundance of food was a major factor in the success of their empire.

PREPARING FOR THE REGENTS

The development of a calendar was an important feature of nearly every early civilization. Calendars were useful in agriculture because they told early peoples when to plant and when to prepare for floods.

THE INCAS

In the 1400s, the **Incas** emerged from the Andes Mountains and conquered a large area that extended over 2,500 miles down the Pacific coast. The Incas ruled an empire made up of many separate conquered peoples.

A Centralized Government

An emperor ruled the Incas. The first emperor was a warrior who led his armies through many successful campaigns of conquest. The emperor held absolute power and owned all of the people, land, herds, and mines. The emperor was also the chief religious leader and claimed divine status as the son of the sun.

The emperor headed a strong central government from the mountain capital at Cuzco. Nobles ran the provinces along with local chieftains from the conquered people of each area. Other officials collected taxes, enforced laws, and performed routine government business. The Incan government strictly controlled the lives of the millions of people within its empire. Everyone had to speak the same language, Quechua, and practice the Incan religion.

An Empire Linked by Roads

The emperor could not have imposed this centralized rule over such a large area without a remarkable system of roads. Runners used these roads to carry news swiftly from far-off provinces to the emperor in the capital. This arrangement allowed him to keep a close watch on his empire. If necessary, Incan armies could move quickly over the roads to crush any rebellions that formed in distant corners of the empire.

Religion

Incan religion affected all parts of daily life. The people worshiped many gods related to forces of nature as well as guardian spirits in the home. The chief Incan deity was the sun god. A powerful class of priests conducted rituals and led monthly religious festivals that featured sports and games.

Contributions

ENGINEERING AND ARCHITECTURE   The Incan system of roads stands out as a major accomplishment of their civilization. It extended more than 12,000 miles, included hundreds of bridges, and even used tunnels and steps to pass through mountainous terrain.

The capital city of Cuzco was home to other Incan engineering feats. In the city center stood the giant Temple of the Sun, built with huge stone blocks and featuring inner walls lined with gold. The engineering of this temple was so advanced that the building was strong enough to withstand major earthquakes.

PREPARING FOR THE REGENTS

How was the Incan emperor similar to the pharaohs of ancient Egypt?

KEY THEMES AND CONCEPTS

Government The Incan government used military power, local rulers, and an excellent road system to impose a more centralized control over the empire.

AGRICULTURE   Like the Aztecs, the Incas frequently borrowed and built upon ideas from other societies. Incan farmers used stone walls to improve upon **terraces** built by earlier peoples. The improved terraces of the Aztecs held strips of land in place on steep hillsides and prevented rain from washing away the soil. The terraces made it possible to farm effectively in places where flat land was scarce.

COMMUNICATION   Incan government officials kept records by means of a system of knotted, colored strings called **quipus.** Historians believe that quipus may have been used to record dates and events as well as population and crop statistics.

SCIENCE   The Incas had a calendar but were not as advanced in astronomy as the Mayas had been. One area in which the Incas excelled was medicine. They performed successful surgery to treat head wounds. The Incas also had knowledge about diseases and medicines; they used herbs as antiseptics.

SUMMARY

Complex civilizations grew up in the Americas from about 1400 B.C. to A.D. 1500. The Olmecs had the first major American civilization, followed by the Mayas and Aztecs in Mexico and Central America and by the Incas in South America. For all these civilizations, agriculture was a primary economic activity that allowed populations to grow. Religion unified the empires. The later Mesoamerican civilizations developed complex government systems and trade networks. Mesoamerican societies made advances in agriculture, medicine, mathematics, engineering, and other areas.

KEY THEMES AND CONCEPTS

Culture and Intellectual Life Like many other groups throughout history, the Incas built upon the work of earlier civilizations to achieve even greater progress.

 PREPARING FOR THE REGENTS

List three ways in which the Incan and Roman empires were similar.

1.

2.

3.

SECTION 2

The Ming Dynasty in China

During the Ming Dynasty, the Chinese:

- restored Chinese rule and reaffirmed belief in Chinese superiority.

- achieved economic and cultural growth.

- after a brief period of exploration, sought to limit contact with most outsiders.

- continued to influence neighboring Asian countries culturally and intellectually.

SECTION OVERVIEW

In the mid-1300s, the Chinese overthrew foreign conquerors, the Mongols, and restored self-rule under the Ming dynasty. Ming China experienced an economic and cultural revival. In the early 1400s, China began voyages of exploration and came into contact with Europe. Later the empire turned inward, seeking to protect itself from outside influences. China did, however, greatly affect nearby Asian lands that fell into its zone of influence. Over time, Chinese culture exerted religious and cultural influence in Korea, Japan, and Southeast Asia.

KEY THEMES AND CONCEPTS

As you review this section, take special note of the following key themes and concepts:

Change How did Chinese government, industry, and trade change after China overthrew its Mongol rulers and established a restored Chinese empire?

Choice Why did China choose to isolate itself from foreign trade after 1433?

Culture What impact did China have on other societies in Asia?

KEY PEOPLE AND TERMS

As you review this section, be sure you understand the significance of these key people and terms:

Zhu Yuanzhang Middle Kingdom Matteo Ricci
Ming dynasty Zheng He

RESTORATION OF CHINESE RULE

In 1368, about 90 years after Mongol leader Kublai Khan had established Mongol rule in China, Chinese rule was restored under the Ming dynasty. Although the Mongols had improved trade and transportation, many Chinese resented foreign rule. In 1368, a peasant leader, **Zhu Yuanzhang,** led a rebellion that successfully overthrew Mongol rule. Zhu then established the **Ming dynasty.**

The Middle Kingdom

Under the Ming, China was once again ruled by the Chinese. Ming leaders sought to restore the country's greatness and its supremacy in the region. China traditionally thought of itself as the **Middle Kingdom,** the center of the earth and the source of civilization.

Ming Government Reform

Ming rulers enacted reforms to improve the government. They brought back the civil service system. In this system, candidates had to pass a difficult exam. Confucian learning once again became important, because knowledge of Confucian classics was a key part of the exam. Ming leaders also established a board of censors to eliminate corruption in the bureaucracy.

Looking Outward and Turning Inward

During the first several decades of the 1400s, the Chinese admiral **Zheng He** established trade links with many distant commerce centers and brought exotic animals back to China for the imperial zoo. After Zheng He's death in 1433, the Ming emperor banned the building of large oceangoing ships, and China, as a result, suddenly halted its voyages of exploration. The reasons for this abrupt change in policy were both economic and cultural. Zheng's voyages had not brought profits to the empire, and his fleets were costly to maintain. Also, Confucian scholars taught that China had the most advanced civilization in the world. Limiting contact with foreign influences therefore seemed the best way to preserve ancient traditions.

ECONOMIC AND CULTURAL CONTRIBUTIONS

Agriculture

Advances in agriculture, such as better fertilization methods, made it possible for farmers on China's eastern plains to produce enough food to support a large population. In the 1500s, corn and sweet potatoes were introduced from the Americas, further improving food production by Chinese farmers.

Industry and Trade

The Chinese also made advances in industry during the Ming period. They utilized new technologies to increase manufacturing production. Industries such as the making of porcelain, tools, and paper thrived in Chinese cities. The Ming also repaired their neglected canal system to improve trade links across the country.

KEY THEMES AND CONCEPTS

Change The Mongol Yuan dynasty, instituted by Kublai Khan, declined after his death. This decline, coupled with the fact that many Chinese hated their Mongol rulers, led to the uprisings that ended in the formation of the Ming dynasty.

PREPARING FOR THE REGENTS

To learn more about Zheng He and global trade, see Unit 3, Section 3.

PREPARING FOR THE REGENTS

Why did China's attitude toward commercial contacts with foreign lands change after 1433?

Arts and Literature

The arts flowered during the Ming dynasty. Artists developed new styles of landscape painting and created beautiful porcelain jars and vases. Chinese silks were much admired by Europeans.

Confucian scholars produced classical poetry; other writers wrote popular fiction. Dramatic artists developed new art forms that combined drama, music, and dance.

CHINA AND THE WEST

European Interest in China

When Portuguese and other European merchants reached East Asia in the 1500s, they were impressed by Chinese goods. European visitors to China wrote enthusiastically about the exquisite silks and porcelains they found there. Europeans were also fascinated with Chinese production of guns and gunpowder.

Chinese Indifference

Ming leaders severely restricted foreign trade, believing European goods to be inferior. However, they allowed limited trade at the coastal outpost of Macao, near present-day Guangzhou. Imperial officials supervised this trade strictly.

Some European scholars, such as the Jesuit priest **Matteo Ricci,** did gain acceptance among the Ming. In the 1580s, the Chinese welcomed Ricci, who shared with them his knowledge of European arts and sciences. Although the Chinese were open to learning about European technology, they had little interest in the religious beliefs that Ricci and the Jesuits sought to promote.

CHINA'S IMPACT WITHIN ASIA

Over time, Chinese civilization exerted a cultural influence over its neighbors in Asia. Korea, Japan, and Southeast Asia were affected by China's customs and values.

Korea

Throughout history, China's civilization has influenced its smaller neighbor, Korea. At times, China even took political control of Korea. China affected Korea in many ways.

Korea continued to maintain its own culture, however. Sometimes, as with the Chinese civil service system, Korea made adaptations that fit its own traditions. After learning to make porcelain from the Chinese, Koreans developed a distinctive blue-green glaze called celadon. Korea also developed its own system of writing. The Korean language is unrelated to Chinese.

China Influences Korea

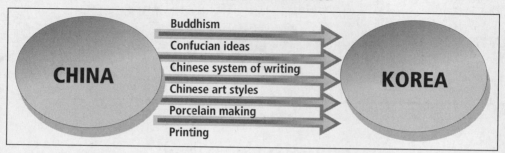

CHINA → Buddhism → KOREA
Confucian ideas
Chinese system of writing
Chinese art styles
Porcelain making
Printing

Japan

Korea served as a cultural bridge linking China with the Japanese islands. In the A.D. 500s, missionaries from Korea introduced Buddhism and other aspects of Chinese culture to Japan. In the centuries that followed, Japanese nobles studied in China, returning with Chinese ideas and technology. Later, however, the Japanese became less interested in China and began to blend Chinese ideas with their own.

Japanese paintings were often influenced by Chinese landscape techniques. Japanese artists developed their own styles, however, re-creating historical events on magnificent scrolls. During Japan's feudal age, Japanese samurai increasingly adopted the beliefs of a Buddhist sect from China known in Japan as Zen. Zen Buddhism greatly influenced Japanese society, including its theater, literature, and art.

Southeast Asia

The diverse cultural region of Southeast Asia consists of a mainland area and scattered islands. It was greatly influenced by traders from China and India, who often passed through Southeast Asian ports. Buddhism, Hinduism, and Islam all entered the region.

Indian influences prevailed in much of Southeast Asia. In Vietnam, however, China exerted a greater influence. China had conquered Vietnam by the first century B.C., and it ruled the region for 1,000 years. Vietnam absorbed the Confucian civil service system and established a bureaucracy that resembled China's. Even so, Vietnam retained a strong cultural identity of its own.

SUMMARY

The Ming dynasty restored Chinese rule and remained in power for more than 250 years. During this period, China prospered economically and culturally. After 1433, however, the Chinese sought to limit contact with the outside world. Europeans established some trading posts in China, but the Chinese saw little value in products from the West. Chinese culture continued to exert a strong influence over Korea, Japan, and much of Southeast Asia, especially Vietnam.

 PREPARING FOR THE REGENTS

To learn more about Japan's feudal age and Zen Buddhism, see Unit 3, Section 1.

 PREPARING FOR THE REGENTS

List two ways in which China influenced each of the following areas.

Korea:

1.

2.

Japan:

1.

2.

Southeast Asia:

1.

2.

★ **THE BIG IDEA**
The Ottoman Empire:

- expanded across a vast area in the 1400s and 1500s, from southeastern Europe through the Middle East and North Africa.

- extended Muslim influence.

- made contributions in the arts, architecture, and literature.

- forced Europeans to begin seeking new routes for trade with Asia.

SECTION OVERVIEW

In 1453, the Ottomans captured Constantinople and overthrew the Byzantine empire. Over the next 200 years, backed by military advances, the Ottomans built a large and powerful empire in Europe and the Middle East. During the reign of Suleiman, the Ottomans strengthened their government and military while spreading Islamic culture over a large area. Various religious beliefs, however, were tolerated within the empire. The Ottoman empire created impressive works of architecture, art, and literature. Ottoman expansion into Eastern Europe and the eastern Mediterranean disrupted European trade. As Europeans began to search for new trade routes in the 1400s, Ottoman domination was gradually weakened. This weakening, along with other factors, led to the decline of the empire.

KEY THEMES AND CONCEPTS

As you review this section, take special note of the following key themes and concepts:

Places and Regions What lands came under control of the Ottoman empire?

Belief Systems How did the Ottoman empire extend Muslim influence and permit freedom of worship for people of other religions?

Culture What contributions did the Ottomans make to the arts and literature?

Change Why did Europeans seek new trade routes to East Asia?

KEY PEOPLE AND TERMS

As you review this section, be sure you understand the significance of these key people and terms:

Constantinople	sultan	janissaries
Suleiman	millet	mosque

THE RISE OF THE OTTOMAN EMPIRE

By the 1400s, the once mighty Byzantine empire had been in decline for nearly two centuries. In the 1400s, it faced a growing threat from the Ottomans, a nomadic Turkish-speaking group that had migrated from central Asia into Asia Minor. In the previous century, the Ottomans had moved through Asia Minor and into the Balkans.

In 1453, Ottoman armies surrounded the Byzantine capital of **Constantinople.** During a two-month siege, Ottoman cannons pounded Constantinople's defensive walls, eventually allowing the attackers to break through and capture the city. The Ottomans changed the city's name to Istanbul and made this ancient Christian city the capital of their Muslim empire.

Geographic Expansion

The Ottoman empire greatly expanded its territory in the century that followed the fall of Constantinople. With its well-armed forces and effective military strategies, the Ottoman empire grew quickly. After 1453, the empire made spectacular gains, conquering lands south to Mecca as well as along the Nile River in Egypt. The Ottomans also expanded further north into the Balkans and into Russia, capturing the Crimean peninsula. The Ottomans even laid siege to Vienna in 1529, causing great fear among Europeans. Ottoman forces failed to capture Vienna, however. Even so, by the 1500s, the Ottomans had built the largest, most powerful empire in the Middle East and Europe. At its peak, the Ottoman empire reached across three continents, from southeastern Europe through the Middle East and North Africa.

Reasons for Ottoman Success

The success of the Ottomans was due in large part to new military technology. In addition to the cannons that smashed Constantinople's defenses, the Ottoman army equipped its foot soldiers with muskets. This strategy increased the soldiers' battlefield effectiveness and reduced the importance of mounted soldiers. The new military technology allowed Ottoman leaders to consolidate their rule within the empire as well as to conquer new lands.

EUROPEAN SEARCH FOR NEW TRADE ROUTES

As the Ottoman empire expanded into Eastern Europe and the eastern Mediterranean, European trade routes were disrupted. For example, Ottoman control of the eastern Mediterranean interfered with Western Europe's trade with East Asia.

No longer able to depend on the old trade routes to Asia, Portuguese sailors sent explorers out over the oceans in search of new trade routes. They were followed later by other Europeans.

♀ KEY THEMES AND CONCEPTS

Power Many factors can contribute to a nation's power. At Constantinople, military technology helped the Ottomans bring about the final collapse of the Byzantine empire.

 PREPARING FOR THE REGENTS

Describe the extent of Ottoman territory at the height of the empire.

♀ KEY THEMES AND CONCEPTS

Movement of People and Goods In the 1400s, Europeans wanted to get around the Muslim and Italian "middlemen" and gain direct access to Asian trade. Portugal, then Spain, and eventually other European nations sought a route to Asia that bypassed the Mediterranean.

OTTOMAN ACHIEVEMENTS AND LASTING IMPACT

The Byzantine Heritage

The Ottoman empire absorbed many influences from the conquered Byzantine empire. As you know, the Byzantine heritage was itself a mingling of Greco-Roman and Middle Eastern influences. The Ottomans blended Byzantine culture with Muslim culture. Byzantine influences could be found in Ottoman government, social life, and architecture.

Suleiman's Golden Age

Suleiman, called Suleiman the Magnificent by westerners, ruled the Ottoman empire from 1520 to 1566. Suleiman was a **sultan,** the name Turks gave to their rulers. An effective military leader who further modernized the army, Suleiman continued to add new territories to the empire.

The years of Suleiman's rule are considered the golden age of Ottoman history. A wise leader, Suleiman strengthened the government and improved the system of justice in his empire. As a Muslim, he based his law on the Sharia, the Islamic system of law. In fact, he was known to his subjects as Suleiman the Lawgiver. Although Suleiman held absolute power, he did consult with an advisor and a council in governing the empire. He also chose able officials to run the large bureaucracy he needed to supervise everyday matters of government.

A Diverse Society

The Ottomans ruled a vast area that included many diverse peoples with many religions. Nevertheless, the Ottomans held their empire together successfully for hundreds of years, thus making Islam the dominant cultural force throughout the region.

SOCIAL CLASSES Ottoman society had four classes:

- **Men of the Pen** At the top of the social structure were highly educated people, such as scientists, lawyers, judges, and poets.
- **Men of the Sword** Also ranked high were members of the military.
- **Men of Negotiation** Below the elite classes were businesspeople, such as moneychangers, tax collectors, and artisans.
- **Men of Husbandry** A fourth class included farmers and herders.

The top two classes were made up almost entirely of Muslims; the two lower classes included people from all backgrounds. This class structure helped make Islam the dominant cultural force in the empire.

MILLETS Non-Muslims in the Ottoman Empire were organized into religious communities called **millets.** Each millet was allowed to maintain its own religious traditions and educate its people—as long as it obeyed Ottoman law.

JANISSARIES Ottoman leaders furthered Muslim influence by recruiting military and government officers from conquered groups. Some Christian families in the Balkans were required to turn their young sons over to the government. The boys were converted to Islam and trained for service. The best soldiers became **janissaries,** members of an elite force in the Ottoman army.

Arts and Literature

Throughout the empire, Muslim architects built many palaces as well as Muslim houses of worship, or **mosques.** Muslim religious structures promoted the further spread of Muslim culture into the Christian areas of southeastern Europe.

Ottoman arts reflected Persian influences. Painters used Persian styles to create detailed miniatures and beautiful illuminated manuscripts. Ottoman writers and poets used Persian and Arab models to produce great works in the Turkish language.

THE DECLINE OF THE OTTOMAN EMPIRE

Although the Ottoman empire survived into the twentieth century, it began to decline much earlier than that. The reasons for this decline came from both within and outside the empire.

Internal Disorder

Problems developed within the Ottoman empire. Slowly, over time, nations were able to break free from foreign Ottoman rule. The empire also experienced government corruption and poor leadership in its later years.

European Advances

The rising power of European nations was the major external reason for the Ottoman decline. In 1571, Spain and its Italian allies defeated an Ottoman fleet at Lepanto. Even while the Ottomans were adding to their empire in the 1400s and 1500s, they were increasingly being cut out of global trade.

By the 1700s, European commercial and military technology had surpassed that of the Ottomans. Also, industrially based European economies became stronger than the Ottoman economy, which was still based on agriculture. The commercial revolution in Europe, therefore, was a strong factor in Ottoman decline.

SUMMARY

During the 1400s and 1500s, the powerful Ottoman empire arose in Asia Minor. The empire expanded over time to cover a vast area, extending the influence of Islam. Ottoman architecture, literature, and other art forms flourished. The Ottoman empire dominated trade for many years, forcing European countries to begin seeking new routes to Asia. However, European advances in technology and internal disorder all contributed to the fall of the empire.

KEY THEMES AND CONCEPTS

Diversity Although the Ottoman empire was ruled by Muslims, other religious beliefs were tolerated in the empire. For example, when restrictions on Jews in Europe became severe in the 1500s, many Jews fled to the Ottoman empire, where they were allowed to prosper.

PREPARING FOR THE REGENTS

Describe at least one other example of a powerful empire that was weakened by internal rebellions, government corruption, or poor leadership.

PREPARING FOR THE REGENTS

What factors contributed to the rise and fall of the Ottoman empire?

4 Explorations, Encounters, and Imperialism

⭐ **THE BIG IDEA**

Between the late 1400s and 1700s, Western Europeans:

- benefited from technology in mapmaking, navigation, shipbuilding, and weaponry.

- found new sea routes and dominated trade with Asia, Africa, and the Americas.

- competed with each other to establish profitable colonies.

- began global interactions that greatly affected people around the world.

SECTION OVERVIEW

In the 1400s, seeking a greater share of the rich Asian spice trade, Europeans began to make oceanic voyages of exploration. Benefiting from new technology, the Portuguese and the Spanish were the first to establish global trade empires in the 1500s. The Dutch, English, and French soon joined them, competing for colonies in Asia, the Americas, and Africa during the 1600s and 1700s. These interactions had a great global impact as food, people, plants, animals, technology, and diseases passed from continent to continent.

KEY THEMES AND CONCEPTS

As you review this section, take special note of the following key themes and concepts:

Movement of People and Goods How did global trade patterns change between the late 1400s and the 1700s?

Science and Technology What types of technology allowed Western Europeans to explore the oceans?

Interdependence What motives did Europeans have for establishing colonies between 1500 and 1700?

Change What major changes did the European expansion bring to peoples around the world?

KEY PEOPLE AND TERMS

As you review this section, be sure you understand the significance of these key people and terms:

Reconquista

cartographer

astrolabe

Vasco da Gama

Christopher Columbus

imperialism

Ferdinand Magellan

sepoy

conquistador

plantation

Middle Passage

encomienda

Columbian

    exchange

mercantilism

THE EVE OF EXPLORATION

As Europeans were looking for new routes to the riches of Asia, two nations in Western Europe, Portugal and Spain, took the lead. Both of these nations had the technology, resources, and political unity to support sea travel. Both of these nations had also struggled with Muslim rule in their countries and had created Christian kingdoms.

Reconquista and Expulsions

The marriage of Ferdinand of Aragon to Isabella of Castile in 1469 brought together two powerful Spanish kingdoms. In 1492, Ferdinand and Isabella forced the Muslims from Granada, their last stronghold in Spain. This victory completed the **Reconquista,** a campaign begun by Christians in the 700s to recapture Spain from the Muslims. After achieving political unity in Spain, Isabella sought to establish religious unity. She launched a brutal crusade against Muslims and Jews who refused to convert to Christianity. Many people were killed, and about 150,000 were forced into exile.

Reasons for European Exploration

Although Europeans had long traded in Asian countries, travel to the east had been disrupted by Ottoman control of the eastern Mediterranean, a situation that interfered with Western Europe's trade with Asia. By the 1400s, seeking to gain access to the Asian spices so highly valued on their continent, Europeans looked to reopen global trade links. Italian and Muslim merchants, however, controlled the routes between Asia and Europe. Muslim traders brought goods to the Mediterranean, and Italian traders carried the goods to the rest of Europe. Each time the goods changed hands, they became more expensive. To gain direct access to Asian trade, Portugal and Spain looked for new oceanic routes.

Impact of Technology

Advances in technology greatly aided Europeans in their quest to explore the oceans.

THE PRINTING PRESS   In the mid-1400s, German printer Johann Gutenberg became the first person to use a printing press to print a book. Through the use of movable metal type, the printing press enabled people to make books quickly and cheaply. As a result, books became more readily available. Europeans were able to gain access to new ideas and information on a broad range of topics, including geography.

GUNPOWDER   European explorers also benefited from advances in military technology. Since Arab traders had brought gunpowder to Europe in the 1200s, Europeans had been making advances in weaponry. By the late 1400s, the Portuguese were equipping their

 **PREPARING FOR THE REGENTS**

Why did Portugal and Spain pursue sea exploration?

 PREPARING FOR THE REGENTS

To learn more about the impact of the printing press on life in Europe, see Unit 3, Section 4.

PREPARING FOR THE REGENTS

What technologies made European overseas expansion possible?

KEY THEMES AND CONCEPTS

Science and Technology
This instrument, the astrolabe, was used to calculate the exact latitude of a ship.

ships with sturdy cannons. Eventually, the use of cannons helped the Portuguese win control of the Indian Ocean trade network.

NAVAL TECHNOLOGY Mapmakers, or **cartographers,** created better maps and charts of the sea. Moreover, European sailors learned to use the magnetic compass to determine direction and the **astrolabe,** an instrument perfected by the Arabs, to figure out their latitude at sea. Europeans also built bigger and better ships. The Portuguese used caravels, ships whose sails, masts, and rudders allowed explorers to sail across or against the wind.

EARLY EXPLORATIONS AND ENCOUNTERS

Around Africa to Asia

In 1415, Prince Henry, the son of the Portuguese king, carried out a plan to improve his country's navy. Known to later generations as Henry the Navigator, this prince gathered experts in science, mapmaking, and shipbuilding. Their work led to a fleet of ships that explored the coast of West Africa. In 1488, Bartholomeu Dias rounded the Cape of Good Hope at the southern tip of Africa.

About a decade later, **Vasco da Gama** followed Dias's route around Africa and traveled across the Indian Ocean to an Indian port. Although he lost half his ships, Da Gama returned home with Asian spices that he sold at a high profit. The Portuguese had established a successful all-water trade route to Asia and would soon expand their empire.

Columbus Reaches the Americas

The success of the Portuguese inspired Ferdinand and Isabella of Spain to try to gain a share of the rich spice trade in the East. Furthermore, Isabella sought to spread Christianity.

In 1492, an ambitious Italian sailor from Genoa convinced the Spanish monarchs to finance his plan to reach Asia by sailing across the Atlantic Ocean. **Christopher Columbus** and his crew thus sailed west for India in three small ships, striking land after two months. Although he landed at an island in the Caribbean Sea, Columbus thought that he had reached islands off the coast of Asia. Later explorers realized that he had reached the Americas, a continent they had not known existed.

Spain and Portugal soon both claimed the islands that Columbus had explored in his voyages. In 1493, to settle the issue, Pope Alexander VI established the Line of Demarcation, which divided the non-European world into two zones. Spain could trade and explore west of the line; Portugal had the same rights east of the line. One year later, with the Treaty of Tordesillas, the two nations agreed to move the line.

EUROPEANS COMPETE FOR COLONIES

The domination by one country of the political and/or economic life of another country is called **imperialism.** Europe's activities in Asia, Africa, and the Americas from the 1500s through the 1700s foreshadowed the major era of European imperialism in the 1800s.

Imperialism in Africa

In the 1400s, the Portuguese explored the coasts of Africa, establishing a string of forts in the west and capturing several port cities in the east. The Portuguese, however, were unsuccessful in their attempts to push into the African interior. As a result, the Portuguese gained little profit from their victories.

In the mid-1600s, the Dutch arrived at the southwestern tip of Africa and established the Cape Town settlement. At Cape Town, Dutch sailors could repair their ships as they traveled to or from the East Indies. The Dutch farmers who settled in and around Cape Town were called Boers. The Boers ousted or enslaved many Africans, whom they considered their inferiors.

Imperialism in Asia

Soon after European powers had established direct trading links with Asia, they sought to gain more permanent control there. First Portugal and then other nations set up colonies in Asia, creating competition in the region.

PORTUGAL   In the early 1500s, the Portuguese took control of the Indian trade network from the Muslims. The Portuguese seized the port of Malacca on the Malay Peninsula in the Indian Ocean, the most important Arab trading city. They also conquered cities on the east

PREPARING FOR THE REGENTS

Practice your map skills by listing three places controlled by Europeans in each of the following areas.

Africa:

India:

East Asia:

European Trade in the East, 1700

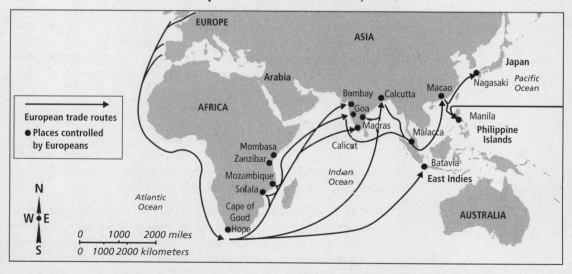

coast of Africa and destroyed Arab ships at sea. For most of the 1500s, Portugal controlled the spice trade between Europe and Asia.

Although the Portuguese were powerful at sea, they were not able to conquer much territory on land. Also, they caused much resentment with their intolerant policies. Portuguese missionaries and traders destroyed Hindu temples, massacred Muslims, and sank pilgrim ships. By the late 1500s, Portuguese power in the Indian Ocean was declining.

THE DUTCH   The first Europeans to challenge Portuguese domination of the Asian spice trade were the Dutch. In the late 1500s, Dutch fleets had established their own trade links with Asia. Soon their sea power surpassed that of the Portuguese. A group of wealthy Dutch merchants formed the Dutch East India Company in the early 1600s. In 1641, the Dutch seized Malacca from Portugal and began trading with China. The Dutch established closer ties with local leaders and stirred less resentment among Asians than had the Portuguese. Soon they dominated the Asian spice trade. Their trading empire did not begin to decline until the 1700s.

SPAIN   Spain also founded colonies in Southeast Asia in the 1500s. Spain financed the voyage of Portuguese noble **Ferdinand Magellan** that completed the first circumnavigation of the world. To circumnavigate something is to go completely around it. During this voyage Magellan claimed the island chain that today is called the Philippines for Spain in 1521. (The islands were named for the Spanish king, Philip II.) This island group gave Spain a base from which to trade with China and spread Catholic teachings to East Asia.

ENGLAND AND FRANCE   In the 1700s, England and France became competing forces in the Asian trade network, concentrating on India. The Mughal dynasty in India had been rich and powerful in the 1600s, but weak rulers and civil wars early in the next century weakened the kingdom. The British and French East India Companies made alliances with local rulers, and each company organized its own army of **sepoys,** or Indian troops. In the 1750s, the British East India Company and its sepoys pushed the French out of their trading posts. The British East India Company forced the Mughal emperor to allow it to collect taxes in northeast India. Before long, the company was the real power in the region.

Imperialism in the Americas

After Christopher Columbus landed in the West Indies, friendly relations existed between the Spanish and the Native Americans for a while. However, these friendly feelings did not last.

SPANISH CONQUISTADORS   Many Spanish **conquistadors,** or conquerors, traveled to the Americas in the years following Columbus's voyages. Some of these adventurers came in search of gold; others wanted to convert the inhabitants of the land to Christianity.

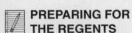

PREPARING FOR THE REGENTS

Describe differences between Portuguese and Dutch trading activity in Asia.

One of the earliest conquistadors, Hernan Cortés, landed in Mexico in 1519. Two years later, having formed alliances with discontented peoples within the Aztec empire, Cortés had conquered the empire. In 1532, another conquistador, Francisco Pizarro, destroyed the Incan empire in Peru.

REASONS FOR SPANISH SUCCESS   The Spanish were able to conquer these empires so quickly for several reasons.

- The Spanish used armor, horses, and powerful weapons that the Indians had never seen before.
- The Spanish found allies among Native American groups who hated being ruled by the Aztecs or Incas.
- Diseases brought by Europeans killed millions of native people, causing them to believe that their own gods had deserted them.

BATTLE FOR NORTH AMERICA   Spain's profitable American empire attracted the attention of other European powers. Dutch, English, and French explorers had long searched North America for a Northwest Passage to Asia. By the 1600s, these nations had planted permanent colonies on the continent.

In the 1600s, the French settled Canada. Naming their colony New France, the French sent over fur trappers and missionaries and established forts and trading posts from Quebec to Louisiana.

In 1607, the English established their first permanent colony in North America at Jamestown. Throughout the 1600s, large numbers of English settlers followed. Some came for profit, others hoped to own land, and still others, such as the Puritans, came seeking religious freedom. The English monarch asserted control over his 13 American colonies, but they still had more self-government than the French or Spanish in North America.

Spain, France, England, and the Netherlands frequently clashed over territory and trade in North America. In the mid-1700s, the British defeated the French in the French and Indian War. The French then had to give up Canada, leaving much of North America to England.

TRIANGULAR TRADE AND SLAVERY

Causes of the Slave Trade

In the 1500s, Europeans came to view African slaves as the most valuable African trade goods. At that time, Europeans began buying large numbers of Africans to satisfy the labor shortage on American **plantations,** or large estates. The slave trade eventually grew into a huge and profitable business. The trade that involved Europe, Africa, and the Americas was sometimes referred to as "triangular trade" because the sea routes among these three continents formed vast triangles.

KEY THEMES AND CONCEPTS

Science and Technology One of the reasons for the relatively swift Spanish conquest of the Americas was the military technology of European powers.

KEY THEMES AND CONCEPTS

Government English monarchs allowed their colonists more self-government than the French or the Spanish did. English political traditions of representative government and limited monarchy took root in the English colonies.

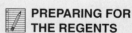 **PREPARING FOR THE REGENTS**

To learn more about the slave trade, see the map of Atlantic Trade Routes, 1750, in the Questions for Regents Practice at the end of this unit.

The Middle Passage

The voyage from Africa to the Americas on the slave ships was called the **Middle Passage.** Conditions were terrible on these ships. Hundreds of people were crammed onto a single ship. In fact, millions of Africans died on the way from disease, brutal mistreatment, or suicide. Those who survived were forced to work on plantations in the American colonies.

Effects of the Slave Trade

By the 1800s, when the slave trade ended, an estimated 11 million Africans had been sent to the Americas. The slave trade caused local wars to develop in Africa. As a result, traditional African political structures were undermined. Through slavery, many African societies were deprived of the talents of strong, intelligent people. West Africa especially lost many young men and women. Some societies and small states disappeared forever. Other states formed, some of them dependent on the slave trade.

THE SPANISH EMPIRE

During the 1500s, the Spanish empire in the Americas stretched from California to South America and brought great wealth to the nation. In return, the Spanish brought their government, religion, economy, and culture to the Americas.

- **Government** Spain maintained a strict control over its distant empire. The king ran the colonial government through his representatives, or viceroys, who ruled the provinces.
- **Religion** The Catholic Church was very important in the colonies. Church leaders helped run the government and worked to convert thousands of Native Americans to Christianity.
- **Encomienda System** Spanish law allowed its colonies to trade only with Spain. Growing sugar cane on large plantations became an important business activity in the colonial empire. Because plantations needed so many workers, the Spanish created the **encomienda** system. A conquistador, under this system, was granted land along with permission to demand labor or tribute from Native Americans in the area. After many of the overworked Indians died, the Spanish brought slaves from Africa to do the work.
- **Culture** Over time, the people in the colonies developed a new culture that combined European, Native American, and African traditions. These people spoke Spanish but also used Native American and African words. The art, architecture, and daily life in the empire were influenced by all three cultures.
- **Social Classes** A social structure developed that placed people in a hierarchy. The Spanish-born people at the top of the class structure were known as *peninsulares. Creoles* was the name given to those of European descent who were born in the colonies. *Mestizos* were people of mixed Native American and European descent, and *mulattoes* was the term for those of mixed African and European descent.

Social Structure of the Spanish Colonies

Most Power — **Fewest People**

Peninsulares
People born in Spain

Creoles
People of European descent born in the colonies

Mestizos
People of mixed Native American and European descent

Mulattoes
People of mixed African and European descent

Native Americans and People of African descent

Least Power — **Most People**

THE COLUMBIAN EXCHANGE: PLANTS, ANIMALS, PEOPLE, AND DISEASES

A global exchange of people, plants, animals, ideas, and technology began during this time, leading to profound changes for people in Asia, the Americas, Africa, and Europe. Because it started with Columbus, it is called the **Columbian exchange.**

Plants, including maize (corn) and potatoes, traveled to Europe, Africa, and Asia. Other plants, such as bananas and rice, traveled back to the Americas. From Africa and Asia, goats and chickens came to the Americas. Unfortunately, other exchanges occurred: diseases such as measles and typhus devastated populations in the Americas.

EUROPEAN CAPITALISM AND MERCANTILISM

Increased trade with the colonies encouraged European capitalism, the investment of money to make a profit. Joint stock companies grew in significance, since they allowed Europeans to gather the capital necessary to finance overseas voyages. Moreover, European nations adopted a new policy of **mercantilism.** This policy involved building up national wealth by exporting more goods than the nation imported.

⚷ KEY THEMES AND CONCEPTS

Movement of People and Goods The introduction of American crops such as corn and potatoes to other continents contributed to population growth in Europe, Africa, and Asia in the 1700s.

 **PREPARING FOR THE REGENTS**

Describe two positive and two negative aspects of the Columbian exchange.

The Columbian Exchange

From the Americas to Europe, Africa, and Asia

maize (corn)
potato
sweet potato
beans
peanut   tomato
squashes chili pepper
pumpkin avocado
          pineapple
          cocoa
          tobacco
          quinine (a medicine)

wheat
sugar
banana   cattle
rice   goat
grape (wine) sheep
dandelion chicken
horse   smallpox
pig   measles
           typhus

From Europe, Africa, and Asia to the Americas

Colonies supplied the parent nation with raw materials and served as a market for its exports.

The expansion of capitalism and mercantilism affected the lives of many Europeans. Nobles became less powerful because their wealth was based in the land they owned. On the other hand, many merchants, whose wealth was based in trade, grew richer. A middle class developed on the continent during this period. The lives of peasants did not change significantly in the 1500s and 1600s.

SUMMARY

From 1500 to 1700, European nations set off on voyages of exploration, establishing empires and trade links around the world. Western European countries competed for colonies and trade in Asia, Africa and the Americas. Slave trade between Africa and the Americas developed into a huge and profitable business. This European expansion had an enormous impact, resulting in many exchanges that altered the lives of people around the world.

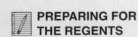 **PREPARING FOR THE REGENTS**

In what ways were the voyages of Columbus a major turning point in global history?

5 Absolutism and the Puritan Revolution

SECTION OVERVIEW

In the 1500s and 1600s, several rulers in Asia and Europe sought to centralize their political power. Claiming divine right, or authority from God, leaders such as Philip II in Spain and Louis XIV in France gained complete authority over their governments and their subjects. England resisted the establishment of absolutism. After a civil war, England's Parliament enacted a Bill of Rights that limited the English monarch's powers.

KEY THEMES AND CONCEPTS

As you review this section, take special note of the following key themes and concepts:

Government How did monarchs in India, Spain, France, and Russia work to increase their political power in the 1500s and 1600s?

Power What ideas did absolute monarchs use to justify their power?

Political Systems In what ways was England's experience of absolutism different from that of other European countries?

Choice What choices did Parliament make in England to assure a check on absolutism?

KEY PEOPLE AND TERMS

As you review this section, be sure you understand the significance of these key people and terms:

absolutism	Jacques Bossuet	Oliver Cromwell
Akbar the Great	Ivan the Terrible	Glorious Revolution
Philip II	Peter the Great	English Bill of Rights
divine right	Puritans	limited monarchy
Louis XIV	*The Leviathan*	

★ THE BIG IDEA
In the 1500s and 1600s:

- monarchs acted to establish absolute power.

- monarchs used the divine right theory and similar ideas to justify their power.

- Parliament and the Puritans in England resisted absolutism.

- a limited monarchy was established in England.

GLOBAL ABSOLUTISM

In the 1500s and 1600s, monarchs in Europe and Asia sought to centralize their power. This trend led to **absolutism,** in which autocratic rulers had complete authority over the government and the lives of the people in their nation.

Absolutism in Mughal India

One place where absolutism appeared in the 1500s was India. In the last half of the 1500s, **Akbar the Great** ruled the powerful Mughal empire in India. Akbar strengthened the central government and made his empire larger and stronger than any in Europe at the time. He modernized the army, encouraged trade, and introduced land reforms. Akbar solidified his reign by recognizing India's diversity and promoting religious tolerance. Akbar's successors were not as strong. Mughal rulers in the late 1600s were much less tolerant, and Mughal power declined, allowing France and England to spread their influence in the region.

Absolutism in Spain

In the 1500s, Spain became the most powerful nation in Europe. Wealth from its empire in the Americas helped Spain's power to grow.

CHARLES V   From 1519 to 1556, Charles V, the grandson of Ferdinand and Isabella, was king of Spain as well as Holy Roman Emperor. Ruling such a large and diverse area in Europe took its toll on Charles, however. He faced military threats from the French, from German Protestant princes, and from the Ottoman empire under Suleiman. In 1556, an exhausted Charles gave up his titles and divided his empire. His brother Ferdinand became Holy Roman Emperor, and his son Philip ruled Spain, the Netherlands, and the vast Spanish overseas empire.

PHILIP II   Ruling from 1556 to 1598, **Philip II** expanded his own power as well as the influence of the Catholic Church and the Spanish empire. Philip wanted to control all aspects of government, believing that he ruled by **divine right.** According to this way of thinking, the king is an agent of God, and his authority to rule comes directly from God. Philip was a hard-working ruler, and he did much to promote a golden age in Spain.

In the 1600s, however, Spanish power slowly declined as rulers spent too much money on wars overseas. The Spanish relied on gold and silver from their colonies and as a result neglected business at home. The middle class felt that they were being taxed too heavily and stopped supporting the government.

Absolutism in France

By the late 1600s, France had replaced Spain as the most powerful European nation. It, too, was ruled by absolute monarchs.

THE INCREASE OF ROYAL POWER In 1589, Henry IV inherited the throne. Henry IV laid the foundations of absolutism by increasing the influence of the government and reducing the power of the nobles. The appointment of Cardinal Armand Richelieu as chief minister by Henry's young son, Louis XIII, continued the trend of increasing royal power. Richelieu subdued or defeated the two groups that did not bow to royal authority: the nobles and the Protestant Huguenots. Meanwhile, Louis XIII strengthened the government and made his army the strongest in Europe.

THE SUN KING Inheriting the throne in 1643 as a five-year-old child, **Louis XIV** ruled France for 72 years. He continued to strengthen the monarchy, taking the sun as the symbol of his power and commanding complete loyalty from his subjects. Louis's claim to absolute power was strengthened by a court preacher, Bishop **Jacques Bossuet.** Bossuet argued that as God's representative on Earth, the king was entitled to unquestioning obedience. During his reign, Louis:

- expanded the bureaucracy, appointing officials to collect taxes, recruit soldiers, and carry out his rule in the provinces.
- built the lavish, immense Palace of Versailles outside of Paris.
- organized a highly disciplined army, the strongest in Europe.
- persecuted the Protestant Huguenots, depriving the nation of many of its most hard-working and prosperous citizens.

LOUIS'S LEGACY Under Louis XIV, France was a wealthy, powerful state with great cultural influence. However, Louis's extravagant parties at Versailles and his costly wars left France in debt, and there was social unrest among the starving peasants. The French monarchy would not survive even a century after Louis XIV's death in 1715.

Absolutism in Russia

During the 1400s, the city of Moscow became the center of power in Russia. The driving force behind Moscow's rising power was Ivan III, known as Ivan the Great. Ruling from 1462 to 1505, Ivan the Great built the framework for absolute rule in Russia. Following Ivan the Great, a long series of absolute rulers dominated Russia.

IVAN THE TERRIBLE Czar Ivan IV centralized royal power and introduced Russia to extreme absolute power. His harsh ruling style and fits of violence earned him the title **"Ivan the Terrible."** To enforce his will, Ivan organized a personal police force. Dressed in black robes, these agents of terror slaughtered rebellious nobles and destroyed towns suspected of disloyalty.

PETER THE GREAT **Peter the Great** ruled Russia as czar from 1682 to 1725. Peter worked to centralize royal power and bring all Russians under his authority. He reduced the power of the nobility and gained control of the Russian Orthodox Church.

◦ KEY THEMES AND CONCEPTS

Power Armand Richelieu was a Roman Catholic cardinal. His role as advisor to the king—and virtual ruler of France—shows the power of the Catholic Church at that time.

PREPARING FOR THE REGENTS

Why did Louis XIV consider himself the "Sun King"? How is that name an example of his belief in absolutism?

WESTERNIZATION UNDER PETER   Peter wanted to modernize Russia. He traveled to Western European cities to study western technology and brought back ideas on how to westernize Russia. For example, he simplified the Russian alphabet and developed mining and textiles. His capital at St. Petersburg served as a symbol of the new modern Russia. However, Peter sometimes resorted to force and terror to achieve his goals.

PETER'S STRONG FOREIGN POLICY   Peter created the largest army in Europe in the late 1600s and used it to expand Russian territory and gain ports on the Baltic Sea. Russia also extended eastward, sending explorers across the Bering Strait into North America.

Peter failed at one of his goals, however: to gain a port that would not be closed due to freezing in winter. He fought the Ottoman Turks to gain a warm-water port on the Black Sea but did not succeed. However, Catherine the Great, another absolute ruler of Russia, would successfully acquire Black Sea ports in 1795.

KEY THEMES AND CONCEPTS

Political Systems The tradition of sharing political power dates back to the Greek and Roman periods. In England, the Magna Carta of 1215 limited the ruler's power by protecting certain basic legal rights of English citizens and by forcing the monarch to consult an English council before raising taxes. To learn more about the Magna Carta, see Unit 3, Section 4.

REACTION TO ABSOLUTISM IN ENGLAND

While other nations turned to absolutism in the 1500s and 1600s, England moved in a different direction. England's Parliament managed to resist successfully the consolidation of royal power.

The royal Tudor family ruled England from 1485 to 1603. These monarchs, who included Henry VIII and Elizabeth I, generally worked well with Parliament. Even though the Tudors believed in divine right, they saw great value in maintaining good relations with Parliament.

In 1603, however, the English throne passed to the Stuarts. Lacking the diplomatic skills of the Tudors, the Stuarts with their absolutist tendencies came into conflict with Parliament.

The Stuart Monarchs

The first Stuart king, James I, sought to increase his power, using divine right as his justification. Needing money for his wars and extravagant court life, he frequently clashed with Parliament over financial issues and foreign policy. Angering leaders in the House of Commons, James eventually dissolved Parliament and imposed his own taxes. The king also conflicted with **Puritans,** who were seeking to "purify" the church of England by eliminating Catholic practices.

The Stuart monarchs received support in their struggles with Parliament from the English thinker Thomas Hobbes. In *The Leviathan,* Hobbes wrote that people were by nature selfish and greedy and would fall into chaos unless ruled by a strong government that could suppress rebellion. Hobbes believed that an absolute monarchy—one that could command obedience—was needed to maintain order.

James's son Charles I inherited the throne in 1625. He continued his father's absolutist policies. Charles created problems during his reign by:

- putting his enemies in prison without trials.
- imposing very high taxes.
- angering the Puritans.
- dissolving Parliament.

Charles, however, had to summon Parliament back in 1640 to obtain funds to put down a Scottish rebellion. As a result, civil war broke out between Charles I and Parliament.

The English Civil War

The English Civil War, sometimes called the Puritan Revolution, pitted Charles's supporters, the Cavaliers, against Parliament's forces, the Roundheads. The Roundheads, a group consisting of Puritans, country landowners, and town-based manufacturers, were led by the skilled military commander **Oliver Cromwell.** Cromwell's disciplined army won several battles against the Cavaliers and captured the king in 1647. Parliament put Charles I on trial and beheaded him in 1649.

Charles I was the first king ever to be tried and executed by his own subjects. This event shocked other European monarchies and signified that absolutism would not prevail in England.

Cromwell and the Commonwealth

After Charles's execution, Parliament's House of Commons abolished the monarchy, the House of Lords, and the official Church of England. England became a republic, called the Commonwealth, with Oliver Cromwell as its leader. England's years as a republic were troubled, however. Supporters of Charles II, the uncrowned heir to the throne, attacked England from Ireland and Scotland. Cromwell led forces into Ireland to crush the uprising. In 1653, Cromwell took the title of Lord Protector and ruled through the army. By the time of his death in 1658, many people had become tired of Puritan rule.

KEY THEMES AND CONCEPTS

Change The English Civil War was an important turning point in the history of constitutional government in England. The ideas of the Puritans also shaped the development of the colonies that became the United States in the 1700s.

Revolution in England

1649 English execute Charles I

1688 In Glorious Revolution, William and Mary become king and queen

A.D.

| 1600 | 1610 | 1620 | 1630 | 1640 | 1650 | 1660 | 1670 | 1680 | 1690 |

1603 Stuart dynasty takes power in England

1625 Charles I becomes king

1642–9 English Civil War takes place

1660 England restores the monarchy

1685 James II becomes king

The Restoration

In 1660, Parliament invited Charles II, son of Charles I, to become king of England. This marked the restoration of the Stuart monarchy. In 1685, his brother, James II, inherited the throne. James quickly became unpopular because of his Catholicism and his absolutist policies.

The Glorious Revolution

PARLIAMENT OVERTHROWS JAMES II   Parliament, in 1688, fearing the return of Catholic dominance, took strong measures. Parliament asked James's daughter, Mary, and her Dutch husband, William, to take the English throne. William and Mary, both Protestants, arrived in England as James II fled to France, completing a bloodless transfer of power. This nonviolent overthrow is known as the **Glorious Revolution.**

KEY THEMES AND CONCEPTS
Political Systems Parliament imposed regulations that ensured its supremacy over the monarch with the English Bill of Rights.

ENGLISH BILL OF RIGHTS   Before they could take power, William and Mary were forced to accept the **English Bill of Rights,** a set of acts passed by Parliament to ensure its superiority over the monarchy. This Bill of Rights:

- stated that the king must work regularly with Parliament.
- stated that the king must give the House of Commons financial control.
- abolished excessive fines and cruel or unusual punishment.
- affirmed habeas corpus, meaning that no person could be held in jail without first being charged with a crime.

With this Bill of Rights, England became a **limited monarchy,** a government in which a legislative body limits the monarch's powers.

TOLERATION ACT   The Toleration Act of 1689 granted Protestant dissenters, such as Puritans and Quakers, limited toleration. Catholics, however, were denied toleration.

PREPARING FOR THE REGENTS
Outline the main points of the two competing political ideologies, absolutism and limited monarchy, described in this section.

SUMMARY

Through the 1500s and 1600s, absolutism became dominant through much of Europe and parts of Asia. In India, Akbar the Great consolidated his power. In Spain, France, and Russia, absolutist monarchs claimed that they ruled by divine right and sought to extend their political power. While other nations accepted absolutism, England stood as a contrast to this trend. After the Puritan Revolution and the Glorious Revolution of the mid-1600s, the English Bill of Rights was passed, establishing England as a limited monarchy.

Questions for Regents Practice

Review the Preparing for the Regents section of this book. Then answer the following questions, which include multiple-choice questions, a thematic essay, and a series of document-based questions.

MULTIPLE CHOICE

Directions

Circle the *number* of the word or expression that best completes the statement or answers the question.

1 One way in which the civilizations of the Sumerians, the Phoenicians, and the Mayas were similar is that all
  1 developed extensive writing systems
  2 emphasized equality in education
  3 established monotheistic religions
  4 encouraged democratic participation in government

2 An effect of a mountainous topography on Incan and Chinese civilizations was the development of
  1 industrialization
  2 a single-crop economy
  3 desalinization projects
  4 terrace farming

3 "The challenges of the Andes helped the Incas develop a thriving civilization." Based on this statement, what does the author believe?
  1 Language and religion are important to national unity.
  2 Cultural diversity flourishes in areas of agricultural prosperity.
  3 People can overcome the limitations of their environment.
  4 Natural resources are necessary for economic independence.

4 The Incas, the Romans, and the Mongols were similar in that all
  1 developed systems of writing
  2 extended control over neighboring peoples
  3 established industrial economies
  4 adopted democratic political systems

5 One factor that accounted for Chinese influence on traditional Japanese culture was the
  1 continuous warfare between the countries
  2 geographical location of the countries
  3 refusal of western nations to trade with Japan
  4 annexation of Japan into the Chinese empire

6 An observation that could be made about the Ottoman empire in the 1400s and 1500s is that the empire
  1 originated in Hungary
  2 had a strategic location between Europe and Asia
  3 was totally landlocked
  4 had control over most of Western Europe

7 Which was the characteristic of Western European nations that *most* enabled them to establish colonies in Asia and Africa?
  1 rigid social class structures
  2 self-sufficiency in natural resources
  3 frequent political revolutions
  4 advanced technology

8 One reason the Spanish conquistadors were able to conquer the Aztec and Inca empires rapidly is that
  1 these empires had no standing armies
  2 the Spanish had better weapons than the Aztecs and Incas did
  3 the Spanish greatly outnumbered the Aztecs and Incas
  4 the Aztecs and Incas joined together to fight the Spanish

9 In Latin America during the early period of Spanish colonialism, the deaths of large numbers of the native people led to
  1 a decline in Spanish immigration to the Americas
  2 the removal of most Spanish troops from the Americas
  3 the importation of slaves from Africa
  4 improved health care in the colonies

10 One major effect of the European slave trade on Africa was that the slave trade
  1 strengthened the traditional African economic systems
  2 led to a rapid decrease in tribal warfare
  3 hastened the decline of African kingdoms
  4 increased the number of trade routes across the Sahara

11 According to the theory of mercantilism, colonies should be
  1 acquired as markets and sources of raw materials
  2 considered an economic burden to the colonial power
  3 granted independence as soon as possible
  4 encouraged to develop their own industries

12 A major result of the European Age of Exploration was
  1 a long period of peace and prosperity for the nations of Western Europe
  2 extensive migration of people from the Western Hemisphere to Africa
  3 the fall of European national monarchies and the end of the power of the Catholic Church
  4 the end of regional isolation and the beginning of a period of European global domination

Base your answer to question 13 on the chart below and on your knowledge of world history.

Social Structure of the Spanish Colonies

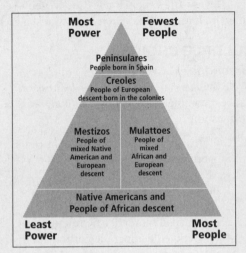

13 Based on the chart, which conclusion can be drawn about the social structure of the Spanish colonies?
  1 Power was evenly distributed among many people
  2 Native Americans ruled over the Spanish
  3 Native Spaniards dominated society
  4 Creoles represented a majority of the population

14 In English history, the Magna Carta (1215) and the Bill of Rights (1689) both reinforced the concept of
  1 a limited monarchy
  2 religious toleration
  3 a laissez-faire economy
  4 universal suffrage

15 During the Age of Absolutism (1600s and 1700s), European monarchies sought to
  1 increase human rights for their citizens
  2 centralize political power in their nations
  3 develop better relations with Muslim rulers
  4 encourage the growth of cooperative farms

THEMATIC ESSAY

Directions

Read the following instructions that include a theme, a task, and suggestions. Follow the instructions to create a well-organized essay that has an introduction with a thesis statement, several paragraphs explaining the thesis, and a conclusion.

Theme: Political Systems

Several empires and nations throughout global history have been ruled by strong leaders who have followed policies of absolutism.

Task

* Define the term *absolutism,* and identify the characteristics of absolutist rule.
* Select a nation or empire you have studied that was ruled according to the principles of absolutism. Identify the specific characteristics of absolutist government that existed in this nation or empire.
* Describe the major positive and/or negative effects that absolutism had on this empire or nation.

Suggestions

You may discuss any nation or empire that you have studied. Some suggestions you may wish to consider are the Incan empire; the Byzantine empire; the Ming empire in China; the Ottoman empire of Suleiman the Great; Spain (Philip II); France (Louis XIV); or Russia (Peter the Great). You are not limited to these suggestions.

QUESTIONS BASED ON DOCUMENTS

The following exercise asks you to analyze three historical documents and then write an essay using evidence from those documents. This exercise is similar to the document-based question that you will see on the Regents Examination, which may include six or more documents. For additional practice with historical documents, see the Preparing for the Regents section and the sample examinations in this book.

This task is based on the accompanying documents. Some of these documents have been edited for the purposes of this task. This task is designed to test your ability to work with historical documents. As you analyze the documents, take into account both the source of each document and the author's point of view.

Directions

Read the documents in Part A and answer the question or questions after each document. Then read the directions for Part B and write your essay.

Historical Context

Throughout history there has been widespread interaction among cultures. Sometimes the effects of this interaction have been positive, and at other times the effects have been negative.

Task

Evaluate both the positive and the negative effects that exchanges between cultures have had on the groups involved.

Part A: Short Answer

Directions: Analyze the documents and answer the question or questions that follow each document, using the space provided.

DOCUMENT 1

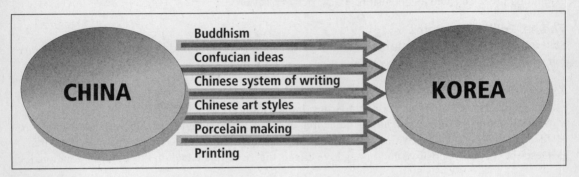

Buddhism
Confucian ideas
Chinese system of writing
Chinese art styles
Porcelain making
Printing

CHINA

KOREA

1 What were some of the effects of the interaction between China and Korea?

_____

_____

_____

_____

DOCUMENT 2

That which led the Spaniards to these terrible deeds was the desire for gold, to make themselves suddenly rich. . . . In a word their greed, their ambition gave occasion to their barbarism. For the Spaniards so little regarded the health of their souls that they allowed this great multitude to die without the least light of religion. The Indians never gave them the least cause to offer them violence until the excessive cruelties of the Spaniards, the torments and slaughters of their countrymen, moved them to take arms against the Spaniards.

—**Bartolomé de Las Casas,** *Brief Report on the Destruction of the Indians,* **1542**

2 Summarize the point of view of this writer concerning the interaction between Spaniards and Native Americans in the 1500s.

_____

_____

_____

_____

DOCUMENT 3
Atlantic Trade Routes, 1750

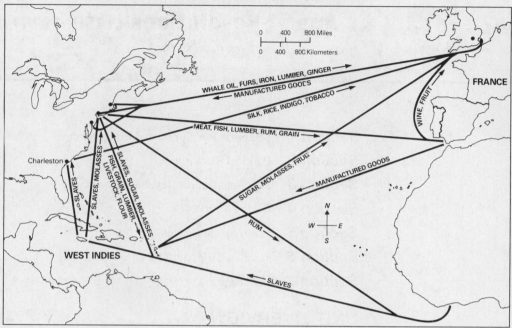

3 What negative effect did the Atlantic trade have on Africans? How did the Atlantic trade benefit Europeans?

_____

_____

Part B: Essay
Directions:
- Write a well-organized essay that includes an introduction, several paragraphs, and a conclusion.
- Use evidence from the documents to support your response.
- Do not simply repeat the contents of the documents.
- Include specific, related outside information.

Historical Context
Throughout history there has been widespread interaction among cultures. Sometimes the effects of this interaction have been positive, and at other times the effects have been negative.

Task
Using information from the documents and your knowledge of global history and geography, write an essay that evaluates the major effects that exchanges between cultures have had on the groups involved. Examine both positive and negative effects.

Be sure to include specific historical details. You must also include additional information from your knowledge of global history.

Note: **The rubric for this essay appears in the Preparing for the Regents section of this book.**

UNIT 5 An Age of Revolutions (1750–1914)

UNIT OVERVIEW

The years between 1750 and 1914 were years of enormous change. The Scientific Revolution and the Enlightenment brought a completely new way of looking at the world. Monarchies were overthrown, and representative forms of government emerged. In some areas, people tried to return to previous ways. In other areas, however, feelings of nationalism arose that led to the growth of nations. During this same time, enormous changes were occurring in Europe and Japan. The Industrial Revolution brought changes in social structure and created new ways of living and working. Industrialization also spurred nations to build empires in Africa and Asia, creating an economy that spanned the globe.

THEMATIC TIME LINE ACTIVITY

Some of the many themes developed in Unit 5 are:

change	political systems	science and technology
nationalism	conflict	culture and intellectual life
power	imperialism	

Choose one of the themes listed above. As you review Unit 5, create a thematic time line based on the theme you have chosen. Your time line should stretch from 1750 to 1914 and include major developments and key turning points having to do with your theme.

1 Scientific Revolution and Enlightenment

SECTION OVERVIEW

In the 1500s and 1600s, the Scientific Revolution changed the way Europeans looked at the world. People began to make conclusions based on experimentation and observation instead of merely accepting traditional ideas. During the 1600s and 1700s, belief in the power of reason grew. Writers of the time sought to reform government and bring about a more just society. Despite opposition from government and church leaders, Enlightenment ideas spread. Some absolute rulers used their power to reform society. Over time, concepts of democracy and of nationhood developed from Enlightenment ideas and contributed to revolutions.

KEY THEMES AND CONCEPTS

As you review this section, take special note of the following key themes and concepts:

Science and Technology How did the Scientific Revolution change the way Europeans looked at the world?

Culture and Intellectual Life How did the Scientific Revolution lead to the ideas of the Enlightenment?

Government What reforms did Enlightenment thinkers want to bring to government in the 1600s and 1700s?

Change What impact did the Enlightenment have on Europe?

KEY PEOPLE AND TERMS

As you review this section, be sure you understand the significance of these key people and terms:

Scientific Revolution	scientific method	Baron de Montesquieu
Nicolaus Copernicus	René Descartes	Voltaire
heliocentric	natural laws	Jean-Jacques Rousseau
Galileo Galilei	Enlightenment	enlightened despot
Isaac Newton	John Locke	Joseph II

⭐ **THE BIG IDEA**
From the 1500s through the 1700s, Europeans:

- experienced the Scientific Revolution, which caused people to change their views about the universe.

- entered the Enlightenment, in which philosophers applied reason to society and government.

- developed ideas about basic human rights and proper government.

- began to consider democratic ideas and the concept of nationalism.

PREPARING FOR THE REGENTS

In what ways was the Scientific Revolution a rejection of traditional authority?

KEY THEMES AND CONCEPTS

Science and Technology
Scientists of the mid-1500s used observation and mathematical calculation to prove their theories of a heliocentric universe.

NEW IDEAS ABOUT THE UNIVERSE

Throughout the Middle Ages, European scholars believed that Earth was the center of the universe. This idea was based on Greco-Roman theories and the teachings of the Church. However, European scientists began to think differently in the 1500s. Influenced by the critical spirit of the Renaissance, they questioned the old ideas about the world. This period of change was called the **Scientific Revolution.**

Copernicus

In the mid-1500s, Polish scholar **Nicolaus Copernicus** challenged the belief that Earth was at the center of the universe. Using mathematical formulas, Copernicus suggested that the universe was **heliocentric,** or sun-centered. He said that the planets revolved around the sun. Most scholars rejected Copernicus's theory.

Galileo

In the early 1600s, an Italian astronomer, **Galileo Galilei,** provided further evidence to support the heliocentric theory. He did this by observing the skies with a telescope he had constructed. Galileo's conclusions caused an uproar because they contradicted Church teachings about the world. Church leaders put Galileo on trial. Threatened with death, Galileo was forced to take back his ideas publicly.

Newton

English scholar **Isaac Newton** built on the knowledge of Copernicus and Galileo. He used mathematics to prove the existence of a force that kept planets in their orbits around the sun. Newton called the force gravity, the same force that made objects fall toward Earth. Newton eventually theorized that nature follows uniform laws.

 PREPARING FOR THE REGENTS

The Scientific Revolution in Europe, with its emphasis on observing, experimenting, investigating, and speculating, was a new approach to solving problems and thinking about the world. This philosophy came to define modern thought.

NEW WAYS OF THINKING

The Scientific Method

A new approach to science had emerged by the 1600s. It relied on experimentation and observation rather than on past authorities. This new way of thinking was called the **scientific method.**

Descartes and Human Reasoning

Frenchman **René Descartes** challenged the idea that new knowledge should be made to fit existing traditional ideas. Descartes emphasized the power of human reason. He believed that reason, rather than tradition, should be the way to discover truth. The ideas of Descartes and other thinkers of the Scientific Revolution paved the way for other changes that would occur in Europe in the 1700s.

SCIENCE AND THE ENLIGHTENMENT

During the Scientific Revolution, scientists used reason to explain why things happened in the physical universe. This success inspired great

The Scientific Method

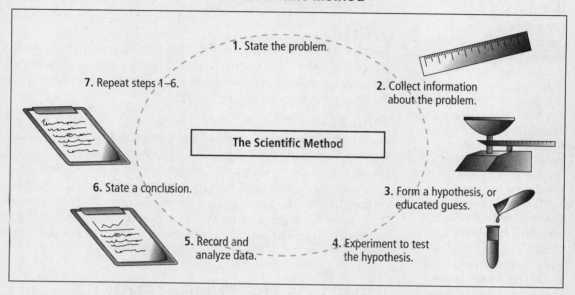

1. State the problem.

2. Collect information about the problem.

3. Form a hypothesis, or educated guess.

4. Experiment to test the hypothesis.

5. Record and analyze data.

6. State a conclusion.

7. Repeat steps 1–6.

The Scientific Method

confidence in the power of reason. By the early 1700s, writers sought to use reason to discover **natural laws,** or laws that govern human behavior. By applying the scientific method of investigation and observation, scholars thought that they could solve the problems of society.

This way of thinking led to the **Enlightenment,** the period in the 1700s in which people rejected traditional ideas and supported a belief in human reason. The belief that logical thought can lead to truth is called rationalism. The Enlightenment introduced new ways of viewing authority, power, government, and law.

LEADING THINKERS OF THE ENLIGHTENMENT

Four of the most influential Enlightenment philosophers were John Locke, Baron de Montesquieu, Voltaire, and Jean-Jacques Rousseau.

Locke

John Locke, an English thinker of the late 1600s, believed that all people possess natural rights. These rights, he said, include the rights to life, liberty, and property. According to Locke, people form governments to protect their rights. If a government does not protect these rights, people have the right to overthrow it.

Montesquieu

In the 1700s, French thinker **Baron de Montesquieu** wrote that the powers of government should be separated into three branches: legislative, executive, and judicial. This separation of powers would prevent tyranny

PREPARING FOR THE REGENTS

How did the Scientific Revolution prepare the way for the Enlightenment?

PREPARING FOR THE REGENTS

How did Europeans try to apply the scientific method to society?

KEY THEMES AND CONCEPTS

Government Locke's ideas about natural rights and the obligations of government later influenced both Thomas Jefferson's writing of the Declaration of Independence and the French revolutionaries.

KEY THEMES AND CONCEPTS

Government Enlightenment thinkers sought to use reason to improve government and society. Although they were able to influence only a few leaders of their day, they created a whole new set of assumptions about the proper use of power, who had authority, and what made up a good and lawful government.

 PREPARING FOR THE REGENTS

Thomas Hobbes was an Enlightenment thinker, even though his philosophy favored absolutism. To learn more about absolutism, see Unit 4, Section 6.

PREPARING FOR THE REGENTS

Contrast Locke's theory of natural rights with the thinking of Thomas Hobbes and the theory of divine right. To learn more about divine right and Thomas Hobbes, see Unit 4, Section 5.

by creating what is called a system of checks and balances. Each branch could keep the other two from gaining too much power.

Voltaire

Voltaire was a French thinker of the 1700s who believed in free speech. He used his sharp wit to criticize the French government and the Catholic Church for their failure to permit religious toleration and intellectual freedom.

Rousseau

Jean-Jacques Rousseau, another French philosopher of the 1700s, put forth his ideas in a book titled *The Social Contract.* He believed that people are naturally good but are corrupted by the evils of society, such as the unequal distribution of property. In agreeing to form a government, he felt, people choose to give up their own interests for the common good. Rousseau believed in the will of the majority, which he called the general will. He believed that the majority should always work for the common good.

IMPACT OF THE ENLIGHTENMENT

The ideas proposed by Enlightenment thinkers had a great impact throughout Europe in the 1700s. Greater numbers of people began to question established beliefs and customs. Enlightenment beliefs affected leaders and the development of nations.

Government Censorship

As Enlightenment ideas gained in popularity, government and Church leaders worked to defend the established systems. They started a campaign of censorship to suppress Enlightenment ideas. Many writers, including Voltaire, were thrown into prison, and their books were banned and burned.

Thinkers of the Enlightenment

Thomas Hobbes	John Locke
People are greedy and selfish. Only a powerful government can create a peaceful, orderly society.	People have natural rights. It is the job of government to protect these natural rights. If government does not protect these rights, the people have the right to overthrow it.
Baron de Montesquieu	**Jean-Jacques Rousseau**
The powers of government should be separated into three branches. Each branch will keep the other branches from becoming too powerful.	In a perfect society, people both make and obey the laws. What is good for everyone is more important than what is good for one person.

Enlightened Despots

Some monarchs accepted Enlightenment ideas. They were known as **enlightened despots,** absolute rulers who used their power to reform society.

MARIA THERESA Austrian ruler Maria Theresa implemented several reforms during her reign in the 1700s. She improved the tax system by forcing nobles and the clergy to pay taxes. This measure eased the tax burden on peasants. Maria Theresa also absorbed Enlightenment ideas on education and made primary education available to children in her kingdom.

JOSEPH II Maria Theresa's son, **Joseph II,** continued and expanded many of his mother's reforms. The most radical of the enlightened despots, Joseph modernized Austria's government, chose officials for their talents rather than because of their status, and implemented legal reforms. He also practiced religious toleration, ended censorship, and abolished serfdom. However, many of Joseph's reforms were later overturned.

CATHERINE THE GREAT Catherine II, who became empress of Russia in 1762, read Enlightenment works and even corresponded with Voltaire and Montesquieu. As a result of her exposure to Enlightenment ideas, Catherine asked for the advice of nobles, free peasants, and townspeople. Never before had Russian citizens been allowed to advise the government. Catherine also built schools and hospitals, promoted the education of women, and extended religious tolerance. Unfortunately, many of Catherine's reforms were short-lived. Later in her reign, Catherine grew more repressive after a peasant uprising.

Democracy and Nationalism

Enlightenment ideas inspired a sense of individualism, a belief in personal freedom, and a sense of the basic equality of human beings. These concepts, along with challenges to traditional authority, became important in the growth of democracy. Nationalism also grew. As people in a country drew together to fight for a democratic government, strong feelings of nationalism arose. In the late 1700s, Enlightenment ideas would contribute to an age of revolution.

SUMMARY

Beginning in the 1500s, the Scientific Revolution introduced a way of thinking based on observation and experimentation instead of acceptance of traditional authority. These changes inspired intellectuals to apply reason to the study not only of science but also of human society. The thinkers of the Enlightenment used this emphasis on reason to suggest reforms in government and society. Many Europeans, including several monarchs, were influenced by these ideas and sought to change the old order. These changes had an impact on all of Europe as democratic and nationalistic ideas grew and contributed to revolutions.

KEY THEMES AND CONCEPTS

Change The term *enlightened despot* almost seems like a contradiction. These rulers believed in absolute power but also saw the value of reforms in government.

PREPARING FOR THE REGENTS

What policies did enlightened despots have in common?

KEY THEMES AND CONCEPTS

Nationalism In both the American and French Revolutions, Enlightenment ideas contributed to democratic movements as well as strong nationalistic feelings. To learn more about the American and French Revolutions, see Section 2 of this unit.

2 Political Revolutions

⭐ **THE BIG IDEA**
Revolution brought change to Europe and the Americas in the 1700s and 1800s.

- People in Britain's 13 colonies applied Enlightenment ideas to the fight for independence from Britain.

- French revolutionaries rebelled against absolute monarchy and reformed the French social order.

- Napoleon spread democratic ideals and nationalism across Europe.

- The revolutionary spirit brought independence to Latin American nations.

SECTION OVERVIEW

In the late 1700s and early 1800s, revolutions shook Europe and the Americas. In North America in 1776, Britain's 13 colonies, inspired by Enlightenment ideals, declared their independence. They then fought the American Revolution to throw off British rule. In France, economic misery and social discontent led to a revolt against the absolute monarchy in 1789. Periods of chaos and reform were followed by the rise of Napoleon Bonaparte. Napoleon built an empire that was short-lived, but his military victories fanned French nationalistic feelings and spread the revolution's ideals. Inspired by the American and French Revolutions, revolutionaries in Latin America threw off Spanish rule.

KEY THEMES AND CONCEPTS

As you review this section, take special note of the following key themes and concepts:

Culture and Intellectual Life What role did Enlightenment ideas play in the major revolutions of the late 1700s and early 1800s?

Conflict Why did the French people rebel against King Louis XIV?

Change What short-term and long-term effects did the revolutions of the late 1700s and early 1800s have on Europe and the Americas?

KEY PEOPLE AND TERMS

As you review this section, be sure you understand the significance of these key people and terms:

Declaration of Independence	coup d'état
Estates General	Napoleonic Code
National Assembly	Toussaint L'Ouverture
Maximilien Robespierre	Simón Bolívar
Napoleon Bonaparte	José de San Martín

THE AMERICAN REVOLUTION

By 1750, the British empire included 13 colonies along the eastern coast of North America. In 1776, the colonies declared their independence from Britain. Britain sent troops to crush the rebellion. However, with the aid of the French as well as the Dutch and Spanish, American forces defeated the British army and gained their independence. In their struggle, the colonists were inspired by Enlightenment ideals and by the traditions of British government. They established a new nation based on representative government and a guarantee of rights and freedoms.

Influence of British Traditions

MAGNA CARTA AND PARLIAMENT   The Magna Carta had limited the power of English monarchs. For example, it stated that the king could not raise new taxes without consulting the body that would later become Parliament. The American colonists interpreted this idea to mean that any taxation without representation was unjust. Because colonists had no representative in Britain's Parliament, they felt that Parliament had no right to tax them. They protested by using the slogan "No taxation without representation."

ENGLISH BILL OF RIGHTS   The English Bill of Rights inspired colonists to fight for the creation of their own bill of rights.

Influence of the Enlightenment

The theories of thinkers such as Locke, Montesquieu, and Rousseau helped inspire the colonists' opposition to British policies after 1763.

PAINE'S COMMON SENSE   Influenced by Enlightenment ideas about a limited, representative government, Thomas Paine wrote in his pamphlet *Common Sense* that the colonists should no longer be the subjects of a distant monarch. Paine appealed to reason and natural law in his arguments for breaking away from Britain. His ideas were widely read in the colonies in 1776.

THE DECLARATION OF INDEPENDENCE   Influenced by Locke and other Enlightenment thinkers, Thomas Jefferson drafted the **Declaration of Independence.** Jefferson wrote that governments rule only with the consent of the governed and that they should protect the unalienable rights of their citizens. The declaration also stated that people have a right to throw off governments that are unjust and that do not protect their citizens. After listing specific grievances against the British monarch, Jefferson wrote that the colonists were justified in forming their own government, independent of Britain.

THE CONSTITUTION   Like the Declaration of Independence, this document reflected the influence of Enlightenment ideas.

- **Social Contract** The Constitution of the United States set up a government by social contract. The government was established by

⚷ KEY THEMES AND CONCEPTS

Human Rights The Declaration of Independence reflects many of Locke's Enlightenment ideas. These ideas include people's natural rights to life and liberty, the role of the government in protecting those rights, and the right of people to overthrow unjust governments.

KEY THEMES AND CONCEPTS

Government and Change
The United States Constitution contributed to change in other parts of the world. It was a model for many other nations that formed new governments in the years that followed.

PREPARING FOR THE REGENTS

Describe some Enlightenment ideas that inspired the American Revolution and influenced the founders of the United States of America.

PREPARING FOR THE REGENTS

Why was the American Revolution an important turning point in global history?

the consent of the governed. The Constitution begins with these words: "We the People of the United States . . ."

- **Separation of Powers** Influenced by the ideas of Montesquieu, the Constitution created a republic in which power was to be divided between the federal government and the states. In addition, the writers of the Constitution established a government that divided powers among an executive, a legislative, and a judicial branch. Each branch could provide checks and balances on the other branches.
- **Protection of Rights** The Bill of Rights was added to the Constitution to protect the basic rights of American citizens, including freedom of speech and freedom of religion. The Constitution stated that it was the duty of the government to protect these rights.

Impact of the American Revolution

The American Revolution had a great impact around the world.

- The American republic stood as a symbol of freedom to both Europe and Latin America.
- The United States Constitution created the most liberal government of its time. Other nations would copy the ideas in this document.
- The success of the American Revolution would soon inspire major global changes as other peoples challenged the power of absolute monarchs.

THE FRENCH REVOLUTION

Soon after the American Revolution, a major revolution broke out in France. Starting in 1789, the French Revolution had a deep and lasting impact on France, Europe, and other areas of the world. The French Revolution went through many stages, caused by changes in leadership and shifts in power.

Causes of the Revolution

Political, social, and economic factors combined to bring about the French Revolution.

ABSOLUTE MONARCHY   On the eve of revolution, France was an absolute monarchy. Under absolutism, most people in France were denied basic rights and any say in government.

 KEY THEMES AND CONCEPTS

Economic Systems Much of the unrest in France was rooted in the unequal distribution of wealth as well as the unequal tax burden.

SOCIAL INEQUALITY   Since the Middle Ages, everyone in France had belonged to one of three social classes called estates. The clergy were the First Estate; the titled nobility composed the Second Estate. These two classes held enormous wealth, did not have to pay taxes, and enjoyed other special rights and privileges. The Third Estate made up most of French society and included a bourgeoisie (middle class), poor city workers, and rural peasants, the largest group. The Third Estate, which resented its heavy tax burden and lack of rights, grew increasingly discontent.

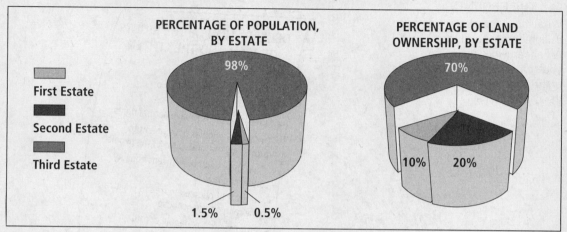

Population and Land Ownership in France, 1789

PERCENTAGE OF POPULATION, BY ESTATE

First Estate
Second Estate
Third Estate

98%
1.5% 0.5%

PERCENTAGE OF LAND OWNERSHIP, BY ESTATE

70%
10% 20%

ECONOMIC INJUSTICES The situation in France became worse because of economic conditions in the late 1780s. The government, with its lavish court and expensive wars, spent more money than it earned. This debt added to the tax burden of the Third Estate. Bad harvests in 1789 caused food prices to rise. Peasants and city dwellers often did not have enough to eat and began to riot, demanding bread.

ENLIGHTENMENT Through the 1600s and 1700s, Enlightenment thinkers were critical of France's absolute monarchy and called for democratic reforms. Enlightenment ideas led many French to question the traditional way of ordering society. It was not reasonable, they felt, for the First and Second Estates to have privileges at the expense of the Third Estate.

ENGLISH AND AMERICAN EXAMPLES England's Glorious Revolution provided an example of how existing authority could be challenged. In addition, the French were inspired by the American colonies' successful fight for liberty and equality in the American Revolution.

Stages of the Revolution

THE REVOLUTION BEGINS As conditions grew worse in France, demands for reform increased. In 1789, King Louis XVI finally called the **Estates General,** a body made up of representatives of all three estates, into session. After this, change came swiftly.

- **National Assembly** The Third Estate, the only elected group in the Estates General, declared itself the **National Assembly.** The National Assembly vowed to write a new constitution for France.
- **Seizure of the Bastille** Working-class people, already rioting over the price of bread, stormed a prison called the Bastille on July 14, 1789. Fighting broke out through city and countryside. In a period known as the Great Fear, peasants attacked nobles and destroyed their homes.

 PREPARING FOR THE REGENTS

Practice your graph skills by writing one or two sentences that state the main point of the graphs on this page.

 PREPARING FOR THE REGENTS

List three factors that led to the French Revolution.

1.

2.

3.

 PREPARING FOR THE REGENTS

As you study the French Revolution, take note of the roles played by individual citizens. Members of the Third Estate formed the National Assembly. Working-class people stormed the Bastille, and peasants attacked the homes of nobles.

PREPARING FOR THE REGENTS

What influences from the Enlightenment and the American Revolution can you see in the Declaration of the Rights of Man and the Citizen?

The French Declaration of Rights

DECLARATION OF THE RIGHTS OF MAN AND THE CITIZEN

- Written in 1789
- Uses American Declaration of Independence as model
- States that all men have natural rights
- Declares the job of government to protect the natural rights of the people
- Guarantees all male citizens equality under the law
- States that people are free to practice any religion they choose
- Promises to tax people according to how much they can afford

- **Declaration of the Rights of Man** The National Assembly abolished the privileges of the First and Second Estates and adopted the Declaration of the Rights of Man and the Citizen. Based partly on the Declaration of Independence, it contained many Enlightenment ideas.

A LIMITED MONARCHY By 1791, the Assembly had written a constitution. The Constitution of 1791 defined the role and purpose of a new government.

- It set up a limited monarchy and a representative assembly.
- It declared that people had natural rights and that it was the job of the government to protect those rights.
- It put the Church under state control.

News about the French Revolution quickly spread across Europe. Many European rulers and nobles feared that revolutionary ideas would spread to their own countries. They threatened to intervene—with military force, if necessary—to save the French monarchy. In 1792, to fight tyranny and spread the revolution, France declared war on Austria, Prussia, Britain, and several other states.

RADICALS IN POWER The war with the other European nations went badly for France. In 1792, radicals took control of the Assembly, ended the monarchy, and declared France a republic. Their slogan was "Liberty, Equality, Fraternity." In 1793, the king was executed for treason. This event was followed by a period in France called the Reign of Terror, led in part by **Maximilien Robespierre,** a radical revolutionary. During this time, tens of thousands of people were executed. Thousands more were put into prison. Within a year, however, the violence turned back on itself. Robespierre himself was executed, and the Reign of Terror ended.

KEY THEMES AND CONCEPTS

Change During the course of the revolution, the people in power changed, and ideas of those in power changed. At first, moderates were in power, and the constitution called for a limited monarchy. By 1793, the radicals were in control, and the king had been executed.

MODERATES RETURN   Beginning in 1795, a five-man "Directory" supported by a legislature held power in France. This government was weak and inefficient. Rising bread prices brought the threat of riots. Into this chaotic situation stepped an ambitious military leader, Napoleon Bonaparte.

Napoleon in Power

HIS RISE TO POWER   When the revolution started, **Napoleon Bonaparte** was a low-level military officer with dreams of glory. Bonaparte rose in the ranks and won important victories against the British and Austrians. A popular general by 1799, Napoleon helped overthrow the weak Directory in a **coup d'état,** or revolt by military leaders to overthrow a government. He organized a new government and put himself in charge. Three years later, he took the title "Emperor of the French." Napoleon now had absolute power. The French people, hoping for stability, supported Napoleon at each step in his rise.

HIS ACHIEVEMENTS   Much of Napoleon's popularity came from his effective policies.

- **Economy** Napoleon controlled prices, supported new industry, and built roads and canals.
- **Education** Napoleon established a government-supervised public school system.
- **Napoleonic Code** The **Napoleonic Code** was a legal code that included many Enlightenment ideas, such as the legal equality of citizens and religious toleration.

NAPOLEON'S EMPIRE   From 1804 to 1814, Napoleon ruled an empire. He conquered much of Europe. Napoleon often replaced the monarchs of defeated nations with his friends and relatives.

PREPARING FOR THE REGENTS

How did Napoleon gain popularity and rise to power?

KEY THEMES AND CONCEPTS

Power Despite Napoleon's reforms, order and authority were still higher priorities for him than individual rights. The Napoleonic Code included many Enlightenment ideas, such as the equality of citizens under the law. However, it also undid some reforms of the revolution, such as rights that had been granted to women.

Napoleon in Europe, 1812

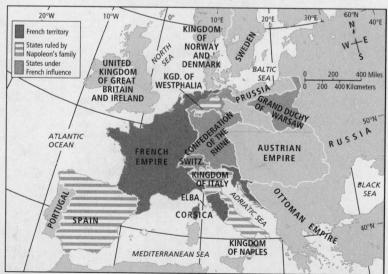

PREPARING FOR THE REGENTS

How did nationalism help Napoleon to build his empire? How did nationalism lead to Napoleon's defeat?

Of the European powers, only Britain and Russia remained beyond Napoleon's reach. Britain was shielded from French troops by a powerful navy and the English Channel.

NAPOLEON'S FALL   Napoleon's empire began to crumble for several reasons. First, most people in conquered states looked on Napoleon's armies as foreign oppressors. Inspired by nationalism, people across Europe revolted against French rule.

Another factor was Napoleon's invasion of Russia in 1812. As Napoleon's armies invaded from the west, the Russians retreated eastward. The "scorched earth" policy of the Russians, in which they burned crops and villages as they retreated, left the French troops hungry and cold. Most of Napoleon's army was lost during the long Russian winter.

The following year, an alliance of Russia, Britain, Austria, and Prussia defeated Napoleon, forcing him to step down in 1814. Napoleon returned to power in 1815, but the British and Prussians defeated him at the decisive Battle of Waterloo. This battle ended Napoleon's reign, and he lived the rest of his life in exile.

Effects of the French Revolution

The French Revolution and the reign of Napoleon transformed both France and Europe in many ways.

 PREPARING FOR THE REGENTS

Create a chart that outlines the causes and lasting effects of the French Revolution.

DEMOCRATIC IDEALS   Napoleon's conquests spread the ideals of democracy throughout Europe. Groups struggled to achieve the goals of the French republic: "Liberty, Equality, Fraternity." People wanted liberty from absolute monarchs and unjust governments. They pursued equality by opposing social inequality and injustice. They expressed fraternity, or brotherhood, by working together for a common cause.

NATIONALISM   Among the French, the revolution and the conquests of Napoleon inspired feelings of national pride. This pride and sense of

 PREPARING FOR THE REGENTS

Practice interpreting political cartoons by answering these questions.

1. What do the scepter (staff) and the globe with the cross on it represent?

2. What is the cartoonist saying about the reasons for Napoleon's fall by including Russian buildings at the lower right of the cartoon?

national identity replaced earlier loyalty to local authority and the person of the monarch.

The conquests of Napoleon also increased nationalistic feeling across Europe and around the world. His conquests had a part in the eventual unification of both Italy and Germany. His weakening of Spain led to the Latin American independence movements.

LATIN AMERICAN INDEPENDENCE MOVEMENTS

In the late 1700s, Enlightenment and revolutionary ideas spread from Europe and the United States to Latin America. Educated Latin Americans read works by Enlightenment writers. They debated about political and social reform. Thomas Jefferson's Declaration of Independence and the Constitution were eagerly read. The success of the American Revolution showed that foreign rule could be thrown off. Latin Americans also were inspired by what the French Revolution had accomplished. Beginning in the 1790s, they struggled to gain independence as well as other rights and freedoms.

Toussaint L'Ouverture

The French colony of Haiti was the first Latin American colony to revolt against European rule. In Haiti, French planters owned large sugar plantations. Here nearly half a million enslaved Africans lived and worked in terrible conditions. Moreover, the French gave few rights to free mulattoes (persons of mixed ancestry) living on the island.

In 1791, a self-educated former slave named **Toussaint L'Ouverture** led a revolt. Toussaint was familiar with the works of the Enlightenment thinkers and wanted to lead his people to liberty. Toussaint proved to be an effective military leader and gained control of much of the island. Haitian slaves won their freedom in 1798.

In 1802, Napoleon sent an army to Haiti to reestablish French dominance. Toussaint led a guerrilla war to gain Haitian independence. The French captured Toussaint, but yellow fever took a heavy toll on their forces. In 1804, Haitians declared their independence. Napoleon then abandoned the island. Haiti became a republic in 1820.

Simón Bolívar

In South America in the early 1800s, an educated creole named **Simón Bolívar** led resistance movements against the Spanish. Bolívar had become an admirer of Enlightenment ideas and the French Revolution during a stay in Europe. He was also inspired by the American Revolution. He vowed to fight Spanish rule in South America. Called "the Liberator," Bolívar became one of the greatest Latin American nationalist leaders of this period.

STRUGGLE FOR INDEPENDENCE   In 1810, Bolívar started his long struggle against the Spanish. Over the next 12 years, he led a series

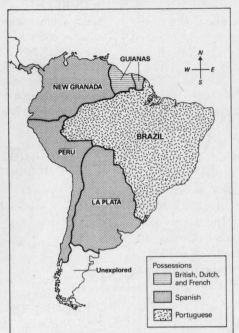

South America, 1790

South America, 1828

of military campaigns that won independence for Venezuela, New Granada (present-day Colombia), Ecuador, Peru, and Bolivia. He then joined forces with **José de San Martín,** who had defeated the Spanish in Argentina and Chile in the 1810s.

DIFFICULTIES AHEAD   Despite his victories against the Spanish, Bolívar failed in his attempt to create a large, united Latin American state. Spain's former empire thus became divided into a number of separate independent states. These nations faced a long struggle to gain stability, achieve social equality, and eliminate poverty.

SUMMARY

Enlightenment ideas about natural rights and rejection of absolutist authority inspired major revolutions in the late 1700s and early 1800s. Colonists in America declared independence from Britain in 1776 and created a government based on the ideas of Locke and Montesquieu. Influenced by the American Revolution, revolutionaries in France overturned the monarchy and created a new social order. Napoleon helped spread revolutionary ideals across Europe. Both the American and French Revolutions contributed to revolutions in Latin America in the early 1800s. Leaders such as Toussaint L'Ouverture and Simón Bolívar led popular movements to overthrow European rule.

3

Reaction Against Revolutionary Ideas

SECTION OVERVIEW

After the French Revolution, there was a reaction against revolutionary ideals. In 1815 at the Congress of Vienna, the leaders of the nations of Europe restored the old monarchies. In the following decades, conflicts between revolutionary ideals and the desire to maintain the old order would cause uprisings and repression. Although some reforms slowly took hold in Western Europe, absolutism remained strong in Russia. In Latin America as well, democratic reforms were slow to develop. In the early 1900s, however, Mexico experienced a political and social revolution accompanied by the growth of nationalistic feelings.

KEY THEMES AND CONCEPTS

As you review this section, take special note of the following key themes and concepts:

Power How did leaders react to revolutionary ideas in Europe after the French Revolution and the reign of Napoleon?

Political Systems What barriers to reform existed in Russia and Latin America in the 1800s?

Change What reforms occurred in Mexico in the early 1800s?

KEY PEOPLE AND TERMS

As you review this section, be sure you understand the significance of these key people and terms:

Congress of Vienna	Russification
Prince Clemens von Metternich	pogrom
balance of power	oligarchy
conservatism	caudillo
liberalism	cash crop economy
nationalism	Porfirio Díaz

★ **THE BIG IDEA**
After the French Revolution, there was a reaction against revolutionary ideals.

- Conservative leaders at the Congress of Vienna opposed such ideals.

- New uprisings across Europe were largely unsuccessful.

- Russian czars remained absolute rulers.

- Reform movements faced difficult obstacles in Latin America.

KEY THEMES AND CONCEPTS

Power The leaders at the Congress of Vienna wanted to keep France from dominating the continent. They also wanted to restore monarchs to power.

THE CONGRESS OF VIENNA

After Napoleon's defeat, European diplomats met at the **Congress of Vienna** in 1815 to devise a peace settlement. As a result of the meeting in Vienna, European leaders agreed to restore order and stability to Europe.

Key Participants and Their Views

Representatives of four important nations brought differing ideas and aims to the Congress of Vienna.

- **Prince Clemens von Metternich** of Austria, the dominant figure at the conference, wanted to restore Europe to the way it was before the French Revolution.
- Alexander I of Russia wanted to create an alliance of Christian monarchs to suppress future revolutions.
- Lord Castlereagh of England wanted to prevent France from rebuilding its military forces.
- Maurice Talleyrand of France wanted to obtain equal footing for France with the rest of the nations.

Balance of Power and Restored Monarchs

Despite their sometimes different goals, the leaders at the Congress of Vienna accomplished a great deal. Much of what the leaders did at the Congress of Vienna occurred for two reasons. First, they wanted to establish a **balance of power,** or a distribution of military and economic power that prevents any one nation from becoming too strong. They also wanted to restore power to monarchs. The Congress of Vienna was the first of many reactions in Europe against the revolutionary ideas of the 1700s and 1800s. It was also a victory for conservatives. **Conservatism** was a set of beliefs held by those who wanted to preserve traditional ways. As conservatism clashed with the ideals of the French Revolution, revolutions would occur throughout Europe and Latin America.

 PREPARING FOR THE REGENTS

Explain how the Congress of Vienna was a reaction against revolutionary ideas.

The Congress of Vienna

GOAL	ACTION
To prevent France from going to war again	Strengthen countries around France • Add Belgium and Luxembourg to Holland to create the kingdom of the Netherlands • Give Prussia lands along the Rhine River • Allow Austria to take control of Italy again
To return Europe to the way it was in 1792, before Napoleon	Give power back to the monarchs of Europe
To protect the new system and maintain peace	Create the Concert of Europe, an organization to maintain peace in Europe

NEW REVOLUTIONS IN EUROPE

The Vienna settlement helped to maintain peace among nations in Europe for almost 100 years. Revolutions did occur within nations, however. Revolutionaries were not happy with the results of the Congress of Vienna. They opposed the Congress's policy of trying to restore Europe to the way it had been before the French Revolution.

Causes

Revolts occurred in many places across Europe from the time of the Congress through about 1850. There were two main causes of these revolutions.

- **Liberalism** People opposed the power of monarchs and sought democratic reforms.
- **Nationalism** People wanted independent nation-states that were free from foreign rule.

Revolutions of 1830

Several revolutions occurred in the 1830s.

- **France** The restoration of the Bourbons, the ruling family in France, by the Congress of Vienna led to attempts to restore absolutism in France. However, Bourbon monarch Charles X was toppled by a revolt in 1830 and replaced by Louis Philippe.
- **Belgium** Revolutionaries demanded independence from the Dutch. Belgium gained independence in 1831.
- **Italy** The Congress of Vienna had divided Italy among several ruling families, including those of Austria and France. In the 1830s, revolutionaries in northern Italy rose up to throw off foreign domination. They were put down by Austrian troops.
- **Poland** Most of Poland was under Russian rule. In 1830, nationalists in Poland staged an uprising. They failed to gain widespread support, however, and were eventually crushed by Russian forces.

Revolutions of 1848

Additional revolutions occurred in 1848.

- **France** King Louis Philippe's government was denounced as corrupt, prompting another revolution in 1848. Louis Philippe stepped down, and a republic was established. Within months of the uprising, upper- and middle-class interests gained control of the government and violently put down a workers' rebellion in Paris. The fighting left bitter feelings between the working class and the middle class.
- **Austrian Empire** When students revolted in Vienna in 1848, Metternich tried to suppress them. He resigned when workers rose up to support the students. As revolution quickly spread to other areas of the empire, the Austrian government agreed to certain reforms. However, the Austrian army soon regained control, and many revolutionaries were imprisoned, executed, or sent into exile.

PREPARING FOR THE REGENTS

Note that nationalism has its roots in the Enlightenment and the French Revolution.

KEY THEMES AND CONCEPTS

Interdependence As had occurred in 1789, a revolution in 1830 in France affected the other nations of Europe.

PREPARING FOR THE REGENTS

How do the events of 1848 reflect the long-term impact of the French Revolution?

Revolutions in Europe, 1830 and 1848

- **Italy and Germany** Rebellions in Italy were successful just for short periods of time. In Germany, student protesters who were backed by peasants and workers demanded reforms. Although an assembly was formed, it was later dissolved as the revolutionaries turned on each other.

Impact of the Revolutions

The revolutions that occurred in 1830 and 1848 frightened many of Europe's rulers. As a result, some agreed to reforms. For the most part, however, the revolts of 1830 and 1848 failed. There were several reasons for these failures.

- Most revolutionaries did not have widespread support.
- Sometimes the revolutionaries themselves were divided.
- Powerful government forces often crushed the revolts.

ABSOLUTISM IN CZARIST RUSSIA

Impact of the French Revolution

While the countries of Western Europe were profoundly changed by the French Revolution, Russian czars strove to keep the ideals of the French

Revolution—liberty, equality, and fraternity—from reaching their people. Unlike the countries of Western Europe, Russia changed very little throughout the 1800s.

Political Conditions

Russian czars resisted reforms, fearing that change would weaken their control. Czars refused to introduce elements of democracy into their societies, although democratic ideas were gaining strength in Western European countries at that time.

Social Conditions

A FEUDAL SOCIETY   Russia had a rigid feudal social structure. Landowning nobles were powerful and resisted any change that would weaken their position. The middle class was too small to have any influence. Although serfdom had gradually disappeared in Western Europe by the 1700s, it had continued in Russia. Serfs were bound to the land, and the owner of the land had almost total power over the serfs who worked it.

FREEING OF THE SERFS   Russia became involved in the Crimean War after trying to seize Ottoman lands along the Danube. Russia suffered a defeat in this war, making its leaders aware of the country's need to modernize and industrialize. Demands for reform, including freedom for the serfs, followed.

In 1861, during the reign of Alexander II, the serfs were freed. Freeing the serfs brought problems, however. Former serfs had to buy the land they had worked, and many were too poor to do so. Even those who could buy land often did not have enough to support their families. Discontent continued.

Many freed serfs moved off their land and into the cities, where they took jobs in industries. These freed serfs were sometimes part of the pressure for reform in Russia.

RUSSIFICATION   Russia, as a vast empire, contained many ethnic minorities. The czars aimed to maintain tight control over these people as well as to encourage feelings of Russian unity. This policy of **Russification** was an attempt to make all groups think, act, and believe as Russians.

For example, Russian czar Alexander III persecuted non-Russians, including Poles, Ukrainians, and Armenians. He insisted on one language, Russian, and one church, the Russian Orthodox Church. Alexander also persecuted Jews, restricting the jobs they could have and even where they could live. These policies encouraged violent attacks on Jews, called **pogroms.** The authorities stood by and watched as the homes of Jews were burned and their businesses looted.

Imperialism in Asia

In the 1700s, Russia had expanded to the Baltic Sea, to the Black Sea, and into Eastern Europe, occupying much of Poland. The Russians also

PREPARING FOR THE REGENTS

How did conditions in Russia in the late 1800s contribute to the revolutions that occurred in the early 1900s?

KEY THEMES AND CONCEPTS

Change Despite the problems faced by freed serfs, their emancipation in 1861 marked a major turning point in Russian history. A similar development occurred in the United States a few years later, when the enslaved African Americans were freed.

KEY THEMES AND CONCEPTS

Diversity Russian czars fought diversity in their nation. They tried to force minorities to abandon their own cultures and adopt Russian culture.

KEY THEMES AND CONCEPTS

Change There were a number of obstacles to change in Russia, including resistance by absolutist czars, a rigid class structure, and a lack of economic growth in the region.

expanded eastward across Siberia and beyond the Bering Strait, into Alaska. During the early 1800s, the Russians began their practice of exiling convicts to Siberia.

Czars in the 1800s added lands in central Asia. This territory gave Russia the largest and most diverse empire in Europe and Asia. The construction of the Trans-Siberian Railway, begun in the 1890s, extended Russian economic and political control over the region.

INSTABILITY IN LATIN AMERICA

As you have learned, revolutionaries in Latin America had thrown off Spanish rule in the early 1800s. Life, however, did not improve for most people after they achieved independence. Revolts and civil wars broke out while poverty and prejudice continued. Many factors made it difficult for Latin American nations to benefit from the revolutions that had occurred.

Geographic Barriers

The Latin American nations that gained independence in the 1800s covered a vast area, from Mexico to the southern tip of South America. This area included numerous geographic barriers, such as the Andes Mountains, that hindered attempts at creating a unified Latin America. Fights between various leaders and nationalistic feelings within different groups also kept Latin Americans from uniting.

Social Injustice

Despite the establishment of Latin American republics with constitutions, democracy did not follow. One problem was that the colonial class structure remained largely intact. Creoles replaced peninsulares as the ruling class, and land and wealth remained in their hands. This kind of system, in which ruling power belongs to a small, powerful elite, is known as an **oligarchy.** Mestizos, mulattoes, Indians, and Africans gained few rights and still faced racial prejudice. Most had to work as peasants on the large estates of the landowners.

Military Rulers

Because of the strong rule that colonial empires had exerted in Latin America, people of these countries had little experience with self-government. Local military strongmen called **caudillos** put together their own armies and challenged central governments. Some caudillos were strong enough to gain control of governments. These dictators were repressive, usually ignoring existing constitutions. Their policies usually favored the upper class.

Power of the Church

The Roman Catholic Church had acted as a stabilizing influence in Latin America. It also promoted education. But the Church had an interest in preserving the old order in Latin America. As in colonial days, the

PREPARING FOR THE REGENTS

To learn more about colonial society in Latin America, see Unit 4, Section 4.

KEY THEMES AND CONCEPTS

Political Systems Three centuries of strong Spanish rule left most Latin Americans with little practical knowledge of how to establish a representative democracy.

Church still owned large amounts of land. Liberals in Latin America hoped to end the Church's power over education and reduce its vast landholdings.

Economic Problems

CASH CROP ECONOMIES   Under colonial rule, Latin American economies had become dependent on trade with Spain and Portugal. Latin Americans relied on a **cash crop economy.** The colonies sent raw materials such as sugar, cotton, and coffee to Europe and had to import manufactured goods. Dependence on just one crop or even a few crops makes a nation's economy very unstable. If a drought or crop failure occurs, or if prices for the products fall, the economy can be devastated.

ECONOMIC IMPERIALISM   In the mid-1800s, some Latin American economies began to grow. Foreign investment allowed them to develop mining and agriculture. Foreigners also invested in transportation improvement, such as the development of ports and the building of railroads. Even so, there were few benefits for the majority of Latin Americans. The rigid class structure limited economic gains to the few at the top of the social structure. In general, only the upper classes and the foreign investors profited.

 PREPARING FOR THE REGENTS

In both Russia and Latin America, there were obstacles to reform. Which obstacles were shared by Russia and Latin America? Which obstacles were unique to Latin America?

PREPARING FOR THE REGENTS

What economic problems can result from dependence on a cash crop economy?

THE MEXICAN REVOLUTION (1910–1930)
Causes

General **Porfirio Díaz** ruled Mexico as a dictator in the late 1800s and early 1900s. Díaz brought economic advances to Mexico. Railroads were built and industry grew. However, the wealth went to a small upper class as well as to foreign investors. The rule of Díaz, who brutally suppressed opposition, left most Mexicans uneducated, landless, and poor. In 1910, the discontent boiled over into a revolution that forced Díaz from power.

 PREPARING FOR THE REGENTS

Compare the causes of the Mexican Revolution to those of the French Revolution.

Key Figures

No one person led the revolution. Several local leaders gathered their own armies, destroying railroads and estates.

- Emiliano Zapata, an Indian, was one of the most famous leaders. He led a large peasant revolt in the south, calling for land reform.
- Francisco "Pancho" Villa, a rebel leader in the north, won the loyalty of a large number of peasants. When the United States supported the Mexican government against Villa, conflict erupted across the border between Villa and the United States government in 1916.
- Venustiano Carranza was elected president of Mexico in 1917. He approved a new constitution that, with amendments, is still in force today.

Effects of the Revolution

THE CONSTITUTION OF 1917   The new constitution agreed to by Carranza in 1917 called for land reform, gave the government control of Church estates, and guaranteed more rights to workers and to women.

SOCIAL REFORMS   Reforms were eventually carried out in the 1920s, making Mexico the first Latin American nation to achieve social and economic reform for the majority of its people. For example, the government set up libraries and schools. Some Indian communities were given the opportunity to regain land that had been taken from them in the past.

ECONOMIC NATIONALISM   Mexico, along with other countries of Latin America, experienced strong feelings of nationalism in the early 1900s. Much of the nationalistic spirit was aimed at ending economic dependence on industrial powers. Mexico became determined to develop its own economy. The Mexican government brought industries under government control or took over foreign-owned industries.

CULTURAL NATIONALISM   In the 1920s and 1930s, nationalistic feeling caused writers in Mexico and other parts of Latin America to reject the influences of Europe. They began to take pride in Latin American culture, which displayed a mixture of Western European and Indian traditions. In Mexico, mural painting, which had been a common art form in the Aztec empire, was revived. Muralists such as Diego Rivera and José Clemente Orozco created works of great beauty. Many showed the struggles of the Mexican people for freedom.

SUMMARY

After the defeat of Napoleon, conservative leaders sought to suppress the ideas of the French Revolution and restore monarchy. In 1830 and 1848, uprisings against the old order occurred all across Europe. Although these revolts were mostly unsuccessful, the ideals behind them continued to have an impact on Europe. In Russia and in Latin America, numerous barriers to reform existed. In Mexico, however, reforms took place that benefited the majority of the population.

♀ KEY THEMES AND CONCEPTS

Nationalism In Mexico, nationalism had economic and cultural aspects. Mexicans wanted to end their economic dependence on foreign powers. They also wanted to show their pride in Latin American culture.

PREPARING FOR THE REGENTS

Compare the reactions against revolutionary ideas in Europe, in Russia, and in Latin America in the 1800s.

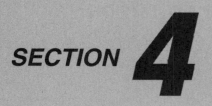

SECTION 4 Global Nationalism

SECTION OVERVIEW

During the French Revolution, people in France expressed great pride in their nation. Nationalism later spread to other peoples, inspiring uprisings across Europe and in Latin America. In the 1860s, nationalism led to the unification of Italy. By 1871, Germany had also united. Outside Europe, nationalist movements took root in India, Turkey, and elsewhere. Among Jews, a movement arose to create a separate Jewish state in Palestine. As the 1800s drew to a close, nationalistic forces created tensions in the Balkans that set the stage for a world war.

KEY THEMES AND CONCEPTS

As you review this section, take special note of the following key themes and concepts:

Nationalism How did nationalism cause revolutions?

Nation-State How did nationalism lead to the creation of nation-states in Italy and Germany?

Change How did nationalism affect Indians, Turks, and Jews?

Diversity How did nationalism cause conflict in the Balkans?

KEY PEOPLE AND TERMS

As you review this section, be sure you understand the significance of these key people and terms:

Giuseppe Mazzini
Count Camillo Cavour
Giuseppe Garibaldi
Otto von Bismarck
kaiser

Zionism
Indian National Congress
Muslim League
Young Turks
Pan-Slavism

⭐ **THE BIG IDEA**
The force of nationalism:

- inspired revolutions in Europe and Latin America.

- led to a united Italy and a united Germany in the late 1800s.

- arose among Indians, Turks, and Jews.

- created conflict in the Balkans by the early 1900s.

KEY THEMES AND CONCEPTS

Nationalism Nationalism is a feeling of pride in and devotion to one's nation. It is a feeling that develops among people who may share a common language, history, set of traditions, or goal. Nationalism often causes people to join together to choose their own form of government, without outside interference.

📝 **PREPARING FOR THE REGENTS**

To learn more about both Napoleon and the independence movements in Latin America, see Section 2 of this unit.

NATIONALISM AND REVOLUTION

As you have learned, nationalism is a feeling of strong devotion to one's country. This feeling often develops among people who share a common language and heritage. Nationalism played an important role in political revolutions of the 1800s.

Revolution and war in the 1790s created a strong sense of national unity in France. This feeling inspired French armies to battlefield success as they sought to spread the ideals of their revolution. Napoleon also inspired nationalism among the nations he conquered. However, nationalistic feelings encouraged conquered peoples to rise up against Napoleon. In the years following the French Revolution, nationalism led to upheaval in Europe and elsewhere.

- **Greece** In 1821, nationalists in Greece revolted against the Ottoman empire. Britain, France, and Russia gave support to Greece. By 1830, Greece was independent.
- **Poland** Nationalists in Poland revolted in 1830, but their revolution was crushed by Russian forces.
- **Belgium** Nationalists in Belgium, who wanted to separate themselves from the Dutch, won independence in 1831.
- **Revolutions of 1848** In 1848, revolutions occurred in parts of the Austrian empire, Italy, and Germany. Throughout the continent of Europe, people sought to develop unified, independent nation-states.
- **Latin America** In the late 1700s and early 1800s, feelings of dissatisfaction led to a number of independence movements that ended European rule throughout Latin America. After gaining independence in the 1800s, groups in Latin America developed into many separate nation-states.

Nationalism Changes the Map of Europe

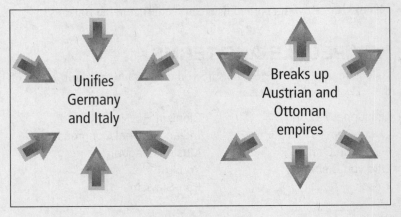

UNIFICATION MOVEMENTS IN EUROPE

Nationalistic feeling became an increasingly significant force for self-determination and unification in Europe.

Italy

Ever since the Roman empire had fallen in the 400s, Italy had been divided into many small states. After Napoleon invaded Italy, he united some of the Italian states into the Kingdom of Italy. The Congress of Vienna, however, redivided Italy and put much of it under Austrian or Spanish control.

The three great leaders of Italian nationalism were Giuseppe Mazzini, Count Camillo Cavour, and Giuseppe Garibaldi. **Giuseppe Mazzini** formed the Young Italy national movement in 1831, but he was exiled for his views. His writings and speeches provided inspiration to the nationalist movement, however. **Count Camillo Cavour,** prime minister of the Italian state of Sardinia, shrewdly formed alliances with France and later with Prussia. He used diplomacy and war to drive Austrian power from Italy. **Giuseppe Garibaldi** was a soldier who led the forces that won control of southern Italy and helped it to unite with the north. By 1861, Victor Emmanuel of Sardinia was crowned king of a united Italy. Rome and Venetia, at first not part of Italy, were included by 1870.

With no tradition of unity, the new nation faced conflicts. The urban north quarreled with the rural south. Also, the Catholic Church resisted the new government. Despite economic growth, unrest grew in the late 1800s.

Germany

Another national unification movement occurred in Germany. In the early 1800s, most German-speaking people lived in small states, to which they felt loyalty. During Napoleon's conquests, feelings of nationalism stirred in those Germans who wanted to be free of French rule. After Napoleon's defeat in 1815, some nationalists called for a united Germany. Metternich, however, blocked this idea at the Congress of Vienna.

THE RISE OF PRUSSIA   In the 1830s, Prussia set up a trade union among German states called the Zollverein. This agreement ended trade barriers between the states and was a step toward unity. More important, it established Prussia as a leader among the states.

In 1862, **Otto von Bismarck** was appointed chancellor of Prussia. Over the next decade, Bismarck, a strong and practical leader, guided German unification. Bismarck was not driven by a feeling of German nationalism, however. His loyalty was to the Prussian king. Unification was merely a means for him to make the Prussian king the ruler of a strong and united German state.

PREPARING FOR THE REGENTS

Explain one way in which each of the individuals listed here helped to unite Italy.

Mazzini:

Cavour:

Garibaldi:

KEY THEMES AND CONCEPTS

Nationalism In both Italy and Germany, the conquests of Napoleon inspired nationalism.

PREPARING FOR THE REGENTS

What role did Prussia and Bismarck play in German unification?

"BLOOD AND IRON" Bismarck believed that the only way to unify Germany was through a policy he called "blood and iron." Bismarck had no faith in speeches and representative government. He believed that the only way to unite the German states was through war. In seven years, Bismarck led Prussia into three wars. Each war increased Prussia's prestige and moved the German states closer to unity.

- **Danish War** In 1864, Prussia allied with Austria to seize land from Denmark.
- **Austro-Prussian War** In 1866, Prussia turned against Austria to gain more land. Prussia overwhelmed Austria in just seven weeks. Several German states were united with Prussia in the North German Confederation.
- **Franco-Prussian War** In 1870, Bismarck used nationalism and the bitter memories of Napoleon's conquests to stir up support for a war against France. Prussia and its German allies easily defeated France. During the war, southern German states agreed to unite with Prussia.

In 1871, the German states united under the Prussian king, William I. As their ruler, William called himself the **kaiser,** a title that was derived from the name *Caesar* and meant "emperor."

 PREPARING FOR THE REGENTS

The anti-Semitism that grew in Europe during the 1800s is an example of the negative effects of a group's nationalism on other peoples. Can you think of other examples of nationalism causing discrimination and violence against religious or ethnic minorities?

ZIONISM

The rise of nationalism in Europe had led to an intensification of anti-Semitism in the late 1800s. As citizens grew more patriotic about their own nations, they often grew more intolerant of those whom they saw as outsiders, including Jews. The pogroms that occurred in Eastern Europe and Russia are one example of this trend.

As anti-Semitism grew in Europe, some Jews moved to Palestine, the ancient Jewish homeland, buying land that they organized into farming communities. A Jewish journalist named Theodor Herzl became alarmed by the strong anti-Semitism he witnessed in France. In 1896, Herzl called for Jews to establish their own state. Herzl's writings helped to build **Zionism,** the movement devoted to building a Jewish state in Palestine. In 1897, he organized the first world congress of Zionists, which met in Switzerland. Herzl's dream of an independent Israel was realized a little more than 50 years later.

NATIONALISM IN ASIA

National movements were also at work outside of Europe.

India

Since the 1700s, the British had maintained control of the Indian subcontinent. Under British rule, nationalistic feelings began to stir among Indians, especially those who had been educated in the West. As

Indian students learned about democracy and natural rights, they called increasingly for self-rule.

INDIAN NATIONAL CONGRESS   In 1885, nationalist leaders in India formed the **Indian National Congress,** which became known as the Congress party. This group was made up mainly of Hindu professionals and business leaders. At first, the Congress party called merely for equal opportunity to serve in the government of India. They called for greater democracy and western-style modernization, looking ahead to self-rule.

MUSLIM LEAGUE   Initially, Muslims and Hindus cooperated in their campaign for self-rule. However, Muslims grew distrustful of the Indian National Congress because the organization was mostly Hindu. The increasing strength of Hindu nationalism alarmed Muslims. In 1906, Muslim leaders formed the **Muslim League** to protect their own rights and interests. They even talked about setting up a separate Muslim state. After World War I, calls for Indian self-rule increased, followed by demands for independence. This goal would finally be achieved in 1947.

Turkey

In the 1800s, the multinational Ottoman empire faced challenges from the various ethnic groups in the empire.

YOUNG TURKS   A group of liberals in the 1890s established a movement called the **Young Turks.** This group wanted to strengthen the Ottoman empire and end the threat of western imperialism. In 1908, they overthrew the sultan and took control of the government.

THE ARMENIAN MASSACRE   The Young Turks supported Turkish nationalism. They abandoned traditional Ottoman tolerance of diverse cultures and religions. Muslim Turks turned against Christian Armenians who were living in the Ottoman empire. Accusing the Armenians of plotting with Russia against the Ottoman empire, the Turks unleashed a massacre that resulted in the death of over a million Armenians over the next 25 years.

NATIONALISM AND CONFLICT IN THE BALKANS

Nationalism was a source of conflict in the Balkan peninsula of southeastern Europe. In the 1800s, the Ottoman empire still ruled much of the area, which was home to many groups. Among these were Serbs, Greeks, Bulgarians, and Romanians. During the 1800s, nationalist groups in the Balkans rebelled against foreign rule. From 1829 to 1908, Greece, Montenegro, Serbia, Romania, and Bulgaria all gained their independence.

The nations of Europe viewed the Ottoman empire as "the sick man of Europe." They hoped to gain land from the Ottoman empire. Russia,

KEY THEMES AND CONCEPTS

Change Western education introduced Indians to the ideals of democracy, nationalism, and basic human rights. This kind of thinking led eventually to self-rule for India. Western education brought change to other nations as well.

KEY THEMES AND CONCEPTS

Diversity Religion and cultural differences made it difficult for Hindus and Muslims to unite in a single national movement. Eventually, two nations—predominantly Muslim Pakistan and predominantly Hindu India—were created. Conflicts between the two groups still exist today.

PREPARING FOR THE REGENTS

How has nationalism been a force that divides as well as a force that unifies? Give examples to support your answer.

 PREPARING FOR THE REGENTS

Practice your map skills by listing the nationalities that existed in the Ottoman empire in 1870.

 PREPARING FOR THE REGENTS

By the 1800s, the Ottoman empire was becoming weaker. How did European nations react to the decreasing power of the Ottomans?

 PREPARING FOR THE REGENTS

Choose one of the regions discussed in this section. Explain how nationalism remains a force in that region today.

Nationalities in Eastern Europe Around 1870

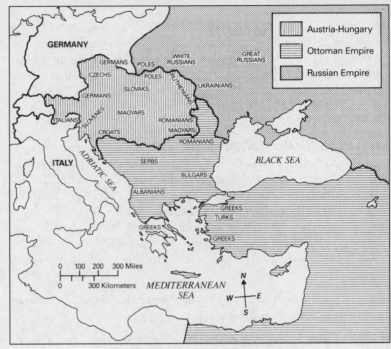

Austria-Hungary, Britain, and France all entered into alliances and wars that were designed to gain territory from the Ottoman empire.

Russia sponsored a nationalistic movement called **Pan-Slavism,** based on the idea that all Slavic peoples shared a common nationality. Serbia had a large Slavic population and was supported by Russia. Austria-Hungary, however, feared Serbian nationalism and angered Serbia by taking control in 1908 of two provinces that would have given Serbia access to the Adriatic Sea.

In the early years of 1900, crisis after crisis broke out on the Balkan peninsula. By 1914, the Balkans were the "powder keg of Europe." Tensions soon exploded into a full-scale global conflict: World War I.

SUMMARY

Starting in the late 1700s, nationalism became a major force that helped inspire uprisings across Europe and Latin America. In the mid-1800s, nationalism led to the creation of two strong, united nations: Italy and Germany. Nationalistic sentiments also spread among Indians, Turks, Jews, and other peoples. Nationalism did not always draw people together, however. In the early 1900s, nationalism created conflicts in southeastern Europe that drove the continent to the brink of war.

5

Economic and Social Revolutions

SECTION OVERVIEW

Starting around 1750, Europe experienced a series of major changes. They began with improvements in farming that led to an increase in population. These changes contributed to the Industrial Revolution. With the Industrial Revolution, social classes, people's roles, working conditions, and city life changed greatly. When the new conditions led to problems, differing thinkers wanted to solve them in different ways. Some groups emphasized the rights of individuals. Socialists and others stressed the needs of society as a whole. A period of reforms followed. By the early 1900s, the world had changed even more: Global migration occurred and movement toward a global economy accelerated.

KEY THEMES AND CONCEPTS

As you review this section, take special note of the following key themes and concepts:

Change What changes occurred during the Agrarian Revolution?

Science and Technology What role did technology play in the Industrial Revolution?

Economic Systems What economic and social developments occurred as part of the Industrial Revolution?

Political Systems What parliamentary reforms came about as a result of the Industrial Revolution?

KEY PEOPLE AND TERMS

As you review this section, be sure you understand the significance of these key people and terms:

Agrarian Revolution	laissez faire	Thomas Malthus
enclosure	Adam Smith	socialism
Industrial Revolution	liberalism	Karl Marx
factory	conservatism	suffrage

⭐ **THE BIG IDEA**
In the 1700s and 1800s in Europe:

- the Agrarian Revolution led to population growth.

- the Industrial Revolution eventually transformed economic systems and social conditions around the world.

- people proposed different ways to deal with the problems created by industrialization.

- economic life became more global, and mass migrations of people occurred.

THE AGRARIAN REVOLUTION

In 1750, most people still lived in small villages and made their own clothing and tools. In the century that followed, dramatic changes took place in the ways people lived and worked.

Increased Food Production

The movement away from rural life began with the **Agrarian Revolution,** a change in methods of farming.

TECHNOLOGY   The Dutch led the way by building dikes to protect their farmland from the sea and using fertilizer to improve the soil. The British discovered ways to produce more food. Jethro Tull invented the seed drill, which planted seeds in rows.

ENCLOSURE MOVEMENT   Landowners found a new purpose for **enclosure,** taking over and fencing off land that once had been shared by peasant farmers. The purpose of the enclosure movement was to replace the many small strip farms with larger fields. This practice made farming more efficient, improving agricultural production.

Population Explosion

The Agrarian Revolution led to rapid population growth. With a better diet, women had healthier and stronger babies. In addition, improved medical care and sanitation helped people live longer. During the 1700s, Europe's population increased from 120 million to about 190 million.

THE INDUSTRIAL REVOLUTION

The **Industrial Revolution** was the period, beginning around 1750, in which the means of production of goods shifted from hand tools to complex machines and from human and animal power to steam power. During this period, technology developed rapidly and production increased. The Industrial Revolution brought great changes into people's lives.

Causes of the Industrial Revolution

Industrialization began in Britain. Belgium, France, Germany, the United States, and Japan would all industrialize by the end of the 1800s. In time, the Industrial Revolution would spread throughout the world. It happened first in Britain for several reasons.

GEOGRAPHY   Britain had plenty of the coal and iron ore needed for industrialization. As an island, Britain had many natural harbors for trade. Rivers served both as means of transportation and as sources of power for factories.

POPULATION GROWTH AND CHANGE   Growth in population, resulting from the Agrarian Revolution, led to more available workers.

Ⴓ KEY THEMES AND CONCEPTS

Change As larger areas were enclosed, farm yields rose. Profits grew because fewer people were needed to work the farms. Unemployed farmers moved to cities.

PREPARING FOR THE REGENTS

How did the Agrarian Revolution of the 1700s contribute to the Industrial Revolution?

Because of the enclosure movement, fewer farm laborers were needed. Many people moved to the cities, where they could work in factories.

CAPITAL FOR INVESTMENT   The British overseas empire had made the economy strong. As a result, the middle class had the capital to invest in mines, railroads, and factories.

ENERGY AND TECHNOLOGY   Britain had experienced an energy revolution. In the 1700s, people used giant water wheels to power new machines. Soon coal was used to power steam engines, which would become an important power source for machines.

Factory System and Mass Production

The textile industry was the first to use the inventions of the Industrial Revolution. Before the Industrial Revolution, families spun cotton into thread and then wove cloth at home. By the 1700s, new machines were too large and expensive to be operated at home. Spinners and weavers

 PREPARING FOR THE REGENTS

As you study current events, keep in mind that the Industrial Revolution is still occurring in the developing nations of the world.

Causes of the Industrial Revolution

AGRARIAN REVOLUTION
- Dutch build dikes to protect farmland from the sea and use animal fertilizer to improve soil
- British discover ways to produce more food and invent seed drill

BETTER FOOD PRODUCTION

POPULATION EXPLOSION
- People eat better
- Women give birth to healthier babies
- Better medical care slows death rate

MORE DEMAND FOR GOODS

ENERGY REVOLUTION
- Water wheels power new machines
- Coal used to fuel steam engine

FASTER PRODUCTION OF GOODS

INDUSTRIAL REVOLUTION

 PREPARING FOR THE REGENTS

Explain three reasons for the start of the Industrial Revolution.

1.

2.

3.

began to work in long sheds that were owned by the manufacturers. These sheds, which brought workers and machines together in one place, became the first **factories.** At first, these factories were located near rapidly moving streams, which provided water power. Later, machines were powered by steam engines, fueled by coal. The factory system promoted mass production, meaning that goods were produced in huge quantities at lower cost.

Effects of the Industrial Revolution

The Industrial Revolution brought about many economic and social changes.

PREPARING FOR THE REGENTS

To learn more about mercantilism, see Unit 4, Section 4.

LAISSEZ-FAIRE ECONOMICS   The mercantilism of the past had called for government regulation to achieve a favorable balance of trade. However, a theory called **laissez faire** had emerged during the Enlightenment. According to this theory, businesses should operate with little or no government interference. In his book *The Wealth of Nations,* **Adam Smith** promoted laissez-faire ideas. They became the basis of the prevailing economic system during the Industrial Revolution.

RISE OF BIG BUSINESS   With new technology came the need for the investment of large amounts of money in businesses. To acquire this money, business owners sold stocks, or shares in their companies, to investors. Each stockholder therefore owned a part of the company. Stockholders allowed businesses to form corporations and expand into many areas.

NEW CLASS STRUCTURE   In the Middle Ages, the two main classes in Europe had been nobles and peasants. During the 1600s, a middle class had emerged. The Industrial Revolution added more complexity.

- The upper class consisted of very rich industrial and business families. Members of these families often married into noble families.
- A growing upper middle class of business people and professionals—such as lawyers and doctors—emerged. Their standard of living was high. Below them a lower middle class of teachers, office workers, shopowners, and clerks existed.
- At the bottom of this social structure were factory workers and peasants. They benefited least from the Industrial Revolution. People in this class faced harsh living and working conditions in overcrowded cities.

PREPARING FOR THE REGENTS

How did the Industrial Revolution lead to urbanization?

URBANIZATION   People moved from small villages to the towns and cities where factories were located. At first, conditions were very bad. Working-class people lived in crowded buildings. Without a sewage or sanitation system, garbage rotted in the streets. Disease spread.

WORKING CONDITIONS   Factory work hours were long. Men, women, and even children worked 12 to 16 hours a day. Mass production methods led to work that was boring. Many machines were dangerous.

CHANGING SOCIAL ROLES   The roles of men, women, and children changed in the new industrial society. Farming families had all worked the land together. Artisans had worked in their homes. Now the workplace became separated from the home.

The roles of middle-class men and women were redefined. Men worked in the public world of business and government. Women worked at home, where they were responsible for maintaining the dwelling and raising the children, including their moral instruction.

Social class had an impact on family life. Middle-class children had a high standard of living and a better chance at education. Among the working class, on the other hand, children had to work long hours to help support their families. Working-class women also worked long hours, although they were paid less than men. Family life sometimes suffered as women worked 12 hours or more in a factory and then came home to care for their families.

IMPROVED TRANSPORTATION   The growth of industry led to improvements in transportation.

- Roads and canals were built and improved.
- The steam locomotive was invented. Railroads grew.
- Steam engines powered ships at sea.

RISING STANDARDS OF LIVING   Settlement patterns shifted over time. The rich lived in pleasant neighborhoods on the edges of the cities. The poor were crowded into slums in city centers, near factories. Over time, conditions in cities improved, however. In addition, people ate more varied diets and were healthier, thanks to advances in medicine.

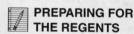

PREPARING FOR THE REGENTS

How did the Industrial Revolution contribute to changing the roles of men and women?

COMPETING PHILOSOPHIES

The hardships and changes brought by the Industrial Revolution inspired many varying solutions. Several different ways of thinking competed against each other.

Liberalism

Liberalism was a strong belief in individual rights to liberty, equality, and property. These concepts had sprung from the Enlightenment ideas that were spread by the French Revolution. According to liberals, the main purpose of government was to protect individual liberty. Most liberals accepted Adam Smith's laissez-faire ideas about economics.

Conservatism

Conservatism was the set of beliefs held by classes who had been in power previously—monarchs, nobles, and church leaders.

⚲ **KEY THEMES AND**
🕈 **CONCEPTS**
Political Systems
Liberalism was expressed by the leaders of the Enlightenment and the French Revolution. Conservatism was expressed by the leaders of the Congress of Vienna.

Conservatives wanted social and political structures to return to what they had been before the various revolutionary movements. Many persons who had been members of the noble class became business leaders. These individuals formed a new business aristocracy.

Conservative thinker **Thomas Malthus** in 1798 published his "Essay on the Principle of Population." In it he concluded that the poor would continue to suffer as long as the population kept increasing. He urged families to have fewer children.

Social Darwinism

Other new ideas of the 1800s challenged long-held beliefs. In 1859, British naturalist Charles Darwin caused an uproar by saying that humans had evolved over millions of years. This theory of evolution, as it was called, stirred conflicts between religion and science.

Part of Darwin's theory involved the idea of natural selection. Using the ideas of Thomas Malthus, Darwin said that species naturally produced more offspring than the food supply could support. Members of each species had to compete to survive. Thus, natural forces selected the most able members, producing an improved species.

Later thinkers used Darwin's ideas to develop a theory known as Social Darwinism. According to Social Darwinism, successful businesspeople were successful because they were naturally more "fit" to succeed than others. War allowed stronger nations to weed out weaker ones. Social Darwinism played a part in racism, the belief that one race is superior to another. It also contributed to the rise in imperialism.

Social Reformism

Many types of social reformism arose. Jeremy Bentham stated that the goal of society should be the happiness of its people. John Stuart Mill believed that government should improve the lives of the poor. Reform movements attempted to correct the abuses of child labor. Trade unions grew in power among the working class and also worked for social reform.

Socialism

Socialism concentrated less on the interests and rights of individuals and more on the interests of society. Industrial capitalism, the socialists claimed, had created a large gap between rich and poor. Under socialism, farms and businesses would belong to all the people, not to individuals. Different types of socialism emerged.

UTOPIAN SOCIALISM   Early socialists called Utopians sought to create self-sufficient communities, where all property and work would be shared. Since all would have equal wealth, Utopians believed that fighting would end. In Scotland, Robert Owen set up a Utopian factory community.

 PREPARING FOR THE REGENTS
Create a chart listing and briefly explaining the competing philosophies that emerged during and after the Industrial Revolution.

MARXIST SOCIALISM   German philosopher **Karl Marx** promoted a more radical theory, "scientific socialism." In 1848, Marx and German economist Friedrich Engels explained their ideas, listed here, in *The Communist Manifesto.*

- History was a class struggle between wealthy capitalists and the working class, or proletariat.
- In order to make profits, the capitalists took advantage of the proletariat.
- The proletariat would eventually rise up and overthrow the capitalist system, creating their own society.
- The proletariat society would take control of the means of production and establish a classless, communist society, in which wealth and power would be equally shared.

In the Soviet Union in the 1900s, Marx's ideas would lead to a communist dictatorship and a command economy, in which government officials made all economic decisions.

EDUCATION AND THE ARTS
Artists, musicians, and writers also took new directions during the Industrial Revolution.

Advances in Education
Governments had begun to set up public schools and require basic education for all children by the late 1800s. Schools not only taught subjects such as reading, writing, and mathematics but encouraged obedience to authority and punctuality as well.

Romanticism
From about 1750 to 1850, a movement known as romanticism thrived. The romantics appealed to emotion rather than to reason. In this way romanticism was a rebellion against the ideas of the Enlightenment. It was also a reaction against the impersonal nature of industrial society.

Realism
The mid-1800s brought an artistic movement known as realism to the West. Realists sought to show the world as it was. They often looked at the harsh side of life, showing poverty and cruel working conditions. Many writers, such as Charles Dickens, were critical of the abuses of industrial society and hoped to contribute to ending them.

Impressionism
In the 1870s, impressionism began in Paris. In this movement, artists worked to capture a fleeting impression of a scene. This was a movement away from realism in painting. Impressionism often achieved a fresh view of familiar subjects.

PREPARING FOR THE REGENTS

Compare and contrast Utopian socialism with Marxist socialism.

PREPARING FOR THE REGENTS

Discuss one important characteristic of each of these artistic movements.

Romanticism:

Realism:

Impressionism:

PREPARING FOR THE REGENTS

1. Describe a reform law that helped women.

2. Describe a law that helped children.

REFORM LEGISLATION

In the early 1830s, British lawmaker Michael Sadler persuaded Parliament to investigate the horrible conditions faced by child laborers in factories. The Sadler Report led to the Factories Regulations Act of 1833. This act prohibited children under 9 years old from being employed in textile mills and limited the working hours of children under 18. This is just one of many types of reforms introduced in Britain in the 1800s. France and Germany enacted labor reforms as well.

British Reform Laws

DIRECTION OF REFORM	LAWS ENACTED
Toward greater human rights	1884: Slavery is outlawed in all British colonies.
Toward more representative government	1832: Reform Act of 1832 gave representation to new industrial towns. 1858: Law ended property qualifications for members of Parliament. 1911: Law restricted powers of House of Lords; elected House of Commons became supreme.
Toward universal **suffrage** (the right to vote)	1829: Parliament gave Catholics the right to vote and to hold most public offices. 1867: Reform Act gave vote to many working-class men. 1884: Law extended voting rights to most farmers and other men. 1918: Women won the right to vote.
Toward more rights for workers	1825: Trade unions were legalized. 1840s to 1910s: Parliament passed laws • limiting child labor. • regulating work hours for women and children. • regulating safety conditions in factories and mines. • setting minimum wages. • providing for accident and unemployment insurance.
Toward improved education	1870: Education Act set up local elementary schools run by elected school boards. 1902: Law created a system of state-aided secondary schools. Industrial cities, such as London and Manchester, set up public universities.

GLOBAL IMPACT OF INDUSTRIALIZATION

Global Migrations

A WAVE OF MIGRATIONS   Improvements in transportation, population growth, and social and political conditions led to a wave of global migrations from about 1845 through the early 1900s.

- Polish nationalists fled Poland for Western Europe and the United States after the Russian army crushed the revolt of 1830.
- Several thousand Germans moved to cities in the United States after the failed revolutions of 1848.
- Russian Jews, escaping pogroms, left Eastern Europe.
- Italian farmers, seeing economic opportunity, also traveled to the Americas.

MASS STARVATION IN IRELAND   Another migration occurred from Ireland. Under British rule, the majority of Irish farmland had been used to grow crops, such as wheat and oats, which were sent to England. The Irish themselves used the potato as their main food crop. This system supported the Irish population until 1845, when a disease destroyed the potato crop. Other crops were not affected. Still, the British continued to ship the other products out of Ireland. Four years later, 1 million Irish had died of starvation or disease. Millions of others moved to the United States and Canada.

PREPARING FOR THE REGENTS

How did British policy contribute to starvation in Ireland and mass migration from Ireland?

Movement Toward a Global Economy

By the mid-1800s, the Industrial Revolution had moved beyond Britain. New powers were emerging. As they became strong industrially, they competed for a share of the wealth in markets around the world. In addition, manufacturers traded with other countries for resources they needed. Steamships and railroads, and then automobiles and airplanes, made global trade easier and quicker. As markets expanded around the world and global trade increased, a new imperialism developed.

PREPARING FOR THE REGENTS

To learn more about the new imperialism, see Section 7 of this unit.

SUMMARY

In the mid-1700s, the Agrarian Revolution in Europe contributed to an increase in population. The Agrarian Revolution led to the Industrial Revolution, which began in Britain and then spread to other countries. Economic and social conditions around the world changed dramatically as a result of the Industrial Revolution. Many new ideas about how to deal with the problems of industrialization developed, and reforms were enacted. Eventually, industrialization led to mass migration and increased global trade.

PREPARING FOR THE REGENTS

Compare the ways in which the Neolithic Revolution, the Industrial Revolution, and the Computer Revolution changed human life.

Japan and the Meiji Restoration

SECTION OVERVIEW

In 1853, an American fleet sailed to Japan and ended over 200 years of isolation by opening Japan to trade. Soon afterward, Japan's ruling shogun was overthrown, and the Meiji Restoration began. During this period, Japan underwent a rapid period of modernization and industrialization. Changes took place within government, the economy, and social life. Within decades Japan became a modern industrial power and began to build an overseas empire.

KEY THEMES AND CONCEPTS

As you review this section, take special note of the following key themes and concepts:

Change What political, social, and economic changes occurred in Japan in the late 1800s?

Interdependence How did Japan use western ideas to modernize and industrialize?

Power How did Japan become a global power by the early 1900s?

KEY PEOPLE AND TERMS

As you review this section, be sure you understand the significance of these key people and terms:

Matthew Perry

Treaty of Kanagawa

Meiji Restoration

zaibatsu

Sino-Japanese War

Russo-Japanese War

THE OPENING OF JAPAN

In 1853, United States ships sailed into Edo (now Tokyo) Bay, ending more than 200 years of Japanese isolation. This contact led to changes that had a great impact on Japan.

Tokugawa Isolation

European traders had first arrived in Japan in the 1500s. In the 1600s, the Tokugawa shoguns had gained control of Japan. They brought stability to Japan but also banned almost all contact with the outside world. Limited trade was allowed only with the Dutch at Nagasaki.

Commodore Matthew Perry

In 1854, American warships commanded by Commodore **Matthew Perry** sailed to Japan. Perry presented a letter to the Japanese from the United States president, asking that Japan open its ports to trade. Europeans and Americans were not only offended by the Tokugawa isolation but resentful at not being able to use Japanese ports to resupply or repair their ships.

Impressed by the American show of strength, the shogun agreed to the Treaty of Kanagawa, ending his country's long period of isolation. It was the first of many treaties Japan would sign with foreign powers.

The Treaty of Kanagawa

In the **Treaty of Kanagawa,** the shogun agreed to open two Japanese ports to American ships. The United States soon won other trading rights with Japan. In time, Britain, France, and Russia gained similar trading rights.

The Treaty of Kanagawa had a powerful impact on Japan.

- Some Japanese felt that the shogun had shown weakness in front of the foreigners by agreeing to the treaty.
- Some Japanese felt that Japan needed to modernize in order to compete with the industrialized West.
- A rebellion overthrew the shogun, restored the emperor to power, and launched Japan on the road to modernization and industrialization.

Japanese Exports and Imports

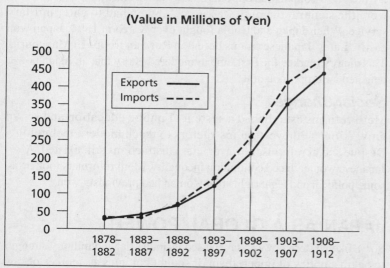

(Value in Millions of Yen)

Exports ———
Imports ------

| | 1878–1882 | 1883–1887 | 1888–1892 | 1893–1897 | 1898–1902 | 1903–1907 | 1908–1912 |

KEY THEMES AND CONCEPTS

Science and Technology
Since the Tokugawa shoguns banned contact with the West, Japan was cut off from the advances of industrialization and fell behind Europe in science and technology.

PREPARING FOR THE REGENTS

What effects did the visit of Commodore Perry and the Treaty of Kanagawa have on Japan's development?

PREPARING FOR THE REGENTS

Practice your graph skills by answering the following questions.

1. During which five-year period did Japanese trade increase the most?

2. Why was Japanese trade increasing so much in the late 1800s?

MODERNIZATION AND INDUSTRIALIZATION

In 1867, daimyo and samurai led a rebellion that removed the Tokugawa shogun from power. In 1868, the emperor was established as the leader of Japan. The period from 1868 to 1912 is known as the **Meiji Restoration.** *Meiji* means "enlightened rule." During this time, the emperor and his advisors implemented a series of reforms that changed Japan forever.

Borrowing From the West

The Meiji reformers were determined to strengthen Japan against the West. Members of the government traveled abroad to learn about western government, economics, technology, and customs. In addition, foreign experts were invited to Japan.

Economic Development

The Meiji government used western methods and machinery to develop an industrial economy in Japan. The government built factories and then sold them to wealthy families. These families became powerful in banking and industry and were known as **zaibatsu.**

The government supported the economy by developing a banking system and a postal system. It also built railroads and improved ports. By the 1890s, the economy was flourishing. The population grew, and peasants migrated to the cities in search of jobs.

Strong Central Government

Meiji reformers wanted to create a strong central government. They chose the government of Germany as their model. A constitution gave the emperor autocratic power and created a two-house legislature. Only one of the houses was elected, and suffrage was limited.

Military Power

By the 1890s, Japan had a modern army and a strong navy. No longer were the samurai the only warriors: All men had to enter military service. When Japan and China fought over Korea in 1894, Japan won easily. Later, Japanese troops defeated Russian troops in Manchuria. This victory marked the first time in modern history that an Asian power defeated a European nation.

Social Change

Meiji reforms established a system of public education and set up universities with western instructors to teach modern technology. Despite social reforms, however, class distinctions still existed. Also, Japanese women faced continuing inequality. Meiji reformers took away some political and legal rights that women had previously won.

JAPAN AS A GLOBAL POWER

Soon, like western powers, Japan used its industrial and military strength to begin a policy of imperialism. It sought colonies as sources of raw

PREPARING FOR THE REGENTS

Why did the Industrial Revolution occur earlier in Japan than in African and other Asian nations?

KEY THEMES AND CONCEPTS

Choice How did choosing a German model for government affect the development of Japan?

PREPARING FOR THE REGENTS

What changes were made in society during the Meiji Restoration? What group did not experience greater personal freedom?

materials and as markets for finished products. Colonies were gained through war.

Sino-Japanese War

In 1894, Japan's territorial ambitions in Korea led to war with China. The conflict, which lasted from 1894 to 1895, was called the **Sino-Japanese War.** Japan quickly won, gaining Formosa (later Taiwan) and treaty ports in China from the Chinese. Japan later made Korea a Japanese protectorate.

Russo-Japanese War

From 1904 to 1905, Japan fought the **Russo-Japanese War** with Russia after the interests of the two nations conflicted in Korea. Japan's modern military defeated Russian troops and crushed Russia's navy. By 1910, Japan had complete control of Korea as well as parts of Manchuria.

Dependence on a World Market

Japan's industrialization drew it increasingly into the global market. Its economy therefore became dependent on trade. An island empire with few natural resources, Japan relied on raw materials from outside the country. It needed foreign markets for its manufactured products. In the years ahead, Japan would continue to compete with other industrialized nations. It would also continue its policy of imperialism.

SUMMARY

In the mid-1800s, Japan ended its long policy of isolation. The Meiji government that took power in 1868 used western ideas to begin a program of modernization that quickly turned Japan into a major industrial power. In the 1890s and 1900s, Japan used its modern military to become a global imperial power.

♀ KEY THEMES AND CONCEPTS

Power Industrialization contributed to Japan's strong military. In turn, a strong military contributed to the nation's imperialistic success.

♀ KEY THEMES AND CONCEPTS

Geography Japan, an island nation with few natural resources, had industrialized rapidly in the 1800s. How did geography affect Japan's decision to follow a policy of imperialism?

SECTION 7 Imperialism

SECTION

The imperialism that emerged in the mid-1800s had a lasting impact on the world.

- Powerful industrialized nations sought to gain power and economic might by building empires.

- Through economic and military power, Britain colonized and dominated India.

- European nations divided up the continent of Africa.

- Western powers and Japan established spheres of influence in China.

- Imperialism has had short-term and long-term effects on various regions of the world.

SECTION OVERVIEW

From the mid-1800s through the first decades of the 1900s, western nations pursued an aggressive policy of expansion. European powers were motivated by economic, political, and social factors as well as by a strong sense of nationalism. During this time, Britain took control of India. In Africa, several European nations engaged in a scramble for colonies. Meanwhile, imperialistic nations forced unequal trade agreements on China. Imperialism had many immediate and long-term effects on the colonial nations and also had an impact on Europe and the rest of the world. Imperialism led to increased competition and conflict.

KEY THEMES AND CONCEPTS

As you review this section, take special note of the following key themes and concepts:

Imperialism What factors led to the new imperialism of the 1800s?

Power How did imperialistic countries gain power over the peoples of Africa and Asia?

Change What were the effects of imperialism?

Nationalism How did imperialism lead to nationalistic feelings in China and other nations of Asia and Africa?

KEY PEOPLE AND TERMS

As you review this section, be sure you understand the significance of these key people and terms:

imperialism	Opium War	Taiping Rebellion
Sepoy Mutiny	Treaty of Nanjing	Boxer Rebellion
Boer War	sphere of influence	Sun Yixian

Causes of the New Imperialism

Economy	Politics and the Military	Society	Science and Invention
• Need for natural resources • Need for new markets • Place for growing populations to settle • Place to invest profits	• Bases for trade and navy ships • Power and security of global empire • Spirit of nationalism	• Wish to spread Christianity • Wish to share western civilization • Belief that western ways are best	• New weapons • New medicines • Improved ships

THE NEW IMPERIALISM

Imperialism is the domination by one country of the political, economic, or cultural life of another country. Historians often divide imperialism into two periods.

- **The Old Imperialism** Between about 1500 and 1800, European nations established colonies in the Americas, India, and Southeast Asia and gained territory on the coasts of Africa and China. Still, European power in these regions of the world was limited.
- **The New Imperialism** Between 1870 and 1914, nationalism had produced strong, centrally governed nation-states. The Industrial Revolution had made economies stronger as well. During this time, Japan, the United States, and the industrialized nations of Europe became more aggressive in expanding into other lands. The new imperialism was focused mainly in Asia and Africa, where declining empires and local wars left many states vulnerable. In Africa, many states had been weakened by the legacy of the slave trade.

Causes of Imperialism

Several important factors combined to lead to the development of the new imperialism.

Nationalism and Social Darwinism

A spirit of nationalism was one cause of the new imperialism. Because nationalism promotes the idea of national superiority, imperialists felt that they had a right to take control of countries they viewed as weaker. Social Darwinism also encouraged imperialism. This idea applied Darwin's theory of survival of the fittest to competition between nations. Social Darwinists argued that it was natural for stronger nations to dominate weaker ones.

Military Motives

Military motives were linked to nationalism, since military power was a way to promote a nation's goals. Colonies were important as bases for resupply of ships. A nation with many colonies had power and security.

KEY THEMES AND CONCEPTS

Imperialism The strong central governments and thriving economies of industrialized nations gave them the confidence to expand through imperialism.

PREPARING FOR THE REGENTS

How did the Industrial Revolution lead to imperialism?

Economic Motives

Imperialists needed raw materials to supply their factories. They needed foreign markets in which to sell their finished products. They needed places to invest their profits. Colonies could provide all these things.

White Man's Burden

Rudyard Kipling's poem "White Man's Burden" offered a justification for imperialism. Kipling expressed the idea that white imperialists had a moral duty to educate people in nations they considered less developed. Missionaries spread western ideas, customs, and religions to people in Africa and Asia.

BRITISH IN INDIA

British East India Company

The British East India Company had established trading rights in India in the early 1600s. By the mid-1800s, with the decline of the Mughal empire and the defeat of French rivals, this company controlled three fifths of India. The company employed Indian soldiers, called sepoys.

PREPARING FOR THE REGENTS

To learn more about the early period of British trade in India, see Unit 4, Section 4

The Sepoy Mutiny

In 1857, tensions rose. The British had angered the sepoys by demanding that soldiers follow rules that were against their religious beliefs. The **Sepoy Mutiny,** or the Sepoy Rebellion, called for Hindus and Muslims to unite against the British. The British, however, crushed the revolt.

PREPARING FOR THE REGENTS

To learn more about the effects of British rule in India, see the chart at the end of this section.

The Sepoy Mutiny left bitter feelings. It also caused the British to change their policies. In 1858, Parliament ended the rule of the East India Company. The British government took direct command of India.

THE SCRAMBLE FOR AFRICA

In the 1870s, King Leopold of Belgium sent a mission to the interior of Africa to establish trade agreements with leaders in the Congo River basin. The Belgian presence in the Congo set off a scramble among other European powers to establish their presence on the continent.

The Berlin Conference

In 1884, to avoid conflict among themselves, European leaders met in Berlin, Germany, to set up rules for colonizing Africa. European powers divided Africa with little regard for the people who lived there. The new imperialism affected Africa strongly. In 1850, most of Africa had been free. Seventy years later, most of the continent was under European rule.

Battle for Southern Africa

THE ZULU EMPIRE   In the early 1800s in southern Africa, an African leader named Shaka organized Zulu warriors into a fighting force. He used his power against European slave traders and ivory hunters. Through conquest of other African groups, he united the Zulu nation.

The Scramble for Africa, 1880–1914

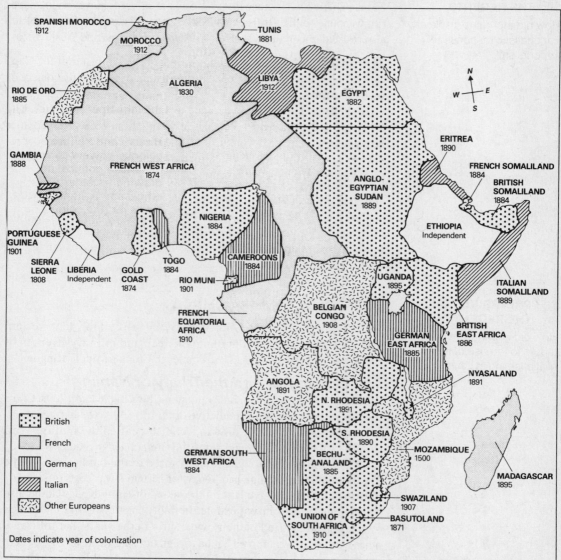

Dates indicate year of colonization

ARRIVAL OF EUROPEANS   Dutch farmers, called Boers, had settled in southern Africa in the mid-1600s. They had built Cape Town as a supply station. In the 1700s, Dutch herders and ivory hunters began to move north. They fought African groups, such as the Zulus. In the early 1800s, the British acquired the Cape Colony from the Dutch.

ZULU RESISTANCE   Large numbers of Boers, resenting British rule, migrated north during the 1830s, coming into conflict with Zulus. Fighting between the Boers and the Zulus continued until late in the century.

PREPARING FOR THE REGENTS

Practice your map skills by identifying the colonial power that occupied each of the following areas: Algeria in 1830, Togo in 1884, and the Union of South Africa in 1910.

PREPARING FOR THE REGENTS

How did the Zulus display a nationalistic response to imperialism?

The Zulus eventually came into conflict with the British as well. The Zulus experienced victory in 1879. Soon afterward, however, the superior weaponry of the British crushed the Zulu resistance. Others in Africa also resisted imperialism, including groups in Ethiopia and West Africa.

THE BOER WAR   Cecil Rhodes became prime minister of the Cape Colony in 1890. Under his leadership, Britain expanded its control of southern Africa.

In the late 1800s, Britain decided to annex the Boer republics. The Boers resisted and the **Boer War** began, lasting from 1899 to 1902. After heavy losses, the British won. In 1910, the British combined the Boer republics with the Cape Colony to form the Union of South Africa. The bitter struggles left a legacy of distrust and hatred.

ANTI-SLAVE TRADE LEGISLATION   Most European powers had abolished the slave trade before the scramble for African colonies began. For example, Denmark passed anti-slave trade legislation in 1803, followed by Britain in 1807, and France in 1818. Illegal slave trading, however, continued throughout the 1800s.

 PREPARING FOR THE REGENTS

How did imperialism contribute to the rise of nationalistic feeling in China?

IMPERIALISM IN CHINA

Since 1644, rulers of the Qing dynasty had refused to adopt western ways. As a result, the economic, political, and military strength of European imperialists was able to challenge China's Middle Kingdom.

The Opium War and the Treaty of Nanjing

British merchants began to trade opium in China in the late 1700s. China tried to halt imports of the addictive drug. In 1839, to keep trade open, the British fought with China in a conflict called the **Opium War.** Britain's superior military and industrial strength led to a quick victory.

In 1842, Britain forced China to agree to the harsh terms of the **Treaty of Nanjing.** China had to pay for Britain's war costs, open ports to British trade, and give Britain the island of Hong Kong. China also had to grant British citizens extraterritoriality, the right to live under their own laws and be tried in their own courts.In the years that followed, other western powers forced China to sign unequal treaties. The western powers carved out **spheres of influence,** areas in which an outside power claimed exclusive trade privileges.

Chinese Reactions to Imperialism

Foreign imperialism led to further clashes between the imperialist powers and China—and among the Chinese themselves.

THE TAIPING REBELLION   From 1850 to 1864, Chinese peasants, angry at their poverty and at corrupt Qing officials, rose up in revolt. The **Taiping Rebellion** resulted in millions of Chinese deaths and weakened China.

THE BOXER REBELLION   In 1900, a group known to westerners as the Boxers assaulted foreign communities across China in a conflict known as the **Boxer Rebellion.** Armies from Japan and the West, however, soon crushed the uprising and forced China to grant more concessions to foreign powers. After this defeat, greater numbers of Chinese called for western-style reforms.

SUN YIXIAN AND THE CHINESE REVOLUTION   In the first decade of the 1900s, Chinese nationalism blossomed. Many reformers called for a new government. **Sun Yixian,** also called Sun Yat-sen, led the movement to replace the Qing dynasty. He had three goals:

- To end foreign domination
- To form a representative government
- To create economic security for the Chinese people

In 1911, workers, peasants, students, and warlords toppled the monarchy. Sun Yixian was named president of the Chinese Republic.

IMPACT OF IMPERIALISM: MULTIPLE PERSPECTIVES

The new imperialism had a major impact on the European nations and on their colonies.

Spheres of Influence in China to 1914

PREPARING FOR THE REGENTS

Compare Japanese and Chinese responses to western industrial power and western imperialism.

PREPARING FOR THE REGENTS

Practice your map skills by describing Japan's sphere of influence in Asia in 1914. How do you think this influence benefited Japan?

Effects on the Colonies

Imperialism had a number of short-term and long-term effects on the colonies themselves. Some were negative; others were positive.

SHORT-TERM EFFECTS   Some effects were immediate.
- Large numbers of Asians and Africans came under foreign rule.
- Local economies became dependent on industrialized powers.
- Some nations introduced changes to meet imperialist challenges.
- Individuals and groups resisted European domination.
- Western culture spread to new regions.
- Traditional political units were disrupted or destroyed.
- Famines occurred in lands where farmers grew export crops for imperialist nations in place of food for local use.

LONG-TERM EFFECTS   Other effects took longer to emerge.
- Western culture continued to influence much of the world.
- Transportation, education, and medical care were improved.
- Resistance to imperial rule evolved into nationalist movements.
- Many economies became based on single cash crops grown for export.

Effects on Europe and the World

The West also changed because of imperialism.
- The West discovered new crops, foods, and other products.
- Westerners were introduced to new cultural influences.
- Competition for empires created and increased conflict between imperial powers. These conflicts sometimes led to war.
- The industrial nations controlled a new global economy.

SUMMARY

In the 1800s, industrialized powers greatly expanded their empires. Britain took control of India, and European nations occupied much of Africa. Imperial powers also forced China to grant trading concessions. This led to the growth of nationalism in China. Other effects of imperialism included the emergence of a global economy, the spread of western culture, and conflict between imperial powers.

The Effects of British Rule in India

GOOD EFFECTS	BAD EFFECTS
• New roads and railroads link parts of India. • Telegraph and postal systems unite people. • Irrigation systems improve farming. • New laws mean justice for all classes. • British schools offer education. • Customs that threaten human rights are ended.	• Indian resources go to Britain. • British-made goods replace local goods. • Farms grow cash crops rather than food crops; Indians go hungry. • Top jobs go to the British. • Indians are treated as inferiors. • Britain tries to replace Indian culture with western ways.

Questions for Regents Practice

Review the Preparing for the Regents section of this book. Then answer the following questions, which include multiple-choice questions, a thematic essay, and a series of document-based questions.

MULTIPLE CHOICE

Directions

Circle the *number* of the word or expression that best completes the statement or answers the question.

1 John Locke and Jean-Jacques Rousseau would be most likely to support
   1 a return to feudalism in Europe
   2 a government ruled by a divine monarchy
   3 a society ruled by the Catholic Church
   4 the right of citizens to decide the best form of government

2 The writers and philosophers of the Enlightenment believed that government decisions should be based on:
   1 fundamental religious beliefs
   2 the concept of the divine right of kings
   3 laws of nature and reason
   4 traditional values

3 A primary cause of the French Revolution in 1789 was the
   1 increasing dissatisfaction of the Third Estate
   2 rise to power of Napoleon Bonaparte
   3 actions of Prince Metternich
   4 execution of Louis XVI

4 In a number of European countries in the 1800s, which situation occurred as a result of the influence of the French Revolution?
   1 increase in religious conflict
   2 rise of nationalistic movements
   3 decentralization of governmental power
   4 economic depression

5 During the early 1800s, which was a major influence on the struggles for political independence in Latin America?
   1 poor conditions in urban centers in Latin America
   2 the American and French Revolutions
   3 the desire of the Roman Catholic Church in Latin America to escape European control
   4 demands by Latin American workers to own their own factories

6 Nationalism is most likely to develop in an area that has
   1 land suited to agriculture
   2 adequate industry to supply consumer demands
   3 a moderate climate with rivers for irrigation
   4 common customs, language, and history

7 Which statement about nationalism is most accurate?
   1 It becomes a unifying force among a people.
   2 It encourages diversity within nation-states.
   3 It prevents the rise of militarism.
   4 It eliminates the ethnic identities of different groups.

8 Which term refers to the Jewish movement to establish a homeland in Palestine?
   1 Zionism
   2 Marxism
   3 animism
   4 secularism

9 The theory of laissez-faire capitalism advocates
   1 government control of the economy
   2 noninvolvement of the government in the economy
   3 government regulation of big business
   4 government sponsorship of labor unions

10 An important result of the Industrial Revolution was the
   1 concentration of workers in urban areas
   2 increased desire of the wealthy class to share its power
   3 formation of powerful craft guilds
   4 control of agricultural production by governments

11 The arrival of Commodore Matthew Perry in Japan in 1853 signaled the end of Japanese
   1 cultural contacts with the West
   2 policies of isolationism
   3 militarism in Southeast Asia
   4 trade relations with the United States

12 In Japan, the period of the Meiji Restoration was primarily characterized by
   1 strict isolation
   2 feudal government
   3 religious revival
   4 reform and modernization

13 Russia in the 1700s and Japan in the 1800s were similar in that both countries
   1 began the process of modernization after a long period of isolation
   2 developed democratic governments after years under absolute monarchies
   3 refused to accept western technological ideas
   4 adopted socialist economic systems after capitalism had failed

14 "All great nations . . . have desired to set their mark upon barbarian lands, and those who fail to participate in this great rivalry will play a pitiable role in time to come."

This quotation supports the concept of
   1 socialism
   2 human rights
   3 revolution
   4 imperialism

15 The Treaty of Tordesillas (1494), concerning Latin America, and the Berlin Conference (1884–1885), concerning Africa, were similar in that each agreement
   1 provided for self-government by native peoples
   2 declared that in these areas, monarchs rule by divine right
   3 divided an area into European-controlled segments
   4 suppressed revolts by native peoples against European imperialists

16 The Boxer Rebellion of the early twentieth century was an attempt to
   1 eliminate poverty among Chinese peasants
   2 bring western-style democracy to China
   3 restore trade between China and European nations
   4 remove foreign influences from China

THEMATIC ESSAY

Directions

Read the following instructions that include a theme, a task, and suggestions. Follow the instructions to create a well-organized essay that has an introduction with a thesis statement, several paragraphs explaining the thesis, and a conclusion.

Theme: Revolution

Throughout global history, there have been major political, economic, social, and cultural revolutions. These revolutions have had complex causes and left lasting impacts on people's lives.

Task

- Define the term *revolution*.
- Select a specific revolution that you have studied, and describe three of the factors that helped to bring about that particular revolution.
- Identify and explain at least one immediate effect and at least one long-term effect of this revolution on people's lives.

Suggestions

You may discuss any revolution from your study of global history, except the American Revolution. Some suggestions you may wish to consider are: the Commercial Revolution, the Reformation, the Enlightenment, the French Revolution, the Industrial Revolution, the Mexican Revolution, and the Russian Revolution. You are not limited to these suggestions.

QUESTIONS BASED ON DOCUMENTS

The following exercise asks you to analyze three historical documents and then write an essay using evidence from those documents. This exercise is similar to the document-based question that you will see on the Regents Examination, which may include six or more documents. For additional practice with historical documents, see the Preparing for the Regents section and the sample examinations in this book.

   This task is based on the accompanying documents. Some of these documents have been edited for the purposes of this task. This task is designed to test your ability to work with historical documents. As you analyze the documents, take into account both the source of each document and the author's point of view.

Directions

Read the documents in Part A and answer the question or questions after each document. Then read the directions for Part B and write your essay.

Historical Context

Throughout history, imperialism has been interpreted from multiple perspectives. Some have seen it as a beneficial influence, while others have seen it as a harmful influence.

Task

Evaluate both the positive and the negative effects of imperialism.

Part A: Short Answer

Directions: Analyze the documents and answer the question or questions that follow each document, using the space provided.

DOCUMENT 1

Modern progressive nations lying in the temperate zone seek to control "garden spots" in the tropics, [mainly in Africa, Latin America, and Asia]. Under [the progressive nations'] direction, these places can yield tropical produce. In return, the progressive nations bring to the people of those garden spots the food-stuffs and manufactures they need. [Progressive nations] develop the territory by building roads, canals, railways, and telegraphs. They can establish schools and newspapers for the colonies [and] give these people the benefit of the blessings of civilization which they have not the means of creating themselves.

—O.P. Austin, "Does Colonization Pay?" *The Forum,* **1900**

1 What nations does the author probably consider to be the "modern progressive nations"? Explain the reason for your answer.

_____

_____

DOCUMENT 2

When the whites came to our country, we had the land and they had the Bible. Now we have the Bible and they have the land.

—African proverb

2 Does this proverb express a positive or negative viewpoint toward the white missionaries? Explain.

_____

_____

DOCUMENT 3

"Learning civilized ways is hard work!"

3 According to this cartoon, how does imperialism affect the lives of native people living under foreign rule?

_____

_____

DOCUMENT 4

To begin with, there are the exporters and manufacturers of certain goods used in the colonies. The makers of cotton and iron goods have been very much interested in imperialism. Their business interests demand that colonial markets should be opened and developed and that foreign competitors should be shut out. Such aims require political control and imperialism.

Finally, the most powerful of all business groups are the bankers. Banks make loans to colonies and backward countries for building railways and steamship lines. They also make loans to colonial plantation owners, importers, and exporters.

—Parker T. Moore, *Imperialism and World Politics*, 1926

4 Based on this passage, explain two ways in which European businesspeople hoped to profit from imperialism.

_____

_____

Part B: Essay

Directions:
- Write a well-organized essay that includes an introduction, several paragraphs, and a conclusion.
- Use evidence from the documents to support your response.
- Do not simply repeat the contents of the documents.
- Include specific, related outside information.

Historical Context

Throughout history, imperialism has been interpreted from multiple perspectives. Some have seen it as a beneficial influence, while others have seen it as a harmful influence.

Task

Using information from the documents and your knowledge of global history and geography, write an essay that evaluates the positive and negative impacts of imperialism. Develop a position either in favor of or against imperialism.

   Be sure to include specific historical details. You must also include additional information from your knowledge of global history.

   Note: **The rubric for this essay appears in the Preparing for the Regents section of this book.**

6 Crises and Achievements (1900–1945)

UNIT OVERVIEW

Science and technology brought many benefits to society in the late 1800s and early 1900s. In most industrialized countries, life expectancy increased and standards of living rose. People became hopeful, for they had experienced peace for many years. However, the forces of nationalism, militarism, and imperialism were moving the world toward war. By the time World War I was over, people understood how science and technology could change their lives in negative ways. The war caused new social and economic problems. In Russia, a communist revolution produced a totalitarian state. Perhaps worst of all, the problems that had led to World War I remained unresolved. A second global conflict erupted in 1939, resulting in even greater destruction than the first.

THEMATIC TIME LINE ACTIVITY

Some of the many themes developed in Unit 6 are:

change	nationalism	human rights
science and technology	political systems	economic systems
culture and intellectual life	power	

Choose one of the themes listed above. As you review Unit 6, create a thematic time line based on the theme you have chosen. Your time line should stretch from 1900 to 1945 and include major developments and key turning points having to do with your theme.

Scientific and Technological Achievements

SECTION OVERVIEW

In the late 1800s and early 1900s, advances in science and technology led to dramatic changes in daily life. Medical discoveries and better sanitation allowed people to live longer, contributing to a population explosion. New inventions revolutionized energy production, communications, and transportation. Scientific discoveries led to new knowledge about the universe and the workings of the human mind.

KEY THEMES AND CONCEPTS

As you review this section, take special note of the following key themes and concepts:

Change How did medical advances in the late 1800s affect life expectancy and population growth?

Science and Technology How did the scientific discoveries of the late 1800s and early 1900s change the way people lived?

Culture and Intellectual Life How did new theories affect the ways in which people thought about their world?

KEY PEOPLE AND TERMS

As you review this section, be sure you understand the significance of these key people and terms:

Louis Pasteur	dynamo	Marie Curie
germ theory	Thomas Edison	Albert Einstein
antibiotic	radioactivity	Sigmund Freud

ADVANCES IN MEDICINE

In the late 1800s and early 1900s, a series of discoveries revolutionized the field of medicine. These medical advances greatly improved health care and increased human life expectancy.

⭐ **THE BIG IDEA**
In the late 1800s and early 1900s:

- new medical technology increased life expectancy.

- inventions and reforms improved the standard of living and made daily life easier.

- scientific discoveries led to new ways of thinking about the universe and the human mind.

The Germ Theory and Disease

Before the mid-1800s, the cause of disease was not clear, even to physicians. However, by the late 1800s, scientists were making great progress in this area.

LOUIS PASTEUR In the 1600s, a Dutch scientist named Anton van Leeuwenhoek had discovered the existence of microbes, or germs, by using a microscope. He did not, however, recognize the role of these tiny organisms in causing disease.

In 1870, French scientist **Louis Pasteur** made two very important discoveries. He showed clearly the link between germs and disease. He also proved that killing certain germs stops the spread of certain diseases.

ROBERT KOCH In the 1880s, the German physician Robert Koch discovered the bacteria that caused tuberculosis. His discovery started the long process of developing a cure for this deadly disease. The work of Pasteur and Koch established the **germ theory** of disease, the idea that many diseases are caused by the action of microorganisms. After people learned about the germ theory, they washed more often and made other lifestyle changes to limit the spread of disease.

Joseph Lister and Antiseptics

Before the mid-1800s, even a very minor surgical operation might be followed by infection and even death. An English surgeon named Joseph Lister became convinced that germs caused these infections. Lister insisted that doctors use antiseptics—substances that destroy or inhibit the growth of germs—on their hands, on their instruments, and on wounds. Lister's discoveries were a turning point in medicine, and they greatly reduced the number of deaths from infection in hospitals.

Antibiotics

In 1928, another turning point in medicine occurred. English scientist Alexander Fleming discovered that a mold called *Penicillium* killed germs. This discovery paved the way for the development of a class of drugs called **antibiotics** that attacked or weakened the bacteria that cause many diseases. Antibiotics were not widely developed and used, however, until the 1940s.

KEY THEMES AND CONCEPTS

Change The acceptance of the germ theory was a great step forward for medical science. Once microscopic organisms were recognized as a major cause of disease, scientists could move ahead in curing and preventing many deadly diseases.

IMPROVED STANDARD OF LIVING

The advances of the late 1800s and early 1900s extended beyond the field of medicine. The standard of living of most Europeans began to rise.

Better Wages and Working Conditions

In the early years of the Industrial Revolution, workers had found it difficult to improve their harsh job conditions. By the late 1800s, however, labor unions became legal in many countries of Europe.

 PREPARING FOR THE REGENTS

How did reforms of the late 1800s and early 1900s affect the average quality of people's lives?

Unions, reformers, and working-class voters pushed for better working conditions and higher wages. Over time, wages improved. People ate more varied diets and lived in cleaner, safer homes. Reform laws regulated working conditions and provided social benefits to the elderly and the unemployed.

Better Housing

Urban conditions were improving in the late 1800s and early 1900s. City governments paved their streets, making cities better places to live. Housing improved. Architects began to use steel to construct stronger, taller buildings.

Improved Sanitation

Underground sewage systems, introduced first in London and Paris, made cities healthier places to live. With underground systems, waste no longer ran through the streets, spreading disease and polluting sources of drinking water. A supply of clean water was necessary to combat diseases such as tuberculosis and cholera. Death rates were dramatically cut after the introduction of the new sewer systems.

New Inventions

A tremendous number of new inventions appeared in the late 1800s and early 1900s. These inventions improved daily life in many ways.

USE OF ELECTRICITY Early in the 1800s, Alessandro Volta and Michael Faraday had discovered how to produce small amounts of electricity. The later development of the **dynamo** enabled the generation of large amounts of electricity and made electricity a useful source of power. In 1879, an American inventor named **Thomas Edison** developed the first practical light bulb. Soon cities had electric street lights. By the 1890s, factories were powered by electricity. In homes, people used electricity to run appliances that made their lives more comfortable.

 PREPARING FOR THE REGENTS

Describe an effect on daily life of each of these inventions.

Electricity:

Telephone:

Radio:

Automobile:

Technology of the Industrial Age

INVENTOR OR DEVELOPER	NATION	INVENTION OR DEVELOPMENT	YEAR
Henry Bessemer	Britain	Process to turn iron ore into steel	1856
Alexander Graham Bell	United States	Telephone	1876
Thomas Edison	United States	Electric light bulb	1879
Gottlieb Daimler	Germany	Automobile	1887
Henry Ford	United States	Mass-produced automobile	1903
Orville & Wilbur Wright	United States	Airplane	1903

THE TELEPHONE   In 1876, Alexander Graham Bell patented the telephone. His machine changed the human voice into electrical impulses, sent them through a wire, and then changed them back into sounds at the other end. The invention of the telephone transformed long-distance communication.

RADIO   The telephone was an important means of communication, but it depended on wires. Guglielmo Marconi, in 1895, sent radio signals directly through the air. The first radios transmitted Morse code signals. The year 1906 marked the first voice broadcast over radio.

THE AUTOMOBILE   Inventions also transformed transportation in the last half of the 1800s. In the 1870s, Nikolaus Otto developed a gasoline-powered internal combustion engine. In the 1880s, Gottlieb Daimler used Otto's engine to power the first automobile. By 1900, thousands of automobiles were on the roads of Europe and North America. Henry Ford's development of the assembly line for the mass production of automobiles made the United States a strong leader in the auto industry.

THE AIRPLANE   The internal combustion engine also allowed humans to fly. In 1903, Orville and Wilbur Wright made the first powered flight.

POPULATION EXPLOSION

In many ways, new technology made life healthier, safer, and easier. As a result, fewer children died, and the average life expectancy increased. In other words, people lived longer. Because of these changes, populations grew dramatically.

✐ PREPARING FOR THE REGENTS

Practice your graph skills by answering the following questions.

1. About how many people lived in Great Britain in 1801?

2. What was the approximate population of Great Britain in 1901?

3. What were the causes of the population changes shown in these two graphs?

Western Populations in the Late 1800s

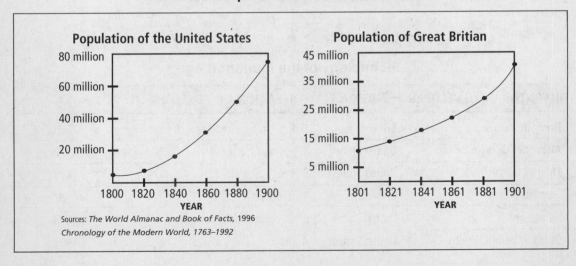

Sources: *The World Almanac and Book of Facts,* 1996
Chronology of the Modern World, 1763–1992

NEW SCIENTIFIC THEORIES

While some scientists were developing knowledge and inventions that improved the quality of daily life, others were exploring the universe and the workings of the human mind.

The Curies and Radioactivity

Just before the turn of the century, French scientist Marie Curie was experimenting with **radioactivity,** a powerful form of energy released by certain substances. Working with her husband, Pierre, **Marie Curie** discovered two new radioactive elements that the Curies called radium and polonium. The discoveries of these scientists had enormous effects on fields such as energy production, medicine, and military technology.

Einstein and Relativity

In 1905, the German-born physicist **Albert Einstein** announced his theory of relativity. This theory revolutionized scientific thought. It proposed that space and time measurements are not absolute but are determined by many factors, some of which are not known. Einstein's work caused many people to question the common view of the universe as a machine that worked by easily understood laws.

Freud and the Human Mind

During the same period, an Austrian physician named **Sigmund Freud** was questioning basic ideas about the human mind. He believed that a part of the mind, which he called the unconscious, drives much of human behavior. Freud felt that the tension between the drives of the unconscious mind and the demands of civilized society caused psychological and physical illness. Freud pioneered psychoanalysis, a new way of thinking about and treating mental illness.

SUMMARY

Scientific and technological advances brought many changes in the late 1800s and early 1900s. Improvements in medicine and sanitation led to a higher life expectancy, which caused an increase in population. People's lives were made easier by inventions such as electrical appliances, the telephone, and automobiles. In other areas of science, theories about the universe and the human mind shook ideas that had once been commonly accepted.

 PREPARING FOR THE REGENTS

What benefits have resulted from the use of radioactive elements? What problems have resulted?

 PREPARING FOR THE REGENTS

The theories of both Einstein and Freud had an unsettling effect on many people of the time. The idea of a powerful unconscious mind or a universe without absolute laws disturbed many.

 PREPARING FOR THE REGENTS

Write a short paragraph about whether you think that science and technology bring more problems or more benefits into people's lives.

SECTION 2 World War I

⭐ THE BIG IDEA
World War I:

- was caused by nationalism, militarism, imperialism, and alliance systems.
- was sparked in the Balkans and blossomed into a global war.
- was fought with highly destructive weapons, made possible by modern technology.
- resulted in enormous human and economic losses.

SECTION OVERVIEW

As the 1900s began, the people of Europe had enjoyed nearly a century of relative peace. At the same time, forces were pushing the continent toward war. Nationalistic feeling, a glorification of the military, imperial rivalries, and tangled alliances led to unrest. War was sparked in the Balkans, where the Ottoman empire had once maintained control. Soon all of Europe was at war. Industrialization and technology had allowed nations to develop more destructive weapons that resulted in millions of deaths. As Russia left the war and the United States entered, the Allies gained control and an armistice was signed. The costs of World War I were enormous.

KEY THEMES AND CONCEPTS

As you review this section, take special note of the following key themes and concepts:

Nationalism and Imperialism What role did nationalism and imperialism play in causing World War I?

Diversity How did ethnic diversity in the Balkans contribute to starting the war?

Science and Technology What impact did innovations in science and technology have on World War I?

KEY PEOPLE AND TERMS

As you review this section, be sure you understand the significance of these key people and terms:

militarism	total war
Bosnia	propaganda
Archduke Francis Ferdinand	neutral
Central Powers	armistice
Allied Powers	reparations
trench warfare	

CAUSES

Although the world seemed at peace in the early 1900s, powerful forces were pushing Europe toward war. These forces included nationalism, militarism, imperial rivalries, alliance systems, and the decline of the Ottoman empire.

Nationalism

As you have learned, nationalism can bring people together. It can also, however, be a source of conflict. In Europe in the early 1900s, aggressive nationalism was a source of tension.

GERMANY AND FRANCE Nationalism was strong in both Germany and France. Germany, now unified, was proud of its growing military and industrial strength. France, meanwhile, wanted to regain its position as a leading European power. It had lost the Franco-Prussian War in 1871. Besides having to pay money to Germany, France lost the provinces of Alsace and Lorraine. Many of the French people wanted revenge on Germany.

PAN-SLAVISM Russia had encouraged a form of nationalism in Eastern Europe called Pan-Slavism. The movement tried to draw together all Slavic peoples. Russia was the largest Slavic country, and it was ready to defend Serbia, a young Slavic nation in the Balkans. Throughout the Balkans, in fact, small Slavic populations looked to Russia for leadership in their desire for unity. The multinational empire of Austria-Hungary opposed Slavic national movements.

Militarism

During the late 1800s, **militarism,** the glorification of military power, arose in many nations of Europe. This development led to fear and suspicion as nations became more willing to use military force to attain their national goals. There was an arms race, in which the great powers competed with each other to expand their armies and navies. One of the fiercest rivalries was between Britain and Germany.

Imperialism and Economic Rivalry

Britain, France, Germany, and other nations competed for colonies and economic power. France and Germany competed especially for colonial gains in Africa. Britain and Germany competed industrially. Germany had industrialized rapidly, and the British felt threatened by this. Because of their mutual competition with Germany, Britain and France began to form close ties with each other.

Alliance Systems

Increased tensions and suspicions led nations to form alliances. Nations agreed to defend each other in case of attack. By 1914, there were several alliances. The two most important were the Triple Alliance and

**♀ KEY THEMES AND
⊩ CONCEPTS**
Nationalism National rivalry between Germany and France contributed to tensions in Europe. Nationalist movements in the diverse Ottoman empire also created unrest, especially in the Balkan peninsula of southeastern Europe.

**♀ KEY THEMES AND
⊩ CONCEPTS**
Conflict European nations competed for territory in Africa and Asia. This competition led to added rivalries between European nations.

the Triple Entente. The triple Alliance consisted of Germany, Austria-Hungary, and Italy. The Triple Entente consisted of Britain, France, and Russia.

Decline of the Ottoman Empire

Other situations also set the stage for war. The Ottoman empire had become weak. British relations with the empire became strained after Britain signed an agreement with Russia. Germany, on the other hand, had taken an interest in establishing good relations with the Ottoman empire.

THE ARMENIAN MASSACRES   Nationalistic feelings had caused periodic waves of violence against Armenians since the 1890s. New violence was a brutal result of the rivalry between Turkey, which ruled the Ottoman empire, and Russia. The Muslim Turks distrusted the Christian Armenians, believing that they supported Russia against the Ottoman empire. When Armenians protested oppressive Ottoman policies, the Turks unleashed a massacre on the Armenians. Additional massacres leading to the deaths of a million or more Armenians occurred over the next 25 years.

THE BALKAN POWDER KEG   The Ottoman empire's control over the Balkans had weakened over time. Serbia declared its independence in 1878, hoping to build a Slavic state in alliance with Russia. Serbia wanted control of **Bosnia** and Herzegovina, two provinces that would give landlocked Serbia an outlet to the Adriatic Sea. These provinces, however, were Ottoman provinces administered by Austria-Hungary. Austria opposed Serbian ambitions, fearing that the same kind of nationalism would spread to its own multinational empire. Also, Austria-Hungary feared Russian expansion.

Tensions grew, and in 1912, Serbia and its allies attacked the Ottoman empire. The great European powers were all interested in gaining lands from the crumbling empire. By 1914, the Balkans were known as the "powder keg of Europe." Any small spark was likely to lead to an explosion.

THE WAR BEGINS

The Balkan Crisis

Not surprisingly, World War I began in the Balkans. Although many Serbs lived in Bosnia, it was still ruled by Austria-Hungary. Serb nationalists felt that Bosnia belonged to Serbia.

Archduke Francis Ferdinand was the heir to the Austrian throne. On June 28, 1914, the duke and his wife were traveling through Sarajevo, the capital of Bosnia. Gavrilo Princip, a member of a radical Slavic nationalist group that opposed Austrian rule, shot and killed the archduke and his wife.

PREPARING FOR THE REGENTS

Summarize how each of the following contributed to World War I.

Nationalism:

Militarism:

Imperialism and economic rivalry:

Alliance systems:

Decline of the Ottoman empire:

A Chain Reaction

After the assassination, the major nations of Europe responded. Each hostile action led to another hostile action.

1. Austria-Hungary blamed Serbia for the murders of the archduke and his wife and made harsh demands in Serbia.

2. Serbia refused to comply with any of the demands.

3. Austria-Hungary declared war on Serbia on July 28.

4. Russia, a Slavic nation and a friend of Serbia, mobilized its forces in preparation for war.

5. Germany, an ally of Austria-Hungary, declared war on Russia.

6. Germany declared war on France, an ally of Russia.

7. Germany invaded Belgium on August 3, 1914, so that German forces could enter France more easily.

8. Britain declared war on Germany.

Central Powers and Allied Powers

The two opposing sides in World War I were the Central Powers and the Allied Powers. The **Central Powers** were Germany, Austria-Hungary, and the Ottoman empire (later joined by Bulgaria). On the other side were the **Allied Powers:** Britain, France, and Russia. Italy at first remained neutral, but it eventually joined the Allies. Other nations, including the United States, also joined the Allies later.

There were three major fronts in Europe where fighting occurred. The Western Front extended across Belgium and northeastern France to the border of Switzerland. The Eastern Front ran from the Baltic Sea to

KEY THEMES AND CONCEPTS

Diversity Serb nationalism led to the assassination of Archduke Francis Ferdinand. Slavic groups in the Ottoman empire hoped to unite and throw off the rule of Austria-Hungary.

PREPARING FOR THE REGENTS

Study the graphic organizer and review the chain reaction of events that occurred in 1914. Which nation or group do you think was to blame for World War I? Explain.

World War I: Who Was to Blame?

Germany
• Felt it must stand behind its ally, Austria-Hungary

Austria-Hungary
• Blamed Serbia for terrorism
• Wanted to crush Serbian nationalism

Russia
• Supported Slavic people
• Feared Austria-Hungary wanted to rule Slavic people

Who was to blame for World War I?

Britain
• Felt a duty to protect Belgium
• Feared power of Germany just across English Channel

France
• Backed Russia
• Felt it might someday need Russian support against Germany

PREPARING FOR THE REGENTS

List the members of the Central Powers and the Allied Powers.

Central Powers:

Allied Powers:

the Black Sea. The Southern Front ran between Italy and Austria-Hungary. Fighting also took place in Africa and the Middle East.

AN INDUSTRIALIZED WAR

World War I was a war between groups of major industrial powers. New technology made this war an enormously destructive one. For example, Swedish chemist Alfred Nobel had invented dynamite in 1867. Used in mining and construction, it also became important in weaponry. Many of the other recent inventions of the time—the internal combustion engine, the airplane, and communications devices—were also put to military use.

Trench Warfare

Heavy fighting took place along the Western Front, a 600-mile stretch from the English Channel to Switzerland. The Germans hoped to win an early victory there, but French and British troops stopped them. For four years, neither side could make any significant gains.

Trench warfare began, so called because the troops dug trenches along the front. Very little ground was gained by either side in this way, and many soldiers were killed.

 PREPARING FOR THE REGENTS

What role did technology play in World War I?

New Air and Sea Weapons

World War I was the first war to make full use of modern technology and machinery. Technology changed methods of warfare greatly.

Technology Changes Warfare

Invention	Description	Use in World War I
Automatic machine gun	Mounted gun that fires a rapid, continuous stream of bullets.	Made it possible for a few gunners to mow down waves of soldiers.
Tank	Armored vehicle that travels on a track and can cross many kinds of land.	Protected advancing troops as they broke through enemy defenses. Early tanks were slow and clumsy.
Submarine	Underwater ship that can launch torpedoes, or guided underwater bombs.	Used by Germany to destroy Allied ships. Submarine attacks helped bring United States into war.
Airplane	One- or two-seat propeller plane equipped with machine gun or bombs.	At first, mainly used for observation. Later, flying "aces" engaged in air combat.
Poison gas; gas mask	Gases that cause choking, blinding, or severe skin blisters; gas masks can protect soldiers from poison gas.	Lobbed into enemy trenches, killing or disabling troops. Gas masks lessened the importance of poison gas.

CIVILIAN LIFE AND TOTAL WAR

The war was fought at home as well as on the battlefield. A war fought in this way is called a **total war.** In a total war, all of a nation's resources go into the war effort.

- Governments drafted men to fight in the war.
- Governments raised taxes and borrowed money to pay for the war.
- Governments rationed, or limited the supply of, goods at home so that the military could be provided for.
- Governments used the press to print **propaganda,** the spreading of ideas to promote a cause or to damage an opposing cause.
- Women at home took jobs that the soldiers had left behind. Some women joined the armed services. Other women went to the fronts as nurses.

MAJOR TURNING POINTS OF THE WAR

Several events that took place during World War I are seen as major turning points. They include the withdrawal of Russia from the war and the entry of the United States into the war.

Entry of the United States

Although the United States had allowed American ships to carry supplies to the Allies, the country had tried to remain **neutral** (not supporting either side) in the war. In 1917, however, Germany used unrestricted submarine warfare, meaning that it attacked any ships on the Atlantic, even if they were carrying American passengers. This policy brought the United States into the war in April 1917. The entry of the Americans helped the Allies win the war.

Russian Withdrawal

In Russia, low morale contributed to a revolution in 1917. Early in 1918, Russia's new leader signed a treaty with Germany that took Russia out of the war.

COSTS OF THE WAR

On November 11, 1918, an **armistice,** or an agreement to end the fighting, was declared. The costs of World War I were enormous. It would take many years for people and nations to recover.

Human Casualties

The costs of the war in terms of human lives were staggering.
- More than 8.5 million people had died.
- More than 17 million had been wounded.
- Famine threatened many regions.
- Disease was widespread in many regions.

KEY THEMES AND CONCEPTS

Interdependence Why did the United States enter World War I? How was the entry of the United States a turning point?

PREPARING FOR THE REGENTS

To learn more about the Russian Revolution, see Section 3 of this unit.

PREPARING FOR THE REGENTS

Based on the pie graph, which nation or groups of nations among the Allies spent the most money on World War I?

Percentage of Money Spent by Allies

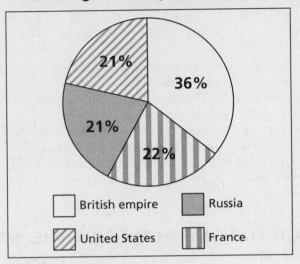

Economic Losses

All over the world, there were also economic and political losses.

- Factories, farms, and homes had been destroyed.
- Nations had huge war debts to repay.
- The Allies, bitter at the destruction, insisted that the Central Powers make **reparations,** payments for war damage they had caused.

 PREPARING FOR THE REGENTS

In what way was World War I a turning point in global history?

SUMMARY

Nationalism, militarism, imperialism, and political rivalries led to World War I. In the Balkans, what began as a local incident blossomed into a global war. Industrialization and new technology made the weapons of World War I much more destructive than any that had been used before. The war caused great human and economic losses.

3 Revolution in Russia: Causes and Impacts

SECTION OVERVIEW

Factors such as dissatisfaction with czarist rule, peasant unrest, and economic difficulties created long-term discontent in Russia. After a revolution in 1905, Czar Nicholas II agreed to reforms, but they failed to solve underlying problems. Hardships caused by World War I sparked a revolution that ended Nicholas's reign. Promises of peace, land, and bread allowed Vladimir Lenin and his Bolsheviks, later called Communists, to gain control of the country. After Lenin's death, Joseph Stalin created a communist dictatorship that controlled every aspect of people's lives. He brought the economy completely under government control. Stalin industrialized the country, focusing on heavy industry. Stalin also brought agriculture under state control, causing mass starvation in the process.

KEY THEMES AND CONCEPTS

As you review this section, take special note of the following key themes and concepts:

Change Why did the Russian people demand change in 1917?

Power How did the Bolsheviks take control of the Russian government from the czar?

Human Rights What was life like in Stalin's totalitarian state?

Economic Systems How did Stalin's command economy affect the Soviet Union's industry and agriculture?

KEY PEOPLE AND TERMS

As you review this section, be sure you understand the significance of these key people and terms:

soviet	New Economic Policy	command economy
Vladimir Lenin	Joseph Stalin	five-year plan
Bolshevik	totalitarian state	collective

⭐ **THE BIG IDEA**
Revolution brought major changes to Russia. In the early 1900s:

- dissatisfaction with czarist rule, peasant unrest, and economic problems led to revolution.

- Bolsheviks under Lenin took control of the Russian government during World War I.

- Stalin created a communist dictatorship that controlled every aspect of its citizens' lives.

- Stalin's economic policies brought industrialization and widespread starvation to Russia.

LONG-TERM CAUSES OF REVOLUTION

A variety of factors had been leading up to revolution in Russia for a long time. Through the 1800s and early 1900s, discontent grew as Russian czars resisted needed reforms.

Czarist Rule

In the late 1800s, Alexander III and his son, Nicholas II, sought to industrialize the country and build Russia's economic strength. Although these czars wanted to import western industrialization, they hoped to block the ideals of the French Revolution. Still, Russian liberals called for a constitution and reforms that would eliminate corruption in government. Both Alexander and Nicholas used harsh tactics, such as the use of secret police, to suppress reform.

Peasant Unrest

A rigid system of social classes still existed in Russia at the beginning of World War I. Landowning nobles, priests, and an autocratic czar dominated society. A small middle class was prevented from gaining power.

Peasants faced many difficulties. Most were too poor to buy the land they worked. Even those who owned land often did not have enough to feed their families. Even though industrialization had proceeded slowly, it had angered some peasants. Some opposed it because they feared the changes it brought and preferred the old ways.

Problems of Urban Workers

Some peasants had moved to cities and found jobs in new industries. They worked long hours, and their pay was low. Most lived in slums that were nests of poverty and disease. It was among these workers that socialists spread ideas about revolution and reform.

Diversity and Nationalism

Russia ruled a vast and diverse empire. It included many ethnic minorities. The czars maintained strict control over these groups. Under the policy of Russification, czars attempted to make all in their empire think, act, and believe as Russians. However, ethnic minorities did not want their native cultures destroyed. Pockets of nationalism remained.

REVOLUTION OF 1905

On Sunday, January 22, 1905, a march occurred in St. Petersburg. The peaceful marchers hoped to influence the czar for reform. Nicholas II, fearing an uprising, called in soldiers. The soldiers shot and killed many of the marchers. "Bloody Sunday," as it was called, destroyed the people's faith and trust in the czar. After Bloody Sunday, strikes and revolts exploded across Russia's cities and countryside.

PREPARING FOR THE REGENTS

To learn more about the czars' policies in the 1800s, see Unit 5, Section 3.

KEY THEMES AND CONCEPTS

Economic Systems Russia had not industrialized fully enough to enjoy the benefits that industrialization can bring. Partial industrialization had not brought economic prosperity or a better standard of living to most people. The Russian middle class remained small and relatively powerless.

PREPARING FOR THE REGENTS

Within each of the categories listed below, describe one specific condition that contributed to revolutionary feelings in Russia.

Czarist rule:

Peasant unrest:

Problems of urban workers:

Diversity and nationalism:

The Russian Revolution of 1905

CAUSES
- Low spirits after defeat in 1904 war with Japan
- Poverty and bad working conditions
- Corrupt government
- Persecution of minority groups
- "Bloody Sunday" killings

Russian Revolution of 1905

RESULTS
- The "October Manifesto"– Czar Nicholas II announces reforms and new freedoms
- Nicholas II sets up the Duma, which must approve all laws
- Nicholas II dissolves the first Duma when its leaders criticize the government
- Pogroms continue
- New voting laws limit powers of later Dumas

 PREPARING FOR THE REGENTS

The 1904 war referred to in this chart is the Russo-Japanese War. How did the Russo-Japanese War contribute to revolution in Russia? To learn more about this conflict, see Unit 5, Section 6.

In the face of this chaos, Nicholas made some changes. He agreed to reforms and promised to grant more rights, such as freedom of speech. He agreed to set up an elected national legislature, the Duma. However, the Duma had limited powers and did little to relieve peasant and worker discontent.

WORLD WAR I AND THE END OF CZARIST RULE

A Nation in Chaos
As you have learned, Russia was one of the Allied Powers in World War I. With little industry, however, Russia was not ready to fight a modern war. Russian soldiers lacked adequate weapons and supplies, and Russia suffered a series of battlefield defeats. Food was scarce. Many soldiers lost confidence in Russia's military leadership and deserted.

The March Revolution
In March 1917, military defeats and shortages of food, fuel, and housing in Russia sparked a revolt. In the capital city, St. Petersburg, rioters in the streets demanded bread. The czar's soldiers sympathized with the demonstrators and refused to fire on them. With no control over his

troops and with the country nearing anarchy, Czar Nicholas II abdicated, or gave up his rule, in March 1917.

Failure of the Provisional Government

After the removal of the czar, Duma officials set up a provisional, or temporary, government. Middle-class liberals in the government planned to write a constitution and promised democratic reforms. However, the provisional government continued the war against Germany, an unpopular decision that drained away men and resources. The new government implemented only moderate reforms that did little to end unrest among peasants and workers.

THE BOLSHEVIK REVOLUTION

The provisional government's slowness to bring about meaningful change led revolutionary socialists to plot further actions. They set up **soviets,** or councils of workers and soldiers, in Russian cities. At first, these soviets worked within the system set up by the government. Soon, however, they were taken over by a radical socialist party.

Lenin Gains Support

Following the March Revolution, an exiled Russian revolutionary named **Vladimir Lenin** returned home. Lenin and Leon Trotsky headed a revolutionary socialist party, the **Bolsheviks.** Lenin and Trotsky followed the ideas of Karl Marx, but they adapted them to the Russian situation. For example, Marx had said that the urban workers would rise on their own to overthrow the capitalist system. Russia, however, did not have a large urban working class. Lenin therefore suggested that an elite group of reformers—the Bolsheviks—would guide the revolution in Russia.

Lenin gained the support of many people by making promises of "Peace, Land, and Bread." The Bolsheviks promised an end to Russia's involvement in the war. They promised land reform and an end to food shortages.

Lenin Takes Over

The provisional government had lost the support of the people. In November 1917, the Bolsheviks led soldiers, sailors, and factory workers in an uprising that overthrew the government. The Bolsheviks, now called Communists, distributed land to the peasants and gave workers control of the factories and mines. The Communists, however, still faced a struggle to maintain control over Russia.

LENIN RULES RUSSIA

Withdrawal From World War I

Lenin moved quickly to end Russian involvement in World War I. In March 1918, Russia signed the Treaty of Brest-Litovsk. The agreement was costly for Russia, giving Germany a large amount of Russian territory. Lenin, however, believed that he needed to make peace with Germany at any price so that he could deal with his enemies at home.

Russia's Civil War

From 1918 to 1921, Lenin's Red Army battled against forces loyal to the czar, called the Whites. Nationalist groups in the Russian empire also rose up against the Red Army at this time, winning independence for Estonia, Latvia, Lithuania, and Poland.

Both sides used brutal tactics during the war. The Whites slaughtered Communists and tried to assassinate Lenin. The Communists employed a secret police force to root out their enemies. They executed thousands who were suspected of opposing the revolution. To eliminate a potential rallying symbol for the Whites, Communists executed Czar Nicholas II and his entire family.

Britain, France, and the United States sent troops to help the Whites. This foreign intervention, however, stirred Russian nationalism. An inspired Red Army, under Trotsky's leadership, defeated its enemies by 1921.

One-Party Government

Lenin's government had a constitution and an elected legislature. However, the Communist Party, not the people themselves, had the real

KEY THEMES AND CONCEPTS

Nationalism Long-term Russian repression of nationalist groups created an anti-Russian reaction during Russia's civil war, when nationalist groups rose up to demand their own nation-states.

PREPARING FOR THE REGENTS

Lenin is the figure with the broom at the top of this poster. What is the point of the poster? Whom do the other figures represent?

ТОВ. Ленин ОЧИЩАЕТ ЗЕМЛЮ ОТ НЕЧИСТИ.

KEY THEMES AND CONCEPTS

Political Systems How is communist government different from democratic government?

KEY THEMES AND CONCEPTS

Economic Systems The private ownership allowed by the New Economic Policy helped the Soviet economy to recover. Even in the early years, socialist economic policies met with limited success in the Soviet Union.

PREPARING FOR THE REGENTS

Describe five specific ways in which Stalin failed to respect the human rights of Russians and minority national groups in the Soviet Union.

1.

2.

3.

4.

5.

power. The Communist Party was the only legal party, and only its members could run for office. The Party enforced its will through the military and a secret police force.

New Economic Policy

During Russia's civil war, Bolshevik leaders had taken over banks, mines, factories, and railroads. This takeover had resulted in economic disaster. In 1921, Lenin adopted the **New Economic Policy.** Under this plan, also called the NEP, the government still controlled banks, large industry, and foreign trade. Some privately owned businesses were allowed, however. These helped the economy to recover.

The Soviet Union

By 1922, Lenin and the Communists had gained control over much of the old Russian empire. The Communist government then created the Union of Soviet Socialist Republics, also called the Soviet Union. It was made up of diverse European and Asian peoples. Russia, the largest republic, controlled the other states in the Soviet Union.

STALIN AND COMMUNIST DICTATORSHIP

Lenin died in 1924, ending the reign of Russia's first Communist leader. A new Soviet leader, **Joseph Stalin,** emerged. Stalin ruled through terror and brutality. In the 1930s, for example, out of fear that other Communist Party members were plotting against him, Stalin launched the Great Purge. During the Great Purge, Stalin accused thousands of people of crimes against the government. Many of the accused were executed; others were exiled or sent to prison camps. For the next 20 years, he pursued ruthless policies that created a totalitarian state in the Soviet Union.

Totalitarian Rule

Stalin turned the Soviet Union into a **totalitarian state.** In this form of government, a one-party dictatorship attempts to regulate every aspect of the lives of its citizens.

Russification

Early in his rule, Stalin promoted individual local cultures. By the end of the 1920s, however, he had changed this policy. Stalin became a strong Russian nationalist. He began to create a Russian ruling elite throughout the Soviet Union. Like the czars before him, Stalin pursued a policy of Russification.

- He promoted Russian history, language, and culture, sometimes forbidding the cultural practices of native peoples.
- He appointed Russians to key posts in the government and secret police.
- He redrew the boundaries of many republics to ensure that non-Russians would not gain a majority.

Life in a Totalitarian State

Economics	Politics	Arts	Religion	Society
• Growth of industry • Growth of military • Low standard of living • Shortage of foods and consumer goods	• One-party dictatorship • Total government control of citizens • Total government control of industry and agriculture • Use of propaganda to win government support	• Censorship of books, music, art • Purpose of all art to praise communism • Observation of artists, writers, and musicians by secret police	• Government war on religion • Takeover of houses of worship • Secret police control religious worship • Communist ideals replace religious ideals	• Fear of secret police • An upper class of Communist Party members • Free education and health care • Public transportation and recreation • Jobs for women

A Command Economy

Stalin established a **command economy,** in which government officials made all basic economic decisions. Under Stalin, the government controlled all factories, businesses, and farms.

INDUSTRIALIZATION   One of Stalin's chief goals was to make the Soviet Union strong by turning it into a modern industrial power. In 1928, Stalin launched the first of a series of **five-year plans** to build industry and increase farm output. Emphasis was placed on heavy industry, while consumer goods were neglected. In the 1930s, Soviet production in oil, coal, steel, mining, and military goods increased. Across the nation, factories, hydroelectric power stations, and railroads were built.

Despite this progress, however, most Russians remained poor and endured a low standard of living. Soviet central planning created shortages in consumer goods. Also, to meet high production quotas, many factories mass-produced goods of low quality.

COLLECTIVIZATION   Stalin forced peasants to give up their small farms and live on state-owned farms or on **collectives,** which were large farms owned and operated by peasants as a group. The collective owned all farm animals and equipment. The government controlled prices and farm supplies and set production quotas. Stalin's plan was for the collectives to grow enough grain for the workers in the cities and to produce surplus grain to sell abroad.

Many peasants resisted collectivization. They killed farm animals, destroyed tools, and burned crops. Stalin responded with a ruthless policy aimed at crushing all who opposed him. The government seized the land of those who resisted and sent the farmers to prison labor camps. There, many died from overwork or were executed.

FORCED FAMINE   The results of Stalin's policies were devastating. Some peasants continued to resist by growing just enough grain to feed

⚲ KEY THEMES AND CONCEPTS

Economic Systems In a command economy, the state controls all factories and businesses and makes all economic decisions. In a capitalist economy, businesses are privately owned and operated for a profit. The free market controls economic decisions.

⚲ KEY THEMES AND CONCEPTS

Power When peasants resisted Stalin's plan of collectivization, he ruthlessly eliminated them through starvation.

First Leaders of the Soviet Union

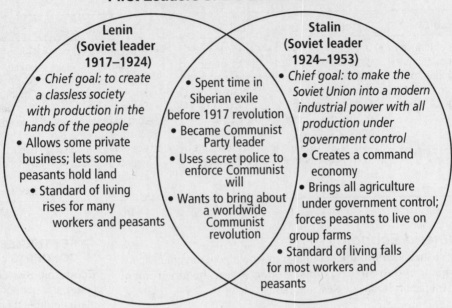

Lenin
(Soviet leader
1917–1924)

- *Chief goal: to create a classless society with production in the hands of the people*
- Allows some private business; lets some peasants hold land
- Standard of living rises for many workers and peasants

- Spent time in Siberian exile before 1917 revolution
- Became Communist Party leader
- Uses secret police to enforce Communist will
- Wants to bring about a worldwide Communist revolution

Stalin
(Soviet leader
1924–1953)

- *Chief goal: to make the Soviet Union into a modern industrial power with all production under government control*
- Creates a command economy
- Brings all agriculture under government control; forces peasants to live on group farms
- Standard of living falls for most workers and peasants

PREPARING FOR THE REGENTS

Practice your chart-reading skills by answering the following questions.

1. What were two goals or practices that Lenin and Stalin held in common?

2. How did Stalin's chief goal differ from Lenin's?

PREPARING FOR THE REGENTS

To what extent was the Russian Revolution a turning point in global history?

themselves. The government then seized all the grain of some of those communities. Mass starvation resulted. In the Ukraine, where opposition to collectivization was especially strong, more than five million people died from starvation. Millions more died in other parts of the Soviet Union.

SUMMARY

In the late 1800s and early 1900s, autocratic rule and poor economic conditions caused many Russians to demand political and social reforms. In 1917, this discontent led to a revolution that ended czarist rule in Russia. Bolshevik leader Vladimir Lenin gained power by promising better economic conditions and an end to Russian involvement in World War I. He then set up a communist government. After Lenin's death, Joseph Stalin took over and established a totalitarian state, in which every aspect of life was controlled. Stalin's five-year plans boosted industry but did little to improve the life of the average worker. His collectivization of agriculture angered peasants, whose resistance resulted in mass starvation.

SECTION 4   Between the Wars

SECTION OVERVIEW

After World War I, global problems remained. The Treaty of Versailles punished Germany. The League of Nations had little power. Old empires had collapsed, and new nations had come into being. Nationalism continued to cause conflict. World War I had disillusioned many, altered society, and prompted new forms of expression. In Europe and the United States, women struggled to gain the right to vote. Then, in 1929, the global economy crashed, leading to a worldwide depression. During this time, fascism, a new kind of dictatorship, rose in Italy and Germany. In Japan, aggressive military leaders gained power.

KEY THEMES AND CONCEPTS

As you review this section, take special note of the following key themes and concepts:

Interdependence   How did the major powers try to resolve troublesome issues after World War I?

Nationalism   What factors led to the nationalist movements of the 1920s and 1930s?

Human Rights   What rights did women gain after World War I?

Economic Systems   What were the causes and effects of the world economic crisis of the 1930s?

Political Systems   What are the major characteristics of fascism?

KEY PEOPLE AND TERMS

As you review this section, be sure you understand the significance of these key people and terms:

Treaty of Versailles	Pan-Arabism	fascism
League of Nations	Mohandas Gandhi	Benito Mussolini
Kemal Atatürk	civil disobedience	Adolf Hitler
Reza Khan	Guomindang	
mandate	Great Depression	

★ **THE BIG IDEA**
After World War I:

- the Treaty of Versailles severely punished Germany.

- new nations formed and old empires collapsed.

- nationalist movements struggled to throw off foreign domination.

- women gained the right to vote in many countries.

- the global economy experienced a severe downturn.

- fascist powers took control in Italy and Germany.

- militarists took power in Japan.

TREATY OF VERSAILLES

World War I had a lasting impact on international politics. In January 1919, the victorious Allies gathered at the palace of Versailles, outside Paris, to work out the terms of peace. United States President Woodrow Wilson and Prime Minister David Lloyd George of England joined French leader Georges Clemenceau. They were known as the "Big Three" of the meeting that would be called the Paris Peace Conference. These men had differing goals. Wilson stressed self-determination, by which people would choose their own government. He also hoped to create a world organization that would guarantee peace in the future. Britain and France wanted to punish Germany and be sure that it would never again become a threat.

Harsh Provisions for Germany

In the end, Britain's and France's ideas guided the **Treaty of Versailles.**

TERRITORIAL LOSSES   Land was taken from Germany. Some of it was used to help create the new country of Poland. Alsace and Lorraine were returned to France. Germany also lost many of its overseas colonies.

MILITARY RESTRICTIONS   Germany's army and navy were limited. Germany had to remove its troops from the Rhineland, an industrial area along the French border.

WAR GUILT   Germany had to accept full responsibility for the war and pay huge reparations, or large sums of money to help undo war damage. Accepting the blame and paying the reparations caused bitterness in Germany.

The League of Nations

The Treaty of Versailles also formed the **League of Nations,** a group of over 40 countries that hoped to settle problems through negotiation, not war. The countries that joined the League of Nations promised to take cooperative economic and military action against any aggressor state. Although the league had been Woodrow Wilson's concept, the United States never joined. Many Americans were afraid that participation in it would drag the United States into future European wars. In refusing to join, the United States weakened the League of Nations.

COLLAPSE OF EMPIRES

World War I caused the collapse of the Austro-Hungarian and Ottoman empires. New nations were carved out of their former territories.

Breakup of Austria-Hungary

As a result of the war, the government in Austria-Hungary had collapsed. Several new nations were created out of the former empire. Austria and

PREPARING FOR THE REGENTS

The Treaty of Versailles did not resolve the issues that had led to World War I. Nationalism continued to be a cause of conflict. German discontent with the Treaty of Versailles would help lead to World War II.

KEY THEMES AND CONCEPTS

Conflict How did the League of Nations plan to deal with international conflict in the future?

Europe After World War I

Hungary became independent nations. Czechoslovakia and Yugoslavia, two multinational states, were formed. Italy and Romania each gained land.

Breakup of the Ottoman Empire

The Ottoman empire, one of the defeated Central Powers, collapsed in 1918. Most of the Arab lands of the Ottoman empire were placed under the control of Britain and France. In theory these countries were being prepared for self-determination. In practice, however, the Allies added to their own overseas empires by creating a system of territories administered by western powers. The remainder of the empire became the country of Turkey.

UNFULFILLED NATIONAL GOALS

Many nations were dissatisfied with the results of World War I. Various groups felt that their goals had not been achieved.

 PREPARING FOR THE REGENTS

Practice your map skills by listing five nations that were created as a result of World War I.

1.

2.

3.

4.

5.

- Germany was horrified by the terms of the Treaty of Versailles.
- Italy had hoped to gain more land than it received. It had made a secret treaty with the Allies that was not fulfilled.
- Japan was angry because the Allies did not recognize its claims in China.
- China was angry that Japan had been given control over former German possessions in China.
- Russia was angry over the reestablishment of Poland and the creation of independent Estonia, Latvia, and Lithuania on lands that had been part of the Russian empire.

Nations and groups, however, waited and watched, hoping for a chance to change events in their favor.

NATIONAL MOVEMENTS

The spirit of nationalism continued after World War I. Nations in the Middle East, Africa, and Asia struggled for self-determination. In many cases, nationalists were influenced by western ideas. Even so, they were determined to throw off western rule.

Turkish Nationalism

KEMAL ATATÜRK Mustafa Kemal was a general and a war hero in Turkey. After World War I, he led a Turkish nationalist movement. He overthrew the sultan, defeated western occupation forces, and declared Turkey a republic. Mustafa Kemal later called himself **Kemal Atatürk.** The name *Atatürk* meant "father of the Turks."

WESTERNIZATION AND MODERNIZATION Atatürk wanted to modernize and westernize Turkey. He believed that Turkey had to change to survive. In accomplishing his goals, he introduced great changes.

- Islamic law was replaced with a new law code, based on European models.
- The Muslim calendar was replaced with the western (Christian) one.
- People were required to wear western dress.
- State schools were set up. Arabic script was replaced with the western (Latin) alphabet.
- Women no longer had to wear veils and were allowed to vote. They could work outside their homes.
- Turkey was industrialized. Atatürk built roads, railroads, and factories.

Iranian Nationalism

Nationalists in Iran followed Turkey's lead. In Iran, the British and the Russians had carved out spheres of influence. In 1925, **Reza Khan,** an army officer, overthrew the ruler of Iran, called the shah. He set up his

KEY THEMES AND CONCEPTS

Nationalism Mustafa Kemal wanted to unite Turks and throw off European domination. At the same time, he felt that Turkey must modernize and westernize to survive in the twentieth century.

PREPARING FOR THE REGENTS

Some Turkish Muslims rejected westernization, believing that it was a betrayal of Islam. This conflict continues today. The government of Turkey remains secular, but some Islamic groups work strongly for a return to traditional ways. For more information on Turkish Muslims today, see Unit 7, Section 5.

own dynasty and proclaimed himself shah. Reza Khan quickly tried to modernize and westernize Iran and make it fully independent. Factories, roads, and railroads were built. The army was strengthened. The western alphabet and western dress were adopted, and secular schools were set up. Islamic law was replaced by secular law, and women were encouraged to take part in public life. Reza Khan had the support of wealthy urban Iranians but not of Muslim religious leaders.

Arab Nationalism

During World War I, many Arabs had helped the Allies. In return they had been promised independence. After the war, however, Britain and France divided up the Ottoman lands between themselves. They set up **mandates,** territories administered by European powers. France had mandates in Syria and Lebanon. Britain had mandates in Palestine and Iraq.

In the 1920s and 1930s, Arab nationalists sought to be free of foreign control. Arab nationalism gave rise to **Pan-Arabism.** This movement sought a unity of all Arab peoples based on their shared heritage.

Zionism

Zionism, as you have learned, had arisen during the 1890s in Europe and the Middle East. Jewish people wanted to establish a Jewish state in Palestine. The situation was complex, however, since Arab peoples were already living there. The Allies had made conflicting promises during World War I. They had promised Arabs land that included Palestine. They had also pledged to set up a Jewish nation in the same region. As more Jews moved to Palestine to escape persecution in the 1930s, tensions grew.

Indian Nationalism

Nearly 1 million Indians had served the Allied cause in Europe during World War I, and many had died. At home, however, Indians had few rights. During World War I, Britain had promised India greater self-government. After the war was over, Britain failed to fulfill these promises.

THE AMRITSAR MASSACRE A turning point came in 1919. There were riots and attacks on British citizens in the city of Amritsar. In response, public meetings were banned. When a large group of Indians assembled on April 13, British troops fired on them without warning, killing about 400 people and wounding about 1,200 more. The incident convinced many Indians that British rule must be ended.

GANDHI In the 1920s and 1930s, a leader named **Mohandas Gandhi** headed the Indian nationalist movement. He taught that nonviolent resistance and **civil disobedience** (the refusal to obey unjust laws), rather than bloodshed, were the way to win rights. He used tactics such as boycotting, or refusing to buy, British goods. Gandhi embraced

 KEY THEMES AND CONCEPTS

Change In Iran—unlike Turkey—modernization eventually led, in 1979, to an Islamic revolution in which the government turned from secularism.

 PREPARING FOR THE REGENTS

What are the similarities among Pan-Slavism, Pan-Arabism, and Zionism? What are some differences?

PREPARING FOR THE REGENTS

Write a brief statement about the historical importance of each of these figures.

Kemal Atatürk:

Reza Khan:

Mohandas Gandhi:

western ideas of democracy and nationalism. He rejected the caste system and urged equal rights for all, including women. India, however, did not achieve independence until 1947, one year before Gandhi's death.

Chinese Nationalism

Chinese civilization was in great disorder during and after World War I. After Sun Yixian (also known as Sun Yat-sen), founder of the Chinese Republic, stepped down, rival warlords fought for power. The economy collapsed, and peasants faced great economic hardship. During this time, foreign powers—especially Japan—increased their influence in China.

RIVAL GROUPS IN CHINA   During this time, several movements emerged.

- **May Fourth Movement** This was a student movement. Its supporters wanted to make China stronger through modernization. The movement turned to western science and to ideas such as democracy and nationalism.
- **Communists** Some Chinese turned to the ideas of Marx and Lenin. A Chinese Communist party was formed.
- **Nationalists** Sun Yixian had formed a nationalist party, the **Guomindang.** After Sun Yixian's death, an army officer named Jiang Jieshi (also known as Chiang Kai-shek) took over the Guomindang.

CIVIL WAR   At first, the Nationalists and the Communists had worked together to unite China. Over time, however, Jiang Jieshi began to see the Communists as a threat. A civil war began between the Nationalists and the Communists that would last for 22 years.

LITERATURE AND ARTS: THE LOST GENERATION

World War I had produced disquiet in social as well as political arenas. The war had shaken many people's long-held beliefs. Scientific discoveries—such as those of the Curies, Einstein, and Freud—had brought new understanding, but they had also cast doubt on the ideas of the past.

The war itself had left scars on those who survived it. Writers, artists, and musicians throughout the 1920s and 1930s expressed a loss of hope, rejecting former rules and moral values. They became known as the "Lost Generation."

Writers such as Ernest Hemingway expressed a loss of faith in western civilization. Poet T. S. Eliot portrayed the modern world as spiritually empty and barren. Some painters stopped trying to reproduce the real world. In an attempt to express their feelings of loss of meaning, they experimented with color and distorted shapes.

PREPARING FOR THE REGENTS

To learn more about Sun Yixian, see Unit 5, Section 7.

PREPARING FOR THE REGENTS

To learn more about the Nationalist Revolution in China, see Unit 5, Section 7. To learn more about the Chinese Communist Revolution, see Unit 7, Section 3.

PREPARING FOR THE REGENTS

How did World War I affect the literature and arts of the 1920s and 1930s?

WOMEN'S SUFFRAGE MOVEMENT

In the mid-1800s in western democracies, women had begun to demand greater rights. These included property rights and suffrage, or the right to vote. The first country in which women won the right to vote was New Zealand in 1893. In Britain, Parliament finally granted women over 30 the right to vote in 1918. By 1928, Britain had granted suffrage to all women over the age of 21. In the United States, President Wilson proposed the Nineteenth Amendment in 1918. This amendment gave American citizens over the age of 21 the right to vote, regardless of gender. Congress adopted the amendment two years later in 1920. Women also gained the right to vote in Canada, Finland, Germany, and Sweden in the early 1900s.

WORLDWIDE DEPRESSION

After World War I, economic problems emerged in Europe. Soldiers, returning from the war, needed jobs. Nations had war debts to pay and cities to rebuild. In the decade following the war, the economies of many European countries began a shaky recovery. Middle-class families enjoyed a rising standard of living.

The United States, on the other hand, experienced an economic boom after the war. It became the world's leading economic power and made investments in Europe to promote recovery. These came to an end, however, with the crash of the American stock market in 1929. This event triggered the **Great Depression** of the 1930s, a time of global economic collapse.

Causes of the Depression

Weaknesses in the economies of the United States and other nations around the world led to the Great Depression.

Industrial Unemployment Rates

Industrial Unemployment Rates		
Country	1921–1929	1930–1938
United States	7.9	26.1
United Kingdom	12.0	15.4
France	3.8	10.2
Germany	9.2	21.8

Source (of statistics): Peter Temin, *Lessons from the Great Depression* (Massachusetts Institute of Technology, 1989), page 3.

KEY THEMES AND CONCEPTS

Justice and Human Rights World War I brought great progress for women. Women kept the economy going at home by taking on jobs left vacant by men who became soldiers. Some joined the armed forces. This independence gave them a new sense of pride and confidence. After the war, women in various western democracies gained the right to vote.

 PREPARING FOR THE REGENTS

Practice your chart skills by describing the general trend that this chart shows.

 **KEY THEMES AND CONCEPTS**

Economics and Interdependence Global economic interdependence was an important factor in the Great Depression. Because the United States economy was part of a network of trade and finance, the American stock market crash of 1929 had a worldwide effect.

LESS DEMAND FOR RAW MATERIALS The war had increased the demand for raw materials from Africa, Asia, and Latin America. Demand lessened after the war, and prices fell. Farmers, miners, herders, and other suppliers of raw materials suffered economic loss.

OVERPRODUCTION OF MANUFACTURED GOODS Industrial workers had won high wages, which increased the price of manufactured goods. However, farmers and other people who had suffered economically could not afford these goods. Factories kept producing them anyway.

THE STOCK MARKET CRASH Investors bought stock on margin, meaning that they paid only part of the cost and borrowed the rest. In the fall of 1929, brokers began to call in the loans. When investors could not pay them, financial panic followed and stock prices crashed.

Impact of the Depression

During the Great Depression, banks and businesses closed, putting millions of people out of work and drastically decreasing production of goods. Millions came to rely on soup kitchens as a main source of food. Worldwide, countries raised import tariffs to protect their own markets, causing a decline in global trade.

As the Great Depression continued, some people lost faith in democracy and capitalism. Extreme ideas of many types arose. Communists celebrated what they saw as the failure of capitalism. Strong leaders supported intense nationalism, militarism, and a return to authoritarian rule.

PREPARING FOR THE REGENTS

While reading the section on fascism, think of specific examples of how Hitler and Mussolini carried out some of the fascist policies shown on this chart.

THE RISE OF FASCISM

Widespread economic despair paved the way for the rise of dictators. Strong leaders in Italy and Germany promised solutions.

The Fascist State

Common Ideals of Fascism

Fascism is the rule of a people by dictatorial government that is nationalistic and imperialistic. Fascist governments are also anti-communist. Fascism emerged in both Italy and Germany after World War I.

Mussolini in Italy

Italy was troubled after World War I. Treaties had given away land that the Italians had expected to control. In addition, many war veterans could not find jobs. Trade was slow and taxes were high. Furthermore, workers went on strike.

Benito Mussolini took advantage of the unrest, gathering a following of war veterans and other unhappy Italians. He called his group the Fascist party and pledged to solve the nation's problems and strengthen Italy. Mussolini promised to end unemployment and gain more land for Italy. He also vowed to outlaw rebellion among workers and stamp out all threats of communism.

In 1922, the Fascists used force and terror to gain control of Italy. They ended free elections, free speech, and the free press. They killed or jailed their enemies. Grasping desperately for order, Italians put the goals of the state above their individual rights.

Hitler in Germany

THE WEIMAR REPUBLIC   After World War I, the kaiser stepped down. Germany was in chaos. The new democratic government, called the Weimar Republic, was politically weak. Inflation created major economic problems. The troubles of the time led to the Nazi rise to power.

KEY THEMES AND CONCEPTS

Political Systems
Describe several ways in which fascism differs from democracy.

Germany: Cost of Living

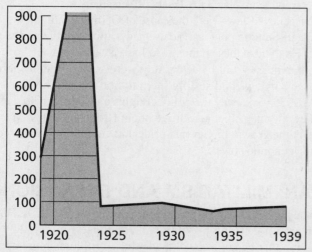

PREPARING FOR THE REGENTS

Practice your graph skills by identifying the years during which the cost of living in Germany was the highest. What impact do you think this had on Hitler's rise to power?

NAZI RISE TO POWER

World War I
- German war debts
- Loss of German colonies
- Wish for revenge

Weak Government
- Doubts about Weimar Republic
- Political quarrels
- Wish to return to strong leader

Economic Problems
- Inflation
- Worldwide depression
- Unemployment

Leadership
- Use of terror and force
- Idea of a super race
- Shift of blame to minority groups

PREPARING FOR THE REGENTS

How did war and economic depression lead to the rise of fascism?

KEY THEMES AND CONCEPTS

Power and Human Rights
Both Mussolini in Italy and Hitler in Germany improved the economies of their nations and brought order. The price of order, however, was loss of personal freedoms and human rights.

Adolf Hitler promised to provide jobs and rebuild German pride. He stated that the Germans were a superior race who were destined to build a new empire. In 1920, he headed the National Socialist German Workers, or Nazi, party. His party grew. In 1933, Hitler was appointed chancellor.

HITLER AS DICTATOR   Hitler's Germany, called the Third Reich, was a totalitarian state. He built a one-party government, ended civil rights, silenced his enemies with force, put businesses under government control, and employed many people in large public works programs. Germany's standard of living rose. Hitler rearmed Germany and rebuilt its military, which violated the Treaty of Versailles.

Hitler believed Jews were the cause of Germany's problems. He instituted anti-Semitic policies. He used education and the arts as propaganda tools to push these policies. At first, Nazis organized boycotts of Jewish businesses, but by 1938 they were seizing the property and businesses of Jews and selling them to non-Jews. The Nuremburg Laws of 1935 took away the political rights and German citizenship of Jews. Few German citizens worried about Hitler's policies. Most were pleased at the growth of German pride and Germany's increased military and economic power.

JAPAN: MILITARISM AND EXPANSION

Japan had moved toward greater democracy during the 1920s. However, there were underlying problems in Japanese society. The Great Depression that began in 1929 made these problems more apparent. Militarists and extreme nationalists gained power.

Japanese Militarists of the 1930s

CAUSES

- Unhappiness over loss of traditions
- Loss of foreign markets due to Great Depression
- Unemployment
- Poverty among peasants
- Feelings of nationalism
- Demand for expansion of Japanese empire

Rise of Militarists in Japan

EFFECTS

- 1931 attack on Chinese province of Manchuria
- Withdrawal from League of Nations
- Anti-western feelings
- End of many democratic freedoms
- Renewed practice of traditions
- Increased honor for emperor
- Renewed expansion and efforts to control China

 PREPARING FOR THE REGENTS

The militarists in Japan were determined to restore Japan to greatness, rid themselves of western influence, and gain foreign territories. Answer the following questions.

1. What economic problems led to the rise of militarism in Japan?

2. What were the political effects of the rise of militarism in Japan?

SUMMARY

After World War I, conflict and turmoil continued. The Treaty of Versailles gave some nations self-determination, punished Germany severely, and created the League of Nations. New nations formed and old empires collapsed. Change occurred as nationalist groups struggled to overthrow foreign domination. Society and culture changed after the war, and people lost faith in old ideas. In 1929, the global economy plunged into a terrible depression. Fascism in Italy and Germany threatened the peace in Europe, while aggressive militarism by Japan caused tension in Asia.

5

World War II

★ THE BIG IDEA
World War II:

- began when aggressive empire building by Germany, Italy, and Japan was opposed by Britain and France.

- was very destructive because of the technological power of new weaponry.

- was a total war that involved civilians as well as the military.

- created political and geographical divisions within Europe.

- affected global politics and culture for many years.

SECTION OVERVIEW

During the 1930s, Italy, Germany, and Japan sought to build new empires. At first, the democratic powers did not stop them. When German aggression became impossible to ignore, in 1939, World War II began. With advanced technology, the war covered a larger area and was more destructive than any before. Civilians became involved on a larger scale as well. At first, the Axis powers—Germany, Italy, and Japan—won major victories. After the entry of the United States and the Soviet Union into the war on the Allied side, however, the tide began to turn. The war finally ended in 1945. It had many lasting effects. There were enormous losses of life and property. The United Nations was formed to try to maintain peace. Europe became divided, with communist governments in Eastern Europe and democratic governments in Western Europe.

KEY THEMES AND CONCEPTS

As you review this section, take special note of the following key themes and concepts:

Power What events led up to World War II?

Science and Technology How did new weapons technology affect the course of the war?

Citizenship How were the lives of individuals affected by the war?

Change What were the major turning points of the war that helped determine its outcome?

KEY PEOPLE AND TERMS

As you review this section, be sure you understand the significance of these key people and terms:

appeasement	Hiroshima	concentration camp
Charles de Gaulle	blitz	Holocaust
Franklin Roosevelt	Winston Churchill	Bataan Death March
Pearl Harbor	genocide	United Nations

CAUSES OF THE WAR

In the 1930s, Italy, Germany, and Japan aggressively sought to build new empires. The League of Nations was weak. Western countries were recovering from the Great Depression and did not want any more war. As a result, acts of aggression occurred and were allowed to go un-checked.

Japan Invades China

The militaristic leaders of Japan wanted to build a Japanese empire. In 1931, Japan seized the Chinese territory of Manchuria. When the League of Nations condemned the action, Japan merely withdrew its membership from the League.

This incident strengthened militarism in Japan. In 1937, the Japanese army invaded the Chinese mainland. They established a puppet govern-ment in the former Chinese Nationalist capital of Nanjing. Their inva-sion of this city was so brutal that it became known as the "rape of Nanjing." Japan continued to gain territory during the period of war with China.

Italy Attacks Ethiopia

In 1935, the Italian army invaded the African country of Ethiopia. The Ethiopians resisted the attack, but their weapons were no match for the armored vehicles, aircraft, and poison gas of the Italians. The Ethiopian king appealed to the League of Nations. The league agreed to stop the sale of weapons and other war materials to Italy. However, the agreement was not honored by all nations.

German Aggression in Europe

Hitler glorified war as a means of restoring German national pride. This philosophy led to a policy of expansion.

- Hitler rebuilt the German army, in violation of the Treaty of Versailles.
- In 1936, Hitler sent troops into the Rhineland. This was an area lo-cated on Germany's border with France. The Treaty of Versailles had required that Germany remove its troops from this border region.
- In 1938, Hitler made Austria part of the German empire. In the same year, he also forced Czechoslovakia to give Germany a border area called the Sudetenland, where many Germans lived.

Appeasement

Western democracies adopted a policy of **appeasement.** Under this policy, nations gave in to aggressive demands to maintain peace. The western democracies responded weakly to German aggression. At the Munich Conference in 1938, western democracies agreed that Germany would seize control of the Sudetenland from Czechoslovakia.

KEY THEMES AND CONCEPTS

Power Militarists had gained great power in Japan. Japan's successful aggression increased their political power.

KEY THEMES AND CONCEPTS

Political Systems Leaders of Britain, France, and the United States knew that their citizens were reluctant to get involved in another costly war. This factor and others kept them from re-sponding immediately to the aggression of Germany, Italy, and Japan.

WORLD WAR II BEGINS

In the face of this weakness, Japan, Italy, and Germany formed the Rome-Berlin-Tokyo Axis. These nations agreed to fight Soviet communism and not to stop each other from making foreign conquests.

It began to be clear that appeasement had failed. Several events led to a declaration of war. In March 1939, Hitler took over the rest of Czechoslovakia. In August 1939, he made a pact with Joseph Stalin, the leader of the Soviet Union. In the Nazi-Soviet Pact, the two enemies agreed not to fight each other. In September 1939, Germany invaded Poland. Finally, Britain and France responded by declaring war on Germany. World War II had begun.

THE AXIS POWERS ADVANCE

The war was fought between the Axis powers (Germany, Italy, and Japan) and the Allied powers (France and Britain). The Allies were later joined by the Soviet Union, China, and the United States. At first, Germany and its allies prevailed. Nazi forces conquered Poland in a swift, massive attack known as blitzkrieg, or lightning warfare. In April 1940, Hitler overran Norway, Denmark, the Netherlands, and Belgium. By June 1940, the Germans had entered Paris. **Charles de Gaulle** formed a French government in exile, calling on French forces to

The World at War: World War II

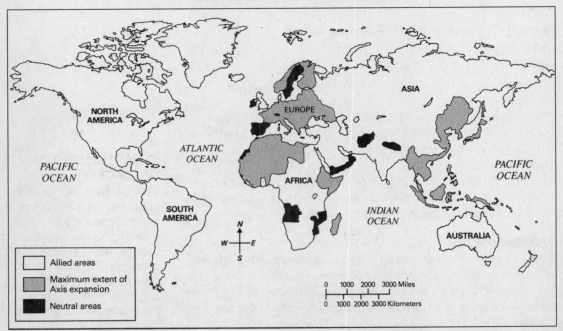

- Allied areas
- Maximum extent of Axis expansion
- Neutral areas

continue fighting Germany. These "Free French" worked from England to liberate their homeland.

TURNING POINTS OF THE WAR

The Axis powers won quick victories in the first several years of the war. Several events after 1940, however, are seen as turning points for the Allies.

The Entry of the United States (1941)

Although the United States had declared its neutrality in the war, President **Franklin Roosevelt** met with England's prime minister, Winston Churchill, in August 1941, and they declared their common desire to end Nazi tyranny. Roosevelt continued to supply arms to the Allies. To stop Japanese aggression, the United States banned the sale of war materials to Japan. Angered by the ban, Japan launched a surprise attack on American military bases at **Pearl Harbor,** Hawaii, on December 7, 1941. More than 2,400 people were killed, and many ships and planes were destroyed. In response, Franklin Roosevelt asked Congress to declare war on Japan. The entry of the United States into the war gave the Allies added strength.

Battle of Stalingrad (1942–1943)

The Germans invaded the Soviet Union in 1941. After steadily advancing, they became stalled outside Moscow and Leningrad. Hitler turned south in 1942 to try to take Stalingrad. Russian troops and a freezing winter caused the German invaders to surrender in 1943. The Red Army drove the Germans out of the Soviet Union. Soon Soviet troops were advancing toward Germany.

El Alamein (1942)

The Germans, under General Erwin Rommel, gained many victories in North Africa in 1941 and 1942. British forces in Egypt finally stopped Rommel's advance during the Battle of El Alamein in 1942. With the help of American forces advancing from the west, the Allies trapped Rommel's army in 1943, and he surrendered.

Invasion of Italy (1943)

The victory in North Africa allowed the British and Americans to land in Italy in July 1943. Hitler was forced to send troops to Italy, weakening his forces in Western Europe.

Invasion of Normandy (1944)

The Allies invaded France on June 6, 1944. Allied troops were ferried across the English Channel, landing on the beaches of Normandy. They broke through German defenses to advance toward Paris and freed France from German control. The Allies then moved from France into Germany.

 PREPARING FOR THE REGENTS

Describe the importance of each of the following turning points of the war.

Entry of the United States:

Battle of Stalingrad:

Battle of El Alamein:

Invasion of Italy:

Invasion of Normandy:

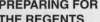
PREPARING FOR THE REGENTS

Describe the significance of each of the following leaders.

Hitler:

Mussolini:

Stalin:

Churchill:

Roosevelt:

THE WAR ENDS

The war in Europe ended on May 7, 1945, with the Germans' surrender. Fighting in the Pacific would continue until the Japanese surrendered in August 1945.

Yalta Conference

In February 1945, Roosevelt, Churchill, and Stalin met at a Soviet resort called Yalta. They knew then that the war was close to an end. The three leaders decided that at war's end, they would divide Germany temporarily. British, French, American, and Soviet forces would each control a zone of Germany. They agreed that Stalin would oversee the creation of new governments in Eastern Europe.

Victory in the Pacific

Japan was greatly weakened, and the United States took the offensive after two Japanese fleets were severely damaged by Americans in 1942. Gradually, American forces recaptured Japanese-held islands south of Japan and advanced north. By 1944, the Americans had begun to bomb Japanese cities. The Japanese, however, refused to surrender.

Hiroshima and Nagasaki

With no war in Europe, the Allies poured resources into the Pacific. By mid-1945, most of the Japanese navy and airforce had been destroyed. Japan's army was still strong, however. On August 6, 1945, an American plane dropped an atomic bomb on the Japanese city of **Hiroshima.** The bomb flattened 4 square miles of the city and killed 70,000 people. They dropped another bomb on Nagasaki, killing 40,000 people. Some militarists wanted to hold out, but on August 10, Japanese emperor Hirohito forced his government to surrender. Japan signed a peace treaty on September 2, 1945.

TECHNOLOGY AND WORLD WAR II

Throughout the war, advanced technology led to more power, greater speed, and better communications. Technological innovation resulted in more widespread destruction than ever before.

CIVILIAN LIFE AND TOTAL WAR

Both the Allied powers and the Axis powers had engaged in total war. Cities became targets of bombing. In 1940, Germany began a **blitz,** or massive bombing, of London using warplanes. **Winston Churchill,** prime minister of Britain, rallied his people.

Democratic governments increased their power during the war. They ordered factories to produce war materials instead of civilian products. Prices and wages were fixed, and consumer goods were rationed.

PREPARING FOR THE REGENTS

How did World War II affect civilian life? How did civilians contribute to the war effort?

Modern Warfare of World War II

- Sonar to detect submarines
- Machine guns
- Improved airplanes
- Improved submarines
- **MODERN WARFARE OF WORLD WAR II**
- Radar to detect airplanes
- Walkie-talkies
- Deadlier bombs
- Aircraft carriers
- Fast-moving armored tanks
- Medical advances to treat wounds

Democratic governments sometimes limited the rights of individuals. In the United States and Canada, some people of Japanese descent were forced into internment camps. The British took similar action with those of German ancestry.

As men joined the war, women worked in the factories. They helped produce planes, ships, and ammunition. British and American women served in the armed forces by driving trucks and ambulances, decoding messages, and serving as nurses at field hospitals.

THE HOLOCAUST

One of Hitler's goals was to create "living space" for Germans who he considered racially superior. He planned to destroy people he found inferior. Jews were the main target, but he also wanted to destroy or enslave others, including Slavs, Gypsies, and the mentally or physically disabled.

The attempt to destroy an entire ethnic or religious group is called **geno-cide.** Hitler committed genocide against the Jews. He began by limiting the rights and encouraging violence against Jews. On November 8, 1938, called Kristallnacht, organized violence began. Thousands of Jewish synagogues, businesses, cemeteries, schools, and homes were destroyed. The next day, 30,000 Jews were arrested for being Jewish and more restrictive laws on Jews and Jewish businesses began. Jews were forced to live in separate areas. Then, Hitler set up **concentration camps.** At death camps, like Auschwitz, Jews were starved, shot, or gassed to death. By 1945, over 6 million Jews died in what became known as the **Holocaust.**

KEY THEMES AND CONCEPTS

Human Rights The Holocaust as well as other atrocities committed during World War II were extreme violations of human rights.

OTHER WARTIME ATROCITIES

The Holocaust stands as the starkest example of wartime inhumanity. Several other incidents, however, also stand out as especially brutal aspects of World War II.

- The Japanese invasion of Nanjing in 1937 involved mass shootings and terrible brutality. As many as 250,000 Chinese were killed.
- In the Philippines, Japanese soldiers forced American and Filipino prisoners of war on a march up the Bataan peninsula. Along the way, prisoners were beaten, stabbed, and shot. This event became known as the **Bataan Death March.**
- In Poland, Soviet troops subjected thousands of Poles to imprisonment, torture, and execution.

IMPACT OF WORLD WAR II

Human Losses

World War II had killed as many as 75 million people. In European countries alone, about 38 million people died. The Soviets, however, had suffered the heaviest losses, with more than 22 million dead. The Holocaust had inflicted death and misery on millions of Jews and others in the Nazi concentration camps.

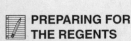

PREPARING FOR THE REGENTS

List five effects of World War II.

1.

2.

3.

4.

5.

Economic Losses

Throughout Europe and parts of Asia, cities were in ruins. Aerial bombardment had been very destructive. Coventry in England; Hamburg and Dresden in Germany; and Tokyo, Hiroshima, and Nagasaki in Japan were some of the hardest-hit cities. The European countryside was devastated as well. The economies of war-torn countries took many years to recover.

War Crime Trials

At meetings during the war, Allied leaders had agreed to punish those responsible for "crimes against humanity." Trials were held in Nuremberg, Germany, from November 1945 through September 1946. Hitler was already dead, but 22 surviving Nazi leaders were tried at the Nuremberg trials. Some received the death penalty; others were imprisoned. Additional trials were held in Italy and Japan. The trials demonstrated that leaders could be held accountable for their actions during war.

Occupied Nations

In order to prevent another world war and to promote democracy, western nations occupied West Germany and Japan. They built new governments with democratic constitutions, which protected individual rights and liberties.

However, Soviet forces occupied East Germany and most of Eastern Europe. They established communist governments in these nations, backed by the power of the Soviet Union. Thus, Europe was divided in two—between democracy in the West and communism in the East.

The United Nations

World War II resulted in the formation of a new international body. In April 1945, representatives from nations around the world met in San Francisco to establish the **United Nations.** The purpose of the United Nations is to provide a place to discuss world problems and develop solutions. The two main bodies of the United Nations are:

- the General Assembly, which includes representatives from all member nations; each representative has one vote.
- the Security Council, with 15 member nations, 5 of which are permanent: the United States, Russia, France, Great Britain, and China.

Literature and the Arts

World War II had a long-term effect on literature and the arts in Europe and the United States. Some writers examined the nature of totalitarianism. George Orwell's *Animal Farm* (1945) is one of the best known of these works. Other writers searched for moral and religious significance amid the destruction of the war. Still others became concerned with the human capacity for evil. William Golding explored this idea in his 1954 novel, *Lord of the Flies*.

Realistic war novels and poetry also emerged. These works examined the human costs of the war; they were often drawn from direct battlefield experiences of the writers.

Many books and films dealt with the horrors of the atomic bomb. Others examined what life might be like in the aftermath of a nuclear war. *On the Beach* by Nevil Shute, written in 1957, is one of the earliest of these works.

 PREPARING FOR THE REGENTS

To learn more about the work of the United Nations after World War II, see Unit 8, Section 2.

SUMMARY

Germany, Italy, and Japan tried in the 1930s to build world empires. When Germany invaded Poland in 1939, World War II began, and the world faced the most devastating conflict in human history. During World War II, new weapons with massive power caused the loss of millions of lives. Civilians were greatly affected by the war, facing rationing, military attacks, and sometimes severe repression. The conflict continued until 1945. World War II resulted in millions of deaths, heavy economic losses, and brutality on a scale such as the world had not seen before. After 1945, the world became divided between communist and democratic forms of government.

Questions for Regents Practice

Review the Preparing for the Regents section of this book. Then answer the following questions, which include multiple-choice questions, a thematic essay, and a series of document-based questions.

MULTIPLE CHOICE

Directions

Circle the *number* of the word or expression that best completes the statement or answers the question.

Base your answer to question 1 on the graph below and on your knowledge of social studies.

World Population 1800–1900

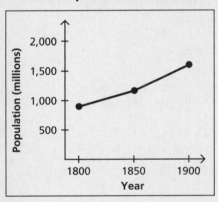

1 What factors would best account for the rise in population shown on this graph after 1850?
1 lack of public sewer systems
2 the end of World War I
3 medical advances and improved diets
4 the decline of feudalism

2 A major cause of World War I was
1 a decline in the policy of imperialism
2 the existence of opposing alliances
3 an increase in acts of aggression by England
4 the spread of communism throughout Europe

3 In Eastern Europe after World War I, the greatest obstacle to national unity in many nation-states was the
1 great ethnic diversity found in the region
2 economic dependence of Eastern Europe on Japan
3 acceptance of democratic traditions by most Eastern Europeans
4 expansion of United States influence in the region

4 The Russian peasants supported the Bolsheviks in the 1917 revolutions mainly because the Bolsheviks promised to
1 establish collective farms
2 maintain the agricultural price-support system
3 bring modern technology to Russian farms
4 redistribute the land owned by the nobility

5 The French Revolution of 1789, the Chinese Revolution of 1911, and the Bolshevik Revolution of 1917 were similar in that these revolutions
1 were led by ruthless dictators
2 were motivated by a desire to overthrow a monarch
3 led directly to the establishment of communism
4 established a higher standard of living for the middle class

6 Which statement best describes the political situation that existed in the Soviet Union immediately after the death of Lenin in 1924?
1 The nation adopted a constitutional monarchy.
2 Trotsky and his followers assumed full control of the Communist Party.
3 Popular elections were held to choose a new general secretary.
4 A power struggle developed among Communist Party leaders.

7 ". . . The organizations of the revolutionaries must consist first, foremost, and mainly of people who make revolutionary activity their profession. . . . Such an organization must of necessity be not too extensive and as secret as possible. . . ."
—V. I. Lenin, 1917

This quotation refers to Lenin's plan to
1 defeat Germany in World War I
2 establish representative democracy in Russia
3 maintain Communist power in Western Europe
4 overthrow the Russian government

8 Under Joseph Stalin, the Soviet Union emphasized centralized economic planning and five-year plans primarily to
1 produce more consumer goods
2 expand exports
3 create an increased demand for high-quality imports
4 develop heavy industry

9 A significant effect of Joseph Stalin's policy of collectivization on Soviet agriculture was
1 a widespread food shortage
2 an increase in the export of agricultural products
3 a surplus of agricultural products
4 the immediate creation of many small private farms

10 One similarity between Russia under the czars and the Soviet Union under Joseph Stalin is that in both types of government, these leaders
1 tried to reduce their nation's influence in world affairs
2 developed policies to limit industrial growth
3 supported the creation of a national church
4 established an authoritarian form of government

11 A study of the causes of the American, French, and Russian Revolutions indicates that revolutions usually occur because the
1 society has become dependent on commerce and trade
2 society has a lower standard of living than the societies around it
3 existing government has been resistant to change
4 lower classes have strong leaders

12 The harsh conditions imposed by the Treaty of Versailles after World War I helped lay the foundation for the
1 rise of fascism in Germany
2 uprisings during the French Revolution
3 division of Korea along the 38th parallel
4 Bolshevik Revolution in Russia

13 Mohandas Gandhi is best known for his
1 use of passive resistance to achieve Indian independence
2 desire to establish an Islamic nation
3 opposition to Hindus holding public office
4 encouragement of violence to end British rule

14 Which situation contributed to Adolf Hitler's rise to power in Germany after World War I?
1 support of Hitler's radical policies by the Social Democrats in the Reichstag
2 strong feelings of resentment and nationalism built up by economic and political crises
3 refusal by the League of Nations to admit Germany as a member
4 violence and terrorism promoted by Germany's former enemies

15 Which was characteristic of France under Napoleon's rule and Germany under Hitler's rule?
 1 Democratic ideas and diversity were encouraged.
 2 Authoritarian control and a strong sense of nationalism prevailed.
 3 Peaceful relations with neighboring countries were fostered.
 4 Artistic and literary freedom flourished.

16 Which policy best demonstrates appeasement?
 1 British policy toward Germany during the 1930s
 2 Japanese policy toward China in the 1930s
 3 Spanish policy toward Native Americans in the 1500s
 4 German policy toward the French during World War I

17 Which series of events is arranged in the correct chronological order?
 1 The Treaty of Versailles is signed. Adolf Hitler becomes chancellor of Germany. German troops invade Poland.
 2 German troops invade Poland. The Treaty of Versailles is signed. Adolf Hitler becomes chancellor of Germany.

3 Adolf Hitler becomes chancellor of Germany. The Treaty of Versailles is signed. German troops invade Poland.
 4 The Treaty of Versailles is signed. German troops invade Poland. Adolf Hitler becomes chancellor of Germany.

18 The treatment of the Jews in Europe during World War II and of the Armenians in the Ottoman empire are examples of
 1 cultural diffusion
 2 fundamentalism
 3 modernization
 4 genocide

19 Which was a major result of the Nuremberg trials?
 1 National leaders were held personally responsible for war crimes against humanity.
 2 The State of Israel was created as a home for victims of the war.
 3 Soldiers were required to pay for the property damages they caused during the war.
 4 Prisoners from all countries were immediately released from captivity.

THEMATIC ESSAY

Directions
Read the following instructions that include a theme, a task, and suggestions. Follow the instructions to create a well-organized essay that has an introduction with a thesis statement, several paragraphs explaining the thesis, and a conclusion.

Theme: Nationalism
Throughout global history, nationalism has had positive and negative effects.

Task
- Define the term *nationalism*.
- Select one country or region you have studied, and describe two specific examples of nationalism within that country or region.
- Explain how each of the two examples had either a positive or negative impact on the future development of the country or region.

Suggestions

You may use any nation or region from your study of global history, except the United States. Some suggestions you may wish to consider are: Latin America (1800s), Italy (1800s and 1900s), China (1900s), India (1900s), Kenya (post-World War II), and the Balkans (1900s). You are not limited to these suggestions.

QUESTIONS BASED ON DOCUMENTS

The following exercise asks you to analyze four historical documents and then write an essay using evidence from those documents. This exercise is similar to the document-based question that you will see on the Regents Examination, which may include six or more documents. For additional practice with historical documents, see the Preparing for the Regents section and the sample examinations in this book.

This task is based on the accompanying documents. Some of these documents have been edited for the purposes of this task. This task is designed to test your ability to work with historical documents. As you analyze the documents, take into account both the source of each document and the author's point of view.

Directions

Read the documents in Part A and answer the question or questions after each document. Then read the directions for Part B and write your essay.

Historical Context

Throughout history, leaders have viewed power in many different ways. There have been a variety of viewpoints on the acquisition and use of power.

Task

Examine several viewpoints on the attainment and use of power. Evaluate positive and negative effects that the various viewpoints have had on people in different countries.

Part A: Short Answer

Directions: Analyze the documents and answer the question or questions that follow each document, using the space provided.

DOCUMENT 1

> *Under the leadership of the working class and the Communist party, these classes [the working class, the peasantry, the petty bourgeoisie, and the national bourgeoisie] unite to create their own state . . . so as to enforce their . . . dictatorship over the henchmen of imperialism—the landlord class and bureaucratic capitalist class. . . . The people's government will suppress such persons.*
>
> **—Mao Zedong, speech on the anniversary of the founding of the Communist party, 1949**

1 According to Mao Zedong, do all classes share power in a communist state? Explain.

_____

_____

2 Describe one goal that Mao thought a communist government should strive to achieve.

_____

_____

DOCUMENT 2

The Fascist State

3 According to this chart, what methods have fascist leaders used to acquire and maintain power?

_____

_____

DOCUMENT 3

> *Passive resistance is a method of securing rights by personal suffering; it is the reverse of resistance by arms. When I refuse to do a thing that is repugnant to my conscience, I use soul-force.*
>
> **—Mohandas Gandhi, *Hind Swaraj*, 1938**

4 What did Gandhi mean by the term "passive resistance"?

_____

_____

DOCUMENT 4

> *The nation has placed its destiny in the hands and heads and hearts of its millions of free men and women; and its faith in freedom. . . . Freedom means the supremacy of human rights everywhere. Our support goes to those who struggle to gain those rights or keep them.*
>
> **—Franklin D. Roosevelt, address to Congress in January 1941**

5 According to President Roosevelt, who or what is the ultimate source of power in the United States?

_____

_____

6 For what purpose did Roosevelt promise to use the power of the United States?

_____

_____

Part B: Essay

Directions:
- Write a well-organized essay that includes an introduction, several paragraphs, and a conclusion.
- Use evidence from the documents to support your response.
- Do not simply repeat the contents of the documents.
- Include specific, related outside information.

Historical Context

Throughout history, leaders have viewed power in many different ways. There have been a variety of viewpoints on the acquisition and use of power.

Task

Using information from the documents and your knowledge of global history and geography, evaluate the differing views that leaders have had on the attainment and use of power. Discuss how the views of at least two leaders have affected people of their own nations and people of other nations.

Be sure to include specific historical details. You must also include additional information from your knowledge of global history.

Note: **The rubric for this essay appears in the Preparing for the Regents section of this book.**

UNIT 7

The Twentieth Century Since 1945
(1945–the present)

UNIT OVERVIEW

After World War II, many nations participated in a struggle called the Cold War. On one side were communist states led by the Soviet Union and China. On the other side were non-communist nations led by the United States. The Cold War finally ended in the 1980s with the collapse of the Soviet Union and the end of communism in Eastern Europe.

During the Cold War, imperialism ended and new nations were born. In the Middle East, there were many conflicts. Elsewhere, newly independent nations had to establish workable economic and political systems. In Latin America, there was political unrest.

THEMATIC TIME LINE ACTIVITY

Some of the many themes developed in Unit 7 are:

change	economic systems	diversity
political systems	conflict	belief systems
human rights	nationalism	

Choose one of the themes listed above. As you review Unit 7, create a thematic time line based on the theme you have chosen. Your time line should stretch from 1945 to the present and include major developments and key turning points having to do with your theme.

SECTION  1   Cold War Balance of Power

SECTION OVERVIEW

After World War II, Japan and West Germany adopted constitutions that built democratic governments. Two major powers emerged from the war: the United States and the Soviet Union. Political and economic differences between the two led to a division of Europe that would last more than 40 years. The conflict between democracy and communism also spread around the globe, resulting in a buildup of arms as well as a race to explore space. The United Nations experienced both failure and success in its quest to maintain peace in the years after 1945.

KEY THEMES AND CONCEPTS

As you review this section, take special note of the following key themes and concepts:

Change   What impact did World War II have on the development of democracy in Germany and Japan?

Political Systems   How did differing political systems help cause the Cold War between the United States and the Soviet Union?

Conflict   How did the rivalry between the United States and the Soviet Union involve other nations around the world?

Justice and Human Rights   What role does the United Nations play in the struggle for justice and human rights?

KEY PEOPLE AND TERMS

As you review this section, be sure you understand the significance of these key people and terms:

iron curtain	satellite	NATO
asylum	Truman Doctrine	Warsaw Pact
superpower	containment	surrogate
Cold War	Marshall Plan	nonaligned nation

★ THE BIG IDEA
After World War II:

- West Germany and Japan developed democratic governments.

- the United States and the Soviet Union emerged as superpowers with differing political and economic systems.

- the Cold War developed, and the superpowers confronted one another throughout the world.

- the United Nations tried to maintain peace.

PREPARING FOR THE REGENTS

How were conditions in Europe after World War II similar to the conditions that existed after World War I? How were the two post-war periods different?

A DIVIDED EUROPE

After World War II, with help from the United States and Great Britain, democracy and free enterprise were restored to the nations of Western Europe. Eastern Europe, however, was occupied by armies of the Soviet Union. Joseph Stalin, the leader of the Soviet Union, wanted to spread communism throughout the area. He hoped to create a buffer zone of friendly governments to prevent possible attacks from Germany and other western nations.

Although Stalin had promised free elections for Eastern Europe, he instead supported the establishment of pro-communist governments throughout the region. Soon Europe was divided by an imaginary line known as the **iron curtain.** In the East were the Soviet-dominated communist countries. In the West were the western democracies, led by the United States.

GERMANY AND JAPAN TRANSFORMED

Both Germany and Japan had been physically and socially devastated by the war. The victorious Allied powers occupied the two countries.

Germany was divided into four zones of occupation. Britain, France, and the United States occupied the three zones in western Germany. The Soviet Union controlled eastern Germany. The United States alone occupied Japan.

Democracy in West Germany

 PREPARING FOR THE REGENTS

Why do you think Germany developed one of Europe's most liberal asylum laws?

Germany's armed forces were disbanded, and the Nazi party was outlawed. Nazi war criminals were tried in the Nuremberg trials, and some were executed. In western Germany, the Allies helped set up political parties. Germans wrote a federal constitution. This constitution set up a democratic government and was approved in 1949. In that year, West Germany also regained self-government as the Federal Republic of Germany.

Germany's constitution included an article that guaranteed political asylum for people who were persecuted for political reasons. **Asylum** is protection from arrest or from the possibility of being returned to a dangerous political situation. For many years, Germany's asylum policy was the most liberal in Europe. Germany's recognition of its role in the persecution of Jews and other groups probably led to this constitutional guarantee. In the late 1990s, Germany began to restrict this right after large numbers of asylum seekers came to Germany for economic rather than political reasons.

THE LESSONS OF THE HOLOCAUST Germany was deeply shaken by the experience of the Holocaust. Germans wanted to be sure that such a thing could not happen again. Today, Germany's relationship with the nation of Israel is very friendly. Germany and Israel have strong diplomatic, economic, and cultural ties. There has also been an attempt to compensate financially some of the victims of the Holocaust.

KEY THEMES AND CONCEPTS

Change Describe two effects that Germany's experience in the Holocaust had on the nation's later development.

Democracy in Japan

Like Germany, Japan was occupied after World War II by Allied troops, most of whom were American. Japan's armed forces were disbanded. Trials were held to punish people who had been responsible for wartime atrocities, and some of these people were executed. General Douglas MacArthur was the supreme commander of the American military government that ruled postwar Japan. The American government wanted to end militarism and ensure democratic government in Japan.

JAPAN'S NEW CONSTITUTION   In Germany, a German council had written the new constitution. Japan's constitution, on the other hand, was drafted by MacArthur and his advisors.

- It created a constitutional monarchy that limited the power of the emperor.
- It promised that Japan would not use war as a political weapon.
- It set up a democratic government. Representatives were elected to the Diet, the Japanese parliament.
- Women gained the right to vote.
- Basic rights, such as freedom of the press and of assembly, were guaranteed.

The Japanese government accepted this new constitution and signed a treaty that took away Japan's overseas empire. In 1952, the Allied occupation officially ended.

TWO SUPERPOWERS

After World War II, several powerful nations of the past were in decline. Germany was defeated and divided. France and Britain were economically drained and needed to concentrate on rebuilding. The United States and the Soviet Union emerged from World War II as the two world **superpowers.** The word *superpower* has been used to describe each of the rivals that came to dominate global politics in the period after World War II. Many other states in the world came under the domination or influence of these powers.

THE COLD WAR BEGINS

The United States and the Soviet Union had cooperated to win World War II. Soon, however, conflicts in ways of thinking and mutual distrust led to the **Cold War**—a continuing state of tension and hostility between the superpowers. This tension was a result of differences in political and economic thinking between the democratic, capitalistic United States and the communist Soviet Union. It was a "cold" war because armed battle between the superpowers did not occur.

The western powers feared the spread of communism. Stalin had forced pro-communist governments in Poland, Czechoslovakia, and

PREPARING FOR THE REGENTS

How were the political conditions in Germany and Japan similar after World War II? How were they different?

PREPARING FOR THE REGENTS

How was the Japanese government after World War II different from the Japanese government that had existed before and during the war?

KEY THEMES AND CONCEPTS

Political and Economic Systems The Cold War was much more than just a military rivalry. It was a struggle between two very different political and economic systems.

PREPARING FOR THE REGENTS

What factors led to the breakup of the alliance between Britain, France, and the United States and the Soviet Union?

 PREPARING FOR THE REGENTS

Practice your map skills by listing the nations that were members of NATO and the nations that were members of the Warsaw Pact in 1955.

elsewhere. These countries came to be known as **satellites** of the Soviet Union. When Stalin began to put pressure on Greece and Turkey, the United States took action.

The Truman Doctrine

In March of 1947, President Harry S. Truman established a policy known as the **Truman Doctrine.** This was an economic and military program designed to help other nations resist Soviet aggression. It was based on the theory of **containment,** which involved limiting communism to areas already under Soviet control. The United States pledged to resist Soviet expansion anywhere in the world. Truman sent military and economic aid to Greece and Turkey so that they could resist the threat of communism.

The Marshall Plan

The **Marshall Plan,** also proposed in 1947, was a massive economic aid package designed to strengthen democratic governments and lessen the appeal of communism. Billions of American dollars helped Western European countries recover from World War II. Although the United

Europe After World War II

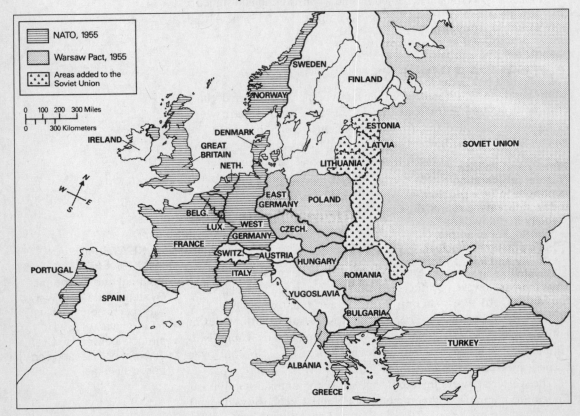

States also offered this aid to Eastern Europe, Stalin forbade these countries to accept it.

Crisis in Germany

The division of Germany into four zones after World War II was supposed to be temporary. Soon Britain, France, and the United States had combined their democratically ruled zones. Tension grew between democratic western Germany and Soviet-controlled eastern Germany. Germany became a major focus of Cold War tension. The Allies were trying to rebuild the German economy, but Stalin feared a strong, united Germany. Berlin, the divided capital, was located in East Germany.

THE BERLIN AIRLIFT   In 1948, Stalin hoped to force the Allies out of Berlin by closing all land routes for bringing essential supplies to West Berlin. In response to the crisis, the western powers mounted a successful airlift. For almost a year, food and supplies were flown into West Berlin. Finally, the Soviets ended the blockade.

A DIVIDED GERMANY   This incident, however, led to the creation of the Federal Republic of Germany (West Germany) in 1949. Germany, like the rest of Europe, remained divided. In 1961, the East German government built a wall that separated East Berlin from West Berlin. East German soldiers shot anyone who tried to escape from East Germany.

Opposing Military Alliances

THE NATO ALLIANCE   After the Berlin airlift and the division of West Germany from East Germany, Western European countries formed a military alliance. It was called the North Atlantic Treaty Organization, or **NATO.** Members of NATO pledged to support each other if any member nation was ever attacked.

THE WARSAW PACT   In 1955, the Soviet Union formed the **Warsaw Pact.** It included the Soviet Union and seven of its satellites in Eastern Europe. This was also a defensive alliance, promising mutual military cooperation.

THE COLD WAR HEATS UP

Repression in Eastern Europe

The Soviet Union kept a tight grip on its Eastern European satellites. Tensions arose in both East Germany and Poland in the 1950s. In East Germany, a revolt was put down with Soviet tanks. In Poland, some reforms were made, yet the country remained under the domination of the Soviet Union. Though Stalin died in 1953, his successors continued his policy of repression.

THE HUNGARIAN REVOLT   In 1956, a revolution began in Hungary. It was led by Imre Nagy, who was a Hungarian nationalist and

 PREPARING FOR THE REGENTS

Briefly describe each of the terms listed below.

Truman Doctrine:

Marshall Plan:

NATO:

Warsaw Pact:

Berlin Airlift:

 PREPARING FOR THE REGENTS

Why were NATO and the Warsaw Pact formed?

KEY THEMES AND CONCEPTS

Conflict The revolts and repression in Hungary and Czechoslovakia were signals to the West that the Soviet Union planned to use military force to ensure the survival of communism in Eastern Europe.

communist. Nagy ended one-party rule, got rid of Soviet troops, and withdrew Hungary from the Warsaw Pact. In response, the Soviet Union quickly sent in troops and tanks. Thousands of Hungarians died, and the revolt against Soviet domination was suppressed.

THE INVASION OF CZECHOSLOVAKIA Another rebellion against Soviet domination occurred in Czechoslovakia in the spring of 1968, when Alexander Dubček called for liberal reforms and the easing of communist controls. The government of Czechoslovakia eased censorship and began to plan for a new constitution. The Soviet Union, however, sent troops to overturn the government and restore a communist dictatorship. Through these incidents, it became clear that the Soviet Union would use force whenever necessary to ensure the survival of communism and Soviet domination in Eastern Europe.

The Arms Race

Both the United States and the Soviet Union armed themselves, each preparing to withstand an attack from the other. The United States had developed the atomic bomb during World War II; Soviet scientists developed their own in 1949.

For 40 years, the two superpowers spent great amounts of money to develop more and more powerful weapons. The arms race raised the level of tension between the two superpowers. It also raised fears among many people that the superpowers might become involved in a conflict that would destroy the world.

PREPARING FOR THE REGENTS

How did the Cold War lead to an arms race?

The Space Race

The superpowers also competed in space. In 1957, the Soviet Union launched *Sputnik*, a satellite, into orbit around the Earth. Congress soon established NASA, the National Aeronautics and Space Administration, to improve American space technology.

The race was on. In 1958, the United States launched its own first satellite. In 1961, the Soviets sent the first man into space. Then, in 1969, the United States was the first nation to put a man on the moon. Both the Soviet Union and the United States explored the military use of space with spy satellites. Many people were concerned about the high cost of space exploration and the extension of the Cold War into space.

PREPARING FOR THE REGENTS

What role did science and technology play in the Cold War?

CONFLICTS AROUND THE WORLD

Although the United States and the Soviet Union did not engage in a war with each other, they did clash through **surrogate,** or representative, states. This meant that the United States and Soviet Union supported opposing forces in many nations throughout the world. These conflicts occurred in East Asia, the Middle East, Africa, and Latin America.

KEY THEMES AND CONCEPTS

Power By supporting governments or rebel groups in other countries, the superpowers could exert their influence without engaging in a major armed combat.

The Cold War in East Asia

Cold War tensions grew into bitter wars in Korea in the 1950s and in Vietnam in the 1960s. In each case, the superpowers supported opposing sides with economic aid, advisors, and troops.

KOREAN WAR   After World War II, Korea was divided into North Korea, occupied by Soviet forces, and South Korea, occupied by American forces. North Korean forces, seeking to unify the country under communist rule, invaded the south in 1950. Commanded by General Douglas MacArthur, UN forces prevented a northern takeover of South Korea. An armistice was signed in 1953.

VIETNAM WAR   In 1954, Vietnam was temporarily divided into a northern half, ruled by communist leader Ho Chi Minh, and a southern half, headed by non-communist Ngo Dinh Diem. Large numbers of American forces were eventually sent to Vietnam to prevent Ho Chi Minh from uniting Vietnam under northern rule. American forces, however, were not able to defeat the communist forces in Vietnam. In 1973, President Richard Nixon ordered a cease-fire and began to pull American forces out of Vietnam. In 1975, the North Vietnamese captured Saigon, reuniting Vietnam.

The Cold War in the Middle East

ARAB STATES AND ISRAEL   In the 1950s, Gamal Abdel Nasser emerged as a leader in the Arab state of Egypt. He was determined to end western power in Egypt. In 1956, he nationalized the Suez Canal, ending British control. He received support from the Soviet Union and used Soviet money to build the Aswan High Dam. Under Nasser's leadership, Egypt took part in two wars against the Jewish state of Israel. While the Soviet Union supported Egypt, the United States supported Israel.

IRAN AND IRAQ   Rivalries over oil resources fueled Cold War tensions in the Middle East. The United States and the Soviet Union both became interested in Iran after vast oil fields were discovered there. An Iranian nationalist leader who had communist support tried to nationalize the oil industry in the early 1950s. The United States helped to keep him from power. The United States then supported the repressive anticommunist shah of Iran with weapons and advisors. An Islamic revolution in 1979 toppled the shah's regime.

The Soviet Union meanwhile supported Iraq, which had become a socialist dictatorship in the 1960s and also had oil reserves. The Soviet Union eventually also supported governments in Syria and Libya.

The Cold War in Africa

CONGO   The Congo, a Belgian colony in Africa, became independent in 1960. The new premier asked for help in dealing with a revolt. The Soviet Union supported him against the rebels. Five years later, a

---

📝 PREPARING FOR THE REGENTS

To learn more about the conflict in Vietnam, see Section 4 of this unit.

 KEY THEMES AND CONCEPTS

Needs and Wants The superpowers interfered in the governments of Iran and Iraq. One reason for their interest in these nations was the presence of oil reserves. Both superpowers needed oil to boost their economies.

strongly anti-communist dictator named Mobutu Sese Seko took control of the country, renaming it Zaire. Because of his anti-communist stance, he received the support of the West, allowing him to stay in power until the late 1990s.

ANGOLA In southwestern Africa, the Portuguese colony of Angola gained independence in 1975, in the midst of a bloody civil war. After that, rival rebel groups continued their conflict with each other. One group, the MPLA, was supported by the Soviet Union and Cuba. The Soviet Union sent advisors and equipment; Cuba sent troops. The MPLA established a communist dictatorship in Angola. The United States tried to undermine this government, and South Africa supported the opposing group, UNITA. This confrontation continued until 1991.

PREPARING FOR THE REGENTS

Describe one way in which the Cold War influenced conflicts or events in each of the following regions.

Asia:

Middle East:

Africa:

Latin America:

The Cold War in Latin America

CUBA Cuba had won independence from Spain in 1898. For 60 years, Cuba was strongly influenced by the United States. In 1952, Fulgencio Batista seized power. His government was repressive and corrupt. Among those who opposed Batista was a young lawyer named **Fidel Castro.** He organized a guerrilla army and fought against Batista. Once gaining victory in 1959, Castro established a communist dictatorship in Cuba.

Castro turned to the Soviet Union for support. Cuba became involved in the rivalry between the United States and the Soviet Union. In 1961, the United States backed a plot by Cuban exiles to invade Cuba at the Bay of Pigs. However, the invading forces were quickly crushed. In 1962, the United States imposed a trade embargo on Cuba.

Angered by American interference, Castro sought closer ties with the Soviet Union. Castro allowed the Soviets to build nuclear missile bases in Cuba, just 90 miles off the coast of Florida. In 1962, however, President Kennedy demanded Soviet removal of nuclear weapons from Cuba. The Soviet Union finally agreed, in exchange for a pledge by Kennedy that the United States would not invade Cuba. Cuba was heavily supported by the Soviet Union until the collapse of communism. Cuba's economy has since suffered greatly from the loss of these trading partners.

Causes and Impact of the Cuban Revolution

Causes of the Cuban Revolution	Impact of the Cuban Revolution
Political Conditions • Rule by a repressive dictatorship • Corruption and bribery among government officials	**Political Changes** • Creation of a communist dictatorship • Denial of basic political rights and freedoms
Economic Conditions • Control of Cuba's sugar plantations by the upper class • Unequal distribution of wealth • Foreign control of many businesses • High unemployment despite prosperity	**Economic Changes** • Establishment of collective farms, jointly operated under government supervision • Government control of business and industry • Seizure of foreign property with little or no compensation

THE NONALIGNED NATIONS

The nations that chose not to ally with either side in the Cold War were known as **nonaligned nations.** Instead, these nations remained neutral. India, Yugoslavia, and many African nations adopted a policy of nonalignment. Their goals were to make economic progress and to avoid involvement in the Cold War.

KEY THEMES AND CONCEPTS

Choice Nonaligned nations did not side with either the Soviets or the United States during the Cold War.

THE ROLE OF THE UNITED NATIONS

During the course of the Cold War, the United Nations provided a forum for the superpowers to air their differences peacefully. While the Cold War was at its peak, however, countries tended to vote in blocs, either as allies of the United States or as allies of the Soviet Union. This practice limited the United Nations' effectiveness.

After the end of the Cold War in 1991, the United Nations expanded several of its traditional roles. Today, it sends international peacekeeping forces to countries in conflict. The United Nations continues to provide many health services to less developed countries. It also supports the struggle for human rights throughout the world.

PREPARING FOR THE REGENTS

What role has the United Nations played in the Cold War and post–Cold War world?

SUMMARY

After World War II, with the help of the United States, democratic governments were established in Japan and West Germany. The United States and the Soviet Union emerged as two rival superpowers with differing political and economic systems. Their rivalry threatened peace around the world in a struggle called the Cold War that went on for more than 45 years. The two superpowers engaged in the buildup of arms, competition in space, and surrogate conflicts in other parts of the world. Despite difficulties, the United Nations remained a force for stability and peace.

PREPARING FOR THE REGENTS

Write a brief essay discussing why the Cold War took place and what impacts it has had on the world.

SECTION 2   Economic Issues

⭐ **THE BIG IDEA**
In the Cold War and post–Cold War eras:

- countries developed market economies, command economies, or mixed economies.

- developing nations struggled to strengthen their economies.

- Western Europe and Japan experienced rapid economic recovery.

- the nations of the world became increasingly interdependent.

SECTION OVERVIEW

In the years after 1945, developing nations chose to develop either a market economy, a command economy, or a mixed economy. Countries in South Asia, Latin America, and Africa struggled to industrialize, improve agriculture, and curb population growth. In Western Europe and Japan, economies recovered and grew rapidly. West Germany and Japan became economic superpowers. The economies of the Pacific Rim, modeled on Japanese success, grew aggressively through trade and industrialization. After 1945, the economic interdependence of the world became clearer. When Middle Eastern oil suppliers limited oil in the 1970s, the economies of the West were hurt.

KEY THEMES AND CONCEPTS

As you review this section, take special note of the following key themes and concepts:

Economic Systems   What are capitalism and communism?

Factors of Production   How have developing nations combined human, natural, and capital resources to promote economic development?

Change   Why did Western Europe and Japan experience great economic growth after 1945?

Needs and Wants   How has the need for petroleum affected international relations?

KEY PEOPLE AND TERMS

As you review this section, be sure you understand the significance of these key people and terms:

developed nation	European Community	zaibatsu
developing nation	Common Market	balance of trade
mixed economy	European Union	Pacific Rim
import substitution	euro	OPEC

Comparison of Market Economies and Command Economies

	Market Economy	Command Economy
Ownership	All property, including the means of production, is privately owned.	The government owns the means of production, distribution, and exchange.
Economic decisions	Private businesses and individuals are free from public control so that they can make basic economic decisions, including what, where, how much, and at what prices goods will be produced.	Government officials make all basic economic decisions, such as what will be produced, when, and where.
Market controls	Prices are determined by supply and demand. Competition promotes high quality and low prices.	The government plans the economy. There is limited production of consumer goods and an emphasis on industrial growth.

MARKET ECONOMIES AND COMMAND ECONOMIES

In the years after World War II, some nations were basing their economic development on the ideas of capitalism. Other countries were adopting command economies, such as that which existed under communism. The choices that countries made were often influenced by the Cold War. The United States and its allies supported market economies. The Soviet Union and its allies supported command economies.

 PREPARING FOR THE REGENTS

Compare and contrast market and command economies.

THE ECONOMIES OF DEVELOPING NATIONS

After World War II, the United States, the Soviet Union, Japan, and the countries of Western Europe came to be called **developed nations.** They had modern agriculture and industries, advanced technology, and strong educational systems. Nations with limited resources and without modern industrial economies were called **developing nations.**

Economic obstacles include overpopulation, natural disasters, and indebtedness. After World War II, many developing nations began to build their economies. Some were just emerging from imperialism. Many had to decide which of the two major economic systems they would follow. Some nations took elements of both.

The issues faced by developing nations were unique to each nation. However, several goals were common:

- Building industry
- Improving agriculture
- Controlling population

PREPARING FOR THE REGENTS

To learn more about the economic progress of developing nations, see Unit 8, Section 1.

KEY THEMES AND CONCEPTS

Economic Systems A mixed economy uses elements of both market and command economies. Developing nations, such as India and some nations of Africa, established mixed economies after 1945.

Case Study: India

After India became independent in 1947, it developed a **mixed economy** that combined elements of market and command economies. Heavy industry was brought under government control, and the nation worked with a series of five-year plans. These plans set economic goals and managed resources. Dams were built to produce hydroelectric power. The government poured resources into heavy industries such as steel production. In addition, crop output was increased with new types of seeds, chemical fertilizers, and improved irrigation.

However, India also faced obstacles. India lacked oil and natural gas, slowing growth. Many government-run businesses were ineffective. Agricultural output was not enough to keep up with population growth. In the 1990s, pressure from lenders forced India to institute reforms. Some industries were privatized, and foreign investment was made easier.

Case Study: Egypt

After Egypt became independent, Gamal Abdel Nasser installed a socialist government and economy. Nasser nationalized banks and businesses and instituted land reform. Peasant farmers were given land.

With the help of the Soviet Union, Egypt built the Aswan Dam. It controlled the flow of the Nile River and provided 2 million acres of additional farmland. However, it also increased the saltiness of the Nile and caused the soil of the Nile Delta to erode.

Nasser's successor, Anwar Sadat, encouraged foreign investment as well as free market practices. Sadat was assassinated in 1981. Sadat's successor, Hosni Mubarak, faced economic problems and a rising population. He also faced criticism from Islamic fundamentalists.

PREPARING FOR THE REGENTS

Describe three economic problems that developing nations of Latin America face.

1.

2.

3.

Case Study: Latin America

After World War II, many Latin American nations experienced unrest. Complex difficulties have sometimes hindered development.

AGRICULTURAL REFORM Many Latin American nations have had to grow more staple crops, such as corn and wheat, in order to feed their growing populations. Because overdependence on any single cash crop is risky, these nations have sought to diversify their agriculture. Some, however, still rely on cash crops. A few countries, believing that uneven distribution of land leads to poverty, have also tried to institute land reform in order to get more land into the hands of a greater number of people.

ECONOMIC NATIONALISM Latin American nations have set up their own industries. Under a policy known as **import substitution,** governments encouraged local manufacturers to produce goods that previously had been imported. Eventually, many governments nationalized foreign-owned companies. They also placed high tariffs on imports.

DEBT CRISIS Often, Latin American nations had to borrow money to build industries. When a worldwide recession hit, demand for goods fell. However, these nations still had to make high interest payments. Money went toward paying off loans rather than building industry.

FREE MARKET REFORMS   Some Latin American governments used free market reforms as a way to recover from their economic crises. Government spending was reduced, and private owners were allowed to buy out state-owned industries. Slowly, economic progress was made.

POPULATION EXPLOSION   Many Latin Americans see the need to control population. Some cultural and religious beliefs, however, work against population control. As a result, populations are still growing rapidly, creating a severe economic burden.

Case Study: Africa

Many of Africa's nations gained independence only after 1945, and more gained independence after 1959. The end of colonialism presented many challenges to the development of the countries of Africa.

Like other developing nations, African countries have focused on building industry and improving agriculture. Although industrial growth has sometimes been successful, many nations remain dependent on imports. Also, money borrowed to build industry created great debts. In some nations, such as Nigeria, people flocked to industrial centers. Food production fell, and rural poverty resulted. Cities could not keep up with population increases.

A continuing reliance on cash crops means that many African nations still need to import food to feed their growing populations. Cash crop economies also have other negative effects. For example, when oil prices fell, the economy of Nigeria—a nation rich in oil—nearly collapsed.

 PREPARING FOR THE REGENTS

Practice your chart reading skills by listing and briefly explaining five obstacles to progress in Africa.

1.

2.

3.

4.

5.

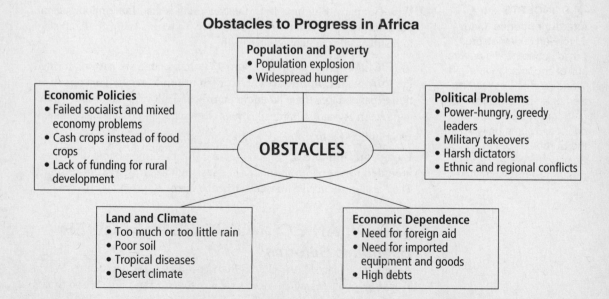

Obstacles to Progress in Africa

Population and Poverty
- Population explosion
- Widespread hunger

Economic Policies
- Failed socialist and mixed economy problems
- Cash crops instead of food crops
- Lack of funding for rural development

OBSTACLES

Political Problems
- Power-hungry, greedy leaders
- Military takeovers
- Harsh dictators
- Ethnic and regional conflicts

Land and Climate
- Too much or too little rain
- Poor soil
- Tropical diseases
- Desert climate

Economic Dependence
- Need for foreign aid
- Need for imported equipment and goods
- High debts

Even so, Africa shows great potential.

- Many African nations have moved from a socialist model to a free market economy, experiencing growth as a result.
- Other nations have expanded mining and manufacturing and built factories to process agricultural products.
- Some nations have improved transportation and communication.

ECONOMIC RECOVERY AND COOPERATION IN EUROPE

After the end of World War II, the United States developed the Marshall Plan to encourage the economic development of Western Europe and to prevent the expansion of communism.

West German Economic Miracle

Capital from the Marshall Plan and the leadership of a democratic government helped West Germany to recover. West Germans rebuilt their cities and factories and developed a strong industrial economy. High-quality German exports were in great demand around the world. The recovery in Germany was so dramatic that it was referred to as an "economic miracle." After Germany was reunited in 1990, difficulties emerged as East Germans made the transition to a market economy.

European Economic Unification

With aid from the Marshall Plan, other Western European countries also recovered quickly from World War II. The countries of Europe promoted their own prosperity through cooperation.

EUROPEAN COAL AND STEEL COMMUNITY In 1952, France, West Germany, Belgium, Italy, the Netherlands, and Luxembourg set up the European Coal and Steel Community to regulate the coal and steel industries and spur economic growth.

THE COMMON MARKET In 1957, these same six nations formed the **European Community** (EC), or **Common Market.** This organization expanded free trade by ending tariffs and allowing labor and capital to move freely across borders. Britain, Denmark, and Ireland later joined.

EUROPEAN UNION The EC expanded further and became the **European Union** (EU). By 2004, the EU had 25 member states. These included former communist countries such as Hungary and Poland. They also introduced a new currency, the **euro.**

JAPAN: AN ECONOMIC SUPERPOWER
Economic Reforms

As you have learned, the United States occupation of Japan after World War II helped to establish democracy in that nation. The United States

PREPARING FOR THE REGENTS

Why do you think West Germany's economy achieved much greater success than East Germany's?

KEY THEMES AND CONCEPTS

Interdependence Many European countries prospered economically as a result of cooperation after World War II. Six Western European nations drew together in 1952 to form an economic community. Today, the European Union is made up of both Western and Eastern European nations.

also brought economic reforms to Japan. Japanese workers were given the right to form unions. Land reform divided up large estates among tenant farmers. The United States tried to break up the **zaibatsu,** the powerful family-owned business concerns that dominated Japanese economic life, but the reform effort achieved only limited success.

Close Ties With the West

As the Cold War intensified, the United States and its allies viewed Japan less as a former enemy and more as a future ally. The outbreak of war in Korea in 1950 reinforced this view. Japan served as a staging area for operations in Korea. The American occupation of Japan ended in 1952. As Japanese industry prospered, the nation engaged in increased trade with the United States and other countries.

How the Japanese Economy Succeeded

Japan rebounded rapidly from the economic devastation that followed World War II. Japan sent many manufactured items to other countries, building a favorable balance of trade. A country that has a favorable **balance of trade** exports more goods than it imports. Why was Japan so successful?

- Japan adapted the latest western technology to its own industries.
- Japan had a well-educated and highly skilled work force.
- Japanese savings gave banks capital to invest in industry.
- The government, prohibited from spending money on defense, poured funds into the economy.
- The government imposed high tariffs and strict regulations to limit foreign competition.

Recently, Japan's economy has not been so healthy. In the late 1980s, Japan was hit by an economic recession. Banks staggered under a mountain of bad debt, companies went bankrupt, and unemployment rose. Japan's government seemed powerless to end the recession.

ECONOMIC DEVELOPMENT OF THE PACIFIC RIM

Southeast Asia and East Asia are part of a region known as the **Pacific Rim,** a group of nations in Asia and the Americas that border the Pacific Ocean. The Pacific began to be an important highway for trade in the 1500s. In the latter half of the 1900s, activity in this area increased dramatically. Some people predict that the 2000s will be the "Pacific century." The size of the area's population makes it a huge market.

Four countries in the area have become known as the "Asian Tigers." They are Taiwan, Hong Kong, Singapore, and South Korea. The Asian Tigers are given this name because of their aggressive economic growth. These countries have followed the Japanese model. They experienced rapid industrialization that led to economic expansion and prosperity.

- **Taiwan** at first set up light industries, such as textile factories. In time, heavy industry developed and created a trade boom, the growth of industrial cities, and a higher standard of living.
- **Hong Kong** is a small island. Formerly a British colony, Hong Kong was returned to communist China in 1997 but was allowed to retain a capitalist economy. Hong Kong is a major financial center with many foreign banks and a busy stock market.
- **Singapore** is a city-state, located on a tiny island at the tip of the Malay Peninsula. Singapore includes one of the world's busiest harbors and is a center of trade.
- **South Korea** initially exported textiles and inexpensive goods. By the 1990s, South Korea was an economic powerhouse, exporting such higher-priced goods as automobiles.

KEY THEMES AND CONCEPTS

Needs and Wants In the 1970s, OPEC nations took advantage of the fact that industrialized countries needed to import oil to keep their economies running. OPEC nations tried to use economic power to gain political power.

OIL, OPEC, AND ECONOMIC INTERDEPENDENCE

Oil became the most important energy resource after World War II. Global economic interdependence is shown in the crises that have developed over oil. Much of the world's oil comes from the Middle East.

The Formation of OPEC

In 1960, Iran, Iraq, Kuwait, Saudi Arabia, and Venezuela formed **OPEC,** whose initials stand for the Organization of Petroleum Exporting Countries. Other oil producers joined later. OPEC's goal was to control the oil industry by setting production levels and prices.

OPEC and Oil Crises

In 1973, OPEC nations halted exports of oil to certain countries. Egypt and Israel were at war, and Arab countries declared the embargo against the United States and other countries that supported Israel. Prices skyrocketed, affecting western economies by slowing growth.

In the 1980s and 1990s, a surplus of oil allowed prices to fall. However, OPEC nations cut oil production in 1998. Oil prices rose sharply around the world.

PREPARING FOR THE REGENTS

How has the global economy changed since 1945?

SUMMARY

In the years after 1945, some countries developed market economies, while others developed command economies. Developing nations struggled to build their economies and deal with economic problems. Western Europe and Japan, with the help of the United States, achieved economic success. Through international trade and finance, tiny Pacific Rim countries became important parts of the global economy. Interdependence characterized the world economy. Oil crises in the Middle East, for example, slowed western economic growth.

3 Chinese Communist Revolution

SECTION OVERVIEW

The establishment of the People's Republic of China in 1949 began a new period in Chinese history. Communists had risen to power during the 1930s and 1940s by appealing to a large part of the population and by achieving military superiority. Under the communist dictatorship of Mao Zedong, however, programs such as the Great Leap Forward and the Cultural Revolution had negative economic results and restricted people's rights and freedoms. The next leader, Deng Xiaoping, made economic reforms but not political ones. The communist government continued to maintain strict control over people's lives.

★ **THE BIG IDEA**
Since 1949, a communist government has ruled China.

- Popular support and military power helped the Communists come to power.
- The programs of Mao Zedong hurt China economically and violated human rights.
- Deng Xiaoping brought economic reforms but not political reforms to China.

KEY THEMES AND CONCEPTS

As you review this section, take special note of the following key themes and concepts:

Conflict How did the Communists come to power in China by 1949?

Human Rights In what ways did the communist government improve the status of women in China? How has the Chinese government violated people's rights?

Change What changes did Mao Zedong bring to China after 1949?

Economic Systems How did Deng Xiaoping reform the economy, and what were the results?

KEY PEOPLE AND TERMS

As you review this section, be sure you understand the significance of these key people and terms:

Mao Zedong	commune	Deng Xiaoping
Long March	Cultural Revolution	Tiananmen Square
Great Leap Forward	Red Guards	

KEY THEMES AND CONCEPTS

Geography China, the largest Asian country and the most populous nation in the world, is located in eastern Asia. Mountains, deserts, and jungles separate China from neighboring lands.

 PREPARING FOR THE REGENTS

To learn more about Jiang Jieshi, see Unit 6, Section 4.

PREPARING FOR THE REGENTS

Why were Mao and the Communists victorious over Jiang and the Nationalists in China's civil war?

KEY THEMES AND CONCEPTS

Change Describe three similarities between the Chinese Communist Revolution and other revolutions you have studied.

1.

2.

3.

TWO CHINAS

Today, China is the most populous nation in the world. There are two Chinas, however. The People's Republic of China is a communist state on the Asian mainland. It has a vast land area and many natural resources. Taiwan, also called the Republic of China, is a small island that today is one of the Asian Tigers. It has a non-communist government. The People's Republic still considers Taiwan a part of China proper. Efforts to reunite the two Chinas have sometimes led to tension because Taiwan values its independence.

COMMUNIST RISE TO POWER

As you recall, Jiang Jieshi (also called Chiang Kai-shek) had taken over the Guomindang, or Nationalist party, after the death of Sun Yixian. In the mid-1920s, Jiang began to strike at the Communist party, which he saw as a threat to his leadership.

Mao Zedong emerged as the leader of the Communists in the 1930s. Along with 100,000 of his followers, Mao fled the Guomindang forces in 1934 in a retreat known as the **Long March.** After traveling more than 6,000 miles, Mao set up a base in northern China with about 20,000 survivors of the march. In the years that followed, the Communists, the Guomindang, and Japanese invaders battled for control of China. After World War II, civil war continued. Finally, in 1949, Mao's Communists were victorious. Jiang and his followers fled to the island of Taiwan.

Reasons for Communist Success

There were several reasons for the victory of Mao and the Communists over Jiang and the Guomindang.

- Mao won the support of the huge peasant population of China by promising to give land to peasants.
- Mao won the support of women by rejecting the inequalities of traditional Confucian society.
- Mao's army made good use of hit-and-run guerrilla warfare.
- Many people opposed the Nationalist government, which they saw as corrupt.
- Some people felt that the Nationalists had allowed foreigners to dominate China.

COMMUNISM UNDER MAO ZEDONG

The Communists set up the People's Republic of China (PRC) in 1949. They wanted to transform China from an agricultural society into a modern industrial nation. Under communism, literacy increased, old landlord and business classes were eliminated, and rural Chinese were provided with health care. However, Mao set up a one-party dictatorship that denied people basic rights and freedoms.

The Changing Role of Women

Traditionally, in China, women were treated as inferior to men. The only role for a woman recognized by the five Confucian relationships was that of wife. As a wife, a woman was considered inferior to her husband. The Nationalists did not change these policies greatly.

In Communist China, however, women gained some rights. Under the new Chinese constitution, women won equality under the law. They were now expected to work alongside men on farms and in factories.

Although Chinese women made progress, they did not have full equality with men. Only a few women had top jobs in government. Women were not always paid the same wages as men for doing the same work. Even so, the position of women improved under the Communists.

The Great Leap Forward

In 1958, Mao launched a program called the **Great Leap Forward.** He called on the people to increase agricultural and industrial output. To make farms more productive, he created **communes,** groups of people who live and work together and hold property in common. Communes had production quotas, which were set amounts of agricultural or industrial output that they were to produce.

The Great Leap Forward failed. Commune-based industries turned out poorly made goods. At the same time, agricultural output declined. Bad weather added to the downturn, creating widespread famine.

The Cultural Revolution

In 1966, Mao launched the **Cultural Revolution** to renew people's loyalty to communism and establish a more equitable society. Mao feared that revolutionary peasants and workers were being replaced by intellectuals in running the country. He shut down schools and universities throughout China and urged Chinese students to experience the revolution for themselves. Students formed groups of fighters called the **Red Guards.** They attacked professors, government officials, and factory managers, many of whom were exiled or executed.

KEY THEMES AND CONCEPTS

Human Rights Chinese women gained some rights under communism. However, they never gained full equality. Very few women were able to acquire top government jobs, and most women did not get paid as much as men who did the same work.

KEY THEMES AND CONCEPTS

Political Systems Describe three similarities between communism in China and communism in the Soviet Union.

1.

2.

3.

Programs of Mao Zedong

Program	The Great Leap Forward	The Cultural Revolution
Goals	• Increase farm and factory output	• Renew communist loyalties
Methods	• Communes • Production quotas	• Red Guards attack professors and other officials
Results	• Program fails • Two years of hunger and low production	• Economy slows • China closes to outside world • People fear arrest • Civil war threatened

United States Recognition

The Cold War was raging in 1949. Consequently, the United States had refused to recognize the People's Republic of China. In the Korean War, Communist China and the United States took opposing sides. By the 1970s, however, this situation was changing. China won admission to the United Nations in 1971, and President Richard Nixon visited Mao Zedong in Beijing in 1972. In 1979, the United States officially recognized the People's Republic of China.

COMMUNISM UNDER DENG XIAOPING

In 1976, Mao Zedong died. **Deng Xiaoping** took control. His leadership brought more economic freedom but little political change.

Economic Reforms: The Four Modernizations

To make China a more modern country, Deng promoted foreign trade and more contact with western nations. He also introduced the Four Modernizations. These were concentrated in four areas.

- **Farming** methods were modernized and mechanized.
- **Industry** was upgraded and expanded.
- **Science and technology** were promoted and developed.
- **Defense** systems and military forces were improved.

LIMITED PRIVATIZATION   Deng got rid of Mao's unpopular communes. He allowed land to be leased to individual farmers. After delivering a certain amount of food to the government, farmers could grow anything they wished and sell it for profit. This system increased agricultural output. The government also allowed some private businesses to produce goods and offer services.

FOREIGN INVESTMENT   Deng also welcomed foreign technology and capital. The government set up special enterprise zones where foreigners could own and operate businesses.

RESULTS OF REFORMS   Deng's policies had both positive and negative results. The economy grew, and some Chinese enjoyed a better standard of living. Foreign relations and trade improved. Crime and corruption grew, however, and the gap between rich and poor widened. Deng's economic changes caused some Chinese to demand greater political freedom.

Tiananmen Square

The government was willing to grant economic reforms but not political ones. In May 1989, demonstrators in Beijing occupied **Tiananmen Square,** demanding more rights and freedoms. When they refused to disperse as ordered, the government sent in troops and tanks. Thousands of Chinese were killed or wounded. The incident showed how important it was for China's communist leaders to maintain control. Order was

PREPARING FOR THE REGENTS

Describe two ways in which Deng Xiaoping's methods differed from Mao Zedong's.

1.

2.

PREPARING FOR THE REGENTS

Why do you think the leaders of China were willing to accept western economic reforms but not western ideas about human rights and political freedom?

LOCKE AND JEFFERSON, PLEASE.

HENRY PAYNE reprinted by permission of United Feature Syndicate, Inc.

PREPARING FOR THE REGENTS

Describe in your own words what this 1989 cartoon says about Chinese leadership and the wishes of the Chinese people.

more important than political freedom. During the 1990s, efforts were made to force China to end human rights violations. However, these efforts had limited effects.

RETURN OF HONG KONG

In 1842, Britain had gained the island of Hong Kong, off the northern coast of China. During the years that Hong Kong was under British rule, it modernized and became wealthy.

In the 1980s, Britain and China decided that Hong Kong would return to Chinese rule in 1997. China agreed not to change Hong Kong's social or economic system for 50 years and to allow the island a degree of self-rule. The island was turned over to China on July 1, 1997.

KEY THEMES AND CONCEPTS
Economic Systems If Hong Kong is allowed to keep a free market economy, how might that affect the rest of China?

SUMMARY

The Communists, under Mao Zedong, rose to power in China after World War II. Their appeal to peasants and to women, their superior army, and lack of support for the Nationalists led to victory for the Communists. The communist government severely restricted the rights and freedoms of most Chinese. Later leaders, such as Deng Xiaoping, allowed free market reforms but little political freedom. Violations of human rights in China have often made relations between China and the United States difficult.

PREPARING FOR THE REGENTS

Create a political cartoon that comments on a major development in China since the 1940s.

4 Collapse of European Imperialism

⭐ **THE BIG IDEA**
After World War II, European imperialism ended, and nations faced difficult challenges as:

- India struggled with social, ethnic, and religious divisions.

- peoples of Asia and Africa used both peaceful and violent means to achieve independence.

- African nations struggled to overcome the legacy of colonial rule.

- Southeast Asia was ravaged by many years of war.

SECTION OVERVIEW

The period after World War II marked the final collapse of European imperialism. India gained independence in 1947 but struggled with ethnic and religious conflicts. In Africa, independence was achieved both through peaceful efforts and through bloody conflicts. In South Africa, years of racial separation ended, and black South Africans gained a voice in government. In Southeast Asia, the struggle for independence came to an end only after many years of civil and international war.

KEY THEMES AND CONCEPTS

As you review this section, take special note of the following key themes and concepts:

Imperialism How did European imperialism collapse?

Nationalism How did nationalistic movements in Asia, Africa, and Southeast Asia result in independence?

Political and Economic Systems What kinds of political and economic systems developed in newly independent nations?

KEY PEOPLE AND TERMS

As you review this section, be sure you understand the significance of these key people and terms:

Mohandas Gandhi	African National Congress
Jawaharlal Nehru	Nelson Mandela
Indira Gandhi	Desmond Tutu
Sikh	F. W. de Klerk
Pan-Africanism	Ho Chi Minh
Kwame Nkrumah	Ngo Dinh Diem
Organization of African Unity	Khmer Rouge
Jomo Kenyatta	Pol Pot
apartheid	Aung San Suu Kyi

INDIAN INDEPENDENCE AND PARTITION

Indian nationalists had been demanding independence since the 1800s. Indians were angered when, during World War II, the British put off granting them independence but expected them to support Britain in the war. **Mohandas Gandhi,** as you have read, played an important part in the independence movement with his policy of passive resistance. Over time, British control of India was weakened. Finally, in 1947, Britain granted independence to India. **Jawaharlal Nehru,** India's first prime minister, celebrated Independence Day with an impassioned speech, full of hope for India's future. Independence, however, brought some difficult problems.

Muslim and Hindu Conflicts

In India, Hindus were the majority and Muslims were the minority. The Muslim League had been demanding a Muslim state. Also, there had been fighting between Muslims and Hindus. In 1947, British officials drew borders that created Hindu India and Muslim Pakistan. Pakistan was made up of West Pakistan and East Pakistan, two widely separated areas that had high Muslim populations. East Pakistan later became the nation of Bangladesh.

The partition, or division, of India did not bring peace. Independence set off mass migrations of Muslims fleeing India and Hindus fleeing Pakistan. Millions were killed crossing the borders. Mohandas Gandhi tried to bring peace, but a Hindu fanatic assassinated him.

Although the worst violence began to lessen after Gandhi's death, conflicts continued to occur. In the years ahead, Indian and Pakistani forces would clash repeatedly over border disputes. Tensions between Hindus and Muslims still exist and continue to erupt into violence today.

Indian Government and Foreign Policy

A DEMOCRATIC NATION   India is the world's largest democracy. It has a federal system of government, with powers divided between a strong central government and smaller local governments. For 40 years after independence, India was led by members of the Nehru family. Jawaharlal Nehru was the first prime minister.

Ethnic and religious conflicts have made democracy difficult for India. After Nehru's death, his daughter, **Indira Gandhi,** became prime minister in 1966. She was assassinated in 1984, and her son, Rajiv Gandhi, became prime minister. He too was assassinated, however, in 1991.

NONALIGNMENT   During the Cold War, India followed a policy of nonalignment. This policy, instituted by Jawaharlal Nehru, allowed India to accept help from both capitalist and socialist nations.

Social Change in India

THE CASTE SYSTEM   The caste system, a system of social stratification, has been a part of Indian life for more than 2,000 years. In the 1900s, the system underwent change.

PREPARING FOR THE REGENTS

To learn more about Mohandas Gandhi, see Unit 6, Section 4.

KEY THEMES AND CONCEPTS

Nationalism In India, nationalism resulted in freedom from colonial rule. Religious conflict led to the creation of two nations: India and Pakistan.

PREPARING FOR THE REGENTS

To learn more about conflict between India and Pakistan, see Unit 8, Section 2.

PREPARING FOR THE REGENTS

To learn more about ethnic and religious divisions in India, see Unit 8, Section 2.

KEY THEMES AND CONCEPTS

Economic Systems Nonalignment allowed developing nations to accept help from both communist and capitalist nations. India was a leader among nonaligned nations.

Obstacles to Progress in India

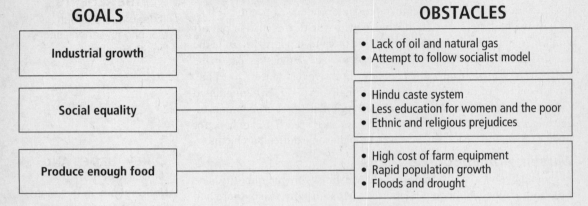

GOALS	OBSTACLES
Industrial growth	• Lack of oil and natural gas • Attempt to follow socialist model
Social equality	• Hindu caste system • Less education for women and the poor • Ethnic and religious prejudices
Produce enough food	• High cost of farm equipment • Rapid population growth • Floods and drought

- Mohandas Gandhi campaigned to end the harsh treatment of the caste called Untouchables.
- The Indian constitution of 1950 banned discrimination against Untouchables.
- The government set aside jobs and places in universities for Untouchables.

In spite of improvements in the legal status of Untouchables, discrimination still exists. Although there are movements for caste reform, the system is still a part of Indian society. It has a stronger effect in rural villages than in urban areas.

THE STATUS OF WOMEN   The Indian constitution of 1950 also granted rights to women. It gave women the right to vote and recognized their right to divorce and inherit property. Indira Gandhi, a woman, became prime minister in 1966. As with the caste system, traditional restrictions on women are more persistent in rural areas.

Sikh Separatism

Sikhism is a religion that began in India in the 1500s by blending elements of Islam and Hinduism. In the 1980s, there was an increased demand for self-rule by Sikhs in the state of Punjab. In the early 1980s, Sikh separatists occupied the Golden Temple in Amritsar to express their demands. Indira Gandhi, still prime minister at the time, sent troops. Many Sikhs died as a result. Not long after that, Gandhi herself was assassinated by two Sikhs who had served as her bodyguards. Continuing tension exists between Sikhs and Hindus.

INDEPENDENT NATIONS IN AFRICA

A movement called Pan-Africanism had been nourishing nationalist movements in Africa since the 1920s. **Pan-Africanism** emphasized the unity of Africans and people of African descent all over the world.

PREPARING FOR THE REGENTS

How is the caste system that exists in India today different from the caste system of the past?

KEY THEMES AND CONCEPTS

Diversity India is a land of diverse peoples with differing religions and languages. The majority of the people is Hindu, but minorities hope to gain power; some even hope to create their own nations.

Although a few African nations had achieved independence before 1945, most gained independence only after World War II. Many Africans had fought in the war. They resented returning home to second-class citizenship. Some Africans had migrated to cities during the war to work in defense industries. There they were exposed to nationalist ideas. In addition, the Atlantic Charter, signed by Franklin Roosevelt and Winston Churchill in 1941, had set forth the goal of self-determination for all nations.

Early Independence Movements

GHANA   The Gold Coast was a British colony. American-educated leader **Kwame Nkrumah,** inspired by Pan-Africanism and by the writings of Mohandas Gandhi, organized a political party. Nkrumah used strikes and boycotts to battle the British. In 1957, the British granted the Gold Coast independence, and Nkrumah became its prime minister. Nkrumah renamed the country Ghana, a name that linked the new nation to its African past. In 1963, Nkrumah created the **Organization of African Unity,** or OAU. This group promoted Pan-Africanism and the end of colonialism in Africa.

KENYA   In the British colony of Kenya, the independence struggle was led by **Jomo Kenyatta.** He was a spokesman for the Kikuyu people, who had been driven off their land by European settlers. When some Kikuyu turned to violent means to gain liberation, the British jailed Kenyatta. Later, however, Kenyatta was released. In 1963, he became the first prime minister of an independent Kenya.

ALGERIA   Algeria, a French colony, had about a million European settlers. A strong Muslim nationalist movement emerged. Fighting between the French army and Algerian nationalists resulted in the deaths of hundreds of thousands of people between 1954 and 1962. Eventually, public opinion in France turned against the war. In 1962, Algeria became a free nation.

Economic Links with Europe

Today, much of Africa suffers from trading patterns that were established during the age of imperialism. European nations had created colonial economies that depended on the export of raw materials and cash crops from Africa. Many African nations still rely on the export of just a few products. When the prices of these products fall, the nations' economies can be devastated. Many African countries also rely greatly on manufactured goods imported from Europe. As a result, these countries have trade deficits and rising debts.

Strong economic links have been maintained between many African nations and the colonial powers that once ruled them. Some former French colonies, for example, have adopted the French currency and many give preference to French products. This also occurs in countries

 PREPARING FOR THE REGENTS

List three ways in which World War II increased the desire for independence among Africans.

1.

2.

3.

 PREPARING FOR THE REGENTS

Describe how nationalism led to independence in Ghana and Algeria.

KEY THEMES AND CONCEPTS

Imperialism The pattern of dependence fostered by imperialism made it difficult for most African nations to build strong economies and stable political systems.

**PREPARING FOR
THE REGENTS**

How did the borders drawn
by colonial powers eventually contribute to civil war in
Africa?

**PREPARING FOR
THE REGENTS**

Use your knowledge of
global history and recent
current events to compare
the genocide that occurred
in Rwanda with another historical example of genocide.

that were once British colonies, especially those that are members of the
Commonwealth, an association of former British colonies.

Ethnic Tensions and Nationalism

Most of the current national boundaries in Africa were established during the
colonial period by Europeans. Unfortunately, the boundaries were made
without consideration for the traditional territories of tribal and ethnic groups.
As a result, some ethnic groups were separated into different nations. Other
ethnic groups were united within nations. Today, therefore, loyalty to one's
tribe is often stronger than loyalty to one's nation.

Nigeria is one of the many nations where tribalism has led to civil
war. More than 200 ethnic groups live within the borders of Nigeria. At
independence, several of the larger groups fought for power. Among
these groups were the Muslim Hausa and Fulani peoples in the north and
the Christian Ibo and Yoruba peoples in the south.

In 1966, a massacre of 20,000 Ibo took place. At the time, Hausa dominated the government. The next year, the Ibo declared their region independent, calling it Biafra. A war raged for several years. Nigeria imposed a
blockade of Biafra that ended the war, but not before nearly a million people had been killed in the war or died starvation.

In Rwanda, ethnic conflict led to genocide. Before 1994, Rwanda
was 85 percent **Hutu** and 14 percent **Tutsi.** In 1994, Hutu extremists,
supported by government officials, launched a murderous campaign
against the Tutsis. According to estimates, more than 500,000 people
were killed in just a few months. The genocide was stopped when a
Tutsi-led rebel army seized control of the government.

In 2002, fifty-three African countries formed a federation, the African
Union (AU). Its goals include solving economic, social, political, and
environmental problems in Africa. AU members deal with issues such as
desertification, AIDS, and famine. Eventually the AU plans to create an
economic bloc, such as the European Union.

The AU also works to control conflicts that spill refugees, violence,
and economic destruction into neighboring countries. Such a conflict
has been occurring in **Darfur,** a region of western Sudan, since 2003.
Arabic militias have killed more than 200,000 black villagers, with the
quiet approval of the Sudanese government. More than two million villagers have become refugees. The UN is trying to get Sudan to agree to
allow a UN peacekeeping force in the country.

End of Apartheid in South Africa

For nearly 350 years, Europeans ruled South Africa. Although South
Africa won independence from Britain in 1910, its white citizens alone
held political power. To control the nation's government and economy,
whites in 1948 made official a system of **apartheid,** or separation of the
races. Apartheid required black Africans and other nonwhites to live in

certain zones, the segregation of public facilities and transportation, and forbade interacial marriage.

THE ANTI-APARTHEID MOVEMENT   In 1912, a political party, later known as the **African National Congress** (ANC), was organized in South Africa. The ANC used boycotts and nonviolent civil disobedience to oppose the apartheid.

In 1960, the police killed 69 people and wounded 180 at a demonstration in Sharpeville. The South African government reacted by outlawing the ANC. In 1964, **Nelson Mandela,** an important ANC leader, was sentenced to prison for life. He became a powerful symbol of the struggle for freedom.

Desmond Tutu was a black Anglican bishop and civil rights leader. Tutu and other activists convinced foreign nations and businesses to limit trade and investment in segregated South Africa. Over time, these nonviolent means of protest had a strong effect.

F. W. de Klerk became president of South Africa in 1989. Knowing reform was necessary, he legalized the ANC, repealed segregation laws, and released Mandela in 1990. In 1994, South Africa held an election in which people of all races could vote. Mandela was elected president. He was succeeded in 1999 by Thabo Mbeki.

DIFFICULT STRUGGLES IN SOUTHEAST ASIA

After World War II, growing nationalist feeling spread through Indochina and other parts of Southeast Asia. Southeast Asians fought against foreign imperialist powers to gain their freedom. They also fought among themselves in bloody civil wars.

Vietnam

Vietnam had been ruled by the French since the mid-1800s. During World War II, the Vietminh, an alliance of nationalist and communist groups, fought the occupying Japanese. After the war, the French hoped to regain Vietnam. Instead, **Ho Chi Minh,** leader of the Vietminh, declared Vietnam free. Defeated by the Vietminh, the French abandoned Vietnam. A 1954 conference in Geneva led to the division of Vietnam into a communist north and a non-commmunist south.

THE VIETNAM WAR   Elections were supposed to be held in 1956 to unite Vietnam. However, the American-supported South Vietnamese government of **Ngo Dinh Diem** did not hold the elections because it

PREPARING FOR THE REGENTS

Describe the role of each of the following figures in the ending of apartheid.

Nelson Mandela:

Desmond Tutu:

F. W. de Klerk:

KEY THEMES AND CONCEPTS

Conflict In Vietnam, a local independence movement became a major Cold War battleground.

Southeast Asia

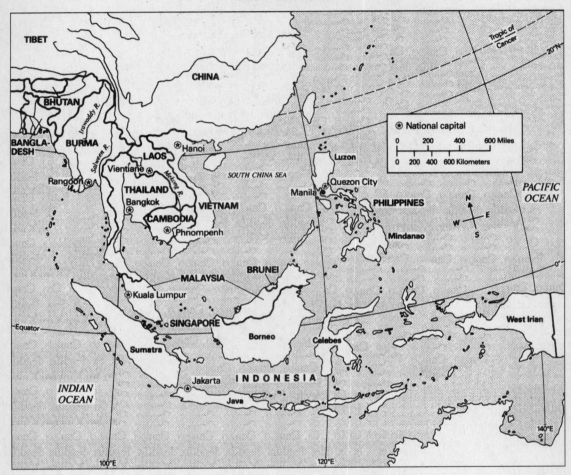

feared that the Communists would win. Ho Chi Minh, now leader of communist North Vietnam, supported the Viet Cong, a group of communist rebels who were trying to overthrow Diem. The United States sent troops to support Diem's government. The Vietnam War lasted from 1959 to 1975. By 1969, more than 500,000 Americans were serving in Vietnam. However, even with this help, the South Vietnamese could not defeat the communist forces. Growing antiwar sentiment in the United States forced President Nixon to withdraw American forces. In 1975, Saigon, the capital of the south, fell. The country was reunited under communist control.

Cambodia

During the Vietnam War, Cambodia served as a supply route for the Viet Cong and North Vietnamese forces. In 1969, American forces bombed and then invaded Cambodia to destroy that route. After the Americans left, Cambodian communist guerrillas, known as the **Khmer Rouge,** took control of the government. Under the leadership of **Pol Pot,** the Khmer Rouge began a reign of terror to remove all western influence from Cambodia. More than a million Cambodians were slaughtered. In 1979, Vietnamese forces invaded Cambodia and occupied the country. In the early 1990s, a settlement was negotiated to end the civil war. UN peacekeepers monitored elections, but some fighting continued.

Myanmar

Myanmar, formerly called Burma, had been a British possession in the 1800s. In the mid-1900s, it gained independence, but it was plagued with ethnic tensions and ruled by a repressive military. Myanmar is a very poor country, and living standards have not improved in recent years.

Opposition to repression by the military rule grew through the 1980s. In 1990, the opposition party, led by **Aung San Suu Kyi**, won an electoral victory. However, the military rejected the election results and put Suu Kyi under house arrest. She was released in 1995, jailed again in 2000, and then released again in 2002.

SUMMARY

European imperialism collapsed throughout the world in the years after World War II. In India, independence was accompanied by conflicts among various ethnic and religious groups. In Africa, nations suffered from the legacy left by colonial rule. Tribal conflicts brought civil war to many nations. In South Africa, the repressive system of apartheid was finally ended. In Southeast Asia, it took years of war to drive out the French. Then another war erupted between communist North Vietnam and non-communist South Vietnam. Despite United States intervention, the communist forces were victorious. In Cambodia, a civil war resulted in the death of approximately 1 million people.

 PREPARING FOR THE REGENTS

List three results of the collapse of European imperialism in the years after World War II.

1.

2.

3.

SECTION 5

Conflicts and Change in the Middle East

<star> **THE BIG IDEA**
In the Middle East, since 1945:

- the creation of Israel has led to conflicts between Jews and Arabs.

- the search for peace between Jews and Arabs has met with some success.

- a revolution in Iran has led to an Islamic republic.

- Iraq has been involved in several international conflicts.

- many Muslims have urged a return to Islamic government and law.

SECTION OVERVIEW

Since 1945, the Middle East has been an area of tension and change. The state of Israel was created in 1948. After years of conflict between Israel and its Arab neighbors, the quest for peace began to achieve some success. In Lebanon, years of civil war ravaged the country. In Iran, an Islamic republic was born. Several international conflicts centered on Iraq, largely because of its dictator, Saddam Hussein. Throughout the Middle East, many Muslims have called for a return to a life based on Islamic law.

KEY THEMES AND CONCEPTS

As you review this section, take special note of the following key themes and concepts:

Diversity How has the diversity of the Middle East affected its recent history?

Conflict What efforts have been made to end conflict between Israel and its Arab neighbors?

Interdependence Why did the Persian Gulf War involve many nations from around the world?

Belief Systems How is Islamic fundamentalism affecting life in the Middle East today?

KEY PEOPLE AND TERMS

As you review this section, be sure you understand the significance of these key people and terms:

Palestine Liberation Organization (PLO)	King Hussein
Yasir Arafat	Ayatollah Khomeini
intifada	Saddam Hussein
Yitzhak Rabin	Persian Gulf War
Camp David Accords	Islamic fundamentalism

Forces Shaping the Middle East

Religious and Ethnic Differences	Natural Resources	Governments	Islamic Traditions
• Muslims, Christians, and Jews • Different sects within religions • More than 30 languages • Religious, racial, and cultural prejudices • Desire for a united Arab state	• Largest oil fields in the world • Oil-rich nations gain wealth and political and economic power • Limited water supply • Arguments over dams and water rights	• Democracy in Israel and Turkey • Rule by royal family in Jordan and Saudi Arabia • Single-party dictators in Iraq and Syria	• Laws of Islam influence government, society, and personal life • Antiwestern feelings • 1990s revival of Islamic traditions

THE IMPACT OF GEOGRAPHY

The Middle East has been a crossroads for people of Africa, Asia, and Europe since ancient times. This fact has led to an enormous diversity of peoples, belief systems, and cultures. These differences have sometimes led to conflict.

The discovery of oil in the region brought power to some Middle Eastern nations. Oil is a vital part of the global economy. Oil resources, however, are not evenly distributed across the region. As a result, Middle Eastern countries have gone to war over control of oil-rich lands. Dependence on oil is one reason why countries around the world take an active interest in conflicts in the Middle East.

A JEWISH STATE AMONG ARAB NATIONS

Jews had begun migrating to Palestine in the late 1800s. After World War II, many Jewish survivors of the Holocaust migrated to Palestine, and the horrors of that time created support for a Jewish homeland. Both Jews and Palestinian Arabs claimed a right to the land of Palestine. Violent clashes between the groups occurred.

Creation of Israel

In 1947, the United Nations drew up a plan to divide Palestine, which was under British rule, into an Arab state and a Jewish state. Jews accepted the plan, but Arabs did not. In 1948, Britain withdrew, and Jews proclaimed the independent state of Israel, which was recognized by both the United States and the Soviet Union.

Israel developed rapidly. Between 1948 and the mid-1980s, nearly 2 million Jews migrated to Israel, some to escape persecution. The government built towns for settlers. A skilled work force expanded the economy. American aid helped Israel as well.

KEY THEMES AND CONCEPTS

Geography What impact has geography had on the culture and history of the Middle East?

KEY THEMES AND CONCEPTS

Movement of People and Goods Since 1948, people have migrated to Israel from all over the world. As Eastern European communism and the Soviet Union collapsed, many Jews moved from Eastern Europe to Israel.

Practice your map skills by answering the following questions.

1. What countries border Israel?

2. What areas were gained by Israel after the 1967 war?

Palestinians and Arab-Israeli Wars

When the state of Israel was created, Arabs vowed to drive the Jews out and restore Palestine as an Arab nation. The first Arab-Israeli war occurred in 1948. After the fighting ended, 700,000 Arabs became refugees. Many went to U. N. refugee camps. Israel had nearly doubled its size and over time, these temporary camps became permanent homes. The poverty and discrimination experienced by these Arab Palestinians fueled anger. Many dreamed of an Arab Palestinian state. Resistance took several forms.

The **Palestine Liberation Organization (PLO)** was led by **Yasir Arafat.** It represented many Palestinian groups. The PLO used terrorist tactics and fought a guerrilla war against Israelis at home and abroad.

Another war was fought in 1956. In 1967, during the Six-Day War, Israel overran the Sinai Peninsula, the Golan Heights on the Syrian border, and East Jerusalem. In 1973, Egypt and Syria launched a war against

Israel's Changing Borders

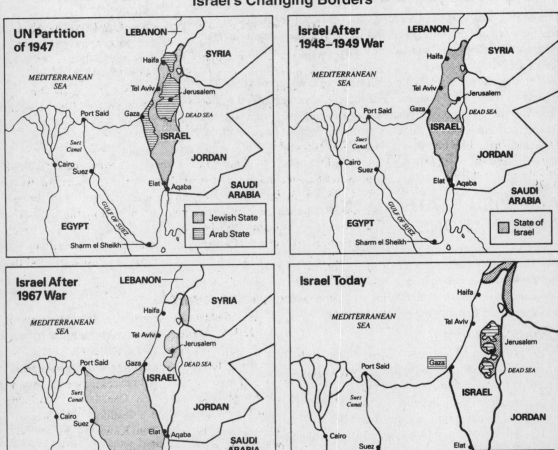

Israel on the Jewish high holy day of Yom Kippur. The Israelis repulsed that attack.

Soon after this Egypt and Israel began to seek peace. In 1979, Egypt and Israel signed the **Camp David Accords,** an agreement to end war between Egypt and Israel.

In 1987, young Palestinians mounted the **intifada,** or uprising. Teenagers defied Israeli soldiers with tactics such as throwing rocks and homemade bombs. Crackdowns on the violence fueled further conflict.

In 1993, direct talks were held for the first time between Israel and the PLO. Yasir Arafat and Israeli prime minister **Yitzhak Rabin** signed a historic agreement that gave Palestinians in Gaza and Jericho limited self-rule but not an independent Palestinian state. In 1994, Jordan, led by **King Hussein,** also made a peace agreement with Israel.

Israelis continued to build settlements in lands that Palestinians claimed while Palestinian riots and suicide bombers began increasing. In 2002, Israeli military forces invaded Palestinian-ruled areas that were centers of terrorist activities. They arrested or assassinated PLO and other Palestinian leaders. Many Palestinian civilians also died. The U.S., UN, EU, and Russia outlined a **roadmap of peace**. This plan would establish a Palestinian state, but the PLO had to make democratic reforms and end the use of terrorism. Peace prospects improved when Palestinian leader, Yasir Arafat, died in 2004.

In February, 2005, cease fire talks began. In summer 2005, Israel withdrew settlers and soldiers from Gaza and four Northern West Bank settlements. In 2006, Palestinians elected members of Hamas to their parliament. Hamas was known for its social services to Palestinians and its terrorist activities. The United States wants Hamas to renounce terrorism. Americans ended diplomatic ties and funding to the Palestinians until this occurs. Ehud Olmert became prime minister of Israel in 2006, following the death of controversial leader Ariel Sharon of a stroke.

CIVIL WAR IN LEBANON

North of Israel, Lebanon had gained independence after World War II. It was a thriving commercial center with a diverse population. Christians and Muslims lived there together peacefully. However, as Palestinian refugees entered Lebanon, especially after 1967, they created a Muslim majority. The PLO became powerful in Palestinian refugee camps.

A civil war between Christians and Muslims began in 1975. Israeli and Syrian forces participated in the conflict. By 1990, a degree of order had returned to Lebanon. In 2000 Israel withdrew its forces, and Syria followed reluctantly in 2005. In May 2005 Lebanon held its first legislative elections since the civil war. In 2006 Hezbollah, a radical Shi'a group, captured 2 Israeli soldiers, leading to a 34-day conflict with Israel.

KEY THEMES AND CONCEPTS

Diversity The diverse population of Lebanon, as well as outside political forces, led to civil war in Lebanon. Diversity has contributed to conflict throughout the Middle East.

THE IRANIAN REVOLUTION

In 1953, Britain and the United States helped Muhammad Reza Pahlavi gain control of the Iranian government. He proclaimed himself the shah. He westernized and modernized the country; he also ruled as a dictator.

In the 1970s, opposition to the shah was led by the exiled **Ayatollah Khomeini.** *Ayatollah* is a title given to learned Shiite legal experts. With protests mounting, the shah fled Iran in 1979. Soon afterward, Khomeini returned, declaring Iran an Islamic republic. In 1989 Khomeini died, more moderate leaders took control. Then, in 2005, elections put conservatives back in power. World concerns grew over Iran's nuclear program, which President Mahmoud Ahmadinejad has refused to curb.

Impact of the Revolution

The Iranian revolution had effects in Iran and beyond.

- The new Iranian government was extremely hostile to the West. Western books, music, and movies were banned.
- The government required strict adherence to Muslim religious tradition.
- Many rights were taken away from women.
- Iranian militants seized the American embassy in Tehran and held a group of Americans hostage for more than a year.
- Iran encouraged Muslims in other countries to work to overthrow secular governments and establish Islamic republics.

ISLAMIC FUNDAMENTALISM

Beginning in the 1970s, increasing numbers of Muslims opposed westernization. They wanted to apply Islamic principles to the problems in their nations. This movement for reform, called **Islamic fundamentalism** by many westerners, has played a key role in the Middle East.

- **Libya** In 1969 Muammar al-Qaddafi's established a government based on Islamic principles. He supported revolutionary organizations and activities in the Middle East and around the world.
- **Algeria** In 1992, the Algerian Islamic political party did well in elections. The ruling party feared that an Islamic revolution might occur. The military therefore seized power and took harsh measures against Islamic activists, resulting in the deaths of thousands of people.
- **Turkey** Throughout the 1900s, the government of Turkey based many of its policies on western models. In the 1990s, however, Islamic political parties gained increasing support and influence. They hoped to restore traditional Islamic government to Turkey.

SADDAM HUSSEIN AND IRAQ

Under the leadership of dictator **Saddam Hussein,** Iraq was involved in several conflicts in the Middle East.

▧ **PREPARING FOR THE REGENTS**

Describe one effect of Islamic fundamentalism on each of the following countries.

Iran:

Algeria:

Afghanistan:

The Middle East and North Africa

A map titled "The Middle East and North Africa" showing countries including TURKEY, TUNISIA, LIBYA, EGYPT, SAUDI ARABIA, IRAQ, IRAN, SYRIA, LEBANON, CYPRUS, ISRAEL, JORDAN, KUWAIT, BAHRAIN, QATAR, UNITED ARAB EMIRATES, OMAN, YEMEN, P.D.R. OF YEMEN, AFGHANISTAN, PAKISTAN, and labeled bodies of water including BLACK SEA, CASPIAN SEA, MEDITERRANEAN SEA, PERSIAN GULF, and ARABIAN SEA.

Iran-Iraq War

In 1980, Hussein's forces seized control of a disputed border area between Iraq and Iran. War broke out between the two nations. When both sides attacked oil tankers in the Persian Gulf, the United States Navy began to protect shipping lanes in the region. The war continued until 1988 and created extreme hardship in both nations.

Persian Gulf War

In 1990, Iraq invaded Kuwait and seized its oil fields. The United States saw the Iraqi action as a threat to Saudi Arabia and to the flow of oil. The first response of the United States was to organize a trade embargo of Iraq. Peacekeeping troops from many western and Middle Eastern countries went to Saudi Arabia. When Iraq refused to withdraw from Kuwait, the 1991 **Persian Gulf War** began. The United States and its allies quickly won the war, and Kuwait was liberated. The United States continued to view Iraqi dictator Saddam Hussein as a very dangerous force. They hoped that the war would topple his dictatorship. He remained in power, however.

SUMMARY

The Middle East is an area of great diversity and economic importance. It is also an area of great conflict. The creation of the state of Israel in 1948 set off years of conflict between Arabs and Jews. A revolution occurred in Iran that created an Islamic republic. A growing influence in the area is that of Islamic fundamentalism, a movement to return to traditional Islamic ways. The aggressive actions of Iraqi leader Saddam Hussein led to a war that involved many countries of the world.

PREPARING FOR THE REGENTS

Which nations border the Persian Gulf?

KEY THEMES AND CONCEPTS

Interdependence
Because the world economy depends so strongly on oil, the Iraqi takeover of Kuwaiti oil fields in 1990 provoked a reaction throughout the world.

KEY THEMES AND CONCEPTS

Conflict What factors have contributed to conflict in the Middle East?

⭐ **THE BIG IDEA**
Between 1970 and 1990, the Soviet Union broke up, and communist control of Eastern Europe ended. During this period:

- the invasion of Afghanistan weakened the Soviet Union.

- Gorbachev's reforms led to the end of the Soviet Union.

- communist governments fell in Eastern Europe.

- ethnic divisions led to civil wars and the creation of new nations.

SECTION OVERVIEW

Eastern Europe underwent great change in the 1980s and 1990s. The Soviet invasion of Afghanistan heightened Cold War tensions and added to Soviet economic problems. Mikhail Gorbachev came to power in the Soviet Union and took steps to reform the economy and allow more openness. His policies contributed to the collapse of communism in Eastern Europe and the breakup of the Soviet Union. By 1989, Germany was reunited. The former Soviet Union and its satellites experienced varying degrees of difficulty as they tried to establish new political and economic systems in their countries. New nations emerged in Eastern Europe, sometimes accompanied by violent ethnic conflict.

KEY THEMES AND CONCEPTS

As you review this section, take special note of the following key themes and concepts:

Change What were the causes and impacts of the collapse of the Soviet Union?

Diversity and Conflict How has ethnic diversity contributed to conflict in Eastern Europe?

Political and Economic Systems What kinds of problems did Eastern European countries face in the transition to democracy and a market economy?

KEY PEOPLE AND TERMS

As you review this section, be sure you understand the significance of these key people and terms:

détente	Vladimir Putin
Mikhail Gorbachev	Lech Walesa
perestroika	Solidarity
glasnost	ethnic cleansing

EASING OF COLD WAR TENSIONS

By the 1970s, the Cold War had been going on for more than 25 years. Both the United States and the Soviet Union realized that the tension could end in mutual destruction. Large amounts of money were spent by both powers on weapons. Under their leaders, Richard Nixon and Leonid Brezhnev, the United States and the Soviet Union promoted a period of **détente,** or lessening of tension. Détente involved:

- arms control talks and treaties.
- cultural exchanges.
- trade agreements.

SOVIET INVASION OF AFGHANISTAN

Détente came to a sudden end with the Soviet invasion of Afghanistan in 1979. The Soviet Union had invaded Afghanistan in order to keep a pro-communist government in power there. This move convinced many in the West that the Soviet Union was still an aggressive force.

Relations between the two superpowers worsened. The United States increased defense spending to match the buildup of Soviet arms that had continued during the period of détente. In the Soviet Union, however, the war in Afghanistan was very unpopular.

The Fall of the Soviet Union

CAUSES

- Leadership of Mikhail Gorbachev
- Openness to democratic ideas (*glasnost*)
- Reshaping of economy and government (*perestroika*)
- Economic problems
- Freedom movement in Eastern Europe

Fall of the Soviet Union

EFFECTS

- Formation of the Commonwealth of Independent States
- Loss of role as world superpower
- End of the Cold War
- Economic hardships
- Conflicts between pro-communist and pro-democratic groups
- Minority revolts and civil conflicts

 PREPARING FOR THE REGENTS

Choose two of the causes shown in this chart and explain briefly how they led to the fall of the Soviet Union.

PREPARING FOR THE REGENTS

Define the following two terms, and tell how they affected the Soviet Union.

Perestroika:

Glasnost:

Effect on the Soviet Union:

GORBACHEV IN THE SOVIET UNION

In 1985, **Mikhail Gorbachev** came to power in the Soviet Union. Gorbachev wanted to end Cold War tensions. He pulled troops out of Afghanistan. He also reformed the Soviet government and economy.

Perestroika

Gorbachev restructured the failing, state-run command economy in a process called **perestroika.** The goals were to stimulate economic growth and to make industry more efficient. Gorbachev also backed free market reforms. Perestroika had some negative effects, however. Inflation increased, and there were shortages of food and medicine.

Glasnost

Gorbachev also called for **glasnost,** or openness. This policy ended censorship and encouraged people to discuss openly the problems in the Soviet Union. Gorbachev hoped to win support for his policies both among ordinary citizens and among members of the Communist party.

BREAKUP OF THE SOVIET UNION

As Gorbachev eased political restrictions, people began to voice their nationalist sentiments. As you have learned, the Soviet Union was a multinational state. People in the non-Russian republics opposed Russian domination. In 1991, the Baltic republics of Estonia, Latvia, and Lithuania regained their independence. Soon, all the Soviet republics declared their independence. The Soviet Union ceased to exist.

In mid-1991, communist hardliners tried to overthrow Gorbachev and restore the previous order. Their attempt failed, but Gorbachev soon resigned. However, Gorbachev's reforms had helped to end communism throughout Eastern Europe. His policies also contributed to the breakup of the Soviet Union.

 PREPARING FOR THE REGENTS

Explain the meaning of the political cartoon on this page.

Reprinted by permission of Bob Englehart, *The Hartford Courant*

DIFFICULT CHALLENGES FOR RUSSIA

Boris Yeltsin became the Russian president. Yeltsin struggled to make the transition from communism to democracy. One of the most difficult challenges was converting the state-run command economy to a market economy. Industries and farms were privatized. Still, economic problems grew worse. Food shortages increased and unemployment rose.

Yeltsin retired in 1999. To succeed him, voters chose **Vladimir Putin.** For the first time in Russian history, power passed peacefully from one elected leader to another. Putin curbed the power of regional leaders and exerted control over the Duma, Russia's legislature. He also sought a new relationship with the West. In 2002, Russia signed a nuclear arms reduction agreement with the United States and began a new era of cooperation with NATO.

EASTERN EUROPE TRANSFORMED

Throughout Eastern Europe, Gorbachev's reforms had sparked demands for democracy and national independence. Poland, East Germany, Romania, Bulgaria, and other countries of Eastern Europe broke away from Soviet control. Through much of the region, there were attempts to enact democratic reforms and make the transition from a command economy to a market economy.

Lech Walesa and Solidarity in Poland

In the 1980s in Poland, economic hardships caused labor unrest. Led by **Lech Walesa,** workers organized **Solidarity,** an independent trade union. With millions of members, Solidarity called for political change.

At first, the Soviet Union pressured the Polish government to suppress Solidarity. The government outlawed the union and arrested Walesa and other leaders. However, communism's power was weakening. International pressure as well as internal pressure led to reform. In 1989, the first free elections in 50 years were held, and Solidarity candidates won. Lech Walesa became president.

East and West Germany United

Since World War II, Germany had been divided into a democratic western state and a communist eastern state. The Berlin Wall had been built in 1961 to keep East Germans from fleeing to the West.

THE FALL OF THE BERLIN WALL   East Germans wanted to share the prosperity and freedom enjoyed by West Germans. By 1989, East German leaders could no longer count on support from the Soviet Union. A rising wave of protests forced the communist government from power. In November 1989, the Berlin Wall was torn down by joyous Germans.

> PREPARING FOR THE REGENTS
>
> Identify and explain three key events in the fall of communism in Eastern Europe.

The Fall of Communism in Eastern Europe

Romania Freedom protests answered with violence, dictator arrested and executed: 1989

Poland Free elections: 1989

Hungary Breakup of Communist party: 1989

East Germany Berlin Wall opened: 1989 Free elections: 1990

Freedom Sweeps Eastern Europe

Czechoslovakia Free elections: 1989

Yugoslavia End of Communist party control, promise of free elections: 1990

Bulgaria Communist leader steps down: 1989

? **KEY THEMES AND**
CONCEPTS

Economic Systems The
reunification of Germany
was a joyous moment for
Germans, but restoring a
market economy to East
Germany created many
problems.

IMPACT OF REUNIFICATION The people of Germany welcomed reunification of their country, but there were problems. West Germans had to pay higher taxes to finance the rebuilding of impoverished East Germany. Unemployment rose in East Germany during the transition to a market economy. Social unrest followed, with some right-wing extremists trying to revive Nazi ideology. Foreign workers, many of whom came from Turkey, were attacked.

ETHNIC TENSIONS SURFACE

Under communism, ethnic tensions in multinational states had been suppressed. With the fall of the Soviet Union, they resurfaced. Czechoslovakia split peacefully into two separate countries, the Czech Republic and Slovakia. Elsewhere, however, ethnic divisions often resulted in open warfare. In the early 1990s, for example, Armenia and neighboring Azerbaijan fought over a small area in Azerbaijan where many Armenians lived. Armenia eventually gained control of the area. In the Balkan peninsula, ethnic conflict ripped the multinational state of Yugoslavia. The Chechen people, whose Muslim culture is very different than that of the Russians, have fought for their independence from Russia for over 150 years. In 1991, when the Soviet Union collapsed, Russia refused to recognize Chechnya as an independent nation. A bitter war began between the Russian army and Chechen separatists. Russian troops and air attacks destroyed sections of Chechnya, while Chechen terrorists conducted deadly attacks on civilians across Russia, including in Moscow theaters. Although Chechnya continues to declare its independence and carry out terrorist attacks, Moscow refuses to recognize the area as an independent nation.

 **PREPARING FOR**
THE REGENTS

To learn more about ethnic
conflicts in what was formerly Yugoslavia, see
Unit 8, Section 2.

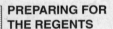 **PREPARING FOR**
THE REGENTS

In what way was the collapse of communism and
the Soviet Union a turning
point in global history?

SUMMARY

Cold War tensions eased in the 1970s, though they flared with the Soviet invasion of Afghanistan. During the 1980s, worker unrest in Poland led to the toppling of the communist government. During the same period, the reforms brought by Mikhail Gorbachev helped bring about the end of the Soviet Union and the collapse of communism throughout Eastern Europe. Germany reunited, and new nations were born. Sometimes these changes led to continuing ethnic conflict. Russia also experienced difficulty in its transition from a command economy to a market economy.

Political and Economic Change in Latin America

SECTION OVERVIEW

Many of the nations of Latin America have experienced periods of unrest since 1945. In Argentina, a series of military regimes and repressive governments finally gave way to democracy in the last decades of the century. Guatemala endured a long civil war and has struggled to rebuild its society. Cuba underwent a revolution in 1959 that led to a communist dictatorship. In Nicaragua, years of strife between communists and counterrevolutionary groups gave way in the 1990s to a democratically elected government. Mexico has experienced more stability but has also had periods of revolt and unrest.

⭐ **THE BIG IDEA**
Many changes have occurred in Latin America as:

- social and political factors have led to unrest.
- nations have struggled to establish democracy and improve their economies.
- drug trafficking has continued to have an impact on the region.

KEY THEMES AND CONCEPTS

As you review this section, take special note of the following key themes and concepts:

Conflict What factors led to continuing conflict in Latin America?

Change What types of political changes occurred in Latin American nations after 1945?

Political Systems What role does democracy play in Latin America today?

KEY PEOPLE AND TERMS

As you review this section, be sure you understand the significance of these key people and terms:

Juan Perón	Fidel Castro
import substitution	Sandinistas
dirty war	contras
desaparecidos	North American Free Trade Agreement
indigenous	cartel

SOURCES OF UNREST

Latin America is a diverse region with a great variety of peoples and cultures. Geographic barriers have discouraged unity, yet the nations of Latin America share similar problems. After World War II, political and social upheavals threatened stability in Latin America. Many Latin American nations looked to authoritarian leaders to provide solutions.

ARGENTINA

By 1900, Argentina was the richest nation in Latin America. The Great Depression of the 1930s devastated the country, however. A military coup brought Juan Perón to power in 1946.

Juan Perón

Juan Perón was a former army colonel. He appealed to Argentine nationalism by limiting foreign-owned businesses and by promoting **import substitution,** in which local manufacturers produce goods at home to replace imported products.

Perón gained popularity by boosting wages, strengthening labor unions, and beginning social welfare programs. Perón's government was repressive, however, and his economic policies led to huge debts. In 1955, he lost power in a military coup.

State Terrorism

PREPARING FOR THE REGENTS

How did individual citizens make a difference in Argentina? What other examples of citizens making a difference can you think of in global history?

Another military government took control in 1976. This government began a program of state terrorism against leftist guerrilla groups. In what came to be known as the **dirty war,** the military arrested, tortured, and killed thousands of people. As many as 20,000 people simply "disappeared."

Many of those who had vanished were young people. Mothers of the *desaparecidos*, or disappeared ones, marched silently every week in Buenos Aires, holding pictures of their children. These protests won worldwide attention.

Democracy Restored

In 1983, Argentina held elections. Voters returned a democratic government to power. The new government worked to control the military and restore human rights. However, economic problems persisted. In 2001, an economic crisis rocked the nation. The hardships led to widespread protests and continued instability.

KEY THEMES AND CONCEPTS

Power The United States has often intervened in the politics of Latin America. This intervention has caused resentment among many Latin Americans.

GUATEMALA

As you have learned, Cold War tensions caused the United States to view certain political movements in Latin America as threats. In Guatemala, the United States helped to overthrow Jacobo Arbenz in 1954, after his land reform program threatened United States business activities in Guatemala. Landowners and the military regained power.

A civil war soon began. The **indigenous** Indians, those who had lived there for years and who were in the majority, suffered. As many as 30,000 were killed in the fighting. Rebels finally laid down their arms in 1996, when a peace accord was reached. The accord brought hope for increased rights for all citizens of Guatemala, including its Indian population.

EL SALVADOR

In El Salvador, civil war raged between left-wing revolutionaries and right-wing forces who murdered anyone they thought sympathized with leftists. The United States provided aid to the repressive government while urging it to make reforms. In 1991, both sides agreed to end their civil war and work to achieve peace.

NICARAGUA

From 1936 to 1979, the Somoza family had governed Nicaragua. The Somozas were repressive but had close ties to the United States because of their anti-communist stance. In 1979, the **Sandinistas,** a group that included both reform-minded nationalists and communists, overthrew the Somoza government.

The Sandinistas in Power

The Sandinistas set up a government under the leadership of Daniel Ortega. Many in the government were Socialists or Communists. The new government introduced some reforms and socialized policies. At the same time, it grew closer to Cuba and other communist nations.

The Contras

In the 1980s, the Sandinistas faced armed opposition from the **contras,** a counterrevolutionary group. Fearing the spread of communism, the United States supported the Contras in their fight against the Sandinistas. A civil war followed, leading to many deaths and weakening the Nicaraguan economy.

Other Central American countries helped both sides reach a compromise. In 1990, the Sandinistas handed over power to a freely elected president, Violeta Chamorro. Nicaragua still had to struggle to rebuild its economy, however.

PREPARING FOR THE REGENTS

Briefly explain causes of unrest in Latin America in each of the categories listed below.

Gap between rich and poor:

Social classes:

Population and poverty:

Urban growth:

MEXICO

Politics in Mexico

After the Mexican Revolution, one party, the Institutional Revolutionary Party (PRI), dominated Mexican politics for 71 years. Between 1960 and 2000, there were periods of upheaval.

- In 1968, students in Mexico protested. The police and the military brutally suppressed the protests.
- In 1994, armed Indian Zapatista rebels in the southern state of Chiapas demanded social and economic reforms. Periodic outbreaks of violence occurred, but the group's goals were not achieved.
- Many groups called for election reforms. In 2000, the PRI lost Mexico's presidential election. Vicente Fox, from the National Action Party (PAN), was elected president. In 2006, Felipe Calderon of the National Action Party won the presidential election in a bitterly contested fight.

Causes of Unrest in Mexico

Gap Between Rich and Poor
- Small group controls most of wealth
- Wealthy people against reforms

Social Classes
- Upper classes descended from Europeans
- Poor majority are mestizo, Native American, and African American

Population and Poverty
- Population explosion
- Not enough land to grow food

Urban Growth
- Migration of peasants to cities
- Slums and urban shacks
- Not enough jobs

Economic Links With the United States

In the 1990s, Mexico, the United States, and Canada signed the **North American Free Trade Agreement,** or NAFTA, a plan to allow free trade among the three nations. Many hoped that it would bring prosperity to Mexico by lowering trade barriers. Some business and investment did come to Mexico, but other manufacturers were hurt by competition from the United States.

Immigration provides another link between Mexico and the United States. Since the 1970s, millions of Mexicans have migrated to the United States, usually in search of better economic opportunities.

PANAMA

In the late 1980s, United States officials suspected that the leader of Panama, Manuel Noriega, was helping criminal gangs called **cartels** smuggle drugs into the United States. United States troops invaded Panama in 1989 and arrested Noriega. Panama experienced greater stability in the 1990s.

The Panama Canal

The Panama Canal was constructed by the United States in the early 1900s. By connecting the Atlantic and Pacific oceans, the canal shortens voyages between the two oceans by thousands of miles. The United States had controlled the canal since it first opened in 1914. Then, in 1977, the United States and Panama signed a treaty designed to gradually turn over control of the canal to Panama. Panama assumed complete control of the Panama Canal on January 1, 2000.

THE ROLE OF RELIGION

The Catholic Church has played a major role in Latin American society since colonial times. Traditionally a conservative force, many church leaders became proponents of social reform during the late 1900s. Outspoken priests and nuns, for example, struggled against the oppressive military regimes that ruled many Latin American countries in the 1970s and 1980s. At the same time, evangelical Protestant groups have gained a growing following with the poor throughout Latin America.

SUMMARY

Many of the nations of Latin America have faced political unrest in the last decades of the twentieth century. Argentina suffered under military rule. Guatemala and Nicaragua experienced civil wars. Cuba was a Cold War battleground. Mexico also experienced unrest. Today, however, democracy is taking hold in the region. Still, some problems remain, including the presence and activity of international drug traffickers.

KEY THEMES AND CONCEPTS

Political Systems In Latin America and elsewhere around the world, drug trafficking causes political upheaval as well as social problems. Drug cartels put pressure on national governments and commit violent acts to gain their ends.

Questions for Regents Practice

Review the **Preparing for the Regents** section of this book. Then answer the following questions, which include multiple-choice questions, a thematic essay, and a series of document-based questions.

MULTIPLE CHOICE

Directions

Circle the *number* of the word or expression that best completes the statement or answers the question.

Base your answers to questions 1 and 2 on the graphs below and on your knowledge of social studies.

Population and Food Production Growth

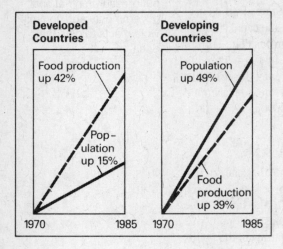

1 Which statement is *best* supported by the data in the graphs?
 1 Food production is rising in both developed and developing countries.
 2 Food production is rising at a faster rate in developing countries than in developed countries.

 3 Population is rising at a faster rate in developed countries than in developing countries.
 4 Population is rising at the same rate in both developing and developed countries.

2 If the trends shown in the graphs continue, it is *most* likely that developing countries will
 1 be able to feed their populations and export food to developed countries
 2 narrow significantly the gap between their population growth and their food production
 3 have a lower birthrate than developed countries
 4 need to import food

3 Which headline concerning the Soviet Union refers to a Cold War event?
 1 **"Yeltsin Assumes Power"**
 2 **"Trotsky Forms Red Army"**
 3 **"Germany Invades Soviet Union"**
 4 **"Warsaw Pact Formed"**

4 "A group of planners makes all economic decisions. The group assigns natural, human, and capital resources to the production of those goods and services it wants. The group decides how to produce them and to whom to distribute them."

This description *best* applies to the
 1 manorial economy of feudal Europe
 2 mercantile economy of the 1700s in Europe
 3 command economy of the Soviet Union
 4 market economy of the United States

Reprinted by permission of Bob Englehart, *The Hartford Courant*

Base your answer to question 5 on the political cartoon above and on your knowledge of social studies.

5 What is the cartoonist saying about the impact of democracy on the Soviet Union?
 1 Democracy covered up hidden problems in the Soviet Union.
 2 Democracy led to the development of the Soviet Union.
 3 Democracy had no impact on the Soviet Union.
 4 Democracy led to the breakup of the Soviet Union.

6 The main reason the Chinese Communists gained control of mainland China in 1949 was that
 1 they were supported by many warlords and upper-class Chinese
 2 the United States had supported the Chinese Communist party during World War II
 3 Mao was a dynamic leader who had the support of the peasant class
 4 they had the support of the Nationalists and of Japan

7 The Tiananmen Square massacre in China was a reaction to
 1 Deng Xiaoping's plan to revive the Cultural Revolution
 2 demands for greater individual rights and freedom of expression
 3 China's decision to seek western investors
 4 Britain's decision to return Hong Kong to China

8 Which statement best explains why India was partitioned in 1947?
 1 The British feared a united India.
 2 One region wanted to remain under British control.
 3 Religious differences led to a political division.
 4 Communist supporters wanted a separate state.

9 From the perspective of the North Vietnamese, the war in Vietnam in the 1960s was a battle between
 1 fascism and liberalism
 2 nationalism and imperialism
 3 republicanism and totalitarianism
 4 theocracy and monarchy

10 One similarity shared by the Meiji emperors of Japan, Peter the Great of Russia, and Shah Reza Pahlavi of Iran was that they all supported policies that
 1 increased the power of the aristocracy
 2 introduced new religious beliefs
 3 kept their nations from industrial expansion
 4 westernized their nations

11 A nation governed by Islamic fundamentalists would be most likely to
 1 allow many different interpretations of the Quran
 2 adopt the values and culture of the West
 3 emphasize the traditional beliefs and values of the religion
 4 promote active participation of women in government

12 "Cuba today is a puppet still dancing after the puppet master's death."

In this 1993 newspaper quotation, which nation is referred to as the "puppet master"?
 1 Haiti
 2 Soviet Union
 3 Spain
 4 United States

13 One similarity between Lenin's New Economic Policy and Gorbachev's policy of perestroika is that both policies
 1 supported collectivization of farms in the Soviet Union
 2 allowed some aspects of capitalism in the Soviet economy
 3 increased citizen participation in the Soviet government
 4 strengthened governmental control over the Soviet republics

14 "Take sides. Neutrality helps the oppressor, never the victim. Silence encourages the tormentor, never the tormented."

—Elie Wiesel, Holocaust survivor

According to this quotation, which situation would have most concerned Elie Wiesel?
 1 formation of the United Nations
 2 the world's initial reaction to ethnic cleansing in Bosnia
 3 Arab reaction to the creation of Israel in 1948
 4 dismantling of the Berlin Wall

THEMATIC ESSAY

Directions
Read the following instructions that include a theme, a task, and suggestions. Follow the instructions to create a well-organized essay that has an introduction with a thesis statement, several paragraphs explaining the thesis, and a conclusion.

Theme: Interdependence
Throughout global history, the world has been growing more and more interdependent. This process has been accelerated in the twentieth century.

Task
• Explain what is meant by *global interdependence*.
• Describe two examples of interdependence.
• Evaluate the positive and negative effects of the examples of interdependence you have chosen on individuals and nations.

Suggestions

You may discuss any nations or regions and any example of interdependence from your study of global history and geography. Some suggestions you may wish to consider are economic interdependence, political interdependence, military interdependence, cultural interdependence, and technological interdependence. You are not limited to these suggestions.

QUESTIONS BASED ON DOCUMENTS

The following exercise asks you to analyze four historical documents and then write an essay using evidence from those documents. This exercise is similar to the document-based question that you will see on the Regents Examination, which may include six or more documents. For additional practice with historical documents, see the Preparing for the Regents section and the sample examinations in this book.

This task is based on the accompanying documents. Some of these documents have been edited for the purposes of this task. This task is designed to test your ability to work with historical documents. As you analyze the documents, take into account both the source of each document and the author's point of view.

Directions

Read the documents in Part A and answer the question or questions after each document. Then read the directions for Part B and write your essay.

Historical Context

After World War II, the world became divided by the Cold War. The Cold War policies of both superpowers affected nations around the world.

Task

Evaluate the ways in which the Cold War affected nations around the world.

Part A: Short Answer

Directions: Analyze the documents and answer the question or questions that follow each document, using the space provided.

DOCUMENT 1

> *A shadow has fallen upon the scenes so lately lighted by the Allied victories. . . . From Stettin in the Baltic to Trieste in the Adriatic, an iron curtain has descended across the Continent. Warsaw, Berlin, Prague, Vienna, Budapest, Belgrade, Bucharest, and Sofia, all these famous cities and populations around them lie in what I must call the Soviet sphere and all are subject to a very high and, in many cases, increasing measure of control from Moscow.*
>
> **—Winston Churchill, from a speech given in Fulton, Missouri, 1946**

1 What image does Churchill use to talk about the division of Europe? Why is this image appropriate?

_____

_____

DOCUMENT 2
Europe After World War II

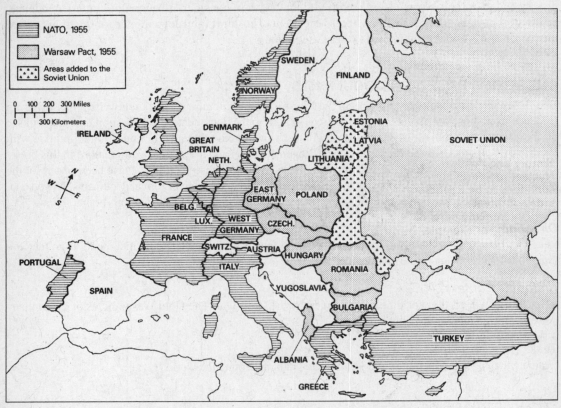

2   Name two European countries that were allies of the Soviet Union during the Cold War.

_____

_____

3   Name two European countries that were allies of the United States during the Cold War.

_____

_____

DOCUMENT 3

The divisive force is international communism. . . . It strives to break the ties that unite the free. And it strives to capture—to exploit [use selfishly] for its own greater power—all forces of change in the world, especially the needs of the hungry and hopes of the oppressed. . . . To counter the threat of those who seek to rule by force, we must pay the costs of our own needed military strength, and help to build the security of others.

—Dwight D. Eisenhower, Second Inaugural Address, January 21, 1957

4   What did President Eisenhower promise to do in response to international communism? Why?

_____

_____

DOCUMENT 4
United States Intervention in Latin America

1965 Dominican Republic
U.S. troops help fight rebel
forces

1983 Grenada
U.S. troops arrive to overthrow
communists

| 1960 | 1970 | 1980 | 1990 |

1973 Chile
U.S. aid helps military
overthrow socialist president

1980s El Salvador
United States aids
military government

1989 Panama
U.S. troops help
remove dictator

5   Explain how one event on this time line was an effect of the Cold War.

_____

_____

Part B: Essay
Directions:
- Write a well-organized essay that includes an introduction, several paragraphs, and a conclusion.
- Use evidence from the documents to support your response.
- Do not simply repeat the contents of the documents.
- Include specific, related outside information.

Historical Context
After World War II, the world became divided by the Cold War. The Cold War policies of both superpowers affected nations around the world.

Task
Using information from the documents and your knowledge of global history and geography, write an essay that describes and evaluates several of the effects of Cold War policies on nations around the world.

   Be sure to include specific historical details. You must also include additional information from your knowledge of global history.

   Note: **The rubric for this essay appears in the Preparing for the Regents section of this book.**

The World Today: Connections and Interactions (1980–the present)

UNIT OVERVIEW

The years since 1980 have been a time of great change. Developing nations face challenges as they strive to progress economically despite rising populations and huge debt. There have been many regional conflicts, and international terrorism remains a great threat to world order. The United Nations addresses many of these issues.

As many nations look to the future, they struggle with the tension between modernization and traditional values. Changes come at a quick pace. Advances in computer technology, space exploration, and medicine have changed the way people live. Still, many problems remain, especially in the global environment. Whatever may be the long-term solutions to these problems, they depend on nations working together toward common goals.

THEMATIC TIME LINE ACTIVITY

Some of the many themes developed in Unit 8 are:

economic systems	urbanization
interdependence	science and technology
movement of people and goods	environment
change	power

Choose one of the themes listed above. As you review Unit 8, create a thematic time line based on the theme you have chosen. Your time line should stretch from 1980 to the present and include major developments and key turning points having to do with your theme.

SECTION  1   Economic Trends

SECTION OVERVIEW

There is an economic division between the more prosperous countries of
the global North and the developing countries of the global South.
Developing countries face many obstacles, such as rapid population
growth, debt, and unrest. In today's world, however, the global North
and South are interdependent. Cooperation among nations can lead to
improvements for all. However, problems in one area of the world may
have powerful effects on the global economy.

KEY THEMES AND CONCEPTS

As you review this section, take special note of the following key themes
and concepts:

Places and Regions   What global economic divisions exist today?

Economic Systems   Why have some developing nations failed to
achieve their goals?

Interdependence   How has economic interdependence affected
the world?

KEY PEOPLE AND TERMS

As you review this section, be sure you understand the significance of
these key people and terms:

post-colonialism	International Monetary Fund
trade deficit	multinational corporation
refugee	Association of Southeast Asian Nations

NORTH AND SOUTH: DIFFERENCES IN DEVELOPMENT

There is an economic division between the relatively rich nations of the
global North and the relatively poor nations of the global South.

★ **THE BIG IDEA**

★ **THE BIG IDEA**
**In the final decades of the
1900s, global economic
trends included the
following:**

- The world became di-
vided economically be-
tween the relatively
prosperous North and
the developing South.

- Developing countries
struggled to overcome
problems such as poor
geographical conditions,
economic dependence,
failed economic policies,
and political unrest.

- Economic interdepen-
dence linked national
economies around the
world.

Wealthy Nations

The global North includes nations of Western Europe and North America, along with Japan and Australia. These nations are highly industrialized and have high literacy rates and high standards of living.

Poor Nations

PREPARING FOR THE REGENTS

What are the differences between the prosperous countries of the global North and the developing countries of the global South?

The global South includes the developing countries of Asia, Africa, and Latin America. Many were once colonies. Much of the area remains poor and industrially undeveloped. Many developing nations are experiencing the problems of **post-colonialism.** Policies established during the age of imperialism continued after 1945. As a result, some nations have remained economically dependent on their former colonial rulers.

OBSTACLES TO DEVELOPMENT
Geography

Several factors have hindered progress in developing countries. Uncertain rainfall, lack of fertile land, and geographic barriers are problems faced by many nations. Some countries are small and have few resources.

Natural disasters such as earthquakes and hurricanes can be devastating to struggling economies. For example, in September 1998, Hurricane Mitch struck Central America. Flooding and mudslides led to deaths and left many survivors homeless. It will take years to rebuild damaged economies.

PREPARING FOR THE REGENTS

Practice your graph reading skills by describing the general trend that this graph shows.

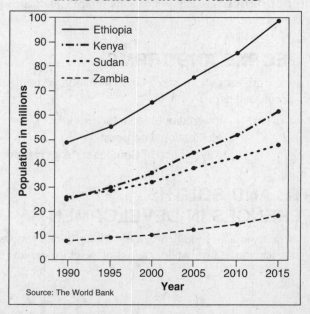

Population Projections for Selected East and Southern African Nations

Source: The World Bank

Population Growth

High birthrates and better medical care in many nations of the global South have led to overpopulation. Problems caused by overpopulation include inadequate food, housing, jobs, and medical care. Many developing nations have tried to reduce population growth. However, few countries other than China are willing to force people to limit family size.

Past Economic Policies

After achieving independence, many new nations imposed socialist economic policies. Over time, socialism hindered economic growth. Beginning in the 1980s, some nations introduced market economies.

Economic Dependence, Trade Deficits, and Debt

The global South is affected by post-colonialism. Much of the labor force is engaged in agriculture. The global South continues to depend on developed nations for manufactured goods and technology while exporting cash crops. These factors have led to trade deficits. A **trade deficit** is a situation in which a nation imports more than it exports.

Economic struggles and the desire to develop quickly have led to heavy borrowing from foreign banks. In the 1980s, interest rates rose, and there was a global economic slowdown. Resources had to be spent on rising interest payments. This spending lowered productivity and increased debt.

Political Instability

Struggles in emerging nations have prevented economic development. In many of these nations, money has been spent on warfare rather than on education or health care. Too often people have become **refugees.**

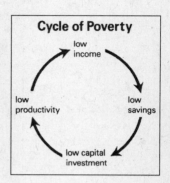

Cycle of Poverty

low income → low savings → low capital investment → low productivity → low income

Labor in Agriculture

	Agricultural workers	Nonagricultural workers
Africa	65%	35%
	Total labor force: 224,920,000	
Asia*	62%	38%
	Total labor force: 1,352,368,000	
Latin America	28%	72%
	Total labor force: 147,254,000	
Australia and Oceania	18%	82%
	Total labor force: 11,549,000	
Europe†	12%	88%
	Total labor force: 373,188,000	
United States and Canada	3%	97%
	Total labor force: 132,495,000	

*Excluding Asian part of the former Soviet Union.
†Including Asian part of the former Soviet Union.
Source: *FAO Production Yearbook, 1987*, Food and Agricultural Organization of the United States. Figures are for 1987, prior to the breakup of the former Soviet Union.

PREPARING FOR THE REGENTS

What evidence does this graph give of the economic division between the global North and the global South? How does having a large percentage of the population in agriculture affect a nation's economic progress?

They flee their homelands to seek safety elsewhere. Economic instability and a labor shortage are the results in some developing nations.

CASE STUDIES
The Congo
In the early 1960s, the Congo was torn by civil war as people from some 200 different ethnic groups competed for power. In 1965, army general Mobutu Sese Seko seized control. He renamed the country Zaire and established a brutal dictatorship. Under Mobutu's rule, Zaire's economy was ruined. Corrupt officials robbed the treasury. Roads were left to decay. Agriculture declined and mines closed.

Finally, in 1997, rebel forces removed Mobutu from power. The nation, renamed the Democratic Republic of the Congo, still faced difficult times as violence between rival groups continued. The country is preparing for its first multiparty election, scheduled for July 2007.

Tanzania
Julius Nyerere, Tanzania's first president, introduced a command economy in the 1960s. Nyerere hoped that nationalizing banks and foreign-owned businesses, setting up a one-party democracy, and promoting collective farming would help the nation. However, many families resisted collective farming. In addition, Tanzania plunged into debt as a result of high oil prices, inflation, and an oversized bureaucracy. In 1985, Nyerere's successor, Ali Hassan Mwinyi, enacted free market reforms. He privatized business and cut government spending. These moves brought some economic improvement to Tanzania.

Brazil

♀ KEY THEMES AND
⸙ CONCEPTS
Environment and Society
Brazil is a good example of the relationship that can occur between economic development and environmental protection. Developing the Amazon region helps Brazil economically. Some nations, however, feel that it has a negative global impact environmentally.

Military rulers controlled Brazil from the 1960s through the 1980s. Under their rule, Brazil experienced a boom. Foreign investment helped the nation develop heavy industry. The Amazon rain forest was exploited for economic profit. By building hydroelectric plants, Brazilians reduced their need for imported oil. However, while the middle and upper classes of Brazil enjoyed prosperity, many workers experienced extreme poverty. The government kept wages low to attract foreign investors and help businesses grow. As a result, working- class people suffered.

In the 1990s, as democracy replaced military rule, Brazil faced serious economic troubles. Much of the country's earnings was used just to make interest payments. The government cut spending to reduce debt. Deforestation in the Amazon continued. Brazilians are searching for ways to have economic growth while reducing destruction of the environment.

ECONOMIC INTERDEPENDENCE
Global Trade
The world has become increasingly interdependent economically. Whatever happens in one part of the world has an effect on other areas.

DEPENDENCE ON OIL   Oil prices affect economies all over the world. When oil supplies are high, prices fall, and many economies benefit. However, when oil supplies are limited, prices rise, and many economies suffer. Inflation brought on by high oil prices has contributed to debt crises in developing nations. On the other hand, falling oil prices are damaging to economies that depend heavily on oil sales.

GLOBAL BANKING AND FINANCIAL MARKETS   Many western banks make loans to developing nations to be used for modernization. As interest rates rose in the 1980s, however, and the world economy slowed, poor nations struggled to repay their loans. The **International Monetary Fund** (IMF) stepped in to work out agreements with debtor nations. Interest rates were lowered and payment schedules were renegotiated. In return, however, debtor nations had to adopt free market policies.

Financial markets are also linked. Changes in one part of the world affect others. When many Asian countries faced economic problems in the 1990s, stock markets in other parts of the world were shaken.

MULTINATIONAL CORPORATIONS   Businesses that operate in many countries are called **multinational corporations.** Many companies based in the global North have made investments in the global South. These enterprises bring new technology. However, local industries may be damaged if they cannot compete with multinational corporations.

Regional Cooperation

In many regions, nations have linked their economies to achieve prosperity and improve regional self-reliance. The **Association of Southeast Asian Nations** (ASEAN), formed in 1967, is made up of ten Southeast Asian countries. It coordinates policies among members in areas such as trade and agriculture. NAFTA (North American Free Trade Agreement) and the European Union are other examples of regional cooperation.

International Drug Trade

Nations in Latin America, Africa, and Asia have been involved in the drug trade. The United States declared a "war on drugs" in the 1980s and pressured many countries to move against drug cartels. There has been some international cooperation to eliminate illegal drug trade. Sometimes the United States has linked this cooperation with trade or aid agreements.

SUMMARY

There is a great economic gulf between the global North and the global South. Developing countries struggle with obstacles that hinder their growth. These include population growth, trade deficits, debt, and instability. Meanwhile, global interdependence has resulted in greater cooperation among nations in banking and trade.

KEY THEMES AND CONCEPTS

Economic Systems How has economic decision making become more global as national economies around the world become increasingly interdependent?

PREPARING FOR THE REGENTS

Describe three policies that could help developing countries achieve greater economic prosperity.

2 Conflicts and Peace Efforts

SECTION OVERVIEW

In the last several decades, some nations and organizations have continued to use violence to achieve political goals. In many areas of the world, ethnic and religious differences have sparked conflict. Even with the end of the Cold War superpower struggles, various areas of the world have become hot spots. In its peacekeeping role, the United Nations (UN) has intervened in many conflicts, with varying degrees of success. The UN also promotes human rights and helps with disaster relief throughout the world.

KEY THEMES AND CONCEPTS

As you review this section, take special note of the following key themes and concepts:

Power For what purposes have various groups used terrorist tactics?

Belief Systems How have religious and ethnic differences contributed to instability and conflict?

Interdependence How does global interdependence cause local conflicts to have potentially global consequences?

Conflict How has the United Nations tried to promote world peace and security?

KEY PEOPLE AND TERMS

As you review this section, be sure you understand the significance of these key people and terms:

terrorism	Slobodan Milosevic
Interpol	Hutu
Irish Republican Army	Tutsi
ethnic cleansing	Universal Declaration of Human Rights

THE THREAT OF TERRORISM
Nature of Terrorism

Terrorism is the deliberate use of unpredictable violence, especially against civilians, to gain revenge or achieve political goals. Terrorism is usually used by groups that do not have their own military power. Terrorists use tactics such as bombings, kidnappings, assassinations, and hijackings. In recent years, new fears about nuclear and chemical terrorism have developed. Terrorism spreads fear throughout the world. It may also lead to more violence if groups attempt to retaliate.

Some recent uses of terrorism have been:

- in conflicts between extreme traditionalist groups and modern western societies (such as the 9/11 attacks by al Qaeda extremists).
- in disputes between nationalist groups over a homeland (as in Palestine and Israel).
- in domestic conflicts between insurgent groups and governments (as in Indonesia).

Efforts to Stop Terrorism

The attacks on New York and Washington, D.C., on September 11, 2001, alarmed government leaders everywhere. The attacks showed how terrorism affects the security and stability of all nations. At the same time, leaders recognized that defeating terrorism will require a lengthy effort. It will bring together nations that are not accustomed to cooperating with each other. They must work together to destroy the ability of terrorist groups to share information, money, weapons, and people.

ETHNIC AND RELIGIOUS TENSIONS

Religious beliefs and ethnic loyalties have united groups and sometimes led to the growth of nations. These forces have also divided peoples and led to persecution and violence. In every conflict, each group involved has its own point of view.

Northern Ireland

Ireland won its independence from Britain in 1922. Britain, however, kept control of the six northern counties, which had a mostly Protestant population. The population of the south was mostly Roman Catholic. Turmoil in Northern Ireland became worse in the 1970s as extremists in both the Catholic and Protestant communities resorted to violence against civilians. The violence continued through much of the 1990s.

The **Irish Republican Army** (IRA) is a Catholic group whose goal was to drive the British from Northern Ireland and unify the country. As the IRA became more active in the 1970s, Protestants formed their own paramilitary groups. Terrorist activity slowed considerably after a cease-fire was declared in 1995, but incidents continued to occur.

KEY THEMES AND CONCEPTS

Conflict List three reasons why groups use terrorist tactics.

1.

2.

3.

KEY THEMES AND CONCEPTS

Belief Systems How have religious differences contributed to the conflict in Northern Ireland?

The Balkans and Ukraine

Yugoslavia was a multinational state created after World War I. In it lived Orthodox Christian Serbs, Roman Catholic Croats, Muslim Albanians, and other ethic groups.

After the fall of communism in Eastern Europe, Croatia, Slovenia, Bosnia and Herzegovina, and Macedonia became independent from Yugoslavia. The breakup of Yugoslavia did not come peacefully. In independent Bosnia and Herzegovina Serbs tried to remove non-Serbs by force. This policy of removing or killing people of a certain ethnic group became known as **ethnic cleansing.**

Observers charged that Yugoslav president **Slobodan Milosevic,** a Serb, supported ethnic cleansing. In the late 1990s, he sent Yugoslav troops against ethnic Albanians in Kosovo. The Serbs mounted a brutal campaign of ethnic cleansing against Muslim Kosovars. NATO (North Atlantic Treaty Organization) forces started a military campaign against Yugoslavia after President Milosevic refused a NATO peace plan. Milosevic was arrested and put on trial for crimes against humanity for the ethnic cleansing in Kosovo.

In 2004, a vicious campaign for president was run in Ukraine. It included intimidation and the alleged poisoning of a major candidate. Observers identified extensive fraud during the election and Ukraine's supreme court declared the results invalid. A new election was held and this time the more pro-western candidate, Victor Yushchenko (who had been poisoned) won.

KEY THEMES AND CONCEPTS

Nationalism Authoritarian communist governments had kept nationalism in check in the years after World War II. After the collapse of communism, nationalism revived and resulted in civil wars.

PREPARING FOR THE REGENTS

Practice your map skills by explaining how this map supports the idea that diversity has led to conflict in the Balkans.

Ethnic Divisions in Yugoslavia Before 1990

South Asia and Southeast Asia

Ethnic and religious conflicts continued on the Indian subcontinent.

- **Muslims, Hindus, and Sikhs** Both Muslims and Sikhs believe they are discriminated against by India's Hindu majority. Incidents of violence between these groups have disturbed India in recent years.

- **Indonesia** Indonesia's population is mostly Muslim, but in East Timor most people are Catholics. When East Timor demanded independence, Indonesia's army responded with force. In 1999, Indonsian forces were replaced with international peacekeepers to allow East Timor to plan its independence. In 2002, Muslim extremists bombed civilains in other Indonesian areas. These extremists seem to be working with al Qaeda. Their goal is to create an Islamic government in Indonesia.

INTERNATIONAL HOT SPOTS

Throughout the world, continuing international tensions have the potential to cause local and global violence.

The Iraq War

At the end of the Persian Gulf War, the United Nations required that Iraq destroy its nuclear, biological, and chemical weapons as well as its missiles. The UN began a series of inspections to ensure compliance. In the late 1990s, Iraq's leader, Saddam Hussein, expelled the UN inspection team and refused to allow further inspections. In response, the United States and Britain staged air strikes against Iraq.

In 2001, the United States accused Iraq of supporting terrorists, such as al Qaeda, and of hiding weapons of mass destruction. UN inspectors continued to search for these weapons. In 2002, the UN denied President George W. Bush's request for military action against Iraq.

In March 2003, without UN support, the United States and its coalition forces invaded Iraq. After 43 days, President Bush declared "major combat operations in Iraq have ended." However, violence continued against the coalition troops, the new Iraqi government, and workers repairing war damage. Saddam Hussein was captured in December 2003. His trial for crimes against humanity began in October, 2005, and went slowly due to many delays. No weapons of mass destruction were located, only evidence of a brutal dictatorship. Some Iraqis, including important religious leaders, supported resisitence to the occupation.

Uncertainty over the future role of Islamic fundamentalism remains a concern. In many countries, like Iraq and Indonesia, groups disagree on whether their nation should westernize or move closer to traditional Islamic principles. Sometimes these disagreements erupt into violence.

VIC HARVILLE/Stephens Media Group

 **PREPARING FOR THE REGENTS**

What political, religious, and social forces led the cartoonist to depict the Iraqi election in this way?

On January 30, 2005, an Iraqi election took place amidst the violence. The transitional government drafted a new constitution, which was approved by voters in October, 2005. The December 15, 2005, parliamentary elections continued a divided parliament, but no longer a Shiite majority. Major disagreements kept the government from forming and parliament from meeting. In April, 2006, a compromise candidate, Jawael al-Maliki, became prime minister and formed a government. The Iraq Study Group, an American bipartisan committee, reported in December 2006 that the situation was "grave and deteriorating." Saddam Hussein was convicted of crimes against humanity and was hanged in December 2006.

The Kurds

Most Kurds are Sunni Muslims, but are not Arabs. Millions live in Turkey, Iraq, Iran, Armenia, and Syria. Kurds have experienced harsh treatment and repression, especially in Turkey and Iraq. Since 1920 they have tried to create a separate independent Kurdish state, with land and people from all these countries. In 2005, they became active participants in the newly elected Iraqi government.

North Korea

While South Korea moved closer to democracy and became more prosperous, North Korea was still ruled by a hard-line communist dictatorship and suffered severe economic hardships. Nevertheless, the North Korean government spent large sums of money on the military. Nations around the world grew more and more concerned about North Korea's nuclear capability, especially after North Korea successfully tested a long-range missile. The Communist government's hope to unite the two Koreas under its rule adds more tension.

China

In the 1990s, China became an industrial power with a rapidly growing economy and expanding trade. However, China's population growth continued to strain its economy. Western nations were concerned about human rights violations in China and China's goal of taking over noncommunist Taiwan.

India and Pakistan

The long-standing hostility between India, with its Hindu majority, and Pakistan, with its Muslim majority, continued into the new century. One hot spot was Kashmir, a region divided between Pakistan and India. In 2001 Islamic terrorists attacked India's parliament. This crisis escalated further, raising fears of a nuclear conflict since both India and Pakistan have tested nuclear weapons.

Afghanistan

Soviet forces invaded Afghanistan in 1979 and for ten years supported a communist government there. During that time, more than 3 million Afghans fled their country. Afghan fighters resisted communist rule and finally forced the Soviets to withdraw. In the mid-1990s, the Taliban imposed an extreme form of Islam on Afghanistan. They also protected the terrorist group al Qaeda, which directed the 2001 attacks on the United States. In response, the United States launched an attack that drove the Taliban from power. The new Afghan government is supported by military from the U.S. and other countries, but the Taliban has continued its resurgence, with 2006 being the deadliest year since 2001.

THE UNITED NATIONS

Structure of the United Nations

The United Nations, or UN, was established in 1945. Its goals are to promote global peace and security as well as economic and social well-being. The UN has the power, through the votes of its more than 170 member nations, to take action against forces that threaten world peace.

The UN has five main bodies. Until 1995, the UN had a sixth body, the Trusteeship Council. It administered trust territories that were not self-governing. The ended in 1994, when the last remaining trust territory became self-governing.

The UN also has a number of specialized agencies. Some, such as the Food and Agriculture Organization (FAO) and the International Fund for Agricultural Development (IFAD), fight hunger through agricultural improvement. Others, such as the United Nations Children's Fund (UNICEF) and the World Health Organization (WHO), are concerned with health issues.

KEY THEMES AND CONCEPTS

Interdependence The United Nations is an international governing body. It is composed of more than 170 nations that cooperate to promote world peace and security.

The United Nations

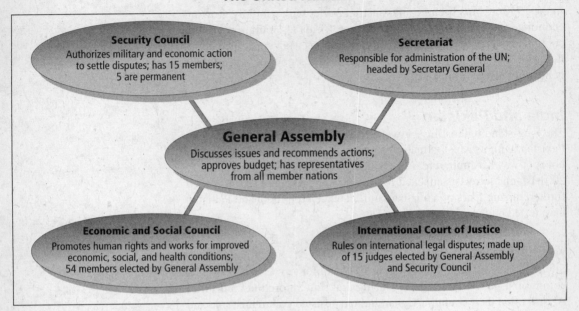

Security Council
Authorizes military and economic action to settle disputes; has 15 members; 5 are permanent

Secretariat
Responsible for administration of the UN; headed by Secretary General

General Assembly
Discusses issues and recommends actions; approves budget; has representatives from all member nations

Economic and Social Council
Promotes human rights and works for improved economic, social, and health conditions; 54 members elected by General Assembly

International Court of Justice
Rules on international legal disputes; made up of 15 judges elected by General Assembly and Security Council

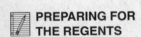 **PREPARING FOR THE REGENTS**

Describe three different types of activities carried out by the United Nations.

1.

2.

3.

Peacekeeping Operations

The United Nations has taken action to maintain peace or restore order in places all over the world.

IRAQ   In August 1990, Iraqi troops invaded oil-rich Kuwait. The United Nations voted to impose economic sanctions on Iraq to force the troops to withdraw. When Iraq did not withdraw, the Security Council voted to allow the use of military force. A multinational force drove Iraq out of Kuwait.

HAITI   From 1957 through 1986, Haiti was ruled by brutal dictators. In 1990, Haiti held free elections. However, Jean-Bertrand Aristide, the victor, was later ousted by a military coup. Several years later, UN forces helped restore Aristide to power and build a functioning democracy in Haiti.

BOSNIA   As you know, the breakup of Yugoslavia in the 1990s was accompanied by violence between various ethnic groups. In Bosnia, Serbs launched a campaign of ethnic cleansing against Croats and Muslims. The Serbs killed or removed many thousands of people. Some criticized the UN for reacting slowly to the situation. UN peacekeepers eventually entered Bosnia to monitor cease-fires and create safe havens for refugees. The UN also charged several Serb leaders with war crimes. A cease-fire agreement came only after NATO forces bombarded Serb strongholds.

The UN has had mixed success in keeping the peace. Although no worldwide conflicts have occurred, the sovereignty of individual nations often makes it difficult for the UN to enforce its wishes.

Copyright © 1994 by Jimmy Margulies, *The Record*, Hackensack, NJ

PREPARING FOR THE REGENTS

How is the UN policy presented in this cartoon similar to the policy of appeasement practiced by the western democracies in the 1930s?

Social and Economic Programs

The UN also promotes social and economic programs.

HUMAN RIGHTS   In 1948, the United Nations adopted the **Universal Declaration of Human Rights.** This document states that human beings are born free and equal with dignity and rights. It goes on to list basic rights and freedoms that all people should have. Nevertheless, human rights are in peril in many parts of the world, including China and the Balkans.

DISASTER RELIEF   The United Nations has responded over the years to famine and other disasters. In the late 1960s, the UN helped save millions in Biafra from starvation during the Nigerian civil war. Other more recent examples of UN disaster relief include the following:

- In the early 1990s, UN forces brought food to Somalians who were caught up in a civil war.
- During the 1990s, the UN provided food to victims of conflict in Sri Lanka.
- Provided relief and recovery aid after December, 2004, Indonesian tsunami and October, 2005 Pakistani earthquake.

KEY THEMES AND CONCEPTS

Needs and Wants At its founding, the United Nations pledged to fight hunger, disease, and ignorance. Its programs to improve agriculture and promote health have accomplished these goals in many regions.

SUMMARY

Terrorists use various tactics, such as bombings and kidnappings, to achieve their political goals. Terrorist activity creates a climate of fear and can lead to further violence. Ethnic and religious differences have sparked conflict in areas such as Northern Ireland and the Middle East. In many areas of the world, local conflicts threaten to become global struggles. The United Nations has intervened in various conflicts around the world to try to bring peace. It has also worked to promote human rights and bring relief to victims of famine and disaster.

PREPARING FOR THE REGENTS

Identify two causes of conflict in the world today.

1.

2.

SECTION 3 Social Patterns and Change

★ THE BIG IDEA
In developing nations to-day, there are pressures for change.

- Strains between modernization and tradition have emerged.
- Overpopulation continues to be a difficult problem to solve.
- Urban areas have grown rapidly and produced social problems.
- People have migrated for better economic opportunities or more favorable political conditions.

SECTION OVERVIEW

Near the end of the twentieth century, modernization and industrialization created tensions. In some countries, these events have brought new opportunities to women; in others they have not. Excessive population growth is a problem facing many nations around the world today. A change that is widespread is rapid urbanization. Another trend is migration—people move to seek economic opportunity or political freedom.

KEY THEMES AND CONCEPTS

As you review this section, take special note of the following key themes and concepts:

Change What are the results of tension between tradition and modernization in societies today?

Culture What are the causes of overpopulation?

Urbanization What changes have resulted from the rapid urbanization that occurred in the late twentieth century?

Movement of People and Goods What patterns of migration have emerged in recent years?

KEY PEOPLE AND TERMS

As you review this section, be sure you understand the significance of these key people and terms:

westernization	urbanization	chador
overpopulation	shantytown	

MODERNIZATION AND TRADITION

In most societies, there is strain between the forces of modernization and those of tradition. This is especially true in nonwestern societies. During the age of imperialism, modernization usually meant **westernization,** or adoption of western ways. Traditions were often weakened.

Many developing nations today hope to find a balance between modernization and tradition. They want to embrace modern technology but preserve traditions and religious beliefs. Two places where this struggle has been going on are Japan and the Middle East.

Japan

Japanese society has always been deeply traditional. The code of behavior that developed during feudal times gave each individual a very clear place in society. People had strictly defined duties toward each other. Families were patriarchal, or dominated by males. Individuals felt a strong sense of responsibility to their families or to a larger group. Personal desires mattered little.

In modern Japan, many of these values have survived. Tensions exist, however, in modern Japanese life.

ROLE OF THE INDIVIDUAL   In the Japanese workplace, the sense of structure, duty, and individual sacrifice for the group remains strong. Japanese companies have always been based on teamwork. Although much was required of the worker, he or she had secure employment and was guaranteed advancement.

Recent economic difficulties, however, have weakened the Japanese economy and resulted in lost jobs. Devotion to the employer declined. At the same time, younger Japanese are less willing to sacrifice their personal lives for their jobs. Some people in Japan express concern about a weakening work ethic.

STATUS OF WOMEN   Laws imposed after World War II ended some of the special legal privileges that were given to males in Japanese families. Women gained many rights, including the right to vote. In the 1970s, they entered the workplace in great numbers. However, traditional views of women keep them in lower positions than men in the workplace. Few women have moved into higher-level jobs in business or government.

The Middle East

Traditionally, Muslim cultures of the Middle East placed great importance on kinship ties and patriarchial families. In some ways, women were subordinate to men. Women were expected to be modest and to remain secluded within their homes. Modernization and movement to cities have created tension regarding some of these traditions.

Today, there are great strains between the forces of westernization and tradition. Many Muslim countries have rejected western values—though not western technology. Some Muslims would like to abolish secular political systems and return to Islamic principles and the Sharia as a basis for government.

- **Saudi Arabia** The oil industry changed Saudi Arabia in many ways. Many people moved to cities, where the traditional extended family structure became weakened. There has been disagreement

KEY THEMES AND CONCEPTS

Culture Nonwestern nations often want modern technology but do not want to lose completely their traditional culture and values.

PREPARING FOR THE REGENTS

For each of the countries listed below, describe one way in which conservative, traditional people have responded to modernization.

Saudi Arabia:

Egypt:

Afghanistan:

Algeria:

over the place of women in society. Some Saudi religious leaders today worry about the influence of western ideas, the education of women, and the effect of such modern technology as television.

- **Egypt** The most heavily populated of the Arab nations, Egypt has experienced a rapid shift in population from rural to urban areas. Social problems have resulted. In response, Muslim reformers in Egypt have called for a return to Islamic laws and customs. Islamic organizations have developed their own schools, medical services, and social services. At the same time, there is a call for a return to traditional practices based on the Quran and a rejection of westernization.

- **Afghanistan** Afghanistan has not experienced a great deal of modernization. From 1979 to 1988, much attention was directed at ousting the Soviet army. Later, Afghanistan came under the control of the Islamic fundamentalist Taliban. Taliban leaders imposed strict religious law on the people of Afghanistan and restricted the roles of women. The Taliban were removed from power after the U.S.-led attack on Afghanistan.

- **Algeria** Once Algeria gained its independence from France, modernization followed, along with a strong desire to rid the country of French cultural influences. Many Algerians began to call for a return to traditional Islamic teachings. A period of intense unrest began in 1991. The army canceled an election when it looked as if a traditional Islamic group would win a strong majority. Violence between the government and Islamic extremists resulted in an estimated 80,000 deaths.

OVERPOPULATION

Overpopulation is an overabundance of people in a region or country that lacks sufficient resources to provide for them. In Asia, China and India face severe problems caused by overpopulation. Many nations in Africa and in Central and South America have very high birthrates, causing them to experience overpopulation problems as well.

Cycle of Overpopulation

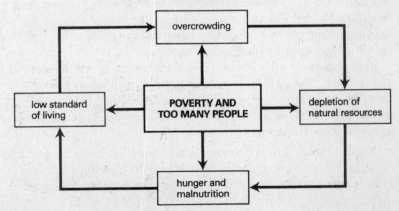

Causes of Overpopulation

Reasons for overpopulation include the following:

- **Religious Beliefs** Some religions teach that it is essential to bring children into the world.
- **Cultural Factors** Some cultures promote the idea that it is necessary to have large families to carry on the family name and provide for parents in their old age.
- **Economic Factors** Some people feel that large numbers of children are necessary to help support the family economically.
- **Lack of Knowledge** Many people lack factual information about reproduction and birth control.

Population Control Efforts

Several solutions to overpopulation have been proposed, foremost among which is family planning. The governments of some countries actively sponsor birth control programs. The Chinese government, for example, provides birth control information as well as financial incentives to couples who limit their offspring to one child. Throughout the world, however, family planning is difficult to achieve wherever cultural tradition or religious beliefs encourage large families.

URBANIZATION

Urbanization, the movement of people to cities, is one of the most significant forces of social change, especially in the developing world.

Reasons for Urbanization

In developing countries, many people have moved to the cities to find jobs and escape the poverty of rural areas. Cities also offer other attractions, such as better health care, educational opportunities, stores, and modern conveniences.

Results of Urbanization

In the developing nations of Africa, South Asia, and Latin America, urbanization has had similar results.

CULTURAL CHANGE   In modern cities, people's traditional values and beliefs are often weakened. The caste system in India, for example, is less strong in urban areas than in rural areas. Women often have more opportunities for change in cities. Some people experience a feeling of being cut off from their earlier communities and customs.

POVERTY   Many people cannot afford to live in cities. They settle around the cities in **shantytowns,** areas of makeshift shacks that lack sewer systems, electricity, and other basic services. Crowded conditions often lead to water pollution and other environmental effects. Lagos in Nigeria, Bombay and Calcutta in India, and Mexico City in Mexico are just some of the cities that have been unable to cope with waves of migration from rural areas.

PREPARING FOR THE REGENTS

What are the dangers of global overpopulation? Why is it difficult to control population growth?

KEY THEMES AND CONCEPTS

Change Industrialization and urbanization are powerful agents of social change in developing nations. Traditional ways are often weakened in large industrial cities.

PREPARING FOR THE REGENTS

Describe two problems that have resulted from urbanization in developing nations.

1.

2.

Percent of Population That is Urban, 1950–2025

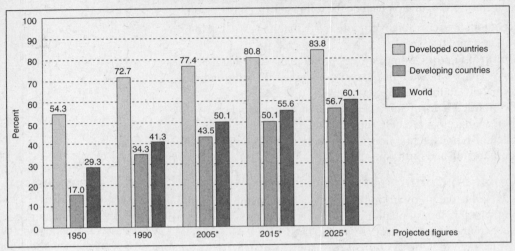

ⓀKEY THEMES AND
CONCEPTS

Decision Making What strategies are developing nations using to overcome the negative aspects of overpopulation and urbanization?

Solving Urban Problems

Developing nations are trying to solve the problems that have resulted from urbanization. Attempts are being made in several areas.

- Developing nations realize the importance of education. Many nations are striving to provide education for all, hoping to give their citizens a chance at better jobs and a better life.
- Religious individuals and groups have set up their own relief agencies. One example is the order founded by Mother Teresa in India, the Roman Catholic Missionaries of Charity.
- Developing nations are working to improve health care in crowded urban centers.

STATUS OF WOMEN

Women's status changed greatly in the 1900s in the West. Women gained the right to vote and entered the work force in large numbers. Some developing countries have also expanded the role of women, but others have limited it.

In the Middle East, the status of women varies greatly from country to country. Israel, for example, includes women in all facets of society. Israeli women are a part of the military forces. Golda Meir was prime minister. The status of women in Muslim countries varies widely. In Turkey, Syria, and Egypt, many urban women have given up some traditional practices, such as the wearing in public of the **chador,** a kind of robe that completely covers the body and most of the face. As you have read earlier in this section, women remain more traditional in other countries such as Saudi Arabia, Iran, and Afghanistan.

In most African nations, women won the right to vote when the countries gained independence. Their social status today often remains low, however. Many of the traditions of the past continue, including a subservient role for women. In rural areas, women traditionally work both at home and in the fields beside men. As men have migrated to the cities to find work in recent years, women have been left with more responsibilities.

PATTERNS OF GLOBAL MIGRATION

The gap between rich and poor nations has continued to grow. This rift has led to migration of people from poor regions to wealthier regions. Many immigrants moved in search of better economic opportunities. Others sought freedom from repressive governments.

- **Immigration to Germany** Until the late 1990s, Germany had a very liberal immigration policy. The German constitution guaranteed food, clothing, and shelter to refugees until their applications for citizenship were accepted or rejected. Many people entered Germany from Eastern Europe or the Middle East. Some were fleeing war-torn areas. Others were seeking jobs. Some Germans felt resentment, especially when the economy faced difficult times. Certain right-wing extremist groups attacked immigrants. The German constitution was amended in 1996 to restrict immigration.

- **Immigration to France** Within French society in the 1980s, more and more people took jobs in management and technology. A wave of immigrants from southeastern Europe and North Africa filled the need for agricultural and other manual labor. In the 1990s, immigrants made up between 5 and 10 percent of the population of France. As in Germany, social and racial tensions emerged. When the economy took a downturn in the mid-1970s, the French government began to restrict immigration.

- **Immigration to the United States** In the 1980s and 1990s, immigration to the United States increased greatly. By 1997, one in every ten people in the United States had been born elsewhere. The majority of these immigrants were from Latin America and Asia. Some were illegal immigrants. The United States took action to halt illegal immigration, deny social benefits to illegal aliens, and return those who had entered the country illegally to their homelands.

SUMMARY

As nations in the developing world have modernized, tensions between modern and traditional ways of living and thinking have emerged. Women have gained new rights and roles in some nations, but they have been kept in traditional roles in others. Throughout the developing world, there has been population growth and movement to cities. Although urbanization has created more opportunities for some individuals, cities have often found it difficult to provide basic services for rising populations. Migrations have occurred as people have sought better economic opportunities and escaped political repression. These migrations have sometimes produced tension and violence.

⚲ KEY THEMES AND CONCEPTS

Movement of People

Answer the following questions about global migration.

1. Give examples to show how ethnic tensions can cause migration.

2. Give examples to show how migration can cause ethnic tensions.

PREPARING FOR THE REGENTS

To what extent are current migrations similar to earlier migrations? How are they different?

★ **THE BIG IDEA**
Science and technology have brought great change as:

- new agricultural methods increase the food supply.

- people are able to obtain, process, and transmit information more quickly than ever before.

- nations are exploring space.

- medical breakthroughs are improving the quality of life.

SECTION OVERVIEW

In the last half of the twentieth century, science and technology have brought great changes. These changes are continuing today. The Green Revolution increased the food supply in developing countries. Computers and advances in telecommunications have brought an explosion of information and, with it, a greater need for education. Technology has allowed exploration of space. Medical breakthroughs have brought better health and longer life.

KEY THEMES AND CONCEPTS

As you review this section, take special note of the following key themes and concepts:

Science and Technology How did science and technology change life in the last half of the twentieth century?

Change What social and economic changes are being produced by the Computer Revolution?

Interdependence In what ways is the world more interdependent than ever before?

KEY PEOPLE AND TERMS

As you review this section, be sure you understand the significance of these key people and terms:

Green Revolution	Information Revolution	clone
Computer Revolution	literacy	AIDS
Internet	genetic engineering	

THE GREEN REVOLUTION
Increasing the Food Supply

Throughout the 1900s, scientists applied technology in a number of ways to increase food production.

- **Irrigation** Farmers installed pumps to bring water from far below the surface of the Earth and used other irrigation systems to distribute water.
- **Machinery** Farmers used machines, especially those powered by gasoline and diesel fuel, to increase yields from their land.
- **Fertilizer and Pesticides** Farmers enriched their soil with fertilizers and eliminated insect pests with pesticides.
- **New Varieties of Grains and Livestock** Scientists developed new, hardier grains and bred livestock that produced more meat or milk.

In the 1960s, farmers in developing countries applied some of these methods to increase their production of wheat and rice. Their efforts were so successful that the result was called the **Green Revolution.** In some countries, such as India and Indonesia, the Green Revolution doubled food output.

Limits of the Green Revolution

The Green Revolution increased the food supply, but it did not solve the problems of world hunger and poverty. In some regions, population is still growing faster than food production. Also, technology has limitations. A region has to have enough water to start with to support new irrigation techniques. Also, irrigation systems, chemical fertilizers, and pesticides cost money that developing nations of the global South do not have. Poorer farmers usually cannot afford these innovations, and some have been forced off their land.

THE INFORMATION AGE

The Computer Revolution

Probably the most revolutionary development since the mid-1900s is the computer. The first computers were enormous machines that filled a

📝 **PREPARING FOR THE REGENTS**

What were the benefits and limitations of the Green Revolution?

KEY THEMES AND CONCEPTS

Science and Technology
The benefits of technology are not enjoyed equally by the global North and the global South. Because technology is expensive, wealthier nations have an added advantage over poorer ones.

New Technology: Benefits and Limits

TECHNOLOGY	BENEFITS (+)	LIMITS (−)
The Computer Revolution	• Creates new jobs • Links people, businesses, nations • Makes more information available	• Threatens some jobs • Available only to those who can afford equipment • Widens gap between global North and global South
Medical breakthroughs	• Prevent illnesses • Wipe out diseases • Increase life span	• Available only to nations and people who can afford them • Present new problems of quality of life and care of the aged
Revolution in agriculture (The Green Revolution)	• Increases food production • Develops new food products	• May succeed only where rainfall is regular • Requires costly chemicals • High cost may force out small farmers

large room and worked slowly. After the invention of the silicon chip, computers were miniaturized. Computers have allowed people to obtain, process, and distribute information very quickly. Businesses today depend on computers for their accounting, word processing, ordering, and many other systems. This great increase in the use of computers is often called the **Computer Revolution.**

The Internet

By the 1990s, the **Internet,** a growing computer network, linked individuals, governments, and businesses all over the world. Many people make connections to the Internet through telephone lines in their homes. With the Internet, people can communicate and do business more rapidly than ever before. At the same time, greater and greater amounts of information are available. The rapid spread of information, which began in the 1950s and increases with each passing year, is sometimes referred to as the **Information Revolution.**

Literacy and Education

The Information Revolution has had a great impact on education and the job market in the global North. In these nations, there has been a gradual decline in the number of jobs in industry and agriculture. New jobs are often based on information and communications services. Such jobs require more education and new types of learning, especially about technology.

Gains continue to be made throughout the world in **literacy,** the ability to read and write. Developing countries have recognized that economic and social progress depends in part on having a literate population. For this reason, most nations of the world provide—and, in fact, require—education through at least age 14.

THE SPACE AGE

Space Exploration

As you have learned, the space age began in the late 1950s with a space race between the United States and the Soviet Union. In the years after the breakup of the Soviet Union, the United States and Russia have cooperated on joint space ventures. Space shuttles circle Earth, and a permanent space station has been set up. Humans have walked on the moon; space probes have been sent to many planets.

Satellites

A satellite is an object that is launched into orbit around the Earth, usually for observation or telecommunications purposes. Satellites can be used to:

- map and forecast weather.
- navigate in ships and aircraft.
- monitor changes in the natural environment.
- aid in rapid worldwide communications.

Satellites are used to transmit television and telephone signals globally. Signals are transmitted from one point on Earth to the satellite. The

PREPARING FOR THE REGENTS

How has the Internet increased global interdependence?

PREPARING FOR THE REGENTS

Why is education so important to progress in today's world?

satellite transmits the signals to another point on Earth. This technology allows rapid reporting of events happening anywhere in the world.

MEDICAL TECHNOLOGY

Since 1945, medical science has achieved amazing successes. Throughout the world, people are living longer, infant mortality rates are lower, and people can enjoy a better quality of life.

Important Advances

- **Antibiotics** Scientists have developed antibiotics to treat diseases.
- **Vaccines** Vaccines have wiped out diseases such as smallpox and prevented the spread of many other diseases.
- **Transplants** Surgeons developed and gradually improved procedures for the transplanting of organs to save lives.
- **Laser Surgery** Lasers, devices that make use of concentrated beams of light, have made surgery safer.

Difficult Challenges

- **Genetic Engineering** The process of **genetic engineering,** which involves changing the chemical codes carried by living things, holds promise for creating new drugs and curing disease. In 1997, the first **clone,** or exact genetic replica of an organism, was announced. Genetic engineering is controversial, however, because it has raised questions about how far science should go to change or create life.
- **New Epidemics** Challenges to medicine have arisen in recent decades. In the 1980s and 1990s, the disease called **AIDS** (acquired immunodeficiency syndrome) resulted in millions of deaths. Scientists searched for a cure for AIDS. Other epidemics include the pneumonic and bubonic plagues in southern India in 1994. Avian influenza (bird flu) was found to infect and kill humans. It spread from domestic and migratory birds to humans across Asia, Europe, and the Middle East.
- **Drug-Resistant Microbes** The widespread use of antibiotics has allowed some types of microbes to become resistant to drugs. Certain diseases that the medical community thought were under control, such as tuberculosis, are becoming a threat again.
- **Destruction of Tropical Rain Forests** The world's tropical rain forests are the source of many medicinal plants. As these forests are being destroyed, scientists worry that valuable drugs in use today, as well as new ones that might have been discovered later, will be lost.

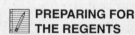

PREPARING FOR THE REGENTS

Ethics are values or moral standards. In what ways have scientific and technological advances, such as genetic engineering, caused ethical conflicts for some people?

SUMMARY

Better food production, an explosion in information and communication, the exploration of space, and medical breakthroughs have changed the world. In many ways, science and technology have benefited people's lives. Many problems, however, remain to be solved.

SECTION OVERVIEW

Many global environmental issues have arisen in the twentieth century. Pollution of water, land, and air threatens the health of all living things. Forests are being destroyed, species are disappearing, and deserts are growing. The safety of nuclear power plants and of nuclear waste disposal methods are additional environmental concerns.

KEY THEMES AND CONCEPTS

As you review this section, take special note of the following key themes and concepts:

Environment and Society What environmental problems exist today?

Interdependence How do these issues affect people globally?

Decision Making How are nations working together to make decisions that will solve environmental problems?

KEY PEOPLE AND TERMS

As you review this section, be sure you understand the significance of these key people and terms:

pollution	ozone layer	deforestation
acid rain	greenhouse effect	desertification
fossil fuel		

POLLUTION

Pollution is the contamination of the environment, including air, water, and soil. Pollution is harmful to humans as well as to plants and other animal life. It takes many forms. Factories and automobiles release gases and soot into the air. These substances can cause respiratory disease. Water can become polluted by human wastes, fertilizers, pesticides, and toxic chemicals. These substances may lead to the development of cancers or even cause death. For this reason, many nations have set standards on both air and water quality. Pollution is resulting in several global problems.

Acid Rain

Acid rain occurs when rain falls through air that is polluted by the burning of fossil fuels. **Fossil fuels** include coal, oil, and natural gas. Factories, automobiles, and other sources release these chemicals. Acid rain damages forests, lakes, and farmland. Because of winds, air pollution in one part of the world can cause acid rain in another. International agreements have been signed to reduce emissions of the substances that cause acid rain.

Depletion of the Ozone Layer

Some scientists are also concerned about depletion of the **ozone layer,** a layer of gases high in the atmosphere that protects the Earth from the dangerous ultraviolet rays of the sun. This layer is becoming thinner, perhaps because of the use of chlorofluorocarbons (CFCs) and other chemical pollutants. Depletion of the ozone layer could expose people to more solar radiation and result in increased skin cancer and eye disease. Ultraviolet rays might also damage crops and marine life. The U.S. and other developed countries have agreed to eliminate production and use of CFCs and other harmful substances. In 2002, a scientific organization found that these limitations were helping reduce harmful pollutants.

Global Warming

Scientists are also concerned about a gradual rise in global temperatures. Many scientists believe that this phenomenon is caused by the **greenhouse effect,** in which warm air becomes trapped in the lower atmosphere. Possible causes of the rising temperatures that have been observed are the use of CFCs, the burning of fossil fuels, and the destruction of forests. Many scientists fear that this overall warming could affect agriculture and cause coastal flooding as polar icecaps melt. They also predict extinction of many plant and animal species. In 1997, a UN summit meeting on global warming set limits on types of emissions that are thought to contribute to the phenomenon. Many countries and some states in the United States have passed legislation requiring businesses to conform to these standards.

DEFORESTATION

Deforestation is the destruction of forests, especially tropical rain forests. Deforestation is usually caused by development as nations harvest lumber or clear land to raise crops, graze cattle, or build homes. Some estimate that the world is losing more than 50 million acres of tropical forest each year. Brazil, India, and Indonesia are the nations where forests are disappearing at the highest rate.

 PREPARING FOR THE REGENTS

Describe the possible causes and impacts of the following environmental problems.

Acid rain:

Depletion of the ozone layer:

Global warming:

Effects of Deforestation

The effects of deforestation include changes in local weather patterns, a buildup of carbon dioxide in the atmosphere (which may lead to the greenhouse effect), soil erosion, and extinction of certain plants and animals.

Global Solutions

One of the challenges in halting deforestation is that many of the world's great forests are in developing nations. These nations need the income they can receive from making use of forested land. Those who want to save the forests say that the economic needs of developing nations must be balanced against needs of the global population. Many nations gathered to debate these and other environmental problems at the UN-sponsored Earth Summit that was held in Rio de Janeiro, Brazil, in 1992.

KEY THEMES AND CONCEPTS
Needs and Wants The economic progress of some developing countries can conflict with the protection of the environment.

ENDANGERED SPECIES
Problems and Effects

A problem related to deforestation is the endangerment of various species of plants and animals. Various by-products of development—the clearing of land, the damming of waterways, and many types of pollution—all threaten to wipe out species of plants and animals.

If species are lost, the balance of the ecosystem of the world could be damaged severely. In addition, resources that people use for food and medicines may disappear.

Global Solutions

Several international agreements have attempted to address the topic of endangered species. Some agreements, for example, have banned the shipment and sale of endangered animals. Some people have suggested that these species can best be protected through preserving their habitats. The 1992 Earth Summit addressed this issue. Other agreements have been made about specific animals, such as whales and tuna, which have been endangered by commercial fishing and other economic practices.

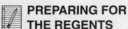
PREPARING FOR THE REGENTS
Why are cooperative solutions needed for international problems such as drug trafficking, deforestation, and the preservation of endangered species?

DESERTIFICATION
Causes and Effects

Desertification is the changeover from arable land (land that can be farmed) into desert. Desertification is caused mostly by human activity, especially the following:

- **Overgrazing** by livestock such as sheep and cattle eliminates the grasses that hold the soil together to prevent erosion.
- **Cutting down forests** robs the land of another barrier to soil erosion.

As grass and trees are eliminated, the soil loses its nutrients. Without plant roots to hold the soil, wind erosion removes the fertile topsoil. The

The Spreading Desert

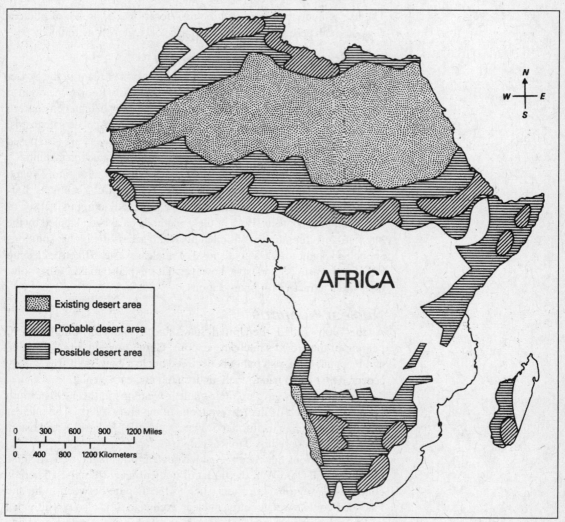

AFRICA

Existing desert area

Probable desert area

Possible desert area

0   300   600   900   1200 Miles

0   400   800   1200 Kilometers

land is then unable to sustain plant life. The Sahara in Africa, for example, is expanding at the rate of about 50 miles per year. The expansion of deserts is one cause of famine.

Controlling Desertification

Methods to control desertification include restricting livestock (to prevent overgrazing) and the planting of new trees to act as a barrier against erosion. These solutions are difficult to put into practice in developing countries, where farmers try to work as much land as possible. However, new farming methods, including improved irrigation, may help solve the problem.

 PREPARING FOR THE REGENTS

Practice your map skills by answering these questions.

1. Where in Africa is the largest area of existing desert?

2. If desertification continues, what social conditions might result?

NUCLEAR PROLIFERATION

The use of nuclear energy and the proliferation, or spread, of nuclear weapons both pose serious potential threats to the global environment.

Accidents and Waste Disposal

In 1986, an accident at the Chernobyl nuclear power plant in the Soviet Union exposed people and crops to deadly radiation. Radiation was also blown across countries in Europe. This accident led to heightened concern about safe use of nuclear energy. Some nations stepped up their safeguards; others scaled back their nuclear power programs. Dangers are also posed by nuclear waste that is created by nuclear weapons production facilities.

Nuclear waste is radioactive and remains that way for many years. Exposure to high levels of radioactivity is very harmful to humans. Earlier methods of disposing of nuclear waste included dumping it at sea or burying it in deep wells. Both of these methods have been banned by the international community. Within nations and across the globe, solutions are being sought for the safe disposal of nuclear waste. Effective cleanup of nuclear waste is expensive, however. This expense makes other solutions more attractive for many nations.

Nuclear Weapons

As the 1900s ended, the United States and Russia controlled over 90 percent of the world's nuclear weapons. China, Britain, France, India, and Pakistan were also publicly declared nuclear powers. It was widely accepted that Israel had a small, undeclared nuclear arsenal.

Several nations gave up their nuclear weapons in the 1990s. South Africa dismantled its nuclear weapons in the early 1990s. The nuclear missiles stationed in the former Soviet republics of Belarus, Kazakhstan, and Ukraine were returned to Russia.

While tensions between the major nuclear powers have eased since the end of the Cold War, the threat of nuclear war still exists. There is concern that regional conflicts, such as the dispute between India and Pakistan, could escalate into a nuclear exchange. It is also possible that additional nations may develop nuclear capabilities. North Korea and Iraq, for example, have both tried to build nuclear weapons. Another danger is that a terrorist group could obtain a nuclear weapon. The world community will continue to closely monitor these threats.

⚲ KEY THEMES AND CONCEPTS

Interdependence How do environmental issues—both problems and solutions—demonstrate the interdependence of the modern world?

SUMMARY

Nations are working together to resolve the environmental issues that face the global community. These issues include air and water pollution, global warming, deforestation, desertification, and nuclear safety. Sometimes making decisions involves balancing the protection of the environment with the needs of individual nations. Only with global cooperation, however, will these problems be solved.

Questions for Regents Practice

Review the Preparing for the Regents section of this book. Then answer the following questions, which include multiple-choice questions, a thematic essay, and a series of document-based questions.

MULTIPLE CHOICE

Directions

Circle the *number* of the word or expression that best completes the statement or answers the question.

Base your answer to question 1 on the graph below and on your knowledge of social studies.

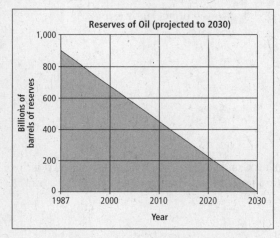

Reserves of Oil (projected to 2030)

y-axis: Billions of barrels of reserves (0, 200, 400, 600, 800, 1,000)
x-axis: Year (1987, 2000, 2010, 2020, 2030)

1   Which action will help slow the trend indicated by the graph?
    1   expanding Green Revolution technology
    2   increasing industrialization in developing countries
    3   using alternative energy sources
    4   lowering worldwide oil prices

2   Bombings, kidnappings, and hijackings are tactics most often used by
    1   imperialists
    2   terrorists
    3   nationalists
    4   absolutists

3   Economic development in Latin American nations has been hindered most by
    1   a scarcity of goods produced for trade and a lack of natural resources
    2   governments that are primarily concerned with preserving the environment
    3   problems of overpopulation, patterns of land distribution, and a lack of investment capital
    4   corporations that are not interested in the use of modern technology

4   Which is the major reason that the United Nations has often been unsuccessful in solving international disputes?
    1   The United Nations does not have sufficient funds to act.
    2   The disputing nations are usually not members of the United Nations.
    3   National sovereignty stands in the way of international cooperation.
    4   The United Nations charter does not provide a means to settle disputes.

5   During the 1990s, Chechens, Sikhs, and Tibetans have all protested their lack of
    1   membership in the European Union
    2   economic stability
    3   independent homelands
    4   representation in the Arab League

6   In many developing nations, rising levels of pollution and continued housing shortages are a direct result of
    1   increased urbanization
    2   a reliance on single-crop economies
    3   changing climatic conditions
    4   increasing nationalism

7   In Middle Eastern societies, women have increasingly been at the center of a conflict between the forces of modernization and the
1   values of traditional Islamic culture
2   pressure for a Palestinian homeland
3   shortage of capital for industrial development
4   need to reduce the birthrate

8   The major goal of the Green Revolution has been to
1   decrease the use of modern farm machinery
2   decrease population growth
3   increase agricultural output
4   increase the number of traditional farms

9   A valid statement about the technology in the 1900s is that technology has
1   eliminated famine and disease throughout the world
2   delayed economic progress in developing countries
3   led to the adoption of free trade policies
4   accelerated the pace of cultural diffusion

10 A study of the accident at the Chernobyl nuclear power plant in the Soviet Union and of the severe air pollution in Mexico City would lead to the conclusion that
1   technology can cause problems throughout the world
2   international trade is more profitable than domestic commerce
3   modern science cannot solve most political problems
4   agricultural nations have caused major world environmental problems

11 A major environmental problem affecting Latin America, sub-Saharan Africa, and Southeast Asia has been
1   air pollution
2   deforestation
3   disposal of nuclear waste
4   acid rain

THEMATIC ESSAY

Directions
Read the following instructions that include a theme, a task, and suggestions. Follow the instructions to create a well-organized essay that has an introduction with a thesis statement, several paragraphs explaining the thesis, and a conclusion.

Theme: Science and Technology
Since 1945, technology has transformed human life. Advances have occurred in many different areas. These changes have had both positive and negative effects on human life.

Task
- Describe one scientific or technological advance made since 1945 that has had a significant impact on global history.
- Give two examples of ways in which this advance has affected you or will have an effect on you in the future.
- Evaluate the positive and negative effects of that scientific or technological advance on the lives of human beings.

Suggestions
You may discuss any scientific or technological advance that has come about since 1945. Some types of advances that you may wish to consider are the discovery of nuclear power, the widespread use of the computer or of Internet technology, and medical advances. You are not limited to these suggestions.

QUESTIONS BASED ON DOCUMENTS

The following exercise asks you to analyze three historical documents and then write an essay using evidence from those documents. This exercise is similar to the document-based question that you will see on the Regents Examination, which may include six or more documents. For additional practice with historical documents, see the Preparing for the Regents section and the sample examinations in this book.

This task is based on the accompanying documents. Some of these documents have been edited for the purposes of this task. This task is designed to test your ability to work with historical documents. As you analyze the documents, take into account both the source of each document and the author's point of view.

Directions

Read the documents in Part A and answer the question or questions after each document. Then read the directions for Part B and write your essay.

Historical Context

People have held differing views about human rights throughout history and in different cultures. In the 1900s, however, there have been movements all over the world to ensure basic human rights for all people.

Task

Examine the progress of justice and human rights in the 1900s.

Part A: Short Answer

Directions: Analyze the documents and answer the question or questions that follow each document, using the space provided.

DOCUMENT 1

Article 1	*All human beings are born free and equal in dignity and rights. . . .*
Article 2	*Everyone is entitled to all the rights and freedoms . . . without distinction of any kind. . . .*
Article 18	*Everyone has the right to freedom of thought, conscience and religion. . . .*
Article 19	*Everyone has the right to freedom of opinion and expression. . . .*
Article 25	*Everyone has the right to a standard of living adequate for the health and well-being of himself and of his family, including food, clothing, housing and medical care. . . .*

—General Assembly of the United Nations,
***The Universal Declaration of Human Rights,* adopted December 10, 1948**

1 Describe one economic right to which Document 1 says all people are entitled.

_____

_____

2 Which article or articles in Document 1 most closely support freedom of speech? Explain the reason for your choice.

_____

_____

DOCUMENT 2

In many parts of the world the people are searching for a solution which would link the two basic values: peace and justice. The two are like bread and salt for mankind. Every nation and every community have the inalienable right to these values. No conflicts can be resolved without doing everything possible to follow that road…

—Lech Walesa, Nobel Peace Prize Lecture, 1983

3   What point was Walesa trying to make by comparing peace and justice to bread and salt?

_____

DOCUMENT 3

4   Explain why some people in this cartoon have been waiting for hours, while others have been waiting for years.

_____

_____

_____

_____

_____

Part B: Essay

Directions:
- Write a well-organized essay that includes an introduction, several paragraphs, and a conclusion.
- Use evidence from the documents to support your response.
- Do not simply repeat the contents of the documents.
- Include specific, related outside information.

Historical Context

People have held differing views about human rights throughout history and in different cultures. In the 1900s, however, there have been movements all over the world to ensure basic human rights for all.

Task

Using information from the documents and your knowledge of global history and geography, write an essay that evaluates justice and human rights in the 1900s. Describe advances in human rights as well as human rights violations. Explain whether you think that the trend is toward greater rights for all.

   Be sure to include specific historical details. You must also include additional information from your knowledge of global history.
   Note: **The rubric for this essay appears in the Preparing for the Regents section of this book.**

Thematic Review

The Regents Examination takes a thematic approach to history. This section of the book will help you to review the themes that are mostly likely to be tested on the thematic essay and document-based parts of the exam.

CHANGE

Change means basic alterations in things, events, and ideas. Throughout global history, major changes have had significant and lasting impacts on human development.

- **Neolithic Revolution** Some 11,000 years ago, people first developed farming methods and lived in permanent settlements. As a result, the first civilizations emerged.
- **Industrial Revolution** This change began in Europe in the 1700s and gradually spread throughout the world. Power-driven machinery in factories became the dominant means of production. The results of this change have included urbanization, a higher standard of living, and pollution of the environment.
- **Chinese Communist Revolution** In 1948, Mao Zedong established a Chinese Communist state. Since then, China has become a world economic power. Today, it works to control its growing population, as well as to adapt communism to modern needs.

Other examples of change are the Crusades, the spread of bubonic plague, the Renaissance, the Scientific Revolution, the Enlightenment, the Agrarian Revolution, the Reformation, African independence movements, and the emergence of Pacific Rim nations.

TURNING POINTS

Turning points are times when decisive changes occur. Turning points often have political, social, and cultural impact.

- **Fall of Constantinople** This event, which occurred in 1453, marked the end of the Christian Byzantine empire and the emergence of the powerful Ottoman empire, a Muslim power that dominated the region for centuries.
- **Voyages of Columbus** The voyages of Columbus began the European race to colonize the Americas. A far-reaching exchange

of people, plants, animals, and ideas occurred between Europe, the Americas, and Africa.

- **French Revolution** The French Revolution of 1789 had a powerful influence well beyond France, spreading democratic ideals and a spirit of nationalism throughout Europe and around the globe.
- **Collapse of Communism in the Soviet Union** The collapse of communism in the Soviet Union initiated years of change in Eastern Europe and brought an end to the Cold War.

Other examples of turning points include the signing of the Magna Carta, the American Revolution, independence movements in Latin America, and the Russian Revolution.

BELIEF SYSTEMS

Belief systems are the established, orderly ways in which groups or individuals look at religious faith or philosophical tenets.

- **Hinduism** A religion more than 3,000 years old, Hinduism has had an enormous effect on India, Southeast Asia, and the rest of the world.
- **Buddhism** A religion founded in the 500s B.C. in India, Buddhism spread throughout Asia.
- **Judaism** The first great monotheistic religion, Judaism has had an important effect on several other world religions.
- **Christianity** Greatly influenced by Judaism, Christianity is a monotheistic religion centered on the teachings of Jesus Christ.
- **Islam** Also greatly influenced by Judaism, Islam is a monotheistic religion and has followers all over the world, especially in the Middle East, Africa, and Asia.

Other examples of belief systems are animism, Confucianism, Taoism, Shintoism, and Sikhism.

GEOGRAPHY AND THE ENVIRONMENT

This theme has to do with relationships among people, places, and environments. Environment means the surroundings, including natural elements and elements created by humans.

- **Early River Civilizations** Early civilizations grew up around rivers. Rivers provided water for crops and for drinking, as well as a means of transportation.
- **Chinese Influence on Japan** Through the bridge of Korea, China had a strong influence on the culture of Japan.
- **Industrialization in Britain** Britain's natural resources, together with such geographical factors as rivers and natural harbors, allowed the Industrial Revolution to begin there.
- **Industrial Revolution: Impact on Environment** The Industrial Revolution had a lasting impact on the natural environment. For

example, new sources of energy often created new types of pollution. Urbanization changed the landscape as cities and their suburbs grew.

Other examples of the impact of geography and the environment are the development of city-states in ancient Greece, the importance of the Middle East as a crossroads between three continents, and environmental problems such as desertification and the destruction of tropical forests.

ECONOMIC SYSTEMS

Economic systems include traditional, command, market, and mixed systems. Each must answer the three basic economic questions: What goods and services are to be produced and in what quantities? How shall these goods and services be produced? For whom shall goods and services be produced?

- **Traditional Economy** An economic system based on farming, often subsistence farming, is a traditional economy.
- **Manorialism** The economic system of Western Europe in medieval times was called manorialism. It was based on the manor, an estate that often included one or more villages and the surrounding lands.
- **Mercantilism** The economic policy in which nations sought to export more than they imported is known as mercantilism. Overseas empires were central to mercantilism, which led to imperialism.
- **Capitalism (Market Economy)** Capitalism is an economic system in which the means of production are privately owned and operated for profit. It developed as an economic system in the 1500s.
- **Marxist Socialism (Command Economy)** Marxist socialism is the economic system found in communist states such as the former Soviet Union and its satellites. It is characterized by ownership of property and operation of businesses by the state rather than by private individuals.

Other examples of topics connected with economic systems are laissez-faire economics, the commercial revolution, cash crop economies, and imperialism.

POLITICAL SYSTEMS

Political systems, such as monarchies, dictatorships, and democracies, address certain basic questions of government such as: What should a government have the power to do? What should a government not have the power to do?

- **Monarchy** In monarchies, a king or queen exercises central power. Monarchies have been common since ancient times, and a few are still in existence today.
- **Feudalism** Feudalism was most prominent in medieval Europe and in Japan from about 1600 to the mid-1800s. It is a decentralized political system. In Europe, it declined with the growth of nation-states.

- **Democracy** Democracy, a system in which the people hold the ruling power—either directly or through elected representatives—had its roots in ancient Greece. It is a primary political system in the countries of the West today.
- **Totalitarianism** In a totalitarian system, a one-party dictatorship regulates every aspect of its citizens' lives. The Soviet Union under Stalin was a totalitarian state.

Other examples of political systems are the limited democracy of Athens, the militarism of Sparta and of Japan, absolutism, theocracy, communism, fascism, and apartheid.

CULTURE AND INTELLECTUAL LIFE

Culture includes the patterns of human behavior (encompassing ideas, beliefs, values, artifacts, and ways of making a living) that a society transmits to succeeding generations to meet its fundamental needs. Intellectual life involves ways of thinking, studying, and reflecting on aspects of life.

- **Roman Civilization** Rome left a great cultural and intellectual legacy to the western world, including a commitment to law and justice, the Latin language, and a body of great literature.
- **Gupta Golden Age** In India, from A.D. 320 through 550, lasting achievements in mathematics, medicine, arts, and architecture occurred, supported by the stable reign of the Gupta dynasty.
- **Islamic Golden Age** Between A.D. 750 and 1350, Islamic empires experienced a golden age. The roots of modern mathematics and science can be traced to this period.
- **African Civilizations** From the mid-1200s through the mid-1500s, Africa was the site of great activity in scholarship and art.
- **Renaissance Europe** The Renaissance in Europe, which began in the mid-1300s, was a time of great cultural and intellectual activity. Humanism—which recognized the importance of individual worth in a secular society—guided the Renaissance.

Other important eras of cultural and intellectual activity included early river civilizations, classical Chinese civilization, Mesoamerican civilizations, and the Enlightenment in Europe.

NATIONALISM

Nationalism is a feeling of pride in and devotion to one's country or the desire of a people to control their own government. It is sometimes a divisive force and sometimes a force that unifies. In many cases, it is a source of conflict.

- **German and Italian Unification** In the mid-1800s, both Germany and Italy experienced unification. In each case, many small states joined into one nation.
- **India** Ideals of western democracy, as well as devotion to traditional Hindu and Muslim culture, sustained Indian nationalism through the first half of the 1900s, leading to independence in 1948.
- **Zionism** Since Roman times, Jews had dreamed of returning to Palestine. This dream grew into an international movement in the 1900s. By 1948, the nation of Israel had been created.
- **African Independence Movements** In 1945, just four European powers controlled nearly all of Africa. Less than 25 years later, a tide of nationalism had liberated many African peoples and set them on the road to self-determination.

Other historical situations in which nationalism had an impact are the development of the nation of Turkey, conflicts in the Balkans, the breakup of the Ottoman empire, Latin America in the 1800s and 1900s, Pan-Africanism, and Pan-Arabism.

IMPERIALISM

Imperialism is the domination by one country of the political and economic life of another country or region. Imperialism has had both positive and negative effects on colonies.

- **British in India** The British controlled India by the late 1700s. Although railroads and the British educational system benefited some Indians, local industries and Indian culture suffered, and Indians were treated as inferiors. India gained its independence in 1948.
- **European Powers in Africa** European nations carved up the continent of Africa in the late 1880s. Africa was a continent made up mainly of colonies until after 1945, when African peoples began to demand independence. The legacy of imperialism still affects Africa today.
- **Japan** An imperialist power from the Meiji period, Japan ruled Korea from 1910 to the end of World War II. It also controlled areas in China and Southeast Asia. Japanese imperialism was a cause of World War II.
- **Imperial Rivalry** Competition between imperial powers was one of the causes of World War I. Germany and France, especially, clashed over territory in Africa. Imperial rivalry was also a cause of many smaller wars.

Other civilizations that practiced imperialism include the Chinese Han dynasty, the Romans, the Byzantines, and the Mongols. The collapse of European imperialism still affects many regions of the world today.

DIVERSITY AND INTERDEPENDENCE

Diversity involves understanding and respecting oneself and others, including differences in language, gender, socioeconomic class, religion, and other human characteristics and traits. It is closely related to interdependence, the reliance upon others in mutually beneficial interactions and exchanges. Sometimes the refusal to accept diversity leads to conflict.

- **Byzantine Empire** The Byzantine empire blended many diverse cultures. This diversity allowed it to preserve many differing traditions.
- **Balkans** This region of Eastern Europe has always been an area of great religious and ethnic diversity. Often this diversity has led to conflict.
- **Global Economy** In the 1900s, the world economy became more interdependent, a process that started during the age of imperialism. Today, the world's economy is truly global.
- **Environmental Issues** The global population shares the Earth, and what occurs in one part of the world often has an impact on many other areas. Increasingly, environmental decisions are reached by many nations working together for mutual benefit.

Other examples of diversity and interdependence include the links between East and West during the time of the Mongol empire, tensions that have arisen as a result of Islamic fundamentalism, and interactions among Muslims, Hindus, and Sikhs in India.

JUSTICE AND HUMAN RIGHTS

Justice is fair, equal, proportional, or appropriate treatment given to individuals in interpersonal, societal, or government interactions. Human rights are those basic political, economic, and social rights to which all human beings are entitled. At times throughout history, justice and human rights have been violated.

- **Code of Hammurabi** Because the Code of Hammurabi was carved on a pillar in Babylon (around 1800 B.C.), all people could see what the laws were. This was the first major collection of laws in history.
- **English Bill of Rights** The English Bill of Rights was an important document because it limited the power of the monarchy and returned traditional rights to English citizens.
- **Irish Potato Famine** A blight that affected the main food crop for the Irish people in the mid-1800s created widespread famine when the British, who ruled the island, continued to export crops that could have fed the Irish. At least a million Irish people died during the famine, also called the Great Hunger.
- **Tiananmen Square** When students in China demanded greater political freedom in the late 1980s, Chinese Communist authorities cracked down, wounding and killing many demonstrators.

Other examples of important developments in justice and human rights include the Laws of the Twelve Tables, Justinian's Code, the Sharia, and the Magna Carta. Violations of human rights include the Armenian massacres, the Holocaust, apartheid, the Khmer Rouge in Cambodia, and international terrorism.

MOVEMENT OF PEOPLE AND GOODS

Cultural diffusion is the constant exchange of people, ideas, products, technology, and institutions from one region or civilization to another. Cultural diffusion has occurred throughout history.

- **Muslim Influence on Africa** Muslim traders spread Islam across Africa. Their contacts with diverse cultures allowed them to spread a great number of other ideas and technologies along with the religion of Islam.
- **Silk Road** This 4,000-mile trade route stretched from western China to the Mediterranean. For centuries, from the A.D. 100s onward, goods, ideas, and technology flowed along this route from East to West and back again.
- **Crusades** From the late 1000s through the late 1200s, Christian and Muslim armies battled for control of Palestine. A great deal of cultural diffusion occurred during and after the Crusades, as Europe increased its interest in goods and ideas from the Middle East.
- **Modern Communication** In today's world, computers, the Internet, and satellite communications allow ideas to be passed in moments over great distances.

Other examples of movement of peoples, goods, and ideas include the spread of belief systems (such as Buddhism and Confucianism to Japan), the Muslim influence on Europe, and patterns of global migration.

SCIENCE AND TECHNOLOGY

Science and technology means the tools and methods used by people to get what they need and want.

- **Neolithic Revolution** When people developed the knowledge and technology for farming and domesticating animals, permanent settlements grew.
- **Invention of the Printing Press** The printing press was a crucial breakthrough in technology, allowing ideas to spread.
- **Computer Revolution** Since the 1950s, our society has become increasingly dependent on computers and on digitized information.
- **Space Explorations** Humans have populated Earth and moved into the solar system. In recent years, space exploration has been a shared venture among major world powers.

Other examples of breakthroughs in science and technology are the improved standard of living that occurred in the 1800s, the Green Revolution, and advances in genetics.

CONFLICT

Conflict has occurred throughout history, and its costs have sometimes been very high. The causes of conflict may be political, social, or economic.

- **Religious Conflicts** Conflicts between peoples of differing belief systems began in ancient times and still exist today in places as widespread as Northern Ireland, India, and the Middle East.
- **Political Revolutions** Violent revolutions occurred within nations from the late 1700s through the 1800s as groups sought democratic reform, national independence, or both.
- **World War I** Sparked by several complex causes, World War I was the first modern, fully industrialized war and the first truly global conflict.
- **The Cold War** After 1945, the United States and its allies were engaged in a global competition with the Soviet Union and its allies. Surrogate conflicts occurred as the two superpowers—the United States and the Soviet Union—exerted their influence throughout the world.

Other examples of conflict include the Crusades, World War II, the Russian Revolution, ethnic disputes in the Balkans and Africa, and Arab-Israeli conflict in the Middle East.

MODERN GLOBAL CONNECTIONS AND INTERACTIONS

Today's world is a web of connections and interactions. On every level, the people of the world meet, connect, interact, and sometimes collide. These interactions involve politics, economics, culture, or the environment.

- **Global Environmental Cooperation** Nations are becoming increasingly interdependent in their decisions about environmental issues, acknowledging that various peoples share one world.
- **Global Migrations** The last half of the 1900s was a time of great migration, especially from Africa, Asia, and Latin America to Europe and North America. Many people migrated to improve their economic conditions.
- **International Terrorism** Modern technology and transportation systems have allowed violent groups to express their frustration and anger globally through random acts of violence.
- **The United Nations** Created after World War II, the United Nations remains an organization through which nations can come together to seek peaceful solutions to global problems and conflicts.

Other examples of modern global connections and interactions include economic interdependence, nuclear proliferation, and the sharing of technology and ideas through the Internet.

Glossary

absolutism: political system in which autocratic rulers have complete authority over the government and the lives of people in their nations

acid rain: toxic mixture that is produced when rain falls through polluted air

African National Congress: group formed by opponents to apartheid in South Africa that encouraged political activism by blacks

Agrarian Revolution: change in farming methods in the 1600s that improved the quality and quantity of farm products

agribusiness: large commercial farm owned by multinational corporation

AIDS: acquired immunodeficiency syndrome

Allied Powers: World War I alliance of Britain, France, and Russia, later joined by Italy, the United States, and others

animism: the belief that every living and nonliving thing in nature has a spirit

antibiotic: drug that attacks or weakens the bacteria that cause many diseases

anti-Semitism: prejudice against Jews

apartheid: South African government policy calling for separation of the races

appeasement: policy of giving in to an aggressor's demands in order to keep the peace

apprentice: young person who is learning a trade from a master

aqueduct: bridgelike stone structure that brings water from hills to cities, first used by ancient Romans

Arabic numeral: type of numeral first developed in India and used by many western countries today (*1, 2, 3,* etc.)

aristocracy: a government ruled by an upper class

armistice: agreement to end fighting

Association of Southeast Asian Nations: formed in 1967, group of nine Southeast Asian countries that coordinate policies among members in areas such as trade and agriculture

astrolabe: instrument used to determine latitude by measuring the position of the stars

asylum: protection from arrest or from being returned to a dangerous place from which one fled

autocrat: a single ruler with complete authority

balance of power: distribution of political and economic power that prevents any one nation from becoming too strong

balance of trade: difference between how much a country imports and how much it exports

Bataan Death March: forced march of Allied prisoners by the Japanese during World War II

Bible: the sacred scriptures of Christianity

blitz: massive bombing

Boer War: war occurring from 1899 to 1902 between the British and the Boers, Dutch farmers; it began after the British tried to annex the Boer republics

Bolshevik: member of 1917 Russian revolutionary group

Boxer Rebellion: event in 1900 in which a group known as Boxers assaulted foreign communities across China

brahman: single unifying spirit of Hindu belief

bubonic plague: a contagious disease that devastated the world in the 1300s

bureaucracy: system of managing government through departments run by appointed officials

bushido: code of conduct for samurai during feudal period in Japan

caliph: successor to Muhammad as political and religious leader of the Muslims

calligraphy: fine handwriting

capitalism: economic system in which the means of production are privately owned and operated for profit

cartel: an association of businesspeople; used to refer to the criminal gangs that produce and smuggle drugs internationally

cartographer: mapmaker

cash crop economy: economy based on the raising and selling of one crop or a small number of crops

caudillo: military dictator in Latin America

Central Powers: World War I alliance of Germany, Austria-Hungary, and the Ottoman empire (later joined by Bulgaria)

chador: cloak worn by some Muslim women

chivalry: the code of conduct followed by knights during the Middle Ages

civil disobedience: the refusal to obey unjust laws

civilization: community characterized by elements such as a system of writing, development of social classes, and cities

clone: exact genetic replica

Cold War: continuing state of tension and hostility between the United States and the Soviet Union after 1945 because of differences in political and economic philosophies

collective: large farm owned and operated by workers as a group

Columbian exchange: global exchange of people, plants, animals, ideas, and technology that began in the late 1400s

command economy: economy in which government officials make all basic economic decisions

commercial revolution: the business revolution that occurred in Europe after the Middle Ages

common law: uniform system of justice, developed in England, based on court decisions that became accepted legal principles

Common Market: See *European Community*

commune: community of people who live and work together and hold property in common

Computer Revolution: great increase in the use of computers

concentration camp: detention centers instituted by Adolf Hitler where Jews and others were starved, shot, or gassed to death

Congress of Vienna: conference held in 1815 among European diplomats that had the purpose of restoring order and stability to Europe

conquistador: name, meaning "conqueror," for certain explorers of the 1500s and 1600s

conservatism: set of beliefs held by those who want to preserve traditional ways

containment: Cold War policy that involved limiting communism to areas already under Soviet control

contras: counterrevolutionary group in Nicaragua that opposed the Sandinistas

Council of Clermont: council of the Christian Church, held in 1095, that sparked the Crusades

coup d'état: a revolt by a small group intended to overthrow a government

Crusades: series of religious wars fought between Christians and Muslims from the late 1000s to the mid-1200s

cultural diffusion: the exchange of ideas, customs, goods, and technologies among cultures

Cultural Revolution: program launched in 1966 by Mao Zedong to renew loyalty to communism and purge China of nonrevolutionary tendencies

cuneiform: wedge-shaped writing formed by pressing a penlike instrument into clay

Czar: term for autocratic ruler of Russia; Russian word for "Caesar"

daimyo: in feudal Japan, warrior lords who held a place below the shogun

decimal system: number system based on 10

Declaration of Independence: document drafted by Thomas Jefferson that declared American independence from Britain

deforestation: destruction of forests, especially tropical rain forests

desaparecidos: word meaning "the disappeared ones," used to describe the thousands of people in Argentina who disappeared during the *dirty war*

desert: dry, barren land

desertification: the changeover of arable land into desert

détente: period in the 1970s during which there was an easing of tensions between the United States and the Soviet Union

developed nation: nation with established agriculture and industry, advanced technology, and a strong educational system

developing nation: nation with limited resources that faces obstacles in achieving modern industrial economies

dharma: in Hinduism, the moral and religious duties that are expected of an individual

diaspora: a scattering of people, as when the Jewish people were forced to leave their homeland in Palestine

direct democracy: system of government in which citizens participate directly rather than through elected representatives

dirty war: period beginning in the late 1970s in Argentina during which the military arrested, tortured, and killed thousands of people

divine right: belief that a ruler's authority comes directly from God

dynamo: mechanism that generates electricity; generator

dynasty: ruling family

empire: group of states or territories governed by one ruler

enclosure: process of taking over and fencing off land once shared by peasant farmers

encomienda: system created by Spanish government in the Americas allowing colonists to demand labor or tribute from Native Americans

English Bill of Rights: a set of acts passed by Parliament to ensure its superiority over the monarchy and guarantee certain rights to citizens

enlightened despot: absolute ruler who used royal power to reform society

Enlightenment: the period in the 1700s in which people rejected traditional ideas and supported a belief in human reason

epidemic: an outbreak of disease that spreads quickly and affects a large number of people

Estates General: a French legislative body made up of clergy, nobles, and common people, such as businesspeople and peasants

ethnic cleansing: policy of forcibly removing or killing people of a certain ethnic group

euro: European currency introduced in 1999

European Community: group of nations established in 1957 to expand free trade in Europe; also called *Common Market*

European Union: expansion of the European Community in the 1980s and 1990s; sometimes abbreviated EU

excommunicate: to exclude from the Roman Catholic Church as a penalty for refusing to obey Church laws

factory: place in which workers and machines are brought together to produce large quantities of goods

fascism: the rule of a people by a dictatorial government that is nationalistic and imperialistic

feudalism: system of government in which local lords control their own lands but owe military service and other support to a greater lord

five-year plan: one of a series of plans instituted by Joseph Stalin to build industry and increase farm output in the Soviet Union

fossil fuels: fuels such as coal, oil, and natural gas

genetic engineering: process of changing the chemical codes carried by living things to produce cures for disease, better drugs, and so on

genocide: attempt to destroy an entire ethnic or religious group

gentry: wealthy landowning class

germ theory: medical theory stating that many diseases are caused by microorganisms

glasnost: period of openness called for in the mid-1980s by Mikhail Gorbachev in the Soviet Union

Glorious Revolution: in Britain, nonviolent overthrow of the government of James II that resulted in the reign of William and Mary

Gothic: style of European church architecture characterized by pointed arches and flying buttresses

Great Depression: global economic downturn that began in 1929

Great Leap Forward: program begun by Mao Zedong in China in 1958 to increase agricultural and industrial output

Green Revolution: development of new varieties of plants and improved agricultural techniques that resulted in greatly increased crop yields

greenhouse effect: process in which excess carbon dioxide in the atmosphere traps heat and causes rising global temperatures

guild: a type of trade association of merchants or artisans that was active in the Middle Ages

Guomindang: Chinese nationalist party formed by Sun Yixian

haiku: form of Japanese poetry that expresses a feeling, thought, or idea in three lines

Hanseatic League: trade association of northern German towns in the mid-1300s

heliocentric: sun-centered

Hellenistic: type of culture, resulting from Alexander the Great's conquests, that blended eastern and western influences

hijra: Muhammad's flight from Mecca to Medina in 622; also spelled *hegira*

Holocaust: act of genocide by the Nazis during World War II in which more than 6 million Jews died

Holy Land: Palestine, a land holy to Jews, Christians, and Muslims

humanism: intellectual movement at the heart of the Renaissance that focused on worldly subjects rather than religious ones

icon: holy image of Jesus, the Virgin Mary, or a saint of the Orthodox Christian Church

imperialism: domination by one country of the political, economic, or cultural life of another country or region

import substitution: government policy of encouraging local manufacturers to produce goods to replace imported products

Indian National Congress: group formed by Hindu nationalist leaders in India in the late 1800s to gain greater democracy and eventual self-rule

indigenous: native to a country or region

Industrial Revolution: period in which production of goods shifted from using hand tools to using power-driven machines and from human and animal power to steam power

Information Revolution: the rapid spread of information that began in the 1950s and increases with each passing year

International Monetary Fund: in the 1980s, group that stepped in to work out agreements to help debtor nations repay their loans

Internet: vast computer network that ties together millions of computers

Interpol: the International Criminal Police Network

intifada: uprising mounted in 1987 by Palestinians in territory held by Israel

iron curtain: the imaginary line through Europe that divided the democracies of the West from the communist countries of the East

Islamic fundamentalism: movement by Muslim reformers who oppose westernization and want to apply Islamic principles to problems in their nations

janissaries: members of an elite force in the army of the Ottoman empire

joint family: family structure in which several generations share a common home

Justinian's Code: code of laws organized by the Byzantine emperor Justinian in the 500s

kabuki: form of Japanese drama developed in the 1600s

kaiser: German word meaning "emperor," used for German kings of the late 1800s and early 1900s

kami: according to Japanese tradition, the spirits in all living and nonliving things

karma: in Hinduism, all the deeds of a person's life that affect existence in the next life

laissez faire: policy allowing business to operate with little or no government interference

Laws of the Twelve Tables: laws of ancient Rome written on twelve tablets and displayed in the marketplace

League of Nations: group of more than 40 countries formed after World War I with the goal of settling problems through negotiation, not war

liberalism: way of thinking that supports personal freedom, democracy, and reform

limited monarchy: government in which a legislative body limits the monarch's powers

literacy: the ability to read and write

Long March: 1934 retreat by Mao Zedong and his followers from the Guomindang

Magna Carta: a charter signed by the English king John in 1215 that placed limits on the king's power

mandate: after World War I, a territory that was administered by a foreign power

Mandate of Heaven: according to Chinese tradition, the divine right to rule

manorialism: an economic system structured around a lord's manor, or estate

Marshall Plan: American aid package for Europe proposed in 1947 to strengthen democratic governments and lessen the appeal of communism

medieval: the name for the period of the Middle Ages, from about 500 to the middle of the 1400s

Meiji Restoration: period from 1868 to 1912 in Japan in which Japan industrialized and modernized

mercantilism: economic policy by which a nation sought to export more than it imported in order to build its national wealth

Messiah: Jewish word for a savior sent by God

Middle Kingdom: traditional name for Chinese civilization, so-called because the Chinese believed China was the center of the Earth

Middle Passage: the voyage from Africa to the Americas on slave ships

militarism: the glorification of military power

millet: within the Ottoman empire, a religious community of non-Muslims

missionary: person dedicated to spreading a religion

mixed economy: economic system with both private and state-run enterprises

monastery: community where men or women focus on spiritual goals

monopoly: complete control of a product or business by one person or group

monotheistic: believing in one god

mosaic: picture or design formed by inlaid pieces of stone or other materials

mosque: Muslim house of worship

multinational corporation: a business that operates in many countries

Muslim League: group formed by Muslims in India in the early 1900s to protect Muslim interests

Napoleonic Code: legal code of Napoleon that included many Enlightenment ideas

National Assembly: group formed mostly by the third estate in France in 1789 with the intention of writing a new constitution

nationalism: a feeling of pride in and devotion to one's country

NATO: acronym for the North Atlantic Treaty Organization, a pact between western nations who pledged to support each other if any member nation was attacked

natural laws: according to some philosophers, rules that govern human nature

Neolithic: the period of human culture characterized by the development of a system of settled agriculture; also called the New Stone Age

neutral: not supporting either side in a conflict

New Economic Policy: plan instituted by Lenin in 1921 that privatized some industries

95 Theses: list of 95 arguments against indulgences, posted by Martin Luther on the door of a church in Wittenberg, Germany, in 1517

nirvana: in Buddhism, union with the universe and release from the cycle of death and rebirth

nomad: person who moves from place to place in search of food

nonaligned nation: nation that does not support either side in a conflict, such as the Cold War

nonalignment: policy of not supporting either side in a conflict, such as the Cold War

oligarchy: government in which ruling power belongs to a few people

OPEC: acronym for the Organization of Petroleum Exporting Countries, a trade group that attempts to set world oil prices by controlling oil production

Opium War: conflict between Britain and China in 1839 over the opium trade

Organization of African Unity (OAU): group founded in 1963 by Kwame Nkrumah to promote Pan-Africanism and the end of colonialism in Africa

overpopulation: overabundance of people in a region or country that lacks sufficient resources to adequately provide for them

ozone layer: layer of gases high in the atmosphere that protects the Earth from the dangerous ultraviolet rays of the sun

Pacific Rim: group of nations in Asia and the Americas that border the Pacific Ocean

pagoda: Buddhist temple with many levels and a roof that curves up at the corners

Palestine Liberation Organization (PLO): group formed in 1964 that represents many Palestinian nationalist groups

Pan-Africanism: movement emphasizing the unity of Africans and people of African descent all over the world

Pan-Arabism: movement emphasizing the unity of all peoples sharing a common Arab cultural heritage

Pan-Slavism: nationalistic movement that sought to unite Slavic peoples

Parliament: representative assembly of England

patriarch: the highest church official in the Orthodox Christian Church

patriarchal: family order in which father or oldest male heads the household

patrician: member of the landholding upper class in ancient Rome

Pax Mongolia: period of stability through much of Asia created by Mongol rule from the late 1200s through the mid-1300s

Pax Romana: term meaning "Roman Peace" for a period covering about 200 years beginning with the reign of Augustus

perestroika: restructuring of the government and the economy in the Soviet Union under Mikhail Gorbachev in the mid-1980s

Persian Gulf War: war in 1991 prompted by the Iraqi invasion of Kuwait in which a coalition of European and Arab powers drove Iraq out of Kuwait

pharaoh: ruler of ancient Egypt

plantation: large estate run by an owner or overseer

plebeian: member of the lower class in ancient Rome, which included farmers, merchants, artisans, and traders

pogrom: violent attack on a Jewish community

polis: city-state in ancient Greece

pollution: contamination of the environment, including air, water, and soil

polytheistic: believing in many gods

porcelain: hard, shiny pottery

post-colonialism: term used to describe conditions shared by nations that were once colonies

propaganda: the spreading of ideas to promote a certain cause or to damage an opposing cause

Protestant Reformation: period when Europeans broke away from the Roman Catholic Church and formed new Christian churches

Puritans: group in England in the 1600s who sought to purify the church of England by eliminating Catholic practices

quipus: knotted strings used by Incan officials for keeping records

Quran: the sacred scriptures of Islam

radioactivity: powerful form of energy released by certain substances

Reconquista: a campaign begun by Christians in the 700s to recapture Spain from the Muslims

Red Guards: groups of radical students formed in China during the Cultural Revolution

refugee: person who flees his or her homeland to seek safety elsewhere

reincarnation: in Hinduism, the rebirth of the soul in a new body

Renaissance: period of great creativity and change in Europe from the 1300s through the 1600s; the word means "rebirth"

reparations: payment for war damages

republic: system of government in which officials are chosen by the people

Russification: attempt by Russian rulers to make all groups under Russian rule think, act, and believe as Russians

Russo-Japanese War: war occurring from 1904 to 1905 between Japan and Russia; won by Japan

samurai: member of the warrior class in Japanese feudal society

Sandinistas: group of revolutionaries that overthrew the Nicaraguan government in 1979

satellite: a smaller country that is economically or politically dependent on a more powerful country

savanna: grassy plain

schism: permanent split

scientific method: a method of discovering truth based on experimentation and observation rather than on past authorities

Scientific Revolution: period in the 1500s and 1600s in which scientific thinkers challenged traditional ideas and relied on observation and experimentation

secular: having to do with worldly rather than religious matters

Senate: the most powerful governing body of ancient Rome

sepoy: Indian soldier serving in the army set up by the British or French East India Companies

Sepoy Mutiny: rebellion fought by Hindu and Muslim sepoys against British rule in India in the mid-1800s

serf: in medieval Europe, peasant bound to the lord's land

shantytown: area of shacks that grows up around a city that is experiencing rapid growth

Sharia: the system of Islamic law

Shiite: one of the two main divisions of Islam

Shinto: traditional Japanese religion

shogun: in Japanese feudal society, top military commander

Silk Road: ancient trade route that linked China with lands to the west

Sino-Japanese War: war that lasted from 1894 to 1895 between Japan and China

socialism: system in which the people as a whole rather than private individuals own all property and operate all businesses

Solidarity: independent trade union formed in Poland in 1980

soviet: council of workers and soldiers set up by Russian revolutionaries in 1917

sphere of influence: area in which an outside power claims exclusive trade privileges

stupa: large dome-shaped Buddhist shrine

suffrage: the right to vote

sultan: Muslim ruler

Sunni: one of the two main divisions of Islam

superpower: name after 1945 for both the United States and the Soviet Union, the two nations that dominated global politics for more than four decades

surrogate: word for a representative state; used to describe smaller countries whose actions represented the interests of either the United States or the Soviet Union during the Cold War

Swahili: language that mixed Arabic words with Bantu, an African language

Taiping Rebellion: peasant rebellion in China occurring between 1850 and 1864

technology: tools and skills people use to meet their basic needs

terrace: a flat area of land on a steep hillside

terrorism: deliberate use of unpredictable violence, especially against civilians, to gain revenge or achieve political goals

Torah: the most sacred scriptures of Judaism

totalitarian state: form of government in which a one-party dictatorship attempts to regulate every aspect of the lives of citizens

total war: the channeling of all of a nation's resources into a war effort

trade deficit: a situation in which a nation imports more than it exports

trade fair: site of regular trading activity in medieval Europe

trench warfare: type of warfare in which troops dig trenches and fight from them

tributary state: independent state that must acknowledge the supremacy of another state and pay tribute to its ruler

Truman Doctrine: an economic and military program of the United States designed in 1947 to help other countries resist Soviet aggression

United Nations: international group formed in 1945 to provide a place to discuss world problems and develop solutions

Universal Declaration of Human Rights: document adopted in 1948 by the United Nations that sets out the basic human rights of all individuals

Untouchables: within the ancient Indian caste system, outcasts who lived harsh lives

Upanishads: philosophical dialogues about Hindu beliefs

urbanization: movement of people to cities

Warsaw Pact: defensive alliance among the Soviet Union and its satellites promising mutual military cooperation

westernization: process of adopting western ways

Young Turks: movement established by Turks in the late 1800s to reform the Ottoman empire

zaibatsu: Japanese families that became powerful in banking and industry

Zen Buddhism: sect of Buddhism that spread throughout Japan

Zionism: movement dedicated to building a Jewish state in Palestine

Index

Regents Examination–June 2007

This section contains an actual Regents Examination in Global History and Geography that was given in New York State in June 2007.

Circle your answers to Part 1. Write your responses to the short-answer questions in the spaces provided. Write your thematic essay and document-based essay on separate sheets of paper. Be sure to refer to the test-taking strategies in the front of this book as you prepare to answer the test questions.

Part I

Answer all questions in this part.

Directions (1–50): For each statement or question, write on the separate answer sheet the *number* of the word or expression that, of those given, best completes the statement or answers the question.

Base your answer to question 1 on the map below and on your knowledge of social studies.

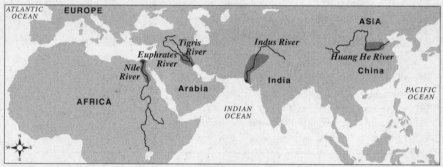

Source: Charles F. Gritzner, *Exploring Our World, Past and Present*, D. C. Heath and Company (adapted)

1 The main purpose of this map is to illustrate the location of
   (1) overseas trade routes
   (2) early belief systems
   (3) river valley civilizations
   (4) burial sites of ancient rulers

---

2 Which social scientist specializes in studying issues such as the scarcity of resources and availability of goods?
   (1) anthropologist   (3) economist
   (2) sociologist   (4) archaeologist

3 Which feature would most likely be shown on a physical map?
   (1) population density   (3) climate
   (2) vegetation zones   (4) mountain ranges

4 Which society practiced direct democracy?
   (1) ancient Athens   (3) Gupta Empire
   (2) dynastic China   (4) early Egypt

5 The caste system in India was characterized by
   (1) toleration for various religious beliefs
   (2) equality between men and women
   (3) a lack of social mobility
   (4) the right of people to choose their occupations

6 Which belief is most closely associated with the philosophy of Confucianism?
   (1) nirvana   (3) prayer
   (2) reincarnation   (4) filial piety

7 What was one result of large armies traveling great distances during the Crusades?
   (1) Europe's population severely declined.
   (2) Democracy in the Middle East grew.
   (3) Cultural diffusion increased.
   (4) Slavery was eliminated.

8 Constantinople was a thriving city in the 1200s mainly because of its location on a major trade route between
   (1) China and southern Africa
   (2) the Atlantic Ocean and the Baltic Sea
   (3) the Inca Empire and the Aztec Empire
   (4) Asia and eastern Europe

Base your answer to question 9 on the pictures below and on your knowledge of social studies.

9 These architectural achievements best indicate that
 (1) advanced technology existed in early civilizations
 (2) religion was of little importance
 (3) entertainment was important to these ancient societies
 (4) trade routes existed between China and the Americas

Base your answer to question 10 on the map below and on your knowledge of social studies.

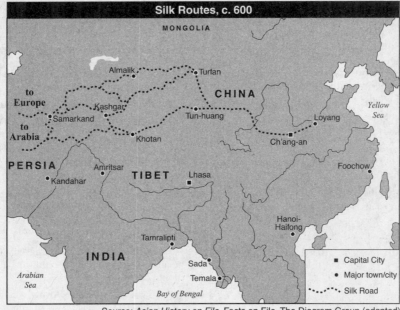

Source: *Asian History on File,* Facts on File, The Diagram Group (adapted)

10 This map shows that the Silk Road
 (1) crossed both Africa and Asia   (3) followed a single route
 (2) was located primarily in Asia   (4) started in Khotan

Base your answer to question 11 on the map below and on your knowledge of social studies.

West Africa, 800–1500

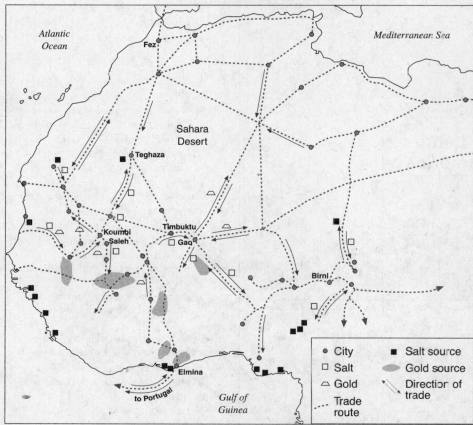

Source: Patrick K. O'Brien, ed., *Oxford Atlas of World History*, Oxford University Press (adapted)

11 Based on the map, which conclusion can best be drawn about this region?

(1) The Sahara Desert acted as a barrier to trade.
(2) Rivers served as the primary trade routes for the entire region.
(3) The economy of the region was influenced by extensive trade connections.
(4) Goods from the Gulf of Guinea were exchanged directly with English cities.

12 The terms *Bushido, samurai,* and *daimyo* are most closely associated with which group in Japanese history?

(1) emperors
(2) warriors
(3) peasants
(4) merchants

13 In 1453, the Ottoman Empire rose to power by defeating the

(1) Holy Roman Empire
(2) European crusaders
(3) Byzantine Empire
(4) Mongol invaders

Base your answers to questions 14 and 15 on the map below and on your knowledge of social studies.

Latin America

Source: *American History, Historical Outline Map Book*, Prentice Hall (adapted)

14 Which letter identifies the region in the Andes Mountains where many Inca settlements were located?

(1) *A*   (3) *C*
(2) *B*   (4) *D*

15 The letter *C* indicates an area of Latin America that was colonized mostly by the

(1) Dutch   (3) English
(2) Portuguese   (4) French

16 • Pope Leo authorizes the sale of indulgences, 1515
   • Martin Luther posts the Ninety-five Theses, 1517

These events are most closely associated with the

(1) Protestant Reformation
(2) Crusades
(3) Age of Reason
(4) Puritan Revolution

17 One contribution that John Locke made to Enlightenment philosophy was the idea that

(1) absolute monarchies should continue
(2) the punishment should fit the crime
(3) individual rights should be denied
(4) governments should be based on the consent of the people

18 What was a major result of the Glorious Revolution?

(1) Napoleon was restored to power.
(2) England further limited its monarchy.
(3) Oliver Cromwell became the leader of England.
(4) The Spanish Armada was defeated.

19 A study of the revolutions in Latin America in the 19th century would show that

(1) religion was a major cause of the conflicts
(2) Spanish-born peninsulares led most of the Latin American uprisings
(3) nationalism had little influence on the outcome
(4) events in North America and Europe influenced Latin Americans

20 A major reason the Industrial Revolution began in England was that England possessed

(1) a smooth coastline
(2) abundant coal and iron resources
(3) many waterfalls
(4) numerous mountain ranges

21 What was an immediate result of the mass starvation in Ireland in the late 1840s?

(1) expansion of the Green Revolution to Ireland
(2) acceptance of British rule by the Irish
(3) migration of many Irish to other countries
(4) creation of a mixed economy in Ireland

22 Which individual is associated with the phrase *blood and iron* as related to the unification of Germany?

(1) Otto von Bismarck
(2) Giuseppe Garibaldi
(3) Kaiser Wilhelm II
(4) Count Camillo di Cavour

23 Which statement would Social Darwinists most likely support?

(1) Universal suffrage is a basic human right.
(2) Political equality strengthens the effectiveness of government.
(3) Stronger groups have the right to rule and control weaker groups.
(4) Public education should be guaranteed to all members of a society.

24 One similarity between the Sepoy Mutiny and the Boxer Rebellion is that they

(1) opposed European imperialism
(2) ended an established dynasty
(3) resulted in the redistribution of land
(4) instituted communist governments

25 What was a direct result of World War I?

(1) Nicholas II was named czar of Russia.
(2) Germany lost its colonies in Africa and Asia.
(3) Archduke Franz Ferdinand was assassinated by a terrorist.
(4) The Ottoman Empire expanded.

26 Which statement about both the Bolshevik Revolution in Russia and the rise of fascism in Germany and Italy is accurate?

(1) Economic conditions led to political change.
(2) Industrialization hindered national development.
(3) Goals were achieved by peaceful means.
(4) Communist ideals fueled both movements.

27 The term *appeasement* is best defined as

(1) an attempt to avoid conflict by meeting the demands of an aggressor
(2) a period of peace and prosperity, resulting in cultural achievement
(3) a declaration of war between two or more nations
(4) an agreement removing economic barriers between nations

Base your answer to question 28 on the map below and on your knowledge of social studies.

1937–1938

Source: Peter Stearns et al.,
World Civilizations: The Global Experience,
Pearson Longman (adapted)

28 What is the best title for this map?

(1) Dominance of Manchukuo
(2) Japanese Imperial Expansion
(3) East Asian Trade Routes
(4) Natural Resources of China and Japan

29 **"Mussolini Attacks Ethiopia" (1935)
"Germany Takes the Rhineland Back" (1936)
"Germany and Russia Divide Poland" (1939)**

These headlines might be used to illustrate the weakness of the

(1) United Nations
(2) Congress of Vienna
(3) Warsaw Pact
(4) League of Nations

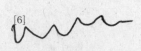

Base your answer to question 30 on the time line below and on your knowledge of social studies.

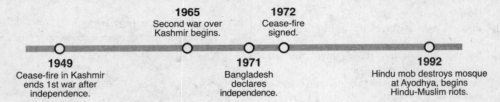

1965
Second war over
Kashmir begins.

1972
Cease-fire
signed.

1949
Cease-fire in Kashmir
ends 1st war after
independence.

1971
Bangladesh
declares
independence.

1992
Hindu mob destroys mosque
at Ayodhya, begins
Hindu-Muslim riots.

30 Which nations have been most directly involved in the events illustrated in this time line?

(1) Mongolia and China
(2) India and Pakistan
(3) Burma and Thailand
(4) Cambodia and Laos

31 Which communist nation is most closely associated with the leadership of Ho Chi Minh and the surrender of Saigon?

(1) North Korea
(2) Soviet Union
(3) Vietnam
(4) People's Republic of China

32 A similarity between the Polish group Solidarity in 1980 and the Chinese protesters in Tiananmen Square in 1989 is that both groups

(1) supported movements for democracy
(2) succeeded in ending communism
(3) encouraged military occupation by the Soviet Union
(4) favored increases in military spending

33 The status of Hong Kong changed in July 1997 when the city

(1) was returned to China
(2) was closed to international trade
(3) became an independent nation
(4) adopted a capitalist economy

34 Mikhail Gorbachev's reforms of perestroika and glasnost resulted in

(1) an era of world peace and Soviet prosperity
(2) conditions that helped lead to the breakup of the Soviet Union
(3) a successful transition to a command economy in Russia
(4) censorship of the news media in Russia

35 The governments of Augusto Pinochet, Saddam Hussein, and Slobodan Milosevic are examples of

(1) absolute monarchies
(2) oppressive regimes
(3) democratic republics
(4) Islamic theocracies

36 One way in which wars, religious conflict, and natural disasters are similar is that these situations may result in

(1) the mass migration of people
(2) economic stability
(3) an increase in life expectancy
(4) global warming

Base your answers to questions 37 and 38 on the passage below and on your knowledge of social studies.

. . . Above all, we want equal political rights, because without them our disabilities will be permanent. I know this sounds revolutionary to the Whites in this country, because the majority of voters will be Africans. This makes the White man fear democracy.

But this fear cannot be allowed to stand in the way of the only solution which will guarantee racial harmony and freedom for all. It is not true that the enfranchisement [right to vote] of all will result in racial domination. Political division, based on colour, is entirely artificial and, when it disappears, so will the domination of one colour group by another. The ANC [African National Congress] has spent half a century fighting against racialism. When it triumphs it will not change that policy. . . .

— Nelson Mandela, Speech at Rivonia Trial, 1964

37 This passage describes the opposition of the African National Congress to the

(1) revival of colonialism
(2) rivalries between tribes
(3) practice of apartheid
(4) introduction of a coalition government

38 Which generalization can be supported by this passage?

(1) Racism has disappeared in South Africa.
(2) The African National Congress has changed its social goals.
(3) Giving the vote to black Africans will result in racial domination.
(4) Nelson Mandela opposed political division based on color.

39 Kim Jong Il and Fidel Castro are 21st-century leaders who believe in the ideas of

(1) Karl Marx
(2) Adam Smith
(3) Siddhartha Gautama
(4) Jean-Jacques Rousseau

Base your answers to questions 40 and 41 on the cartoon below and on your knowledge of social studies.

Source: Jeff Koterba, *Omaha World Herald*, 2003 (adapted)

40 What is the main idea of this 2003 cartoon?

(1) There are problems to resolve on the road to peace.
(2) Colin Powell has removed the stumbling blocks to peace.
(3) Both groups have reached agreement on the road map for peace.
(4) The road to peace has been carefully mapped.

41 This 2003 cartoon illustrates the struggle between Palestinians and

(1) Iraqis   (3) Egyptians
(2) Hamas   (4) Israelis

42 Which heading best completes the partial outline below?

I. _____
A. Unification of Italy
B. Formation of the Indian National Congress
C. Founding of the Muslim League
D. Breakup of Austria-Hungary

(1) Tensions of the Cold War
(2) Effects of Nationalism
(3) Causes of World War II
(4) Results of Economic Revolutions

43 A. Crusades
    B. Fall of the Roman Empire
    C. Golden Age of Greece
    D. Renaissance

Which sequence of letters places these events in the correct chronological order?

(1) $A \rightarrow B \rightarrow C \rightarrow D$
(2) $D \rightarrow C \rightarrow B \rightarrow A$
(3) $C \rightarrow B \rightarrow A \rightarrow D$
(4) $C \rightarrow D \rightarrow B \rightarrow A$

44 One way in which Asoka, Mansa Musa, and Suleiman the Magnificent are similar is that they

(1) established republics
(2) led nationalist movements
(3) ruled during times of prosperity
(4) discouraged scientific advancements

Base your answers to questions 45 and 46 on the passage below and on your knowledge of social studies.

. . . The power of God can be felt in a moment from one end of the world to the other: the royal power acts simultaneously throughout the kingdom. It holds the whole kingdom in position just as God holds the whole world.

If God were to withdraw his hand, the entire world would return to nothing: if authority ceases in the kingdom, all lapses into confusion. . . .

— Bishop Jacques-Benigne Bossuet

45 This passage describes the idea of

(1) divine right rule
(2) parliamentary democracy
(3) Marxism
(4) totalitarianism

46 Which historical era is most closely associated with this passage?

(1) Industrial Revolution
(2) Agricultural Revolution
(3) Age of Imperialism
(4) Age of Absolutism

Base your answer to question 47 on the cartoon below and on your knowledge of social studies.

Capitalism Will Crush Russia!

Source: Student Artwork, Shaneekwa Miller, Fashion Industries High School (adapted)

47 Which period of history is depicted in this cartoon?

(1) Industrial Revolution
(2) Age of Enlightenment
(3) Age of Imperialism
(4) Cold War

48 Which situation best illustrates the concept of isolationism?

(1) The Spanish government required that gold found in its colonies be brought directly to Spain.
(2) Japan closed its ports to trade with other nations.
(3) France, Germany, Belgium, and Great Britain negotiated to divide various areas of Africa into colonies.
(4) The British ruled much of India through the control of local rulers.

49 "Bombardment, barrage, curtain-fire, mines, gas, tanks, machine-guns, hand-grenades — words, words, but they hold the horror of the world."

— Erich Maria Remarque,
All Quiet on the Western Front

This quotation best describes the effects of the

(1) technological developments used during World War I
(2) formation of alliances in World War II
(3) tension between the superpowers during the Cold War
(4) protests against reforms during the Indian independence movement

50 One similarity in the leadership of Simón Bolívar and Jomo Kenyatta is that both leaders

(1) promoted European control over the Americas
(2) became religious leaders of their countries
(3) controlled large areas of land in the Americas
(4) fought for independence from European control

Answers to the essay questions are to be written in the separate essay booklet.

In developing your answer to Part II, be sure to keep these general definitions in mind:

(a) <u>describe</u> means "to illustrate something in words or tell about it"

(b) <u>explain</u> means "to make plain or understandable; to give reasons for or causes of; to show the logical development or relationships of"

(c) <u>discuss</u> means "to make observations about something using facts, reasoning, and argument; to present in some detail"

Part II

THEMATIC ESSAY QUESTION

Directions: Write a well-organized essay that includes an introduction, several paragraphs addressing the task below, and a conclusion.

Theme: Political Change

> Often, governments implement policies in an attempt to change society.

Task:

> Choose *one* example from global history where a government attempted to change society and
> - Describe the change the government wanted to bring about
> - Explain why the government wanted to make this change
> - Describe *one* specific policy the government used to try to bring about this change
> - Discuss the extent to which this change was achieved

You may use any example of governmental change from your study of global history. Some suggestions you might wish to consider include efforts to strengthen the Empire of Mali under Mansa Musa, Reformation in England under Henry VIII, westernization of Russia under Peter the Great, Reign of Terror during the French Revolution under Robespierre, Meiji Restoration in Japan under the Emperor Meiji, modernization of Turkey under Atatürk, five-year plans in the Soviet Union under Joseph Stalin, fascism in Italy under Benito Mussolini, and oil policies in Venezuela under Hugo Chávez. **Although you are *not* limited to these suggestions, you may *not* use communism under Mao Zedong or Deng Xiaoping as your example of governmental change.**

Do *not* use an example of governmental change in the United States as your answer.

Guidelines:

In your essay, be sure to
- Develop all aspects of the task
- Support the theme with relevant facts, examples, and details
- Use a logical and clear plan of organization, including an introduction and a conclusion that are beyond a restatement of the theme

NAME _____ SCHOOL _____

In developing your answers to Part III, be sure to keep these general definitions in mind:

    (a) <u>describe</u> means "to illustrate something in words or tell about it"

    (b) <u>discuss</u> means "to make observations about something using facts, reasoning, and argument; to present in some detail"

Part III

DOCUMENT-BASED QUESTION

    This question is based on the accompanying documents. The question is designed to test your ability to work with historical documents. Some of these documents have been edited for the purposes of this question. As you analyze the documents, take into account the source of each document and any point of view that may be presented in the document.

Historical Context:

> Throughout history, different economic systems have influenced specific nations, regions, and peoples. These systems include **manorialism** during the Middle Ages in Western Europe, **mercantilism** during the Age of Exploration, and **communism** in post–World War II China.

Task: Using the information from the documents and your knowledge of global history, answer the questions that follow each document in Part A. Your answers to the questions will help you write the Part B essay in which you will be asked to

> Choose **two** of the economic systems mentioned in the historical context and for **each**
> - Describe the characteristics of the economic system
> - Discuss the impact of the economic system on a specific nation **or** region **or** on a group of people

Part A
Short-Answer Questions

Directions: Analyze the documents and answer the short-answer questions that follow each document in the space provided.

Document 1

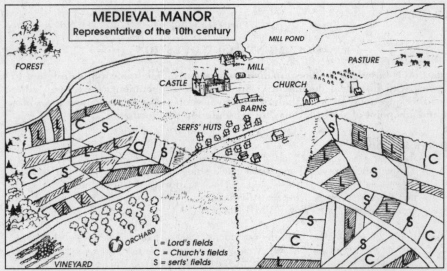

Source: Kime and Stich, *Global History and Geography,* STAReview, N & N Publishing Company

1 Based on this diagram, state *one* economic characteristic of the medieval manor. [1]

_____

_____

Score ☐

Document 2

Tenants on a manor owed services to their lord. Some of these services are listed below.

> . . . To carry manure for two days, with a cart and two oxen, receiving food as before [3 meals each day];
>
> To find a man to mow for two days receiving food as above; it is estimated that he can mow 1 1/2 acres in the two days;
>
> To gather and lift the hay so mown, receiving 2 meals for one man;
>
> To carry the lord's hay for one day with a cart and three of the tenant's own beasts, receiving 3 meals as before;
>
> To carry beans or oats for two days in the autumn, and wood for two days in the summer, in the same manner and with the same food as before; . . .

Source: S. R. Scargill-Bird, ed., *Custumals of Battle Abbey in the Reigns of Edward I and Edward II (1283–1312),* The Camden Society (adapted)

2a Based on the *Custumals of Battle Abbey,* state **one** benefit the lord received under manorialism.   [1]

_____

_____

Score ☐

b Based on the *Custumals of Battle Abbey,* state **one** benefit that tenants received under manorialism.   [1]

_____

_____

Score ☐

Document 3

> . . . Of necessity, the manor was a self-sufficient economic unit in view of the overwhelming difficulties of transportation in the period. International trade was carried on only to serve the demands of the wealthy, and it was largely in the hands of aliens [different peoples]—Greeks, Jews, Moslems. Local society made almost no use of money. To the extent that local exchange was carried on, it was conducted by barter. The small amount of international trade precluded [ruled out] the need for gold coinage. The Carolingians minted only silver coins, which were all that was usually necessary when the smallest silver coin could buy a cow. When gold coins were needed, Byzantine and Moslem currency was used. . . .

Source: Norman F. Cantor, *The Civilization of the Middle Ages*, Harper Perennial

3 According to Norman Cantor, what are *two* ways manorialism influenced the economy of Europe? [2]

(1)_____

_____

Score ☐

(2)_____

_____

Score ☐

Document 4

The Mercantilist Argument for Colonial Expansion

Source: Philip Dorf, *Our Early Heritage: Ancient and Medieval History,*
Oxford Book Company (adapted)

4 According to this cartoon by Philip Dorf, what is **one** characteristic of mercantilism from the perspective of the mother country? [1]

_____

_____

Score [ ]

Document 5

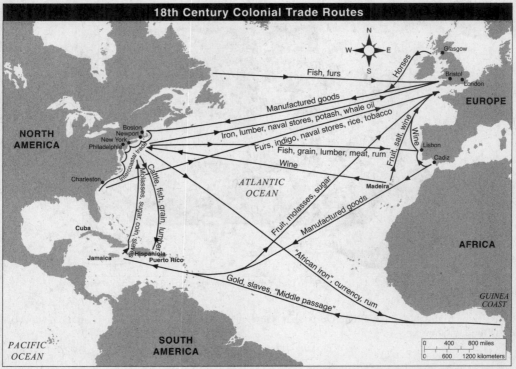

18th Century Colonial Trade Routes

Source: *Historical Maps on File*, Revised Edition (adapted)

5 Based on this map, state **one** effect of the Atlantic trade. [1]

_____

_____

Score ☐

Document 6

This is an excerpt from a letter written in 1559 by Michele Soriano about Spain's interactions with its colonies in the Americas.

> . . . From New Spain are obtained gold and silver, cochineal, (little insects like flies,) from which crimson dye is made, leather, cotton, sugar and other things; but from Peru nothing is obtained except minerals. The fifth part of all that is produced goes to the king, but since the gold and silver is brought to Spain and he has a tenth part of that which goes to the mint and is refined and coined, he eventually gets one-fourth of the whole sum, which fourth does not exceed in all four or five hundred thousand ducats, although it is reckoned not alone at millions, but at millions of pounds. Nor is it likely that it will long remain at this figure, because great quantities of gold and silver are no longer found upon the surface of the earth, as they have been in past years; and to penetrate into the bowels of the earth requires greater effort, skill and outlay, and the Spaniards are not willing to do the work themselves, and the natives cannot be forced to do so, because the Emperor has freed them from all obligation of service as soon as they accept the Christian religion. Wherefore it is necessary to acquire negro slaves [enslaved Africans], who are brought from the coasts of Africa, both within and without the Straits, and these are selling dearer [more expensive] every day, because on account of their [enslaved Africans'] natural lack of strength and the change of climate, added to the lack of discretion [care] upon the part of their masters in making them work too hard and giving them too little to eat, they fall sick and the greater part of them die. . . .

Source: Merrick Whitcomb, ed., "The Gold of the Indies — 1559," *Translations and Reprints from the Original Sources of European History*, The Department of History of the University of Pennsylvania

6 According to Michele Soriano, what is *one* influence that gold and silver had on Spain? [1]

_____

_____

Score ☐

Document 7

This is an excerpt from Chapter 1, General Principles, of the 1954 "Constitution of the People's Republic of China."

> **Article 1** The People's Republic of China is a people's democratic state led by the working class and based on the alliance of workers and peasants. . . .
>
> **Article 6** The state sector of the economy is the socialist sector owned by the whole people. It is the leading force in the national economy and the material basis on which the state carries out socialist transformation. The state ensures priority for the development of the state sector of the economy.
>
> All mineral resources and waters, as well as forests, undeveloped land and other resources which the state owns by law, are the property of the whole people.
>
> **Article 7** The co-operative sector of the economy is either socialist, when collectively owned by the masses of working people, or semi-socialist, when in part collectively owned by the masses of working people. Partial collective ownership by the masses of working people is a transitional form by means of which individual peasants, individual handicraftsmen and other individual working people organize themselves in their advance towards collective ownership by the masses of working people. . . .

Source: *Constitutions of Asian Countries*, N. M. Tripathi Private

7   Based on these articles from the "Constitution of the People's Republic of China," state *two* characteristics of the communist economic system in China.   [2]

(1)_____

_____

Score [ ]

(2)_____

_____

Score [ ]

Document 8

In an attempt to break with the Russian model of Communism and to catch up with more advanced nations, Mao proposed that China should make a "great leap forward" into modernisation. He began a militant Five Year Plan to promote technology and agricultural self-sufficiency. Overnight, fertile rice fields were ploughed over, and factory construction work began. Labour-intensive methods were introduced and farming collectivised on a massive scale. The campaign created about 23,500 communes, each controlling its own means of production. But former farmers had no idea how to actually use the new factories and what was once fertile crop land went to waste on a disastrous scale. The Great Leap Forward was held responsible for famine in 1960 and 1961. Twenty million people starved, and Mao Zedong withdrew temporarily from public view.

Source: BBC News, Special Reports, China's Communist Revolution

8 Based on this BBC News article, what is **one** effect the Great Leap Forward had on China's economy? [1]

_____

_____

Score ☐

Document 9

This is an excerpt from the speech "We Shall Speed Up Reform" given by Deng Xiaoping on June 12, 1987.

> ... China is now carrying out a reform. I am all in favour of that. There is no other solution for us. After years of practice it turned out that the old stuff didn't work. In the past we copied foreign models mechanically, which only hampered [blocked] the development of our productive forces, induced [caused] ideological rigidity and kept people and grass-roots units from taking any initiative. We made some mistakes of our own as well, such as the Great Leap Forward and the "cultural revolution" [Mao's policies], which were our own inventions. I would say that since 1957 our major mistakes have been "Left" ones. The "cultural revolution" was an ultra-Left mistake. In fact, during the two decades from 1958 through 1978, China remained at a standstill. There was little economic growth and not much of a rise in the people's standard of living. How could we go on like that without introducing reforms? So in 1978, at the Third Plenary Session of the Eleventh Central Committee, we formulated a new basic political line: to give first priority to the drive for modernization and strive to develop the productive forces. In accordance with that line we drew up a series of new principles and policies, the major ones being reform and the open policy. By reform we mean something comprehensive, including reform of both the economic structure and the political structure and corresponding changes in all other areas. By the open policy we mean both opening to all other countries, irrespective [regardless] of their social systems, and opening at home, which means invigorating [quickening] the domestic economy. . . .

Source: Deng Xiaoping, *Fundamental Issues in Present-Day China*, Foreign Languages Press, 1987

9 According to Deng Xiaoping, what were **two** ways Mao Zedong's economic policies influenced China? [2]

(1)_____

_____

Score ☐

(2)_____

_____

Score ☐

Part B
Essay

Directions: Write a well-organized essay that includes an introduction, several paragraphs, and a conclusion. Use evidence from *at least **four*** documents in your essay. Support your response with relevant facts, examples, and details. Include additional outside information.

Historical Context:

Throughout history, different economic systems have influenced specific nations, regions, and peoples. These systems include **manorialism** during the Middle Ages in Western Europe, **mercantilism** during the Age of Exploration, and **communism** in post–World War II China.

Task: Using the information from the documents and your knowledge of global history, write an essay in which you

Choose ***two*** of the economic systems mentioned in the historical context and for ***each***

- Describe the characteristics of the economic system
- Discuss the impact of the economic system on a specific nation ***or*** region ***or*** on a group of people

Guidelines:

In your essay, be sure to

- Develop all aspects of the task
- Incorporate information from *at least **four*** documents in the body of the essay
- Incorporate relevant outside information
- Support the theme with relevant facts, examples, and details
- Use a logical and clear plan of organization, including an introduction and conclusion that are beyond a restatement of the theme

The University of the State of New York

REGENTS HIGH SCHOOL EXAMINATION

GLOBAL HISTORY AND GEOGRAPHY

Wednesday, June 13, 2007 — 1:15 to 4:15 p.m., only

ANSWER SHEET

Sex: ☐ Male ☐ Female

Student ....

Teacher ....

School ....

Write your answers for Part I on this answer sheet, write your answers to Part III A in the test booklet, and write your answers for Parts II and III B in the separate essay booklet.

FOR TEACHER USE ONLY	
Part I Score	————
Part III A Score	————
Total Part I and III A Score	[ ]
Part II Essay Score	————
Part III B Essay Score	————
Total Essay Score	[ ]
Final Score (obtained from conversion chart)	[ ]

Part I

1.........	26.........
2.........	27.........
3.........	28.........
4.........	29.........
5.........	30.........
6.........	31.........
7.........	32.........
8.........	33.........
9.........	34.........
10.........	35.........
11.........	36.........
12.........	37.........
13.........	38.........
14.........	39.........
15.........	40.........
16.........	41.........
17.........	42.........
18.........	43.........
19.........	44.........
20.........	45.........
21.........	46.........
22.........	47.........
23.........	48.........
24.........	49.........
25.........	50.........

No. Right [ ]

The declaration below should be signed when you have completed the examination.

I do hereby affirm, at the close of this examination, that I had no unlawful knowledge of the questions or answers prior to the examination and that I have neither given nor received assistance in answering any of the questions during the examination.

———————————————————————

Signature

Tear Here

Tear Here

Regents Examination–January 2007

This section contains an actual Regents Examination in Global History and Geography that was given in New York State in January 2007.

Circle your answers to Part 1. Write your responses to the short-answer questions in the spaces provided. Write your thematic essay and document-based essay on separate sheets of paper. Be sure to refer to the test-taking strategies in the front of this book as you prepare to answer the test questions.

Part I

Answer all questions in this part.

Directions (1–50): For each statement or question, write on the separate answer sheet the *number* of the word or expression that, of those given, best completes the statement or answers the question.

1 Which aspect of social science would a geographer most likely study in depth?

(1) how beliefs influence the behavior of a group of people
(2) how economic events influence history
(3) how location influences the way people live
(4) how people influence governmental decisions

2 One similarity between the ancient civilizations in Egypt and in China is that they developed

(1) nomadic lifestyles
(2) monotheistic belief systems
(3) democratic governments
(4) written forms of communication

3 What effect did the geography of ancient Greece have on its early development?

(1) The mountainous terrain led to the creation of independent city-states.
(2) A lack of natural seaports limited communication.
(3) An inland location hindered trade and colonization.
(4) Abundant natural resources encouraged self-sufficiency.

4 One contribution of ancient Roman culture was the development of

(1) the concept of zero
(2) the process of making silk
(3) a republican form of government
(4) the printing press

5 What is considered one of the Byzantine Empire's greatest contributions to western European society?

(1) spreading Hinduism throughout the region
(2) supporting the Catholic Church
(3) defeating the Mongols at Kiev
(4) preserving Greek and Roman culture

Base your answer to question 6 on the diagram below and on your knowledge of social studies.

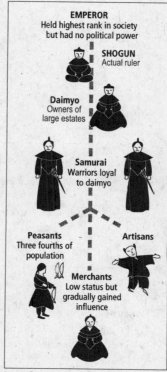

Source: *Guide to the Essentials of World History*, Prentice Hall, 1999 (adapted)

6 Which type of political and social order is shown in this diagram?

(1) theocratic   (3) fascist
(2) tribal   (4) feudal

Base your answer to question 7 on the map below and on your knowledge of social studies.

First Empires in India, 600 BC–AD 500

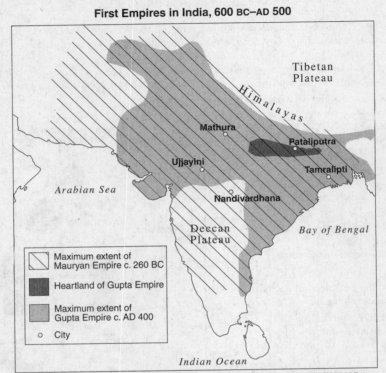

Source: Patrick K. O'Brien, ed., *Oxford Atlas of World History*, Oxford University Press, 1999 (adapted)

7 Which statement can best be supported by the information shown on this map?

   (1) By 260 B.C., the Mauryan Empire extended north into Central China.

   (2) The Mauryan Empire controlled more of the Indian subcontinent than the Gupta Empire did.

   (3) Most of the Gupta Empire was located on the Deccan Plateau.

   (4) The economies of India's early empires were based on trade.

8 Which circumstance best describes a long-term result of the Crusades?

   (1) Muslim control of Jerusalem ended.

   (2) Feudalism began in western Europe.

   (3) Cultural exchanges between the Middle East and Europe grew.

   (4) Christians and Muslims achieved a lasting peace.

9 Which statement about the geography of Japan is most accurate?

   (1) Location has made it easy to invade.

   (2) The irregular coastline has many natural harbors.

   (3) Large plains are its primary physical feature.

   (4) Earthquakes do not threaten the islands.

Base your answer to question 10 on the passage below and on your knowledge of social studies.

. . . He who, being of weak faculties [abilities], develops the wisdom of the first path with a dull insight is reborn seven times at most; after seven rebirths in states of bliss he will make an end of misery: he who develops it with medium faculties and insight is a roamer; after two or three rebirths he will make an end of misery: he who develops it with keen faculties and insight takes root but once, only one human birth will he pass through and make an end of misery. . . .

— Charles W. Eliot, ed., *Sacred Writings*, Vol II, P.F. Collier & Son, 1910

10 Which belief system is described in this passage?

(1) Buddhism (3) Islam
(2) Christianity (4) Confucianism

11 Which description best characterizes the city of Timbuktu?

(1) port on the water route to East Asia
(2) major urban and industrial center on the Silk Road
(3) commercial and cultural center of West Africa
(4) inland city of the Hanseatic League

12 What was one long-term impact of Marco Polo's visit to China?

(1) The Chinese began construction of the Great Wall.
(2) The principle of divine right was introduced to China.
(3) Christianity rapidly spread throughout the Yuan Empire.
(4) Europeans increased trade with China.

13 Which statement best expresses an idea held by many Renaissance humanist philosophers?

(1) People should study worldly subjects as well as sacred matters.
(2) Governments should establish overseas empires.
(3) Individuals should withdraw from the world and study religion.
(4) Scholars should dedicate themselves to the study of life after death.

14 Which document limited the power of the English monarchy during the Middle Ages?

(1) Magna Carta (3) Justinian Code
(2) Twelve Tables (4) Rig Veda

15 • Martin Luther stresses the central role of faith.
• The belief of predestination spreads throughout Switzerland.
• The Council of Trent clarifies the teachings of the Roman Catholic Church.

These statements describe ideas and events that

(1) brought religious unity to Europe
(2) shaped the Reformation and the Counter Reformation
(3) ended the Glorious Revolution
(4) expanded the importance of the Orthodox Church

16 Which nation had the most influence on the colonization of Latin America in the 1500s?

(1) Spain (3) England
(2) France (4) Netherlands

17 What was one goal of mercantilism?

(1) removal of trade barriers
(2) elimination of private property
(3) establishment of subsistence agriculture
(4) creation of a favorable balance of trade

18 According to John Locke, the chief role of government was to

(1) protect natural rights
(2) fight territorial wars
(3) ensure the wealth of citizens
(4) redistribute land

19 In England, which circumstance was a result of the other three?

(1) availability of labor
(2) abundance of coal and iron
(3) waterpower from many rivers
(4) start of the Industrial Revolution

Base your answer to question 20 on the cartoon below and on your knowledge of social studies.

The Rhodes Colossus

Source: *Punch*, 1892 (adapted)

20 Which slogan best reflects the point of view of Cecil Rhodes as shown in this cartoon?

(1) "Imperialism is a Glorious Pursuit."
(2) "Embrace African Diversity."
(3) "Unite All Africans."
(4) "Connecting Constantinople to Cairo."

21 What was the primary reason that large numbers of people left Ireland in the 1840s and 1850s?

(1) The people faced mass starvation.
(2) A political revolution had started.
(3) A smallpox epidemic broke out in the country.
(4) The people sought better educational opportunities.

22 During the 19th century, European nations established spheres of influence in China mainly to

(1) profit from the ivory trade
(2) introduce Islam to the Chinese people
(3) gain commercial advantages in China
(4) obtain human rights for Chinese citizens

23 Porfirio Díaz, Francisco "Pancho" Villa, and Emiliano Zapata are all associated with the revolution in

(1) Haiti   (3) Bolivia
(2) Mexico   (4) Nicaragua

24 One effect of industrialization on Meiji Japan was that it

(1) strengthened the power of the Shogunate
(2) decreased the level of pollution
(3) modernized transportation
(4) increased the number of small farms

25 What was a major cause of World War I?

(1) rebellions in colonial lands in Africa and Asia
(2) expansion of communism into western Europe
(3) militarism in the nations of Europe
(4) inability of the League of Nations to keep the peace

26 What was one reason that totalitarian dictatorships gained power in Europe between World War I and World War II?

(1) Famine and AIDS spread throughout Europe.
(2) Trade was banned between western and eastern Europe.
(3) Governments failed to meet the needs of the people.
(4) Monarchies were reinstated in many nations.

Base your answer to question 27 on the map below and on your knowledge of social studies.

Source: Goldberg and DuPré, *Brief Review in Global History and Geography*, Prentice Hall, 2002 (adapted)

27 The countries shown in dark gray on this map can best be described as

(1) Triple Alliance members before World War I
(2) European countries formed immediately after World War I
(3) Axis powers during World War II
(4) Common Market members after World War II

28 The policy of appeasement helped cause World War II because this policy

(1) reduced the armaments of major European powers
(2) gave too much power to the United Nations
(3) increased sea trade between England and the United States
(4) allowed the aggressive actions of Germany to go unchecked

29 One reason for the construction of the Berlin Wall in 1961 was to

(1) promote reunification of East Germany and West Germany
(2) keep East Germans from fleeing to the Western sector of Berlin
(3) complete the post–World War II rebuilding of Berlin
(4) meet the requirements of the North Atlantic Treaty Organization (NATO)

Base your answers to questions 30 and 31 on the chart below and on your knowledge of social studies.

Production Levels in the Soviet Union (1932–1937)

Industry	1932	1937
Electricity (billion kw)	13.5	36.2
Coal (million tons)	64.4	128.0
Crude Oil (million tons)	21.4	28.5
Rolled Steel (million tons)	4.4	13.0

Source: R.W. Davies, ed., et al., *The Economic Transformation of the Soviet Union,1913–1945*, Cambridge University Press, 1994 (adapted)

30 Which policy is illustrated in this chart?

(1) pogroms   (3) Russification
(2) five-year plans   (4) nuclear arms

31 The data in this chart illustrate the

(1) benefits of foreign trade
(2) successful development of heavy industry
(3) availability of consumer goods
(4) effects of inflation on the economy

32 In China, Deng Xiaoping's Four Modernizations led to

(1) a decrease in industrialization
(2) a decreased interest in investments by foreign businesses
(3) an increase in the emphasis on collective farming
(4) an increased use of free-market practices

33 Border conflicts between India and Pakistan have most often occurred in

(1) Kashmir   (3) Tibet
(2) East Timor   (4) Afghanistan

Base your answer to question 34 on the map below and on your knowledge of social studies.

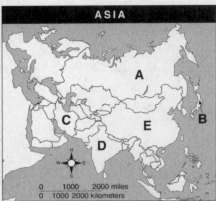

Source: *American History: Historical Outline Map Book With Lesson Ideas,* Prentice Hall, 1998 (adapted)

34 Which letter identifies the nation most closely associated with Mohandas Gandhi?

(1) A   (3) C
(2) B   (4) D

35 One reason Mikhail Gorbachev implemented the policies of glasnost and perestroika in the Soviet Union was to

(1) eliminate freedom of speech and press
(2) destroy the power of the opposition party
(3) dominate the governments of Eastern Europe
(4) encourage political discussion and economic reform

reasons did these allies give for this invasion?

(1) | Iraq was threatening war with Saudi Arabia.
Iraq had not had free elections for a number of years. |

(2) | Iraq had oil needed by the United States and Great Britain.
Iraq was threatening to cut off oil supplies to both countries. |

(3) | Iraq had weapons of mass destruction that threatened nations around the world.
Iraq sponsored world terrorism. |

(4) | Iraq's leader was responsible for the deaths of hundreds of thousands of Americans.
Iraq's army held Americans hostage for almost a year. |

Base your answer to question 37 on the graphs below and on your knowledge of social studies.

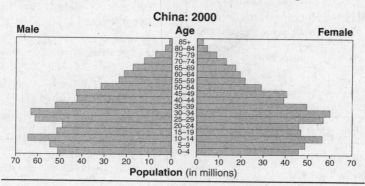

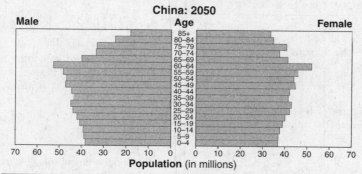

Source: U.S. Bureau of the Census, *International Data Base* (adapted)

37 In 2050, which concern will the Chinese government have to address as a result of the shift in the makeup of its population?

(1) military defense spending   (3) needs of an aging population

(2) production of consumer goods   (4) education of young people

38 "'We Blew It': Nike Admits to Mistakes Over Child Labor"

"UN Envoy Makes Plea for War on Global Poverty"

"International Literacy Decade Targets Women"

Which concern do these 21st-century headlines address?

(1) higher education issues
(2) social and economic issues
(3) cultural literacy
(4) individual responsibility

39 Which problem faces many of the least developed nations today?

(1) Too many varieties of crops are being grown.
(2) An excess of investment capital is available.
(3) High rates of illiteracy are limiting economic development.
(4) A high-calorie diet is causing obesity.

40 Which heading best completes the partial outline below?

I. _____

   A. Surplus of food

   B. Rise of cities

   C. Job specialization

   D. Development of new technology

(1) Results of the Fall of Rome
(2) Effects of the Neolithic Revolution
(3) Reasons for the Puritan Revolution
(4) Causes of the Bantu Migration

41 The ancient cultures of both the Incas and the Chinese adapted to the physical geography of their region by

(1) developing terrace farming on hillsides
(2) building chariots to protect their open plains against invaders
(3) becoming maritime traders
(4) constructing harbors to encourage exploration

42 Which factor best characterizes the art of both ancient Greece and the Renaissance?

(1) emphasis on the human form
(2) focus on biblical themes
(3) dominance of landscape paintings
(4) influence of the West African tradition

43 Which geographic factor played the greatest role in preventing Russia from being conquered by both Napoleon and Adolf Hitler?

(1) deserts   (3) climate
(2) rivers   (4) mountains

44 The unification of Germany (1870–71) and the breakup of Yugoslavia after 1991 both illustrate the influence of

(1) imperialism   (3) westernization
(2) industrialization   (4) nationalism

45 What was a direct result of the Opium War in 19th-century China?

(1) Japan gained control of Hong Kong.
(2) Kublai Khan rose to power in China.
(3) Chinese ports were opened for trade with European powers.
(4) Jiang Jieshi (Chiang Kai-shek) fled to Taiwan.

46 One way in which Peter the Great and Atatürk (Mustafa Kemal) are similar is that they sought to

(1) gain a warm-water port
(2) adopt western-style reforms
(3) limit the role of women in society
(4) return to traditional values

47 Which cause-and-effect relationship is accurate?

(1) The Russian Revolution led to an absolute monarchy.
(2) Enlightenment thoughts led to manorialism.
(3) The Black Plague led to labor shortages.
(4) The Commercial Revolution led to the creation of traditional economies.

48 A major argument used to support the building of the Suez and Panama Canals was that these waterways would

(1) shorten trade routes
(2) strengthen command economies
(3) increase competition for trade
(4) promote the local economy

49 Which pair of leaders used political purges, including the killing of opposition groups, as a means of maintaining control of the government?

(1) Sun Yixian (Sun Yat-sen) and Emperor Hirohito
(2) Joseph Stalin and Mao Zedong
(3) Simón Bolívar and Bernardo O'Higgins
(4) F. W. de Klerk and Indira Gandhi

50 Which heading best completes the partial outline below?

I. _____

A. Market system
B. Profit incentive
C. Entrepreneurs

(1) Forms of Government
(2) Characteristics of Capitalism
(3) Structure of the Guild System
(4) Elements of Culture

Answers to the essay questions are to be written in the separate essay booklet.

In developing your answer to Part II, be sure to keep these general definitions in mind:

(a) <u>describe</u> means "to illustrate something in words or tell about it"

(b) <u>discuss</u> means "to make observations about something using facts, reasoning, and argument; to present in some detail"

Part II

THEMATIC ESSAY QUESTION

Directions: Write a well-organized essay that includes an introduction, several paragraphs addressing the task below, and a conclusion.

Theme: Human Rights Violations

> The human rights of many groups have been violated at different times in various nations and regions. Efforts by governments, groups, and individuals to resolve these human rights violations have met with mixed results.

Task:

> Select *two* groups who have experienced human rights violations in a specific nation or region and for *each*
> - Describe *one* historical circumstance that led to a human rights violation in the nation or region
> - Describe *one* example of a human rights violation in that nation or region
> - Discuss the extent to which a government, a group, or an individual made an attempt to resolve this human rights violation

You may use any group whose rights have been violated from your study of global history. Some suggestions you might wish to consider include Christians under the Roman Empire, indigenous peoples in Latin America, Armenians under the Ottoman Empire, Ukrainians after the Russian Revolution, Jews in Europe, Cambodians under Pol Pot, blacks under apartheid in South Africa, and Kurds in the Middle East.

You are *not* limited to these suggestions.

Do *not* use any human rights violations from the United States in your answer.

Guidelines:

In your essay, be sure to
- Develop all aspects of the task
- Support the theme with relevant facts, examples, and details
- Use a logical and clear plan of organization, including an introduction and a conclusion that are beyond a restatement of the theme

NAME _____ SCHOOL _____

In developing your answers to Part III, be sure to keep this general definition in mind:

discuss means "to make observations about something using facts, reasoning, and argument; to present in some detail"

Part III

DOCUMENT-BASED QUESTION

This question is based on the accompanying documents. It is designed to test your ability to work with historical documents. Some of these documents have been edited for the purposes of this question. As you analyze the documents, take into account both the source of each document and any point of view that may be presented in the document.

Historical Context:

The French Revolution (1789–1814), which included Napoleon's reign, is considered a major turning point in world history. This revolution led to major changes in France and other nations and regions of the world.

Task: Using information from the documents and your knowledge of global history, answer the questions that follow each document in Part A. Your answers to the questions will help you write the Part B essay, in which you will be asked to

- Discuss the political, economic, *and/or* social causes of the French Revolution
- Discuss how the French Revolution affected the people of France
- Discuss *one* impact the French Revolution had on the world outside France

Part A
Short-Answer Questions

Directions: Analyze the documents and answer the short-answer questions that follow each document in the space provided.

Document 1

> . . . **Powers of the king.**—The King, Louis XVI, was absolute. He ruled by the *divine right theory* which held that he had received his power to govern from God and was therefore responsible to God alone. He appointed all civil officials and military officers. He made and enforced the laws. He could declare war and make peace. He levied taxes and spent the people's money as he saw fit. He controlled the expression of thought by a strict censorship of speech and press. By means of *lettres de cachet* (sealed letters which were really blank warrants for arrest) he could arbitrarily imprison anyone without trial for an indefinite period. He lived in his magnificent palace at Versailles, completely oblivious to the rising tide of popular discontent. . . .

Source: Friedman & Foner, *A Genetic Approach to Modern European History,*
College Entrance Book Co., 1938

1 According to this document by Friedman & Foner, what is **one** cause of the French Revolution? [1]

_____

_____

Score [ ]

Document 2

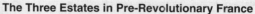

The Three Estates in Pre-Revolutionary France

Source: Jackson J. Spielvogel, *World History,* Glencoe/McGraw-Hill, 2003 (adapted)

2 Based on the information in these graphs, identify *one* cause of the French Revolution. [1]

_____

_____

Score ☐

Document 3

> **July 12, 1789**
> . . . The 12th. Walking up a long hill, to ease my mare, I was joined by a poor woman, who complained of the times, and that it was a sad country; demanding her reasons, she said her husband had but a morsel of land, one cow, and a poor little horse, yet they had a *franchar* (42 lb.) of wheat, and three chickens, to pay as a quit-rent to one Seigneur [noble]; and four *franchar* of oats, one chicken and 1 sou [small unit of money] to pay to another, besides very heavy tailles [taxes on the land and its produce] and other taxes. She had seven children, and the cow's milk helped to make the soup. But why, instead of a horse, do not you keep another cow? Oh, her husband could not carry his produce so well without a horse; and asses are little used in the country. It was said, at present, that *something was to be done by some great folks for such poor ones, but she did not know who nor how,* but God send us better, *car les tailles & les droits nous ecrasent* [because the taxes and laws are crushing us]. —This woman, at no great distance, might have been taken for sixty or seventy, her figure was so bent, and her face so furrowed [wrinkled] and hardened by labour, — but she said she was only twenty-eight. An Englishman who has not travelled, cannot imagine the figure made by infinitely the greater part of the countrywomen in France; it speaks, at the first sight, hard and severe labour: I am inclined to think, that they work harder than the men, and this, united with the more miserable labour of bringing a new race of slaves into the world, destroys absolutely all symmetry of person [balanced proportions] and every feminine appearance. To what are we to attribute this difference in the manners of the lower people in the two kingdoms? To Government . . . .

Source: Miss Betham-Edwards, ed., *Arthur Young's Travels in France During the Years 1787, 1788, 1789*, G. Bell and Sons (adapted)

3 Based on this document of Arthur Young's travels, state **one** reason the French peasants were dissatisfied with their life during this period of French history. [1]

_____

_____

Score [   ]

Document 4

The French Revolution

Date	Ruling Government	Changes
1789–1791	National Assembly	• Constitutional monarchy established • Feudalism abolished • *Declaration of the Rights of Man and the Citizen* adopted
1791–1792	Legislative Assembly	• Constitutional monarchy undermined • Mob forced king to flee to the safety of the Legislative Assembly • War declared against Austria and Prussia
1792–1795	The First Republic and The Convention	• France declared a Republic (Sept. 1792) • France ruled by Committee of Public Safety • Radicals (Jacobins) overcame moderates (Girondins) • Terror used to execute "enemies of the regime" • Robespierre executed
1795–1799	The Directory	• Five directors ruled as executive • Coups d'état attempted by radical and conservative forces • Napoleon overthrew the government in a coup d'état (Nov. 1799)

4 Based on this chart, identify *two* political changes that occurred during the French Revolution. [2]

(1)_____

_____

Score ☐

(2)_____

_____

Score ☐

Document 5

The Declaration of the Rights of Man and the Citizen

Article 1 – Men are born and remain free and equal in rights. Social distinctions may be based only on considerations of the common good. . . .

Article 4 – Liberty consists in being able to do anything that does not harm others: thus, the exercise of the natural rights of every man has no bounds other than those that ensure to the other members of society the enjoyment of these same rights. These bounds may be determined only by Law. . . .

Article 6 – The Law is the expression of the general will. All citizens have the right to take part, personally or through their representatives, in its making. It must be the same for all, whether it protects or punishes. All citizens, being equal in its eyes, shall be equally eligible to all high offices, public positions and employments, according to their ability, and without other distinction than that of their virtues and talents. . . .

Article 11 – The free communication of ideas and of opinions is one of the most precious rights of man. Any citizen may therefore speak, write and publish freely, except what is tantamount [equivalent] to the abuse of this liberty in the cases determined by Law. . . .

Source: *The Declaration of the Rights of Man and the Citizen*

5 Based on this excerpt from *The Declaration of the Rights of Man and the Citizen*, state **two** ways the National Assembly attempted to redefine the relationship between the individual and the government. [2]

(1)_____

_____

Score ☐

(2)_____

_____

Score ☐

Document 6

Helen Williams was a foreigner living in Paris in 1793. She sympathized with those who wanted France to form a republic. She was arrested because her views differed from the views of those in power.

> . . . After two months in our new prison, we were released. A young Frenchman, who has since married my sister, managed to get us released by haunting all the officials he could find and finally by begging the release from Chaumette, the procurer of the Paris Commune, and a tyrant. So we were free but were watched. We could see very few people and went out little, and yet it was a sort of liberty. We feared to go out, in case, without realizing it, we committed some transgression [offense] that would lead to being arrested again. We hardly spoke to anyone, for there were spies everywhere, and we jumped at each knock at the door, fearing arrest. For the prisons were growing more crowded daily, and more and more were going to the scaffold as the Reign of Terror tightened its hold. "Suspicion" was now a warrant for imprisonment, and conspiracy and murder were in the air. One man was arrested because he "looked" noble, another because a total stranger swore that he supported monarchy. Some were arrested for having been rich, others for being clever. Many who were arrested asked for the reason in vain. And the numbers of executions rose, and the horrors increased, and the stories of both courage and cowardice were passed from home to home. Yet it seemed to me that there was more courage than cowardice to be found, which gave us hope for humanity even in these dark days.
>
> Soon after our release from prison, we decided to move from the center of the town to a house in the most remote part of the faubourg [suburb], Saint Germain. Our new home was but a few moments walk from the countryside. But although we were close, we did not dare to walk there. The parks and woods that surrounded us and had once belonged to royalty were now haunted by revolutionaries, despots, police spies, even the conspirators themselves on occasion. So we walked in the common fields near our house, where people put their animals to graze. I have no words to describe how reluctantly we returned from our walks to Paris, that den of carnage, that slaughterhouse of man. The guillotine was claiming both the innocent and the guilty alike, and at such a rate that the gutters seemed to stream with blood. And just when it seemed that things could get no worse, when you thought it was not possible to increase the stream of people flowing to the scaffold, you were proved wrong, and the pace of the flow quickened even more. . . .

Source: Jane Shuter, ed., *Helen Williams and the French Revolution*, Raintree Steck-Vaughn Publishers (adapted)

6 According to Helen Williams, what is **one** impact the Reign of Terror had on the people of Paris in 1793? [1]

_____

_____

Score ☐

Document 7

> . . . By 1799, however, Frenchmen had had the experience of enjoying, at least in theory, freedom of speech and freedom of the press. Education had been reorganized along the lines which it still follows in most modern states—free, compulsory, universal, and secular. The Revolution had given rise to an extensive, if not always great, periodical press. Lack of opportunities had yielded to the "careers open to talents" already mentioned, and such talents were encouraged and brought to fruition through public prizes, state patronage, and similar devices. Moreover, while there had been few museums and libraries prior to 1789, the revolutionaries established many more, planned still additional ones, and endeavored to integrate them with the educational system. . . .

Source: John Hall Stewart, ed., *A Documentary Survey of the French Revolution*, Macmillan

7 According to John Hall Stewart, what is **one** change brought about by the French Revolution by 1799? [1]

_____

_____

Score ☐

Document 8

> . . . The lasting quality of Napoleon's reforms outside France was in direct ratio to the length of time French control had been in effect and to the weakness of the local governments. In the areas annexed before 1804, the Revolutionary changes were put into effect as a whole. Italy was more profoundly transformed than any other part of Europe. The stronger the local governments were, the more able they were to overthrow Napoleonic institutions after his military defeat. But only rarely did the reaction upset the civil principles which to Napoleon were so important Even in Naples King Ferdinand did not abolish the Civil Code or re-establish feudal rights when he returned. All the reactionary forces of Europe combined were not strong enough to restore things as they had been before the outbreak of the French Revolution. They could not, in particular, undo the many-faceted social change that had been set in motion. . . .

Source: Robert B. Holtman, *The Napoleonic Revolution*, J.B. Lippincott Company, 1967

8 According to Robert B. Holtman, what is *one* impact the French Revolution and Napoleon's reforms had on a nation or region outside France? [1]

_____

_____

Score

Document 9

The Ambiguous Legacy of the Revolution

... However, the majority of Europeans and non-Europeans came to see the Revolution as much more than a bloody tragedy. These people were more impressed by what the Revolution accomplished than by what it failed to do. They recalled the Revolution's abolition of serfdom, slavery, inherited privilege, and judicial torture; its experiments with democracy; and its opening of opportunities to those who, for reasons of social status or religion, had been traditionally excluded.

One of the most important contributions of the French Revolution was to make revolution part of the world's political tradition. The French Revolution continued to provide instruction for revolutionaries in the 19th and 20th centuries, as peoples in Europe and around the world sought to realize their different versions of freedom. Karl Marx would, at least at the outset, pattern his notion of a proletarian revolution on the French Revolution of 1789. And 200 years later Chinese students, who weeks before had fought their government in Tiananmen Square, confirmed the contemporary relevance of the French Revolution when they led the revolutionary bicentennial parade in Paris on July 14, 1989. ...

Source: Thomas E. Kaiser, University of Arkansas, encarta.msn.com/encyclopedia

9a According to Thomas E. Kaiser, what is **one** change that resulted within France from the French Revolution? [1]

_____

_____

Score ☐

b According to Thomas E. Kaiser, what are **two** effects the French Revolution had outside France? [2]

(1)_____

_____

Score ☐

(2)_____

_____

Score ☐

Part B
Essay

Directions: Write a well-organized essay that includes an introduction, several paragraphs, and a conclusion. Use evidence from *at least **five*** documents to support your response.

Historical Context:

The French Revolution (1789–1814), which included Napoleon's reign, is considered a major turning point in world history. This revolution led to major changes in France and other nations and regions of the world.

Task: Using the information from the documents and your knowledge of global history, write an essay in which you

- Discuss the political, economic, ***and/or*** social causes of the French Revolution
- Discuss how the French Revolution affected the people of France
- Discuss ***one*** impact the French Revolution had on the world outside France

Guidelines:

In your essay, be sure to
- Develop all aspects of the task
- Incorporate information from *at least **five*** documents
- Incorporate relevant outside information
- Support the theme with relevant facts, examples, and details
- Use a logical and clear plan of organization, including an introduction and conclusion that are beyond a restatement of the theme

Regents Examination–August 2006

This section contains an actual Regents Examination in Global History and Geography that was given in New York State in August 2006.

Circle your answers to Part 1. Write your responses to the short-answer questions in the spaces provided. Write your thematic essay and document-based essay on separate sheets of paper. Be sure to refer to the test-taking strategies in the front of this book as you prepare to answer the test questions.

Part I

Answer all questions in this part.

Directions (1–50): For each statement or question, write on the separate answer sheet the *number* of the word or expression that, of those given, best completes the statement or answers the question.

1 • Height above sea level
 • Distance from the equator
 • Amount of rainfall
 • Average daily temperature

 Which aspect of geography is most influenced by these factors?

 (1) natural boundaries
 (2) climate
 (3) topography
 (4) mineral resources

2 Which activity would be most characteristic of people in a traditional society?

 (1) serving in government assemblies
 (2) working in an industrialized city
 (3) having the same occupation as their parents
 (4) establishing a mercantile system of trade

3 • Large areas in the north and south received less than ten inches of rainfall annually.
 • The presence of waterfalls and rapids slowed river travel.
 • Highlands and steep cliffs limited exploration.

 In which region did these geographic factors have an impact on European exploration and colonization?

 (1) South America
 (2) Southeast Asia
 (3) subcontinent of India
 (4) Africa

4 What is the main reason the Neolithic Revolution is considered a turning point in world history?

 (1) Fire was used as a source of energy for the first time.
 (2) Spoken language was used to improve communication.
 (3) Domestication of animals and cultivation of crops led to settled communities.
 (4) Stone tools and weapons were first developed.

5 Which heading best completes the partial outline below?

I. _____
A. Centralized governments
B. Organized religions
C. Social classes
D. Specialization of labor

 (1) Economic Development in Ancient Egypt
 (2) Cultural Diffusion in Mohenjo-Daro
 (3) Features of the Old Stone Age
 (4) Characteristics of Civilizations

6 The Pillars of Emperor Asoka of the Mauryan Empire and the Code of Hammurabi of Babylon are most similar to the

 (1) ziggurats of Sumeria
 (2) map projections of Mercator
 (3) Great Sphinx of the Egyptians
 (4) Twelve Tables of the Romans

7 A similarity between Bantu migrations in Africa and migrations of the ancient Aryans into South Asia is that both moved

 (1) across the Atlantic Ocean
 (2) from rural lands to urban areas
 (3) in search of additional food sources
 (4) for religious freedom

8 Which factor led to the development of civilizations in ancient Mesopotamia?

 (1) political harmony
 (2) favorable geography
 (3) religious differences
 (4) universal education

9 Which statement most likely represents the view of a citizen of ancient Athens visiting Sparta?

(1) "The government and society in Sparta are so strict. The people have little voice in government."
(2) "I feel as though I have never left home. Everything here is the same as it is in Athens."
(3) "This society allows for more freedom of expression than I have ever experienced in Athens."
(4) "I have never heard of a society like Sparta that believes in only one God."

10 One similarity between animism and Shinto is that people who follow these belief systems

(1) practice filial piety
(2) worship spirits in nature
(3) are monotheistic
(4) are required to make pilgrimages

11 • Buddhist temples are found in Japan.
   • Most Indonesians study the Koran.
   • Catholicism is the dominant religion in Latin America.

These statements illustrate a result of

(1) westernization
(2) cultural diffusion
(3) economic nationalism
(4) fundamentalism

12 Which group introduced the Cyrillic alphabet, Orthodox Christianity, and domed architecture to Russian culture?

(1) Mongols   (3) Jews
(2) Vikings   (4) Byzantines

13 The topography and climate of Russia have caused Russia to

(1) depend on rice as its main source of food
(2) seek access to warm-water ports
(3) adopt policies of neutrality and isolation
(4) acquire mineral-rich colonies on other continents

14 One of the major achievements of Byzantine Emperor Justinian was that he

(1) established a direct trade route with Ghana
(2) defended the empire against the spread of Islam
(3) brought Roman Catholicism to his empire
(4) preserved and transmitted Greek and Roman culture

15 Both European medieval knights and Japanese samurai warriors pledged oaths of

(1) loyalty to their military leader
(2) devotion to their nation-state
(3) service to their church
(4) allegiance to their families

16 What was a significant effect of Mansa Musa's pilgrimage to Mecca?

(1) The African written language spread to southwest Asia.
(2) Military leaders eventually controlled Mali.
(3) Islamic learning and culture expanded in Mali.
(4) The trading of gold for salt ended.

17 A direct impact that the printing press had on 16th-century Europe was that it encouraged the

(1) spread of ideas
(2) beginnings of communism
(3) establishment of democracy
(4) development of industrialization

18 Which technological advancement helped unify both the Roman and the Inca Empires?

(1) astrolabe   (3) gunpowder
(2) road system   (4) wheeled carts

19 Cervantes' literary classic *Don Quixote*, the rule of Isabella and Ferdinand, and the art of El Greco are associated with the

(1) Golden Age in Spain
(2) Hanseatic League in Germany
(3) Glorious Revolution in England
(4) Renaissance in Italy

Base your answer to question 20 on the diagram below and on your knowledge of social studies.

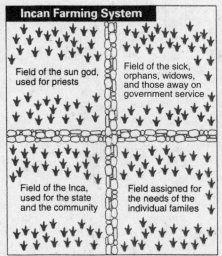

Incan Farming System

Field of the sun god, used for priests

Field of the sick, orphans, widows, and those away on government service

Field of the Inca, used for the state and the community

Field assigned for the needs of the individual families

All land belonged to the community. Farmers grew crops in different fields.

Source: Ellis and Esler, *World History: Connections to Today*, Prentice Hall (adapted)

20 This diagram shows the Incas had a farming system that

(1) provided crops for the entire society
(2) left much of the land unfarmed
(3) set aside fifty percent of the crops for those who farmed the fields
(4) grew crops only for priests and government officials

---

21 Which statement best describes a result of the encounter between Europeans and native populations of Latin America?

(1) Native societies experienced rapid population growth.
(2) European nations lost power and prestige in the New World.
(3) Large numbers of natives migrated to Europe for a better life.
(4) Plantations in the New World used enslaved Africans to replace native populations.

Base your answers to questions 22 through 24 on the speakers' statements below and on your knowledge of social studies.

Speaker A: Although I spread serfdom in my country, I tried to modernize our society by incorporating western technology.

Speaker B: I promoted culture with my support of the arts. Unfortunately, I drained my country's treasury by building my palace at Versailles and involving my country in costly wars.

Speaker C: I gained much wealth from my overseas empire in the Americas. I waged war against the Protestants and lost.

Speaker D: I inherited the throne and imprisoned my foes without a trial. I dissolved Parliament because I did not want to consult with them when I increased taxes.

22 Which speaker represents the view of King Louis XIV of France?

(1) *A*   (3) *C*
(2) *B*   (4) *D*

23 Which nation was most likely governed by *Speaker D*?

(1) Russia   (3) Spain
(2) France   (4) England

24 Which type of government is most closely associated with all these speakers?

(1) limited monarchy
(2) absolute monarchy
(3) direct democracy
(4) constitutional democracy

Base your answer to question 25 on the statements below and on your knowledge of social studies.

. . . The Laws ought to be so framed, as to secure the Safety of every Citizen as much as possible.

. . . The Equality of the Citizens consists in this; that they should all be subject to the same Laws. . . .

— *Documents of Catherine the Great,*
W. F. Reddaway, ed., Cambridge University Press (adapted)

25 These ideas of Catherine the Great of Russia originated during the

(1) Age of Exploration
(2) Age of Enlightenment
(3) Protestant Reformation
(4) French Revolution

Base your answers to questions 26 and 27 on the speakers' statements below and on your knowledge of social studies.

Speaker A: Government should not interfere in relations between workers and business owners.

Speaker B: The workers will rise up and overthrow the privileged class.

Speaker C: Private property will cease to exist. The people will own the means of production.

Speaker D: A favorable balance of trade should be maintained by the use of tariffs.

26 Which two speakers represent Karl Marx's ideas of communism?

(1) *A* and *B*   (3) *B* and *D*
(2) *B* and *C*   (4) *C* and *D*

27 Which speaker is referring to laissez-faire capitalism?

(1) *A*   (3) *C*
(2) *B*   (4) *D*

Base your answers to questions 28 and 29 on the map below and on your knowledge of social studies.

Japanese Imperialism, 1875–1910

Source: Henry Brun et al., *Reviewing Global History and Geography,* AMSCO (adapted)

28 What was a basic cause of the political changes shown on this map?

(1) Russia and Japan formed an alliance.
(2) Korea defeated Japan in the Sino-Japanese War.
(3) The Japanese people wanted to spread the beliefs of Shinto.
(4) Japan needed raw materials for industrialization.

29 Which event is associated with the changes shown on this map?

(1) Opium War
(2) Meiji Restoration
(3) Chinese Nationalist Revolution
(4) rise of the Soviet Union

30 The Bolshevik Party in 1917 gained the support of the peasant class because they promised them

(1) "Peace, Land, and Bread"
(2) "Liberty, Equality, Fraternity"
(3) abolition of the secret police
(4) democratic reforms in all levels of government

Base your answer to question 31 on the map below and on your knowledge of social studies.

Areas lost as a result of the Versailles Treaty

Schleswig Holstein
Polish Corridor
GERMANY
Saarland
Alsace-Lorraine

Source: Geoffrey Barraclough, ed., *Hammond Concise Atlas of World History,* Hammond, 1998 (adapted)

31 Which time period in German history is most accurately represented in this map?

(1) between World War I and World War II
(2) just after the Berlin Conference
(3) immediately after the Congress of Vienna
(4) during unification under Bismarck

32 Which statement describes one major aspect of a command economy?

(1) Supply and demand determines what will be produced.
(2) Most economic decisions are made by the government.
(3) The means of production are controlled by labor unions.
(4) The economy is mainly agricultural.

33 Which area was once controlled by Britain, suffered a mass starvation in the 1840s, and became an independent Catholic nation in 1922?

(1) Scotland   (3) Ghana
(2) India   (4) Ireland

34 Totalitarian countries are characterized by

(1) free and open discussions of ideas
(2) a multiparty system with several candidates for each office
(3) government control of newspapers, radio, and television
(4) government protection of people's civil liberties

35 Which name would best complete this partial outline?

I. African Nationalists of the 20th Century
    A. Leopold Senghor
    B. Jomo Kenyatta
    C. Julius Nyerere
    D. _____

(1) Atatürk [Mustafa Kemal]
(2) Ho Chi Minh
(3) José de San Martín
(4) Kwame Nkrumah

36 Since 1948, a major reason for the conflict between Arabs and Israelis is that each side

(1) wants the huge oil reserves that lie under the disputed land
(2) believes that the United States favors the other side in the conflict
(3) claims sovereignty over the same land
(4) seeks to control trade on the eastern end of the Mediterranean Sea

37 In the 1980s, Mikhail Gorbachev's attempts to change the Soviet Union resulted in

(1) an increase in tensions between India and the Soviet Union
(2) a strengthening of the Communist Party
(3) a shift from producing consumer goods to producing heavy machinery
(4) a series of economic and political reforms

Base your answer to question 38 on the diagram below and on your knowledge of social studies.

Cycle of the Ecological Environment

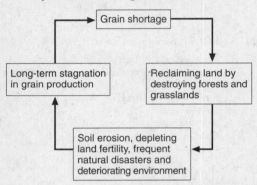

Source: Yan Ruizhen and Wang Yuan,
Poverty and Development,
New World Press, 1992 (adapted)

38 Which conclusion based on the ecological cycle shown in this diagram is most valid?

(1) Grain yields increase as the amount of land reclaimed increases.

(2) The destruction of forests leads to soil erosion.

(3) Grain production has no impact on the environment.

(4) Natural disasters have little effect on grain production.

39 • Egypt builds the Aswan Dam to control flooding and produce hydroelectric power.
• China builds the Three Gorges Dam to control flooding and improve trade.
• Brazil builds the Tucuruí Dam in the tropical rain forest to produce hydroelectric power.

Which conclusion can be drawn from these statements?

(1) Societies often modify their environment to meet their needs.

(2) Monsoons are needed for the development of societies.

(3) Topography creates challenges that societies are unable to overcome.

(4) Land features influence the development of diverse belief systems.

Base your answer to question 40 on the cartoon below and on your knowledge of social studies.

Ziraldo/Rio de Janeiro, Brazil
Cartoonists & Writers Syndicate
Source: Ziraldo Alves Pinto

40 What is the main idea of this Brazilian cartoon?

(1) Relations between Latin America and the United States are mutually beneficial.

(2) The United States wants to cut off political and economic relations with Latin America.

(3) Latin American nations are self-sufficient and need not rely on the United States.

(4) The United States wants to control its relationships with Latin America.

41 **"Tensions Increase Over Kashmir"**
"Hindus and Muslims Clash in Calcutta Riots"
"Threat of Nuclear Conflict Worries World"

These headlines refer to events in which region?

(1) Latin America
(2) sub-Saharan Africa
(3) subcontinent of India
(4) East Asia

Base your answer to question 42 on the cartoon below and on your knowledge of social studies.

Source: Kim Song Heng, *Lianhe Zaobao*, 2002 (adapted)

42 The main idea of this 2002 cartoon is that East Timor is

(1) experiencing massive floods that might destroy the nation
(2) struggling with the arrival of large numbers of freedom-seeking refugees
(3) facing several dangers that threaten its existence as a new nation
(4) celebrating its success as an independent nation

43 One way in which the Tang dynasty, the Gupta Empire, and the European Renaissance are similar is that they all included periods of

(1) religious unity
(2) democratic reforms
(3) economic isolation
(4) cultural achievements

44 What was one similar goal shared by Simón Bolívar and Mohandas Gandhi?

(1) ending foreign control
(2) promoting religious freedom
(3) establishing a limited monarchy
(4) creating collective farms

45 The Armenian Massacre, the "killing fields" of the Khmer Rouge, and Saddam Hussein's attacks against the Kurds are examples of

(1) apartheid
(2) enslavement
(3) human rights violations
(4) forced collectivization

46 In western Europe, the Middle Ages began after the collapse of which empire?

(1) Mughal   (3) Ottoman
(2) Roman   (4) Byzantine

Base your answers to questions 47 and 48 on the chart below and on your knowledge of social studies.

Executions During the Reign of Terror

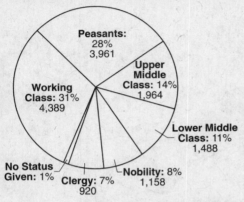

Peasants: 28% 3,961

Upper Middle Class: 14% 1,964

Working Class: 31% 4,389

Lower Middle Class: 11% 1,488

No Status Given: 1%

Clergy: 7% 920

Nobility: 8% 1,158

Source: Dennis Sherman et al., eds., *World Civilizations: Sources, Images, and Interpretations*, McGraw-Hill (adapted)

47 During which revolution did these executions occur?

(1) French   (3) Chinese
(2) Russian   (4) Cuban

48 Which statement is best supported by information found in this chart?

(1) Clergy were spared from the Reign of Terror.
(2) The Reign of Terror affected all classes equally.
(3) The Reign of Terror crossed social and economic boundaries.
(4) Peasants were the most frequent victims of the Reign of Terror.

Base your answer to question 49 on the passage below and on your knowledge of social studies.

. . . Our foundation rests upon trade, because, as you see, we have a large part of our capital invested [in it]. And therefore we shall have little for exchange operations, and we are forced to exert our ingenuity elsewhere. This, however, in my opinion, does not involve greater risk than one incurs in exchanges today, especially when no risks at sea are run [That is, when shipments by sea are insured.]; nor does it bring smaller profits. And [trade operations] are more legal and more honorable. In them we shall so govern ourselves that every day you will have more reason to be content; may God grant us His grace. . . .

Source: Letter to the home office of the Medici from branch office at Bruges, May 14, 1464 (adapted)

49 This passage best illustrates circumstances that characterized the

(1) Crusades
(2) Age of Reason
(3) Commercial Revolution
(4) Scientific Revolution

50 "Germany, Austria-Hungary, and Italy Form Triple Alliance"
"Serbian Nationalism Grows in Balkans"
"Archduke Franz Ferdinand Assassinated in Bosnia"

The events in these headlines contributed most directly to the

(1) beginning of World War I
(2) outbreak of the Cold War
(3) development of communist rule in Europe
(4) strengthening of European monarchies

Answers to the essay questions are to be written in the separate essay booklet.

In developing your answer to Part II, be sure to keep these general definitions in mind:

(a) <u>explain</u> means "to make plain or understandable; to give reasons for or causes of; to show the logical development or relationships of"

(b) <u>discuss</u> means "to make observations about something using facts, reasoning, and argument; to present in some detail"

PART II

THEMATIC ESSAY QUESTION

Directions: Write a well-organized essay that includes an introduction, several paragraphs addressing the task below, and a conclusion.

Theme: Movement of People and Goods: Trade

> Trade routes and trade organizations have had an impact on nations and regions. The effects have been both positive and negative.

Task:

> Identify *two* trade routes *and/or* trade organizations and for *each*
> - Explain *one* reason for the establishment of the trade route or trade organization
> - Discuss *one* positive effect *or* *one* negative effect of the trade route or trade organization on a specific nation or region

You may use any example from your study of global history. Some suggestions you might wish to consider include the Silk Roads, the trans-Saharan trade routes of the African kingdoms, Mediterranean trade routes, the Hanseatic League, the British East India Company, the Organization of Petroleum Exporting Countries (OPEC), and the European Union (EU).

You are *not* limited to these suggestions.

Guidelines:

In your essay, be sure to
- Develop all aspects of the task
- Support the theme with relevant facts, examples, and details
- Use a logical and clear plan of organization, including an introduction and a conclusion that are beyond a restatement of the theme

NAME _____ SCHOOL _____

In developing your answer to Part III, be sure to keep this general definition in mind:

> discuss means "to make observations about something using facts, reasoning, and argument; to present in some detail"

PART III

DOCUMENT-BASED QUESTION

This question is based on the accompanying documents. It is designed to test your ability to work with historical documents. Some of these documents have been edited for the purposes of this question. As you analyze the documents, take into account the source of each document and any point of view that may be presented in the document.

Historical Context:

As World War II came to an end, a new conflict emerged between the United States and the Soviet Union. This conflict, known as the Cold War, affected many regions of the world, including **Europe**, **Asia**, and **Latin America**.

Task: Using information from the documents and your knowledge of global history, answer the questions that follow each document in Part A. Your answers to the questions will help you write the Part B essay in which you will be asked to

> • Discuss how the Cold War between the United States and the Soviet Union affected other nations *and/or* regions of the world

Part A
Short-Answer Questions

Directions: Analyze the documents and answer the short-answer questions that follow each document in the space provided.

Document 1

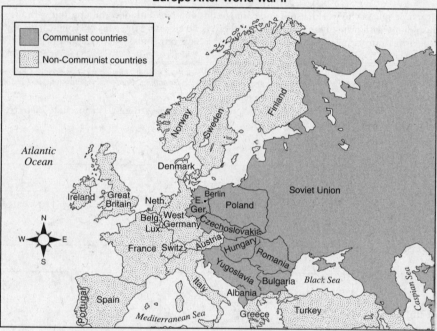

Europe After World War II

Source: Roger B. Beck et al., *World History: Patterns of Interaction*, McDougal Littell (adapted)

1 What does the information shown on this map indicate about the governments of Western Europe and Eastern Europe after World War II? [1]

_____

_____

Score ☐

Document 2a

Imre Nagy, the Hungarian leader, was forced out of office by the Soviet Communist government. The people of Hungary protested his removal from office.

> This is Hungary calling! This is Hungary calling! The last free station. Forward to the United Nations. Early this morning Soviet troops launched a general attack on Hungary. We are requesting you to send us immediate aid in the form of parachute troops over the Transdanubian provinces [across the Danube River]. It is possible that our broadcasts will soon come to the same fate as the other Hungarian broadcasting stations . . . For the sake of God and freedom, help Hungary! . . .
>
> — Free Radio Rakoczi
>
> Civilized people of the world, listen and come to our aid. Not with declarations, but with force, with soldiers, with arms. Do not forget that there is no stopping the wild onslaught [attack] of Bolshevism. Your turn will also come, if we perish. Save our souls! Save our souls! . . .
>
> — Free Radio Petofi

Source: Melvin J. Lasky, ed., *The Hungarian Revolution: The Story of the October Uprising as Recorded in Documents, Dispatches, Eye-Witness Accounts, and World-wide Reactions,* Frederick A. Praeger, 1957 (adapted)

2a Based on these broadcasts from Free Radio Rakoczi and Free Radio Petofi, state *two* reasons the Hungarian people were asking for help in 1956.   [2]

(1) _____

_____

Score ☐

(2) _____

_____

Score ☐

Document 2b

> This morning the forces of the reactionary conspiracy [anti-Soviet plot] against the Hungarian people were crushed. A new Hungarian Revolutionary Worker-Peasant [Communist] Government, headed by the Prime Minister Janos Kadar, has been formed. . . .
>
> — Radio Moscow

Source: Melvin J. Lasky, ed., *The Hungarian Revolution: The Story of the October Uprising as Recorded in Documents, Dispatches, Eye-Witness Accounts, and World-wide Reactions,* Frederick A. Praeger, 1957

2b Based on this broadcast from Radio Moscow, state *one* result of the Hungarian Revolution.   [1]

_____

_____

Score ☐

Document 3a

Berlin, Germany After World War II

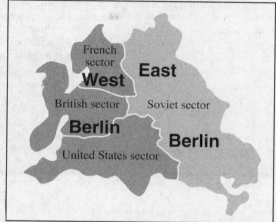

Source: Henry Brun et al., *Reviewing Global History and Geography*, AMSCO (adapted)

Document 3b

Berlin, 1961

Source: Heiko Burkhardt, dailysoft.com

3 Based on this map and the Burkhardt photograph, state **one** way the Cold War affected the city of Berlin. [1]

_____

_____

Score [ ]

Document 4

> . . . The preservation of peace forms the central aim of India's policy. It is in the pursuit of this policy that we have chosen the path of nonalinement [nonalignment] in any military or like pact or alliance. Nonalinement does not mean passivity of mind or action, lack of faith or conviction. It does not mean submission to what we consider evil. It is a positive and dynamic approach to such problems that confront us. We believe that each country has not only the right to freedom but also to decide its own policy and way of life. Only thus can true freedom flourish and a people grow according to their own genius.
>
> We believe, therefore, in nonaggression and noninterference by one country in the affairs of another and the growth of tolerance between them and the capacity for peaceful coexistence. We think that by the free exchange of ideas and trade and other contacts between nations each will learn from the other and truth will prevail. We therefore endeavor to maintain friendly relations with all countries, even though we may disagree with them in their policies or structure of government. We think that by this approach we can serve not only our country but also the larger causes of peace and good fellowship in the world. . . .

Source: Prime Minister Jawaharlal Nehru, speech in Washington, D.C., December 18, 1956

4 According to Prime Minister Nehru, what was India's foreign policy in 1956? [1]

_____

_____

Score ☐

Document 5

Sook Nyul Choi was born in Pyongyang, Korea and immigrated to the United States during the 1950s. She integrates her autobiographical information into a work of historical fiction set in Korea between the end of World War II and 1950.

> . . . Our freedom and happiness did not last long. In June 1950, war broke out. North Korean and Communist soldiers filled the streets of Seoul, and were soon joined by Chinese Communist troops. Russian tanks came barreling through. In the chaos, many more North Korean refugees made their way to Seoul. Theresa and the other nuns finally escaped, and made their way to our house. They told us that the Russians and Town Reds had found out about Kisa's and Aunt Tiger's other activities. They died as all "traitors" did. They were shot with machine guns, and then hanged in the town square to serve as a lesson to others. We never heard any further news about the sock girls, or about my friend Unhi. I still wonder if they are alive in the North.

Source: Sook Nyul Choi, *Year of Impossible Goodbyes,* Houghton Mifflin Company

5 Based on Sook Nyul Choi's description, state **two** ways the beginning of the Korean War affected the people of Korea. [2]

(1)_____

_____

Score ☐

(2)_____

_____

Score ☐

Document 6a

War in Korea, 1950–1953

Document 6b

War in Vietnam, 1954–1973

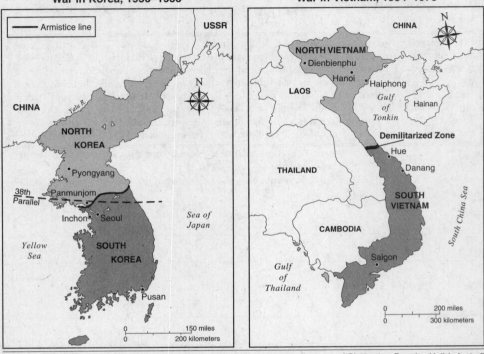

Source: Burton F. Beers, *World History: Patterns of Civilization*, Prentice Hall (adapted)

6 Based on the information shown on these maps, state **one** similarity in the way the Cold War affected Korea and Vietnam.   [1]

_____

_____

Score [ ]

Document 7a

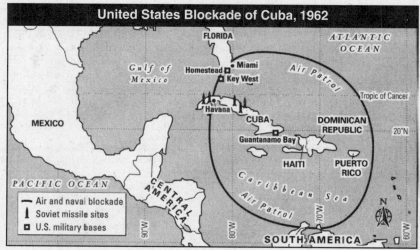

United States Blockade of Cuba, 1962

Source: *World History: Patterns of Interaction*, McDougal Littell (adapted)

Document 7b

   This Government as promised has maintained the closest surveillance of the Soviet military build-up on the island of Cuba.

   Within the past week unmistakable evidence has established the fact that a series of offensive missile sites is now in preparation on that imprisoned island.

   The purpose of these bases can be none other than to provide a nuclear strike capability against the Western Hemisphere.

   Upon receiving the first preliminary hard information of this nature last Tuesday morning at 9 A.M., I directed that our surveillance be stepped up. And having now confirmed and completed our evaluation of the evidence and our decision on a course of action, this Government feels obliged to report this new crisis to you in fullest detail.

   The characteristics of these new missile sites indicate two distinct types of installations. Several of them include medium-range ballistic missiles capable of carrying a nuclear warhead for a distance of more than 1,000 nautical miles.

   Each of these missiles, in short, is capable of striking Washington, D.C., the Panama Canal, Cape Canaveral, Mexico City or any other city in the southeastern part of the United States, in Central America or in the Caribbean area. . . .

Source: President John F. Kennedy, address to the nation on the Soviet arms buildup in Cuba, October 22 1962

7 Based on this map and President John F. Kennedy's address, state *one* way the Cold War affected Cuba. [1]

_____

_____

Score [ ]

Document 8a

. . . Immediately after the revolution, the Sandinistas had the best organized and most experienced military force in the country. To replace the National Guard, the Sandinistas established a new national army, the Sandinista People's Army (Ejército Popular Sandinista—EPS), and a police force, the Sandinista Police (Policía Sandinista-PS). These two groups, contrary to the original Puntarenas Pact [agreement reached by Sandinista government when in exile] were controlled by the Sandinistas and trained by personnel from Cuba, Eastern Europe, and the Soviet Union. Opposition to the overwhelming FSLN [Sandinista National Liberation Front] influence in the security forces did not surface until 1980. Meanwhile, the EPS developed, with support from Cuba and the Soviet Union, into the largest and best equipped military force in Central America. Compulsory military service, introduced during 1983, brought the EPS forces to about 80,000 by the mid-1980s. . . .

Source: Library of Congress, Federal Research Division (adapted)

8a According to this document from the Library of Congress, what effect did the Cold War have on Nicaragua in the 1980s? [1]

_____

_____

Score ☐

Document 8b

Her [Violeta Chamorro] husband's murder sparked a revolution that brought the Sandinistas to power. Now Violeta Chamorro is challenging them in Nicaragua's presidential election.

. . . "Violeta! Violeta! Throw them [Sandinistas] out! Throw them out!"

Surrounded by outstretched hands, Mrs. Chamorro hugs everyone in reach. Then Nicaragua's most famous widow goes straight to her message. This is the town where my husband was born, she tells them. This is where he learned the values of freedom that cost him his life. This is where he would tell us to make a stand against the Sandinista regime.

"I never thought that I would return to Granada as a candidate, raising the banner steeped in the blood of Pedro Joaquín Chamorro, to ask his people once again to put themselves in the front lines," she says. "But Nicaragua must win its freedom once again.

"All across the world," she continues, her voice rising, "people like you are burying Communism and proclaiming democracy. So set your watches! Set them to the same hour as Poland, as Bulgaria, as Czechoslovakia, as Chile! Because this is the hour of democracy and freedom — this is the hour of the people!". . .

Source: Mark A. Uhlig, *New York Times*, February 11, 1990

8b According to Mark A. Uhlig, what political change did Violeta Chamorro hope to bring to Nicaragua? [1]

_____

_____

Score ☐

Part B
Essay

Directions: Write a well-organized essay that includes an introduction, several paragraphs, and a conclusion. Use evidence from *at least **five*** documents to support your response. Support your response with relevant facts, examples, and details. Include additional outside information.

Historical Context:

As World War II came to an end, a new conflict emerged between the United States and the Soviet Union. This conflict, known as the Cold War, affected many regions of the world, including **Europe**, **Asia**, and **Latin America**.

Task: Using the information from the documents and your knowledge of global history, write an essay in which you

> • Discuss how the Cold War between the United States and the Soviet Union affected other nations ***and/or*** regions of the world

Guidelines:

In your essay, be sure to

• Develop all aspects of the task
• Incorporate information from *at least **five*** documents
• Incorporate relevant outside information
• Support the theme with relevant facts, examples, and details
• Use a logical and clear plan of organization, including an introduction and a conclusion that are beyond a restatement of the theme

Regents Examination–June 2006

This section contains an actual Regents Examination in Global History and Geography that was given in New York State in June 2006.

Circle your answers to Part 1. Write your responses to the short-answer questions in the spaces provided. Write your thematic essay and document-based essay on separate sheets of paper. Be sure to refer to the test-taking strategies in the front of this book as you prepare to answer the test questions.

Part I

Answer all questions in this part.

Directions (1–50): For each statement or question, write on the separate answer sheet the *number* of the word or expression that, of those given, best completes the statement or answers the question.

1 Which heading best completes the partial outline below?

> I. _____
>
> A. Seafood makes up a large part of the Filipino diet.
> B. Africans built hydroelectric plants along the Zambezi River.
> C. The majority of Russians live west of the Ural Mountains.
> D. The most densely populated area of India is the Ganges River Valley.

(1) Rivers Are Barriers to Interdependence
(2) Economic Issues Influence National Goals
(3) Geography Affects Human Behavior
(4) Governments Control the Actions of Citizens

2 • Siberian Plain
   • Sahara Desert
   • Amazon Basin
   • Mongolian Steppes

One characteristic common to these areas is that they all

(1) have a low population density
(2) are located between major river valleys
(3) are major religious centers
(4) have large areas of valuable farmland

3 Which pair of belief systems share a belief that spirits reside in natural objects and forms?

(1) Hinduism and Confucianism
(2) Islam and Judaism
(3) Shintoism and animism
(4) Christianity and Buddhism

Base your answer to question 4 on the map below and on your knowledge of social studies.

Source: Ellis and Esler,
World History: Connections to Today,
Prentice Hall, 2003 (adapted)

4 Which generalization about the Maurya and Gupta Empires is supported by the map?

(1) Expansion was limited by geographic factors.
(2) Trade contributed to stable societies.
(3) Extensive road systems unified India.
(4) Southern India was isolated from northern India.

Base your answers to questions 5 and 6 on the illustration below and on your knowledge of social studies.

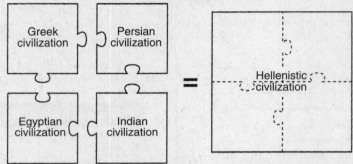

Source: *Guide to the Essentials of World History*, Prentice Hall, 1999 (adapted)

5 Which concept is most closely related to the main idea of the illustration?

(1) isolation   (3) armed conflict
(2) cultural diffusion   (4) urbanization

6 Which leader is most closely associated with the accomplishment shown by the illustration?

(1) Charlemagne
(2) Mansa Musa
(3) Alexander the Great
(4) Suleiman the Magnificent

7 Base your answer to this question on the graphic organizer below and on your knowledge of social studies.

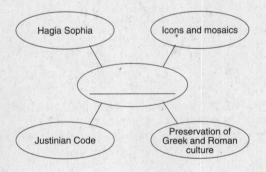

Which title best completes this graphic organizer?

(1) Arab Accomplishments
(2) Achievements of Meso-American Civilizations
(3) Russian Law and Architecture
(4) Byzantine Achievements

8 Which statement about the Tang dynasty is a fact rather than an opinion?

(1) Technical advances would have been greater if the Tang dynasty had lasted longer.
(2) China's best emperors came from the Tang dynasty.
(3) The Tang emperors granted government jobs to scholars who passed examinations.
(4) The culture of the Tang dynasty was superior to that of the Han dynasty.

9 During the feudal period in Europe, power and position in society were based on the

(1) amount of money earned
(2) level of education achieved
(3) number of slaves owned
(4) amount of land possessed

Base your answer to question 10 on the illustration below and on your knowledge of social studies.

Everyone had duties and responsibilities, depending on his or her position in a relationship.

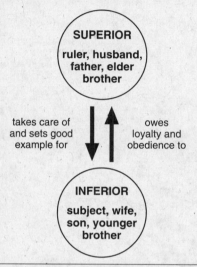

SUPERIOR

ruler, husband, father, elder brother

takes care of and sets good example for

owes loyalty and obedience to

INFERIOR

subject, wife, son, younger brother

Source: *Guide to the Essentials of World History*, Prentice Hall, 1999 (adapted)

10 The illustration shows the relationship between individuals in a society according to the ideas of

(1) Confucius
(2) Moses
(3) Mohammad
(4) Siddhartha Gautama

11 Revival of trade in western Europe, decline of feudalism, revival of interest in learning, and cultural interaction with the Middle East are associated with the

(1) impact of the Crusades
(2) effects of the barter system
(3) growth of the Maya Empire
(4) rise of Charlemagne

Base your answer to question 12 on the quotation below and on your knowledge of social studies.

. . . The circumference of the city of Constantinople is eighteen miles; one-half of the city being bounded by the continent, the other by the sea, two arms of which meet here; the one a branch or outlet of the Russian, the other of the Spanish sea. Great stir and bustle prevails [dominates] at Constantinople in consequence of the conflux [meeting] of many merchants, who resort thither [come there], both by land and by sea, from all parts of the world for purposes of trade, including merchants from Babylon and from Mesopotamia, from Media and Persia, from Egypt and Palestine, as well as from Russia, Hungary, Patzinakia, Budia, Lombardy and Spain. In this respect the city is equalled only by Bagdad, the metropolis of the Mahometans. . . .

— Rabbi Benjamin of Tudela,
Manuel Komroff, ed., *Contemporaries of Marco Polo*,
Boni & Liveright

12 This author would most likely agree with the idea that the

(1) size of Constantinople limited trade
(2) cities of western Europe were more impressive than Constantinople
(3) location of Constantinople contributed to its prosperity
(4) government of Constantinople failed to provide order

13 Much of the wealth of the West African kingdoms of Ghana and Mali was gained from the

(1) sale of slaves to Europeans
(2) creation of colonies on the Mediterranean coast
(3) taxation on goods brought by Indian merchants
(4) control of the trans-Saharan trade in gold and salt

Base your answers to questions 14 and 15 on the map below and on your knowledge of social studies.

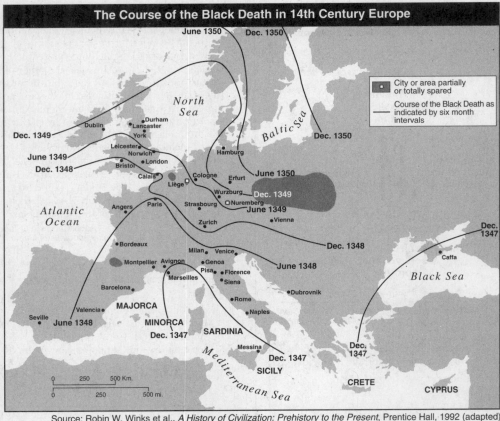

The Course of the Black Death in 14th Century Europe

Legend:
- City or area partially or totally spared
- Course of the Black Death as indicated by six month intervals

Source: Robin W. Winks et al., *A History of Civilization: Prehistory to the Present*, Prentice Hall, 1992 (adapted)

14 Which geographic theme is the focus of this map?

(1) Regions: How They Form and Change
(2) Movement: Humans Interacting on Earth
(3) Location: Position on the Earth's Surface
(4) Place: Physical and Human Characteristics

15 The map shows that the Black Death

(1) began in England and Ireland and then spread eastward
(2) spread slowly over several decades
(3) affected most areas of western Europe
(4) was most severe in Italy

16 What was a long-term impact of Marco Polo's trips to China?

(1) The Silk Roads replaced the all-water route to Asia.
(2) The Chinese forced the Europeans to trade only in Peking.
(3) China was isolated from other countries.
(4) Trade increased between China and Europe.

17 In western Europe, Martin Luther's Ninety-five Theses and Henry VIII's Act of Supremacy led to

(1) an end to Christian unity
(2) a strengthening of economic unity
(3) better relations between peasants and merchants
(4) fewer violent outbreaks between ethnic groups

18 • Leonardo DaVinci used movement and perspective in his work.
   • Machiavelli's *The Prince* advised rulers on how to gain and maintain power.
   • Humanist scholars examined worldly subjects and classical culture.

Which period is associated with these statements?

(1) French Revolution   (3) Early Middle Ages
(2) Renaissance   (4) Enlightenment

19 During the 15th century, which two European countries began sea voyages of exploration?

(1) Germany and Italy
(2) Portugal and Spain
(3) England and France
(4) Russia and the Netherlands

Base your answer to question 20 on the quotation below and on your knowledge of social studies.

. . . Finally, gather together all that we have said, so great and so august [important], about royal authority. You have seen a great nation united under one man: you have seen his sacred power, paternal and absolute: you have seen that secret reason which directs the body politic, enclosed in one head: you have seen the image of God in kings, and you will have the idea of majesty of kingship.

God is holiness itself, goodness itself, power itself, reason itself. In these things consists the divine majesty. In their reflection consists the majesty of the prince. . . .

— Jacques-Benigne Bossuet

20 Which philosophy of government is expressed by this quotation?

(1) oligarchy   (3) democracy
(2) fascism   (4) divine right

Base your answer to question 21 on the diagram below and on your knowledge of social studies.

From the Americas to Europe, Africa, and Asia

maize (corn)   tomato
potato   chill pepper
sweet potato   avocado
beans   pineapple
peanut   cocoa
squashes   tobacco
pumpkin   quinine (a medicine)

wheat   cattle
sugar   goat
banana   sheep
rice   chicken
grape (wine)   smallpox
dandelion   measles
horse   typhus
pig

From Europe, Africa, and Asia to the Americas

Source: Goldberg and Clark DuPré,
Brief Review in Global History and Geography,
Prentice Hall, 2002 (adapted)

21 What is the best title for this diagram?

(1) Encomienda System   (3) Silk Road
(2) Columbian Exchange   (4) Open Door policy

22 The Aztec use of the calendar and the Maya writing system both illustrate that pre-Columbian cultures in the Americas

(1) traded extensively with Africa
(2) flourished prior to European contact
(3) declined because of invasion and disease
(4) converted others to Islam

23 Locke's *Two Treatises of Government,* Rousseau's *The Social Contract,* and Montesquieu's *The Spirit of the Laws* were works written during which time period?

(1) Middle Ages   (3) Enlightenment
(2) Renaissance   (4) Reformation

Base your answer to question 24 on the map below and on your knowledge of social studies.

African Slave Trade

Source: Ellis and Esler, *World History: Connections to Today*,
Prentice Hall, (adapted)

24 Which conclusion about the slave trade in Africa is supported by this map?

(1) Most of the slaves came from eastern Africa.
(2) Few people were taken from Africa to other continents.
(3) Several European countries participated in the slave trade.
(4) The slave trade began in southern Africa.

25 What was a major cause of the French Revolution?

(1) inequalities in the tax structure
(2) economic success of mercantilism
(3) failure of the Congress of Vienna
(4) Continental System in Europe

26 The British government took control of the Suez Canal and Singapore during the 19th century in order to

(1) sell petroleum to these territories·
(2) gain more converts to Christianity
(3) ensure safe passage on strategic waterways
(4) transport laborers directly to the Americas

27 The Sepoy Rebellion was to India as the Boxer Rebellion was to

(1) Russia   (3) Japan
(2) China   (4) Italy

28 One reason for Japan's rapid industrialization during the Meiji Restoration was that Japan had

(1) rejected Western ideas
(2) used its access to the sea for fishing
(3) relied on traditional isolationist policies
(4) reformed its political and economic systems

29 What was the immediate cause of World War I in Europe?

(1) start of the civil war in Russia
(2) sinking of the British liner, *Lusitania*
(3) assassination of the heir to the throne of the Austro-Hungarian Empire
(4) attack on Poland by the German army

30 Under communism in the former Soviet Union, people were required to

(1) reject modern technology
(2) limit the size of their families
(3) honor their ancestors and religious traditions
(4) put the interests of the state before individual gain

31 Many historians believe that the harsh terms found in the Treaty of Versailles helped lead to

(1) Italy's unification
(2) Turkey's modernization
(3) revolutions in Russia
(4) World War II

32 Which economic program was implemented by Joseph Stalin?

(1) Four Modernizations
(2) five-year plans
(3) Great Leap Forward
(4) perestroika

33 One reason the Japanese followed a policy of expansionism before World War II was to gain

(1) warm-water ports
(2) control of Tibet
(3) additional natural resources
(4) control of the Suez Canal

34 **"Korea Divided at 38th Parallel"**
"Hungarian Revolution Crushed"
"Missile Sites Spotted in Cuba"

The events in these headlines contributed to the

(1) development of peacetime alliances
(2) collapse of the Soviet Union
(3) rejection of imperialism by Western nations
(4) tensions between the superpowers

35 One reason the Chinese Communists were able to gain control of China was primarily due to the support of the

(1) peasants   (3) foreigners
(2) landed elite   (4) warlords

36 "India made detailed preparations for war with Pakistan yesterday, although senior officers said offensive operations would have to wait for the end of searing summer temperatures and the monsoon rain which follows. . . ."

— *The Daily Telegraph* (London), May 21, 2002

Which conclusion is based on this passage?

(1) Military offensives often succeed because of monsoons.
(2) Pakistan will be destroyed by flooding and drought.
(3) Geographic factors can influence a nation's military decisions.
(4) Trade has a major impact on political life in India.

Base your answer to question 37 on the photograph below and on your knowledge of social studies.

— Pool Photo by Natalie Behring–Chisholm

Loya jirga **opens:** Female delegates at the Afghan grand council in Kabul [Afghanistan] read an official statement together during the opening session Tuesday. Women make up about 200 of the 1,551 delegates to the council, which will pick the next Afghan government.

Source: Copeland and Komarow, *USA Today*, June 12, 2002

37 What was a direct cause of the event illustrated in this photograph?

(1) defeat of the Taliban-controlled government
(2) rise of the Ayatollah Khomeini
(3) signing of the Camp David Accords
(4) withdrawal of Soviet troops from Afghanistan

Base your answer to question 38 on the map below and on your knowledge of social studies.

JOINING THE CLUB?

NATO faces a November deadline on whether to admit nine hopefuls to the alliance.

■ NATO members

▨ NATO candidates

United States and Canada (not shown) are members

Source: *The Washington Times*, April 15, 2002 (adapted)

38 Which conclusion about the North Atlantic Treaty Organization (NATO) can be drawn from this 2002 map?

(1) NATO was considering including more former Soviet satellite countries as members.
(2) NATO had fewer members than the Warsaw Pact.
(3) NATO does not admit new members.
(4) NATO has included many Asian members.

---

39 How do some Latin American governments justify the destruction of the rain forests?

(1) Cattle raising, farming, and mining in the rain forest will help the economy.
(2) Manufacturers no longer use the latex produced by the trees of the rain forest.
(3) People who live in the rain forest are moving to the cities.
(4) Drug trafficking will decrease when the protection of the rain forests is gone.

40 Which nation had the greatest influence on the recent histories of Taiwan, Hong Kong, and Tibet?

(1) India   (3) China
(2) South Korea   (4) Russia

Base your answer to question 41 on the cartoon below and on your knowledge of social studies.

Source: Ann Telnaes, Tribune Media Services, 2001 (adapted)

41 What is the main idea of this cartoon?

(1) Traditional social and economic patterns are difficult to change.
(2) Women have become outspoken supporters of the government in India.
(3) The United Nations only holds conferences on problems that are easy to solve.
(4) India is the most populated nation in the world.

42 "... We cannot and must not allow ourselves to have the message of Hiroshima and Nagasaki fade completely from our minds, and we cannot allow our vision or ideals to fade, either. For if we do, we have but one course left for us. And that flash of light will not only rob us of our vision, but it will rob us of our lives, our progeny [descendants], and our very existence."

— Tadatoshi Akiba, Mayor of Hiroshima

With which issue is Mayor Akiba most concerned?

(1) depletion of the ozone layer
(2) treatment of infectious diseases
(3) nuclear proliferation
(4) international terrorism

43 Which empire became powerful partly because of its location near the Mediterranean Sea?

(1) German   (3) Ming
(2) Maya   (4) Ottoman

44 One similarity in the rule of Julius Caesar, Genghis Khan, and Catherine the Great is that each leader

(1) required the use of Latin throughout the empire
(2) engaged in territorial expansion
(3) introduced the use of gunpowder in warfare
(4) encouraged the spread of independence movements

45 Both Inca farmers and Japanese farmers adapted a geographic feature of their countries by

(1) engaging in overseas expansion
(2) growing crops suited to desert climates
(3) building terraces into the mountainsides
(4) reclaiming land from the sea by building dikes

Base your answer to question 46 on the passage below and on your knowledge of social studies.

... The history of all hitherto existing society is the history of class struggles.

Freeman and slave, patrician [a person of high birth] and plebeian [common person], lord and serf, guild-master and journeyman, in a word, oppressor and oppressed, stood in constant opposition to one another, carried on an uninterrupted, now hidden, now open fight, a fight that each time ended, either in a revolutionary reconstitution of society at large, or in the common ruin of the contending [competing] classes. ...

46 This passage expresses the ideas of

(1) Napoleon Bonaparte
(2) Karl Marx
(3) Adolf Hitler
(4) Benito Mussolini

47 One similarity in the unification of Italy, the Zionist movement, and the breakup of the Ottoman Empire was that each was influenced by

(1) humanism   (3) nationalism
(2) polytheism   (4) imperialism

Base your answer to question 48 on the map below and on your knowledge of social studies.

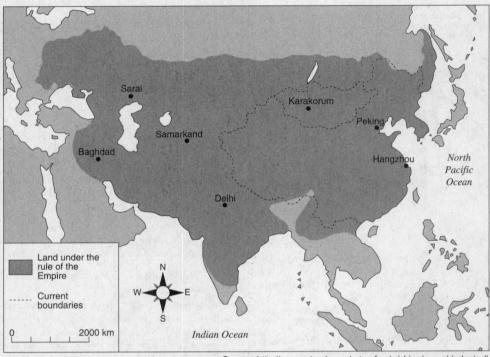

Source: http://www.artsmia.org/arts-of-asia/china/maps/ (adapted)

48 Which empire is the focus of this map?

(1) Mongol   (3) Roman

(2) Songhai   (4) Persian

49 • The Nazi Party controls Germany.
  • Khmer Rouge rules in Cambodia.
  • The Sandinistas control Nicaragua.

Which statement describes a similarity in these situations?

(1) Civil liberties were promoted.
(2) Voting rights were extended to women.
(3) Leaders won the support of all groups.
(4) One group seized power and limited opposition.

50 A comparison of the actions of the Jacobins during the French Revolution and the actions of the Bolsheviks during the Russian Revolution indicates that revolutions sometimes

(1) occur in a peaceful manner
(2) gain the support of wealthy landowners
(3) ignore urban workers
(4) bring radicals to power

Answers to the essay questions are to be written in the separate essay booklet.

In developing your answer to Part II, be sure to keep this general definition in mind:

discuss means "to make observations about something using facts, reasoning, and argument; to present in some detail"

PART II

THEMATIC ESSAY QUESTION

Directions: Write a well-organized essay that includes an introduction, several paragraphs addressing the task below, and a conclusion.

Theme: Conflict

> Conflicts between groups of people have threatened peace in many nations and regions.

Task:

> Identify *one* conflict that has threatened peace in a nation or region and
> * Discuss *one* major cause of that conflict
> * Identify *two* opposing groups involved in the conflict and discuss *one* viewpoint of *each* group
> * Discuss the extent to which the conflict was *or* was *not* resolved

You may use any major conflict from your study of global history. Some suggestions you might wish to consider include the Crusades, the French Revolution, World War I, the Russian Revolution, the Chinese civil war, the partition of India, the policy of apartheid in South Africa, the Rwandan civil war, and the Bosnian War.

You are *not* limited to these suggestions.

Do *not* use conflicts that *occurred* in the United States in your answer.

Guidelines:

In your essay, be sure to
* Develop all aspects of the task
* Support the theme with relevant facts, examples, and details
* Use a logical and clear plan of organization, including an introduction and a conclusion that are beyond a restatement of the theme

NAME _____ SCHOOL _____

In developing your answers to Part III, be sure to keep this general definition in mind:

> <u>discuss</u> means "to make observations about something using facts, reasoning, and argument; to present in some detail"

PART III

DOCUMENT-BASED QUESTION

This question is based on the accompanying documents. The question is designed to test your ability to work with historical documents. Some of these documents have been edited for the purposes of this question. As you analyze the documents, take into account the source of each document and any point of view that may be presented in the document.

Historical Context:

> The Industrial Revolution that began in Europe changed society in many ways. Some of these changes were positive while others were negative.

Task: Using the information from the documents and your knowledge of global history, answer the questions that follow each document in Part A. Your answers to the questions will help you write the Part B essay in which you will be asked to

> • Discuss both the positive effects *and* the negative effects of the Industrial Revolution on European society

Part A
Short-Answer Questions

Directions: Analyze the documents and answer the short-answer questions that follow each document in the space provided.

Document 1a

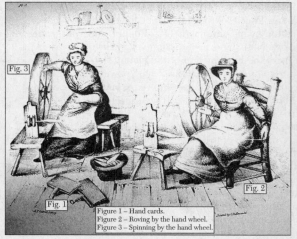

Fig. 3
Fig. 2
Fig. 1
Figure 1 – Hand cards.
Figure 2 – Roving by the hand wheel.
Figure 3 – Spinning by the hand wheel.

Source: R. Guest, *A Compendious History of the Cotton Manufacture*, A. M. Kelley, first published in 1823 (adapted)

Document 1b

At Work in a Woollen Factory

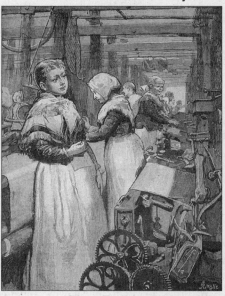

Source: *The Illustrated London News*, August 25, 1883

1 Based on these pictures, state ***two*** changes in how cloth was produced. [2]

(1)____

____

Score ☐

(2)____

____

Score ☐

Document 2

. . . Passing to manufactures, we find here the all-prominent fact to be the substitution of the factory for the domestic system, the consequence of the mechanical discoveries of the time. Four great inventions altered [changed] the character of the cotton manufacture; the spinning-jenny, patented by Hargreaves in 1770; the water-frame, invented by Arkwright the year before; Crompton's mule [spinning machine] introduced in 1779, and the self-acting mule, first invented by Kelly in 1792, but not brought into use till Roberts improved it in 1825. None of these by themselves would have revolutionised the industry. But in 1769—the year in which Napoleon and Wellington were born—James Watt took out his patent for the steam-engine. Sixteen years later it was applied to the cotton manufacture. In 1785 Boulton and Watt made an engine for a cotton-mill at Papplewick in Notts, and in the same year Arkwright's patent expired. These two facts taken together mark the introduction of the factory system. But the most famous invention of all, and the most fatal to domestic industry, the power-loom, though also patented by Cartwright in 1785, did not come into use for several years, and till the power-loom was introduced the workman was hardly injured. At first, in fact, machinery raised the wages of spinners and weavers owing to the great prosperity it brought to the trade. In fifteen years the cotton trade trebled [tripled] itself; from 1788 to 1803 has been called "its golden age;" for, before the power-loom but after the introduction of the mule [spinning machine] and other mechanical improvements by which for the first time yarn sufficiently fine for muslin [a fabric] and a variety of other fabrics was spun, the demand became such that "old barns, cart-houses, out-buildings of all descriptions were repaired, windows broke through the old blank walls, and all fitted up for loom-shops; new weavers' cottages with loom-shops arose in every direction, every family bringing home weekly from 40 to 120 shillings per week." At a later date, the condition of the workman was very different. Meanwhile, the iron industry had been equally revolutionised by the invention of smelting by pit-coal brought into use between 1740 and 1750, and by the application in 1788 of the steam-engine to blast furnaces. In the eight years which followed this latter date, the amount of iron manufactured nearly doubled itself. . . .

Source: Arnold Toynbee, *Lectures on the Industrial Revolution of the 18th Century in England*, Humboldt (adapted)

2 According to this document, what were **two** results of the use of machinery? [2]

(1) _____

_____

Score ☐

(2) _____

_____

Score ☐

Document 3

. . . Steam-engines furnish the means not only of their support but of their multiplication. They create a vast demand for fuel; and, while they lend their powerful arms to drain the pits and to raise the coals, they call into employment multitudes of miners, engineers, ship-builders, and sailors, and cause the construction of canals and railways: and, while they enable these rich fields of industry to be cultivated to the utmost, they leave thousands of fine arable fields free for the production of food to man, which must have been otherwise allotted to the food of horses. Steam-engines moreover, by the cheapness and steadiness of their action, fabricate [produce] cheap goods, and procure [acquire] in their exchange a liberal supply of the necessaries and comforts of life, produced in foreign lands. . . .

Source: Andrew Ure, *The Philosophy of Manufactures: or, an Exposition of the Scientific, Moral, and Commercial Economy of the Factory System of Great Britain*, A. M. Kelley

3 According to this document, what are **two** ways that steam engines helped the economy in Great Britain? [2]

(1)_____

_____

Score [ ]

(2)_____

_____

Score [ ]

Document 4

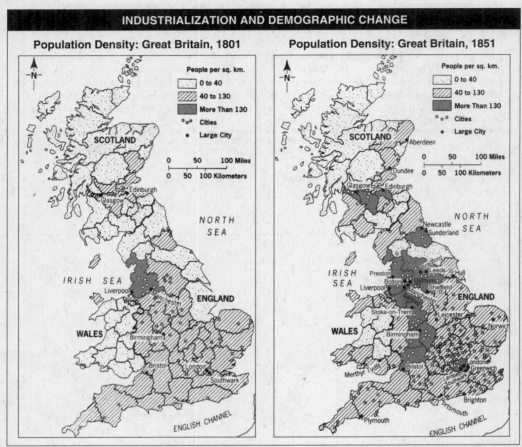

INDUSTRIALIZATION AND DEMOGRAPHIC CHANGE

Population Density: Great Britain, 1801

Population Density: Great Britain, 1851

Source: *World Civilizations: Sources, Images, and Interpretations*, McGraw-Hill (adapted)

4 Based on these maps, state *one* change that occurred in Great Britain during the Industrial Revolution. [1]

_____

_____

Score ▢

Document 5

. . . Every great town has one or more slum areas into which the working classes are packed. Sometimes, of course, poverty is to be found hidden away in alleys close to the stately homes of the wealthy. Generally, however, the workers are segregated in separate districts where they struggle through life as best they can out of sight of the more fortunate classes of society. The slums of the English towns have much in common—the worst houses in a town being found in the worst districts. They are generally unplanned wildernesses of one- or two-storied terrace houses built of brick. Wherever possible these have cellars which are also used as dwellings. These little houses of three or four rooms and a kitchen are called cottages, and throughout England, except for some parts of London, are where the working classes normally live. The streets themselves are usually unpaved and full of holes. They are filthy and strewn with animal and vegetable refuse. Since they have neither gutters nor drains the refuse accumulates in stagnant, stinking puddles. Ventilation in the slums is inadequate owing to the hopelessly unplanned nature of these areas. A great many people live huddled together in a very small area, and so it is easy to imagine the nature of the air in these workers' quarters. However, in fine weather the streets are used for the drying of washing and clothes lines are stretched across the streets from house to house and wet garments are hung out on them. . . .

Source: Friedrich Engels, *The Condition of the Working Class in England,* W. O. Henderson and W. H. Chaloner, eds., Stanford University Press

5 According to the document, what did Friedrich Engels state were *two* characteristics of working class living conditions in England? [2]

(1)_____

_____

Score ☐

(2)_____

_____

Score ☐

Document 6

Edwin Chadwick presented a report to Parliament as secretary to a commission that investigated sanitary conditions and means of improving them.

> . . . *First, as to the extent and operation of the evils which are the subject of the inquiry:* . . .
>
> That the formation of all habits of cleanliness is obstructed by defective supplies of water.
>
> That the annual loss of life from filth and bad ventilation are greater than the loss from death or wounds in any wars in which the country has been engaged in modern times.
>
> That of the 43,000 cases of widowhood, and 112,000 cases of destitute orphanage relieved from the poor's rates in England and Wales alone, it appears that the greatest proportion of deaths of the heads of families occurred from the above specified and other removable causes; that their ages were under 45 years; that is to say, 13 years below the natural probabilities of life as shown by the experience of the whole population of Sweden. . . .

Source: Edwin Chadwick, *Report on an Inquiry into the Sanitary Condition of the Labouring Population of Great Britain,*
W. Clowes and Sons, 1842

6 Based on this document, state *one* negative effect of industrialization on the workers of Great Britain. [1]

_____

_____

Score ☐

Document 7

Flora Tristan was a 19th-century French activist and a member of the lower working class. In 1843, she wrote *The Workers' Union*.

> . . . 1. Consolidation of the working class by means of a tight, solid, and indissoluble [indivisible] Union.
>
> 2. Representation of the working class before the nation through a defender chosen and paid by the Workers' Union, so that the working class's need to exist and the other classes' need to accept it become evident.
>
> 3. Recognition of one's hands as legitimate property. (In France 25,000,000 proletarians have their hands as their only asset.)
>
> 4. Recognition of the legitimacy of the right to work for all men and women.
>
> 5. Recognition of the legitimacy of the right to moral, intellectual, and vocational education for all boys and girls.
>
> 6. Examination of the possibility of labor organizing in the current social state [social conditions].
>
> 7. Construction of Workers' Union palaces [buildings] in every department, in which working-class children would receive intellectual and vocational instruction, and to which the infirm and elderly as well as workers injured on the job would be admitted.
>
> 8. Recognition of the urgent necessity of giving moral, intellectual, and vocational education to the women of the masses so that they can become the moral agents for the men of the masses.
>
> 9. Recognition in principle of equal rights for men and women as the sole [only] means of unifying humankind. . . .

Source: Flora Tristan, *The Workers' Union,* University of Illinois Press (adapted)

7 Based on this document, state **two** changes in society that Flora Tristan believed were needed for the working class. [2]

(1)_____

_____

Score ☐

(2)_____

_____

Score ☐

Document 8

The Devilfish in Egyptian Waters

Source: *The British Empire in the Nineteenth Century*, Highsmith, 2000 (adapted)

8 Which effect of the Industrial Revolution is implied by this cartoon? [1]

_____

_____

Score ☐

Part B
Essay

Directions: Write a well-organized essay that includes an introduction, several paragraphs, and a conclusion. Use evidence from *at least **five*** documents in your essay. Support your response with relevant facts, examples, and details. Include additional outside information.

Historical Context:

The Industrial Revolution that began in Europe changed society in many ways. Some of these changes were positive while others were negative.

Task: Using the information from the documents and your knowledge of global history, write an essay in which you

> • Discuss both the positive effects ***and*** the negative effects of the Industrial Revolution on European society.

Guidelines:

In your essay, be sure to
- Develop all aspects of the task
- Incorporate information from *at least **five*** documents
- Incorporate relevant outside information
- Support the theme with relevant facts, examples, and details
- Use a logical and clear plan of organization, including an introduction and a conclusion that are beyond a restatement of the theme

Part I

Answer all questions in this part.

Directions (1–50): For each statement or question, write on the separate answer sheet the *number* of the word or expression that, of those given, best completes the statement or answers the question.

1 The main purpose of a time line is to show the

(1) causes and effects of wars
(2) location of important places
(3) benefits of modern civilizations
(4) chronological relationship between events

2 Throughout history, people have lived on savannas, in deserts, in mountains, along river valleys, along coastlines, and on islands.

This statement demonstrates that people

(1) adapt their surroundings
(2) develop a common language
(3) organize similar forms of government
(4) prefer to live in isolated areas

3 In a command economy, economic decisions are mostly influenced by

(1) consumer demands
(2) government policies
(3) private investors
(4) banking practices

4 How did the introduction of agriculture affect early peoples?

(1) Societies became nomadic.
(2) Food production declined.
(3) Civilizations developed.
(4) Birthrates decreased rapidly.

5 • If a man has destroyed the eye of a free man, his own eye shall be destroyed.
• If a man has knocked out the teeth of a man of the same rank, his own teeth shall be knocked out.

These rules are based on the

(1) Analects of Confucius
(2) Code of Hammurabi
(3) Ten Commandments
(4) Koran (Qur'an)

6 Which civilization first developed a civil service system, invented gunpowder, and manufactured porcelain?

(1) Aztec   (3) Japanese
(2) Chinese   (4) Roman

7 What was one effect of Alexander the Great's conquests?

(1) expansion of Hellenistic culture
(2) formation of the Christian church
(3) decreased importance of the Silk Roads
(4) increased support of the Mayan leaders

8 Which two belief systems teach that there are spirits in nature?

(1) Shinto and animism
(2) Hinduism and Confucianism
(3) Judaism and Christianity
(4) Islam and Buddhism

9 Constantinople's location on the Bosporus Strait was one reason that the Byzantine Empire was able to

(1) conquer the Russian city of Moscow
(2) spread Judaism throughout western Europe
(3) control key trade routes between Europe and Asia
(4) unite the Eastern Orthodox and Roman Catholic Churches

10 The Justinian Code is considered a milestone because it

(1) preserved many ancient Chinese legal decrees in writing
(2) served as a model for European legal systems
(3) became the first democratic constitution
(4) united Muslim and Roman thought

Base your answers to questions 11 and 12 on the diagram below and on your knowledge of social studies.

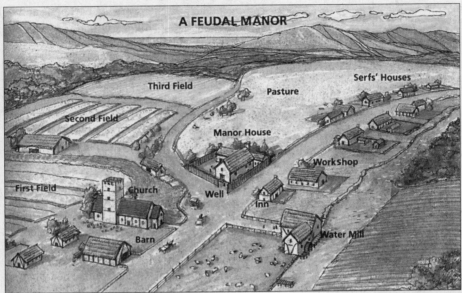

A FEUDAL MANOR

Source: Michael B. Petrovich et al., *People in Time and Place: World Cultures*, Silver, Burdett & Ginn, 1991

11 Most economic activities on this feudal manor were related to

(1) guilds   (3) banking
(2) industry   (4) agriculture

12 Which economic concept can be inferred from this diagram?

(1) self-sufficiency   (3) trade embargo
(2) inflation   (4) competition

13 A major contribution of the Golden Age of Islam was the

(1) development of mercantilism
(2) creation of the first polytheistic religion
(3) spread of democratic ideals
(4) advancement of mathematics and science

14 Which factor most influenced a person's social position in early Indian societies?

(1) education
(2) birth
(3) geographic location
(4) individual achievement

15 Which civilization best completes the heading of the partial outline below?

I. _____

   A. Spread of Islam
   B. Gold and salt trade
   C. Growth of Timbuktu
   D. Pilgrimage of Mansa Musa

(1) Benin   (3) Mali
(2) Kush   (4) Egyptian

16 Historians value the writings of Marco Polo and Ibn Battuta because they

(1) serve as primary sources about trade and culture
(2) provide the basis for European holy books
(3) include advice on how to be a democratic ruler
(4) present unbiased views of life in Africa and Asia

17 Which factor contributed to the beginning of the Renaissance in Italian cities?

(1) occupation by foreign powers
(2) interaction with Latin America
(3) surplus of porcelain from Japan
(4) access to important trade routes

18 • 1340s—Mongols, merchants, and other travelers carried disease along trade routes west of China.
• 1346—The plague reached the Black Sea ports of Caffa and Tana.
• 1347—Italian merchants fled plague-infected Black Sea ports.
• 1348—The plague became an epidemic in most of western Europe.

Which conclusion can be made based on these statements?

(1) The plague primarily affected China.
(2) The interaction of people spread the plague.
(3) Port cities were relatively untouched by the plague.
(4) The plague started in western Europe.

19 Which innovation had the greatest impact on the Protestant Reformation?

(1) movable-type printing press
(2) Mercator map projection
(3) magnetic compass
(4) triangular sail

20 Which statement best describes the concept of mercantilism?

(1) Universal suffrage leads to educated citizens.
(2) Controlling trade is a key to increasing power.
(3) Only the fittest deserve to survive.
(4) Strict social control prevents revolutions.

21 The Magna Carta, the Petition of Right, and the English Bill of Rights were created to

(1) limit the power of English monarchs
(2) establish laws protecting the rights of Protestants
(3) organize England's colonial empire
(4) abolish the role of Parliament

22 The theory justifying a monarch's rule by God's authority is called

(1) laissez faire
(2) totalitarianism
(3) predestination
(4) divine right

23 One similarity in the rule of Peter the Great, Suleiman I, and Louis XIV is that each leader

(1) shared power with a legislature
(2) practiced religious toleration
(3) expanded his territory
(4) decreased the amount of taxes collected

24 Which factors protected Russia from control by Napoleon's army?

(1) religious and cultural similarities
(2) industrialization and modernization
(3) geographic size and location
(4) political and economic instability

25 "To him who wishes to follow me, I offer hardships, hunger, thirst and all the perils of war."

— *Garibaldi's Memoirs*

This quotation from Garibaldi is most closely associated with Italian

(1) exploration
(2) nationalism
(3) imperialism
(4) neutrality

26 During the 1800s, reform legislation passed in Great Britain, France, and Germany led to

(1) formation of zaibatsu, greater equality for men, and establishment of a banking system
(2) legalizing trade unions, setting minimum wages, and limiting child labor
(3) government-owned factories, establishment of five-year plans, and limits placed on immigration
(4) bans on overseas trade, mandatory military service, and universal suffrage for women

Base your answer to question 27 on the map below and on your knowledge of social studies.

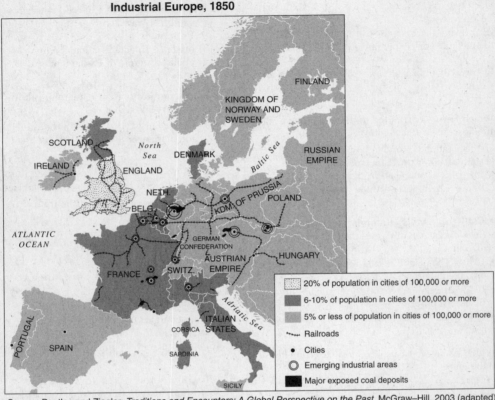

Industrial Europe, 1850

Source: Bentley and Ziegler, *Traditions and Encounters: A Global Perspective on the Past,* McGraw–Hill, 2003 (adapted)

27 Which concept is most closely associated with the pattern of population distribution in England shown on this map?

  (1) urbanization   (3) collectivization

  (2) colonization   (4) globalization

28 Karl Marx and Friedrich Engels encouraged workers to improve their lives by

  (1) electing union representatives

  (2) participating in local government

  (3) overthrowing the capitalist system

  (4) demanding pensions and disability insurance

29 Totalitarian governments are characterized by the

  (1) elimination of heavy industry

  (2) use of censorship, secret police, and repression

  (3) lack of a written constitution

  (4) support of the people for parliamentary decisions

Base your answer to question 30 on the quotation below and on your knowledge of social studies.

". . . I am willing to admit my pride in this accomplishment for Japan. The facts are these: It was not until the sixth year of Kaei (1853) that a steamship was seen for the first time; it was only in the second year of Ansei (1855) that we began to study navigation from the Dutch in Nagasaki; by 1860, the science was sufficiently understood to enable us to sail a ship across the Pacific. This means that about seven years after the first sight of a steamship, after only about five years of practice, the Japanese people made a trans-Pacific crossing without help from foreign experts. I think we can without undue pride boast before the world of this courage and skill. As I have shown, the Japanese officers were to receive no aid from Captain Brooke throughout the voyage. Even in taking observations, our officers and the Americans made them independently of each other. Sometimes they compared their results, but we were never in the least dependent on the Americans. . . ."

— Eiichi Kiyooka, trans., *The Autobiography of Fukuzawa Yukichi*, The Hokuseido Press, 1934

30 Which set of events is most closely associated with the nation described in this passage?

(1) end of the Opium War → creation of European spheres of influence
(2) end of the Tokugawa Shogunate → beginning of the Meiji Restoration
(3) fall of the Manchus → rise of Sun Yixian (Sun Yat-sen)
(4) imperialism in China → start of World War II

31 The famine in Ukraine during the 1930s resulted from the Soviet government's attempt to

(1) end a civil war
(2) implement free-market practices
(3) collectivize agriculture
(4) introduce crop rotation

32 When some European leaders agreed to Hitler's demands concerning Czechoslovakia in 1938, they were supporting a policy of

(1) détente
(2) balance of power
(3) collective security
(4) appeasement

33 One reason Germany's invasion of Poland in 1939 was successful is that Poland

(1) lacked natural barriers
(2) was located along the North Sea
(3) lacked natural resources
(4) was close to the Balkans

34 What was one reason that India was divided into two nations in 1947?

(1) Indian leaders disagreed about India's role in the United Nations.
(2) Great Britain feared a unified India would be a military threat.
(3) The Soviet Union insisted that India should have a communist government.
(4) Differences between the Hindus and the Muslims created religious conflict.

35 • Organization of American States (OAS)
• European Union (EU)
• North American Free Trade Agreement (NAFTA)

These organizations and agreements are examples of

(1) political isolation
(2) military alliances
(3) regional cooperation
(4) collective security

36 Which factor most helped Communist Party forces gain control of China after World War II?

(1) The United States sent weapons to the Communists.
(2) The Japanese gave economic aid to the Nationalists.
(3) The Communists gained the support of China's peasant class.
(4) The Chinese Nationalists set up their own government in Taiwan.

Base your answer to question 37 on the maps below and on your knowledge of social studies.

Independent Africa, 1950–1980

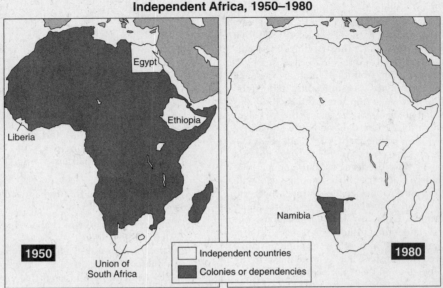

Source: Glenn E. Hughes et al., *Practicing World History Skills*, Scott, Foresman & Co., 1984 (adapted)

37 Based on these maps, which statement is accurate?

(1) Egypt and Ethiopia are no longer part of Africa.
(2) By 1980, most African countries had become independent.
(3) By 1950, most of Africa was controlled by Russia or the United States.
(4) The Union of South Africa was renamed Namibia.

38 Which event illustrates the policy of containment?

(1) Nuremberg trials (1945–1946)
(2) Hungarian revolt (1956)
(3) launching of Sputnik (1957)
(4) naval blockade of Cuba (1962)

39 One similarity between Mikhail Gorbachev's perestroika and Deng Xiaoping's Four Modernizations is that each

(1) allowed elements of capitalism
(2) maintained the democratic process
(3) strengthened communism
(4) increased global tensions

40 One similarity between the Korean War and the Vietnam War is that both wars were

(1) resolved through the diplomatic efforts of the United Nations
(2) fought as a result of differing political ideologies during the Cold War
(3) fought without foreign influence or assistance
(4) caused by religious conflicts

41 Which practice in medieval Europe was most similar to a Japanese warrior's code of bushido?

(1) indulgences   (3) chivalry
(2) serfdom   (4) tribute

Base your answer to question 42 on the photograph below and on your knowledge of social studies.

The Berlin Wall

— Reuters/David Brauchli/Archive Photos
Source: http://imagesrvr.epnet.com/embimages/
imh/archivephoto/full/g1952059.jpg

42 This 1989 photograph symbolizes the

(1) end of the Cold War
(2) importance of the Berlin airlift
(3) creation of a divided Germany
(4) fear of Nazism among Germans

43 In Iran, both the Revolution of 1979 and the rise of Islamic fundamentalism have caused

(1) an increase in women's rights
(2) tension between traditionalism and modernization to continue
(3) foreign control of natural resources to expand
(4) the introduction of a communist form of government

Base your answer to question 44 on the graph below and on your knowledge of social studies.

Average Monthly World Cotton Price
(in cents per pound)

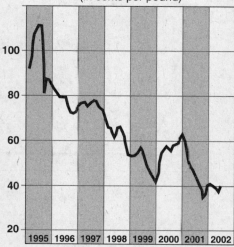

Source: *Wall Street Journal*, June 26, 2002
(adapted)

44 This graph suggests a potential problem for nations

(1) with a favorable balance of trade
(2) with both industrial and agricultural exports
(3) that rely on a cash crop to support their economy
(4) whose economies have been diversified

45 Which sequence of events is listed in the correct chronological order?

(1) Crusades → French Revolution → Renaissance
(2) French Revolution → Crusades → Renaissance
(3) Crusades → Renaissance → French Revolution
(4) Renaissance → Crusades → French Revolution

Base your answer to question 46 on the graph below and on your knowledge of social studies.

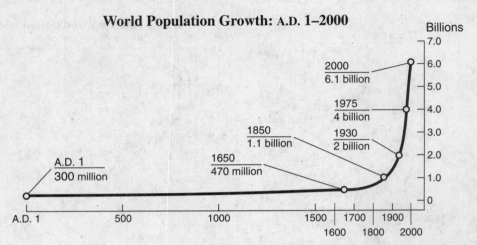

World Population Growth: A.D. 1–2000

Source: Population Reference Bureau and de Blij and Murphy,
Human Geography: Culture, Society, and Space, John Wiley & Sons, 1999 (adapted)

46 Which statement can be supported by the information in the graph?

(1) The population of the world remained the same from A.D. 1 to A.D. 1650.
(2) Most of the world's population growth took place during the period from 1000 to 1500.
(3) The population growth rate decreased during the period from 1650 to 1800.
(4) The world's population tripled between 1930 and 2000.

47 Which period of history had the greatest influence on the Enlightenment ideas of natural law and reason?

(1) Pax Romana
(2) Middle Ages
(3) Age of Exploration
(4) Scientific Revolution

48 During the 20th century, global attention was drawn to the Armenians of the Ottoman Empire, the Tutsis of Rwanda, and the Muslims of Kosovo because these groups were all victims of

(1) nuclear power accidents
(2) human rights violations
(3) environmental disasters
(4) the AIDS epidemic

49 • Maize and potatoes were grown in Europe.
• Millions of Africans suffered during the Middle Passage.
• Smallpox had devastating effects on indigenous peoples.
• Spanish language is used in much of Latin America.

Which global interaction is illustrated by these statements?

(1) Silk Road trade
(2) Crusades
(3) Columbian Exchange
(4) Scramble for Africa

Base your answer to question 50 on the cartoon below and on your knowledge of social studies.

Source: John Trever, *Albuquerque Journal*, Sept. 2001 (adapted)

50 What is the main idea of this 2001 cartoon?

(1) The main task in fighting terrorism is to eliminate nuclear weapons.
(2) The battle against terrorism will be long and difficult.
(3) New equipment is needed to eliminate terrorism.
(4) The methods of dealing with global terrorism have created consensus.

Answers to the essay questions are to be written in the separate essay booklet.

In developing your answer to Part II, be sure to keep these general definitions in mind:

(a) <u>explain</u> means "to make plain or understandable; to give reasons for or causes of; to show the logical development or relationships of"

(b) <u>discuss</u> means "to make observations about something using facts, reasoning, and argument; to present in some detail"

PART II

THEMATIC ESSAY QUESTION

Directions: Write a well-organized essay that includes an introduction, several paragraphs addressing the task below, and a conclusion.

Theme: Change

> The ideas and beliefs of philosophers and leaders have led to changes in nations and regions.

Task:

> Choose *two* philosophers *and/or* leaders and for *each*
> • Explain a major idea or belief of that philosopher or leader
> • Discuss how that idea or belief changed *one* nation or region

You may use any philosophers or leaders from your study of global history. Some suggestions you might wish to consider include Confucius, John Locke, Adam Smith, Simón Bolívar, Otto von Bismarck, Vladimir Lenin, Mohandas Gandhi, Mao Zedong, Fidel Castro, or Nelson Mandela.

You are *not* limited to these suggestions.

Do *not* use a philosopher or leader from the United States in your answer.

Guidelines:

In your essay, be sure to
• Develop all aspects of the task
• Support the theme with relevant facts, examples, and details
• Use a logical and clear plan of organization, including an introduction and a conclusion that are beyond a restatement of the theme

NAME _____ SCHOOL _____

In developing your answers to Part III, be sure to keep this general definition in mind:

discuss means "to make observations about something using facts, reasoning, and arguments; to present in some detail"

PART III

DOCUMENT-BASED QUESTION

This question is based on the accompanying documents. The question is designed to test your ability to work with historical documents. Some of these documents have been edited for the purposes of this question. As you analyze the documents, take into account the source of each document and any point of view that may be presented in the document.

Historical Context:

In the late 1800s and early 1900s, imperialism affected many societies throughout the world. Perspectives on imperialism differed depending on a person's point of view.

Task: Using the information from the documents and your knowledge of global history, answer the questions that follow each document in Part A. Your answers to the questions will help you write the Part B essay in which you will be asked to

- Discuss imperialism from the point of view of the imperialist power
- Discuss imperialism from the point of view of the colonized people

Do *not* use an example of imperialism from United States history in your answer.

Part A

Short-Answer Questions

Directions: Analyze the documents and answer the short-answer questions that follow each document in the space provided.

Document 1

> We must look this matter in the face, and must recognise that in order that we may have more employment to give we must create more demand. Give me the demand for more goods and then I will undertake to give plenty of employment in making the goods; and the only thing, in my opinion, that the Government can do in order to meet this great difficulty that we are considering, is so to arrange its policy that every inducement [encouragement] shall be given to the demand; that new markets shall be created, and that old markets shall be effectually developed. You are aware that some of my opponents please themselves occasionally by finding names for me—and among other names lately they have been calling me a Jingo [extreme nationalist]. I am no more a Jingo than you are. But for the reasons and arguments I have put before you tonight I am convinced that it is a necessity as well as a duty for us to uphold the dominion [power] and empire which we now possess. For these reasons, among others, I would never lose the hold which we now have over our great Indian dependency—by far the greatest and most valuable of all the customers we have or ever shall have in this country. For the same reasons I approve of the continued occupation of Egypt; and for the same reasons I have urged upon this Government, and upon previous Governments, the necessity for using every legitimate opportunity to extend our influence and control in that great African continent which is now being opened up to civilisation and to commerce; and, lastly, it is for the same reasons that I hold that our navy should be strengthened—until its supremacy is so assured that we cannot be shaken in any of the possessions which we hold or may hold hereafter. . . .

Source: Joseph Chamberlain, *Foreign and Colonial Speeches*, George Routledge & Sons, 1897

1 Based on this document, state *one* reason Joseph Chamberlain believed colonies were valuable to Great Britain. [1]

_____

_____

Score ▢

Document 2

. . . The value of the Industrial mission, on the other hand, depends, of course, largely on the nature of the tribes among whom it is located. Its value can hardly be over-estimated among such people as the Waganda, both on account of their natural aptitude and their eager desire to learn. But even the less advanced and more primitive tribes may be equally benefited, if not only mechanical and artisan work, such as the carpenter's and blacksmith's craft, but also the simpler expedients [ways] of agriculture are taught. The sinking of wells, the system of irrigation, the introduction and planting of useful trees, the use of manure, and of domestic animals for agricultural purposes, the improvement of his implements [tools] by the introduction of the primitive Indian plough, etc. — all of these, while improving the status of the native, will render [make] his land more productive, and hence, by increasing his surplus products, will enable him to purchase from the trader the cloth which shall add to his decency, and the implements and household utensils which shall produce greater results for his labour and greater comforts in his social life. . . .

Source: Frederick D. Lugard, *The Rise of Our East African Empire*, Frank Cass & Co., 1893

2 Based on this document, state *two* ways British imperialism would benefit Africans. [2]

(1) _____

_____

Score ☐

(2) _____

_____

Score ☐

Document 3

> . . . Let it be admitted at the outset [beginning] that European brains, capital, and energy have not been, and never will be, expended [spent] in developing the resources of Africa from motives of pure philanthropy [goodwill]; that Europe is in Africa for the mutual benefit of her own industrial classes, and of the native races in their progress to a higher plane; that the benefit can be made reciprocal [equivalent], and that it is the aim and desire of civilised administration to fulfil this dual mandate.
>
> By railways and roads, by reclamation [recovery] of swamps and irrigation of deserts, and by a system of fair trade and competition, we have added to the prosperity and wealth of these lands, and [have] checked famine and disease. We have put an end to the awful misery of the slave-trade and inter-tribal war, to human sacrifice and the ordeals of the witch-doctor. Where these things survive they are severely suppressed. We are endeavouring [trying] to teach the native races to conduct their own affairs with justice and humanity, and to educate them alike in letters and in industry. . . .

Source: Lord [Frederick D.] Lugard, *The Dual Mandate in British Tropical Africa*, Archon Books, 1922

3 According to this document, what were *two* ways the British improved the lives of Africans? [2]

(1)_____

_____

Score [ ]

(2)_____

_____

Score [ ]

Document 4

The Growth of the Japanese Empire
1872–1918

Source: Geoffrey Barraclough, ed., *Hammond Concise Atlas of World History*,
Hammond, 1998 (adapted)

4 Based on the information in this map, state *one* change that occurred in Asia as a result of the
expansion of the Japanese empire. [1]

_____

_____

Score [ ]

Document 5

> . . . The Chief business of the East India Company in its early period, the very object for which it was started, was to carry Indian manufactured goods—textiles, etc., as well as spices and the like—from the East to Europe, where there was a great demand for these articles. With the developments in industrial techniques in England a new class of industrial capitalists rose there demanding a change in this policy. The British market was to be closed to Indian products and the Indian market opened to British manufactures. The British parliament, influenced by this new class, began to take a greater interest in India and the working of the East India Company. To begin with, Indian goods were excluded from Britain by legislation, and as the company held a monopoly in the Indian export business, this exclusion influenced other foreign markets also. This was followed by vigorous attempts to restrict and crush Indian manufactures by various measures and internal duties which prevented the flow of Indian goods within the country itself. British goods meanwhile had free entry. The Indian textile industry collapsed, affecting vast numbers of weavers and artisans. The process was rapid in Bengal and Bihar; elsewhere it spread gradually with the expansion of British rule and the building of railways. It continued throughout the nineteenth century, breaking up other old industries also, shipbuilding, metalwork, glass, paper, and many crafts. . . .

Source: Jawaharlal Nehru, *The Discovery of India*, John Day Company, 1946

5 According to Jawaharlal Nehru, what were *two* ways Great Britain exploited the Indian economy? [2]

(1) _____

_____

Score ☐

(2) _____

_____

Score ☐

Document 6

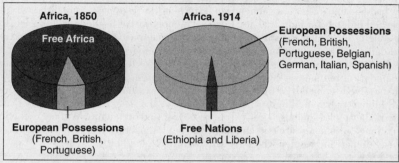

Amount of African Land Controlled by Europeans

Source: *World History, Connections to Today*, Core Support, Prentice Hall, 2001 (adapted)

6   Based on these graphs, state *one* change that occurred in Africa between 1850 and 1914.   [1]

_____

_____

Score ☐

Document 7

. . . When the great scramble for Africa began in the last quarter of the nineteenth century, colonies had become a necessary appendage [extension] for European capitalism, which had by then reached the stage of industrial and financial monopoly that needed territorial expansion to provide spheres for capital investment, sources of raw materials, markets, and strategic points of imperial defence. Thus all the imperialists, without exception, evolved the means, their colonial policies, to satisfy the ends, the exploitation of the subject territories for the aggrandizement [enhancement] of the metropolitan [imperialistic] countries. They were all rapacious [greedy]; they all subserved the needs of the subject lands to their own demands; they all circumscribed [limited] human rights and liberties; they all repressed and despoiled [violated], degraded and oppressed. They took our lands, our lives, our resources, and our dignity. Without exception, they left us nothing but our resentment, and later, our determination to be free and rise once more to the level of men and women who walk with their heads held high. . . .

Source: Kwame Nkrumah, *Africa Must Unite*, International Publishers, 1970

7 According to the document, what is **one** criticism made about the European imperialist? [1]

_____

_____

Score ☐

Document 8

Japanese Treatment of Koreans during World War II

> . . . In order to make Koreans just like the Japanese, the Korean people were forced to change their family names into Japanese names. In religion [religious] life, Japan forced the Korean people to worship the Japanese gods as a part of their duty.
>
> This policy was aimed at erasing the Korean nation [cultural identity] from the earth forever and to nurture [treat] them as colonial subjects and slaves obedient only to the Japanese.
>
> Ultimately, the Japanese drew countless Korean youths and women to the battle fields, factories, and mines to aid in their conquests and wars. . . .

— Radio Korea International, 2003
Source: http://rki.kbs.co.kr/src/history/hok_contents.asp

8 Based on this document, state *two* effects of Japanese occupation on the Korean people. [2]

(1) _____

_____

Score ☐

(2) _____

_____

Score ☐

Part B

Essay

Directions: Write a well-organized essay that includes an introduction, several paragraphs, and a conclusion. Use evidence from *at least five* documents in your essay. Support your response with relevant facts, examples, and details. Include additional outside information.

Historical Context:

In the late 1800s and early 1900s, imperialism affected many societies throughout the world. Perspectives on imperialism differed depending on a person's point of view.

Task: Using the information from the documents and your knowledge of global history, write an essay in which you

> * Discuss imperialism from the point of view of the imperialist power
> * Discuss imperialism from the point of view of the colonized people

Do *not* use an example of imperialism from United States history in your answer.

Guidelines:

In your essay, be sure to
* Develop all aspects of the task
* Incorporate information from *at least five* documents
* Incorporate relevant outside information
* Support the theme with relevant facts, examples, and details
* Use a logical and clear plan of organization, including an introduction and a conclusion that are beyond a restatement of the theme

Regents Examination–August 2005

This section contains an actual Regents Examination in Global History and Geography that was given in New York State in August 2005.

Circle your answers to Part 1. Write your responses to the short-answer questions in the spaces provided. Write your thematic essay and document-based essay on separate sheets of paper. Be sure to refer to the test-taking strategies in the front of this book as you prepare to answer the test questions.

Part I

Answer all questions in this part.

Directions (1–50): For each statement or question, write on the separate answer sheet the *number* of the word or expression that, of those given, best completes the statement or answers the question.

1 • Oceans are an important source of food in Japan.
  • Terrace farming is used in many parts of China.
  • Irrigation systems are widely used in India.

Which conclusion can best be drawn from these statements?

(1) Many civilizations use irrigation to improve crop production.
(2) People adapt to meet the challenges of their geography.
(3) Fish provide adequate protein for the Japanese.
(4) Most nations are dependent on the same food source.

2 Which social scientists are best known for studying the physical artifacts of a culture?

(1) geographers   (3) economists
(2) archaeologists   (4) sociologists

3 Which statement most accurately describes how geography affected the growth of the ancient civilizations of Egypt and Mesopotamia?

(1) River valleys provided rich soil to grow plentiful crops.
(2) Large deserts provided many mineral deposits.
(3) Access to the Atlantic Ocean provided trade routes.
(4) Large savanna areas provided protection from invaders.

4 One way in which the Five Relationships, the Ten Commandments, and the Eightfold Path are similar is that they

(1) promote polytheism
(2) establish gender equality
(3) provide codes of behavior
(4) describe secularism

5 The Phoenicians are often referred to as the "carriers of civilization" because they

(1) introduced Islam and Christianity to Central Africa
(2) established colonies throughout northern Europe
(3) developed the first carts with wheels
(4) traded goods and spread ideas throughout the Mediterranean region

6 The exchange of silks and spices and the spread of Buddhism along the Silk Roads are examples of

(1) cultural diffusion   (3) ethnocentrism
(2) self-sufficiency   (4) desertification

Base your answer to question 7 on the passage below and on your knowledge of social studies.

1. *In the name of Allah, Most Gracious, Most Merciful.*
2. Praise be to Allah, The Cherisher and Sustainer of the Worlds;
3. Most Gracious, Most Merciful;
4. Master of the Day of Judgement.
5. Thee do we worship, And Thine aid we seek.
6. Show us the straight way,
7. The way of those on whom Thou hast bestowed Thy Grace, Those whose (portion) Is not wrath, And who go not astray.

— 'Abdullah Yūsuf 'Alī, ed.,
The Meaning of The Holy Qurān,
Amana Publications, 1999

7 Which concept is best reflected in this passage?

(1) baptism   (3) monotheism
(2) karma   (4) animism

8 Which accomplishments are associated with the Gupta Empire?

(1) adoption of democracy and construction of the Pantheon
(2) defeat of the Roman Empire and adoption of Christianity
(3) establishment of Pax Mongolia and founding of a Chinese dynasty
(4) use of Sanskrit language and development of the concept of zero

9 Kievian Russia adopted the Eastern Orthodox religion, the Cyrillic alphabet, and different styles of art and architecture through contact with

(1) traders from South Asia
(2) conquering invaders from Mongolia
(3) crusaders from western Europe
(4) missionaries from the Byzantine Empire

10 Which statement about the Golden Age of Islam is a fact rather than an opinion?

(1) Islamic art was more abstract than Greek art.
(2) Muslims were the best early mathematicians.
(3) Islamic society preserved Greek and Roman culture.
(4) Muslim artists had more talent than European artists.

11 Which economic activity was the basis for most of the wealth and power of the West African empires of Ghana and Mali?

(1) hunting and gathering
(2) farming and cattle ranching
(3) trading in salt and gold
(4) working in bronze and brass

12 What was one reason that some Italian cities developed into major commercial and cultural centers during the 13th and 14th centuries?

(1) unified central government
(2) isolationist economic policies
(3) geographic location
(4) system of social equality

13 Which two cultures most influenced the development of early Japan?

(1) Greek and Roman
(2) Chinese and Korean
(3) Egyptian and Mesopotamian
(4) Indian and Persian

Base your answers to questions 14 and 15 on the quotation below and on your knowledge of social studies.

". . . Finally, gather together all that we have said, so great and so august [important], about royal authority. You have seen a great nation united under one man: you have seen his sacred power, paternal and absolute: you have seen that secret reason which directs the body politic, enclosed in one head: you have seen the image of God in kings, and you will have the idea of majesty of kingship.

God is holiness itself, goodness itself, power itself, reason itself. In these things consists the divine majesty. In their reflection consists the majesty of the prince. . . ."

— Jacques-Benigne Bossuet

14 Which concept is associated with this quotation?

(1) direct democracy   (3) socialism
(2) imperialism   (4) divine right

15 Which individual most likely opposed the form of government described in this quotation?

(1) Ivan the Terrible   (3) John Locke
(2) Thomas Hobbes   (4) Louis XIV

16 The foreign policy of many Russian rulers supported the country's desire for

(1) access to inland cities
(2) more mineral resources
(3) extensive canal systems
(4) warm-water ports

Base your answer to question 17 on the map below and on your knowledge of social studies.

Spread of the Black Death

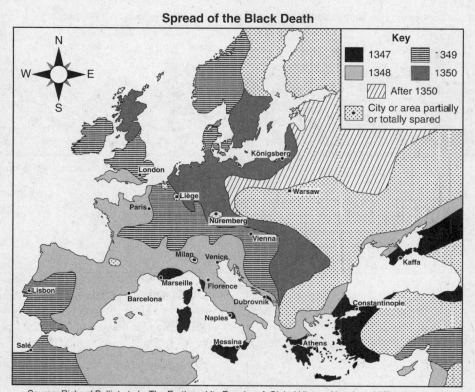

Source: Richard Bulliet et al., *The Earth and Its Peoples: A Global History*, Houghton Mifflin, 2001 (adapted)

17 Which area of Europe was *least* affected by the Black Death?

    (1) southwestern Europe   (3) eastern Europe

    (2) Mediterranean Coast   (4) British Isles

18 One way in which the Magna Carta, the Petition of Right, and the Glorious Revolution are similar is that each

    (1) strengthened the power of the pope

    (2) led to the exploration of Africa

    (3) limited the power of the English monarchy

    (4) settled religious conflicts

19 The encomienda system in Latin America was a direct result of the

    (1) Crusades

    (2) Age of Exploration

    (3) Reformation

    (4) Age of Reason

Base your answer to question 20 on the illustrations below and on your knowledge of social studies.

Aztec Civilization (A.D. 1200 to 1535)

Inca Civilization (A.D. 1200 to 1535)

Source: Sue A. Kime, *World Studies: Global Issues and Assessments*, N & N Publishing, 1995 (adapted)

20 These illustrations suggest that early Latin American civilizations

(1) were based on European societies
(2) used advanced technology to build complex structures
(3) incorporated early Roman architectural design
(4) were strongly influenced by Renaissance humanism

---

21 Sir Isaac Newton, Galileo Galilei, and Johannes Kepler are all directly associated with the

(1) Industrial Revolution
(2) Scientific Revolution
(3) English Revolution
(4) Agricultural Revolution

22 The Enlightenment and the American Revolution were both major influences on 19th-century uprisings in

(1) Latin America   (3) Vietnam
(2) the Middle East   (4) Japan

23 Before the French Revolution, the people of France were divided into three estates based mainly on their

(1) education level   (3) social class
(2) geographic region   (4) religious beliefs

24 One similarity in the leadership of Jomo Kenyatta, José de San Martín, and Sun Yixian (Sun Yat-sen) is that they

(1) supported nationalistic movements
(2) organized communist rebellions
(3) opposed trade with other nations
(4) established democratic rule in their countries

25 The Opium Wars in China and the expedition of Commodore Matthew Perry to Japan resulted in

(1) the economic isolation of China and Japan
(2) an increase in Chinese influence in Asia
(3) the beginning of democratic governments in China and Japan
(4) an increase in Western trade and influence in Asia

26 What was a direct result of the Meiji Restoration in Japan?

(1) Japan became a modern industrial nation.
(2) The Tokugawa Shogunate seized control of the government.
(3) Russia signed a mutual trade agreement.
(4) Japan stayed politically isolated.

27 Which statement best describes a mixed economy?

(1) The government determines the production and distribution of goods and services.
(2) The products that consumers demand determine what goods are produced.
(3) Some industries are owned by the state, and others are privately owned.
(4) People produce the same goods, but in different amounts, every year.

Base your answer to question 28 on the cartoon below and on your knowledge of social studies.

Source: Arcadio Esquivel, *La Nación*,
Cartoonists & Writers Syndicate (adapted)

28 This 2001 cartoon implies that nations in Central America are

(1) defeating enemies and overcoming all obstacles
(2) requesting assistance in the battle against drought
(3) facing several serious problems at the same time
(4) waiting patiently until the economic crisis is over

---

29 Which leader based his rule on the ideas of Karl Marx and Friedrich Engels?

(1) Neville Chamberlain
(2) Vladimir Lenin
(3) Adolf Hitler
(4) Jiang Jieshi (Chiang Kai-shek)

30 One reason for the outbreak of World War II was the

(1) ineffectiveness of the League of Nations
(2) growing tension between the United States and the Soviet Union
(3) conflict between the Hapsburg and the Romanov families
(4) refusal of the German government to sign the Treaty of Versailles

31 Which United States foreign policy was used to maintain the independence of Greece and Turkey after World War II?

(1) containment   (3) nonalignment
(2) neutrality   (4) militarism

32 Which important principle was established as a result of the Nuremberg trials?

(1) Defeated nations have no rights in international courts of law.
(2) Individuals can be held accountable for "crimes against humanity."
(3) Soldiers must follow the orders of their superiors.
(4) Aggressor nations must pay war reparations for damages caused during wars.

33 Which statement about the European Union (EU) is most accurate?

(1) The European Union dissolved because of disagreements among its members.
(2) The goal of the European Union is to improve the economic prosperity of Europe.
(3) Some nations are now being forced to become members of the European Union.
(4) The European Union has recently expanded to include North African nations.

Base your answer to question 34 on the cartoon below and on your knowledge of social studies.

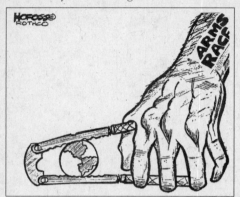

Source: Ellis and Esler, *World History: Connections to Today*, Prentice Hall, 2001 (adapted)

34 What is the main idea of this cartoon?

(1) Proliferation of military weapons could destroy the world.
(2) The world's population is growing faster than its food supply.
(3) The land masses of the Northern and Southern Hemispheres are shifting.
(4) Military technology is making the world a smaller place.

35 "... I saw that the whole solution to this problem lay in political freedom for our people, for it is only when a people are politically free that other races can give them the respect that is due to them. It is impossible to talk of equality of races in any other terms. No people without a government of their own can expect to be treated on the same level as peoples of independent sovereign states. It is far better to be free to govern or misgovern yourself than to be governed by anybody else...."

— Kwame Nkrumah, *Ghana: The Autobiography of Kwame Nkrumah*, Thomas Nelson & Sons, 1957

Which idea is expressed in this statement by Kwame Nkrumah?

(1) free trade
(2) collective security
(3) self-determination
(4) peaceful coexistence

36 Most of the world's known oil reserves are located near which geographic area?

(1) Persian Gulf   (3) Ural Mountains
(2) North Sea   (4) Gulf of Mexico

37 The policy of strict racial separation and discrimination that was implemented in the Republic of South Africa is called

(1) collectivization   (3) intifada
(2) apartheid   (4) communism

38 Which statement best describes a problem facing India today?

(1) Democracy has failed to gain popular support.
(2) Religious and ethnic diversity has continued to cause conflict.
(3) A decrease in population has led to labor shortages.
(4) Lack of technology has limited military capabilities.

Base your answer to question 39 on the cartoon below and on your knowledge of social studies.

Teamwork

Source: Jim Morin, *The Miami Herald*, King Features Syndicate, 1989

39 Which concept is illustrated by the cartoon?

(1) scarcity   (3) revolution
(2) capitalism   (4) interdependence

40 **"India Strives for Grain Self-Sufficiency by 1970"**
    "New Wheat Variety Grows in Arid Climate"
    "Chemical Fertilizer Use Rises 10% in 1960"
    "Sri Lanka's Rice Production Increases 25% in Three Years"

These newspaper headlines from the 1960s and 1970s describe some of the results of the

(1) Sepoy Mutiny
(2) Kashmir crisis
(3) Green Revolution
(4) Computer Revolution

Base your answer to question 41 on the diagram below and on your knowledge of social studies.

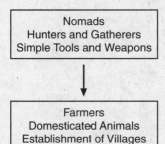

41 What is the best title for this diagram?

(1) Elements of Belief Systems
(2) Characteristics of Classical Civilizations
(3) Benefits of the Counter Reformation
(4) Changes during the Neolithic Revolution

42 The treatment of the Armenians by Ottoman Turks in the late 19th and early 20th centuries and the treatment of Muslims by the Serbs of Yugoslavia in the 1990s are both examples of

(1) coalition rule
(2) liberation theology
(3) universal suffrage
(4) human rights violations

43 The doctrines of the Roman Catholic, Eastern Orthodox, and Protestant churches are all based on the

(1) concept of reincarnation
(2) principles of Christianity
(3) teachings of Muhammad
(4) leadership of the pope

44 Which factor contributed to the success of the Hanseatic League, the Kingdom of Songhai, and the British East India Company?

(1) location in the Middle East
(2) imperialism in Europe
(3) development of trade with other regions
(4) growth of the Ottoman Empire

45 Heavy military losses in World War I, food and fuel shortages, and opposition to the czar led to the

(1) French Revolution
(2) Russian Revolution
(3) Chinese Revolution
(4) Cuban Revolution

46 Which geographic factor in Russia played a role in Napoleon's defeat in 1812 and Hitler's defeat at Stalingrad in 1943?

(1) Siberian tundra   (3) arid land
(2) Caspian Sea   (4) harsh climate

47 • Scholars take civil service examinations for government positions.
    • Students form Red Guard units to challenge counterrevolutionaries.
    • Students demonstrate for democratic reforms in the capital and are killed by government troops.

These statements describe the changing role of students in which nation?

(1) Japan   (3) Russia
(2) China   (4) India

Base your answer to question 48 on the map below and on your knowledge of social studies.

Source: Ellis and Esler, *World History: Connections to Today,* Prentice Hall, 2005 (adapted)

48 Which time period is represented in this map of Europe?

(1) before the Congress of Vienna
(2) during the Age of Imperialism
(3) between World War I and World War II
(4) during the Cold War

Base your answers to questions 49 and 50 on the quotation below and on your knowledge of social studies.

"... The daily tasks of the women are to milk the cattle in the morning and evening, and to fetch water as required. By using their donkeys it is possible for them to bring back enough water to last two or three days. When the settlement moves, on average about once every five weeks, each woman is responsible for moving her hut and rebuilding it. All the necessary movables, including hides, wooden containers and important struts in the framework of the hut, can normally be carried by two donkeys. Older women rely on their daughters, their younger co-wives, and their sons' wives for help in all these tasks. ..."

Source: Paul Spencer, *The Samburu*, University of California Press, 1965

49 Which type of economy would most likely be found in this society?

(1) command   (3) free market
(2) traditional   (4) manorial

50 Based on this passage, the Samburu people would be classified as

(1) commercial farmers   (3) nomads
(2) urban dwellers   (4) serfs

Write the answer to the essay question on the lined sheets in this booklet.

In developing your answer to Part II, be sure to keep these general definitions in mind:

(a) <u>describe</u> means "to illustrate something in words or tell about it"

(b) <u>discuss</u> means "to make observations about something using facts, reasoning, and argument; to present in some detail"

PART II

THEMATIC ESSAY QUESTION

Directions: Write a well-organized essay that includes an introduction, several paragraphs addressing the task below, and a conclusion.

Theme: Change

> Throughout history, the actions of leaders have changed the society in which they lived.

Task:

> Identify *two* leaders who changed the society in which they lived and for *each*
> - Describe *one* situation the leader attempted to change
> - Describe *one* action the leader took to change this situation
> - Discuss the impact of that action on the society in which the leader lived

You may use any leader from your study of global history and geography *except* **Johann Gutenberg** and **James Watt**. Some suggestions you might wish to consider include Martin Luther, Queen Elizabeth I, Toussaint L'Ouverture, Napoleon Bonaparte, Simón Bolívar, Otto von Bismarck, Mohandas Gandhi, Mao Zedong, Ho Chi Minh, Fidel Castro, and Nelson Mandela.

You are *not* limited to these suggestions.

Do *not* use a leader from the United States in your answer.

Guidelines:

In your essay, be sure to
- Develop all aspects of the task
- Support the theme with relevant facts, examples, and details
- Use a logical and clear plan of organization, including an introduction and a conclusion that are beyond a restatement of the theme

NAME _____   SCHOOL _____

Write the answer to the essay question on the lined sheets in this booklet.

In developing your answers to Part III, be sure to keep these general definitions in mind:

(a) <u>explain</u> means "to make plain or understandable; to give reasons for or causes of; to show the logical development or relationships of"

(b) <u>discuss</u> means "to make observations about something using facts, reasoning, and argument; to present in some detail"

PART III

DOCUMENT-BASED QUESTION

   This question is based on the accompanying documents. It is designed to test your ability to work with historical documents. Some of these documents have been edited for the purposes of this question. As you analyze the documents, take into account the source of each document and any point of view that may be presented in the document.

Historical Context:

Throughout history, changes in technology have had a great influence on society. Development of the **printing press**, **steam-powered machinery**, and the **atomic bomb** had a major impact on specific societies and the world.

Task: Using the information from the documents and your knowledge of global history, answer the questions that follow each document in Part A. Your answers to the questions will help you write the Part B essay in which you will be asked to

> Identify *two* of the technological changes mentioned in the historical context and for *each*
>
> • Explain how the new technology changed the existing technology
> • Discuss the impact of this new technology on a specific society *or* the world

Part A

Short-Answer Questions

Directions: Analyze the documents and answer the short-answer questions that follow each document in the space provided.

Document 1a

Medieval Scriptorium

Source: www.hrc.utexas.edu/exhibitions/permanent/
gutenberg/2a.html

Document 1b

The Book Before Gutenberg

> The earliest books were written on scrolls. From the Second Century A.D. to the present time, however, most books have been produced in the familiar codex format—in other words, bound at one edge. During the Middle Ages, manuscript books were produced by monks who worked with pen and ink in a copying room known as a scriptorium. Even a small book could take months to complete, and a book the size of the Bible could take several years. . . .

Source: www.hrc.utexas.edu/exhibitions/permanent/gutenberg/2a.html

1 According to these documents, how were books made before the development of the Gutenberg press? [1]

_____

_____

Score ☐

Document 2

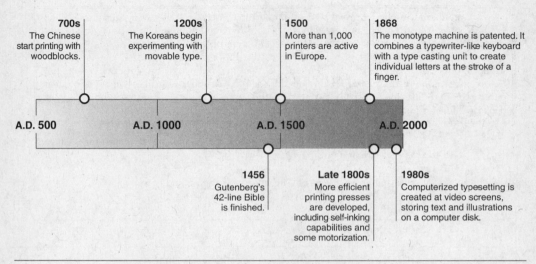

700s The Chinese start printing with woodblocks.	**1200s** The Koreans begin experimenting with movable type.

1500
More than 1,000 printers are active in Europe.

1868
The monotype machine is patented. It combines a typewriter-like keyboard with a type casting unit to create individual letters at the stroke of a finger.

A.D. 500   A.D. 1000   A.D. 1500   A.D. 2000

1456
Gutenberg's 42-line Bible is finished.

Late 1800s
More efficient printing presses are developed, including self-inking capabilities and some motorization.

1980s
Computerized typesetting is created at video screens, storing text and illustrations on a computer disk.

Source: Stephen Krensky, *Breaking Into Print, Before and After the Invention of the Printing Press*, Little, Brown and Company, 1996 (adapted)

2   Based on this document, state *two* advances in printing technology that took place between 500 and 2000.   [2]

(1) _____

_____

Score [   ]

(2) _____

_____

Score [   ]

Document 3

> . . . Gutenberg's methods spread with stunning rapidity. By 1500 an estimated half million printed books were in circulation: religious works, Greek and Roman classics, scientific texts, Columbus's report from the New World. An acceleration of the Renaissance was only the first by-product of the Gutenberg press. Without it, the Protestant movement might have been stillborn [failed], as well as the subsequent political and industrial revolutions. Gutenberg, however, got none of the glory. His brainchild [idea] bankrupted him; the year his Bible was published, a creditor took over his business. Little more is known of the inventor — in part because he never put his own name into print. . . .

Source: Robert Friedman, ed., *The Life Millennium:*
The 100 Most Important Events & People of The Past 1,000 Years,
Time, 1998

3 Based on this document, state *two* effects of Gutenberg's invention. [2]

(1)_____

_____

Score [ ]

(2)_____

_____

Score [ ]

Document 4

Woman Spinning

Source: *The Costume of Yorkshire*, Richard Jackson, Publisher

4 According to this document, what technology was used in cloth production in the early 1700s? [1]

_____

_____

Score ☐

Document 5a

Invention	Description
Improved steam engine (James Watt)	Improved version of steam engine that used coal rather than water power. First used to pump water from mines and to forge iron. By the late 1780s, powered machines in cotton mills.

Source: Ellis and Esler, *World History: Connections to Today*, Prentice Hall, 1999 (adapted)

Document 5b

Power Loom Weaving

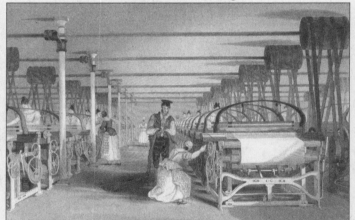

Drawn by T. Allom   Engraved by J. Tingle

Source: Edward Baines, *History of the Cotton Manufacture in Great Britain*, Fisher, Fisher, and Jackson, 1835 (adapted)

5 According to these documents, how did the steam engine promote the growth of the factory system? [1]

_____

_____

Score [ ]

Document 6

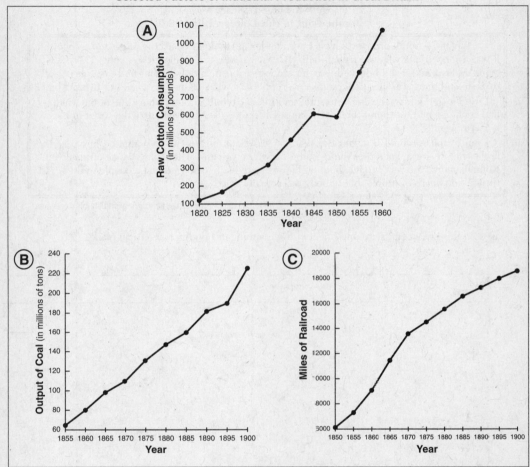

Selected Factors of Industrial Production in Great Britain

Source: Brian Mitchell, *Abstract of British Historical Statistics*, Cambridge University Press, 1962 (adapted)

6 What do these graphs imply about the effect of steam-powered machinery on industrial production in Great Britain? [1]

_____

_____

Score ☐

Document 7

This is an excerpt from a tape-recorded conversation of Kathleen Brockington in August 1994.

Kathleen's Story
Bombed out in the London Blitz, 1940

> . . . When the bomb dropped I wasn't even under the table! I heard the plane and recognised it was a Jerry (that's what we called them) [Germans] because I'd heard so many. There was a tremendous BANG! and I ducked. All the windows came in and the ceiling and a couple of walls came in and there was incredible smoke everywhere. I was shaking like a leaf but I wasn't hurt.
>
> I tried to get out but the door was stuck and I had to climb through where one of the windows had been. I could see there were lots of houses affected, glass everywhere in the street so I knew it was a big'un.
>
> I ran to the Air Raid Post but the Warden said "look missus, we're gonna be busy digging bodies out, if you've got a roof you're better off where you are. There's lots worse off than you". Funnily enough he was wrong; about 50 houses were badly damaged and a couple of them just turned into heaps of rubble, but nobody was actually killed. . . .

Source: http://timewitnesses.org/english/blitz.html (adapted)

7 Based on this document, state *one* effect of the bombing of London by German planes. [1]

_____

_____

Score ☐

Document 8

> . . . In both cities the blast totally destroyed everything within a radius of 1 mile from the center of explosion, except for certain reinforced concrete frames as noted above. The atomic explosion almost completely destroyed Hiroshima's identity as a city. Over a fourth of the population was killed in one stroke and an additional fourth seriously injured, so that even if there had been no damage to structures and installations the normal city life would still have been completely shattered. Nearly everything was heavily damaged up to a radius of 3 miles from the blast, and beyond this distance damage, although comparatively light, extended for several more miles. Glass was broken up to 12 miles.
>
> In Nagasaki, a smaller area of the city was actually destroyed than in Hiroshima, because the hills which enclosed the target area restricted the spread of the great blast; but careful examination of the effects of the explosion gave evidence of even greater blast effects than in Hiroshima. Total destruction spread over an area of about 3 square miles. Over a third of the 50,000 buildings in the target area of Nagasaki were destroyed or seriously damaged. The complete destruction of the huge steel works and the torpedo plant was especially impressive. The steel frames of all buildings within a mile of the explosion were pushed away, as by a giant hand, from the point of detonation. The badly burned area extended for 3 miles in length. The hillsides up to a radius of 8,000 feet were scorched, giving them an autumnal appearance. . . .

Source: "The Atomic Bombings of Hiroshima and Nagasaki," Manhattan Engineer District, United States Army, June 29, 1946

8 Based on this document, state *two* effects of the atomic bombings on Hiroshima and Nagasaki. [2]

(1) _____

_____

Score ☐

(2) _____

_____

Score ☐

Document 9a

Nuclear Countries – November 2002

Declared Nuclear States	Estimates of Nuclear Weapons Stockpiled
United States	10,640
Russia	8,600
China	400
France	350
United Kingdom	200
Israel	100–200
Pakistan	24–48
India	30–35
North Korea*	1–2

Source: Natural Resources Defense Council (NRDC), 2002
(adapted); *Bulletin of Atomic Scientist, 2003

Document 9b

Countries with Nuclear Power Reactors in Operation or Under Construction – December 2002

Argentina	Finland	Korea, Republic of	Slovenia
Armenia	France	Lithuania	South Africa
Belgium	Germany	Mexico	Spain
Brazil	Hungary	Netherlands	Sweden
Bulgaria	India	Pakistan	Switzerland
Canada	Iran	Romania	Ukraine
China	Japan	Russian Federation	United Kingdom
Czech Republic	Korea, Dem. Peoples Rep. of	Slovakia	United States

Source: "Nuclear Technology Review," International Atomic Energy Agency (IAEA), 2003 (adapted)

9 Based on these charts, state *two* ways countries have used nuclear technology. [2]

(1) _____

_____

Score ☐

(2) _____

_____

Score ☐

Part B

Essay

Directions: Write a well-organized essay that includes an introduction, several paragraphs, and a conclusion. Use evidence from *at least **four*** documents to support your response.

Historical Context:

> Throughout history, changes in technology have had a great influence on society. Development of the **printing press**, **steam-powered machinery**, and the **atomic bomb** had a major impact on specific societies and the world.

Task: Using the information from the documents and your knowledge of global history, write an essay in which you

> Identify ***two*** of the technological changes mentioned in the historical context and for ***each***
> * Explain how the new technology changed the existing technology
> * Discuss the impact of this new technology on a specific society ***or*** the world

Guidelines:

In your essay, be sure to

* Develop all aspects of the task
* Incorporate information from *at least **four*** documents
* Incorporate relevant outside information
* Support the theme with relevant facts, examples, and details
* Use a logical and clear plan of organization, including an introduction and conclusion that are beyond a restatement of the theme